Andrew
SCHULMAN

UNAUTHORIZED WINDOWS 95™

DEVELOPER'S RESOURCE KIT

An International Data Group Company
Foster City, CA • Chicago, IL • Indianapolis, IN • Braintree, MA • Dallas, TX

Unauthorized Windows 95™

Published by
IDG Books Worldwide, Inc.
An International Data Group Company
155 Bovet Road, Suite 310
San Mateo, CA 94402

Copyright

Library of Congress Catalog Card No.: 94-72739

ISBN 1-56884-305-4

Printed in the United States of America
First Printing, October, 1994
10 9 8 7 6 5 4 3 2 1

Distributed in the United States by IDG Books Worldwide, Inc.

Limit of Liability/Disclaimer of Warranty

Trademarks

Published in the United States of America

Credits

Vice President and Publisher
Christopher J. Williams

Publishing Director
Trudy Neuhaus

Brand Manager
Amorette Pedersen

Project Editor
Susan Pink

Manuscript Editor
Teresa Frazier

Technical Editor
James Finnegan

Editorial Assistants
Berta Hyken
Kate Tolini

Production
Beth A. Roberts
Ronnie K. Bucci

Proofreader
Seth Maislin

Indexer
Elizabeth Cunningham

Book Design
Scally Design

Cover Design
Kavish + Kavish

For More Information

For general information on IDG Books in the U.S., including information on discounts and premiums, contact IDG Books at 800-434-3422 or 415-312-0650.

For information on where to purchase IDG's books outside the U.S., contact Christina Turner at 415-312-0633.

For information on translations, contact Marc Jeffrey Mikulich, Director, Rights and Licensing, at IDG Books Worldwide; fax number: 415-286-2747.

For sales inquires and special prices for bulk quantities, contact Tony Real at 800-434-3422 or 415-312-0644.

For information on using IDG books in the classroom and ordering examination copies, contact Jim Kelley at 1-800-434-2086.

Unauthorized Windows 95: A Developer's Resource Kit is distributed in the United States by IDG Books Worldwide, Inc. It is distributed in Canada by Macmillan of Canada, a Division of Canada Publishing Corporation; by Computer and Technical Books in Miami, Florida, for South America and the Caribbean; by Longman Singapore in Singapore, Malaysia, Thailand, and Korea; by Toppan Co. Ltd. in Japan; by Asia Computerworld in Hong Kong; by Woodslane Pty. Ltd. in Australia and New Zealand; and by Transword Publishers Ltd. in the U.K. and Europe.

International Data Group's Publications

IDG Books Worldwide, Inc. is a subsidiary of International Data Group. The officers are Patrick J. McGovern, Founder and Board Chairman; Walter Boyd, President. ARGENTINA'S Computerworld Argentina, Infoworld Argentina; AUSTRALIA'S Computerworld Australia, Australian PC World, Australian Macworld, Network World, Mobile Business Australia, Reseller, IDG Sources; AUSTRIA'S Computerwelt Oesterreich, PC Test; BRAZIL'S Computerworld, Gamepro, Game Power, Mundo IBM, Mundo Unix, PC World, Super Game; BELGIUM'S Data News (CW); BULGARIA'S Computerworld Bulgaria, Ediworld, PC & Mac World Bulgaria, Network World Bulgaria; CANADA'S CIO Canada, Computerworld Canada, Graduate Computerworld, InfoCanada, Network World Canada; CHILE'S Computerworld Chile, Informatica; COLOMBIA'S Computerworld Colombia, PC World; CZECH REPUBLIC'S Computerworld, Elektronika, PC World; DENMARK'S Communications World, Computerworld Danmark, Macintosh Produktkatalog, Macworld Danmark, PC World Danmark, PC World Produktguide, Tech World, Windows World; ECUADOR'S PC World Ecuador; EGYPT'S Computerworld (CW) Middle East, PC World Middle East; FINLAND'S MikroPC, Tietoviikko, Tietoverkko; FRANCE'S Distributique, GOLDEN MAC, InfoPC, Languages & Systems, Le Guide du Monde Informatique, Le Monde Informatique, Telecoms & Reseaux; GERMANY'S Computerwoche, Computerwoche Focus, Computerwoche Extra, Computerwoche Karriere, Information Management, Macwelt, Netzwelt, PC Welt, PC Woche, Publish, Unit; GREECE'S Infoworld, PC Games; HUNGARY'S Computerworld SZT, PC World; HONG KONG'S Computerworld Hong Kong, PC World Hong Kong; INDIA'S Computers & Communications; IRELAND'S ComputerScope; ISRAEL'S Computerworld Israel, PC World Israel; ITALY'S Computerworld Italia, Lotus Magazine, Macworld Italia, Networking Italia, PC Shopping, PC World Italia; JAPAN'S Computerworld Today, Information Systems World, Macworld Japan, Nikkei Personal Computing, SunWorld Japan, Windows World; KENYA'S East African Computer News; KOREA'S Computerworld Korea, Macworld Korea, PC World Korea; MEXICO'S Compu Edicion, Compu Manufactura, Computacion/Punto de Venta, Computerworld Mexico, MacWorld, Mundo Unix, PC World, Windows; THE NETHERLANDS' Computer! Totaal, Computable (CW), LAN Magazine, MacWorld, Totaal "Windows"; NEW ZEALAND'S Computer Listings, Computerworld New Zealand, New Zealand PC World, Network World; NIGERIA'S PC World Africa; NORWAY'S Computerworld Norge, C/World, Lotusworld Norge, Macworld Norge, Networld, PC World Ekspress, PC World Norge, PC World's Produktguide, Publish& Multimedia World, Student Data, Unix World, Windowsworld; IDG Direct Response; PAKISTAN'S PC World Pakistan; PANAMA'S PC World Panama; PERU'S Computerworld Peru, PC World; PEOPLE'S REPUBLIC OF CHINA'S China Computerworld, China Infoworld, Electronics Today/Multimedia World, Electronics International, Electronic Product World, China Network World, PC and Communications Magazine, PC World China, Software World Magazine, Telecom Product World; IDG HIGH TECH BEIJING'S New Product World; IDG SHENZHEN'S Computer News Digest; PHILIPPINES' Computerworld Philippines, PC Digest (PCW); POLAND'S Computerworld Poland, PC World/Komputer; PORTUGAL'S Cerebro/PC World, Correio Informatico/Computerworld, Informatica & Comunicacoes Catalogo, Macln, Nacional de Produtos; ROMANIA'S Computerworld, PC World; RUSSIA'S Computerworld-Moscow, Mir - PC, Sety; SINGAPORE'S Computerworld Southeast Asia, PC World Singapore; SLOVENIA'S Monitor Magazine; SOUTH AFRICA'S Computer Mail (CIO),Computing S.A.,Network World S.A., Software World; SPAIN'S Advanced Systems, Amiga World, Computerworld Espana, Communicaciones World, Macworld Espana, NeXTWORLD, Super Juegos Magazine (GamePro), PC World Espana, Publish; SWEDEN'S Attack, ComputerSweden, Corporate Computing, Natverk & Kommunikation, Macworld, Mikrodatorn, PC World, Publishing & Design (CAP), Datalngenjoren, Maxi Data,Windows World; SWITZERLAND'S Computerworld Schweiz, Macworld Schweiz, PC Tip; TAIWAN'S Computerworld Taiwan, PC World Taiwan; THAILAND'S Thai Computerworld; TURKEY'S Computerworld Monitor, Macworld Turkiye, PC World Turkiye; UKRAINE'S Computerworld; UNITED KINGDOM'S Computing /Computerworld, Connexion/Network World, Lotus Magazine, Macworld, Open Computing/Sunworld; UNITED STATES' Advanced Systems, AmigaWorld, Cable in the Classroom, CD Review, CIO, Computerworld, Digital Video, DOS Resource Guide, Electronic Entertainment Magazine, Federal Computer Week, Federal Integrator, GamePro, IDG Books, Infoworld, Infoworld Direct, Laser Event, Macworld, Multimedia World, Network World, PC Letter, PC World, PlayRight, Power PC World, Publish, SWATPro, Video Event; VENEZUELA'S Computerworld Venezuela, PC World; VIETNAM'S PC World Vietnam.

Contents

Preface xiii
Industry Update: The Impact of Windows 95 1

Chapter One

Welcome to Windows 95 1

Bypassing COMMAND.COM 5
...But Bypassing DOS, Too? 9
Why Bother Refuting Microsoft's Claims? 19
Those Ubiquitous Microsoft Diagrams 20
Claiming Integration 23
Windows 95 and DOS 26
Sidebar: *Just one little callback* 39
Who's Afraid of MS-DOS? 42
WfW 3.11: The Neglected Operating System 44

Chapter Two

Watching Chicago Boot 49

From WINBOOT.SYS to WIN.COM 49
Sidebar: *A complete rewrite?* 52
From the Registry to XMS 55
Sidebar: *Pushing aside real-mode drivers?* 57
From IFSHLP.SYS to WIN.COM 60
From WIN.COM to KRNL386.EXE 62
Inside the Virtual Machine Manager 66
VxDs: TSRs of the 1990s 78
From KRNL386.EXE to CAB32.EXE 84
Exploring the Explorer 91

Chapter Three

The Windows-DOS Connection 95

Windows INT 2Fh Broadcasts 97
Instance Data 101
Embedded VxDs 103

FAKEWIN Caveats ... 105
Inside FAKEWIN ... 107
FAKEWIN.C ... 107

Chapter Four

A Marriage Made in Redmond ... **115**
TSRLDR.ASM ... 117
DOS Instance Data and the SDA ... 119
Sidebar: *What was WINA20.386?* ... 122
DOS's IN_WIN3E Flag ... 123
TEST1684.C ... 124
V86 Mode ... 127
Global EMM Import ... 128
The DOSMGR Broadcast API ... 129
FAKEVXD.C ... 130
TSR Identify Function ... 132
FAKETSR.C ... 132

Chapter Five

The Two Faces of Windows ... **139**
The Inner Core of Windows ... 139
DOS Extenders and the Future of DOS ... 140
DOSX: A General-Purpose DOS Extender and DPMI Server ... 146
USEDPMI.C ... 146
RUNDOSX ... 152
RUNDOSX.BAT ... 154
Using the DPMI Shell Library ... 156
USEDPMI2.C ... 156
MEMLOOP ... 157
MEMLOOP.C ... 157

Chapter Six

Protected-Mode DOS: WIN386 and MSDPMI ... **161**
GOWIN386.INI ... 162
GOWIN386.BAT ... 163
Sidebar: *What mode is KRNL386 loaded in?* ... 167

DPMIINFO 167
DPMIINFO.C 168
Sidebar: *WIN386 really, really is a memory manager* 170
MSDPMI 173

Chapter Seven

Where Do 32BFA and LFN Come From? 177

Onward to Windows 95: VMM32 182
RUNVMM32.BAT 188
Long Filename Support in Windows 95 193
Sidebar: *The eleven kinds of Windows disk/file drivers* 197
LFN.C 201
The DblSpace VxD Saga 204
Four Steps Toward DOS Nirvana 207

Chapter Eight

The Case of the Gradually Disappearing DOS 161

Bypassing DOS 210
TEST21.C 211
Sidebar: *32BFA versus disk cache performance* 221
Getting and Setting the Current Drive 223
TEST_1 224
CURRDRIV.ASM 230
Windows 95: Still Bypassing DOS, but Supporting TSRs 234
INTVECT: Another Sample VxD INT 21h Hooker 238
INTVECT.ASM 239
Global and Local INT 21h Hookers 242
The Role of IFSHLP.SYS and V86 Callbacks 244
VXD86API.C 252
WINBP.C 259
32BFA and Networks, CD-ROM, and Floppies 274
Replacing Real-Mode Code: It's Not New 277
TEST1600.C 278
Another Old Example: TEST1600 281
TEST2F16.C 282
Interrupts 101: IDT versus the IVT 284

Chapter Nine

Who's in Charge: Windows or DOS? 293

"A Thing on a Thing"? 293
Running DOS in Protected Mode........ 296
The Virtual Machine Monitor (VMM)........ 298
V86 Mode and the PE Bit 302
PE.C 305

Chapter Ten

How Windows Runs DOS 307

V86TEST........ 307
V86TEST.C........ 309
Sidebar: *Switching from V86 mode to real mode* 317
IOPL and the Interrupt Flag 319
CLITEST.C (Windows version)........ 325
CLITEST2.C (DPMI version) 326
CLISTI.C........ 328
Running DOS in a Virtual Machine 331
Simulating versus Reflecting Interrupts 333
Options for Controlling DOS 336

Chapter Eleven

Who Needs DOS? 339

What Does V86TEST Actually Show?........ 340
Windows at Work?........ 342
Sidebar: *VxD callouts*........ 347
The Top Windows INT 21h Calls 352
Bouncing Back into Windows 356
The Effect of 32-Bit File Access 359
What about BIOS Calls? 363

Chapter Twelve

Exploring with WV86TEST........ 371

Breaking All Ties with DOS? 373

WinWord and DOS 380
The Windows 95 Explorer and DOS 383
PSPs and Other DOS Data in Windows 95 385
Win32 FindNextFile Is INT 21h Function 714Fh 396
MYDIR.C 404
The WV86TEST Code 409
Windows 95 and Protected-Mode DOS 415

Chapter Thirteen

Thunk! KERNEL32 Calls KRNL386 417

Launching a Win16 App from the Explorer 420
CAB32: KERNEL32 Uses the Win16 KERNEL 425
DYNLINK32.C 433
Sidebar: *Win32 and the PSP* 437
WINPSP.C 438
Who's Calling INT21h? 441
Where's the Windows 95 Current Directory? 444
CHGDIR.C 446
WALKWIN.C 453
From Explorer to Create PSP in Six Easy Steps 460
The WSPY21 Code 472
WSPY21.C 474
Sidebar: *The DOS extender: Still a great pretender?* 483
DOSMEM.C 484
KERNEL's INT 21h Handler and KernelDosProc 488

Chapter Fourteen

Clock: Mixing 32-Bit and 16-Bit Code 497

16/16: The Win16 Clock under WfW 3.11 497
32/16: The Windows 95 Clock under Win32s 500
Sidebar: *Thunking: Mixing 16- and 32-bit code with CALL FWORD PTR* 505
FWORD.C 505
INTSERV.C 506
32/32: The Windows 95 Clock 510
Does Windows 95 Really Call Down to DOS? And What Does It Do When It Gets There? 515
Sidebar: *The magic of Call_Priority_VM_Event* 526

Win32 File Handles and Thunking 529
Reading the PSP from Win32 530
TH32.C 530
WIN32PSP.C 533
Using Win32 File Handles 536
W32HAND.C 538
FILETEST.ASM 543
Really Bypassing DOS: Executable Loading and Memory-Mapped Files 545
MAPFILE.C 545
W16LOCK.C 553
WIN16 Everywhere: The Saga of Win16Lock 549

EPILOG **559**

APPENDIX A **565**

APPENDIX B **573**

FOR FURTHER READING **577**

INDEX **581**

LICENSE AGREEMENTS **589**

PREFACE

> No one is surprised more often by the dynamic behavior of a program than its author.
>
> — Russ Blake, *Optimizing Windows NT*

Microsoft Corp. is the author of not only Windows 95 ("Chicago") but also virtually all materials regarding this operating system. Microsoft has released a 300-page *"Chicago" Reviewer's Guide*, almost monthly articles in *Microsoft Systems Journal*, and several articles in *Microsoft Developer Network News*. Microsoft Press, which recently started describing itself in its ads as "The Knowledge Division of Microsoft," has published a 475-page book, *Inside Windows 95*, by a former director of systems software products at Microsoft, Adrian King.

Almost all other descriptions of Windows 95 in the computer trade press have been based heavily on such Microsoft-provided resources. Moreover, we — like all non-Microsoft book publishers — are required by Microsoft's publisher relations program to include the following notice:

> This book is based on information on Windows 95 made public by Microsoft as of 10/19/94. Since this information was made public before the release of the product, we encourage you to visit your local bookstore at that time for updated books on Windows 95.
>
> If you have a modem or access to the Internet, you can always get up-to-the-minute information on Windows 95 direct from Microsoft on WinNews:
>
> On CompuServe: *GO WINNEWS*
> On the Internet: *ftp://ftp microsoft.com/PerOpSys/Win_News/Chicago*
> *http://www.microsoft.com*

On AOL:	keyword *WINNEWS*
On Prodigy:	jumpword *WINNEWS*
On Genie:	*WINNEWS* file area on Windows RTC

You can also subscribe to Microsoft's WinNews electronic newsletter by sending Internet email to enews@microsoft.nwnet.com and put the words SUBSCRIBE WINNEWS in the text of the email.

Interestingly, the publisher's note (September 16, 1994) to Microsoft Press's own *Inside Windows 95* starts off with a somewhat different disclaimer:

> As we went to press, some aspects of Windows 95 were still under a general nondisclosure agreement, but Microsoft had made public a great deal of information about Windows 95. *This book offers an interpretation of that information, and the author's conclusions are based on his exploration of Beta-1.* [italics added]

Similarly, *Unauthorized Windows 95* also offers an interpretation of the information Microsoft provides on Windows 95, and the conclusions are similarly based on my exploration of Chicago's Beta-1 (May 1994). In addition, I examined the commercially-released Windows for Workgroups (WfW) 3.11, whose 32-bit file access is said by Microsoft's advertisements to be "powered by 32-bit technology from our 'Chicago' project," and I examined Microsoft's 32-bit add-in to Windows 3.1, Win32s, which bears a far closer resemblance to Windows 95 than representatives for Microsoft claim (and apparently believe).

Microsoft representatives also claim, and no doubt sincerely believe, that Windows 95 is "integrated," is not based on MS-DOS, has been rewritten from the ground up, and has a 32-bit kernel. Microsoft seeks by these statements to position Windows 95 head-to-head against the Apple Macintosh (whose ease of use is widely perceived to stem from its "integration") and to a far lesser extent against IBM's OS/2 operating system, the avid supporters of which make much ado about the fact that OS/2 is a complete, "from the ground up" operating system, not a "thing on a thing" like Windows.

But, just as an author is often surprised by the behavior of his or her own program, likewise a company is often misinformed — and hence a source of misinformation — as to the nature of its own products. This is why educated car buyers generally pay more attention to *Consumer Reports* than to the manufacturer's advertising or the salesman's pitch. Similarly, you would no more want to learn about an operating system straight from the horse's mouth than you would expect to learn about a book by asking its author. An author is generally the *last* person you would ask for an objective perspective on his or her work.

Not surprisingly then, many of Microsoft's statements on Windows 95 have been ill-informed. This book shows that Windows 95 is no more integrated than its predecessors, and does not represent a "complete rewrite" of Windows.

However, although this book pokes several large holes in Microsoft's claims for Windows 95, I do not join the IBM OS/2 contingent nor the equally small contingent marching behind Microsoft's high-end Windows NT. The OS/2 and NT enthusiasts (who sound remarkably alike) pounce on any proof of architectural compromises in Windows 95 — such as the continuing use of 16-bit code in the kernel, or the continuing reliance on MS-DOS — as proof that Windows 95 isn't a genuine operating system. But Windows 95 is likely to be a shockingly successful operating system *precisely because* of such compromises.

This book will show you that Windows 95 continues to rely on DOS, that its Win32 kernel continues to rely on the Win16 kernel, and that surprise! — this is *okay*. My goal is not to prove that Windows 95 continues to use DOS and therefore isn't a genuine operating system. Instead, my goal is to show that even though Windows 95 does use DOS, Windows 95 (like Windows 3.*x* Enhanced mode before it) is not some "thing on a thing," but employs a reasonable, legitimate operating system architecture, the foundation of which is Intel's Virtual-8086 (V86) mode.

One of my hopes is that this book will help overcome some common prejudices as to what constitutes a proper operating system architecture. Windows and DOS are by far the most successful operating systems in the history of computing. That they don't conform to certain principles of operating system design might tell us that there is something wrong with these principles. Most general-purpose computers on the planet are running DOS and possibly Windows. Thus, like it or not, Windows and DOS together define what operating systems *actually look like* in the world today.

My goal in puncturing some of Microsoft's claims about Windows 95 is not to find fault with Windows 95. By understanding that Windows 95 is not a complete rewrite, is still partially based on DOS, has 16-bit code in its kernel, and so on, you will better understand how Windows 95 actually works.

In particular, I hope this book will help you see that the coolest new features of Windows 95 have their roots in Windows 3.0 Enhanced mode, first made available to paying customers on the fateful day of May 22,

1990 (The Day the Software Industry Changed). Windows 95 should have been predictable from a careful reading of the Windows 3.0 Device Driver Kit's description of VMM services such as Hook_V86_Int_Chain, Set_PM_Int_Vector, Allocate_V86_Call_Back, Install_V86_Break_Point, and Call_Priority_VM_Event.

This VMM layer, which is a genuine operating system, and plug-in add-ons to this operating system, called VxDs, have been around for five years, yet only now is it likely that the typical Windows programmer will encounter them. Unfortunately, I suspect that few Windows developers could tell you much about the components of the Windows operating system such as VMM, IFSMgr, VPICD, DOSMGR, VWIN32, or IOS. Likewise, Windows programming books likewise say hardly anything about this layer of Windows.

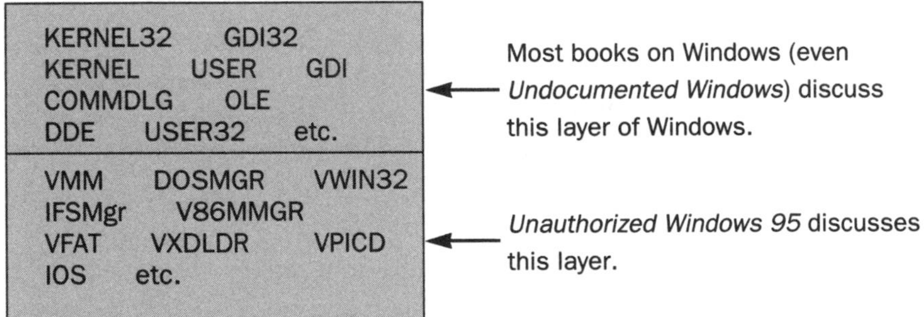

Although Windows is frequently referred to as an *environment* rather than an operating system, a little-known part of Windows really and truly is a full-blown operating system. This book covers this operating system component of Windows.

Although *Unauthorized Windows 95* is largely a book about VMM and VxDs in Windows 95, it is not a book for device driver writers. Even though I hope someone writing a device driver will find a lot of valuable information here, my assumption throughout is that the reader has no intention of writing device drivers. And although I discuss some important undocumented functions — most notably undocumented Win32 APIs provided by KERNEL32.DLL, such as VxDCall and GetpWin16Lock — my intention is simply to give you a taste of how Windows 95 actually works.

Another thing I've tried to do in this book is to "integrate" (as Microsoft would put it) minute technical details of Windows 95 with an overview of Microsoft's role in the PC software industry and the likely impact of Windows 95 on the industry. I've never been interested in details for their own sake. Examining the Windows code, in some cases down to the instruction level, is important only because this code is running on tens of millions of machines every day. I don't think it would be worth subjecting a less ubiquitous operating system, such as OS/2 or NT, to the same scrutiny.

Well, so much for what you can expect from *Unauthorized Windows 95*. Now for my favorite part of the book, where I get to give thanks for all the help I received.

First, there's my editor, Trudy Neuhaus. For five years, Trudy edited the back of *PC Magazine*, where authors such as Douglas Boling, Ray Duncan, Charles Petzold, and Jeff Prosise regularly appeared. Well-known as the finest editor in the computer-writing business, Trudy joined IDG Books as Senior Editor of its new Programmers Press division, and is now Publishing Director of Programmers Press Professional. I was incredibly fortunate to have Trudy as the editor for this book.

Richard Smith, president of Phar Lap Software, not only was tremendously useful to talk with both about technical and business issues, but also was very supportive.

Jim Finnegan, a contributing editor to *Microsoft Systems Journal* (check out his absolutely brilliant articles, cited in the "For Further Reading" section at the end of this book) was the technical editor for this book. Jim's eagle eye and ready wit saved me from making a fool of myself in numerous places.

Geoff Chappell is largely responsible for my understanding of the inner workings of VMM and 32-bit file access. Paul Bonneau, Ron Burk, Tim Farley, Bill Lewis, David Markun, Klaus Mueller, Thomas Olsen, Walter Oney, Matt Pietrek, Brett Salter, Murray Sargent, Alex Shmidt, Mike Spilo, and Kelly Zytaruk all helped me through phone conversations and over email.

Geoff, Klaus, Tom, Alex, and Kelly provided me with huge amounts of material on VMM and VxDs, most of which unfortunately did not make it into *Unauthorized Windows 95*. Doug Boling wrote a wonderful second-generation version of the WINIO library, which also did not end up in this book. I promise, guys, that all this stuff *will* get into print!

Nu-Mega Software makes the incredible Soft-ICE/Windows debugger, which made this book possible.

My friend Chris Williams, Vice President and Publisher of IDG Programmers Press, came up with the title *Unauthorized Windows 95*, and often seems to have understood the point of this book better than I did.

Amy Pedersen was aggressively marketing this book long before I had written it. Thanks, Amy!

Teresa Frazier and Susan Pink transformed my chaotic manuscript into a readable, understandable book. I was very fortunate to have them on the *Unauthorized Windows 95* team.

Desktop publishing wizards Ronnie Bucci and Beth Roberts produced the entire book, including the screen shots and diagrams, and made corrections to corrections of corrections with good humor and accuracy.

Seth Maislin proofread the book, and Liz Cunningham compiled the index, both in record time. Thanks for your sharp eyes!

Kate Tolini made reservations, tracked down books, arranged couriers, and did all sorts of other essential things. By providing an emergency supply of samosas and pakoras, Berta Hyken kept me from complete spicy-food withdrawal.

Jon Erickson, my long-time editor, let me wriggle out of two months worth of my "Undocumented Corner" column in *Dr. Dobb's Journal*, and at the same time taught me Erickson's Second Law of the Conservation of Prose, thereby extending my life by the two articles I now owe him.

Larry Seltzer, Wendy Goldman Rohm, Stephen Manes, Paul Andrews, and John Markoff sometimes called me up for some background to articles they were writing — and I always got far more out of the conversation than they did.

Gene Landy of Shapiro, Israel, and Weiner (and author of the superb *Software Developer's and Marketer's Legal Companion*), Richard De Bodo of Irell and Manella, Dan Silver at the U.S. Federal Trade Commission, and Stuart Taylor of *The American Lawyer* all helped me try to understand U.S. antitrust and trade-practices law.

Ray Valdés, in addition to having taught me C programming in the mid-1980s, is a great friend, and his totally brilliant pieces in *Dr. Dobb's Developer's Update* are an inspiration.

Claudette Moore of the Moore Literary Agency put me together with IDG Books. Back when I was a lowly engineer at Lotus, Claudette got me started writing computer books.

My son, Matthew Jacob Schulman, had to put up with my absence for almost two months while I finished this book. Matthew, I'm sorry, and I promise I will never again be away for that long.

My wife, Amanda Susan Claiborne, during what was already a difficult time, had to be a single mom for two months. Thanks for that, for eleventh-hour revising of this preface, and for reminding me that there are more important things in life than VxDs.

Occidental, CA
October 23, 1994

INDUSTRY UPDATE

The Impact of Windows 95

> "If someone thinks we're not after Lotus and after WordPerfect and after Borland, they're confused. My job is to get a fair share of the software applications market, and to me that's 100 percent."
>
> — Mike Maples, senior vice president for applications, Microsoft (quoted in Jane Morrissey, "Microsoft applications unit seeks market dominance," *PC Week*, November 18, 1991).

In typical Microsoft fashion — like a very late gangbuster — Windows 95 is coming. When Microsoft chairman Bill Gates announced that the next version of Windows, codenamed "Chicago," would be about five months late, coming out probably in April, 1995, instead of December, 1994, Microsoft's stock immediately shot up almost three points.

Bill Gates announces the product will be late and the stock goes up? Yes, because Gates also declared that Chicago will be "more of a phenomenon than any new piece of systems software we or anyone else has ever done" (*New York Times*, July 23, 1994). That's all Wall Street needed to hear. Microsoft's Windows 3.0 announcement in May 1990 — sometimes called "the mother of all rollouts" — changed the face of the PC software industry. Microsoft spent about $2 million on the Windows 3.0 rollout; apparently it is planning a $40 million campaign for Windows 95. This is nothing compared to the potential billion dollars in revenues that Microsoft expects to make over a two-year period from Windows upgrades alone (Paul Andrews, "The Winds of Chicago," *Marketing Computers*, May 1994).

Windows 95 will have a tremendous impact on the PC software industry, and almost certainly will be more of a phenomenon than any previous piece of systems software. Yet the product's significance, and its likely impact on the industry, are somewhat different from what Microsoft portrays. Microsoft says that its Windows 95 product is a brand-new operating system that completely replaces MS-DOS and has been rewritten "from the ground up." But the fact is Windows applications running under Windows 95 will still end up using MS-DOS. Windows 95 is based on the same architecture as Windows 3.*x* Enhanced mode, which has been available since 1990 (we might as well call it Windows 90). From a technical perspective, Windows 95 is not a revolutionary product. It's just Windows 90+5.

Although the architecture of Windows 95 isn't brand new, the product will have a major impact on the PC software industry, similar to the impact Windows 3.0 had five years ago. Unlike Windows 3.0, though, Windows 95 doesn't need to be a revolutionary product. The industry's experience with both OS/2 and Windows NT is that, when offered an entirely new operating system, the overwhelming majority of PC users opt instead for the old devil they know: the combination of MS-DOS and Windows. The Windows 90 Enhanced mode architecture was a far more radical departure from the old real-mode DOS operating system than most of us realized at the time. It is okay for Windows 95 to keep it.

Microsoft also says that Windows 95 is "integrated." This isn't accurate either. Windows 95 isn't integrated; instead, it "just grew." Windows 95 does have many more features and capabilities than its predecessors, performing many tasks that until now required applications and utilities produced by vendors other than Microsoft. But there isn't much genuine integration at a technical level. It could very well turn out that the only integration we'll see with Windows 95 will be Microsoft's *vertical integration*, that is, the company's further expansion throughout the software industry.

In fact, this is occurring right now. The inclusion of more applications/utilities in Windows 95, the increasing ties between Microsoft Windows and Microsoft Office, the merger and acquisition fever that has taken hold of the PC software business, the limited U.S. Department of Justice (DOJ) antitrust settlement with Microsoft — these are all signs of a maturing industry; of the restructuring of an industry from one that once had hundreds, if not thousands, of firms of all sizes, to one with a small number of large firms.

The PC software industry is going through a shakeout and consolidation, similar to what happened in previous technology-based industries. For example, in the early 1920s, there were 75 automobile manufacturers in the U.S. alone. Today, there are a handful. Nothing makes the software industry immune from similar consolidation.

There is another aspect to this maturation of the PC software industry — the movement from a technology-based industry into a consumer product-based industry — and the very name Windows 95 suggests this product will play a leading role. If a Windows program queries the GetVersion function in Windows 95, it will get back 4.0 as the answer; a DOS program will get back the answer 7.0. Indeed, Windows 95 is Windows 4.0 plus MS-DOS 7.0. But in its marketing, Microsoft has decided to trade in the nerdy major.minor version-numbering scheme (version *x*.0 has always given the company trouble, anyway) for a new product-naming scheme based on that used by automobile manufacturers and vineyards. Windows 95 isn't foremost a technology or an operating system; it's a product. It is targeted not at developers or end-users but at consumers.

What does Microsoft Windows 95 mean to you as a participant in the PC software business?

If you are a software developer or entrepreneur, the brief answer is that Windows 95 should make you nervous (unless you work for Microsoft, or have invested in Microsoft stock, or both). At the very least, Windows 95 will change how you sell software and what sort of software you develop.

Windows users (I mean, consumers) should welcome Windows 95 as a big improvement over previous versions. But this is short-term; users too ought to worry about the long-term effect of Microsoft's growing dominance over the software industry. Windows 95 is a big step towards Microsoft's stated goal of supplying 100 percent of your software needs. Even if, as the Department of Justice (DOJ) apparently found, Microsoft is not in serious violation of the antitrust laws of the U.S., and even if the company's goal of owning 100 percent of the industry is merely what every other company in a similar position would want, nonetheless software developers and entrepreneurs ought to fully realize the special role that Microsoft plays in the software industry: Microsoft is not only the supplier of your operating system. It is also your competition.

The Ever-Expanding Operating System

Microsoft not only makes the Windows and MS-DOS operating systems upon which most of the world's commercial software runs, it also makes applications such as Microsoft Word, Excel, PowerPoint, Access, and Mail, which comprise the Microsoft Office suite. These compete directly with non-Microsoft applications such as 1-2-3, WordPerfect, Quattro Pro, and dBASE. The makers of these applications — companies such as Lotus, Novell, and Borland — worry whether Microsoft's ownership of the operating system (OS) gives its applications an advantage, and if so, whether that advantage is unfair.

However, this is just one part of the problem. Even the Microsoft Windows and MS-DOS operating systems themselves compete with the third-party applications and utilities that require them. At least since the incorporation of several major third-party utilities into MS-DOS 5.0 in June 1991, Microsoft has been putting features that once were the turf of vendors other than Microsoft into its operating systems. Windows 95 is the clearest expression of this trend.

In other words, Microsoft competes with its own customers. The Independent Software Vendors (ISVs) that make Windows applications and utilities are essentially customers of Microsoft. They depend on Microsoft for the tools and information necessary to write Windows software.

Microsoft intends to greatly expand Windows at the expense of the ISVs it is supposed to be assisting. Here are just a few of the features Microsoft is including in Windows 95:

- Networking
- InfoCenter universal in-box (electronic mail, fax)
- Explorer (a vastly improved shell)
- WordPad (a full-featured word processor)
- Microsoft Paint (a full-featured paint program)
- Hyperterminal (a full-featured telecommunications package)

The operating system is growing and the application domain is shrinking. Future operating systems will incorporate even more functionality that today we associate with applications such as word processors and databases.

Now, Bill Gates will never present his vision using the late Nikita Khrushchev's approach of banging his shoe on the podium and announcing to assembled ISVs, "We will bury you!" Instead, Gates will say, "look at all the work we are doing for you." In Microsoft's eyes, the expansion of the operating system does not entail the contraction of the application domain. Instead, by taking on more and more work, Microsoft's operating systems will let developers be innovative.

However, an impartial observer might instead interpret Microsoft's approach not so much as "look at all the work we are doing for you," but instead as "look at all the avenues we are closing for you."

The relationship between applications and the operating system need not be a zero-sum game, in which functionality taken on by one is necessarily lost to the other. And there's nothing particularly nefarious about Microsoft's goals to have Windows do more and more. I am sure that any one of us in Mr. Gates's position would similarly seek global domination, or at least total control of the software industry. Even so, understanding Microsoft's larger goals helps put Windows 95 in context.

The president of one important software company, while reading about all these new features in Microsoft's *"Chicago" Reviewer's Guide*, started to make a list of the companies he expected to go out of business shortly after Windows 95 ships. Okay, that's a bit melodramatic, but even staid *Business Week* states that Windows 95

> will do far more to shape the destiny of Microsoft and the computer industry than anything the trustbusters [in the U.S. Justice Dept.] could cook up....
>
> If makers of other operating systems have only a glimmer of hope, other software makers have next to none. With Chicago, Microsoft steps up its effort to build in more features that used to be sold separately —

> such as electronic-mail software. When Gates described Chicago's features to the Electronic Mail Assn., the mood was somber. "It was like a wake," says [Steven] Holdschild [director of developer relations] of Lotus, which sells cc:Mail. "A lot of people believe that when Chicago ships, the messaging industry as we know it is gone."
>
> — Amy Cortese, "Next Stop, Chicago," *Business Week,* August 1, 1994.

In an *InfoWorld* article titled, "ISVs: Wake up," (June 27, 1994), Windows 95 enthusiast Steve Gibson paints a similar picture of the impact Windows 95 will likely have on some Independent Software Vendors (ISVs):

> A system equipped with nothing more than Chicago can be used to perform really useful work right out of the box. Today I'm still using a trusty old DOS version of cc:Mail Remote, a crusty old version of Procomm for DOS, and Delrina Corp.'s excellent WinFax Pro software. None is hooked together or has any hooks into the operating system. Consequently, I'm forced to jump through hoops with these applications to do what Chicago will do with far more ease from day one.
>
> For the providers of yesterday's solutions, this should be a loud wakeup call. Product developers must begin taking Chicago seriously right now to determine how to best leverage their opportunities in this new area of Chicago. Those who don't, face sure and certain extinction."

Windows 95 is the loudest and clearest delivery of this wakeup call. The PC software industry is quickly reducing itself to just three major players: Microsoft, Novell, and Lotus. Back when Novell purchased WordPerfect, a writer for *PC Week* took a look around and saw that ISVs were feeling trapped in the PC software business and looking for escape routes:

> Novell's $1.5 billion deal brought into sharp reflief the trends that are remaking the software industry — and forcing many ISVs to perform death-defying feats of survival. Not only are the big players — Microsoft, Novell, and Lotus — bigger than they used to be, they have come to dominate the office productivity scene the way Ford, GM, and Chrysler once dominated the auto industry.... The object lesson: The PC software business is toast. "The business model from the past is unsustainable," says Roger McNamee, a money manager who specializes in technology investments.
>
> But take heart. Despite a continuing wave of consolidations, there are alternatives to just selling out....
>
> Have a word processor? Kill it. Instead of going up against the Big Three, modify the product into a pop-up notepad for sending messages on the Internet. Afraid of suites? Relax. Think of them as a platform for a host of symbiotic products. Being kicked around on the desktop? Look to the server. Utilities makers such as Symantec and McAffee

> Associates are — especially as Microsoft adds more and more functionality to the operating system.
>
> — Bill Snyder, "The Great Escape," *PC Week*, April 4, 1994.

The article goes on to note that Symantec's "core utility business is being undercut by the ever lengthening list of functions built into the OS."

Now, it's important to slightly qualify these fire-and-brimstone warnings of toast and wakeup calls. Most of the functionality Microsoft is putting into Windows 95 isn't built into the operating system. Bundled, yes. But built in or integrated? Not really. Microsoft has outsourced much of the work on these extra features to third parties. Many of Microsoft's bundled utilities are not as full-featured as the separate, commercially available products.

However, even if Windows 95 doesn't do everything that available third-party products can do, consider that most customers probably don't want full-featured products; something that does what they need and that comes ready to use with their machine, will do just fine. So if you were the maker of a fax, email, Internet, or communications package, even a stupendously good one, you would need to start worrying — and I mean lose-sleep worrying — about the inclusion of these capabilities in every copy of Windows 95.

Lessons from History: MS-DOS 5.0 and 6.0

If the PC software business as we know it is toast, Microsoft started slicing the bread (so to speak) back in June 1991, when it released MS-DOS 5.0. That version of DOS included 386 memory management, somewhat similar to what Quarterdeck and Qualitas had been selling as third-party add-ins to DOS, and a number of disk utilities that Microsoft "licensed" from Central Point Software (now part of Symantec). I put licensed in quotation marks because apparently all Central Point received in exchange for its software was a license from Microsoft allowing use of the DOS shell's "look and feel" (*Newsbytes*, June 12, 1991).

As an interesting commentary on the need for competition in the operating systems market, Microsoft produced MS-DOS 5.0 largely because Digital Research's DR-DOS 5.0 had been released in August 1990 and was doing quite well. DR-DOS 5.0 was being sold through normal retail channels, which Microsoft had never tried with MS-DOS. It is likely that, without competition from Digital Resarch, MS-DOS would have continued to stagnate (it had been years since the awful DOS 4.0 release). On the other hand, the MS-DOS 5.0 feature set, including the bundled memory manager and disk utilities, was borrowed wholesale from DR-DOS 5.0. So perhaps it is the late Digital Research that we should blame (or thank) for the initial expansion of the operating system.

It's interesting to examine the concerns expressed when MS-DOS 5.0 was released regarding the effect it would have on companies making memory managers, such as Quarterdeck. Let's go back in time and see how the then-impending DOS 5 looked. If you wonder why I'm dredging up this stuff, remember: Those who do not remember history are doomed to repeat it. There are many close parallels between the expected impact of Windows 95 and the known impact of MS-DOS 5.0. Let's see if we can learn something from history:

> As you read through what's new and great in DOS 5.0, you have to wonder what happens to the third-party utility makers who have made millions filling the gaps in DOS — companies such as Qualitas (386-MAX), Quarterdeck (QEMM-386), Symantec (The Norton Utilities), and Central Point Software (PC Tools), and others. The short-term answer is that they'll be hurt, some worse than others, but the smart utility designers have already upgraded their products to capitalize on the new features of DOS 5.0.... Symantec and Central Point may actually profit from the emergence of DOS 5.0....
>
> Makers of 386 memory managers will take a harder hit. DOS 5.0's EMM386.EXE memory manager won't do everything 386MAX or QEMM-386 will do, for example, swap out slow ROM for fast RAM to boost system performance or automatically optimize your system's configuration to take advantage of upper memory, but the truth is that it does the two most important things that these products do: load TSRs and drivers high and emulate LIM 4.0 expanded memory with extended memory. If you buy any 386 memory manager right now, you're paying good money just for incremental features, but like the utilities makers, the memory management vendors are currently enhancing their products to provide extra benefits.
>
> — Jeff Prosise, "DOS 5: what's in it for you?", *PC Magazine*, September 24, 1991.

Central Point has since been bought by Symantec. Meanwhile, Symantec lost $11.5M in sales in 1993.

As for memory-management vendors such as Quarterdeck and Qualitas, there were hopes that DOS 5 would help them by legitimizing the market for their products, as Paul Sherer noted at the time in *PC Week*:

> Memory-management software vendors facing imminent competition from Microsoft Corp.'s DOS 5.0 say they are confident that the new system's shortcomings will work to their advantage.
>
> DOS 5.0 fails to duplicate the automatic ability of existing memory products to move device drivers and memory-resident programs into upper memory and place them into optimal regions of memory, according to beta testers and the DOS 5.0 manual.
>
> Slated to be announced June 11, DOS 5.0 will perform these tasks only on a manual basis. However, it will improve on existing memory

> managers by loading portions of the operating system into the 64K-byte High Memory Area just above 1M byte, the beta testers said.
>
> Even though other vendors' products currently don't match this loading capability of DOS 5.0, vendors say DOS 5.0's capabilities will help expand the market for memory managers. It will also encourage users to piggyback DOS 5.0 with the existing programs.
>
> "DOS 5.0 legitimizes what we have been doing all along," said Mary Stanley, president of Qualitas Inc. in Bethesda, Md. More than a million people use Qualitas' memory-management technology, either through 386Max or OEM products, she said.
>
> "Our biggest issue all along has been market education. Microsoft [will] introduce people to this" technology, Stanley added....
>
> Existing vendors claim that once users get a taste of DOS 5.0, they will move to the more complete solutions offered by third parties.
>
> — Paul M. Sherer, "DOS 5.0 shortcoming may help memory-management vendors," *PC Week*, May 20, 1991.

Contrary to the rosy predictions in 1991, Quarterdeck is seriously hurting today. As another *PC Week* article (this one dated 1994) reports:

> After three successive quarters of declining sales and mounting losses, Quarterdeck Office Systems Inc. is undergoing drastic cost-cutting measures in hopes of returning to profitability.
>
> The cuts — which so far have resulted in the layoff two weeks ago of 25 percent of its U.S. work force, or 55 employees — also prompted the resignation of founder, President, and CEO Terry Myers.
>
> Analysts said Quarterdeck is in a precarious position, given the erosion of its flagship QEMM memory manager.
>
> "That market has dried up a lot," said Richard Davis, an analyst with Louis Nicoud Associates in San Francisco. Davis said he is not convinced that the company's Internet strategy [a Mosaic front-end and World-Wide Web server products] will be enough to turn it around.
>
> Overseeing the turnaround efforts is industry veteran King Lee, who joined Quarterdeck's board August 1 and is serving as interim chief operating officer. Lee pledged to get back to the basics and has already closed several of the company's offices, cutting $1 million from the quarterly U.S. run rate....
>
> Although Lee has had past success building, or rebuilding, utility companies such as Fifth Generation Systems Inc. and XTree Co. — both of which were later sold — Quarterdeck officials claimed no sell-off is planned.
>
> — Jane Morrissey, "Quarterdeck CEO resigns over drastic cost-cutting," *PC Week*, August 29, 1994.

It's not Microsoft's fault that Quarterdeck chose to spend several years working on its DESQview/X project. But at one time it looked like this was part of an intelligent strategy for competing with Microsoft. Back in 1991, *Forbes* ran a story on what it called Quarterdeck's "buggy whip marketing":

> Quarterdeck Office Systems, a little ($48 million sales) firm in Santa Monica, Calif., makes a living filling in gaps in the Microsoft product. Why does Microsoft leave room for this tiny competitor? How does Quarterdeck survive? The answers to these questions provide a case study in how little firms compete with big ones....
>
> Unfortunately for Quarterdeck, both DESQview and QEMM have been eclipsed by a competing Microsoft product....
>
> Obvious question: How is it that Quarterdeck is still able to sell its products at all? How is it that the firm's profit margin is a fat 23%? The answer is that [Quarterdeck founder Gary] Pope's programs work much better than Windows 3.0 with the older version of application programs. Windows 3.0, in contrast, works best with the latest versions of spreadsheets, word processors and other application programs, versions specifically made compatible with Windows.
>
> Thus, Quarterdeck is selling to users who are beefing up older computer systems rather than starting over with spanking new machines and applications. Quarterdeck sells new, improved buggy whips while the bigger firm busies itself with the much larger market for horseless carriages....
>
> Buggy whips are a nice niche for a while, but what do you do when the last customer has traded in his horse for a car? Quarterdeck is looking for other niches. Its next product, now in customer testing, allows PC users to run application programs created for Unix workstations while running MS-DOS programs in separate windows. Years hence, when DOS is passe and new machines all run on some new operating system, it's quite possible that Quarterdeck will still be selling this product. No doubt some entrepreneur out there is still selling replacement parts for the Model T, and making a decent living at it.
>
> — Julie Pitta, "Buggy whip marketing: tiny Quarterdeck sells enhancements to giant Microsoft's operating systems. How does it survive?," *Forbes*, November 25, 1991.

Let's now turn the clock forward to September 1992, when news of the forthcoming MS-DOS 6.0 (which would not be released until April 1993) was appearing in the computer trade press:

> Microsoft Corp. is once again using its operating system prowess to march into territory held by other software developers. This time the battleground is utilities.
>
> The upcoming DOS 6.0, due later this year or in early 1993, is expected to include anti-virus software, a more sophisticated backup program,

and a disk defragmenter for optimizing disk space and data compression, according to sources briefed on the upgrade.

These utilities are part and parcel of Microsoft's Windows strategy as well, sources said. All of this is part of a trend that began in June 1991 with the introduction of DOS 5.0, which is equipped with a built-in keystroke and macro editor, a DOS shell, a robust text editor, and backup and recovery tools.

Given the utility horsepower of today's — and tomorrow's — operating systems, many corporate sites are diminishing their reliance on third-party products in an effort to reduce costs.

If the level of utilities functionality in DOS 6.0 comes within 15 percent to 20 percent of that in third-party packages, "I'll use DOS 6.0 as my standard and make an exception for the handful of users who want full-featured utilities," said Bill Ramage, a systems architect in the San Francisco office of Bechtel Corp., an engineering and construction firm with 6,000 PCs worldwide.

"Frankly, it's free [in DOS 6.0]," Ramage said. "Also, I'd prefer to have the tighter integration of utilities in the operating system."

Ramage speaks from experience. Bechtel decided against standardizing on Quarterdeck Office Systems Inc.'s QEMM memory-management program last year simply because DOS 5.0 offered similar capabilities.

Microsoft officials, however, denied they are trying to overtake the utilities market, claiming the company doesn't want to be everything to everybody.

"We'll provide 80 percent [of utilities' capabilities]," said Brad Chase, general manager of MS-DOS for the Redmond, Wash., company. "There will be an opportunity for utility vendors to add value as well." ...

Companies like Stac Electronics and Qualitas Inc. have fared reasonably well with one principal utility, but many industry observers say that times are about to change.

"Clearly, the one-trick ponies are at risk," said Bernd Harzog, program director of personal computing for Gartner Group Inc., a market-research firm in Stamford, Conn. "System software will continue to include many things that today we think of as applications, and people in business on that fringe should be nimble ... and find new things to move upstream."

— Paula Rooney and Paul M. Sherer, "DOS 6.0 threatens utility developers; users, however stand to benefit," *PC Week*, September 14, 1992.

Sound familiar? True, Brad Chase's desire for 80 percent of the market sounds better than Mike Maples's desire for 100 percent, but otherwise the concerns surrounding the introduction of MS-DOS 6.0 — the OS is coming to include what formerly was application software, one-product companies are at risk, times are about to change — sound like a dress rehearsal for Windows 95.

So, what did happen to these vendors after the release of MS-DOS 6.0 in April 1993? Well, we've already seen that Central Point was bought up by Symantec, and that Symantec and Quarterdeck have been losing sales. As another example, Stac Electronics laid off 40 people, or 20 percent of its work force, in May 1993.

Many of the concerns surrounding Windows 95 have already been played out in MS-DOS 5.0 and 6.0. If these releases are any guide, there's a slim possibility that Windows 95 will "legitimize" the market for Windows email and fax software, for example, and that the next version (Windows 96?) will deliver a fairly serious blow. On the other hand, Microsoft appears to have learned a lot since the releases of MS-DOS 5.0 and Windows 3.0. At least they got that *x*.0 out of the product name. So Microsoft might get it right the first time and cause serious damage to other software companies (who, remember, are not only its competitors but also effectively its customers for the operating system) as soon as Windows 95 is released.

What Belongs in the Operating System?

Now, I'm not asking you to cry over the difficulties that will confront companies such as Symantec and Delrina as their core functionality is bundled for free with Windows 95. When Microsoft put disk compression into MS-DOS 6, leading to nearly immediate layoffs at Stac, the response of most developers (myself included) was "Heck, disk compression belongs in the OS. Stac had a nice ride for a while. Let them find another line of business." Them's the breaks.

Indeed, perhaps everything Microsoft is putting into Windows 95 and everything Mr. Gates wants to see in a future version of Windows really does belong in the OS. As word processors, databases, spreadsheets, and graphics packages all converge toward the same basic well-defined set of standard features, perhaps this software belongs in the OS either as bundled programs or as reusable components in the form of dynamic link libraries (DLLs). Does the world really need so many different word processors? How about C++ compilers? Telecommunications programs? Disk repair utilities? If you're an ISV, wouldn't the world be a better place if the functionality of your product were provided free with every copy of Windows 95?

If an ISV makes an application or utility product that it thinks most PC users should buy, then — almost by definition — it seems that product's functionality belongs as part of the OS. Just as a database should not include any duplicated data, likewise the software base ideally should not include any duplicated code. For any general-purpose application or utility that is widely used, it's probably only a matter of time before Microsoft considers putting that product or its functionality where it "belongs": in Windows. Windows supports general-purpose non-Microsoft applications in the same way that a rope can be said to support someone who will soon be hanged. Your product may be a Microsoft DLL just waiting to happen.

But one reason behind this expansion of Windows has to do with an early aberration of the PC software market. Microsoft's operating systems started out supplying users with the bare minimum necessary to use their PCs. A large third-party industry formed to fill the many holes Microsoft left in DOS and later in Windows. All sorts of programs, such as as shells, file managers, disk-repair programs, debuggers, and memory managers, that would on most other computers have simply been part of the OS from day one were on the PC sold as separate products by third-party vendors.

This aberration played a large part in the explosion of the PC market. As one example, competition over who could produce the best disk-compression software undoubtedly led to the production of better disk-compression software than would have occurred if it had simply been bundled with the OS from day one. The flipside is "you get what you pay for" — that if you don't pay for something, you probably won't get much either. Software bundled with the OS is likely to suffer from complacency. (Well, the software isn't, but you know I mean.) The high quality and low price of most PC software is largely due to the fact that it wasn't bundled with the operating system.

Thus, even if a piece of software "belongs" in the OS in some narrow technical sense, the economics of how to produce the best software most efficiently leads to a more complicated idea of where it belongs. The decision about whether a piece of software should be integrated (or at least bundled) into the OS, or instead handled by third-party vendors through the marketplace, is similar to a "make or buy?" decision. Just as "make or buy?" should not be answered according to some narrow technical criteria, similarly you should not jump to the conclusion that, say, disk compression, disk repair utilities, or even a command shell belongs in the OS.

For Microsoft, the question of whether something belongs in the OS is not an entirely technical issue, but also a business decision. Windows is sold as a retail product; Microsoft continuously needs major new features to display on the outside of the box. In addition, as we'll see later (in "Is Microsoft Office the Operating System?"), Microsoft is not above adding features to DOS and Windows that will make them into better platforms for the Microsoft Office applications suite.

So, for a variety of reasons, Microsoft now wants to bring a lot of extra functionality into Windows. This is understandable. At least in a purely technical sense (though, again, that's only part of the story), most of the features that Microsoft is putting into Windows 95 *do* belong there. But the incorporation of these features into the OS is bound to have a major impact on the software industry. Windows 95 is indeed a wake-up call.

Commenting on the utilities bundled with MS-DOS 6.0, *PC Magazine* (September 14, 1993) noted that, "by adding these utilities, Microsoft has clouded the definition of exactly what an operating system should be." If Microsoft's definition of the OS was clouded at the time of the DOS 6 announcement, certainly by the time Windows 95 is released there will be few doubts: Microsoft not only has a near-monopoly on the operating system but is also constantly expanding the definition of what belongs in the operating system. Maybe it's just 80 percent today, but ultimately Microsoft wants 100 percent of the market.

Some commentators see this outward expansion and the Department of Justice's seeming refusal to touch it as a good thing. For example, Stewart Alsop was quoted in the *New York Times* (July 18, 1994) as saying, "If you really care about improving the personal computer, you want Microsoft to take over all the pieces of the pie."

There is a certain logic in this. For example, one reason the Apple Macintosh was for so long much easier to use than a PC was that Apple had a closed architecture and completely dominated the market, guaranteeing that almost everything came from a single vendor. Monopoly has some clear benefits. In certain situations, such as public utilities, monopoly may be the only viable industry structure, leading to a so-called *natural monopoly.*

Speaking of which, the superb biography *Gates* by Stephen Manes and Paul Andrews (p. 202) quotes a 1981 statement by Microsoft chairman Bill Gates in which he noted that volume and standards in PC software can lead to a natural monopoly:

> Why do we need standards? ... It's only through volume that you can offer reasonable software at a low price. Standards increase the basic machine you can sell into....
>
> I really shouldn't say this, but in some ways it leads, in an individual product category, to a natural monopoly: where somebody properly documents, properly trains, properly promotes a particular package and through momentum, user loyalty, reputation, sales force, and prices builds a very strong position within that product.

Gates probably understood this connection between volume and quality earlier than anyone else in the PC software industry (which industry, of course, he largely defined in the first place). Still, it is worrisome to hear Gates speaking of monopoly even back in 1981. If the PC operating system is a natural monopoly, if Microsoft should take over all the pieces of an increasingly-valuable pie, remember that companies in such favored positions generally are forced to make an important tradeoff: So-called natural monopolies are generally regulated, are prevented from expanding their monopoly into new areas, and so on.

Microsoft already has MS-DOS installed on about 120 million PCs in the world and Windows on about 50 million. Having reached a very favorable antitrust settlement with the Department of Justice, Microsoft can move even more rapidly towards its goal of becoming an unregulated, non-public utility providing total one-stop shopping for all your software needs.

The Windows 95 Compatible Logo

It's long been observed that Microsoft keeps raising the stakes for staying in the software business. For example, a *New York Times* (December 14, 1992) article that started off, "Can anyone besides the Microsoft Corporation make money in software anymore?" (answer: yes, as long as you find a niche "in which Microsoft is not a player"), went on to quote one financial analyst's explanation for why he was not currently recommending any software stocks:

> User expectations for shrink-wrapped software are being reset very low in terms of price and very high in terms of functionality.... The problem is the marketing expense to get share of mind is so high, and Microsoft keeps raising the ante."

In Windows 95, Microsoft is quite literally raising the ante to stay in the Windows application development game. In what might be the first tentative steps towards a Nintendo-style certification program, Microsoft has published new guidelines on what applications must do to qualify for the *Windows 95 Compatible* logo on their product and ads. As spelled out in an article on "How to adapt an app for Chicago" (*Microsoft Developer Network News*, July 1994), the requirements are quite strict. There are too many to quote in full here, but some highlights follow:

- The application must be a Win32 executable.
- The program must run successfully on Windows NT 3.5 in addition to Windows 95.
- If the program deals with files, it must have OLE 2.0 support.
- If the program deals with files, it must be mail enabled, supporting at least a Send or Send Mail command on the File menu.

According to the manager of the Windows logo program at Microsoft, "we are raising the stakes by saying not only do these products [with the Windows 95 logo] work, but they create a valuable synergy with the operating system" *(InfoWorld*, August 29, 1994, p. 27). The question is, valuable for whom? Most of the requirements seem to have more to do with Microsoft's desires than with the potential end-user's. For example, although the Win32 application programming interface (API) is nice, many programs simply get larger when ported to use 32-bit code. The NT requirement seems like nothing more than an attempt to leverage Microsoft's control over the upcoming Windows 95 market to assist its lacklustre Windows NT product. The OLE 2.0 requirement is odd, given that Microsoft itself hasn't used OLE for the Windows 95 shell (see Chapter 2).

Microsoft is simply raising the cost of developing Windows applications, and not necessarily in ways that will benefit end-users.

Is Microsoft Office the Operating System?

Besides the expansion of Windows to include functionality that once was the domain of third-party applications, a similar trend is represented by the increasing integration between Microsoft Office and Microsoft Windows. Most PCs today come with not only MS-DOS and Windows but also Microsoft Office preinstalled on the hard disk. Office was the top-selling software package in 1993, with revenues just under $500 million, according to Dataquest; it outsold its closest competitor, Lotus SmartSuite, by 4 to 1 in 1993. In turn, Microsoft estimates that 50 percent of its revenue comes from Office (*InformationWeek,* June 27, 1994).

Microsoft Office seems more and more like part of Windows. Or is it the other way around? The Windows 95 user interface appears to borrow heavily from that of Microsoft Office:

> The Justice Department may not have seen a connection between the way Microsoft develops its operating systems and its applications, but Windows users will see a clear connection once Chicago makes it to market....Many of the changes in the user interface that Microsoft is pushing can already been seen in Office 6.0....
>
> One example of the changes in the operating system that were taken directly from Office is the use of the right mouse click as a property inspector....
>
> In the next version of windows, dialog boxes will resemble the tab-centric designs used in the Office suite.
>
> — Randall C. Kennedy, "Like Office? You'll Love Chicago!", *Windows Sources*, October 1994, pp. 23-24.

Windows 95 is not some nefarious Trojan horse for Microsoft Office. (One wild rumor had it that Microsoft was deliberately delaying Windows 95 to let the Windows apps division finish its next version of Office!) But in the past it has sometimes seemed as if Windows was just a platform for Microsoft Office.

Microsoft has even added features to DOS and Windows to make them into better platforms for the Microsoft Office applications suite. For example, during the *Stac v. Microsoft* trial, it came out that one of the main reasons Bill Gates urged the MS-DOS group to include disk compression was that, without it, Microsoft would have a harder time selling the disk-hungry Office suite. MS-DOS 6.0 needed disk compression not only to compete with DR-DOS 6.0 (which included disk compression) and not only to to have a nice starburst on the box saying "The easiest way to double your hard disk," but also to grease the skids (or at least the hard disks) for Microsoft Office.

As another example, Microsoft Windows much-hyped (but not necessarily very practical) Object Linking and Embedding (OLE) feature always seems to show up earlier in the components of Microsoft Office than in any non-Microsoft applications. Brian Livingston (*More Windows 3.1 Secrets*, p. 194) reports that Microsoft PowerPoint 2.0, which was shipping to customers in June 1990, included support for OLE — six months before OLE documentation was released to developers. On a broader scale, OLE appears to have been designed largely for the convenience of Microsoft Office.

With the Office Developers Kit (ODK) and Visual Basic for Appliations (VBA), Microsoft is encouraging developers to write Windows applications targeted specifically at Office. Of course, Lotus and Novell have similar programs to encourage applications targeted specifically at their suites. But given Office's market share — particularly the fact that it comes bundled together with Windows on most new PCs — Microsoft, unlike Lotus and Novell, has a good chance of convincing developers to view its suite as a major development platform.

Similar to the Windows 95 Compatible logo, Microsoft also has an Office Compatible logo. Paul Bonner, who has written extensively on customizing Windows, had some interesting observations about this:

> If you're living within a suite, and selecting applications and utilities based on how well they work with that suite, you can't even think of Windows as your operating environment anymore. The suite is your operating environment, meaning, among other things, that both you and your applications have to live by the suite's rules, not those of Windows....
>
> This year, Microsoft introduced the Office Compatible logo program. For a fee of $1,000, third-party vendors gain the right to adopt the look and feel of Office applications such as Word and Excel, including their toolbars and menu structures...
>
> There's only one catch: If your software application competes with any application or tool Microsoft itself offers, you aren't eligible to take part in the Office Compatible program.
>
> Maybe that's not surprising. The Microsoft Office and Office Compatible labels are, after all, the trademarked property of Microsoft Corp. The Office Compatible program lets participants use all kinds of copyrighted icons and toolbar designs, and all kinds of otherwise proprietary information about Office. Microsoft shouldn't have to extend those privileges to competitors' products, right?
>
> Wrong. Microsoft Office is not just another application, and Office Compatible programs are not simple add-ins. When Office compatibility becomes a checklist item for buyers, determines the look and feel of applications, and extends otherwise unavailable capabilities to them, then Microsoft Office becomes an operating system unto itself, complete with a proprietary application programming interface...

> Once you begin to think of Microsoft Office as an operating system, the Office Compatible program takes on a whole new light.... The non-competition clause in the Office Compatibility contract ensures that the only applications that will be available for use with Office will be those Microsoft wants to have available. That means only applications that complement Redmond's core applications, not any that compete with them....
>
> Microsoft will undoubtedly convince scores of independent developers and small software companies to produce Office Compatible applications, if only because of the marketing support it can offer.
>
> — Paul Bonner, "Will the real operating system please stand up?", *Computer Shopper*, October 1994.

A friend of mine who is president of a medium-sized software company keeps telling me, "Microsoft Office is now the operating system, and Visual Basic is its API." I think there's a large element of truth to this: Microsoft really is intent on grabbing a much larger share of the applications business, and Windows 95 is a key part of this strategy, so it follows that customizing Office will be a growth industry, in much the same way that customizing 1-2-3 and dBASE was once a major form of software development. An interesting question, which we'll take up later (see "Windows 95: Dangers and Opportunities"), is whether a viable software industry can be based on writing add-ins for Microsoft Office.

Microsoft and the Justice Department

Now, you may recall that Microsoft was under investigation for possible antitrust violations, first by the U.S. Federal Trade Commission (FTC) and then, when the FTC became hopelessly deadlocked, by the Antitrust Division of the U.S. Department of Justice (DOJ). You might have expected the trustbusters to in some way address Microsoft's increasing hold over an increasingly important industry. Well, they did address this: After what appears to have been a very thorough, aggressive, and expensive four-year investigation, the trustbusters ended up telling Microsoft to change a few minor practices. In essence, the U.S. government gave Microsoft the green light.

On July 15, 1994, Microsoft signed a consent decree with the Antitrust Division of the DOJ, ending a four-year government investigation into Microsoft's trade practices. At the same time, Microsoft signed a nearly identical settlement with the Directorate-General for Competition of the European Commission. The judgment lasts for 6 1/2 years in the United States, 4 1/2 years in Europe.

Microsoft agreed to immediately abandon several arrangements for licensing the MS-DOS and Windows operating systems to PC hardware vendors, and also agreed to halt some "unnecessarily restrictive" clauses in its non-disclosure agreements (NDAs) for the Chicago beta test. The consent decree explicitly excludes Windows NT.

The consent decree was first viewed as a victory for the DOJ and Microsoft's competitors. *The New York Times* (July 17) carried a front-page headline, "Microsoft's Grip on Software Loosened by Antitrust Deal," and crowed that "the pact could reshape the world of computing.... The accord could undermine Microsoft's near total control of the market for operating systems." *The Boston Globe's* headline was equally enthusiastic: "Microsoft accord to create competition in US, Europe."

Indeed, the consent decree sounds at first as if it should cramp Microsoft's style and lead to more competition in PC software. For years, Microsoft has provided PC hardware manufacturers (original equipment manufacturers, or OEMs) with per-processor licenses to MS-DOS and Windows, in which the vendor pays Microsoft based on the number of machines it think it will ship rather than the number of copies of DOS or Windows it actually uses. In 1993, such per-processor agreements accounted for about 60 percent of MS-DOS OEM sales, and 43 percent of Windows OEM sales.

According to the DOJ, "Microsoft's per processor contracts penalize OEMs, during the life of the contract, for installing a non-Microsoft operating system. OEMs that have signed per processor contracts with Microsoft are deterred from using competitive alternatives to Microsoft operating systems." The consent decree put an immediate stop to this practice, leading to the hope that non-Microsoft operating systems would now have a shot at the desktop.

But the morning after, nearly everyone realized that, in fact, the DOJ's abortion of *US v. Microsoft* was a victory for Microsoft. Directly contradicting the previous day's headline, a *New York Times* (July 18) news analysis by John Markoff spoke of "Microsoft's Barely Limited Future": "Rather than reining in the Microsoft Corporation, the consent decree ... frees the company to define the computer industry's ground rules through the rest of the decade."

In the first day of trading after the settlement, Wall Street made its statement on the consent decree: Microsoft stock rose $1.87, to $50.50. Rick Sherlund, an analyst for Goldman Sachs, stated that with the settlement, Microsoft "should dominate the market for desktop software for the next 10 years." Another frequently-quoted analyst, Richard Shaffer, announced that "The operating system wars are over — Microsoft is the winner.... Microsoft is the Standard Oil of its day."

Windows 95 needs to be viewed in the context of Microsoft's victory over the DOJ: Windows 95 and its successors will be the primary mechanism through which Microsoft exercises its control over the desktop and defines the industry's ground rules.

But how could a ban on an important Microsoft trade practice be viewed as cementing Microsoft's hold on the industry?

First, the change from per-processor to per-copy licensing probably comes several years too late. Anne Bingaman acknowledges this: "I wish it were five years ago. I know it's late" (*InfoWorld*, August 15, 1994, p. 46). Despite some brave words from IBM and Novell following the consent decree, it seems unlikely that the change will lead to a larger presence for OS/2. For its part, Novell almost immediately followed the DOJ settlement by ditching Novell DOS 7; this was in any case a smart move. As a spokesman for Compaq (which already offers OS/2 to its customers) noted, "Windows is the standard — not much will change."

More important, the consent decree doesn't address the key questions about Microsoft's role in the PC software industry. Companies such as Lotus and Borland that compete with Microsoft in the market for word processors, spreadsheets, and other applications have long asserted that Microsoft leverages its control of the operating system to unfairly benefit its applications — particularly Microsoft Office — at the expense of non-Microsoft applications and suites.

Microsoft continues to deny that it monopolozies the PC software industry. Nor has it admitted to any guilt by consenting to the court's final judgment. The consent is explicitly "without trial or adjudication of any issue of fact or law; and without this Final Judgment constituting any evidence or admission by any party with respect to any issue of fact or law."

Nonetheless, the PC software industry has been treated to some enjoyable denunciations of Microsoft trade practices from high government officials. After the signing of the consent decree, U.S. Attorney General Janet Reno said, "Microsoft's unfair contracting practices have denied other U.S. companies a fair chance to compete, deprived consumers of an effective choice among competing PC operating systems, and slowed innovation."

The Assistant Attorney General for Antitrust, Anne Bingaman, noted that "Microsoft is an American success story but there is no excuse for any company to try to cement its success through unlawful means, as Microsoft has done with its contracting practices."

"Microsoft has used its monopoly power, in effect, to levy a 'tax' on PC manufacturers who would otherwise like to offer an alternative system." said Bingaman. "As a result, the ability of rival operating systems to compete has been impeded, innovation has been slowed and consumer choices have been limited." According to a DOJ press release, Bingaman noted that Microsoft has maintained the price of its operating systems even while the price of other components has fallen dramatically, and that since 1988, Microsoft's share of the market has never dropped below 70 percent.

This is quite amazing: The chief U.S. trustbuster saying exactly what many in the PC software industry have said for several years: that there's a Microsoft "tax," and that Microsoft — despite the perception among consumers that its prices are low — has in essence engaged in price gouging.

But for all the pleasure many PC software developers might take in reading the accusations in the abortive *US v. Microsoft complaint*, the fact remains that the consent decree addresses only a narrow issue: OEM sales represent less than 25 percent of Microsoft revenue.

The complaint notes that "At least 50,000 applications now run on MS-DOS and over 5,000 have been written to run on Windows. Microsoft sells a variety of its own very successful and profitable applications." But that is all it has to say about applications!

The complaint also notes that "All versions of Windows released to date require the presence of an underlying operating system, either MS-DOS or a close substitute," but says nothing about alleged tying arrangements between Windows and MS-DOS (see *Undocumented DOS*, 2nd edition, pp. 3-18).

Similarly, the complaint mentions "critical information about the interfaces in the operating system that connect with applications — information which the ISVs need to write applications that run on the operating system." But the complaint doesn't address the charge that Microsoft unfairly withholds some of this critical information to try to give its own developers exclusive use of undocumented interfaces.

Now, it's not as if the DOJ was unaware of these issues. From my own meeting with DOJ attorneys Sam Miller, Don Russell, and Larry Frankel, I know that they were extremely interested in the issues surrounding undocumented interfaces. We spoke for several hours about possible remedies, including what they referred to as "mandatory interface disclosure."

Similarly, a Civil Investigative Demand I received from the DOJ requested "All correspondence, including electronic mail messages, to and from Microsoft Corporation... that discusses or relates to competition in the development or sale of personal computer operating systems or graphical user interfaces; the compatibility or incompatibility of any Microsoft product or any non-Microsoft product; or the disclosure or non-disclosure of information relating to software interfaces." I was able to supply them with some fascinating email from Microsoft VP Brad Silverberg. My favorite is Brad's explanation from October 1993 of why he must keep on expanding the Windows API: "Once Windows is frozen and no longer moving forward, it can easily be cloned and thus be reduced to a commodity. Microsoft doesn't want to be in the BIOS business."

The DOJ was well aware of, and quite interested in, the issues surrounding Microsoft's ownership of the vastly important DOS and Windows standards. Yet none of this is addressed in the consent decree, which ends up looking similar to what Microsoft probably could have received from the FTC a year earlier. Even Bill Gates, who apparently denounced even the mildest FTC and DOJ questions as "communistic" and "socialistic," had to admit that the final settlement was no big deal. After years of investigation, he says, "This is what they came up with."

Why did the DOJ settle for so little? How could they seemingly ignore the entreaties of so many PC software vendors?

One theory is that the Clinton administration views Microsoft as a "national treasure," and put pressure on DOJ to leave Microsoft alone. The press made much of a May 25 meeting between Bill Gates and Clinton's chief economic advisor, Robert Rubin. The date is significant because just one week later, Gates testified under oath before the DOJ. According to one anonymous source, Gates pointed out to Rubin that Microsoft is responsible for a substantial portion of U.S. software exports *(Information Week*, June 27, 1994).

But it's difficult to buy Clinton administration pressure as an explanation for the DOJ's limited settlement. Microsoft may be highly visible, but it simply isn't that important to the U.S. economy, at least when compared to companies such as IBM or GM that make tangible goods. Although software is a crucial part of the world economy, consider that even "giant" Microsoft has only about 15,000 employees. Its quarterly sales are about $1.25 billion, compared to $13.3 billion for IBM and even $2.5 billion for Apple.

What makes Microsoft different is that it has almost obscenely low costs. This is very nice for Microsoft, but it's hard to see what it does for the U.S. economy, especially when 45 percent of Microsoft's stock is owned by insiders. The DOJ could have made a moderately plausible case to the American public that Microsoft, far from being a "national treasure," is simply a grossly profitable monopolist, with few employees and few stockholders, that gives back little to the public.

Another explanation is that the DOJ feared a repeat of *US v. IBM*, which dragged on for thirteen years, only to be dropped as "without foundation." But while you could easily imagine lawyers for the DOJ not wanting to stake their careers on a losing battle, I wonder whether *US v. IBM* was such a complete washout, after all. Even though the case was eventually dropped, for years it had a serious effect on IBM.

According to a recent book on the fall of IBM and the rise of its one-time suppliers, Microsoft and Intel, it was the supposedly unsuccessful antitrust case that caused IBM to unbundle software from hardware. This opened the way for an independent software market, making room for software upstarts including a company called Microsoft:

> The 1969 suit has been expected for a long time, and IBM had already begun to unbundle the pricing of its systems, making it easier for other companies to sell comptible devices and software....
>
> Many of IBM's actions in the 1970s and 1980s, particularly its supine attitude toward small suppliers of PC components and software, can be explained as the reflexes ingrained by a decade in the courtroom's harsh glare....

> After a brief negotiation, [IBM] agreed that Gates would own the system and that they would pay him on a royalty basis, instead of with a lump sum. (Because of the still-pending antitrust action, IBM was wary of owning operating system software for fear of suits from software writers.)
>
> — Charles Ferguson and Charles Morris, *Computer Wars: The Fall of IBM and the Future of Global Technology*, 1993, pp. 10-11, 26.

In other words, Microsoft was a direct beneficiary of *US v. IBM*, and "the next Microsoft" could have been a beneficiary of a *US v. Microsoft* case. Well, it's too late for that now.

Ultimately, I think that the DOJ didn't push for more against Microsoft for the simple reason that it felt it couldn't win anything else. Responding to widespread criticism of the settlement as a DOJ sell-out, Anne Bingaman protests, "folks, we looked at every aspect of this. We brought the case that was there to bring." According to the DOJ, the Microsoft settlement was "everything we could have hoped for in a fully litigated case, and possibly more."

Unfortunately, this is probably true. Law, like politics, is an art of the possible. Although the settlement gives Microsoft's ever-expanding monopoly the green light, it's hard to see what the DOJ could have done differently. The DOJ's job is to enforce the antitrust laws, not to make industries more competitive — and the two are not the same thing.

What all this means is that the Microsoft practices studied by the DOJ but not covered in the settlement are either not illegal or (what is much the same thing) too difficult to prove illegal.

Microsoft must be feeling emboldened by the limited scope of the consent decree. The company should be able to go full-steam ahead with its plans to greatly expand the operating system's dimensions in Windows 95. Microsoft Office will increasingly seem like an essential part of Windows.

Windows 95: Dangers and Opportunities

Given that the DOJ apparently saw little wrong in Microsoft's role in the software industry, the company's hegemony is likely to last until some time in the next century. Windows 95 will be the platform and Win32 will probably be the API, in the same way that Windows 3.*x* was the platform and the API that defined the industry in the first half of the 1990s. Or Microsoft will be the platform and Visual Basic for Applications will be the API. Either way, Microsoft runs the show for at least the next five years.

Microsoft's goal is clear: Provide all general-purpose software for the desktop. Microsoft's strategy for attaining this goal is to keep moving functionality into

Windows and to keep pushing Microsoft Office as the "integrated" application layer for Microsoft Windows.

How should the rest of us deal with the changes in the PC software industry?

It is probably stating the obvious, but there is little point in trying to compete with Microsoft. Novell figured this out almost immediately after the DOJ settlement and decided to drop products and projects such as Novell DOS 7, OpenDoc, and AppWare that put it in direct competition with Microsoft.

Similarly, general-purpose applications and application suites look like a bad area to be in. Particularly because of its bundling with Windows on many new machines, Microsoft Office is rapidly becoming a quasi part of Windows itself. Even Lotus probably has little chance in this area. Microsoft Office is everywhere and everything.

So forget writing the next great word processor. After all, word processing is not really an application; preparing legal documents or quarterly sales reports is. A database is not really an application; the accounts payable/receivable system for a dental office is. In some ways, then, it is natural for one company — it happens to be Microsoft — to have a virtual monopoly on general-purpose horizontal-market programs, and for these programs to move into the operating system.

Perhaps there is still some room in graphics and personal finance software. Microsoft Money suffered a much-publicized defeat at the hands of Intuit's Quicken product, for example, and CorelDraw! is doing well.

What other PC software companies are doing well? Bill Gates, during a presentation he gave in late 1993, rattled off a list of small software companies that he felt represented the opportunities available to software vendors today:

Altamira	Composer image editor financed by AutoDesk; acquired recently by Microsoft
Caligar	TrueSpace 3-D illustration/modeling software
EJ Bilingual	EZ Japanese
Insoft	Communique teleconferencing
ShapeWare	Visio graphics software; Visio add-in for Microsoft Office
ReportSmith	Client/server report writer; acquired by Borland
Watermark	Providing image-enabled capabilities for Microsoft Exchange; image server for NT

The best bet is to find areas where Microsoft doesn't have a product and where there is a chance of a several-year window of opportunity before it does have a product. On the other hand, the only market I've ever heard that Microsoft didn't want to get into was pornographic screen savers and adult multimedia. As one company employee told me, "We looked carefully at adult software, and decided to leave that money on the table." It's difficult to think of any other area where Microsoft plans to leave money on the table.

As noted earlier, one big hope is that so-called "downsizing" will expand the market and produce new opportunities in the client/server market. Many in the computer industry view downsizing and reengineering the corporation as a direct product of advances in computing technology, and expect the PC industry to be a direct beneficiary of this corporate change. (For example, see the book *Client/Server Strategies: A Survival Guide for Corporate Reengineers* by Microsoft's director of enterprise-wide computing, David Vaskevitch.)

However, this might be extremely shortsighted. Reengineering the corporation stems not only from the rapidly dropping cost of PCs but at least as much from the long-term downturn in the U.S. economy. Downsizing is often just a euphemism for lay-offs and budget cuts — probably not a good long-term foundation for growth in the PC software industry. At any rate, it is far from obvious that replacing a mainframe with a network of PCs really saves a company money: one report claims that buying and installing a PC network accounts for less than ten percent of the system's total cost.

How about the home market? There has been an increase in computer and software purchases for the home. But unfortunately, the industry's excitement over the home market stems less from an actual rise in the number of families that have decided to computerize their recipes, stamp collections, and checkbooks, and more from wishful thinking and a desperate need for some fresh blood in the market.

But let's suppose that the home market does take off. Is this really the holy grail that the industry has sought? The profit margin on a home software product is very low. As one Microsoft speaker put it in a talk about marketing multimedia titles, the margin is so low that if you take a single tech-support call, your margin's gone. (His suggestion: Put phone numbers for every hardware vendor you can think of in big letters on the package; put your own phone number in as small a font as possible.) One can have tremendous successes in this area — look at the popularity of Doom — but this doesn't necessarily translate into profitability.

One last point about the home market: Microsoft is already there. As noted earlier, Microsoft Home is shipping one title per week. The company expects to have over thirty titles available (including the appropriately titled Microsoft Dangerous Creatures) before the 1994 holiday shopping season.

Enough about the general state of the industry. What are the business dangers and opportunities from Windows 95, and what is the proper response?

The dangers of Windows 95 should be fairly clear: The incorporation of many features in Windows 95 will make some current third-party products (and the third parties themselves) obsolete.

As for opportunities, it appears that Windows 95 will provide a large number of small opportunities.

First, there's the upgrade business. Many software vendors are expecting an increase in sales when Windows 95 is released and they can come out with a

Windows 95 upgrade of their product. Microsoft's delays in getting Windows 95 out the door have cost not only Microsoft but also many other vendors, whose revenue stream is stalled while customers wait for Windows 95 before purchasing any further Windows software. When Windows 95 is released, there will be a large spurt of pent-up demand.

Whether this will translate into profitability for anyone except Microsoft is less clear. Recall Roger McNamee's point quoted earlier that the upgrade business seems based on the Milo Minderbinder business model: Sell at a loss, but make it up on volume.

As always, another interesting area is plugging holes in the operating system. Several computer journalists have been extremely enthusiastic about the opportunities Windows 95 will provide in this area. For example, Jesse Berst says "For developers, Chicago is a city of golden opportunity" (*PC Week*, August 29, 1994):

> Even though the new interface will disappoint experienced users, it will be a dream come true to utility vendors. It gives them dozens of opportunities for extensions, improvements, and mini-utilities.

As one example of these opportunities, Berst mentions the need for a font-management utility. And in a later article ("Chicago's a great place to build products on," *PC Week*, September 5, 1994), Berst writes that "Chicago's biggest opportunity lies in computer telephony."

Maybe it's just me, but I don't see how computer telephony has yet to emerge from the "gee whiz, that's cool" fad phrase. If this unproven area is truly Windows 95's biggest basis on which to build products, the future is truly bleak.

As for utilities, Windows 95 certainly does present dozens of opportunities to extend the shell, improve the registry, and so on. But these are likely short-term opportunities (Microsoft will simply take over anything really vital in its next release). And in any case, you can't sustain a 1000- or even 50-person company on $79.95 utilities and add-ins. (Perhaps a 10-person company, though.)

The Virtual Device Driver (VxD) interfaces discussed in this book provide numerous ways to extend Windows 95. Perhaps some third-party vendor will see among the hundreds of VxD functions the ingredients for an important, profitable Windows extension that for some reason Microsoft won't jump into for a few years. The DOS extender business was like that: companies such as Phar Lap prospered because Microsoft for a variety of reasons didn't want to move MS-DOS into protected mode.

Steve Gibson provides an excellent example of the ways that existing utilities vendors will need to adapt to Windows 95. Following the discussion quoted earlier about how Chicago lets him "perform really useful work right out of the box," and how, "for the providers of yesterday's solutions, this should be a loud wakeup call," Gibson notes,

> This doesn't mean that opportunities for Chicago add-ons are gone. There is a wide variety of ways to hook things into Chicago. But opportunities have changed. Delrina, for example, recently announced a fax mailbox and store-and-forward services. Executives there must know that their sales of WinFax Pro will be impacted sharply by Chicago, so Delrina is evolving into a fax service provider, tapping into the features that every Chicago user will discover in their box.
>
> — Steve Gibson, "ISVs: Wake up," *InfoWorld*, June 27, 1994.

From a technical perspective, this sounds like exactly the right thing to do. My only question is whether providing add-ins to Windows 95 is really a sound basis for a company's existence. In an article quoted earlier, *PC Week* said that if you make a word processor, turn it into an Internet popup notepad. The article went on to point to Q+E and Shapeware as perfect examples of companies that have successfully turned their standalone products into components.

Indeed, there is a lot of excitement about component building in the software industry. Jon Udell has written some superb articles about this in *Byte* ("Visual Basic Custom Controls Meet OLE," March 1994, and "Componentware," May 1994). As Udell points out, one of the most interesting things about this development is that a true component industry came not from C++ or other object-oriented languages but from Visual Basic, of all things. Similar to what 1-2-3 and dBASE did in the 1980s, Visual Basic Custom Controls (VBXs) have spawned a subindustry of component builders. A survey of "VBX Controls as Software Components" in *PC Techniques* (October-November 1994) lists a number of companies who have made VBXes their business, including Crescent Software, Desaware, FarPoint Technologies, MicroHelp, and Sheridan.

This is indeed an exciting development. However, it's not yet proven what sort of business can be sustained on components, at least ones without license fees. Equally important, recall that what Microsoft giveth, Microsoft can take away. Because of deficiencies in the VBX architecture, Microsoft is promoting a new interface, OLE custom controls (OCX), which is incompatible with the old VBX interface. If VBX or OCX component building becomes a big business, don't expect Microsoft to stay out of it. Already, Visual Basic Professional Edition 3.0 includes a large number of third-party VBXs from Sheridan, Crescent, MicroHelp, and others.

As noted earlier, there are also some fascinating opportunities for customizing Microsoft Office, which effectively is the operating system for more and more users. Roger McNamee's *Upside* article on PC software economics spelled this out nicely:

> Most software executives view Microsoft as the meanest shark in the ocean. That is a mistake. Microsoft is no longer a shark. Microsoft is

> the ocean itself, in which all the other fish must live.... If I were an application software vendor, I would look upon Microsoft products as platforms on which to build my business. I think back to the business that Funk Software built on the 1-2-3 platform — or that the utilities vendors built around MS-DOS — and recognize that it is only a matter of time before entrepreneurs build businesses on top of Word, Excel and the other Microsoft products.
>
> — Roger McNamee, "Sobering Up," *Upside*, March 1993.

Recall that this also was the advice provided by *PC Week*: "Afraid of suites? Relax. Think of them as a platform for a host of symbiotic products." The idea of writing add-ins, macros, vertical-market products, and so on for application suites, primarily Microsoft Office, dovetails nicely with the current enthusiasm in business books for something called mass customization. (See, for example, William H. Davidow and Michael S. Malone, *The Virtual Corporation*, pp. 40-42, which discusses the ever-popular example of ASICs, application-specific integrated circuits.)

Again, however, it is not clear that viable companies can be built around the customization of mass-market products. As McNamee points out, 1-2-3 did spawn Funk Software. But the only large by-product of dBASE that I can think of is SBT, makers of accounting modules written in dBASE. Did HyperCard on the Mac spawn any big successes? It generated tons of software, but any major companies? Well, Ross Perot's EDS started off essentially in the customization business, so perhaps there's some hope.

Aside from these specifics, what larger lessons can be drawn from the past few years of life under Windows?

First, accept the fact that Microsoft runs the show. I've seen developers make business decisions, such as using Borland's OWL rather than Microsoft's MFC, simply because they dislike Microsoft. Then there's the company whose sole product was a CASE tool for AppWare; or companies whose products are based entirely around OpenDoc or OS/2. Unfortunately, this just doesn't make sense. It's okay to resent Microsoft, I suppose, but don't cut off your nose to spite your face.

Second, for the vast majority of us in the PC software business, it's important to realize that systems such as Windows 95 will be important and that systems such as Windows NT won't be. Evolutionary changes are much easier for the market to accept. For a revolutionary upset to be accepted, it must be an order of magnitude better than what it seeks to replace. Not 25 percent better or 33 percent better, but at least 10 times better. Otherwise, change had better be gradual, like Windows 95. Specifically, products such as NT and Daytona (NT 3.5), and perhaps even Cairo, speak to too small a niche to be interesting. And even the NT sales that do occur don't lead anywhere: Right now I'm running on a network with an NT server, but no software is likely to ever be bought for that server. It sits in a closet that no one touches for weeks at a time. This is not the sort of platform on which to base your fortunes.

Third, if you're choosing platforms for which to develop software, remember that what ultimately matters is not technical excellence but market penetration. The two rarely go hand-in-hand. This is not simply a matter of bowing to the foolish whims of the market, however: Market penetration leads to standardization, and standards have tangible benefits that are more important than the coolest technical feature. Yes, Windows 95 still uses MS-DOS; no, it's not a pure Win32 system; no, it's not particularly integrated; no, it hasn't been rewritten from the ground up; and yes, it is lacking some nice features found in Windows NT or OS/2. But none of these compromises will hurt Windows 95's chances for success and some will actually help make Windows 95 a success. Windows 95 will be the standard desktop computing platform for the next five years, and that by itself is worth far more than the coolest technology.

Chapter 1

Welcome to Windows 95

When you turn on a PC running MS-DOS version 6, possibly with the intention of running Windows 3.1, one of the first things you see on the screen is the message "Starting MS-DOS...".

When you turn on a PC running Windows 95, the message that greets you is "Starting Windows...".

This is a dramatic demonstration (well, as dramatic as a PC sign-on message can get) of how Microsoft wants you to think of Windows. Microsoft wants you to view Windows, not MS-DOS, as the operating system: you turn on your PC, and it tells you you're starting Windows.

One goal behind Windows 95 ("Chicago") is to turn the PC into a machine that no longer makes you wonder why you're not using a Macintosh (especially now that Apple's prices have come down far enough that the Mac competes in the same market as the PC). One of the stated missions for Windows 95 is to create what Microsoft calls a "no excuses" standard for PC hardware. Adrian King states hopefully in his *Inside Windows 95* (p. xxviii) that with Windows 95 "Apple Computer won't be able to run those Windows commercials any longer." He's referring, of course, to Apple's TV commercials portraying Windows as difficult to set up and use. This ad campaign apparently had a big impact on Microsoft, possibly even providing the impetus behind the so-called "Plug and Play" effort.

Many reviewers have been impressed with how close Windows 95 comes to this goal of turning the PC into a high-volume, low-price Windows appliance. In its August 1994 issue (p. 130), *PC World* stated:

> Starting a Chicago PC is like turning on a toaster: Just hit the button. Sure, you'll still see BIOS information and other machine-specific hieroglyphics scroll by, but far fewer than under Windows 3.1. And then, instead of pausing at the nasty old C> prompt, your PC will charge directly into Chicago's Desktop. At the bottom left, your eyes are immediately drawn to a button emblazoned with the Windows logo and the word Start. I say *drawn* because an arrow attached to a text message — "Click here to begin" — floats in from the right, gently bouncing off the Start button. This pervasive cuteness gets stale in a hurry, but new users will never be left wondering what to do next.

Indeed, the ability to boot seemingly seamlessly into Windows is impressive. So too, as Figure 1-1 shows, is the work that Microsoft has obviously put into the Windows 95 user interface. However, having used Windows 95 nearly full time since May 1994, I confess that I *still* envy my seven-year-old son Matthew's Macintosh Quadra 660 AV (a beautiful machine that cost less than $2,000 U.S.). Windows 95 won't turn the proletarian PC into a yuppie Mac. But Windows 95 definitely *will* improve the PC's longevity, health, image, and reputation. And the simple matter of booting right into Windows when you turn on the machine is obviously an important part of this effort to turn the PC into a computing appliance or at least make it seem like one.

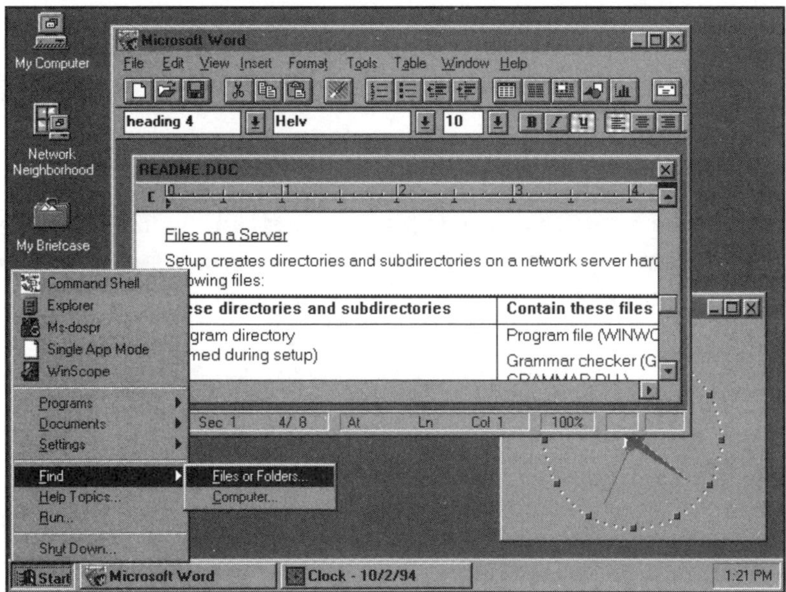

Figure 1-1: As seen from the Chicago shell, the Chicago user interface is substantially nicer than that in previous versions of Windows. Even old Windows applications, such as Microsoft Word 2.0 (shown here), look better in Chicago.

Now, what does this ability to boot right into Windows tell us about the architecture of Windows 95?

Even though you could make a PC appear to boot right into earlier versions of Windows merely by putting the command WIN as the last line of AUTOEXEC.BAT, Windows 95 must be doing a lot more than this. In fact, it appears that Windows is no longer stitched onto DOS with a batch file, but rather that Windows has replaced DOS entirely. After all, the machine doesn't say "Starting MS-DOS..." any more; almost from the moment it starts up, the machine now says "Starting Windows...".

The old "Starting MS-DOS..." message is produced by a hidden MS-DOS file called IO.SYS. IO.SYS and a second file called MSDOS.SYS form the kernel of the real-mode MS-DOS operating system:


```
C:\>dir *.sys /a:h

IO       SYS         40,566 09-30-93   6:20a
MSDOS    SYS         38,138 09-30-93   6:20a
```

As you see in the following annotated hex dump from the DOS DEBUG utility, the *startup record* (or *boot record*, as it's often referred to in books on the DOS file and disk system) occupies the first sector of the DOS bootable disk partition and contains code to load IO.SYS:

```
C:\WINDOWS>debug
-l 100 2 0 1            ;;; load drive C: sector 1 into address 100h
-d 100 300              ;;; now dump out address 100h
7431:0100  EB 3C 90 4D 53 44 4F 53-35 2E 30 00 02 10 01 00   .<.MSDOS5.0.....
...
7431:02E0  61 64 79 0D 0A 00 49 4F-20 20 20 20 20 20 53 59   ady...IO      SY
7431:02F0  53 4D 53 44 4F 53 20 20-20 53 59 53 00 00 55 AA   SMSDOS   SYS..U.
```

In Windows 95, the "Starting Windows..." message is produced by a file called WINBOOT.SYS, a much larger file that plays a role in Windows 95 similar to the one played by IO.SYS and MSDOS.SYS in earlier versions of MS-DOS:

```
C:\>dir *.sys /a:h

WINBOOT  SYS        288,030 06-10-94   4:22a
```

And, sure enough, the startup/boot record in Windows 95 looks for WINBOOT.SYS rather than for IO.SYS and MSDOS.SYS:

```
C:\Windows>debug
-l 100 2 0 1
-d 100 300
77AB:0100  EB 3C 90 4D 53 57 49 4E-34 2E 30 00 02 08 01 00   .<.MSWIN4.0.....
...
77AB:02F0  00 57 49 4E 42 4F 4F 54-20 53 59 53 00 00 55 AA   .WINBOOT SYS..U.
```

Notice that not only has WINBOOT.SYS replaced the hidden kernel files IO.SYS and MSDOS.SYS, but the OEM name (as Microsoft calls it) in the boot record has changed too, from "MSDOS5.0" to "MSWIN4.0". (See *Undocumented DOS*, 2d ed., pp. 408-411, for a fuller discussion of the boot record.)

These are just two examples of how, wherever you look in Chicago, the name DOS has been crossed off and the name Windows written in. This — along with the whole Windows 95 "look and feel" — has suitably impressed the computer trade press, as seen in its reaction to Beta-1 (May 1994) of Chicago:

> When you boot Chicago — without DOS, because it's a complete operating system in its own right — you see that you are dealing with a very different kind of Windows.
>
> — *Windows Magazine*, July 1994, pp. 184-185.

> Chicago bypasses DOS and runs completely in protected mode, although on startup it can stop briefly in real mode to process the now-optional CONFIG.SYS and AUTOEXEC.BAT for loading TSRs and old device drivers.
>
> — *PC/Computing*, July 1994, p. 60.

> First of all, there is no DOS hiding under Windows anymore. For the sake of compatibility with legacy applications, Chicago will read and respect CONFIG.SYS and AUTOEXEC.BAT files, but it doesn't require them.
>
> — Steve Gibson, *InfoWorld*, July 4, 1994, p. 45.

Whereas previous versions of Windows merely hid real-mode DOS, Windows 95 appears to abolish it. As the statements above indicate, in Windows 95 you don't need CONFIG.SYS or AUTOEXEC.BAT to run Windows. Windows 95 can automatically load all the files necessary to run Windows — not only WIN.COM, but also two DOS device drivers, HIMEM.SYS and IFSHLP.SYS — without any instruction from CONFIG.SYS or AUTOEXEC.BAT.

This is analogous to the introduction in MS-DOS 6.0 of the ability to silently and automatically "preload" DoubleSpace disk compression. All previous disk compression, such as Stacker, required assistance (sometimes a lot of assistance) from DOS initialization files. Similarly, until Windows 95, CONFIG.SYS and AUTOEXEC.BAT were needed to get Windows up and running. And just as DOS 6.0's undocumented preload interface (over which Microsoft and Stac Electronics got into an interesting court battle) made disk compression transparent, likewise Windows 95's ability to autoload HIMEM.SYS, IFSHLP.SYS, and WIN.COM makes Windows transparent. You turn on the PC, and it boots into Windows.

Bypassing COMMAND.COM...

If you have Windows 95, you can try out its ability to transparently boot Windows, even if you normally use a CONFIG.SYS or AUTOEXEC .BAT file, by pressing F5 for a moment when the machine starts. F5 initiates a so-called "fail safe" mode, in which WINBOOT.SYS ignores CONFIG.SYS and AUTOEXEC.BAT, and loads HIMEM.SYS, IFSHLP.SYS, and in some circumstances, SETVER.EXE and EMM386. EXE. WINBOOT.SYS then loads WIN.COM which, in Windows 95 just as in previous versions of Windows, loads the Windows Virtual Machine Manager (VMM) and Virtual Device Driver (VxD) layer, which in turn loads the Windows graphical user interface.

Of all the files loaded by WINBOOT.SYS, one well-known file is missing: the DOS command interpreter, COMMAND.COM. Indeed, WINBOOT.SYS only requires COMMAND.COM to process AUTOEXEC.BAT, so if you boot Windows 95 without an AUTOEXEC.BAT, WINBOOT.SYS will directly load Windows — without a copy of the DOS command interpreter sitting under it!

This feature is sufficiently important to make it worth confirming with a simple experiment. On a machine running Windows 95, if there's an AUTOEXEC.BAT file, temporarily rename it to something like AUTOEXEC.FOO. Whether or not there was one to begin with, create a dummy AUTOEXEC.BAT file with just one line, such as "ECHO Hello world!", and then reboot the machine. It's not strictly necessary for this experiment, but it makes a more forceful demonstration if you also temporarily rename the CONFIG.SYS file, if there is one, to something like CONFIG.FOO.

Once Windows is up and running, open a DOS box and run Microsoft's MEM utility. See Figure 1-2. (Notice, by the way, that the C:\> prompt in the DOS box has Windows with an initial cap, not WINDOWS. In addition to providing long filenames and directory names, the Windows 95 file system also preserves case.)

There's a lot going on here. First, if you've followed along and removed or renamed CONFIG.SYS, observe that we've booted Windows without providing any instructions on how to do so. WINBOOT.SYS (whose name, interestingly — and significantly — MEM reports as MSDOS) clearly took care of loading HIMEM.SYS, IFSHLP.SYS, and SETVER.EXE. Next, we see that COMMAND.COM was loaded into memory before WIN (and before vmm32, which we'll be discussing in detail in Chapter 2). There's another copy of COMMAND.COM loaded after WIN: this is the copy in the DOS box from which we ran the MEM utility. Finally, look at the amount of available memory: 592K.

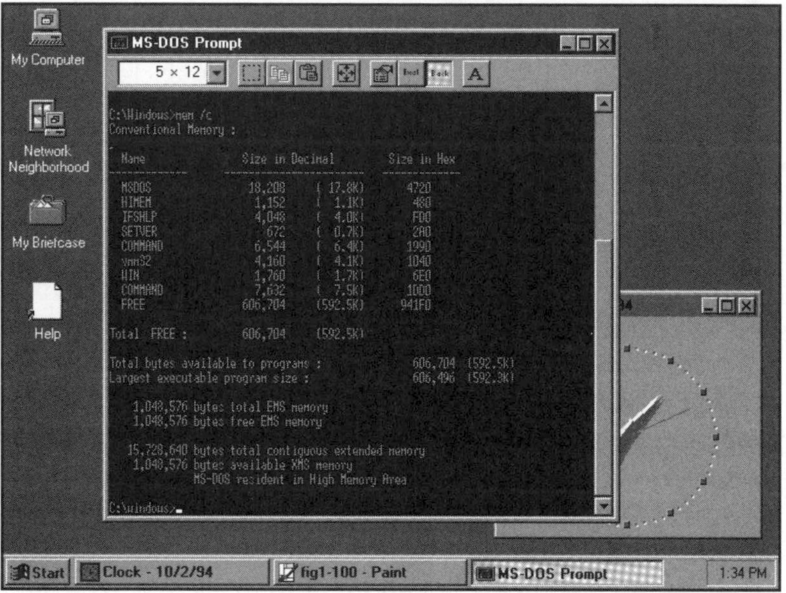

Figure 1-2: Running Microsoft's MEM utility in a DOS box under Windows 95 shows some of the DOS software used to boot Windows. There was an AUTOEXEC.BAT file in this configuration, so COMMAND.COM was loaded to process it.

Now, start Windows 95 without an AUTOEXEC.BAT file: delete the one-line AUTOEXEC.BAT file, boot with F5, or press F8 for "interactive boot," and answer Y to the question "Load Graphical User Interface?". When Windows 95 comes up, open a DOS box and run MEM /C again. The results are shown in Figure 1-3.

Note carefully what happened. By deleting the one-line dummy AUTOEXEC.BAT file, the first copy of COMMAND no longer appears: MEM shows that MSDOS loaded HIMEM, IFSHLP, and SETVER, and then started WIN, which loaded this vmm32 thing we'll look at in Chapter 2. Again, the copy of COMMAND loaded after WIN and vmm32 represents the DOS box from which we've run MEM /C. There's now 601K available DOS memory: another 9K of conventional memory.

So, eliminating AUTOEXEC.BAT gets rid of COMMAND.COM. But there's a problem with this little experiment: we had to open a DOS box and load a copy of COMMAND.COM just to run MEM /C. It's obviously confusing to load COMMAND.COM in order to run a test that tries to prove that Windows doesn't need COMMAND.COM. We could run MEM from a PIF file and thereby eliminate the need for COMMAND.COM. But you may suspect that the very act of opening an DOS box to run the test might still have some other effect that distorts the results we're seeing. It would be a lot better to have a *Windows* program that examines DOS memory, so we wouldn't have to open a DOS box.

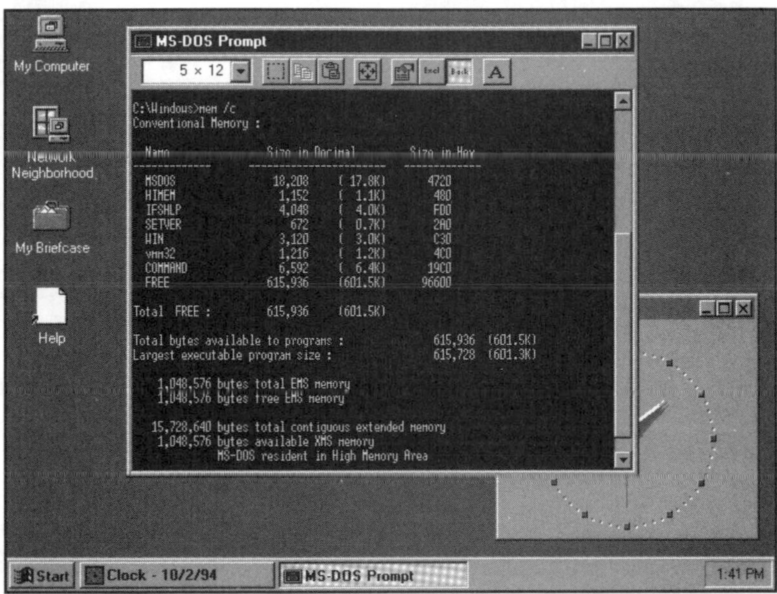

Figure 1-3: If AUTOEXEC.BAT is missing, Windows 95 can boot its graphical user interface without loading an initial copy of COMMAND.COM.

The WINPSP program from Chapter 13 is perfect for this. The PSP (Program Segment Prefix) is a real-mode DOS data structure; every running real-mode DOS program has a PSP, and the real-mode address of a program's PSP acts as its process identifier. At any given time in real-mode DOS there's a single *current* PSP, and DOS performs file I/O and memory allocation in the context of this current PSP: each file handle is stored in a Job File Table, a pointer to which is stored in the PSP, and each DOS memory block is stamped with the PSP of its owner.

WINPSP is a protected-mode Windows program that prints out some information about each PSP, such as its real-mode address and the name of its owner (see the WINPSP.C source code in Chapter 13 for a fuller explanation). Figure 1-4 shows output from WINPSP when Windows 95 has been booted with a dummy AUTOEXEC.BAT file; COMMAND.COM is plainly visible.

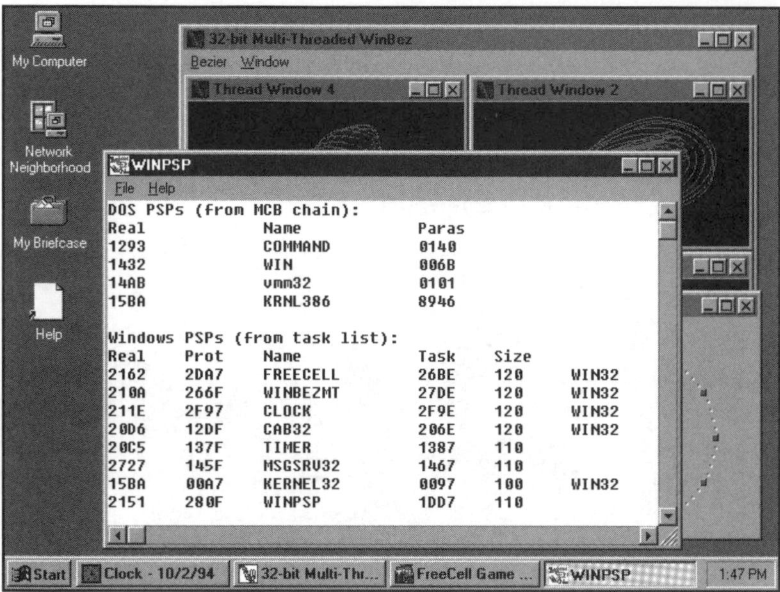

Figure 1-4: WINPSP, a 16-bit Windows program, reveals the DOS Program Segment Prefix (PSP) structures present in Windows 95. In this example, Windows 95 was booted with an AUTOEXEC.BAT file, so COMMAND.COM is present in memory.

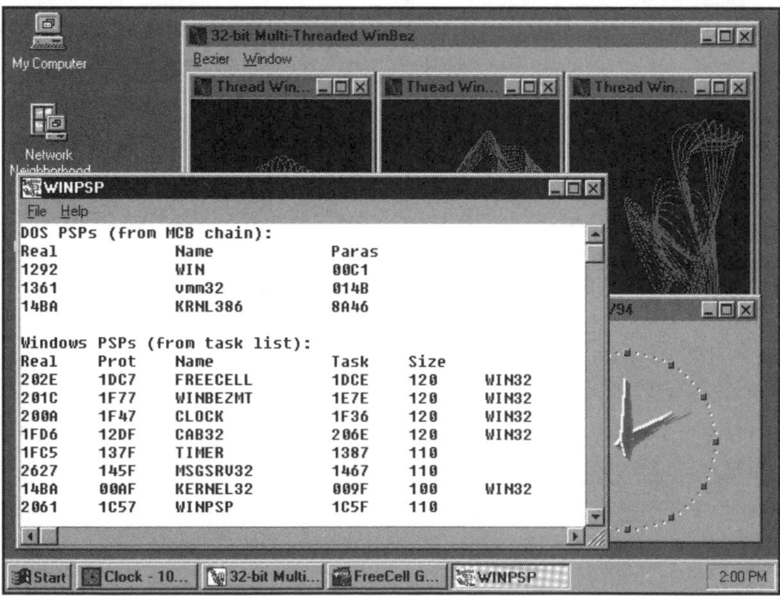

Figure 1-5: WINPSP again shows DOS PSPs on a Windows 95 system. This time, however, there was no AUTOEXEC.BAT, so COMMAND.COM was not needed to start Windows.

Figure 1-5 shows WINPSP output when there's no AUTOEXEC.BAT; COMMAND.COM is gone.

The Windows loader, WIN.COM, has replaced the DOS command interpreter, COMMAND.COM: whereas COMMAND.COM was loading in at address 05F7h, WIN is now loading in at the nearly identical address 05F9h.

This is great!

...But Bypassing DOS, Too?

Windows 95's capability to dispense with COMMAND.COM has been the source of much confusion. For example, one particularly ill-informed writer claimed, before Windows 95 was even in beta, that:

> If no real-mode DOS device drivers or TSRs have been loaded in CONFIG.SYS or AUTOEXEC.BAT, Windows 4 should be able to remove itself entirely from real-mode DOS, relying on the VMM/VxD operating system.
>
> — Andrew Schulman, *Dr. Dobb's Journal*, February 1994, p. 108.

Leaving aside the curiously inelegant phrase, "remove itself entirely from," and the way he hedged his bets with that word "should," this writer was obviously deeply confused. COMMAND.COM is *not* MS-DOS; it is merely the DOS command interpreter. If there's no AUTOEXEC.BAT file, Windows 95 can dispense with COMMAND.COM, but this hardly means that Windows 95 can dispense with real-mode DOS.

Even though it's well known that COMMAND.COM and the C:\> prompt are not synonymous with MS-DOS — you can replace them simply by naming some other program in the CONFIG.SYS SHELL= statement — many people who *do* know the difference between MS-DOS and COMMAND.COM nonetheless persist in viewing Windows 95's capability to bypass COMMAND.COM as somehow synonymous with bypassing the real-mode DOS code. For example, responding to a reader's letter that took exception to its July 1994 assertion that Windows 95 is "a complete operating system in its own right," *Windows Magazine* (October 1994, p. 20) offered the following substantiation for this assertion:

> Here's a test anyone with a Chicago beta system can perform: Rename your AUTOEXEC.BAT and CONFIG.SYS to AUTOEXEC.OLD and CONFIG.OLD; then shut down and restart Windows 95. It will boot back up — into Windows. You will see no command prompt.... That looks to me like a full-up operating system, not an "environment" that runs on top of such a system.

Windows 95's capability to boot right into Windows is certainly impressive. But because the C:\> prompt isn't part of the real-mode DOS kernel, this impressive feat tells us nothing about Windows 95's status as a "full-up operating system."

As a final example of this persistent confusion about Windows 95's relation to DOS, one reader of the draft manuscript for this book noted that "Chicago ships with MS-DOS 7.0, which apparently gets executed if the user has a CONFIG.SYS and/or an AUTOEXEC.BAT file (meaning that the user needs support for non-Chicago, DOS-based device drivers and TSRs)." Several hours of experimentation (and several beers) later, we discovered that Windows 95 *always* uses MS-DOS 7.0, and that it is nothing more (but also nothing less) than the use of COMMAND.COM that is conditional upon the presence of AUTOEXEC.BAT.

Windows 95's capability to bypass COMMAND.COM must, in part at least, be responsible for the popular notion that in the absence of any real-mode TSRs or device drivers, Windows 95 can "push" real-mode DOS off the machine. For example, on page 71 in his semi-official *Inside Windows 95*, Adrian King (former director of systems software products for Microsoft and a darned good writer) says:

> Windows 95 is subtly different from Windows 3.1 during this initialization phase. With Windows 3.1, it's up to the user to enter the *win* command and start the initialization of the Windows system. Windows 95 immediately gains control and switches to protected mode to complete the initialization process after loading — no *win* command is needed. In either case, when Windows switches to protected mode, it pushes the real mode code aside and takes control of the machine.

Other than the capability to skip COMMAND.COM, it's hard to know what "pushes the real mode code aside" means. But evidently this is also what computer journalists mean when they say (as we've seen earlier) that "Chicago bypasses DOS and runs completely in protected mode" or that "there is no DOS hiding under Windows anymore."

Certainly it's great not having Windows resting on top of COMMAND.COM. And booting Windows right out of WINBOOT.SYS (duh, that must be where the name comes from!) makes a big difference to a user's perception of their PC. But the idea that Windows 95 "pushes the real mode code aside," "bypasses DOS and runs completely in protected mode," or "should be able to remove itself entirely from real-mode DOS," has no foundation in any version of Chicago that has shipped to date and is extremely unlikely to have any foundation in the final shipping Windows 95 retail.

As I stated earlier, COMMAND.COM is *not* MS-DOS. It is merely the MS-DOS user interface, the provider of the familiar but contemptible C:\> prompt. Windows 95 makes it possible to run Windows without ever seeing a C:\> prompt. Great!

But does this mean, as Adrian King puts it in *Inside Windows 95* (p. 112), that in Windows 95 "if you run only Windows applications, you'll never execute any MS-DOS code" and that "Windows 95 finally breaks all ties with the real mode MS-DOS code"? No, it doesn't.

There are numerous ways to quickly see that Windows 95 neither pushes real-mode DOS aside, nor bypasses DOS, nor runs completely in protected mode, nor breaks all ties with the real-mode DOS code, nor removes itself entirely from real-mode DOS (whatever *that* was supposed to mean).

For example, as a quick test you can run the Microsoft MEM utility again, this time with the /D (debug) command-line option. The following was generated on a pure Windows 95 system, without CONFIG.SYS or AUTOEXEC.BAT. COMMAND.COM wasn't present either, because MEM was run from a Windows PIF file:

```
Address     Name        Size      Type
-------     --------    ------    ------
000000                  000400    Interrupt Vector
000400                  000100    ROM Communication Area
000500                  000200    DOS Communication Area

000700      IO          000360    System Data
            CON                     System Device Driver
            AUX                     System Device Driver
            PRN                     System Device Driver
            CLOCK$                  System Device Driver
            A: - C:                 System Device Driver
            COM1                    System Device Driver
            LPT1                    System Device Driver
            LPT2                    System Device Driver
            LPT3                    System Device Driver
            CONFIG$                 System Device Driver
            COM2                    System Device Driver
            COM3                    System Device Driver
            COM4                    System Device Driver

000A60      MSDOS       0014E0    System Data

001F40      IO          003F30    System Data
              HIMEM     000480     DEVICE=
                XMSXXXX0            Installed Device Driver
              IFSHLP    000FD0     DEVICE=
                IFS$HLP$            Installed Device Driver
              SETVER    0002A0     DEVICE=
```

```
                SETVERXX                   Installed Device Driver
                          000220
                          000130
                          000CC0        FILES=
                          000100        FCBS=
                          000200        BUFFERS=
                          0008F0        LASTDRIVE=
                          000BA0        STACKS=
005E80     MSDOS          000040      System Program

005ED0     WIN            0000A0      Environment
005F80     WIN            000B90      Program
006B20     vmm32          0000C0      Environment
006BF0     vmm32          000400      Program
007000     MEM            0000B0      Environment
0070C0     MEM            014550      Program
01B620     MSDOS          0839D0      -- Free --

   651,264 bytes total conventional memory
   651,264 bytes available to MS-DOS
   622,384 largest executable program size
```

On this purest of pure Windows 95 systems (well, except for the fact that in order to run MEM we've had to open a DOS box — but we'll get to that in a moment), MEM /D shows that not only has DOS *not* been pushed off the machine, but it can't even be said to be hanging on for dear life:

- MEM (and this is the version of Microsoft's MEM utility that comes with Windows 95) refers to "IO" and "MSDOS". WINBOOT.SYS is the old IO.SYS and MSDOS.SYS pasted together with some new code, a fancy ray-traced logo, and a new name. WINBOOT.SYS contains the real-mode DOS INT 21h handler. To a DOS program, Windows 95 is MS-DOS 7.0 (both INT 21h function 30h and function 3306h return 7).
- The usual DOS device drivers, such as CON, AUX, PRN, CLOCK$, and so on, are present. Running any sort of hex-dump or strings-dump utility on WINBOOT.SYS confirms that these device drivers are built into WINBOOT.SYS, just as in previous versions of DOS they were built into IO.SYS. There's also a new built-in DOS device, CONFIG$, which works with the Plug and Play configuration manager (the CONFIGMG VxD).
- IFSHLP.SYS is a real-mode DOS device driver *required* by the Windows 95 Installable File System Manager (IFSMgr) VxD, which is the foundation for 32-bit file access (32BFA), long filenames, and Windows 95's built-in networking support. Chapter 8 discusses IFSHLP.SYS in detail.

For now, just note that one of the most vital VxDs in Windows 95 absolutely depends on a real-mode DOS device driver: If IFSMgr cannot find IFSHLP.SYS, it fails with the error message "The Microsoft Installable File System (IFSMgr) cannot find the helper driver. Please ensure that IFSHLP.SYS has been installed."

- The MEM /D display for FILES=, LASTDRIVE=, and so on indicates that the traditional real-mode DOS data structures are present. A little snooping around with DEBUG showed, for example, that the DOS Current Directory Structure (CDS), whose size can be set with the LASTDRIVE= command, was located in this test at 049E:0000. And the real-mode DOS CDS was tracking the current directory. I know this because while I was using a Windows application to browse a folder on A: called "This is a long directory name on a floppy", I started a DOS box and used DEBUG to examine the CDS at 049E:0000. Sure enough, it reflected the current directory on A: at the time the DOS box was started:

```
-d 49e:0
  049E:0000  41 3A 5C 54 48 49 53 49-53 41 4C 00 00 00 00 00   A:\THISISAL
```

Of course, the real-mode DOS CDS doesn't know how to handle long directory (sorry, I mean *folder*) names, but at any rate the data structure is still present and in reasonably good working order.

But running MEM requires a DOS box; prehaps we're seeing real-mode because we're running a DOS application. However, if you've ever run Windows NT or OS/2, you know that you can have a DOS box, and the DOS INT 21h programming interface, without having real-mode DOS.

So maybe what we're seeing when we run MEM is just the illusion of real-mode DOS. After all, if you run MEM from a DOS box in Windows NT or OS/2, you'll see this kind of stuff, too! For example, here's MEM/D output from Windows NT 3.1:

```
Address     Name        Size      Type
-------     --------    ------    ------
000000                  000400    Interrupt Vector
000400                  000100    ROM Communication Area
000500                  000200    DOS Communication Area

000700      IO          000370    System Data
                CON                 System Device Driver
                AUX                 System Device Driver
                PRN                 System Device Driver
                CLOCK$              System Device Driver
                COM1                System Device Driver
                LPT1                System Device Driver
                LPT2                System Device Driver
```

```
                LPT3                        System Device Driver
                COM2                        System Device Driver
                COM3                        System Device Driver
                COM4                        System Device Driver

000A70      MSDOS         0015C0      System Data

002030      IO            001C90      System Data
              KBD         000C10       System Program
              HIMEM       0004E0       DEVICE=
                XMSXXXX0                Installed Device Driver
                          000200       FILES=
                          000090       FCBS=
                          0000E0       LASTDRIVE=
                          0007D0       STACKS=
003CD0      COMMAND       000950      Program
004630      MSDOS         000070      -- Free --
0046B0      COMMAND       000150      Environment
004810      MEM           000170      Environment
004990      MEM           017550      Program
01BEF0      MSDOS         0840F0      -- Free --
09FFF0      SYSTEM        028000      System Program

0C8000      MSDOS         000170      -- Free --
0C8180      MSCDEXNT      0001C0      Program
0C8350      REDIR         000A60      Program
0C8DC0      DOSX          008950      Program
0D1720      DOSX          000080      Data
0D17B0      MSDOS         00E830      -- Free --
0DFFF0      SYSTEM        008000      System Program

0E8000      IO            003620      System Data
              MOUSE       003610       System Program
0EB630      MSDOS         0049C0      -- Free --

  655360 bytes total conventional memory
  655360 bytes available to MS-DOS
  636496 largest executable program size

 1048576 bytes total contiguous extended memory
       0 bytes available contiguous extended memory
  925696 bytes available XMS memory
         MS-DOS resident in High Memory Area
```

It sure looks as if, here too, real-mode MS-DOS is present. Yet we *know* in the case of Windows NT that it's not. So maybe the same thing is true of Windows 95. Maybe Windows 95 is emulating DOS, just as NT and OS/2 do.

In the course of this book, we'll see that Windows 95 *does* emulate DOS to a large extent. But we'll also see that this emulation is neither complete nor new. To the large but incomplete extent that Windows 95 emulates rather than relies on the real-mode DOS code, exactly the same is true of Windows for Workgroups (WfW) 3.11 with 32-bit file access.

Even more significant than the strong similarities between Windows 95 and WfW 3.11 is the fact that the technology behind Windows 95's impressive (albeit partial) emulation of DOS goes all the way back to Windows 3.0 Enhanced mode, introduced in 1990 (we might as well call it Windows 90). Although 32-bit file access is the most visible manifestation of Windows' capability to emulate DOS, the seeds for 32-bit file access and Windows 95 were sown in a well-documented but little-known VMM service named Hook_V86_Int_Chain. This book will spend a lot of time looking at Hook_V86_Int_Chain and spinning out its implications. In 25 words or less, however, Hook_V86_Int_Chain is the chief means by which Microsoft is turning MS-DOS into a 32-bit protected-mode operating system. And this has been going on, under our noses, since the debut of Windows 90 — I mean, Windows 3.0 Enhanced mode.

Although Windows can emulate some DOS functions in protected mode, we still need to see whether or not Windows 95 rests on real-mode DOS. Let's close the DOS box and return to the WINPSP program shown earlier. This is a Win16 program. If "Windows 95 bypasses DOS" and "there is no DOS hiding under Windows anymore," this ought to be reflected in WINPSP's output. But it's not. I didn't say anything about it earlier, but when we used WINPSP to show that Windows 95 can run without COMMAND.COM, it also happened to show that all Windows programs running under Windows 95 have real-mode DOS PSPs:

```
Windows PSPs (from task list):
Real    Prot    Name            Task    Size
1314    1FFF    CAB32           2006    120     WIN32
12E1    12EF    TIMER           12F7    110
1943    13CF    MSGSRV32        13D7    110
1347    1E57    GROWSTUB        1E5F    110
07D7    00A7    KERNEL32        0097    100     WIN32
1379    2687    WINPSP          241F    110
```

It's particularly revealing that both a Win32 program like the Windows 95 Cabinet/Explorer (CAB32) and the Win32 kernel (KERNEL32) should have real-mode DOS PSPs. Microsoft says, "If you run only Windows applications, you'll never execute any MS-DOS code" — well, here we're running only Windows applications, but who do you think is creating those PSPs? We'll see in Chapter 13 that DOS is creating them, and that the Win16 KERNEL is asking DOS to create them by calling an undocumented DOS function, INT 21h function 55h (Create PSP).

This finding, though surprising at first, actually follows logically from other well-known aspects of the Windows 95 architecture:

- Microsoft has said quite explicitly that the windowing and messaging system in Windows 95, even for Win32 applications, uses the Win16 USER module: "Most of the code in the 32-bit User DLL is little more than a layer that accepts 32-bit API calls and hands them to its 16-bit counterpart for processing" (King, *Inside Windows 95*, p. 148). All WM_XXX messages, even those intended for Win32 applications, are first processed in the Win16 USER module.
- The Win16 USER messaging system in turn depends on a Win16 KERNEL data structure called the Task Database (TDB). For example, the TDB contains a pointer to the application message queue (see *Undocumented Windows*, pp. 379-385). Even the most cursory examination of Windows 95 shows that every process — including every Win32 process — has an associated Win16 TDB.
- The TDB, in turn, depends on the DOS PSP. In his book *Windows Internals* (pp. 254-256), Matt Pietrek shows that the CreateTask function in the Win16 KERNEL calls an internal BuildPDB function, which in turn calls INT 21h function 55h. (PDB, meaning Process Data Block, is another name for PSP.)

Put these three points together, and it makes perfect sense that Windows 95 depends on the DOS INT 21h interface for PSP management if for nothing else, and that this has nothing to do with whether or not you run any DOS programs.

However, just because Windows 95 is making an INT 21h call does *not* necessarily mean that Windows 95 is calling the real-mode DOS code. You need to get used to the fact that in Windows, an INT 21h call — even one coming from a real-mode DOS program, device driver, or TSR — isn't necessarily handled by the real-mode DOS code. Just because KERNEL's task-creation routine calls INT 21h function 55h, it doesn't necessarily mean that KERNEL calls down to the real-mode DOS code.

There are two reasons why INT 21h ain't necessarily real-mode DOS:

- Windows runs the real-mode DOS code in Virtual-8086 (V86) mode. This is not a pedantic point. As seen in Chapter 9, V86 mode is hardly at all like real mode. In fact, it more closely resembles 1MB protected mode. The best way to wrap your mind around Windows' relationship to DOS is to keep telling yourself that Windows runs the real-mode DOS code in protected mode. Chapter 10 explains this admittedly bizarre notion in detail.
- Windows avoids sending most INT 21h calls down to the real-mode DOS code (which, as just mentioned, Windows is effectively running

in protected mode), because these calls — whether coming from a DOS program running in a DOS box, or from some piece of DOS software loaded before Windows, or from a Windows application — are handled by VxDs. As noted earlier, the Hook_V86_Int_Chain service provided by VMM, and used by VxDs, is the basis for 32-bit protected-mode emulation of the DOS interface. This book spends a lot of time looking at the far-reaching implications of Hook_V86_Int_Chain and of another VMM service, Set_PM_Int_Vector. These services let a variety of VxDs — the most important being IFSMgr — keep most INT 21h calls away from the real-mode DOS code.

You'll see throughout this book that the DOS PSP management services, including functions 50h (Set PSP), 51h and 62h (Get PSP), and 55h (Create PSP), are *not* among those INT 21h services that the Windows 95 VxDs currently emulate in protected mode. A third-party vendor could write a VxD, using VMM services that have been available and documented since 1990, that does handle these calls entirely in protected mode. It's interesting to ponder whether such an imaginary PSP.VXD, while further cutting Windows 95 off from the real-mode DOS code base, would really qualitatively change the nature of Windows 95.

At any rate, every time you start up an application in Windows, be it a DOS program, a Win16 program, or even the newest Win32 application, Windows asks DOS (in the case of Win32, via a complicated process discussed in detail in Chapter 13) to create a PSP.

I don't see anything wrong with this reliance on DOS (incidentally, PSP management is just one example of this reliance). But the very idea that Windows 95 does rely on DOS is so different from what both Microsoft and the trade press have been saying about Windows 95 that you surely must doubt that it's true.

Well, let's see. Perhaps the WINPSP output shown a few moments ago reflects some sort of DOS emulation layer. We've already seen that the MEM utility, when run under Windows NT, produces results fairly similar to those that MEM produces when run under Windows 95. Yet we know for a fact that Windows NT doesn't rest atop DOS. So what happens if we run WINPSP on Windows NT? Perhaps every process in NT is trotted out with some sort of fake PSP, and the same thing is true of Windows 95. Well, here is output from WINPSP running on a heavily used Windows NT 3.1 server:

```
DOS PSPs (from MCB chain):
Real            Name            Paras
05B2            COMMAND         0095
067E            KRNL386         9981
```

```
Windows PSPs (from task list):
Real     Prot     Name             Task    Size
139F     0B57     WINPSP           0B1F    220
1D95     03B7     WOWEXEC          03AF    220
```

Yes, a few Win16 tasks in NT do have DOS PSPs. But meanwhile, running Microsoft's PSTAT utility from the Win32 NT SDK shows that over thirty different processes are running, including CSRSS (Client Server Runtime Subsystem, which services window and graphics requests), LMSVCS (redirector), SFMSVC (File Server for Macintosh), SFMPRINT (Print Server for Macintosh), MSGSVC (Messenger), NETDDE, and RASMAN (Remote Access Connection Manager):


```
C:\WINNT>pstat | find "pid"
pid:  0 pri: 0 (null)
pid:  7 pri: 8 (null)
pid: 1c pri:11 SMSS.EXE
pid: 14 pri:13 CSRSS.EXE
pid:  d pri:13 WINLOGON.EXE
pid: 46 pri:13 SCREG.EXE
pid: 41 pri:10 LSASS.EXE
pid: 3f pri: 7 SPOOLSS.EXE
pid: 2f pri: 7 EVENTLOG.EXE
pid: 68 pri: 7 LMSVCS.EXE
pid: 63 pri: 7 NETDDE.EXE
pid: 5b pri: 8 (null)
pid: 71 pri: 7 CLIPSRV.EXE
pid: 6c pri: 7 SFMSVC.EXE
pid: a5 pri: 7 SFMPRINT.EXE
pid: a3 pri: 8 (null)
pid: 97 pri: 7 MSGSVC.EXE
pid: 93 pri: 7 RASMAN.EXE
pid: 90 pri: 7 ATSVC.EXE
pid: 8c pri: 7 UPS.EXE
pid: c8 pri: 7 RASSRV.EXE
pid: b5 pri:13 NDDEAGNT.EXE
pid: ad pri:13 PROGMAN.EXE
pid: ab pri: 7 NTVDM.EXE
pid: e3 pri: 7 PRINTMAN.EXE
pid: b1 pri:24 OS2SRV.EXE
pid: 82 pri: 8 OS2SS.EXE
pid: b7 pri: 7 CMD.EXE
pid: cd pri: 7 NTBACKUP.EXE
pid: 35 pri: 7 WINFILE.EXE
pid:105 pri: 7 CMD.EXE
pid: d4 pri: 7 PSTAT.EXE
```

None of these services showed up in WINPSP. Well, why would they? Why would Win32 services in the NT operating system require real-mode DOS PSPs? Obviously, they don't. Equally obvious, I hope, Win32 processes in Windows 95 *do* require real-mode DOS PSPs.

What we're left with, then, is that Windows 95 can dispense with COMMAND.COM, purveyor of the nasty C:\> prompt. This is terrific. A Windows 95 machine can boot right into Windows without a CONFIG.SYS or AUTOEXEC.BAT. Fantastic! But is this what everyone means when they say that Windows 95 "doesn't require DOS"? It would appear so.

We'll soon see that WINBOOT.SYS contains the old real-mode DOS code, and that Windows 95 calls down to this code quite frequently (albeit in V86 mode which, you'll recall, you need to keep telling yourself is really protected mode). Now, the VxD layer in Windows 95 *does* handle most INT 21h calls entirely in 32-bit protected mode, without calling DOS. This, too, deserves two and possibly even three cheers. But 32-bit file access in WfW 3.11 did the same thing and met with considerably less fanfire than Windows 95. In fact we'll see in Chapter 8 that the trade press generally *complained* that WfW 3.11's "bypassing DOS" for 32BFA was some sort of *bug* that caused all sorts of DOS compatibility problems.

So what could the "Windows 95 completely bypasses DOS" claim possibly mean?

Perhaps it simply refers to the *packaging* of Windows 95. For example, the *Microsoft Windows "Chicago" Reviewer's Guide* (p. 275) says "Chicago will be a complete, integrated protect-mode operating system that does not require or use a separate version of MS-DOS." Note Microsoft *doesn't* say that Chicago will not require or use DOS. Microsoft says Chicago won't require or use a *separate* version of MS-DOS. Perhaps Microsoft is just telling us that all the functionality formerly associated with MS-DOS will now be brought out under the Windows brand name. If everything formerly thought to be part of MS-DOS is by executive fiat now part of Windows, then the "you'll never execute any MS-DOS code" claim makes sense, I suppose.

Why Bother Refuting Microsoft's Claims?

I hadn't intended to spend so long here looking at DOS PSP usage in Windows 95. This is just one part of the Windows 95 architecture. However, the contrast between Windows 95's true relationship with DOS and Microsoft's claims that Windows 95 bypasses DOS is representative of Microsoft's more general claims about Windows 95. For example, Microsoft also asserts that the Win32 kernel, KERNEL32.DLL, "is completely independent of its

16-bit ally. There is some communication from the 16-bit side to the 32-bit side, but the 32-bit Kernel never calls across to the 16-bit side" (*Inside Windows 95*, p. 148). As with the assertions regarding Windows 95's independence from DOS, this one regarding KERNEL32's independence from the Win16 kernel (KRNL386.EXE) is quite far from the truth.

The point here is not to poke holes in Microsoft's claims for Windows 95. Few adults expect "truth in advertising," even when this advertising is packaged as technical documentation, architectural descriptions, or industry white papers. It would be pointless to expect readers to wade through a 500 page refutation of Microsoft's marketing hype and its reflection in the computer trade press.

Instead, by taking a good hard look at just a few of these claims, which we'll visit and revisit from several different angles throughout this book, we'll get a good idea of how Windows 95 works, and how it's different from and similar to previous versions of Windows and MS-DOS.

An in-depth examination of a few selected aspects of Windows 95 — particularly the relationship of Windows to DOS, and of the Win32 kernel to the Win16 kernel — will illuminate many aspects of the product, such as Windows' poorly-understood VMM/VxD layer, the Win32 API, thunking, 32-bit file access, executable loading, and memory-mapped files.

If we ask just a few very specific (maybe even overly specific) hard questions about Windows 95, perhaps in the end some sort of architectural overview will emerge. It might not be as ordered or coherent as Microsoft's architectural overview, but it might have the benefit of accuracy.

Those Ubiquitous Microsoft Diagrams

Such a focused examination is a good alternative to the usual look at Microsoft-supplied architectural diagrams, which have an unfortunate tendency to induce either sleep or a state known as MEGO ("my eyes glazeth over").

At the same time, I guess we'd better take a moment to look at two of these diagrams. I'm sure you've already seen them or something like them because they appear, more or less as stamped-out boilerplate, in nearly every computer magazine article on Windows 95. However, it's worth actually *examining* and pondering these diagrams for a few moments because the tendency of most people (certainly, my tendency) on encountering one of them in a magazine is to just let the soothing waves of technological bliss induced by those arrows and boxes wash over you. Such diagrams, in other words, are largely a "feel good" exercise, meant to induce a feeling that the software has been *designed* — as opposed to what is more likely, that the software "just grew."

Figure 1-6 shows the first Microsoft diagram. This diagram seems to be appearing everywhere, like some software-engineering form of kudzu. (The same diagram appears verbatim in *Windows Magazine*, July 1994, p. 187; with a prettier presentation but the same content in *PC Magazine*, April 12, 1994, p. 193; and with a very pretty presentation but the same content in *PC World*, August 1994, p. 134.)

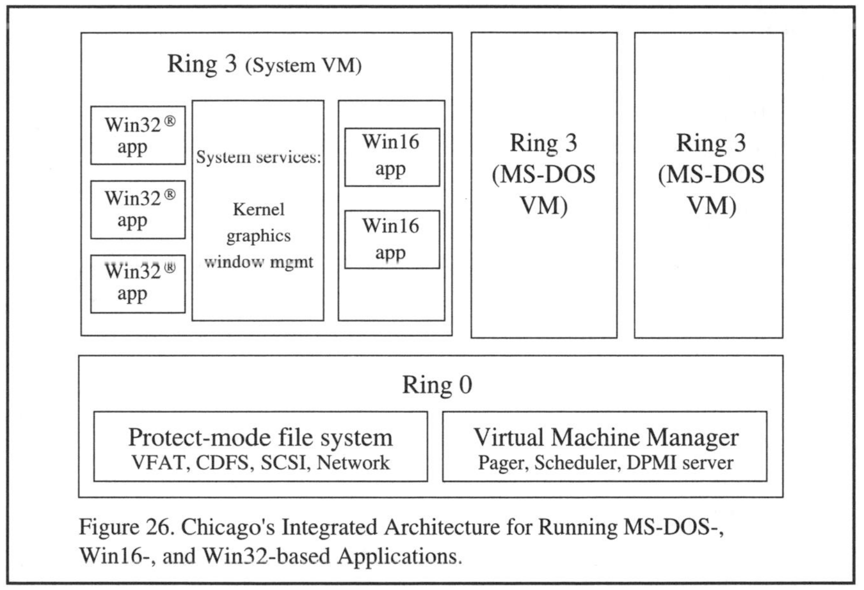

Figure 1-6: Microsoft's boilerplate diagram of the Windows 95 architecture.

Now, Microsoft's own caption for this diagram is a little different from the one I've supplied. One place this diagram appears is in the *Microsoft Windows "Chicago" Reviewer's Guide* (May 1994), a compelling and well-written 300-page document Microsoft has made publicly available (and, quite deliberately, without any copyright notice, which means that in the next six months we should see about 20 books published containing a largely-recycled regurgitation of Microsoft's *Windows "Chicago" Reviewer's Guide*). There, Microsoft's caption (p. 59) is "Chicago's Integrated Architecture for Running MS-DOS-, Win16-, and Win32-based Applications."

We're going to have to come back to this "integrated" phrase, because it's a tremendously important part of the hype surrounding — sorry, I mean technical documentation regarding — Windows 95.

In the meantime, there's one very noticeable feature of this diagram: MS-DOS is missing. Now, the diagram does show two DOS boxes, but I'm referring to MS-DOS itself, or, if you prefer, WINBOOT.SYS. Where is it? I hope Microsoft (and those who recycle its artwork) isn't suggesting that WINBOOT is *just* for booting Windows (200K is a *lot* of bootstrap code), and that it somehow drops out of sight (or perhaps is pushed aside) when Windows starts up. I hope the output from MEM presented earlier showed that the real-mode WINBOOT.SYS code (which Microsoft's own MEM program persists in calling IO and MS-DOS) is still in memory while Windows is running. So where's WINBOOT in the diagram? Similarly, where's IFSHLP.SYS (which, as noted earlier, is a real-mode DOS device driver that is *required* by the IFSMgr)? These important V86-mode components are conveniently absent from Microsoft's architectural diagram.

Of course, a diagram is an abstraction. It cannot, and should not, show every detail. A lot of other things are also missing from this diagram: at Ring 0, there's no mention of the crucial hardware-related VxDs such as VPICD, VDMAD, VKD, VDD, VMD, and VTD (that's Virtual Programmable Interrupt Control Device, Virtual Direct Memory Access Device, Virtual Keyboard Device, Virtual Display Device, Virtual Mouse Device, and Virtual Timer Device). There's no mention of the DOSMGR or SHELL or VWIN32 VxDs; VWIN32 in particular plays an absolutely vital role in Windows 95. Nor does the diagram show that the System VM rests atop 16-bit Windows device drivers (totally different from VxDs), such as KEYBOARD, MOUSE, DISPLAY, or SYSTEM. But obviously there's only so much that can be crammed into a single diagram without inducing more than the intended amount of MEGO.

Still, I think the omission of WINBOOT, aka MS-DOS, from this diagram is significant. Not only does Microsoft intend to convince end users that DOS is gone and that software on a Windows 95 PC has been stamped out in one piece like an integrated circuit, but also to convince developers of the same thing. Programmers are people too, and they want to feel good about the operating system they develop for. So Microsoft will let developers feel good by showing them lots of pretty diagrams in which MS-DOS has been wished away.

The second boilerplate diagram is shown in Figure 1-7. It too appears to have become industry standard in the computer trade press (see, for instance, the verbatim copy in *Windows Magazine*, July 1994, p. 186) and comes from the Chicago *Reviewer's Guide*.

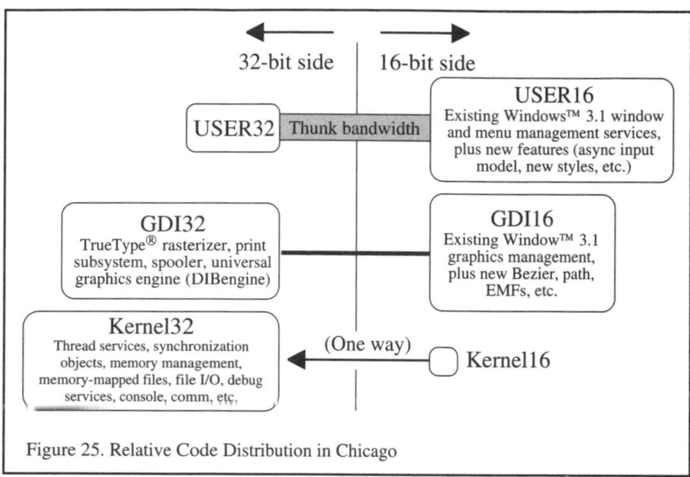

Figure 1-7: Microsoft's boilerplate diagram of 32-bit and 16-bit thunking in Windows 95.

Now, the key here is the bottom layer, showing a supposed one-way flow from Kernel16 to Kernel32 (the actual names are KRNL386.EXE and KERNEL32.DLL). Chapter 13 shows that, in fact, communication between the Win16 and Win32 kernels is a two-way street, just as is communication between the Win16 and Win32 USER and GDI modules. And, as noted earlier, the reliance of KERNEL32 upon KRNL386 for some functionality in any case flows logically from USER32's reliance upon Win16 USER.

The version of this diagram in *InfoWorld* (July 4, 1994, p. 46) goes Microsoft one better, stating that "All kernel functions are on the 32-bit side, so all 16-bit calls are thunked up to 32 bits." Microsoft has never made such a claim, and even the quickest examination of the Win16 KERNEL code (employing a debugger to glance at a few Win16 KERNEL functions such as GlobalAlloc or LoadModule or LoadResource) shows that it is not true.

Claiming Integration

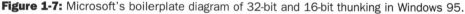

Now, why this great desire, not only by Microsoft but also by intelligent and knowledgeable computer journalists, to believe that Windows 95 is a brand-new operating system that doesn't employ MS-DOS except perhaps as a short-lived bootstrap loader?

Certainly, there's nothing radically wrong with the Windows 95 architecture as it actually exists. Other chapters will make the point that, because V86 mode is really a form of protected mode, the employment of DOS doesn't undermine Windows 95's status as a genuine operating system. Similarly, there's nothing wrong with KERNEL32's reliance on the Win16 KERNEL for some functionality. Adrian King notes (*Inside Windows 95*, p. 148) that USER32's use of Win16 USER API is "a sensible way of using tried and trusted code." Well, the same basic point applies to KERNEL32 and the Win16 KERNEL.

So if there's nothing radically wrong with the Windows 95 architecture, and if Microsoft has made fundamentally the right compromises and tradeoffs, then why this false vision of Chicago as some sort of magic land from which DOS has been banished and where 32-bit kernel code never employs 16-bit kernel code?

The answer, I think, lies in the persistent use of the nebulous term *integrated* to describe Windows 95. Like some school board trying to wriggle out of a court order, Microsoft keeps telling everyone that Chicago is "integrated." For example, Microsoft's own caption for Figure 1-6 refers to "Chicago's Integrated Architecture." Elsewhere (p. 275), the *Reviewer's Guide* says, "Chicago will be a complete, integrated protect-mode operating system that does not require or use a separate version of MS-DOS"; it also says (p. 54):

> The first thing that users of Windows 3.1 and MS-DOS will see when they turn their computer on (or perhaps won't see) is the lack of an MS-DOS command prompt from which they would need to invoke Windows. Chicago is a tightly integrated operating system that features a preemptive multitasking kernel that boots directly into the graphical user interface, yet provides full compatibility with the MS-DOS operating system.

The word integrated is used so frequently to describe Windows 95 that you quickly stop thinking about what it could possibly mean, and simply accept and repeat it. Integration is one of those grand words that just feels good to repeat.

Apart from being yet another feel-good exercise (a frequent occurrence among us supposedly rational engineering types in the software business), what else is going on with this annoying "tightly integrated" drumbeat?

Actually, I think it's pretty simple. The "tightly integrated" theme is part of Microsoft's response to the Mac. As noted at the beginning of this chapter, a major goal of Chicago is to change the perception of Windows and the PC. By claiming that Windows 95 is integrated — which I guess means that Windows 95 is supposed to be a self-contained whole that doesn't require MS-DOS — Microsoft can give the impression that the PC has been turned into a seamless Windows machine.

We've seen that when you turn on a PC, Windows 95 does an excellent job of taking you right into Windows. We've also seen that this doesn't constitute independence from the real-mode DOS code. Microsoft has taken the code formerly known as MS-DOS, modified it to run HIMEM, IFSHLP, and WIN (much as it was earlier modified to run DBLSPACE), renamed it WINBOOT, and put it in the same package as Windows. This is a perfectly reasonable implementation, but it's not what I would call seamless or integrated, and it certainly doesn't push DOS out of the way. The automatic loading of the graphical user interface in Windows 95 doesn't need to be seamless or integrated, and it doesn't need to push DOS out of the way.

So why pretend otherwise? Because, if Microsoft admits that Windows 95 relies on MS-DOS 83, even in perfectly acceptable ways, then it's a bit harder to say with a straight face that the PC is a Windows "toaster" or that after Windows 95 ships, "there will be no reason to buy an Apple Macintosh," as Bill Gates reportedly said in a memo (*Computer Reseller News*, March 21, 1994).

There are additional reasons for Microsoft to claim that Windows 95 is an integrated, seamless, complete operating system. Far less important in Microsoft's eyes than the Apple Macintosh, I think, is OS/2. OS/2 is not much of a threat to Microsoft, but it must be mildly annoying to have the OS/2 contingent deride Windows-DOS as "a thing on a thing."

Perhaps the tightly integrated theme is also a subtle way of beating the drum for Microsoft Office. In addition to the usual spiel that any applications-suite vendor would deliver regarding the benefits of integration, Microsoft has its own special theme here: the desirability of getting *all* your software from one place, Microsoft.

The funny thing is, *lack* of software integration (depending, of course, on what this term is really supposed to mean) was once thought to be a good thing. Back then, this lack of software integration was called *modularity*. In this sense Windows 95, like previous versions of Windows Enhanced mode, is not particularly integrated, and is actually fairly modular.

We'll see in Chapter 13 that there are two layers in Windows that know almost nothing about each other: the VMM/VxD layer down below and the KERNEL/USER/GDI layer up above. The benefit of this modularity is that it's possible to run one layer without the other. The negative side of this modularity, or lack of integration, is that the Win16 KERNEL in particular has to frequently second-guess and fake-out the VxD layer. For example, while IFSMgr maintains the current directory on a per-virtual machine (VM) basis, this does absolutely no good for the multiple Win16 and Win32 applications (each of which require their own current directory) in the System VM. Windows 95 does little or nothing to tie together these two parts of Windows.

On the other hand, Chapters 3 and 4 show that, long before Windows 95, there was already a surprising degree of integration between DOS and Windows. The README.WRI file included with Windows 3.1 and 3.11 states that "Microsoft Windows and MS-DOS work together as an integrated system." There's that "integrated" term again, but this time it refers to the combination of DOS and Windows. If DOS-Windows was integrated, and Windows 95 is integrated, what's the difference?

In a letter to *Dr. Dobb's Journal* (January 1994, p. 10), responding to an earlier article "Examining the Windows AARD Detection Code" (*Dr. Dobb's Journal*, September 1993), Microsoft vice president Brad Silverberg wrote:

> Windows is tightly coupled to the underlying MS-DOS operating system. It relies on a number of very precise behavioral characteristics of MS-DOS...

In private conversation, Brad several times used the word "seamless" to describe how Windows and DOS work together. Chapters 3 and 4 show that this, and even the term "integrated" from the Windows README.WRI, is a fairly accurate way of describing the relationship between Windows 3.1 Enhanced mode and MS-DOS 5 and 6. Windows was not just some arbitrary application that ran "on top of" MS-DOS.

But if Windows 3.1 and DOS 6 were "integrated," "tightly coupled," and part almost of a single "seamless" product, then what's Windows 95 bring to the DOS-Windows integration party? Merely that the two components are now shipped in a single box?

Windows 95 and DOS

Well, enough snide remarks. We've seen that Windows 95 doesn't bypass DOS, push DOS aside, or remove itself entirely from DOS. How then *does* Windows 95 relate to MS-DOS? What is the division of labor in Windows 95 between Windows and DOS?

That, of course, depends on what you mean by "DOS." If you just mean the INT 21h interface, then Windows 95 *expands* the role of DOS, because long filenames in Windows 95 are based on an entire new suite of INT 21h calls, using function 71h.

However, the expanded role of INT 21h in Windows 95 tells us surprisingly little about Windows 95's relationship to MS-DOS because INT 21h is just an interface: as noted earlier, for example, any VxD can use the Hook_V86_Int_Chain or Set_PM_Int_Vect VMM services to provide its own 32-bit protected-mode emulation of INT 21h or any other interrupt-based interface. This is how the IFSMgr VxD provides 32-bit file access. In fact, this is also how Windows 95 provides the new INT 21h function 71h calls: IFSMgr's INT 21h handlers, installed with Hook_V86_Int_Chain and Set_PM_Int_Vect, look for calls to function 71h and handle them entirely in protected mode.

Rather than focus on the INT 21h interface, then, it's much more useful to ask how Windows 95 relates to the real-mode MS-DOS code base.

But what does the phrase "the real-mode MS-DOS code base" mean? Any real-mode code that Windows 95 does use *never* runs in real mode; Windows 95 always uses — all together now! — *a 1MB form of protected mode called virtual-8086 mode*. What "the real-mode MS-DOS code base" refers to is the actual code that for years has been part of MS-DOS. For example, if a program running under real-mode DOS calls INT 21h function 62h to get the current PSP, there is a block of code somewhere in MSDOS.SYS that handles this call.

So, what's happened to that block of code in Windows 95? Is it part of Windows 95? Is it ever used after Windows 95 initializes, while the graphical user interface is running? Is it ever used in a "pure" Windows 95 system that has been booted without CONFIG.SYS, AUTOEXEC .BAT, or COMMAND.COM, and in which the user is running only Windows applications? Is the DOS code ever used in a super "pure" Windows 95 system in which the user is running only new Win32 applications? And if so, why? For which particular INT 21h functions do Win16 and Win32 applications depend on the real-mode DOS code?

To intelligently answer these questions, we first need to understand the real-mode DOS code a little better. The second edition of *Undocumented DOS* devoted a chapter to this code, particularly its INT 21h dispatch function (see "Disassembling DOS," pp. 265-341). The INTCHAIN program included with *Undocumented DOS* is useful for locating DOS's INT 21h dispatch function, even when it's at the end of a long chain of other INT 21h handlers. When you tell INTCHAIN to issue some INT 21h call, the program traces through the execution of the INT 21h, and reports back on all the different INT 21h handlers it encountered. For example, the following INTCHAIN output was produced under MS-DOS 6.2; I asked INTCHAIN to issue an INT 21h function 62h (Get PSP) call:

```
C:\UNDOCDOS>intchain 21/6200

1DD3:16B4   SMARTDRV
105D:0498   IFS$HLP$
0019:40F8   DOS
```

The last line of the INTCHAIN output most likely represents MS-DOS's INT 21h dispatch function. In this particular configuration, this function appears to be at 0019:40F8. We can use DEBUG or any similar debugger to examine the code at this address which, it turns out, *is* the MS-DOS INT 21h dispatch function. I've added a few comments to the DEBUG disassembly shown here:


```
C:\UNDOCDOS>debug
-u 19:40f8
0019:40F8 FA            CLI
0019:40F9 80FC6C        CMP AH,6C  ;;; 6Ch is max DOS function in DOS 6
0019:40FC 77D2          JA  40D0   ;;; if more than 6Ch, error
0019:40FE 80FC33        CMP AH,33
0019:4101 7218          JB  411B
0019:4103 74A2          JZ  40A7
0019:4105 80FC64        CMP AH,64
0019:4108 7711          JA  411B
0019:410A 74B5          JZ  40C1
0019:410C 80FC51        CMP AH,51   ;;; Get PSP
0019:410F 74A4          JZ  40B5
0019:4111 80FC62        CMP AH,62   ;;; Get PSP
0019:4114 749F          JZ  40B5
0019:4116 80FC50        CMP AH,50   ;;; Set PSP
0019:4119 748E          JZ  40A9
...
```

We can readily see that the two DOS Get PSP functions (51h and 62h) are both handled at 0019:40B5 in this configuration and that the Set PSP function (50h) is handled at 0019:40A9. Let's look at the real-mode DOS code for these functions:

```
-u 19:40a9                                ;;; look at 21/50 (Set PSP)
0019:40A9 1E            PUSH    DS
0019:40AA 2E            CS:
0019:40AB 8E1EE73D      MOV DS,[3DE7]    ;;; get DOS DS out of DOS CS
0019:40AF 891E3003      MOV [0330],BX    ;;; put new PSP into DOS:[330h]
0019:40B3 1F            POP DS
0019:40B4 CF            IRET

-u 19:40b5                                ;;; look at 21/51,62 (Get PSP)
0019:40B5 1E            PUSH    DS
0019:40B6 2E            CS:
0019:40B7 8E1EE73D      MOV DS,[3DE7]    ;;; get DOS DS
0019:40BB 8B1E3003      MOV BX,[0330]    ;;; return DOS:[330h] in BX
0019:40BF 1F            POP DS
0019:40C0 CF            IRET
```

This is the code that's executed whenever a program running in real-mode DOS sets or gets the current PSP. We can see that the code is quite simple: setting the PSP involves nothing more than ramming the caller's BX into a variable at offset 330h in the DOS data segment, and getting the PSP involves nothing more than returning the value of this same variable. Offset 330h in the DOS data segment happens to be offset 10h in the Swappable Data Area (SDA), a DOS data structure that all versions of Windows Enhanced mode, including Windows 95, declare as *instance data* (see Chapter 4).

Now, the question is whether this same code is also part of Windows 95, and more importantly, whether it plays any role in Windows 95 beyond that necessary for compatibility with real-mode DOS programs and drivers.

Let's first verify whether it's in Windows 95 at all. The easiest way to do this is to run INTCHAIN and DEBUG again, this time inside a Windows 95 DOS box (yes, we'll get rid of the DOS box in just a minute):

```
C:\UNDOCDOS>intchain 21/6200

00A6:0FAC    DOS
0748:41E4    DOS

C:\UNDOCDOS>debug
-u 748:41e4
0748:41E4 FA            CLI
0748:41E5 80FC73        CMP AH,73   ;;; 73h is max DOS function in Windows 95
0748:41E8 77D2          JA  41BC    ;;; if more than 73h, error
0748:41EA 80FC33        CMP AH,33
0748:41ED 7218          JB  4207
0748:41EF 74A2          JZ  4193
0748:41F1 80FC64        CMP AH,64
0748:41F4 7711          JA  4207
0748:41F6 74B5          JZ  41AD
0748:41F8 80FC51        CMP AH,51    ;;; Get PSP
0748:41FB 74A4          JZ  41A1
0748:41FD 80FC50        CMP AH,50    ;;; Set PSP
0748:4200 7493          JZ  4195
0748:4202 80FC62        CMP AH,62    ;;; Get PSP
0748:4205 74F4          JZ  41FB     ;;; JZ JZ 41A1
...
```

This is nearly identical to the MS-DOS 6.20 code, except that Windows 95 supports INT 21h functions up to 73h. Now let's see what the DOS Get/Set PSP functions look like in Windows 95:

```
-u 748:4195                                ;;; look at 21/50 (Set PSP)
0748:4195 1E            PUSH    DS
0748:4196 2E            CS:
0748:4197 8E1E273F      MOV DS,[3F27]    ;;; get DOS DS out of DOS CS
```

```
0748:419B 891E3003      MOV [0330],BX   ;;; put new PSP into DOS:[330h]
0748:419F 1F            POP DS
0748:41A0 CF            IRET

-u 748:41A1                             ;;; look at 21/51,62 (Get PSP)
0748:41A1 1E            PUSH    DS
0748:41A2 2E            CS:
0748:41A3 8E1E273F      MOV DS,[3F27]   ;;; get DOS DS
0748:41A7 8B1E3003      MOV BX,[0330]   ;;; return DOS:[330h] in BX
0748:41AB 1F            POP DS
0748:41AC CF            IRET
```


Not surprisingly, this is nearly identical to the DOS 6.2 MSDOS.SYS implementation. A little poking around with DEBUG shows that in Windows 95 this DOS code is part of the WINBOOT.SYS file:

```
C:\windows>debug \winboot.sys
-s 0100 ffff fa 80 fc 73        ;;; search in file for CLI / CMP AH,73
1E73:E8C1                       ;;; DEBUG found it
-u 1e73:e8c1
1E73:E8C1 FA            CLI
1E73:E8C2 80FC73        CMP AH,73
1E73:E8C5 77D2          JA  E899
...
1E73:E8DA 80FC50        CMP AH,50
1E73:E8DD 7493          JZ  E872
...
-u 1e73:e872                    ;;; handler for 21/50 (Set PSP)
1E73:E872 1E            PUSH    DS
1E73:E873 2E            CS:
1E73:E874 8E1E273F      MOV DS,[3F27]
1E73:E878 891E3003      MOV [0330],BX
1E73:E87C 1F            POP DS
1E73:E87D CF            IRET
```

We could look at the code for some more INT 21h functions, but this should be sufficient to establish that the same real-mode DOS code that previous versions of the operating system stored in MSDOS.SYS, Windows 95 stores in WINBOOT.SYS.

So the real-mode DOS code *is* part of Windows 95. I've run the above tests from a DOS box inside Windows, so it's obvious that this WINBOOT code is used for more than just booting Windows and is not "pushed aside" by Windows. The name WINBOOT is therefore somewhat misleading, because it seems to suggest that the code's *only* purpose is to boot Windows.

In fact, WINBOOT.SYS plays a much larger role in Windows 95. For example, a Microsoft document on Plug and Play refers in passing to "the real mode operating system kernel," and this is a good way of describing WINBOOT.SYS: it's the real-mode portion of the Windows 95 kernel. It's odd that all mention of it should be so conspicuously absent from the Microsoft documents and diagrams intended for a wider audience. How come WINBOOT.SYS doesn't show up in Figure 1-6? You'd almost get the impression that Microsoft is embarrassed about it. That isn't a very nice way to treat a piece of code that has earned Microsoft *billions* of dollars.

So we know that Windows doesn't push WINBOOT aside; WINBOOT is present for the duration. But even though WINBOOT sticks around to handle certain DOS calls in certain circumstances, on the other hand these tests were conducted from a DOS box, in which we ran the real-mode DOS DEBUG program. Although what we've seen already raises questions about the absence of WINBOOT.SYS from Microsoft's diagrams, it is perhaps still consistent with one theory, which is that Windows 95 only uses the real-mode DOS code for compatibility with DOS programs.

As pointed out earlier, there is no necessary connection, one way or the other, between MS-DOS and the ability to run DOS programs. MS-DOS might be necessary to support the needs of non-DOS (for example, Win16 and Win32) programs. On the other hand, you can also have real-mode DOS programs running on an operating system other than DOS, as long as that operating system emulates the INT 21h interface. We'll see in later chapters that, for many DOS functions, both Windows 95 and WfW 3.11 are perfect examples of such an operating system: with 32-bit file access, even INT 21h calls coming from real-mode DOS software are in many cases handled in 32-bit protected mode. So the idea that DOS must hang around to support the running of DOS programs is pretty ridiculous. However, the assumed association between MS-DOS and DOS compatibility, while fallacious, is so widely accepted that for the sake of argument we'd better temporarily accept it.

Okay, then, here's the question rephrased: To what extent is the real-mode DOS code present and operational in Windows 95, when running only Windows (Win16 and Win32) applications and when Windows 95 has been booted without CONFIG.SYS or AUTOEXEC.BAT? There are no DOS boxes, no special real-mode drivers or TSRs: Is the DOS code still part of Windows 95? And, if so, what role does DOS play in a "pure" Win32 system?

Take the code that was shown earlier, where WINBOOT (nee MS-DOS) handles INT 21h function 50h: If this code is ever executed in a pure Windows 95 system — if a debugger breakpoint on this code is ever triggered — Windows 95 uses the real-mode DOS code and that's that.

It turns out, even when only running Win32 applications in Windows 95, this real-mode DOS code *is* executed. Using Nu-Mega's superb

Soft-ICE/Windows debugger (which Microsoft distributes with the Windows 95 Device Driver Kit), I placed a breakpoint on the WIN-BOOT Set PSP code:

```
:bpx &748:4195
```

Even when running only Win32 applications such as the Cabinet/ Explorer, WinBezMT, and Clock, this breakpoint was triggered so frequently that I couldn't actually *do* anything in Windows 95 until I changed the breakpoint to only trigger every 50 times:


```
:bpx &748:4195 c=50
```

Even so, Soft-ICE/Windows still popped up so frequently I could only stand to run this test for few minutes. Again, this was on a "pure" Windows 95 system only running Win32 applications. I didn't start a DOS box, and I didn't even start any Win16 applications. There were no real-mode device drivers or TSRs installed.

Ah, but I did run the Soft-ICE/Windows debugger, though. This loads before Windows, and thus appears to Windows to be something like a TSR. Since WINBOOT.SYS wants to jump directly into WIN .COM, I used F8 to do an interactive boot, declined to load the graphical user interface, and from the C:\> prompt loaded WINICE, which in turn loads WIN.COM and the Windows GUI. Thus, this doesn't look like such a pure Win32 system after all. As with Werner Heisenberg's hypothetical "gamma-ray microscope," the mere use of which *changes* what's under the microscope, it's conceivable that the very presence of Soft-ICE/Windows is somehow causing Windows 95 to pass INT 21h calls down to the real-mode DOS code inside WINBOOT.SYS, and that Windows 95 wouldn't be calling this real-mode DOS code were the debugger not present.

Well, this is certainly a plausible concern. Let's use one more program, then, to show up the Windows-DOS relationship. Here's a review of what we've done so far:

- We've used a DOS box to see that Windows 95 rests atop DOS, then decided that the DOS box might be influencing the outcome;
- We've used a Win16 application, only to decide that Windows 95 might simulate DOS the same way NT does;
- We've used a debugger and decided that the debugger acts as a DOS TSR, the very presence of which might cause Windows to send down to real-mode DOS calls that it otherwise would not send down.

Having gone through all that, let's turn to one final (at least for this first chapter) demonstration of the Windows-DOS relationship in Windows 95: WLOG212F is a Win16 program that lets us see which INT 21h and 2Fh calls are generated on the Windows side of the fence, and then see which ones pop up on the V86 side of the fence. By counting the number of calls to each INT 21h and INT 2Fh function generated in Windows and comparing this with the number of calls seen down in V86 mode, WLOG212F provides a good idea of which calls a given Windows environment such as Windows 95 or WfW 3.11 passes down to V86 mode and which ones it emulates in protected mode. Figure 1-8 shows WLOG212F running in Windows 95.

On the Windows side, WLOG212F installs its hooks with the DPMI Set Protected Mode Interrupt Vector function (INT 31h function 0205h) and with an undocumented Windows API called GetSetKernelDosProc (see Chapter 13). Though it can see calls down in V86 mode, WLOG212F contains no real-mode code and does not employ a DOS box. WLOG212F creates its V86-mode hook with another DPMI function, Allocate Real Mode Callback Address (INT 31h function 0303h), and installs it with Set Real Mode Interrupt Vector (INT 31h function 0201h).

For example, in the following fragment of WLOG212F output, an INT 21h handler installed with GetSetKernelDosProc has encountered 15 calls to INT 21h function 0 (Exit). However, the V86 mode hook saw no calls to this function (WLOG212F shows blank white space instead of the number zero), so WLOG212F decides the call is emulated in protected mode, rather than passed down to V86 mode:

```
INT 21h:
Func        Prot mode    KernelDOSProc    V86 mode
00h                          15                       Emulated
```

Reasonable enough. It turns out that the Win16 KERNEL contains an INT 21h handler which, among many other things, changes calls to the obsolete function 0 into calls to the newer function 4Ch. This, too, is reflected in the WLOG212F output:

```
INT 21h:
Func        Prot mode    KernelDOSProc    V86 mode
4Ch                                           15      Passed down
```

Why did WLOG212F decide that function 4Ch is "Passed down"? Because its V86 mode INT 21h handler saw at least as many calls to this function as did its protected-mode INT 21h handlers (which, in fact, saw no such calls). Perhaps the WLOG212F output for the DOS Get Version function will make this clearer:

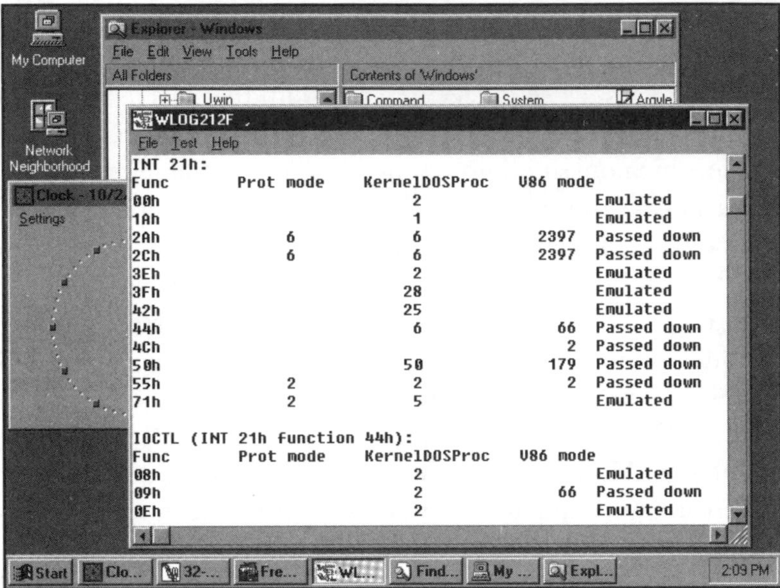

Figure 1-8: The WLOG212F program (running here alongside some Win32 applications under Windows 95) counts INT 21h and (not seen here) INT 2Fh calls generated in protected-mode Windows, and compares these with the number of calls sent down to V86 mode. If a call is seen in protected mode but not in V86 mode, WLOG212F indicates that the call is "Emulated." On the other hand, if at least as many calls are seen in V86 mode as were generated in protected mode, WLOG212F indicates the call is "Passed down."

```
INT 21h:
Func        Prot mode    KernelDOSProc   V86 mode
30h            10            33             33       Passed down
```

Here, the KernelDosProc handler (see Chapter 13 for a full explanation of GetSetKernelDosProc) saw 33 DOS Get Version calls, and so did the V86 mode INT 21h handler. Thus, at least in this situation, Windows passes all calls to this function down to V86 mode. Simple, eh?

I'll discuss the implementation of WLOG212F a little later in this chapter (and the WLOG212F.C source code is provided on the *Unauthorized Windows 95* disk), but first let's examine the output from WLOG212F and see what it can tell us about the Windows-DOS relationship in Windows 95. It's important to note that, according to Microsoft, the behavior revealed by WLOG212F never happens in Windows 95, or only happens in the presence of special real-mode drivers for which there is no currently available protected-mode replacement. According to King's authorized *Inside Windows 95* (p. 79):

> Windows applications on Windows 95 never use virtual 8086 mode. They execute in protected mode all the way down to the bare hardware.

We're about to run some Windows applications in Windows 95, and WLOG212F will show that they *frequently* use V86 mode. Ah, but the categorical statement we just saw is qualified with a footnote (King, *Inside Windows 95*, p. 79n):

> This isn't strictly true since Windows 95 still runs MS-DOS device drivers in virtual 8086 mode if there's no protected mode driver available. But real mode drivers are an endangered species.

This qualification doesn't apply here, though, because the following WLOG212F output was produced (in Windows 95 Beta-1 from May 1994) without CONFIG.SYS, AUTOEXEC.BAT, COMMAND.COM, or a DOS box. Since Beta-1 didn't ship with VxDs to support Microsoft's DoubleSpace disk compression — and thus the MS-DOS DBLSPACE .BIN driver would fall into King's "endangered species" list — it's important to add that this system wasn't using disk compression either. On this pure-as-the-driven-snow Windows 95 system, then, I ran Microsoft Office 4.2, plus other parts of the Windows operating system, such as the Explorer, and the WinBezMT and Clock Win32 applets, and, of course, WLOG212F itself. Here's part of the WLOG212F output:


```
Elapsed: 897 seconds
Calls: 15723
17 calls/second

INT 21h:
Func        Prot mode     KernelDOSProc    V86 mode
00h                               15                    Emulated
0Eh             189             1147           1182     Passed down
19h             228             1162           3526     Passed down
1Ah              18            13410                    Emulated
1Ch                                1                    Emulated
25h              32               20                    Emulated
2Ah               7              330           5555     Passed down
2Ch               7             6313          11538     Passed down
2Fh               7             5182                    Emulated
30h              10               33             33     Passed down
32h               7                7                    Emulated
35h              12               10                    Emulated
36h               2                6                    Emulated
...
```

Rather than bore you with the entire output from WLOG212F, it makes more sense to look at just a few of the emulated calls, and then focus on the calls labeled as "Passed down." But you can already notice that, in this test under Windows 95 (where, you'll recall, Windows applications supposedly *never* use V86 mode unless some unusual real-mode driver is loaded), the V86 mode INT21 handler is seeing some calls. In the case of function 2Ch (Get Time), for instance, it's seeing a ton of calls.

In the almost 15 minutes that WLOG212F was running, its protected-mode INT 21h handler saw almost 7,800 calls, its KernelDosProc handler saw over 80,000 calls, and its V86 mode handler saw over 26,000 calls.

In this particular test, in other words, almost one-third of the INT 21h calls from Windows applications ended up going down to V86 mode. In a Windows 95 system such as this with no CONFIG.SYS, no AUTOEXEC.BAT, no real-mode DOS drivers (other than the ones that Windows 95 requires and loads itself), no TSRs, no DOS box, no nuthin' except Windows applications, this is not supposed to happen.

The only explanation I can think of is that WINBOOT.SYS itself needs to be considered a real-mode driver (though you'll recall its conspicuous absence from the Microsoft diagram), and that part of this driver (such as Get Time) qualifies as functionality for which "there's no protected mode driver available." In other words, no one happens to have written a VxD to replace the parts of WINBOOT.SYS (such as the Get Time function) that are still employed by Windows 95.

This would be a quite reasonable statement — the CURRDRIV.386 and INTVECT.386 examples in Chapter 8 demonstrate how the Hook_V86_Int_Chain service provided by VMM makes it easy to write VxDs to handle INT 21h functions in 32-bit protected mode — but I'm pretty sure it's not what Microsoft or the trade press have in mind when they say that Windows 95 doesn't require DOS. For one thing, if this is all that the hoopla surrounding Windows 95's supposed liberation from DOS really means, then the same statement could, and should, have been made years ago, when Windows first acquired a VMM that provided a Hook_V86 _Int_Chain service. The implementation of that function, and not its apparently more extensive use in Windows 95, was the real watershed in Windows' relation with DOS. If Windows 95 is a genuine operating system, then so was Windows 3.0 Enhanced mode, in which Hook_V86_Int _Chain first appeared.

As noted earlier, if WLOG212F sees calls to a function on the Windows side but no calls to this function down in V86 mode, the program decides that, as far as it can tell, the function has to be emulated. For example, here's what WLOG212F shows for the Open (3Dh), Close (3Eh), Read (3Fh), and Write (40h) file I/O calls in Windows 95:

```
Func        Prot mode     KernelDOSProc    V86 mode
3Dh                          698                              Emulated
3Eh                          1320                             Emulated
3Fh                          10816                            Emulated
40h                          1817                             Emulated
```

WLOG212F shows that Windows 95 handles these crucial INT 21h functions entirely in protected mode. This is pretty amazing. Don't let our focus on the situations in which Windows 95 still calls down to DOS detract in any way from the fact that, for many key DOS functions, it *doesn't* call down to DOS. In fact, the whole point of my harping on the cases where Windows 95 still calls down to V86 mode DOS is to heighten your appreciation for those cases where it doesn't. By assessing Windows 95's relation to DOS on a function-by-function basis, rather than by uncritically parroting Microsoft's claims that Windows 95 runs Windows applications entirely in protected mode, my praise for Windows 95 will actually carry some weight.

Whether Windows 95 emulates or passes down an INT 21h function is not an exclusive either/or choice, of course. Sometimes WLOG212F's protected-mode handlers see more calls to a function than does its V86 mode handler, yet the V86 mode handler still sees *some* calls. In this case, WLOG212F just displays the statistics without any commentary. A good example is the DOS IOCTL (I/O Control) function:

```
Func        Prot mode     KernelDOSProc    V86 mode
44h            338          7112               23
```

IOCTL function 44h is really an umbrella for a large number of subfunctions. I was sufficiently curious about Windows 95's IOCTL handling that I had WLOG212F break the function 44h results out by subfunction:

```
Func        Prot mode     KernelDOSProc    V86 mode
00h            338           347                          Emulated
08h                         2255                          Emulated
09h                         2255               23
0Eh                         2255                          Emulated
```

Function 4409h is the Check if Block Device is Remote request. We can see that, once in a blue moon, Windows 95 passes this request down to V86 mode. Now, DOS itself handles IOCTL calls by creating device-driver request packets that it passes to the Strategy and Interrupt routine of the appropriate real-mode DOS device driver. So it's possible that the 32-bit protected-mode code in Windows 95 for INT 21h function 44h is doing the same thing. WLOG212F only spies on INT 21h and INT 2Fh, and won't see any far calls that Windows 95 VxDs might be making to DOS device drivers.

As noted earlier, this WLOG212F test was run in a Windows 95 configuration without a CONFIG.SYS and hence without any user-installed DOS device drivers. But of course there are still the DOS device drivers that are built into WINBOOT.SYS (such as COM1, COM2, LPT1, LPT2, CLOCK$, CONFIG$, and so on), there's the IFSHLP driver installed by IFSHLP.SYS, there's HIMEM.SYS's XMSXXXX0 driver, and there's SETVER.EXE's SETVERXX driver. You'd expect that *some* IOCTL calls would have to be handled by passing them to the appropriate DOS device driver, even one built into WINBOOT.SYS. Indeed, a debugger breakpoint, placed for example on the common Strategy routine shared by the built-in DOS device drivers, *is* triggered under Windows 95.

Finally, we come to the INT 21h functions for which WLOG212F's V86 hook sees at least as many calls as did its protected-mode hook. WLOG212F labels these functions as "Passed down." I hope you've already been convinced that, contrary to Microsoft's claims, Windows applications running under Windows 95 *do* use V86 mode, so we can move on to the more interesting questions about *when* and *why* and *under what circumstances* Windows applications in Windows 95 still use V86 mode. I've edited the WLOG212F output below, replacing the "Passed down" string with the name of each function:

```
INT 21h:
Func    Prot mode    KernelDOSProc   V86 mode
0Eh        189          1147           1182        Set Drive
19h        228          1162           3526        Get Drive
2Ah          7           330           5555        Get Date
2Ch          7          6313          11538        Get Time
30h         10            33             33        Get DOS Version
45h        226           226            226        Dup File Handle
4Ch                                      15        Exit
50h                     3018           3787        Set PSP
51h          1             1              1        Get PSP
55h         15            15             15        Create PSP
5Ah          3             3              3        Create Temp File
65h          2             2              2        International
DCh                        3              3        Novell NetWare Get Station Num
```

Now, perhaps you feel that the only reason Windows 95 is passing these calls down to V86 mode is because my V86 mode callback is installed. (The Heisenberg effect rears its ugly head again!) But if this is the case, how come Windows 95 is so darned selective about it? It doesn't send my V86 mode callback any file I/O calls, for example. Surely if WLOG212F's V86 mode callback were responsible for these passed-down calls, then all INT 21h calls would show up as passed down.

Just one little callback

You might worry that it's a self-fulfilling prophecy for WLOG212F to use a V86 mode callback INT 21h handler to test whether Windows programs in Windows 95 ever use V86 mode.

Let's consider how this callback is installed. The WLOG212F.C source code on disk contains the following function:

```
INTRFUNC GetSetRealInt(int intno, INTRFUNC new, INTRFUNC *pcallback,
    RMODE_REGS **pregs)
{
    INTRFUNC old;
    if ((old = _dpmi_get_rmode_vect(intno)) != 0)
    {
        RMODE_REGS *regs;
        INTRFUNC callback;
        if (! (regs = (RMODE_REGS *) calloc(sizeof(RMODE_REGS), 1)))
            return (INTRFUNC) 0;
        if (! (callback = _dpmi_alloc_rmode_callback(new, regs)))
        {
            free(regs);
            return (INTRFUNC) 0;
        }
        _dpmi_set_rmode_vect(intno, callback);
        *pcallback = callback;
        *pregs = regs;
    }
    return old;
}
```

The _dpmi_xxx functions called by GetSetRealInt are simple C wrappers around the equivalent INT 31h calls; in particular, _dpmi_alloc_rmode_callback is a wrapper around INT 31h function 0303h (Allocate Real Mode Callback Address). To assess what possible Heisenberg-like impact WLOG212F could have on Windows 95's relationship with DOS, we need to understand this DPMI function.

The DPMI server in Windows 95, as in previous versions of Windows Enhanced mode, is provided by VMM. Many of the DPMI INT 31h functions are themselves mere wrappers around VMM functions. This means that, under Windows, DPMI can be seen as a way to call certain VMM functions that are otherwise directly callable only from a VxD.

DPMI function 0303h, which WLOG212F uses to create a protected-mode handler for a V86 mode interrupt, is based on a VMM service called Allocate_V86_Call_Back. A V86 callback is a small piece of code (a very small piece — one byte) that, when called in V86 mode, thunks up to 32-bit protected mode. By allocating a V86 callback and then installing the address of this callback as the V86 mode INT 21h handler, WLOG212F forces all V86 mode INT 21h calls to thunk into VMM, which passes the call to WLOG212F. In other words, the effect of WLOG212F is to take a call that has already appeared in V86 mode, and ship it over to protected mode. There's no way it can cause the call to appear in V86 mode in the first place.

Even without WLOG212F, the INT 21h chain *already* contains some V86 callbacks. In particular, the IFSHLP device uses a V86 callback to communicate with the IFSMgr VxD, and this callback is active even when no DOS programs are running. Calling the GetOpenFileName common dialog triggers the IFSHLP V86 callback, for example.

As shown by the WINBP program in Chapter 8, literally *hundreds* of these V86 call backs are active in any Windows system. These V86 callbacks are constantly triggered, even on the purest Windows 95 system. If Windows applications never execute any V86 mode code, why is the documented V86 callback facility used so heavily in Windows 95, even when you're only running Windows applications?

Here's another interesting thing about DPMI function 0303h: in a sample program that shows how to use this function, the DPMI specification (version 1.0, March 1991, p. 37) contains a comment that is both wrong and enlightening; this comment gets to the root of the confusion surrounding INT 21h handling in Windows:

> *The following code...hooks the DOS Int 21h and returns an error for the delete file function (AH=41h). Other calls are passed through to DOS. This example demonstrates the techniques used to hook a real mode interrupt. Note that since DOS calls are reflected from protected mode to real mode, the following code will intercept all DOS calls from both real mode and protected mode.*

Note the blanket assertion here that "DOS calls are reflected from protected mode to real mode," as if this were some by-definition inherent property of protected-mode DOS calls. But every "Emulated" line output by WLOG212F disproves this assertion. A DOS call generated in protected mode is sent to V86 mode only if the DOS extender *decides* to send it to V86 mode. More than this, in Windows even a DOS call generated in V86 mode (for example, by a program running in a DOS box) is sent back down to V86 mode only if a VxD *decides* to send it back down to V86 mode. Again, there is no inherent connection between INT 21h calls and MS-DOS.

Actually, this confused notion that "DOS calls are reflected from protected mode to real mode" can coexist peacefully with the opposite but equally confused notion that in Windows 95, "if you run only Windows applications, you'll never execute any MS-DOS code." Both ideas are based on the same fundamental misunderstanding, which equates DOS software with MS-DOS. According to this notion, if there's a DOS call it must by definition be handled by MS-DOS, and conversely, if you don't run any DOS applications you'll never execute any MS-DOS code.

The reality, meanwhile, is that (a) you can have DOS software that doesn't require DOS, and that (b) you can have non-DOS software that does require DOS. An example of (a) is that 32-bit file access in WfW 3.11 and Windows 95 enables even real-mode DOS programs to bypass most of the MS-DOS code. An example of (b) is that every Win16 and Win32 application in Windows 95 requires a real-mode DOS PSP; this has nothing to do with whether any DOS applications are running.

We can be quite confident that WLOG212F provides an accurate picture of the situations under which Windows applications in a pure Windows 95 system use V86 mode. Here's a summary of the INT 21h calls that WLOG212F displays as "Passed down":

- Getting and setting the current drive. Chapter 8 explains why the number of function 19h calls in V86 mode is exactly twice the number of function 0Eh calls in V86 mode, plus the number of function 19h calls seen by KernelDosProc; CURRDRIV.386 in Chapter 8 shows how a VxD can handle function 19h entirely in 32-bit protected-mode.
- Getting the current date and time. Chapter 14 shows the path taken in Windows 95 from the Win32 GetSystemTime and GetLocalTime API calls, down to the INT 21h Get Date/Time functions, down to the CLOCK$ device driver, and back up to the Virtual Timer Device (VTD)'s 32-bit protected-mode emulation of the ROM BIOS INT 1Ah time functions.
- Getting, setting, and creating PSPs. Throughout this book, we'll see numerous places where both Win16 and Win32 tasks in Windows 95 rely on the DOS PSP. Chapter 13 shows the path from the Win32 CreateProcess API, down to the BuildPDB routine in the Win16 KERNEL, down to the DOS create-PSP code. Task-switching between Windows applications usually involves getting and setting the DOS current PSP.
- Miscellaneous DOS functions for getting the DOS version number, exiting back to the operating system, duplicating file handles, and so on. When you Paste Link an object from one document into another, for example, the STORAGE.DLL module of OLE calls DOS function 45h to duplicate the file handle.

Now, would it be possible for a VxD to handle each of these INT 21h functions in 32-bit protected mode and not pass the call down to DOS? Yes, it would be possible for a VxD to do this; see CURRDRIV.386 and INTVECT.386 in Chapter 8. So, Windows 95 currently passes a bunch of INT 21h calls down to V86 mode DOS, but there seems to be no *inherent* reason why it must do so. Perhaps even when Windows 95 is commercially released, it won't.

Who's Afraid of MS-DOS?

An interesting question then is this: If *all* INT 21h calls were handled by VxDs in protected mode, would this fundamentally change the nature of Windows 95? In other words, would moving these dozen or so remaining INT 21h calls over to protected mode turn Windows 95 into a genuine, complete, integrated operating system?

I don't think it would. For one thing, much of the VxD code that handles INT 21h in 32-bit protected mode still uses the real-mode DOS data structures. My CURRDRIV.386, for example, manipulates the current-drive variable in the DOS data segment. True, CURRDRIV manipulates this variable entirely from protected mode, but it's still a variable located in DOS's real-mode data segment. When Microsoft claims that "if you run only Windows applications, you'll never execute any MS-DOS code" (*Inside Windows 95*, p. 112), notice that nothing is said about peeking or poking any MS-DOS *data*.

Of course, with long file and directory names, many of the DOS data structures such as the System File Table (SFT) and Current Directory Structure (CDS) become less useful. The Swappable Data Area (SDA), which the Windows 95 instance data manager doles out on a per-VM basis, could be made a lot more useful were it further doled out within the System VM on a per-task basis. But in any event we'll see throughout this book that Windows 95, even when using VxDs to handle DOS calls in 32-bit protected mode, must still quite frequently peek and poke the real-mode DOS data.

However, there's a far more basic reason why providing VxD handlers for the remaining dozen or so INT 21h functions that Windows 95 currently passes down to DOS wouldn't turn Windows 95 into a genuine operating system.

The reason, quite simply, is that Windows 95 is *already* a genuine operating system, and that its reliance upon the real-mode MS-DOS code does not change this. *Windows 95 can be a genuine operating system, and still use DOS for some operations.*

Since, as we've seen, Windows 95 *does* rely on DOS, it's odd for Microsoft to make total independence from DOS into some kind of criteria for operating-system goodness. In its technical propaganda regarding the Windows 95 architecture, I think Microsoft might be making a big mistake by implicitly promoting the idea that an operating environment can't be a complete, integrated operating system if it calls down to

DOS for any reason other than compatibility with DOS applications and drivers. *Employing the real-mode DOS code does not diminish Windows 95's status as a genuine operating system.*

These general statements are probably more surprising than anything I've said about this-or-that particular aspect of Windows 95. How can independence from DOS not be all that important? How can it possibly be okay that Windows 95 uses the DOS Create PSP each time you run a Win32 application, and that task-switching even between two Win32 applications often involves a Set PSP call?

Of course it's important and not okay that Microsoft is selling Windows 95 to the computer trade press and to programmers as an operating system in which the real-mode DOS code is never executed on behalf of Windows applications. But leaving aside Microsoft's apparent confusion regarding its own product, how can Windows 95 possibly constitute a genuine operating system when, as we've seen, it relies on the real-mode DOS code?

Here's how: because Windows 95 runs this DOS code in V86 mode! Recall that V86 mode is a form of protected mode. When Windows calls down to DOS in V86 mode, Windows is in control and DOS is a subservient assistant. The phrase "Windows calls down to DOS," which sounds so final (jeez, I sure hope my INT 21h call is okay down there!), is hardly the end of the story. Once Windows 95 sends an INT 21h call down to the real-mode DOS code, the call can bounce back numerous times into 32-bit protected mode.

For example, if the real-mode DOS code loaded before Windows generates an INT instruction (to call a BIOS function, for instance), this traps immediately into the VMM, because that's what INT does in V86 mode. VMM can pass the INT to some VxD which handles it entirely in protected mode. Chapter 14 provides a good example of this: the INT 21h function 2Ah (Get Date) and 2Ch (Get Time) calls that Windows sends down to the real-mode DOS code are turned by this code into INT 1Ah function 0 calls. All INTs in V86 mode trap into the VMM; VMM hands the INT 1Ah call off to the Virtual Timer Device, which handles the call in protected mode.

As another example of how Windows uses V86 mode to control the execution of the real-mode DOS code, those V86 callbacks mentioned earlier can be patched right on top of an existing piece of real-mode DOS code, thereby forcing any execution of this code to trap into VMM. These V86 callback patches are created with the Install_V86_Break_Point service provided by VMM.

Because of V86 mode, then, Windows — including Windows 95 — doesn't run "on top of" DOS; it essentially uses DOS as a driver. Windows needs someone to implement INT 21h functions 2Ah, 2Ch, 50h, 55h, and so on. Perhaps one day a VxD will do this; in the meantime, a real-mode driver called WINBOOT.SYS implements these calls.

WfW 3.11: The Neglected Operating System

It's important to realize that there's nothing new in Windows 95's relationship to MS-DOS. Windows 95 isn't the first version of Windows to employ the real-mode DOS code as little more than a driver that implements some scattered INT 21h calls. Windows 95 is not even the first version of Windows that deserves to be called a genuine operating system.

As noted several times already, the fundamental transformation of Windows occurs not in 1995 with Windows 95 but occurred already in 1990 with Windows 3.0 Enhanced mode — and perhaps even earlier, in 1988, with Windows/386 2.0.

Windows programmers who've spent most of their time with the upper-level Windows API provided by KERNEL, USER, and GDI would understandably doubt whether any version of Windows prior to Windows 95 deserves to be called an operating system. But Windows 95 can only be plausibly considered a genuine operating system if you look at its lower layer, particularly VMM — and the same applies to earlier versions of Windows. Windows 3.0 Enhanced mode, Windows 3.1 Enhanced mode, and WfW 3.11 all have fundamentally the same architecture as Windows 95. If there's any logic in calling Windows 95 an operating system (and there is, despite its use of real-mode DOS code), then the VMM/VxD layer in Windows 3.*x* Enhanced mode is an operating system too. For years, only a handful of VxD writers were aware of this operating system and how it had basically replaced real-mode MS-DOS. As Chapter 8 points out, we've had a 32-bit protected-mode operating system sitting right under our noses for several years now, but we've barely noticed it.

This 32-bit protected-mode operating system became a lot more difficult to ignore when WfW 3.11 came out with 32-bit file access (32BFA). WfW 3.11 is surely one of the most under-appreciated software products of all time. While Windows 95 clearly has many features (long filenames, threads, memory-mapped files, and so on) that aren't present in WfW 3.11 or that are only partially present in Windows extensions such as Win32s, it's also true that the architectures of Windows 95 and WfW 3.11 are fundamentally the same.

This should come as no surprise, given that Microsoft's ads (late 1993-early 1994) for WfW 3.11 bragged about how 32BFA was based on "the 32-bit file system from our Chicago project." WfW 3.11 includes 32-bit file system VxDs such as IFSMgr, VCACHE, and VFAT, just as Windows 95 does. In other words, a major chunk of Windows 95 went on sale about a year and a half before the rest of the product. While WfW 3.11 sales have been impressive (finally living down WfW 3.10's reputation as "Windows for Warehouses"), the trade press has said little about the fact that we have a 32-bit protected-mode operating system living in our midst.

The inclusion of Windows 95 VxDs such as IFSMgr in WfW 3.11 was a double-edge sword, however. On the one hand (I mean, edge), Microsoft made a large chunk of Windows 95 available to the public long before the rest of Windows 95 was ready to ship. At the same time, it's not clear that the IFSMgr portion of Windows 95 was actually ready to ship. In essence, WfW 3.11 contains *pre-beta* code from Windows 95. It's also worth noting that the only way to get any programmer's documentation for the 32BFA layer in WfW 3.11 was to enlist in the Windows 95 beta: IFSMgr is completely undocumented in WfW 3.11.

Chapter 11 shows that when 32BFA is enabled, WfW 3.11 is really a 32-bit protected-mode version of MS-DOS. It's particularly interesting that 32BFA could be lifted out of Windows 95 and dropped into Windows 3.*x* without fundamental changes to VMM. The services necessary to host 32BFA were already part of VMM and had been since Windows 3.0.

Perhaps it sounds absurd that a product such as WfW 3.11, which Microsoft apparently didn't even deem worthy of more than a .01 version number increase, could possibly have the same relation to MS-DOS as Windows 95, for which Microsoft adopted a whole new version naming scheme. However, by running WLOG212F under WfW 3.11, both with and without 32BFA enabled (WIN /D:C turns off 32BFA), it's fairly easy to see that WfW 3.11 relates to MS-DOS in much the same way that Windows 95 does.

Rather than present two more log files, I've consolidated the WLOG212F results from WfW 3.11 and Windows 95 into Table 1-1.

Table 1-1: INT 21h Function Handling in WfW 3.11 and Windows 95

Function	WfW 3.11 without 32BFA	WfW 3.11 with 32BFA	Windows 95
00h	E	E	E
0Dh	–	P	–
0Eh	P	P	P
11h	P	E	–
19h	P	P	P
1Ah	S	E	E
1Ch	P	E	E
25h	E	E	E
29h	P	–	–
2Ah	P	P	P
2Ch	P	P	P
2Fh	E	E	E
30h	P	P	P
32h	–	E	E
35h	E	E	E
36h	P	E	E
3Bh	P	E	E
3Ch	P	E	E
3Dh	P	E	E
3Eh	P	E	E
3Fh	P	E	E
40h	P	E	E
41h	P	E	E
42h	P	E	E
43h	P	E	E
44h	P	S	S
45h	P	P	P
47h	P	S	E
4Bh	E	E	E
4Ch	P	P	P
4Eh	P	E	E
4Fh	P	E	E
50h	P	P	P
51h	P	P	P
52h	–	P	–
55h	P	P	P
56h	P	E	E
57h	P	S	S
59h	P	P	E
5Ah	–	P	P
5Bh	P	E	E
5Ch	–	–	E
5Dh	P	P	–
60h	–	P	–
62h	P	P	–
65h	–	–	P

68h	–	–	E
71h	–	–	E
DCh	P	P	P
E	5	23	27
P	34	18	13
S	1	3	2
–	9	5	7

P = Passed down
E = Emulated
S = Sometimes passed down
– indicates no data

Earlier, I used WLOG212F mostly to show that Windows 95 passes some INT 21h calls down to V86 mode DOS. Here, the key point is that WfW 3.11 with 32BFA emulates many INT 21h functions in protected mode, without passing them down to V86 mode DOS. As seen in Table 1-1, WfW 3.11 with 32BFA is almost identical to Windows 95. As far as their relationship with MS-DOS is concerned, there seems to be little difference between the two products.

This table makes it appear as if Windows 95 emulates a few more INT 21h calls than WfW 3.11. However, this only reflects the different INT 21h calls that happened to be seen by WLOG212F in each test. For example, WfW 3.11 passed function 0Dh down to DOS, but in Windows 95 WLOG212F happened not to encounter any calls to function 0Dh. We'll see in Chapter 8 that if anything, Windows 95 is a little *more* tied to DOS than was WfW 3.11.

There's not much to say about the difference between WfW 3.11 with and without 32BFA. Clearly, with 32BFA disabled (WIN /D:C), WfW 3.11 passes almost all INT 21h calls down to V86 mode. However, it does emulate a few calls, such as function 4Bh (EXEC) and functions 25h and 35h (Set/Get Interrupt Vector). This apparent emulation is carried out by the INT 21h handler in the Win16 KERNEL; as Chapter 13 discusses, KERNEL special cases a few INT 21h calls. For example, a function 4Bh call from a Windows application is a request to WinExec another Windows application; DOS doesn't know how to execute Windows applications, so KERNEL handles this INT 21h function call, turning the execute into a File Open, Read, Seek, and so on.

For the most part, Windows 95 and WfW 3.11 with 32BFA pass the same INT 21h calls down to V86 mode DOS. These are mostly non-file INT 21h calls such as get Date/Time, Get/Set PSP, and so on. While

Microsoft publicly claims that Windows 95 never, ever passes INT 21h calls down to V86 mode on behalf of Windows applications, a confidential Microsoft document ("Chicago File System Features — Tips & Issues," April 22, 1994) provided with Beta-1 says something very different:

> On default all INT 21 interrupts, except file API INT 21s, are passed down to any hooker present in the system.

This phrase "except file API INT 21s," is consistent with what WLOG212F showed: Windows 95, like WfW 3.11 before it, passes non-file INT 21h calls down to V86 mode. By the colorful phrase "hooker," Microsoft means code that has hooked INT 21h. Since WINBOOT.SYS itself is an INT 21h hooker, Microsoft here acknowledges what it seems so anxious to deny in its more widely publicized statements: DOS functions not related to file I/O *are* passed down to, and handled by, the real-mode DOS code. Jeez, what's so hard about saying that?

If I had to explain how Windows 95 relates to DOS in 25 words or less, I'd say this: *Windows 95 relates to DOS the same way that WfW 3.11 does.* Windows 95 provides 32BFA. For non-file calls, it calls (in V86 mode) the real-mode DOS code in WINBOOT.SYS. Windows 95 is a genuine operating system; so were WfW 3.11, Windows 3.1 Enhanced mode, and Windows 3.0 Enhanced mode.

Chapter 2

Watching Chicago Boot

Having just seen in Chapter 1 how Windows 95 actually relates to real-mode MS-DOS, it's a good time to see how all the pieces of Windows 95 fit together.

Well, the word *all* is perhaps a trifle overambitious, since the Windows 95 setup deposits about a thousand files — at least that's how many were on my hard disk. But we can get a good idea of the various discrete components that make up this "integrated" operating system by watching what happens while Windows 95 boots up.

From WINBOOT.SYS to WIN.COM

In Chapter 1, I mentioned that the Windows 95 boot record looks for WINBOOT.SYS, just as the older DOS boot record looked for IO.SYS and MSDOS.SYS. Once WINBOOT.SYS is loaded, we can start watching the Windows 95 initialization process. An excellent tool for this is the DOS version of Nu-Mega's Soft-ICE debugger. Soft-ICE (the DOS version, not the Windows version) provides a BOOT command that resets the machine while retaining Soft-ICE in memory. You can install some breakpoints and then BOOT; when your machine comes back up, you then use Soft-ICE to trace through the early portions of initialization. As one indication of its usefulness, this Soft-ICE BOOT command was used by Stac Electronics to reverse engineer the undocumented preload interface in MS-DOS 6.0. (Microsoft later claimed in court, under oath and with a straight face, that this use of the Soft-ICE BOOT command constituted "misappropriation of trade secrets"; unfortunately, the jury believed Microsoft, but fortunately the two companies have subsequently settled out of court.)

To watch the early portion of Windows 95 initialization, I set a breakpoint on the DOS File Open function (BPINT 21 AH=3D), the Extended Open/Create function (BPINT 21 AH=6C), the Find First File function (BPINT 21 AH=4E), and EXEC (BPINT 21 AH=4B). Since we've already seen that Windows 95 uses INT 21h while running, it should come as no surprise that it uses INT 21 during its initialization. Each time one of the INT 21h breakpoints was triggered, I examined the string pointed to by the DS:DX register pair.

The DOS version of Soft-ICE loads as a device driver, so I needed a CONFIG.SYS with the single line DEVICE=C:\SICE\S-ICE.EXE. None of the other drivers seen in Figure 2-1 were mentioned in this one-line CONFIG.SYS file.

```
Func    File                             Comment
----    ----                             -------
OPEN    \LOGO.SYS                        failed -- use logo inside WINBOOT.SYS
RENAME  IO.SYS -> IO.DOS                 I watched INT 21h AH=56 too
RENAME  IBMBIO.COM -> IBMBIO.DOS
RENAME  MSDOS.SYS -> MSDOS.DOS
RENAME  IBMDOS.COM -> IBMDOS.DOS
FIND    \DRVSPACE.BIN                    failed -- no DriveSpace
OPEN    C:\DBLSPACE.BIN                  failed -- no DblSpace either
EXEC    C:\WINBOOT.SYS
FIND    C:\SYSTEM.DAT                    registry
OPEN    C:\SYSTEM.DAT
OPEN    CONFIG$                          real-mode portion of Plug and Play
                                         Configuration Manager; after open,
                                         do IOCTL calls to CONFIG$

OPEN    \CONFIG.SYS                      only one line, to load Soft-ICE
OPEN    C:\SICE\S-ICE.EXE
EXEC    C:\SICE\S-ICE.EXE
OPEN    C:\WINDOWS\HIMEM.SYS             this was *not* in CONFIG.SYS!
EXEC    C:\WINDOWS\HIMEM.SYS
OPEN    IFS$HLP$                         failed
OPEN    C:\WINDOWS\IFSHLP.SYS            this was *not* in CONFIG.SYS!
EXEC    C:\WINDOWS\IFSHLP.SYS
OPEN    SETVERXX                         failed
OPEN    C:\WINDOWS\COMMAND\SETVER.EXE    this was *not* in CONFIG.SYS!
EXEC    C:\WINDOWS\COMMAND\SETVER.EXE
OPEN    CON
OPEN    AUX
OPEN    PRN
OPEN    \AUTOEXEC.BAT                    failed -- no AUTOEXEC.BAT; so no
                                         need to load COMMAND.COM either!
FIND    WIN.???
FIND    C:\WINDOWS\WIN.???
OPEN    C:\WINDOWS\WIN.COM
EXEC    C:\WINDOWS\WIN.COM               here we go!
```

```
OPEN    C:\WINDOWS\VMM32.VXD           failed -- it's in \windows\system
OPEN    C:\WINDOWS\SYSTEM\VMM32.VXD
EXEC    C:\WINDOWS\SYSTEM\VMM32.VXD    load VMM and VxDs
```

Figure 2-1: You can watch the early stage of Windows 95 initialization using Soft-ICE's BOOT command.

Figure 2-1 shows only the first stage of Windows 95 initialization. We'll be better able to follow the next stage with the INTRSPY interrupt-logging program rather than with Soft-ICE (see the "From WIN.COM to KRNL386.EXE" section). In the meantime, what's happening during this first period of Windows 95 initialization?

51

As I've noted several times, WINBOOT.SYS serves the same function in Windows 95 that IO.SYS and MSDOS.SYS served in earlier versions of MS-DOS, or that IBMBIO.COM and IBMDOS.COM served in PC-DOS and DR-DOS. Figure 2-1 shows that, every time you start Windows 95, WINBOOT.SYS looks for these old DOS kernel files; if it finds them, it renames them with a .DOS extension. This resurrects Windows 95 following an F4 boot using IO.SYS and MSDOS.SYS to run a previous version of DOS.

Next, WINBOOT.SYS tries to preload a disk-compression driver named either DRVSPACE.BIN (from MS-DOS 6.22) or DBLSPACE .BIN (from MS-DOS 6.0). The phrase "preload" refers to the loading of this driver before DOS processes CONFIG.SYS (and, in Windows 95, before it processes the registry). DBLSPACE.BIN could be Microsoft's own DblSpace or a disk-compression driver such as Stacker that masquerades as DblSpace to get itself preloaded. The DOS preload interface played a part in the Stac v. Microsoft case (for details, see *Undocumented DOS*, 2d ed., pp. 40-42, 269-270; Geoff Chappell, *DOS Internals*, pp. 156-161; and "LA Law," *Dr. Dobb's Journal*, May 1994, pp. 137-139).

After attempting to load a disk-compression driver, WINBOOT.SYS looks for user-definable configuration information. In previous versions of DOS, this meant processing CONFIG.SYS. In Windows 95, the preferred place for configuration information is the registry. Figure 2-1 shows that WINBOOT opens the file C:\SYSTEM.DAT — this is the central registry file. What Figure 2-1 doesn't show (because I was watching only a few INT 21h functions) is that WINBOOT retrieves the registry's path name by calling INT 2Fh function 1613h, which is implemented in another part of WINBOOT. The INT2FAPI.H header file included with the Chicago Device Driver Kit (DDK) refers to INT 2Fh function 16h as W386_Int_Multiplex, and has the following entry for subfunction 13h:

```
#define W386_Get_SYSDAT_Path    0x13
/* IO.SYS service to return path to SYSTEM.DAT */
```

It's interesting that Windows 95 would use the real-mode DOS code in WINBOOT to implement a nominally WIN386 function (we'll see another example of this shortly), and that the DDK header file refers to this, not as a WINBOOT.SYS service but as an IO.SYS service. INT2FAPI.H refers to several other INT 2Fh function 16h IO.SYS services that are new to Windows 95; for example, function 160Eh is the "IO.SYS service for logo management."

A complete rewrite?

If you take a few minutes to ponder the otherwise unimportant description of W386_Get_SYSDAT_Path from INT2FAPI.H, several points emerge:

- Programmers at Microsoft freely use the name IO.SYS when they refer to code located in WINBOOT.SYS. Clearly, they don't see much difference between WINBOOT.SYS and the old combination of IO.SYS and MSDOS.SYS.
- Programmers at Microsoft think nothing of implementing Windows functions (remember, INT 2Fh function 16h is W386_Int_Multiplex) down in real-mode IO.SYS.
- Programmers at Microsoft don't see much difference between Windows 95 and the old Windows/386 product.

This last point requires some explanation. INT2FAPI.H makes constant reference to Windows/386, a product that was released in 1987–88. The first datestamp in INT2FAPI.H is "10-Mar-1989 RAL" (that's Ralph Lipe, now Microsoft's chief architect for Windows 95); the file appears to have been created for what at the time was called version 3.0 of Windows/386. A little over a year later (May 1990), this Windows/386 3.0 became Windows 3.0 Enhanced mode.

INT2FAPI.H is just one of many DDK header files that reveal an unbroken continuity, from Microsoft's planned version 3.0 of Windows/386 all the way to Windows 95. For example, the VPICD.H header file included with the DDK is dated "13-Apr-1988 RAL", VMDA.H is dated "05-May-1988 AAR" (Aaron Reynolds), and the all-important VMM.INC is dated "05-May 1988 RAL". Good chunks of Windows 95 were first written for the Windows/386 3.*x* project.

So what? Well, Microsoft claims that Windows 95 has an entirely new architecture not based on any previous versions of Windows. For example:

> *Windows no longer can be likened to a fancy paint job on an old MS-DOS Yugo. Because the entire operating system is freshly designed from the ground up,*

you now have killer features such as threads, memory-mapped files, and asynch I/O.

— *Dave Edson, "Seventeen Techniques for Preparing Your 16-bit Applications for Chicago,"* Microsoft Systems Journal, *February 1994, p. 20.*

And, of course, the computer trade press — ya gotta believe! — happily chimes in:

Chicago is an operating system with an entirely new architecture.

— PC Magazine, *April 12, 1994, p. 184.*

Chicago uses all-new code, written from the ground up.

— PC/Computing, *March 1994, p. 126.*

[Chicago is] an entirely rewritten 32-bit pre-emptive multitasking operating system.

— InfoWorld, *July 4, 1994, p. 45.*

What's the origin of this idea that Windows 95 is freshly designed from the ground up, is written from the ground up, has an entirely new architecture, has been entirely rewritten, and uses all new code? It must be wishful thinking, because not even the most casual glance at the code, nor even the most cursory examination of the header files included with the Chicago DDK — some of which are even older than INT2FAPI.H — bears out this happy thought.

In truth, I'm not sure how much of a happy thought that really is. Do you want to trust your program to an entirely rewritten-from-the-ground-up — in other words, largely untested — version 1.0 operating system? I didn't think so.

It might seem perverse of me to scrutinize minor points in an obscure DDK header file, especially in light of Microsoft's many carefully worded statements regarding the Windows 95 architecture. It's unlikely that much thought went into INT2FAPI.H. But that's a major reason to examine this obscure file! Just as people are more likely to tell the truth when they're in casual situations than when they carefully consider what they're saying (which was the basis for Freud's brilliant *Psychopathology of Everyday Life*), a corporate entity such as Microsoft is likely to reveal more in off-hand header-file comments than in carefully orchestrated statements for the press. An otherwise unimportant header file such as INT2FAPI.H can tell us more about Windows 95 design and architecture than can a hundred Microsoft press releases.

By looking over files haphazardly thrown on the Chicago DDK, we learn that Windows 95 isn't entirely rewritten from the ground up, but rather is based on the Windows/386 3.0 project, which became Windows 3.0 Enhanced mode. And the VMM core of Windows 95 made its first appearance, under the name Virtual DOS Machine Manager (VDMM), in Windows/386 2.1:

> *A program that runs in the 80386's native 32-bit protected mode and oversees a set of virtual machines is called a 386 control program, or virtual machine monitor. Windows/386 is such a virtual machine monitor; it also provides complete device virtualization for the PC's disk controller, video adapter, keyboard, mouse, timer chip, and 8259 programmable interrupt controllers.*
>
> — *Ray Duncan, "Microsoft Windows/386: Creating a Virtual Machine Environment,"* Microsoft Systems Journal, *September 1987, p. 5.*

In Windows 95, the VMM manages threads as well as virtual machines, but the Windows 95 VMM still has its roots in the Windows/386 VDMM. Unfortunately, few programmers or journalists paid much attention to this VDMM layer in Windows/386, or indeed to the VMM and VxD layer in Windows 3.*x*. This is one reason why Windows 95 appears to be newer, and a more radical break with the past, than it really is.

According to the biographical note in the back of his authorized, semi-official *Inside Windows 95*, ex-Microsoft employee Adrian King "managed the group that developed Windows/386, the product that pioneered the use of software virtual machine technology in Microsoft operating systems." King's work on Windows/386 gives him many insights into Windows 95. For example, how many authors would know that Microsoft not only uses V86 mode but also helped to design it? As King states on page 37, "Microsoft helped Intel design virtual 8086 mode and harnessed that mode initially with the release of Windows/386 in 1987."

Another point King makes is that while Windows/386 provides some of the background to DOS compatibility in Windows 95, "no code is repeated" (p. 4n). A quick look at the WIN386.386 file (dated July 1, 1988) from Windows/386 2.1 seems to bear this out. Although there are many conceptual similarities between Windows/386 2.1 and Windows 95 — which is why Duncan's 1987 *Microsoft Systems Journal* article remains useful reading — Microsoft nonetheless appears to have used Windows/386 2.1 as its "throw one away" testbed for what would two years later become Windows 3.0 Enhanced mode and seven years later, Windows 95.

In particular, Microsoft appears to have engaged in a large rewrite campaign between the Windows/386 2.1 release in 1987-88, and the release of Windows 3.0 Enhanced Enhanced mode in 1990. For example, look at some of the Windows VxD source files included with the DDK:

File	**Description**
VPICD.INC	"13-Apr-1988 RAL Rewrite"
VNETBIOS.ASM	"25-Apr-1988 RAL Complete rewrite of network (used to be VND)"
VKD.ASM	"29-Jul-1988 RAP Started complete rewrite"

So yes, parts of Windows 95 *were* completely rewritten — back in 1988!

From the Registry to XMS

Having discussed how WINBOOT locates the registry, a few words are in order about the registry itself. Unlike CONFIG.SYS, AUTOEXEC.BAT, SYSTEM.INI, and so on — all files that it seeks to replace — the registry is not a readable plain ASCII file. Users can browse and edit the registry with the REGEDIT application. Programs query and change the registry with Windows API functions such as RegOpenKey, RegEnumKey, RegQueryValue, RegCreateKey, and RegSetValue. VMM provides the actual implementation of the registry-access functions; the Windows APIs call VMM's protected-mode API. DOS programs can access the registry with VMM's V86 API.

The registry is a hierarchical database of keys and values, holding everything from Object Linking and Embedding (OLE) settings and File Viewer associations to performance-monitoring statistics and dynamic VxD information. For example, the following tree (produced by recursively calling RegOpenKey, RegEnumKey, RegQueryValue, and RegCloseKey) represents information (stored in HKEY_LOCAL_MACHINE\SOFTWARE\Classes) about Microsoft Word 6.0 documents:

```
Word.Document.6=Microsoft Word 6.0 Document
   shell
      open
         command=C:\MSOFFICE\WINWORD\WINWORD.EXE /w
         ddeexec=[FileOpen("%1")]
      print
         command=C:\MSOFFICE\WINWORD\WINWORD.EXE /w
         ddeexec=[FileOpen("%1")][FilePrint()][DocClose(2)]
            ifexec=[FileOpen("%1")][FilePrint .Background = 0][FileExit(2)]
   CLSID={00020900-0000-0000-C000-000000000046}
   Insertable
   protocol
      StdFileEditing
         verb
            0=Edit
         server=C:\MSOFFICE\WINWORD\WINWORD.EXE
```

To determine the incantation to print a Word 6.0 document, for instance, a program could RegQueryValue these two keys:

```
Word.Document.6\shell\print\command
Word.Document.6\shell\print\ddeexec
```

The value of the first key can be passed to WinExec:

```
C:\MSOFFICE\WINWORD\WINWORD.EXE /w
```

and the value of the second key is a DDE EXEC string:

```
[FileOpen("%1")][FilePrint()][DocClose(2)]
```

Notice that the program requires no hard-wired knowledge other than the names of the keys.

Windows 95 itself uses the registry to store configuration information, for example, regarding dynamic VxDs loaded by the I/O Supervisor:

```
[HKEY_LOCAL_MACHINE\System\CurrentControlSet\Services\Class\fdc\0000]
"DevLoader"="IOS"
"PortDriver"="HSFLOP.pdr"
"DriverDesc"="Standard Floppy Disk Controller"
"Int13ToDrvSelMap"=hex:00,1c,01,2d
```


Mercifully (I've somehow trashed SYSTEM.DAT more than once), Windows 95 can run with a missing or corrupted registry, though it will warn that "Registry services may be inoperative for this session." You can also use the F8 interactive boot to bypass the registry. Without a registry, Windows 95 cannot support features such as OLE or Quick View (a handy Explorer option that we'll use later to examine some components of Windows 95). Each time you shut down Windows 95, it writes known-good registry files named SYSTEM.DA0 and USER.DA0. But I still bet some enterprising third-party vendor will come along with much-needed registry repair tools.

Returning to Figure 2-1, we see that after opening the registry, Windows 95 opens the CONFIG$ device, which is part of WINBOOT.SYS. CONFIG$ is the real-mode portion of the Plug and Play Configuration Manager. The protected-mode portion lives in a VxD called CONFIGMG (it will probably be a while before Microsoft starts using long filenames for core executable files). The CONFIGMG VxD communicates with the real-mode CONFIG$ device via the DOS IOCTL function; CONFIGMG passes CONFIG$ a V86 callback (see the upcoming sidebar "Pushing aside real-mode drivers?") so that CONFIG$ can call up to CONFIGMG. In some ways, CONFIG$ can be viewed as an extension of the DOS 6.0 multi-boot feature.

Aside from the point that the Plug and Play Configuration Manager even has a real-mode component, it's also worth noting that CONFIG$ provides a new interface that lets DOS device drivers and TSRs query configuration information. As described in a Microsoft document, "Plug and Play Device Driver Interface for Windows 3.1 and MS-DOS" (October 5, 1993) — Microsoft and Intel provide a Plug and Play add-in (DWCFGMG.SYS) for non-Windows 95 systems — the interface uses

INT 2Fh function 1684h, with the value 34h in BX. It just so happens that INT 2Fh function 1684h is normally called to retrieve the entry point to a VxD whose ID is given in the BX register; 34h is the VxD ID for CONFIGMG. Once again we see a Windows interface implemented down in the real-mode DOS portion of Windows 95.

Next, if there is a CONFIG.SYS file, WINBOOT processes it. I did need a CONFIG.SYS here to load Soft-ICE, but not to load HIMEM, IFSHLP, or SETVER. WINBOOT.SYS loaded these automatically, in much the same way that MS-DOS 6.*x* (and as we've seen, WINBOOT .SYS, too) would automatically load DBLSPACE.BIN or DRVSPACE .BIN. An important difference is that disk-compression drivers need to be loaded before processing CONFIG.SYS; the XMS and IFSHLP drivers required to run Windows can be loaded after CONFIG.SYS.

There's nothing particularly sophisticated about WINBOOT's ability to find and load file drivers such as HIMEM and IFSHLP. In his discussion of system startup in the brilliant book *DOS Internals*, Geoff Chappell said that DOS 6.0's provisions for loading DBLSPACE.BIN, despite Microsoft's claims of providing integrated (there's that word again!) disk compression, "has the appearance of a hack" (p. 156). Much the same is true of WINBOOT's ability to bootstrap Windows. If you don't look too hard, the ability to load Windows without any configuration files looks quite integrated; however, it involves nothing more than some trivial code (find and execute HIMEM.SYS, IFSHLP.SYS, and WIN.COM) hacked into SYSINIT.

Like previous versions of Windows, Windows 95 requires HIMEM .SYS or some other extended-memory (XMS) driver, the V86MMGR (V86 Memory Manager) VxD supplies its own XMS services once Windows is up and running. V86MMGR's XMS server replaces the one that must be present before Windows starts.

Pushing aside real-mode drivers?

The relationship between V86MMGR and a real-mode XMS server such as HIMEM may help shed some light on another one of Microsoft's confusing claims regarding Windows 95 — that its VxDs "take over" from, and possibly even "push aside," any equivalent real-mode drivers.

Adrian King's explanation of this "take over" idea is quite reasonable:

> *The file system design in Windows 95 allows a protected mode port driver to take control of a real mode driver and bypass it while the system is running in protected mode — Windows 95 can classify the real mode driver as a 'safe' driver. Safe means, essentially, that the protected mode driver can offer functionality identical to the real mode driver's. In such a case, the protected mode driver will simply carry out all the I/O operations and never call the real mode driver.*
>
> — *King,* Inside Windows 95, *p. 307.*

This makes a lot of sense: Many VxDs do provide functionality that replaces what's provided by some real-mode driver (for example, CDFS replaces MSCDEX, and VCACHE replaces SmartDrive). The file IOS.INI contains a list of so-called "safe" real-mode drivers from which a VxD can take over. Here, "take over" simply means never calling — that is, ignoring the presence of — the real-mode driver.

However, Microsoft has at times suggested that Windows 95 will literally unload the safe real-mode driver and reclaim its memory. Ralph Lipe discussed this possibility in his presentation on the Windows 95 architecture at Microsoft's Win32 Professional Developers Conference in 1993. I've also heard the specific claim that the CDFS (CD-ROM file system) VxD will unload MSCDEX from memory. Certainly, this is the image conjured up by the more general claims that Windows "pushes the real mode code aside" (*Inside Windows 95*, p. 71). Ignoring something is not normally equated with pushing it aside.

Presumably Jon Udell of *Byte* magazine heard the same line I did:

> *When protected-mode components like the VFAT (Virtual FAT) and CD-ROM file systems, network redirectors, and 32-bit DoubleSpace driver load, they can, in many cases, unload their corresponding real-mode components from memory. DOS will then be history...."*
>
> — *"Chicago: An Ambitious Compromise,"* Byte, *March 1994, p. 22.*

HIMEM.SYS isn't an I/O driver, but a look at V86MMGR's interaction with HIMEM can help clear up a lot of the confusion about Windows 95 pushing aside real-mode drivers.

Although V86MMGR replaces HIMEM or another real-mode XMS server with its own 32-bit protected-mode XMS server, V86MMGR doesn't "push" the real-mode XMS server off the machine. It doesn't unload HIMEM, reclaim its memory, or anything like that. How could it? Some code that loaded after HIMEM but before V86MMGR might have called INT 2Fh function 4310h (Get XMS Entry Point) and might be hanging on to a function pointer that it thinks is the address of the XMS server. If V86MMGR were somehow to unload HIMEM from memory, the system would most likely hang the intermediate program that called this stale function pointer.

V86MMGR can't unload HIMEM. Instead, as shown in Chapters 8 and 11, V86MMGR uses the VMM Install_V86 _Break_Point service to patch the real-mode XMS driver. If anyone calls the real-mode XMS server, they will immediately encounter a V86 breakpoint that jumps them into V86MMGR.

That V86MMGR will install a V86 breakpoint over HIMEM is a good illustration not only of the fact that Windows 95 doesn't push real-mode code aside but also of the equally important fact that Windows 95 (like previous versions of Enhanced mode) will run this real-mode code in V86 mode and alter it in various ways.

It's difficult to see how Windows 95 could possibly unload any nontrivial real-mode driver or TSR from memory. Another good example is MSCDEX (Microsoft CD-ROM Extensions); it's fairly well-known that MSCDEX patches MS-DOS (see *Undocumented DOS*, 2d ed., p. 463). Unloading MSCDEX would require backing out these patches. This is why the excellent MARK/RELEASE utilities by Kim Kokkonen never quite worked 100% of the time with MSCDEX.

If you think about it, for Windows 95 to truly unload real-mode drivers and TSRs from memory, it would have to include very sophisticated versions of MARK/RELEASE. Unloading drivers and TSRs is not just a matter of unhooking some interrupt vectors. An examination of Kim Kokkonen's comments to MARK.PAS and RELEASE.PAS shows that over the years it has become more and more complicated to safely unload this stuff.

I suppose it's possible that Windows 95 could in time incorporate a facility to release certain specific drivers or TSRs, such as MSCDEX, about which it had intimate knowledge. However, there's no general technique for undoing all the nasty hooks and patches that drivers and TSRs might have inserted into the real-mode DOS code.

The only reason the question of unloading drivers and TSRs comes up is that Windows 95 (specifically, as we'll see in a few minutes, the WIN.COM component of Windows 95) intends for you never to exit Windows and return to MS-DOS. When you shut down Windows 95, you can choose between shutting down the machine, restarting Windows 95, or logging off the network; exiting back to the C:\> prompt is not an option. (This is another way that Windows 95 creates the impression of being seamlessly integrated with the machine, as though it were without any intervening real-mode DOS code.) Since Windows 95 never exits back to DOS, it obviously needn't worry about undoing whatever changes it makes to DOS — such as, hypothetically, unloading redundant real-mode drivers.

But wait a minute! As you might know, for those few DOS programs that won't run in a V86 mode DOS box, Windows 95 offers a Single Application Mode check box in the DOS box properties. In Single Application Mode, Windows 95 saves away its current context, puts the machine into real (not V86!) mode, and runs a DOS command prompt. This is very much like exiting Windows back to DOS or like running a DOS box in Windows 3.*x* Standard mode. VxDs are unloaded, which is why long filename support disappears in Single Application Mode — IFSMgr isn't running. Windows 95 even issues the INT 2Fh function 1606h Windows Exit broadcast, so that software loaded before Windows 95 thinks — pretty much correctly — that Windows is exiting (see Chapter 3). When you exit from Single Application Mode back to Windows, Windows 95 reinitializes, reloads VxDs, issues the function 1605h Windows Startup broadcast, and so on.

Given that Windows 95 really can exit back to DOS, albeit via this odd Single Application Mode, it's hard to see how Windows 95 could possibly unload TSRs and device drivers. Windows 95 would just have to reload them again whenever a user wanted Single Application Mode.

In short, not only does Windows 95 not currently push real-mode code aside, it's unlikely that it ever could. It's much more likely that for those real-mode drivers whose functionality is provided by a VxD and is not required during Windows initialization (MSCDEX is a good example), the phrase "push the real-mode code aside" means little more than that the Windows 95 Setup program could remove any mention of them from CONFIG.SYS and AUTOEXEC.BAT.

How did this humble feature get transubstantiated into the glorious idea that Windows 95 would literally unload the "safe" device drivers and TSRs and reclaim their memory? I think this happened because it's natural — even for programmers and the computer trade press — to hear what you want to hear.

For example, a Microsoft VP once told me that Windows 95 would "shove DOS off the machine," and from the context of our conversation I was sure at the time that he meant Windows 95 would literally unload DOS from memory and load itself at the memory location previously occupied by DOS and by real-mode drivers. That's what I wanted to believe, anyway. In retrospect, I bet he just meant something trivial such as that the Windows 95 setup program removes DEVICE= lines from CONFIG.SYS, or that WINBOOT.SYS replaces IO.SYS and MSDOS.SYS. Or maybe this VP really believed that Windows 95 can plow real-mode code off a running machine, because this is what one of his programmers told him. The programmer, meanwhile, just meant that the Windows 95 setup program removes....

Perhaps Microsoft's incorrect descriptions of the Windows 95 architecture are due to nothing more than a wishful-thinking variant of the game of "telephone."

From IFSHLP.SYS to WIN.COM

After HIMEM.SYS, WINBOOT loads IFSHLP.SYS. As noted in the "...But Bypassing DOS, Too?" section of Chapter 1, the real-mode code in IFSHLP is a key part of Windows 95's installable file system; IFSMgr won't load if it can't locate the IFSHLP driver. IFSMgr calls IFSHLP using the DOS IOCTL function, and passes IFSHLP a pointer to a V86 callback that IFSHLP can later use to communicate with IFSMgr. (See "The Role of IFSHLP.SYS and V86 Callbacks" in Chapter 8.)

WINBOOT.SYS next loads SETVER.EXE (which changes the DOS version number on a per-application basis — sick!) and, under certain circumstances, Microsoft's expanded memory manager, EMM386.EXE.

Note that the V86MMGR VxD not only provides XMS services but is also an EMM.

Next in Figure 2-1, WINBOOT.SYS looks for an AUTOEXEC.BAT file. WINBOOT.SYS loads the DOS command shell (COMMAND.COM) to process AUTOEXEC.BAT. However, as shown earlier, if there's no AUTOEXEC.BAT, there's no need to load COMMAND.COM, and WINBOOT will proceed directly to load WIN.COM. This, of course, is the tight integration we've all been hearing so much about. Well, it's nice and everything, but it's about as integrated as the Boston public school system before court-ordered busing.

Bypassing COMMAND.COM definitely saves some memory, but I don't see any significant architectural difference between WINBOOT .SYS's direct loading of WIN.COM, and putting WIN as the last line of AUTOEXEC.BAT. Now, it *is* a huge difference that end-users don't have to go into AUTOEXEC.BAT (a scary process for many people) and add a WIN command. But this usability enhancement, however important, doesn't constitute a fundamental change in the Windows architecture. In whatever way Windows gets loaded, DOS is still sitting underneath it. It's just a matter of whether COMMAND.COM sits down there too.

Incidentally, to autoload WIN.COM, WINBOOT.SYS must know its location. Although WIN.COM is usually found in C:\WINDOWS, this location is *not* hard-wired (excuse me, I mean "integrated") into WINBOOT.SYS. It comes from the registry (HKEY_LOCAL_MACHINE \Software\Microsoft\Windows\Current Version\System Root).

So, yes, autoloading WIN.COM is a great feature: just don't say it involves changing the Windows architecture. I think some sort of "Technology Rulz" prejudice makes it difficult for many of us in the computer industry to believe that a major usability enhancement can come about without an underlying fundamental change to the software. Well, it can.

But why autoload WIN.COM? As is well known, WIN.COM is not Windows. It is a small (less than 20K) program whose job is to load Windows (see Matt Pietrek, *Windows Internals*, pp. 3-8). Why doesn't WINBOOT.SYS just load Windows directly? Why bother with WIN .COM at all?

We'll see in a moment that, in Windows 95, WIN.COM loads the file VMM32.VXD. In Windows 3.*x* Enhanced mode, WIN.COM loaded WIN386.EXE and, in Standard mode, DOSX.EXE. Chapters 5 through 7 show that executables such as DOSX.EXE, WIN386.EXE, and even VMM32.EXE (if you rename it with an .EXE extension) can be run directly from the C:\> prompt. So it seems that WINBOOT.SYS should be able to directly load VMM32.VXD, and bypass WIN.COM just as it usually bypasses COMMAND.COM.

The file now called VMM32.VXD was called DOS386.EXE in early pre-beta versions of Windows 95. There was a DOS=ENHANCED switch in CONFIG.SYS (such as DOS=HIGH,UMB,ENHANCED) that IO.SYS (as it was still called back then) would interpret as a request to directly load DOS386.EXE. Notice that ENHANCED was a reference, not to Windows, but to DOS! Apparently at one time there was some consideration at Microsoft of having Standard and Enhanced modes of MS-DOS. Standard mode would, presumably, be a real-mode version of MS-DOS, and Enhanced mode would be a V86-mode version, running under DOS386.EXE. Chapter 6 shows how to easily build your own copy of this Enhanced mode of MS-DOS, in the privacy and comfort of your own home.

Thus, some thought did go into bypassing WIN.COM. But WIN.COM plays an important role in Windows 95; namely, it prevents you from exiting back to DOS. When you shut down Windows 95, it is WIN.COM that displays the message, "You can now safely turn off the computer. If you want to restart your computer, press Ctrl-Alt-Del." As we'll see in Chapter 7, if you run VMM32 without WIN.COM, you can exit back to DOS. Clearly, such an ability interferes with the image Microsoft wants to build of a seamless, integrated Windows PC.

From WIN.COM to KRNL386.EXE

The tail end of Figure 2-1 shows that WIN.COM runs VMM32.VXD. This contains, we'll see, the very heart and soul of the Windows operating system (and I do mean operating system, not operating environment).

While the BOOT command in Soft-ICE gave us a ringside seat to the early stages of the Windows 95 boot process, it can be somewhat tedious to interact with the debugger every time Windows 95 triggers a Soft-ICE breakpoint. All we really need is a list of the files that Windows 95 looks for, opens, or executes; such a list is best generated using a non-interactive debugger.

David Maxey's INTRSPY (Interrupt Spy) utility from *Undocumented DOS* (2d ed., pp. 229-263) is perfect for this. INTRSPY can be loaded in AUTOEXEC.BAT. Actually, I've just realized that you don't need AUTOEXEC.BAT (and hence COMMAND.COM) to run TSRs such as INTRSPY, because Windows 95 processes any INSTALL= commands in CONFIG.SYS. But since we already know that the effect of AUTO-EXEC.BAT is fairly minimal (aside from creating a global COMMAND .COM visible in all VMs), we should be okay.

The CMDSPY script compiler can be given a script that tells INTR-SPY to log calls to the DOS File Find, Open, and EXEC functions. For instance, to watch the DOS File Open function (INT 21h function 3Dh), which expects an ASCII filename in DS:DX and which returns either a file handle (if the carry flag is clear) or an error code (carry set) in AX, an INTRSPY script might look like this:


```
intercept 21h
    function 3Dh
        on_entry
            output "OPEN " (ds:dx->byte,asciiz,64)
        on_exit if (cflag == 1)
            sameline " [FAIL " ax "]"
```

Figure 2-2 shows the next stage of the Windows 95 boot process, overlapped slightly with the bottom of Figure 2-1. In addition to File Find, Open, and EXEC functions, the INTRSPY script also logged calls to Extended Open/Create (function 6Ch, shown as XOPEN in Figure 2-2), to File Create, and to the new long filename (LFN) variants of all these functions. However, as long as INTRSPY is a DOS TSR, it will never see these LFN DOS calls.

```
EXEC  C:\WINDOWS\WIN.COM
OPEN  C:\WINDOWS\vmm32.vxd [FAIL 2]
OPEN  C:\WINDOWS\system\vmm32.vxd
EXEC  C:\WINDOWS\system\vmm32.vxd
OPEN  QEMM386$ [FAIL 2]
OPEN  386MAX$$ [FAIL 2]
OPEN  SMARTAAR [FAIL 2]
OPEN  C:\SYSTEM.DAT
OPEN  $DebugDD [FAIL 2]
OPEN  NDISHLP$ [FAIL 2]
OPEN  C:\WINDOWS\SYSTEM.INI
CREAT C:\WINDOWS\WNBOOTNG.STS
FIND  C:\WINDOWS\SYSTEM\VMM32\*.VXD [FAIL 18]
OPEN  C:\WINDOWS\system\nwlink.386
OPEN  C:\WINDOWS\system\wsipx.386
OPEN  C:\WINDOWS\system\vnetsup.386
OPEN  IFS$HLP$
OPEN  C:\WINDOWS\system\ndis.386
OPEN  IFS$HLP$
OPEN  C:\WINDOWS\system\ndis2sup.386
OPEN  NDISHLP$ [FAIL 2]
OPEN  C:\WINDOWS\system\msodisup.386
OPEN  C:\WINDOWS\system\vnetbios.386
```

```
OPEN  C:\WINDOWS\system\wsock.386
OPEN  CONFIG$
OPEN  C:\WINDOWS\system\vserver.386
OPEN  IFS$HLP$
OPEN  C:\WINDOWS\system\vredir.386
OPEN  c:\andrew\vxd.386
OPEN  C:\WINDOWS\system\dva.386
OPEN  C:\WINDOWS\system\vpmtd.386
OPEN  IFS$HLP$
OPEN  SMARTAAR [FAIL 2]
OPEN  C:\WINDOWS\system\ISAPNP.vxd
OPEN  C:\WINDOWS\system\MMDEVLDR.vxd
OPEN  C:\WINDOWS\system\MSSB16.vxd
OPEN  C:\WINDOWS\system\VJOYD.vxd
OPEN  SCSIMGR$ [FAIL 2]
OPEN  C:\WINDOWS\IOS.INI
XOPEN C:\WINDOWS\IOS.LOG
FIND  C:\WINDOWS\system\IOSUBSYS\*.vxd
OPEN  C:\WINDOWS\system\IOSUBSYS\apix.vxd
OPEN  C:\WINDOWS\system\IOSUBSYS\cdfs.vxd
OPEN  C:\WINDOWS\system\IOSUBSYS\cdtsd.vxd
OPEN  C:\WINDOWS\system\IOSUBSYS\cdvsd.vxd
OPEN  C:\WINDOWS\system\IOSUBSYS\disktsd.vxd
OPEN  C:\WINDOWS\system\IOSUBSYS\diskvsd.vxd
OPEN  C:\WINDOWS\system\IOSUBSYS\scsi1hlp.vxd
OPEN  C:\WINDOWS\system\IOSUBSYS\voltrack.vxd
OPEN  C:\WINDOWS\system\IOSUBSYS\rmm.pdr
XOPEN C:\WINDOWS\NDISLOG.TXT
OPEN  C:\WINDOWS\system\ee16.386
OPEN  C:\WINDOWS\system\netbeui.386
OPEN  C:\WINDOWS\WINSTART.BAT [FAIL 2] ;;; look on path for WINSTART.BAT
OPEN  C:\WINDOWS\system\LPTENUM.vxd
OPEN  C:\WINDOWS\system\UNICODE.BIN
OPEN  IFS$HLP$
EXEC  C:\WINDOWS\system\krnl386.exe
```

Figure 2-2: Using INTRSPY, we see the middle stage of Windows 95's initialization.

Although I edited the INTRSPY output in one place — instead of showing all the lines where Windows 95 looks for a WINSTART.BAT file in each subdirectory in my PATH, I've shown only one such line, and added a comment — Figure 2-2 is otherwise all that INTRSPY saw of the Windows 95 boot process. Even if you're only vaguely familiar with the architecture of Windows, you probably suspect that there must be a lot more to Windows 95 than what's shown in Figure 2-2. Where's the Windows 95 Explorer? Where's GDI? What about the Win32 kernel?

Yes, there's a ton of INT 21h file activity missing from the INTRSPY log in Figure 2-2, and no, INTRSPY is not broken. INTRSPY hasn't missed anything seen by real-mode DOS.

Oh, of course: 32-bit file access! Once 32BFA is up and running, Windows 95 won't be sending file I/O calls down to DOS. Consequently, INTRSPY (which, again, is a real-mode DOS TSR) won't see these calls either. INTRSPY gets the same truncated view if you use it to watch WfW 3.11 with 32BFA. There's a way (at least in Beta-1) to make Windows 95 load without 32BFA, and I'll use this loophole later so that INTRSPY can watch Windows 95 boot all the way up. In the meantime, Figure 2-2 has enough material to last us for a while.

The top of Figure 2-2 overlaps slightly with the bottom of Figure 2-1. WINBOOT has run WIN.COM, which turns around to look for and run VMM32.VXD. As noted earlier, VMM32.VXD is the equivalent in Windows 95 of WIN386.EXE in Windows 3.*x* Enhanced mode. However, this might not tell you much. It's amazing how little attention has been paid, until Windows 95, to this crucial lower half of Windows.

Despite its filename extension, VMM32.VXD is not a single Virtual Device Driver (VxD) but a collection of VxDs. Like WIN386.EXE, VMM32.VXD uses the W3 executable file format. The *Unauthorized Windows 95* disk comes with a program, W3MAP, that you can use to examine these W3 files.

W3MAP, I have to admit, is a boring-looking character-mode DOS program. What we really need is a VxD "Quick View" DLL for the Windows 95 Explorer. But that's a different project, for a different book. In the meantime, W3MAP's heart is in the right place, even if its user interface could be better. If you give W3MAP the name of a W3 file, it spits out a list of the VxDs that comprise that file. For example:

```
C:\UNAUTHW>w3map \windows\system\vmm32.vxd
W3          00010000
VMM         00011000
VDD         00058000
VFLATD      00063000
ENABLE      00065000
VSHARE      0006d000
VWIN32      00071000
VFBACKUP    0007c000
VCOMM       00080000
COMBUFF     00089000
VCD         0008c000
IFSMGR      00091000
IOS         000b0000
SPOOLER     000be000
VFAT        000c5000
VCACHE      000d1000
...
```

The Windows 95 setup program builds VMM32.VXD out of loose VxDs, so the file might differ from one machine to another. But VMM32 .VXD generally incorporates about 45 VxDs. The hex number next to each VxD name is the offset within the file where that VxD can be found. However, the first item shown, W3, isn't a VxD, but rather the W3 file-format map for the rest of the file. Everything before it (here, 10000h bytes) is a real-mode DOS program — the program that WIN.COM runs — whose job is to switch to 32-bit protected mode and start the process of loading the VxDs in the rest of the file. DOS doesn't know how to load VxDs; this DOS program at the head of VMM32.VXD includes the VxD bootstrap loader.

Starting with the Virtual Machine Manager (VMM) at offset 11000h in the file, everything else is a VxD. Well, it's not quite accurate to call VMM a VxD, since it really manages all the VxDs in the system. But in terms of its file format, VMM looks like just another VxD. All VxDs, and VMM, use the 32-bit Linear Executable (LE) file format. If you dump out one of the locations displayed by W3MAP, you'll see an LE header:

```
C:\UNAUTHW>dump -offset 0x11000 \windows\system\vmm32.vxd
00011000 | 4C 45 00 00 00 00 00 00 02 00 04 00 00 00 00 00 | LE..............
00011010 | 00 80 02 00 40 00 00 00 04 00 00 00 66 05 00 00 | ....@.......f...
...
```

Well, this isn't terribly interesting. You can get a better idea of what's in VMM32.VXD — or in any other file that uses the W3 format, such as WIN386.EXE from Windows 3.*x* Enhanced mode — if you use W3MAP's -VERBOSE option.

Inside the Virtual Machine Manager

When pointed at VMM32.VXD, W3MAP -VERBOSE spits out almost 2,000 lines of information about the VxDs in the file and the functions they provide. I'm not going to bore you by displaying the full output (which would occupy about fifty pages of this book and which you can easily produce yourself using W3MAP), so let's just look at VMM.

As Adrian King notes (*Inside Windows 95*, p. 67), "The Virtual Machine Manager is the heart of the Windows 95 operating system. It includes software to implement all the basic system primitives for task scheduling, virtual memory operations, program loading and termination, and inter-task communication." The bit about program loading isn't quite true (VMM knows nothing about either the Win16 or Win32 executable file formats), but otherwise this is a good description. VMM is the heart of Windows 95. It also was the heart of Windows 93 (WfW 3.11), Windows 92 (3.1 Enhanced mode), and Windows 90 (3.0 Enhanced mode), but we'll get into that in a moment.

In addition to the various services it provides, VMM also holds the primary interrupt, fault, and exception handlers in the system. For example, all hardware interrupts from the timer, keyboard, mouse, COM ports, and so on first go to VMM, which generally hands them off to the Virtual Programmable Interrupt Controller (PIC) Device (VPICD) VxD. Likewise, general-protection (GP) faults and virtual-memory page faults first go to VMM, which either deals with them itself or doles them out to interested VxDs.

So what's VMM look like? Figure 2-3 shows a small portion of the verbose W3MAP output:

```
Module name: VMM
VMM_DDB @ 0001:0000dc28
Real-mode Init @ 0004:00000566
Device # 0001
Virtual Machine Manager
Version 4.00
Init order: 00000000 (Earliest -- same as VMM)
DDB_Control_Proc @ 000013de
DDB_V86_API_Proc @ 00001a11
DDB_PM_API_Proc  @ 00001a11
DDB_Service_Table @ 0000d644 (179 services)
    010000 @ 00001a08   Get_VMM_Version
    010001 @ 00000e46   Get_Cur_VM_Handle
    010002 @ 00000e4d   Test_Cur_VM_Handle
    010003 @ 00000e54   Get_Sys_VM_Handle
    010004 @ 00000e5b   Test_Sys_VM_Handle
    010005 @ 00000e64   Validate_VM_Handle
    010006 @ 0000312c   Get_VMM_Reenter_Count
    010007 @ 00003133   Begin_Reentrant_Execution
    010008 @ 0000313c   End_Reentrant_Execution
    010009 @ 00000704   Install_V86_Break_Point
    01000a @ 0000078c   Remove_V86_Break_Point
    01000b @ 0000098c   Allocate_V86_Call_Back
    01000c @ 000009de   Allocate_PM_Call_Back
    01000d @ 00000a90   Call_When_VM_Returns
    01000e @ 00001a58   Schedule_Global_Event
    01000f @ 00001ab8   Schedule_VM_Event
...
```

Figure 2-3: A small portion of VMM, as displayed by the W3MAP utility.

In addition to providing a V86 and PM programming interface (accessible to DOS and Windows applications via INT 2Fh function 1684h), we see here that VMM provides 179h (377) services to other VxDs. I've listed just the first few here.

You can examine VMM's code for these services if you have a Windows disassembler (such as my Windows Source product from V Communications) or a debugger such as Soft-ICE/Windows from Nu-Mega Technologies (which is what I've used in most cases for this book). For example, the code for the first few VMM services named is not particularly exciting, but looking at this code is a good way to get acquainted with VMM and 32-bit protected-mode code in general:

```
Get_VMM_Version
0028:C0002A08 B800040000        MOV      EAX,00000400
0028:C0002A0D 33C9              XOR      ECX,ECX
0028:C0002A0F F8                CLC
0028:C0002A10 C3                RET
```

In Figure 2-3, W3MAP said that, in VMM on disk, Get_VMM_Version was located at 1A08h. Soft-ICE shows the function at 28:C0002A08h. Thus, VMM loaded at address 28:C0001000. While a full address such as 0028:C0002A08h requires 48 bits (two bytes for the segment, which is called a selector in protected mode, and four bytes for the offset), 32-bit code usually needs to worry about only the 32-bit offset. (See the discussion of thunking in Chapter 14 for an interesting example in which Win32 code has to manipulate full 48-bit addresses.) Selector 28h, which is the code segment for VMM and all VxDs, and selector 30h, which is the data segment, both have a base address of 0 and a limit (last valid offset) of 0FFFFFFFFh. That's a 4GB address space. VxDs can use a 32-bit offset to manipulate anything within this address space.

This otherwise-boring Get_VMM_Version service helps introduce the 32-bit register set. Instead of the 16-bit AX and CX registers most PC programmers are familiar with, this code is manipulating 32-bit registers called EAX and ECX. EAX, EBX, ECX, and so on are the native registers of the 386 and later microprocessors.

Most of the benefits of 32-bit code involve using these 32-bit registers. For example, to store a 32-bit number, 16-bit code would have to employ a pair of registers such as DX:AX:

```
mov dx, 1234h
mov ax, 5678h
```

In contrast, 32-bit code could store the same quantity in the single EAX register:

```
mov eax, 12345678h
```

This not only uses one instruction instead of two, but because it uses only one register, it leaves open more possibilities for future register use. That's because 32-bit code can generally keep more frequently-used values in registers than can 16-bit code, which must then keep the values in slower memory:

```
mov [102h], 1234h
mov [100h], 5678h
```


Of course, if a program doesn't manipulate any 32-bit quantities, it's unlikely to see any benefits from moving to 32-bit code. In fact, there's a downside to 32-bit code. Notice in Get_VMM_Version that to return the version number (here, 0400h for Windows 4.00; hmm, shouldn't that be 05Fh for Windows 95?) in EAX, the code uses 32-bit numbers. Instead of the three bytes B8 00 04 that 16-bit code would use for MOV AX, 0400h VMM employs the five bytes B8 00 04 00 00 for MOV EAX, 0400h.

The downside to 32-bit code, then, is that it tends to be fatter. This shouldn't be at all surprising, unless you believe in free lunches and the tooth fairy. That 32-bit code is fatter than 16 bit code is a major reason why Windows 95 — which Microsoft decided needed to "run great" in 4MB of memory — is not a 100% 32-bit system. According to Adrian King, "a conversion to 32-bit code would have increased the memory requirement [for Windows 95] by close to 40 percent" (*Inside Windows 95*, p. 150).

Even though we got a fair amount of mileage out of it, Get_VMM_Version is a pretty boring function. Here's the code for the next VMM service whose name W3MAP displayed in Figure 2-3:

```
Get_Cur_VM_Handle
0028:C0001E46 8B1DE40601C0      MOV     EBX,[C00106E4]
0028:C0001E4C C3                RET
```

I noted earlier that VxDs can manipulate anything in a 4GB address space, and VMM's offhand manipulation of [C00106E4] is a good example. It's obvious from the code that in this particular configuration, the four bytes (DWORD) at C00106E4h hold the handle of the current Virtual Machine (VM), which Get_Cur_VM_Handle returns in the EBX register. In VxD code, EBX generally holds a VM handle.

To call Get_Cur_VM_Handle, a VxD writer just includes the VMM .INC header file and uses the macro VMMcall Get_Cur_VM_Handle. When the VxD source code is assembled, this turns into an INT 20h followed by the DWORD 010001h:

```
;;; VMMcall Get_Cur_VM_Handle
int      20h
dd       010001h
```

You can see in the W3MAP output in Figure 2-3 that VMM has VxD ID #1 and that Get_Cur_VM_Handle is function 1; hence the magic number 10001h. Windows uses INT 20h for VxD dynamic linking. VMM contains an INT 20h handler; whenever it encounters an INT 20h, it looks at the magic DWORD following the instruction, uses this to locate the 32-bit address of the function, and replaces the INT 20h DD with a 32-bit CALL to the function:

```
;;; INT 20h DD 010001h
call     [C0001E46h]
```

Actually, I lied. That's what VMM in Windows 3.*x* would do with calls to Get_Cur_VM_Handle. Things are a little different in Windows 95. For a selected set of heavily used small functions such as Get_Cur_VM_Handle and Get_Cur_Thread_Handle (discussed a little later in this chapter), VMM's dynamic linker replaces the INT 20h DD not with a CALL to the function, but with the actual inline contents of the function:

```
;;; INT 20h DD 010001h
mov      ebx, [C00106E4h]
```

Clearly, the DWORD at C00106E4h is the current VM handle:

```
:dd c00106e4
0030:C00106E4 C51200E8
```

Here, the current VM handle is C51200E8h. By itself, this number isn't very interesting. However, a VM handle is a 32-bit pointer to a VM Control Block (VMCB), so C51200E8h must be the VMCB of the currently running VM. Let's see what a VMCB looks like:

```
:dd c51200e8
0030:C51200E8 00008802  C5000000  C0EE6F70  00000002       ........po......
0030:C51200F8 62634D56  000E47B2  00000000  00000008       VMcb.G..........
0030:C5120108 C0FDC898  00000005  00000000  C45200E8       ..............R.
0030:C5120118 C5121A04  00000000  00000000  C0FCEABC       ................
...
```

The first few fields in the VMCB are documented in the VMM.H and VMM.INC header files that come with the Windows DDK:

```
struct cb_s {
    ULONG CB_VM_Status;          /* VM status flags */
    ULONG CB_High_Linear;        /* Address of VM mapped high */
    ULONG CB_Client_Pointer;
    ULONG CB_VMID;
```

```
    ULONG CB_Signature;
};
```

If you treat this C structure as a template and lay it over the hex dump just shown, you'll see that these fields have the following values for this VM:

Field	Value
CB_VM_Status	00008802h
CB_High_Linear	C5000000h
CB_Client_Pointer	C0EE6F70h
CB_VMID	00000002h
CB_Signature	62634D56h ('VMcb')

CB_VM_Status holds up to 32 flags that indicate the status of the virtual machine, such as whether it's running in the background or in exclusive mode, whether there's a protected-mode program running in the VM (and if so, whether it's a 32-bit program), whether the VM is currently blocked on a semaphore or has released its time slice, and so on.

CB_High_Linear (such as C5000000h in this case) is particularly useful to anyone interested in communicating from one VM to another: it's the base of a VM's address space, whether or not that VM is currently running. For example, if a program in another VM wanted to access something at real-mode address 00A6:0330 in this VM, it could do so with the address C5000000h + A60h + 0330h = C5000D90h.

The first four fields in the Windows 95 VMCB are identical to the Windows 3.*x* VMCB. A new field is the 'VMcb' signature at offset 10h. This was introduced in Windows 95 as part of VMM/VxD parameter validation. A service that expected to be passed a VM handle in EBX, for example, could do a CMP [EBX+10], 62634D56h.

While the VMCB has changed quite a bit in Windows 95 from its format in Windows 3.1 (see Kelly Zytaruk, "The Windows 3.1 Virtual Machine Control Block," *Dr. Dobb's Journal*, January 1994 and February 1994), and while this is just one of many changes in VMM, fundamentally the Windows 95 VMM is an improved rather than a rewritten version of the Windows 3.1 VMM.

Indeed, *Microsoft Systems Journal's* first article on Chicago (January 1994, p. 15) noted that "Many aspects of Chicago are similar to what you already know from Windows 3.1, especially regarding virtual machines." This is a far more accurate picture of Windows 95 than, say, the claim that "the entire operating system is freshly designed from the ground up;" which is what *Microsoft Systems Journal* printed the month after.

(See the sidebar, "A complete rewrite?" which was presented earlier in this chapter).

Unfortunately, however, the fact is that very few Windows programmers actually do know about virtual machines in Windows 3.1. Look in the index of several Windows programming books, and the chances are slim that you'll find any mention of virtual machines, VMM, VxDs, or V86 mode. Even in supposedly "heavy metal" books such as the one I coauthored, *Undocumented Windows*, the treatment of these "V" subjects is pathetic. To find out about these topics, you had to turn to books targeted specifically at device-driver writers. Unfortunately, by taking crucial information about the core of the Windows 3.*x* operating system and packaging it as information on how to write device drivers (yawn!), Microsoft effectively excluded the vast majority of Windows programmers.

Inside Windows 95 (p. 129) observes that "The Virtual Machine Manager is the single most important operating system component in Windows 95." Now, the interesting thing about this statement is that the same thing could have been said about the VMM in Windows 3.*x* Enhanced mode. This makes the general neglect of this subject prior to Windows 95 all the more puzzling. We all had a 32-bit protected-mode operating system right in front of our faces and never noticed it!

At the same time, VMM in Windows 95 is substantially larger than VMM in Windows 3.1. We saw in Figure 2-3 that Windows 95's VMM provides 377 services; the one in Windows 3.1 provides only 241 services. So, in one very superficial sense, Windows 95's VMM is almost one-third new. Here are some of the new VMM services in Windows 95:

```
0100f9 @ 00001848   _GetThreadTimeSlicePriority
0100fa @ 000073f4   _SetThreadTimeSlicePriority
0100fb @ 00001b4c   Schedule_Thread_Event
0100fc @ 00001c1c   Cancel_Thread_Event
0100fd @ 00002650   Set_Thread_Time_Out
0100fe @ 0000265c   Set_Async_Time_Out
0100ff @ 00002710   _AllocateThreadDataSlot
010100 @ 00002733   _FreeThreadDataSlot
010101 @ 00000d20   _CreateMutex
010102 @ 00006c65   _DestroyMutex
010103 @ 00006f50   _GetMutexOwner
010104 @ 00007f1a   Call_When_Thread_Switched
010105 @ 00008023   VMMCreateThread
010106 @ 00002754   VMMStartThread
010107 @ 00007f40   VMMTerminateThread
010108 @ 00000e85   Get_Cur_Thread_Handle
010109 @ 00000e8c   Test_Cur_Thread_Handle
01010a @ 00000e93   Get_Sys_Thread_Handle
...
```

You probably aren't shocked to see that many of the new VMM functions relate to threads and to synchronization objects such as mutexes (mutual exclusion). The Win32 thread and synchronization APIs in Windows 95 are based on this VMM functionality. Let's look at the code for two tiny thread-related VMM services:

```
Get_Cur_Thread_Handle
0028:C0001E85 8B3D700601C0       MOV     EDI,[C0010670]
0028:C0001E8B C3                 RET

Get_Sys_Thread_Handle
0028:C0001E93 8B3D740601C0       MOV     EDI,[C0010674]
0028:C0001EA0 C3                 RET
```

Just as VxDs generally use EBX to hold a VM handle, in Windows 95 they generally use EDI to hold a thread handle. We can see that in this configuration, VMM stores the current thread handle at C00010670h and the system thread handle in the DWORD that follows it. Here, the current thread happened to be the system thread:

```
0030:C0010670 C4520298  C4520298
```

A thread handle is a 32-bit pointer to a Thread Control Block (THCB). We can use the debugger to display a THCB:

```
:dd c4520298
0030:C4520298 00000000  C0010C2C  C0010C2C  42434854      ............THCB
0030:C45202A8 C000D18C  C45200E8  012F0001  000011F6      ......R.../.....
0030:C45202B8 000070E8  00000000  00A70117  0000002A      .p..........*...
0030:C45202C8 01000000  00000000  00000000  00100005      ................
0030:C45202D8 00000000  C0FD0D4C  C000D18C  80001000      ....L...........
...
```

Other than the THCB signature at offset 0Ch, it's a little hard to see what's going on here. However, the VMM.H file that comes with the DDK has a C structure for the THCB:

```
struct tcb_s {
    ULONG   TCB_Flags;              /* Thread status flags */
    ULONG   TCB_Reserved1;          /* Used internally by VMM */
    ULONG   TCB_Reserved2;          /* Used internally by VMM */
    ULONG   TCB_Signature;
    ULONG   TCB_ClientPtr;          /* Client registers of thread */
    ULONG   TCB_VMHandle;           /* VM that thread is part of */
    USHORT  TCB_ThreadId;           /* Unique Thread ID */
    USHORT  TCB_PMLockOrigSS;       /* Original SS:ESP before lock stack */
    ULONG   TCB_PMLockOrigESP;
    ULONG   TCB_PMLockOrigEIP;      /* Original CS:EIP before lock stack */
    ULONG   TCB_PMLockStackCount;
    USHORT  TCB_PMLockOrigCS;
    USHORT  TCB_PMPSPSelector;
    ULONG   TCB_ThreadType;         /* dword passed to VMMCreateThread */
```

```
    USHORT  TCB_pad1;               /* reusable; for dword align */
    UCHAR   TCB_pad2;               /* reusable; for dword align */
    UCHAR   TCB_extErrLocus;        /* extended error Locus */
    USHORT  TCB_extErr;             /* extended error Code */
    UCHAR   TCB_extErrAction;       /*      "  "   Action */
    UCHAR   TCB_extErrClass;        /*      "  "   Class */
    ULONG   TCB_extErrPtr;          /*      "   pointer */
};
```

There are a few interesting things here — note, for example, that THCBs are backlinked to VMCBs — but there's one item that really jumps out:


```
USHORT  TCB_PMPSPSelector;
```

Now, I ask you: How can anyone claim that Win32 applications don't use MS-DOS when, in the documented thread structure, there's a field that holds a PSP? We saw in Chapter 1 that Win32 tasks have PSPs. We saw that this flowed logically from USER32's dependence on the Win16 USER module. But, given Microsoft's frequent claims that "Windows 95 finally breaks all ties with the real-mode MS-DOS code," it's something of a shock to see the primary DOS data structure, the PSP, explicitly mentioned in the middle of one of the key Win32 data structures, the thread.

But let's see if it's really a real-mode DOS PSP that each thread is connected to. Laying the VMM.H C structure over the hex dump, we see that, for this particular thread (which, you'll recall, is the system thread), TCB_PMPSPSelector is 00A7h. The name says "PM" and "selector," so it must be a protected-mode selector to a PSP. Let's look at 00A7 in a debugger:

```
:db a7:0
00A7:0000 CD 20 00 9F 00 9A F0 FE-1D F0 82 0C 3C FD F2 0C  . ..........<...
00A7:0010 35 FD 74 01 93 12 D5 17-07 01 01 00 02 03 FF FF  5.t.............
00A7:0020 FF FF FF FF FF FF FF FF-FF FF FF FF B7 00 24 02  ..............$.
00A7:0030 CB 18 80 00 00 00 FC 29-FF FF FF FF 00 00 00 00  .......)........
...
```

Those first two bytes, CD 20, are a dead giveaway: it's a PSP. But just to be sure, let's see if it has an environment segment at offset 2Ch. Here, the WORD at 2Ch is 00B7h:

```
:d b7:0
00B7:0000 4D54 3D50 3A43 575C 4E49 4F44 5357 5400    TMP=C:\WINDOWS.T
00B7:0010 4D45 3D50 3A43 575C 4E49 4F44 5357 5000    EMP=C:\WINDOWS.P
00B7:0020 4F52 504D 3D54 7024 6724 5000 5441 3D48    ROMPT=$p$g.PATH=
...
```

Looks like an environment segment, all right. This is getting good. How about the parent PSP at offset 16h? Hmm, the WORD at offset 16h is 17D5h, which somehow looks like a real-mode paragraph address, not a protected-mode selector. In Soft-ICE, putting an & before an address specifies a real-mode address:

```
:db &17d5:0
17D5:0000 CD 20 80 9F 00 9A F0 FE-1D F0 41 01 5C 17 A1 10  . ........A.\...
17D5:0010 62 14 74 01 93 12 5C 17-01 01 01 00 02 FF FF FF  b.t...\.........
17D5:0020 FF FF FF FF FF FF FF FF-FF FF FF FF C8 17 F2 01  ................
```

Sure enough, another PSP. It's a little strange that the system thread's PSP holds the protected-mode selector of its environment and the real-mode segment of its parent, but otherwise it's a PSP.

Yes, but is it in conventional memory? Were this structure located in extended memory, it wouldn't matter if it looked like a PSP — DOS wouldn't be able to touch it, so it would be a protected-mode structure with the mere form of PSP. To be a genuine DOS data structure, it must be located in conventional memory. To see if this PSP is located in conventional memory, we can use the debugger to examine the Local Descriptor Table (LDT) entry for selector 00A7h:

```
:ldt a7
00A7  Data16    Base=00018BB0  Lim=000000FF  DPL=3  P   RW
```

The address 18BB0h is definitely in conventional memory. Let's just double check that this is a PSP:

```
:d &18bb:0
18BB:0000 CD 20 00 9F 00 9A F0 FE-1D F0 82 0C 3C FD F2 0C  . ..........<...
18BB:0010 35 FD 74 01 93 12 D5 17-07 01 01 00 02 03 FF FF  5.t.............
18BB:0020 FF FF FF FF FF FF FF FF-FF FF FF FF B7 00 24 02  ..............$.
...
```

This structure at real-mode address 18BB:0 looks pretty similar to the structure we dumped out at protected-mode address 00A7:0000. It had better look similar, because it's the exact same structure! Because selector A7h has a base address of 18BB0h, protected-mode address 00A7:0000 and real-mode address 18BB:0000 point to same block of memory. And this block of memory is a DOS PSP. We'll look at these thread PSPs in Chapter 13 (in the "Win32 and the PSP" section). Note, though, that each thread does not have its own PSP. Instead, a PSP goes with a Windows task, and a task can have more than one thread.

Rather than try to figure out what's what in the THCB from a raw hex dump, we can use the Soft-ICE THREAD command:

```
:thread C4520298
Ring0TCB  ID    Context   Ring3TCB  Process   TaskDB  PDB   SZ   Owner
C4520298  0001  C0FD3B7C  8117B314  8117B23C  0097    00A7  32   VM 01
CS:EIP=05FB:000001F8  SS:ESP=0CCB:00000226  DS=0000  ES=FFFF  FS=0000  GS=0000
EAX=C0FD1607  EBX=00010018  ECX=00020004    EDX=00000004
ESI=00000080  EDI=00000090  EBP=00000000  ECODE=C0000004
TLS Offset 00CC = 00000000 VPICD
TLS Offset 00D0 = 00000000 SHELL
TLS Offset 00D4 = C0FD8E48 VMCPD
TLS Offset 00D8 = C0FD1834 VWIN32
TLS Offset 00DC = C0FD1204 PAGESWAP
```


The Soft-ICE output indicates that C4520298h is the Ring 0 THCB for use by VxDs. A Win32 application that called GetCurrentThreadId would get back a different handle: the one Soft-ICE identifies as the Ring 3 THCB. (See the CHGDIR.C Win32 program in Chapter 13 for an odd use of GetCurrentThreadId.)

The TLS referred to by Soft-ICE means Thread Local Storage. We can see that some VxDs such as VPICD, SHELL, and so on, store variables on a per-thread basis. As instance data is to VMs (see Chapters 3 and 4), TLS is to threads.

We were looking at new functions provided by VMM in Windows 95. Besides thread and synchronization services, another interesting set of new VMM services provides the ability to undo some of the older VMM services. For example, VxDs have always been able to hook I/O ports (or, "call this function whenever someone does an IN or OUT to this I/O port"), using VMM's Install_IO_Handler and Install_Mult_IO_Handlers services. Similarly, VxDs could hook the V86 interrupt chain, hook V86 faults, and even hook device services. (In other words, a VxD can intercept all calls to any VMM VxD or service such as Get_Cur_VM_Handle, either to spy on or modify the service.)

But there was never a provision for *removing* these handlers. With Windows 95 there must be such a provision, because dynamic VxDs can be unloaded and reloaded due, for example, to Plug and Play events. So VMM in Windows 95 provides new removal functions such as:

```
010116 @ 00001161   Remove_IO_Handler
010117 @ 000010c5   Remove_Mult_IO_Handlers
010118 @ 00000bee   Unhook_V86_Int_Chain
010119 @ 00001520   Unhook_V86_Fault
01011a @ 00001527   Unhook_PM_Fault
01011b @ 0000152e   Unhook_VMM_Fault
01011c @ 0000004c   Unhook_Device_Service
```

But, wait, there's more! Most of the new Win32 memory management functionality in Windows 95, such as memory-mapped file I/O (which in essence can make a data file into a Windows virtual-memory swap file; see the discussion of memory-mapped files in Chapter 14), is based on a set of new services provided by VMM:

```
01011d @ 000001f0   _MMReserve
01011e @ 00001890   _MMCommit
01011f @ 00001bc7   _MMDecommit
010120 @ 00001b20   _MMRegisterPager
010121 @ 00001b99   _MMQueryPagerInfo
010122 @ 00001bec   _MMDeregisterPager
010123 @ 00000584   _MMCreateContext
010124 @ 0000034b   _MMDestroyContext
010125 @ 000005c0   _MMAttach
010126 @ 00000334   _MMFlush
010127 @ 0000745c   _MMCopy
010128 @ 00001770   _MMCommitPhys
```


All registry access goes through a set of new VMM functions; the Windows registry APIs are just wrappers around calls to VMM:

```
010148 @ 00005066   _RegOpenKey
010149 @ 0000506b   _RegCloseKey
01014a @ 00005057   _RegCreateKey
01014b @ 00005070   _RegDeleteKey
01014c @ 00005075   _RegEnumKey
01014d @ 00005084   _RegQueryValue
01014e @ 000050b3   _RegSetValue
```

Then, there's new scheduler stuff:

```
010160 @ 00008bb2   Time_Slice_Sys_VM_Idle
010161 @ 00008b1c   Time_Slice_Sleep
010162 @ 00008784   Boost_With_Decay
010163 @ 0000864a   Set_Inversion_Pri
010164 @ 000086ab   Reset_Inversion_Pri
010165 @ 000086e8   Release_Inversion_Pri
```

And on, and on.... But with all this new VMM functionality, it's important not to lose sight of the fact that Windows 95's VMM is simply the next iteration of the same VMM that appeared in WfW 3.11, in Windows 3.1 Enhanced mode, and in Windows 3.0 Enhanced mode. It's quite significant that in WfW 3.11, Microsoft could take an early pre-beta version of 32-bit file access from the Windows 95 project and drop it in with an essentially unchanged copy of the Windows 3.1 VMM. The functionality provided by the earlier VMM provided a solid foundation on which to build Windows 95.

VxDs: TSRs of the 1990s

We've just looked at VMM. Remember that about 40 other VxDs are also part of VMM32.VXD. The [386Enh] section of SYSTEM.INI uses asterisks to indicate VxDs that are built into VMM32.VXD (such as device=*vpicd and device=*v86mmgr). These VxDs include the Windows hardware virtualization layer, which provides 32-bit protected-mode emulation of most standard PC and BIOS functionality. Here are just a few examples:

VxD	Description
VPICD	Virtual Programmable Interrupt Controller (PIC) Device
VDMAD	Virtual Direct Memory Access (DMA) Device
VKD	Virtual Keyboard Device
VDD	Virtual Display Device
VMD	Virtual Mouse Device
VTD	Virtual Timer Device
IOS	I/O Supervisor (formerly BLOCKDEV and Virtual Hard Disk Device)

The Windows file system also lives inside VMM32.VXD; for example:

VxD	Description
IFSMgr	Installable File System (IFS) Manager
VCACHE	Virtual Cache
VFAT	Virtual DOS File Allocation Table (FAT) system
VSHARE	VxD replacement for SHARE.EXE

Let's look at just one of these examples in more detail. Here's a small part of the verbose output W3MAP shows for IFSMgr in VMM32.VXD:

```
Module name: IFSMgr
IFSMgr_DDB @ 0001:00002bfc
Real-mode Init @ 0004:00000000
Device # 0040
32-bit file access Installable File System (IFS) Manager
Version 3.00
Init order: A0011000
DDB_Control_Proc @ 000000cc
DDB_V86_API_Proc @ 00001ca7
DDB_Service_Table @ 00002a60 (67 services)
    400000 @ 0000031a   IFSMgr_Get_Version
    400001 @ 00000321   IFSMgr_RegisterMount
    400002 @ 00000367   IFSMgr_RegisterNet
    400003 @ 00000395   IFSMgr_RegisterMailSlot
    400004 @ 000003fa   IFSMgr_Attach
    400005 @ 000003fa   IFSMgr_Detach
```

```
400006 @ 000019e4   IFSMgr_Get_NetTime
400007 @ 0000ef7c   IFSMgr_Get_DOSTime
400008 @ 0000af30   IFSMgr_SetupConnection
400009 @ 00000401   IFSMgr_DerefConnection
40000a @ 00001628   IFSMgr_ServerDOSCall
40000b @ 0000de18   IFSMgr_CompleteAsync
... etc. ...
40005f @ 000099b8   IFSMgr_FSDAttachSFT
400060 @ 00003fdc   IFSMgr_GetTimeZoneBias
400061 @ 000120ec   IFSMgr_PNPEvent
400062 @ 000003c4   IFSMgr_RegisterCFSD
400063 @ 000072c8   IFSMgr_Win32MapExtendedHandleToSFT
400064 @ 00000429   IFSMgr_DbgSetFileHandleLimit
400065 @ 00007464   IFSMgr_Win32MapSFTToExtendedHandle
400066 @ 000099bc   IFSMgr_FSDGetCurrentDrive
```


Given that IFSMgr itself has been publicly available since the introduction of WfW 3.11 in late 1993, it's rather shocking that the programmer's documentation for this vital interface is available only as part of the Chicago beta: Why should a developer sign a Chicago beta NDA to learn about the file system of a released product? Furthermore, as of this writing, the documentation in the Chicago DDK is limited to two rather incomplete header files, IFSMGR.INC and IFS.H. And other parts of 32-bile file access, such as VFAT (which is also part of the released WfW 3.11 product) appear to not be documented at all.

Even though the IFSMgr header files included with the Windows 95 DDK are rather bare-bones, they can still provide us with important information about the relationship of Windows 95 to MS-DOS. IFSMGR.INC has the same references to the SFT (the real-mode DOS System File Table) that we see in the W3MAP output. There's also an interesting reference to IFSMgr_ServerDOSCall, which emulates the odd undocumented INT 21h function 5D00h (see *Undocumented DOS*, 2d ed., p. 295, 723).

We could spend ages looking at each of the VxDs in VMM32.VXD. Besides the ones already mentioned, the following VxDs are also quite important:

VxD	**Description**
VWIN32	VxD to support Win32 applications in Windows 95
VCOND	Virtual CON Device; used for Win32 Console applications
VXDLDR	Dynamic VxD loader/unloader; used in Plug and Play
CONFIGMG	Plug and Play Configuration Manager
DOSMGR	Windows DOS extender; provides protected-mode INT 21h
V86MMGR	V86 Memory Manager; provides XMS, EMS, DOS extender translation
SHELL	VxD to access Windows API; includes "Appy Time"

Well, that's enough about VMM32.VXD for right now. It was a long time ago, but you may dimly recollect that we were walking through the Windows boot process and had encountered these two lines in Figure 2-2:

```
OPEN  C:\WINDOWS\system\vmm32.vxd
EXEC  C:\WINDOWS\system\vmm32.vxd
```

Throughout Figure 2-2, we can see Windows 95 (which at this point in the boot process is just a collection of VxDs) look for various real-mode DOS device drivers, most of which I didn't have installed:

```
OPEN  QEMM386$ [FAIL 2]        Quarterdeck QEMM/386
OPEN  386MAX$$ [FAIL 2]        Qualitas 386Max
OPEN  SMARTAAR [FAIL 2]        SmartDrive
OPEN  $DebugDD [FAIL 2]        WDEB386.EXE (Windows kernel debugger)
OPEN  NDISHLP$ [FAIL 2]        NDISHLP.SYS (for NDIS 2.0)
OPEN  IFS$HLP$                 IFSHLP.SYS
OPEN  CONFIG$                  CONFIG$ in WINBOOT.SYS
OPEN  SCSIMGR$ [FAIL 2]
```

Windows 95 isn't trying to locate these real-mode DOS device drivers so it can push them aside. Instead, Windows 95 is trying to locate these real-mode drivers so that, when it finds one of these drivers, a VxD will communicate with it via DOS IOCTL (INT 21h function 44h) calls, hand it a V86 callback, and so on.

Throughout Figure 2-2, we also see Windows 95 loading a wide variety of additional VxDs (with .386 or .VXD extensions) that aren't located inside VMM32.VXD. In this particular configuration, for example, SYSTEM.INI contained device= directives to load the 32-bit protected-mode networking software:

```
OPEN  C:\WINDOWS\system\vserver.386     Server for peer-to-peer access
OPEN  C:\WINDOWS\system\vredir.386      Network redirector
OPEN  C:\WINDOWS\system\vnetbios.386    Virtual NetBIOS (INT 5Ch, etc.)
OPEN  C:\WINDOWS\system\nwlink.386      Microsoft NetWare-compatible protocol
OPEN  C:\WINDOWS\system\wsipx.386       Windows Sockets for Novell IPX
OPEN  C:\WINDOWS\system\wsock.386       Windows Sockets
OPEN  C:\WINDOWS\system\vnetsup.386     "Win386 Virtual Net Support"
OPEN  C:\WINDOWS\system\netbeui.386     NetBIOS Extended User Interface
OPEN  C:\WINDOWS\system\ndis.386        NDIS 3.0
OPEN  C:\WINDOWS\system\ndis2sup.386    Map between NDIS 2.0 and 3.0
OPEN  C:\WINDOWS\system\msodisup.386    "ODI support mapper for ODI MLID"
OPEN  C:\WINDOWS\system\ee16.386        Intel EtherExpress 16 (NDIS 3.0)
```

The EE16.386 VxD at the bottom of this list is what does actual "work": talking to the network adapter card. As is typical in networking software, a packet of data must negotiate many layers before it is sent over the wire to another machine.

Microsoft's Windows for Workgroups 3.11 Resource Kit contains reasonable descriptions for many of these files and for how they all fit together. Adrian King's *Inside Windows 95* has a complete chapter on Windows 95 networking (pp. 341-380). After leaving Microsoft, King was in charge of development at Artisoft, makers of the famous LANtastic peer-to-peer network, so this stuff is right up his alley.

Returning once again to Figure 2-2: all these .386 and .VXD files use the 32-bit Linear Executable (LE) file format (the LX format used by OS/2 2.*x* 32-bit applications is a variant of the LE format). The LEDUMP utility from the *Unauthorized Windows 95* disk displays the contents of these VxDs. For example, NDIS.386 contains the 32-bit protected-mode implementation of version 3.0 of Microsoft's Network Device Interface Standard (NDIS):


```
C:\UNAUTHW>ledump \windows\system\ndis.386
...
DDB_V86_API_Proc @ 00004512
DDB_PM_API_Proc  @ 00004512
DDB_Service_Table @ 00000eb0 (57 services)
    280000 @ 00000920   NdisGetVersion
    280001 @ 00000cc5   NdisAllocateSpinLock
    280002 @ 00000cf9   NdisFreeSpinLock
    280003 @ 00000cd9   NdisAcquireSpinLock
    280004 @ 00000ced   NdisReleaseSpinLock
    ...
    28002d @ 00000d50   NdisSend
    28002e @ 00000d55   NdisTransferData
    28002f @ 00003d5a   NdisReset
    280030 @ 00003d5f   NdisRequest
    ...
    280039 @ 00000d5a   NdisCompleteSend
    28003a @ 00000d5f   NdisCompleteTransferData
    28003b @ 00003d78   NdisCompleteReset
    28003c @ 00003d7d   NdisCompleteRequest
    ...
```

In addition to showing Windows 95 in the process of loading those VxDs that are explicitly requested with device= statements in SYSTEM.INI, Figure 2-2 also shows the Windows 95 I/O Supervisor (IOS) dynamically loading VxDs from the IOSUBSYS subdirectory. These include the RMM, voltrack, and DiskTSD VxDs. RMM is the Real Mode Mapper, which makes a real-mode disk driver look as though it were a protected-mode FastDisk driver. In Windows 95, 32-bit file access requires 32-bit disk access, so if you actually have a real-mode disk driver (DBLSPACE .BIN will be the best example until Microsoft ships a DblSpace VxD for Windows 95), RMM makes it appear as though it were a VxD. The voltrack VxD takes care of volume tracking for drives with removable media, such as floppy disks or tape backup. DiskTSD is a type specific driver responsible for mapping logical requests to physical disk requests.

Toward the bottom of Figure 2-2, we can see that Windows 95 looks for a batch file called WINSTART.BAT. As noted earlier, I edited the figure at this point, because INTRSPY showed Windows 95 searching for this file in every subdirectory on the PATH. I don't have a WINSTART.BAT, so the search was unsuccessful. When this batch file exists, though, Windows 95 uses it to run DOS software (generally TSRs) in the System VM. There's a brief discussion of WINSTART.BAT at the end of Chapter 6. Note that it is not some vague entity "Windows 95" that looks for WINSTART.BAT, but specifically the DOSMGR VxD within VMM32.VXD.

At the very end of Figure 2-2, we see that Windows 95 executes KRNL386.EXE. This is the Win16 kernel, which we'll look at in a few moments. Again, note that it's not some vague "Windows 95" that loads KRNL386.EXE: the SHELL VxD within VMM32.VXD is what loads KRNL386.EXE. SHELL will load any file called KRNL386.EXE; we'll see in Chapter 6 that this is quite significant.

While we've spent a lot of time looking at the VMM and VxD layer of Windows 95, our examination has obviously been superficial: not a grand tour of Chicago, but a hurried and harried look at a few of its underground passages, plumbing, and sewers. However, hopefully it has at least given you the flavor — or perhaps the smell — of the Windows 95 operating system.

Notice that even though we haven't looked at the Win16 or Win32 kernels yet, I'm already referring to the operating system. That's because VMM is the Windows operating system. It will probably require the remainder of this book to convince you of this. In the meantime, try to remember two things as you read along: first, that the VMM is what makes it possible for Microsoft to call Windows 95 a complete operating system, and second, that the VMM was also in the Windows 3.*x* operating system. Therefore, to the extent that Windows 95 is a complete operating system, the same thing can be said of WfW 3.11, Windows 3.1 Enhanced mode, and even Windows 3.0 Enhanced mode.

Now, if VMM is the operating system, what are these VxDs we've seen such as IFSMgr, DOSMGR, VPICD, and so on? There is very general agreement that VxDs play an enormous role in Windows 95. For example, Microsoft's *"Chicago" Reviewer's Guide* says:

> Most computer system functionality and support is handled by VxDs in Chicago rather than by real-mode code or BIOS routines. (p. 84)

> Chicago's networking components are built as Windows VxDs. (p. 132)
>
> Virtual device drivers are an integral part of the Chicago operating system and have a more important role than in Windows 3.1, as many operating system components are implemented as VxDs. (p. 85)

Indeed, to a large extent VxDs need to be considered alongside VMM as part of the Windows operating system. In another sense, though, VxDs are user-installable extensions to the Windows operating system. As noted earlier, Microsoft implemented 32-bit file access in WfW 3.11 by dropping some VxDs on top of a basically unchanged VMM. This means that some enterprising third-party vendor could have done the same thing, at least in principle.

In other words, then, VxDs are an integral (sorry, I mean "integrated") part of the operating system that can be supplied by anyone with a copy of the Windows Device Driver Kit.

Hmm, VxDs are user-suppliable parts of the operating system. This kind of carte blanche for anyone and their brother to dive in and hack the operating system might remind you of something: the DOS memory-resident program (TSR) craze in the 1980s. Yes, VxDs are to Windows as TSRs were to DOS.

And again, this is true not only in Windows 95, but also in Windows 3.*x*. Consider just two VMM services: Call_Priority_VM_Event and Hook_V86_Int_Chain. Call_Priority_VM_Event is the whole basis for inter-VM communications in Windows. As the Microsoft KnowledgeBase puts it, "Call_Priority_VM_Event is one of the most valuable virtual device (VxD) calls available." Hook_V86_Int_Chain is the whole basis for bypassing DOS. These two services first became available in Windows 3.0, and they remain in Windows 95 essentially unchanged (Windows 95 adds a Call_Priority_Thread_Event service). There's a tremendous amount of power — having nothing to do with devices or device drivers — provided by just these two services, and they are only directly callable from a VxD. (And they *don't* take American Express.)

Seen from this perspective, the names Virtual Device Driver and Device Driver Kit are unfortunate. They automatically turn off most Windows programmers, who quite sensibly feel that device-driver writing is an area they would rather stay away from. More appropriate names would have been "TSRs for Windows" or "Please Hack Our Operating System." As it is, the names VxD and DDK alienate many programmers who would otherwise jump at this stuff. For example, Matt Pietrek — the ultimate operating-system hacker if there ever was one — had the following to say about VxDs in *Microsoft Systems Journal* (August 1994, p. 30):

> These days some developers are in the habit of saying things like "Chicago is all VxDs." But while VxDs play a big role in Chicago, Chicago is not implemented entirely in VxDs. If your programs stay within the Win32 API, most of the system code your programs use will be primarily in Ring 3 system DLLs. Unless you have a special need for things like interrupt handlers, you don't have to write a VxD to run under Chicago. I think large-scale Chicago applications comprised of mostly VxD code will be a rarity rather than the norm.

Admittedly, very few Windows programmers will be using VxDs to write hardware interrupt handlers or to drive devices. But a short time spent with the DDK should convince you that there's a ton of documented functionality available to VxDs that is otherwise difficult or impossible to get to under Windows. Whenever a programmer says that something is "impossible" in Windows, I suspect the correct reply will be "No it isn't. Write a VxD." Just as TSRs allowed DOS programmers to do the otherwise-impossible in the 1980s, VxDs are going to let Windows programmers go anywhere and do anything in what's left of the 1990s. Whether this is ultimately a good thing or a bad thing (remember "TSR RAM cram"?; remember "load me last"?) is of course another question.

From KRNL386.EXE to CAB32.EXE

At the tail end of Figure 2-2, we saw Windows 95 (or to be more precise, the SHELL VxD) execute the Win16 kernel, KRNL386.EXE. The Win16 kernel is obviously a vital part of Windows 95, but I'm not going to say much about it here, because Matt Pietrek — yes, the same one with whom I was disagreeing about VxDs a moment ago — does a superb job discussing the Win16 kernel in his book *Windows Internals*. (Matt's coverage of the kernel is so thorough that the book almost ought to be called *Kernel Internals*.) Chapter 1 of Matt's book ("The Big Bang: Starting Up and Shutting Down Windows," pp. 1-78) covers KRNL386's initialization in great detail.

KRNL386.EXE provides Win16 KERNEL API functions such as (to choose a few at random) GlobalAlloc, LoadLibrary, LoadResource, FindAtom, and SetSelectorBase. KRNL386 uses the 16-bit Segmented Executable or New Executable (NE) file format. In contrast to the situation with the W3 and LE file formats used for VxDs, there are many utilities that know about the NE file format, so there are plenty of tools you can use to examine KRNL386.EXE. For example, Borland C++ comes with TDUMP, various versions of Microsoft C have provided EXEHDR, and my own Windows Source product comes with EXEDUMP. (It's a good thing that Windows 95 has long filenames: the 8.3 name space is starting to get so crowded that it's hard to find reasonable, unique names for utilities that dump out executable headers.)

You can also use the Windows 95 shell to look at KRNL386.EXE or any Win16 executable: just right-click on the executable, and then select Quick View from the pop-up menu. (We'll see in the following "Exploring the Explorer" section that this right-click menu facility works off the Windows 95 registry and is extensible.) Figure 2-4 shows some of the APIs exported from KRNL386.EXE. Not all these APIs are documented; the book *Undocumented Windows*, which I coauthored, was largely about those functions exported from KRNL386.EXE in Windows 3.*x* that weren't mentioned in the Windows programmer's reference or header files.

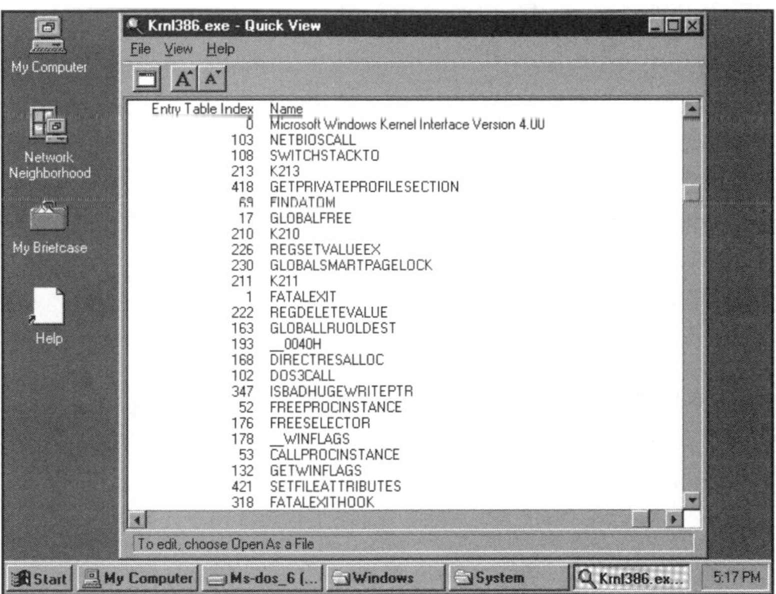

Figure 2-4: Chicago Explorer's Quick View of KRNL386.EXE, showing a few of the more than 200 APIs exported by the Win16 kernel.

Well, we've reached the end of the Windows 95 boot process shown back in Figure 2-2. As I pointed out earlier, Figure 2-2 provides a woefully incomplete picture of the Windows 95 boot process, because once 32-bit file access kicks in, Windows not only bypasses DOS for most file I/O calls but also bypasses the INTRSPY utility (which is a DOS TSR that loads before Windows).

To see everything that happens after the SHELL VxD executes the Win16 kernel, we need to disable 32-bit file access. There's a WIN /D:C command-line option in WfW 3.11 to disable 32BFA, but this has no equivalent in Windows 95. You're not supposed to run Windows 95 without 32BFA. However, I found quite by accident that, in Beta-1 at any rate, if the I/O Supervisor can't find an IOSUBSYS subdirectory, it disables 32-bit disk access in a way that also disables 32-bit file access.

If 32BFA is disabled, INTRSPY sees the entire Windows 95 boot sequence. For example, compare the following with the bottom of Figure 2-2:

```
OPEN  C:\WINDOWS\WINSTART.BAT [FAIL 2] ;; look along path for WINSTART.BAT
OPEN  C:\WINDOWS\system\LPTENUM.vxd
OPEN  C:\WINDOWS\system\UNICODE.BIN
OPEN  IFS$HLP$
OPEN  C:\WINDOWS\system\IOSUBSYS\hsflop.pdr [FAIL 3]
OPEN  C:\WINDOWS\system\IOSUBSYS\esdi_506.pdr [FAIL 3]
OPEN  C:\WINDOWS\system\IOSUBSYS\scsiport.pdr [FAIL 3]
OPEN  C:\WINDOWS\system\VFD.VXD
OPEN  C:\WINDOWS\system\krnl386.exe
OPEN  C:\WINDOWS\USER.DAT
OPEN  C:\WINDOWS\USER.DAT
XOPEN C:\WINDOWS\IOS.LOG
OPEN  C:\WINDOWS\system\KERNEL32.DLL
EXEC  C:\WINDOWS\system\krnl386.exe
OPEN  C:\WINDOWS\system\KERNEL32.DLL
OPEN  C:\WINDOWS\SYSTEM\KRNL386.EXE
```

In particular, note the references to KERNEL32.DLL, which is the Win32 kernel. These references didn't show up in Figure 2-2. Clearly, the call to open the KERNEL32.DLL file wasn't sent down to DOS, and consequently wasn't seen by INTRSPY.

The full INTRSPY log is far too long (about 500 lines of OPENs and FINDs) to show in its entirety, so we'll just look at the highlights here.

As we just saw, KERNEL32.DLL is loaded. INTRSPY doesn't tell us *who* loaded KERNEL32.DLL, though. This is an interesting point because of something that Adrian King says in *Inside Windows 95* (p. 147): "the 16-bit Kernel module will load the VWIN32 VxD the first time there's a call to any 32-bit API. VWIN32 loads the three DLLs and returns to the 16-bit Kernel, which then calls the KERNEL32 DLL initialization function. Once this call is complete, the Win32 subsystem is ready for use."

Given that the SHELL VxD loads the Win16 kernel, it's quite reasonable that the VWIN32 VxD would load the Win32 kernel. And, in fact, it is VWIN32.VXD that loads KERNEL32.DLL. But the statement by King that I've just quoted has the following footnote:

Given that the Windows 95 shell is a 32-bit application, the loading and initialization of the Win32 subsystem will actually occur during the system startup phase.

This implies that if the Windows 95 shell were a 16-bit application, the Win32 subsystem wouldn't load until you ran a Win32 application.

It's easy to make the Windows 95 shell a 16-bit application; all you have to do is change the SHELL=CAB32.EXE or SHELL=CAB32.EXE /NE line in the [boot] section of SYSTEM.INI. For example, Windows is still largely a Solitaire-playing engine, and you can make Windows 95 reflect this fact by temporarily making SOL.EXE (which is a Win16 application) the shell:


```
[boot]
shell=sol.exe
;;; shell=cab32.exe
```

This produces a version of Windows 95 with which you can do nothing but Solitaire. But does it produce a pure Win16 version of Windows 95? No, of course it doesn't. Given that KRNL386.EXE thunks up to KERNEL32.DLL for some operations, it's hard to see how loading KERNEL32 would await the coming of a Win32 shell that (given the ease of changing the shell= statement) might never arrive.

At any rate, the VWIN32 VxD has loaded KERNEL32.DLL. This DLL of course provides the Win32 kernel API, functions generally defined in the WINBASE.H header file such as CreateThread, MapViewOfFile, CreateFile, and so on. As noted earlier, in many cases these Win32 APIs rely on VMM or the VWIN32 VxD.

Win32 executables such as KERNEL32.DLL use the Portable Executable (PE) file format. This is a vast improvement over Microsoft's previous executable-file formats.

Unfortunately, the Windows 95 shell currently doesn't have a Quick View DLL that displays PE files, but there are some character-mode utilities available. The *Unauthorized Windows 95* disk comes with a W32DUMP utility that displays the imports (APIs used) and exports (APIs provided) of a Win32 PE file. Phar Lap's TNT product, which supports the Win32 API under 32-bit protected-mode MS-DOS, comes with a MAPEXE utility. And Microsoft C++ comes with DUMPBIN, a Win32 Console application that not only displays the imports and exports of a Win32 executable but also provides a /DISASM option.

Here's a small fragment of KERNEL32.DLL, as displayed by DUMPBIN; note that I've just shown the Win32 kernel APIs whose names start with Create:

```
C:\MSVC32S\BIN>dumpbin /exports \windows\system\kernel32.dll
...
     3A   39   CreateConsoleScreenBuffer  (0002a8b7)
     3B   3A   CreateDirectoryA  (00012afb)
     3C   3B   CreateDirectoryExA  (00012b2d)
     3D   3C   CreateDirectoryExW  (000303c7)
     3E   3D   CreateDirectoryW  (000303be)
     3F   3E   CreateEventA  (00012198)
     40   3F   CreateEventW  (000303d0)
     41   40   CreateFileA  (00012bf0)
     42   41   CreateFileMappingA  (00012240)
     43   42   CreateFileMappingW  (000303e2)
     44   43   CreateFileW  (000303eb)
     45   44   CreateKernelThread  (000116c7)
     46   45   CreateMailslotA  (00011ebd)
     47   46   CreateMailslotW  (000303d0)
     48   47   CreateMutexA  (00012137)
     49   48   CreateMutexW  (000303c7)
     4A   49   CreateNamedPipeA  (000303f4)
     4B   4A   CreateNamedPipeW  (000303f4)
     4C   4B   CreatePipe  (00011dc1)
     4D   4C   CreateProcessA  (0001230e)
     4E   4D   CreateProcessW  (000303fd)
     4F   4E   CreateRemoteThread  (000303eb)
     50   4F   CreateSemaphoreA  (000121f5)
     51   50   CreateSemaphoreW  (000303d0)
     52   51   CreateTapePartition  (000303d0)
     53   52   CreateThread  (0001169d)
     54   53   CreateToolhelp32Snapshot  (00032b81)
```

That last line is a good excuse for me to point out that KERNEL32 provides a set of Win32 ToolHelp functions to enumerate Win32 processes, threads, heaps, and modules. These functions, such as Toolhelp32-ReadProcessMemory, Process32First, Process32Next, Thread32-First, Thread32Next, and so on, are documented in Microsoft's TLHELP32.H header file.

Naturally, not all functions exported from KERNEL32.DLL are documented (at least in the current SDK). The following are some that I use or discuss in other parts of this book:

```
127  127   GetProcAddress16  (000114eb)
160  15F   GetpWin16Lock  (0001cd32)
1B0  1AF   LoadLibrary16  (00021d52)
1F4  1F3   QT_Thunk  (00001247)
2A5  2A4   VxDCall0  (00001f0c)
2B8  2B7   Win32HandleToDosFileHandle  (00023d94)
```

VxDCall0 is particularly powerful. As shown in Chapter 14 (WIN32-PSP.C), VxDCall0 allows Win32 applications to call a set of Win32 services provided by VxDs such as VWIN32, VMM, and VCOND. Two of the services provided by VWIN32 give Win32 applications an easy way to make

DOS and DPMI calls. This is important because Win32 applications normally cannot use direct INT instructions in Windows 95.

After KERNEL32.DLL loads, the next interesting thing that INTRSPY shows is Windows 95 loading Win16 device drivers (these Win16 drivers should not be confused with 32-bit VxDs):

```
XOPEN C:\WINDOWS\SYSTEM\system.drv
XOPEN C:\WINDOWS\SYSTEM\keyboard.drv
XOPEN C:\WINDOWS\SYSTEM\mouse.drv
XOPEN C:\WINDOWS\MOUSE.INI
XOPEN C:\WINDOWS\system.ini
XOPEN C:\WINDOWS\SYSTEM\framebuf.drv
XOPEN C:\WINDOWS\SYSTEM\DIBENG.DLL
XOPEN C:\WINDOWS\SYSTEM\sound.drv
XOPEN C:\WINDOWS\SYSTEM\comm.drv
```

KRNL386.EXE uses run-time dynamic linking to load these Win16 drivers (see InitFwdRef in *Windows Internals*, pp. 47-50).

It's curious that these Win16 drivers don't appear in Microsoft's architectural diagrams for Windows 95, because they play a crucial role in the Windows messaging system. Much has been written about desynchronized input queues in Windows 95 (Matt Pietrek has a good discussion in "Investigating the Hybrid Windowing and Messaging Architecture of Chicago," *Microsoft Systems Journal*, September 1994) and how this differs from messaging in Windows 3.*x*, but it's also important to note that many aspects of the Windows 3.*x* message system remain relatively unchanged in Windows 95. In particular, Win16 drivers such as MOUSE.DRV, KEYBOARD.DRV, and SYSTEM.DRV are still involved in the process of turning hardware interrupts into WM_XXX messages.

Windows messages like WM_LBUTTONDOWN and WM_KEYDOWN start life as hardware interrupts, of course. Hardware interrupts are handled by the VPICD (the Virtual PIC Device) VxD, and other VxDs such as VMD (Virtual Mouse Device), VKD (Virtual Keyboard Device), or VTD (Virtual Timer Device) call the VPICD_Set_Int _Request service to simulate the hardware interrupt into an appropriate VM.

If the simulated interrupt goes to the System VM, where Win16 and Win32 applications run, it is picked up by a 16-bit Windows device driver such as MOUSE.DRV, KEYBOARD.DRV, or SYSTEM.DRV (which handles the timer). If one of these 16-bit device drivers hooks a hardware interrupt, it might think it's partying with the hardware, but in fact it's just receiving one of VPICD's simulated interrupts. (On the other hand, some of these drivers, like MOUSE.DRV, do talk directly to the appropriate VxD.)

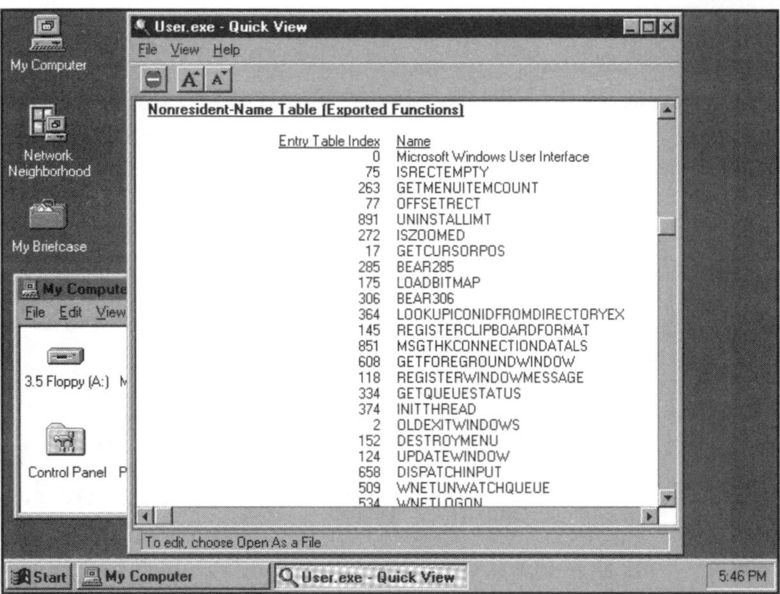

Figure 2-5: Chicago Explorer's Quick View of USER.EXE, showing a few of the more than 400 APIs exported by the Win16 windowing and user interface module.

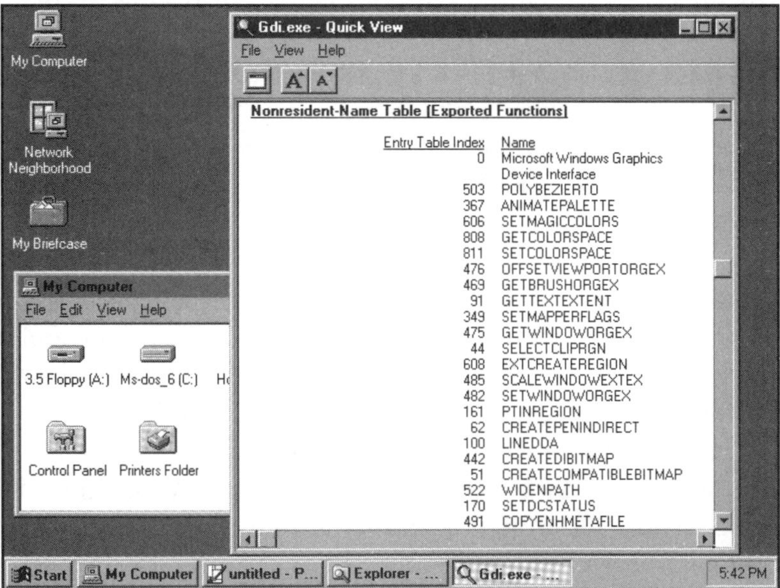

Figure 2-6: Chicago Explorer's Quick View of GDI.EXE, showing a few of the almost 400 APIs exported by the Win16 Graphical Device Interface module.

The device driver's interrupt handler is responsible for invoking a function in USER which, in turn, puts a message on the System Message

Queue. KEYBOARD.DRV's INT 9 handler calls the Keybd_Event routine in USER (*Undocumented Windows*, pp. 467-469). SYSTEM.DRV's INT 8 handler invokes any callback routines installed with CreateSystemTimer (*Undocumented Windows*, pp. 602-607); the SetTimer API provided by USER is based on a callback that USER installs with CreateSystemTimer.

In other words, all hardware events seen even by Win32 applications come from Win16 drivers such as MOUSE and KEYBOARD.

At this point, the INTRSPY log shows Windows 95 loading a huge number of DLLs. These include GDI.EXE, GDI32.DLL, USER.EXE, and USER32.DLL. Figures 2-5 and 2-6 show a few of the many APIs provided by USER.EXE and GDI.EXE. We're not going to plow through all these DLLs; it would take far too long and it's not clear we'd learn anything substantially different from what we already know about Windows 95, anyway. Huge amounts of Windows functionality is provided via DLLs, and in Windows 95 this includes Win32 DLLs. There's not a whole lot else to say.

Exploring the Explorer

Finally, we come to the most visible part of Windows 95. The shell, which is also sometimes called the Explorer or the Cabinet, is shown in Figure 2-7.

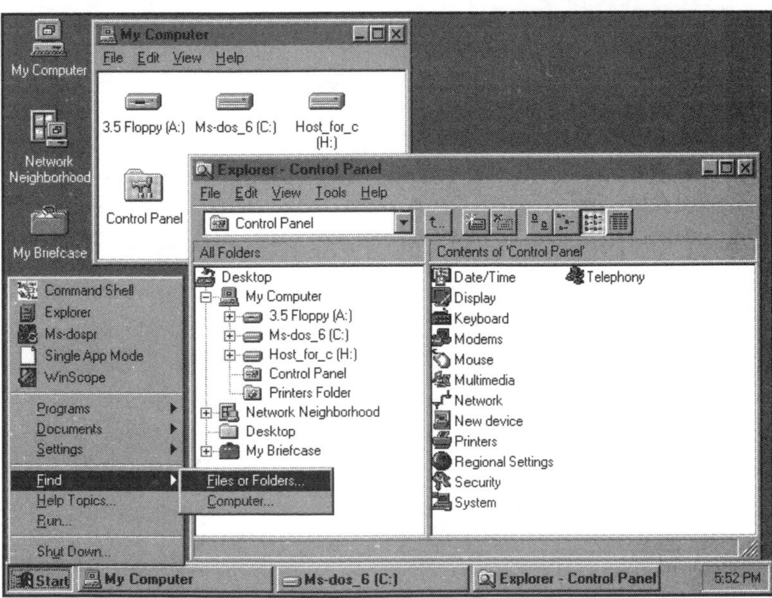

Figure 2-7: The default Chicago shell provided by CAB32.EXE (a Win32 application).

The Windows 95 shell is a Win32 application, CAB32.EXE:

```
XOPEN C:\WINDOWS\CAB32.EXE
XOPEN C:\WINDOWS\SYSTEM\SHELL32.DLL
XOPEN C:\WINDOWS\SYSTEM\shell16.dll
XOPEN C:\WINDOWS\icocache.dat
XOPEN C:\WINDOWS\SYSTEM\DIBENG.DLL
XOPEN C:\WINDOWS\fonts\coure.fon
XOPEN C:\WINDOWS\cabinet.ini
FIND  C:\*.*
FIND  C:\WINDOWS
FIND  C:\Windows\Desktop
FIND  C:\Windows\Desktop\*.*
; ... Explorer loading lots of stuff here ...
XOPEN C:\WINDOWS\SYSTEM\LINKINFO.DLL
XOPEN C:\Windows\Programs\Explorer.lnk
XOPEN C:\Windows\Desktop\Windows 95b.lnk
XOPEN C:\Windows\Programs\Ms-dospr.lnk
FIND  C:\Windows\Recent\*.*
XOPEN C:\Windows\Recent\Relnotes.lnk
...
```

But the Windows 95 shell isn't exactly part of Windows 95. It's ridiculously easy to change SHELL=CAB32.EXE in SYSTEM.INI to SHELL=WINFILE.EXE or SHELL=PROGMAN.EXE or even (as we saw earlier) SHELL=SOL.EXE. At the same time, the highly attractive shell is clearly one of Windows 95's major selling points. Another possible sign that major advances (and the Windows 95 shell is a major advance for the Windows user interface) don't always require a fundamentally new architecture. CAB32 is just an application.

Or is it? Running

```
DUMPBIN /IMPORTS \WINDOWS\CAB32.DLL
```

shows that it appears to use a large number of undocumented Win32 APIs from SHELL32.DLL. (Or at least, they're undocumented at the time of this writing.) For example, here are a few APIs that CAB32 imports from SHELL32:

```
16   RegisterShellHook
1C5   FSNotify_HandleEvents
4C7   SHRegisterDragDrop
1C2   FSNotify_Register
154   SHFindComputer
153   SHFindFiles
```

Running DUMPBIN /EXPORTS on \WINDOWS\SYSTEM\SHELL32.DLL turns up these, plus many other functions. While a few of these do appear in SHELL.H (for example, SHFileOperation and ShellExecuteEx), the majority appear to be undocumented. Running

```
DUMPBIN /IMPORTS \WINDOWS\SYSTEM\ SHELL32.DLL
```

shows that, in turn, SHELL32 seems to use undocumented functionality from KERNEL32, such as MapLS, QT_Thunk, and ThunkConnect32. But of course SHELL32 is part of the operating system, so these are internal interfaces. Well, perhaps CAB32 is part of the operating system too. ("It's Integrated!") Instead of using public interfaces, CAB32 relies on some intimate knowledge of Windows 95. Hmm, perhaps saying that something relies on undocumented features and insider knowledge is just another way of saying that it's integrated?

One thing is conspicuously absent from the DUMPBIN /IMPORTS lists for CAB32 and SHELL32: Object Linking and Embedding (OLE)! Perhaps this will change before the commercial release of Windows 95 but — at least in Beta-1 — the Windows 95 shell doesn't use OLE. This is in sharp contrast to some statements made in the press, such as that "Chicago's shell uses OLE 2.0 extensively" (Ray Valdés, *Dr. Dobb's Developer's Update*, March 1994, p. 6).

Microsoft appears to have been careful not to say this. In an extremely useful article on "Extending the Chicago Shell" (*Microsoft Developer Network News*, July 1994, pp. 10-11), Kyle Marsh says merely that the shell is similar to OLE:

> The design of Chicago's shell extensions is based on the Compound Object Model in Object Linking and Embedding (OLE) version 2.0. The shell accesses objects via interfaces, and applications implement those interfaces as shell extension dynamic link libraries (DLLs), which are similar to the In-Proc Server DLLs in OLE 2.0.

I don't know how significant this is, but besides apparently avoiding anything but the most abstract, conceptual use of OLE 2.0 in the Windows 95 shell, Microsoft seems somewhat down on OLE in general. In *Inside Windows 95*, Adrian King comes right out and says that "Right now, adding full OLE support to an application is an extremely complex engineering project" and "OLE is leading edge technology. Using it now is expensive but could also give you a competitive edge in the Windows 95 applications market" (p. 220). In an interview in the back of the book, Paul Maritz says, "There's a tremendous amount of heat and light about 'things object' at the moment — most of which has nothing to do with the average end user. This is truly an industry-induced storm here, where we're just talking to each other" (p. 421).

While OLE 2.0 itself may amount to nothing more than a very expensive way for the PC software industry to talk to itself, the OLE-like extensions in the Windows 95 shell look like just the ticket. When I used the shell to get a Quick View of KRNL386.EXE and other Win16 executables earlier, I didn't mention that there's nothing particularly built-in about this facility. The ability to handle right-click events and add new "verbs" to the shell's popup menu all works off settings in the registry. Once Windows 95 ships, most of the utilities for this book could be redone as Windows 95 shell extensions.

Chapter 3

The Windows-DOS Connection

According to Microsoft's "Chicago Questions and Answers" white paper (January 1994), Windows 95 "will be a complete, integrated protect-mode operating system that does not require or use a separate version of MS-DOS." Although this, of course, is wonderful news, the technology behind Windows 95 ("Chicago") is actually not all that new:

- Windows 95's much-heralded preemptive multitasking of threads is based on improvements to the old preemptive Virtual Machine (VM) multitasker in the Windows 3.*x* Enhanced mode Virtual Machine Manager (VMM). At the same time, exposing the preemptive multitasker programming interface to mere-mortal application developers — thus lifting it out of its VxD confines — *is* a major step forward.
- Windows 95's 32-bit file access is based on that provided much earlier in Windows for Workgroups (WfW) 3.11. To the foundation laid by WfW, and on top of the venerable DOS FAT file system, Windows 95 adds long file and directory names.
- Windows 95's ability to run Win32 applications is based on improvements to the old Win32s add-in to Windows 3.1.

In many ways, then, Windows 95 simply improves on — and makes users and programmers more aware of — features and capabilities that Windows has had for quite some time (in the case of preemptive multitasking, going all the way back to Windows/386 2.0 in 1988).

That Windows 95 is a "complete" operating system that "does not require or use a separate version of MS-DOS" and yet isn't radically different from previous versions of Windows suggests that perhaps these earlier versions of Windows were also close to being complete operating systems. It also suggests that the connection between these operating systems and MS-DOS was different from what was commonly thought at the time.

Before Windows 95, Windows was frequently described not as an operating system but as an operating environment. After all, Windows 3.*x* ran "on top of" DOS; you started Windows by typing WIN at the DOS C:\> prompt or by putting WIN as the last line of your AUTOEXEC.BAT file. In many ways Windows seemed to be just another DOS application.

Somewhere between Windows 3.0 and 3.1, Microsoft changed the description on the Windows packaging from "graphical environment" to "operating system." But now that it wants to promote Windows 95, Microsoft has suddenly discovered that the previous version of Windows wasn't a genuine operating system after all because it ran on top of DOS.

A peek under the hood shows that, in fact, "operating system" was quite an accurate way to describe Windows 3.*x* Enhanced mode. Certainly, if Windows 95 is to be considered a full-blown operating system, then so must Windows 3.*x* Enhanced mode, because they are not intrinsically different.

In fact, from MS-DOS 5.0 on, Microsoft maintained that Windows 3.*x* was not just some random program that ran on top of DOS, but rather part of a single integrated system with MS-DOS. For example, in a section on "Running Windows with an Operating System Other Than MS-DOS," the README.WRI file included with Windows 3.1 states:

> Microsoft Windows and MS-DOS work together as an integrated system. They were designed together and extensively tested together on a wide variety of computers and hardware configurations. Running Windows version 3.1 on an operating system other than MS-DOS could cause unexpected results or poor performance.

The README.WRI file included with WfW 3.11 adds an explicit note that running Windows with something other than MS-DOS "is not supported by Microsoft." Presumably, "not supported" means that running Windows with another operating system, such as Novell DOS 7 or IBM OS/2, might (in the words of a warning message in a different Microsoft product) "void valuable warranty protection provided by Microsoft on this product."

To fairly assess Microsoft's claims for Windows 95 as a complete operating system, presumably in contrast to Windows 3.*x*'s dependence on

MS-DOS, you first need to understand the relationship between Windows 3.*x* and DOS: What was this "integrated system" that Microsoft was talking about?

This chapter and the next examine an INT 2Fh interface that is just one of the many ways DOS and Windows 3.*x* work together as an integrated system. To explore the DOS-Windows connection, this chapter presents a program called FAKEWIN, which examines how DOS (and DOS-based software such as TSRs and device drivers) reacts when Windows starts up. Using FAKEWIN, I'll establish that MS-DOS 5.0 and 6.0 knew about Windows, and that even before Windows 95, Windows was more than just another pretty face. The next chapter examines the output from FAKEWIN in more detail. Other connections between DOS and Windows, such as Windows's extensive use of undocumented DOS functions and data structures, are discussed in Chapter 1 of *Undocumented DOS* (2d ed.) and need not concern us here.

The FAKEWIN program reveals that, even before Windows 95, Windows (particularly Enhanced mode) and DOS were integrated to such an extent that Windows was *not* just another application that ran on top of DOS. Thanks to the VMM inside WIN386.EXE, it was a true operating system that used real-mode DOS as an assistant. As Geoff Chappell, author of the book *DOS Internals*, puts it, "DOS and its device drivers, TSRs, etc. form a subsystem of 16-bit drivers for Windows." The most you can say is that, in Windows 95, this real-mode subsystem plays a smaller role than it did in Windows 3.1 and WfW 3.11.

Windows INT 2Fh Broadcasts

FAKEWIN, as its name implies, is a DOS program that pretends to be Windows. How does it do this?

When Windows starts up and exits, it issues four separate INT 2Fh broadcasts, called Startup, Startup Complete, Begin Exit, and Exit. DOS device drivers and TSRs loaded before Windows can hook INT 2Fh to receive these notifications of Windows startup and termination. In response to the Startup broadcast (INT 2Fh function 1605h), a device driver or TSR can request that Windows load a Virtual Device Driver (VxD) or allocate *instance data* (you'll see what this is in a few moments).

FAKEWIN pretends to be Windows by issuing the same INT 2Fh broadcasts that Windows would issue. Individual Windows VxDs can also issue broadcasts (INT 2Fh function 1607h), thus allowing them to communicate with software loaded before Windows; FAKEWIN emulates one of these calls, too — namely, the call normally issued by the DOSMGR VxD inside WIN386.EXE. Finally, FAKEWIN emulates a TSR Identify broadcast (INT 2Fh function 160Bh) issued by the Windows USER module; TSRs can use this broadcast to request that Windows load a Windows executable, a dynamic link library (DLL), or a device driver.

These INT 2Fh broadcasts are documented in Microsoft's *Device Driver Adaptation Guide*, included with the Windows Device Driver Kit (DDK), and in an article by David Long on "TSR Support in Microsoft Windows Version 3.1" on the Microsoft Developer Network (MSDN) CD-ROM. But there are two serious problems with this documentation.

First, notice that DOS software developers are expected to look in the Windows DDK, of all places, to find what is basically a DOS interface. It's true that these INT 2Fh calls are issued by Windows, but that doesn't make them part of the Windows API. The Windows INT 2Fh broadcasts are useful only to software loaded *before* Windows, that is, to DOS software. As you'll see, typical users of the INT 2Fh function 1605h interface include the DOSKEY, SMARTDRV, and EMM386 utilities included with MS-DOS. For better or worse, DOS programmers in the 1990s — even ones who resolutely "don't do Windows" — are going to have to become familiar with the Windows DDK. Windows is the operating system now; DOS is just its real-mode 16-bit assistant.

Second, like 99% of the Windows programming documentation, Microsoft's documentation for the INT 2Fh broadcasts explains the interface itself, but not how it's used in the real world. In this case, Microsoft doesn't discuss *which* DOS device drivers and TSRs respond to Windows startup by hooking the INT 2Fh calls. If discussing DOSKEY, SMARTDRV, and EMM386 sounds too implementation-dependent, note that the Windows INT 2Fh broadcasts are hooked not only by an assortment of DOS device drivers and TSRs but more importantly by *MS-DOS itself* (version 5.0 and later).

Let me repeat that: MS-DOS 5.0 and later hook the Windows INT 2Fh broadcast. In other words, *MS-DOS knows about Windows*. DOS behaves differently when Windows Enhanced mode is running. Windows 3.*x* is not just any random DOS application, but (pretty much as Microsoft once claimed, before it was pushing Windows 95) part of an integrated system with MS-DOS.

Using the FAKEWIN program, you'll see exactly what Windows and MS-DOS have to say to each other. FAKEWIN prints any information returned by DOS software that handles the Windows Startup (INT 2Fh function 1605h) broadcast. DOS software that hooks this call can communicate with Windows in the following (fairly unrelated) ways:

- A DOS device driver or TSR can tell Windows not to load (for example, if the software is incompatible with Windows). Employing this part of the function 1605h interface is not recommended.
- A DOS device driver or TSR can ask Windows to load a VxD, possibly a VxD embedded in the same file as the driver or TSR. (Similarly, DOS programs can use INT 2Fh function 160Bh to ask Windows to load Windows executables, DLLs, and 16-bit Windows drivers; as with VxDs, these can be embedded in the same file as the DOS program.)
- A DOS device driver or TSR can declare some number of bytes at some segment:offset address as instance data. Windows normally treats memory allocated before it started (for example, code and data belonging to DOS or to a TSR) as *global* memory: a single copy of the memory is *mapped* (rather than copied) into each virtual machine (VM). However, this is inappropriate for any DOS data that must be separate in each DOS box. For example, the history buffer belonging to a command-line editor such as DOSKEY — if loaded before Windows rather than in a DOS box — must be maintained on a per-VM basis; otherwise, commands typed in one DOS box would leak across to other DOS boxes (a probably unintentional form of interprocess communications). Declaring the history buffer as *instance data* tells Windows to make a separate copy of the buffer for each VM, while keeping the rest of the TSR as global data, a single copy of which is mapped into each VM. Mapping aliases a block of memory to a given reserved linear address. (See Klaus Mueller, "Think Globally, Act Locally: Inside the Windows Instance Data Manager," *Dr. Dobb's Journal*, April 1994.)
- A DOS device driver or TSR can give Windows the address of a function call to turn Virtual 8086 (V86) mode off and on. Expanded memory managers such as EMM386, QEMM, and 386MAX put the machine into V86 mode — a form of protected mode (see Chapter 9) — in order to emulate the EMS interface and to backfill empty Upper Memory Block (UMB) addresses. Meanwhile, Windows wants to switch the machine from real mode to protected mode. It can't do this if the memory manager *already* has the machine in protected mode, so the Windows startup broadcast allows 386 memory managers to tell Windows how it can turn them off when it starts up and back on again when it exits. If

DOS software has allocated memory (EMS, XMS, or UMBs), the memory manager can hand off control of this memory to Windows, using an undocumented interface known as Global EMM Import.

The Windows initialization broadcast is shown in Figure 3-1. This broadcast is similar to the Task Switcher Identify Instance Data function (INT 2Fh function 4B05h) documented in Microsoft's *MS-DOS Programmer's Reference*. Both broadcasts expect the same startup info structure; DOSKEY for example uses a single block of code to handle both calls.


```
Called with:
    AX = 1605h
    CX = 0 if okay to start Windows; nonzero if not okay
    DX = flags (bit 0 clear if Enhanced mode; set if Standard mode)
    DI = Windows major/minor version number (high/low)
    ES:BX -> 0:0, or previous Win386_Startup_Info_Struc
    DS:SI -> 0:0, or (if nonzero) indicates that the V86 enable/disable callback
             already exists
    INT 2Fh

Return:
    CX = 0 if okay to start Windows; nonzero if not okay
    Win386_Startup_Info_Struct -> SIS_Next_Dev_Ptr = previous ES:BX
    ES:BX -> Win386_Startup_Info_Struc (see below)
    DS:SI -> 0:0, or V86 enable/disable callback

typedef struct {
    void far *IIS_Ptr;        // segment:offset of instance data
    WORD IIS_Size;            // number of bytes
    } Instance_Item_Struc;

typedef struct _WINFO {
    WORD SIS_Version;
    struct _WINFO far *SIS_Next_Dev_Ptr;     // next startup info struct
    DWORD SIS_Virt_Dev_File_Ptr;             // name of VxD to load
    DWORD SIS_Reference_Data;                // ref data for VxD
    Instance_Item_Struc far *SIS_Instance_Data_Ptr;
    } Win386_Startup_Info_Struc;
```

Figure 3-1: If a DOS device driver or a TSR loaded before Windows hooks the Windows initialization broadcast (INT 2Fh function 1605h), it can request that Windows load a VxD or allocate instance data.

DOS software that hooks the Windows startup broadcast is responsible for maintaining a linked list of Windows startup info structures. Before setting ES:BX to the address of its own Win386_Startup_Info_Struc, a program hooking this broadcast must first pass it (unchanged) to the previously installed INT 2Fh handler (see TSRLDR.ASM in Chapter 4 for an example).

As shown in Figure 3-1, software that uses this broadcast to return a pointer to a Win386_Startup_Info_Struc must set the SIS_Next_Dev_Ptr field in the structure to the address of the *previous* Win386_Startup_Info_Struct, which is returned from the previous handler.

FAKEWIN walks this linked list, printing each structure. For example, FAKEWIN reveals that if you happen to be running the Qualitas 386MAX memory manager and then start Windows (or FAKEWIN), 386MAX responds to the INT 2Fh function 1605h with the following:

```
Win386_Startup_Info_Struc at 0255:01E2 (386MAX$$)
VxD name: C:\386MAX\386MAX.VxD   (Reference data: 0053DA1E)
Instance_Item_Struc at C001:042E
    C001:0183   0001
V86 Enable/Disable function: 036E:03D4 (386MAX$$)
Global EMM Import @ 00BD9EACh (version 1.11)
```

Here, 386MAX is doing several things. First, it's telling Windows to load a virtual device driver called 386MAX.VXD. Second, it's declaring one byte of instance data at C001:0183. And third, it's giving Windows the address of a 386MAX function to turn V86 mode off and on. 386MAX also supports the Global EMM Import specification, and FAKEWIN prints the address and version of the EMM import structure. (See Taku Okazaki, "The Windows Global EMM Import Interface," *Dr. Dobb's Journal*, August 1994.)

Instance Data

I noted earlier that the DOSKEY command-line editor declares its history buffer as instance data and that FAKEWIN lets you see how DOSKEY communicates this information to Windows. Here's what I was referring to:

```
Win386_Startup_Info_Struc at 2996:024B (DOSKEY)
Instance_Item_Struc at 2996:025D (DOSKEY)
    2996:0000   0288 (DOSKEY)
    2996:0F23   0200 (DOSKEY)
```

FAKEWIN has a -DUMP option that prints the current contents of an instance data block in hex and ASCII. Using this option confirms that DOSKEY's history buffer is instance data:

```
2996:0F23   0200 (DOSKEY)
2996:0F23 | 45 00 63 3A 5C 65 70 73 5C 65 70 73 69 6C 6F 6E | E.c:\eps\epsilon
2996:0F33 | 2E 65 78 65 20 24 2A 00 70 00 66 61 6B 65 77 69 | .exe $*.p.fakewi
2996:0F43 | 6E 20 2D 64 75 6D 70 20 3E 20 74 6D 70 2E 74 6D | n -dump > tmp.tm
2996:0F53 | 70 00 72 6C 6E 6B 00 66 61 6B 65 77 69 6E 20 3E | p.rlnk.fakewin >
```

If you had two DOS boxes open under Windows and you used DEBUG or some other real-mode debugger in each DOS box to display the DOSKEY history buffer, you'd see (as shown here) that each DOS box has its own separate history buffer, even though only a single copy of DOSKEY was loaded before Windows.

```
-d 2996:0f23
2996:0F20           45 00 63 3A 5C-65 70 73 5C 65 70 73 69      E.c:\eps\epsi
2996:0F30  6C 6F 6E 2E 65 78 65 20-24 2A 00 67 72 65 70 20   lon.exe $*.grep
2996:0F40  44 4F 53 4B 45 59 20 66-61 6B 65 77 69 6E 2E 74   DOSKEY fakewin.t

-d 2996:0f23
2996:0F20           45 00 63 3A 5C-65 70 73 5C 65 70 73 69      E.c:\eps\epsi
2996:0F30  6C 6F 6E 2E 65 78 65 20-24 2A 00 64 69 72 00 64   lon.exe $*.dir.d
2996:0F40  69 72 00 6D 65 6D 00 6D-65 6D 00 6D 65 6D 00 67   ir.mem.mem.mem.g
```

That's the general idea behind instance data: it takes a single piece of data and multiplexes it among multiple clients. Knowing the differences between local, global, and instance data is also helpful when trying to understand instance data. These differences are shown in Figure 3-2. I'll be discussing instant data in more detail in the "DOS Instance Data and the SDA" section in Chapter 4.

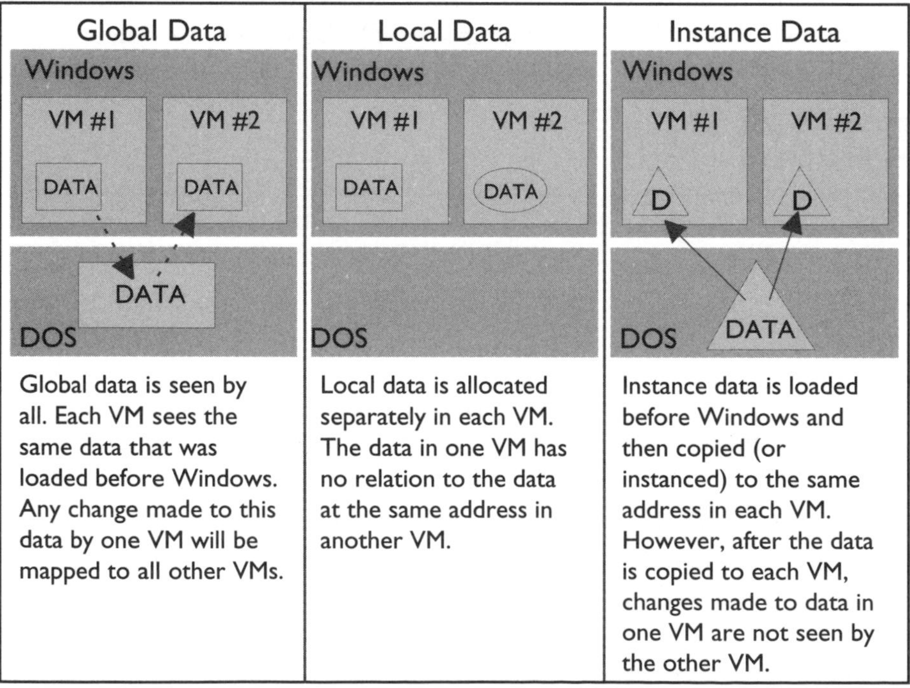

Figure 3-2: The differences between global, local, and instance data.

Embedded VxDs

In the following sample output from FAKEWIN, the SmartDrive disk cache and DoubleSpace disk compression are asking Windows to load VxDs (DriveSpace in MS-DOS 6.22 does the same thing):

```
Win386_Startup_Info_Struc at 2AF4:12EF (SMARTDRV)
VxD name: C:\DOS\SMARTDRV.EXE   (Reference data: 2AF41301)
No instance data

Win386_Startup_Info_Struc at 1551:3F10 (DBLSYSH$)
VxD name: H:\DBLSPACE.BIN   (Reference data: 15513F32)
No instance data
```


But SMARTDRV.EXE and DBLSPACE.BIN don't look like names of Windows VxDs — they're DOS files, right?

As mentioned earlier, DOS programs can have embedded Windows executables. Here, SMARTDRV.EXE and DBLSPACE.BIN both have embedded VxDs. (DRVSPACE.BIN in MS-DOS 6.22 has one, too.) Actually, it's not quite accurate to describe these as DOS programs with embedded Windows executables. They're really Windows executables that, like *every* Windows executable, have an embedded DOS program. Usually that DOS program is a small stub that prints a message like "This program requires Microsoft Windows." However, it's just as easy to make the embedded DOS program do something useful. In the case of SMARTDRV.EXE and DBLSPACE.BIN, the embedded DOS program is part of the DOS system software.

We can use the VXDSHOW utility from the *Unauthorized Windows 95* disk to the VxDs embedded in these DOS utilities. While we're at it, we can also look at another DOS utility with an embedded VxD, EMM386.EXE. Figure 3-3 shows the result.

```
C:\UNAUTHW>vxdshow h:\dblspace.bin
Module name: DSVXD
Description: "Win386 DSVXD Device  (Version 1.0)"
DSVXD_DDB @ 000001d0
Start @ 0000:00000000
Device # 003b
Version 3.00
Init order: 80000000 (Undefined)
DDB_Control_Proc @ 00000000
DDB_V86_API_Proc @ 00000057

C:\UNAUTHW>vxdshow c:\dos\smartdrv.exe
Module name: SDVXD
Description: "Win386 SDVXD Device  (Version 2.0)"
```

```
SDVXD_DDB @ 00000060
Start @ 0000:00000000
Version 3.00
Init order: 80000000 (Undefined)
DDB_Control_Proc @ 00000000

C:\UNAUTHW>vxdshow c:\dos\emm386.exe
Module name: LoadHi
Description: "Win386 LoadHi Device  (Version 1.0)"
LoadHi_DDB @ 000012e4
Start @ 0003:00000000
Device # 001c
Version 1.00
Init order: 00000000 (Earliest -- same as VMM)
DDB_Control_Proc @ 000005a0
DDB_Service_Table @ 000012e0
    1c0000 @ 0000079d   LoadHi_Get_Version
```

Figure 3-3: Running VxDSHOW with DBLSPACE.BIN, SMARTDRV.EXE, and EMM386.EXE reveals the surprise VxD inside.

It so happens that these particular VxDs aren't especially important in Windows 95. For example, the SDVxD embedded in SMARTDRV.EXE does little more than allow Windows to do a SHELL_SYSMODAL_Message in the event of a serious disk error. However, even if SmartDrv is loaded in Windows 95, Windows basically ignores it because its role is taken over by the VCACHE VxD. SMARTDRV.EXE is listed in the "safe driver" list, IOS.INI, which the Windows 95 I/O Supervisor (IOS.386) consults to see which real-mode DOS drivers can be ignored.

Now, if SmartDrv is no longer needed in Windows 95, why bother learning how SmartDrv communicated its needs to earlier versions of Windows? Because the very fact that SmartDrv and other DOS utilities *could* communicate their needs to Windows is significant: it's one more sign that Windows 3.*x* didn't blithely run "on top of" DOS, but instead participated in a dialog with DOS and with DOS utilities like SmartDrv. This point is in turn important because it helps establish that Windows 95's bundling of DOS and Windows in a single package is less of a radical departure from previous DOS-Windows relations than you might otherwise think. If Windows 95 represents the marriage of DOS and Windows, the fact remains that the two have already been living together for many years. It's a big step — but not *that* big a step.

FAKEWIN Caveats

Although FAKEWIN helps reveal the true relationship between Windows and DOS, the program is somewhat invasive because it might interfere with other programs that use the Windows INT 2Fh broadcasts to maintain an internal IN_WINDOWS flag. MS-DOS itself is one such program. For example, while Windows Enhanced mode is running, MS-DOS keeps track of which virtual machine (VM) owns which open file. We'll see in Chapter 4 (see Listing 4-2) that, if DOS thinks Windows is running, DOS can make calls into what it thinks is the DOSMGR VxD. Unfortunately, while FAKEWIN is running, MS-DOS thinks that Windows Enhanced mode is running. There's no way to know how every DOS device driver and TSR will react to FAKEWIN's phony notification that Windows has started. Thus, it's difficult to answer the following question: "How can I use INT 2Fh functions 1605h and 1606h and be sure I'm not messing up DOS?"

It's worth quoting at length from Geoff Chappell's answer to this question, from the Undocumented Corner area in the *Dr. Dobb's Journal* forum (DDJFORUM) on CompuServe:

#: 65821 S3/Undocumented Corner
16-May-94 01:39:01
Sb: #65697-#SmartDrive API
Fm: Geoff Chappell 100043,564
To: Ralph E Griffin 70323,1440 (X)

It's perfectly OK for non-Windows programs to issue int 2Fh functions 1605h and 1606h and pretend to be Windows starting up and closing down — if they don't do anything with external consequences between the two calls.

The situation is less clear if external consequences are involved. Software may, quite reasonably, reconfigure itself for operation under Windows. This software does not know that you are only pretending to be Windows. You could argue that perhaps such software should not make any changes that could have harmful side-effects if in fact the signals were not coming from Windows — in other words, that the software should not assume int 2Fh function 1605h comes from Windows.

Maybe that would be a fair point, but you've been pre-empted by Microsoft, who designed DOS 5 in such a way that the machine ID (word at DOS:033E) is handled differently the moment the DOS kernel sees the int 2Fh function. I am unconvinced that this is a good idea on DOS's part; it may have unwelcome consequences for file sharing in cases where a file consulted by Windows (before DOSMGR is initialised) is already open when Windows is started. This is an unlikely case in the real world where Windows is usually run from the top-level command prompt (its likelihood is, however, sufficiently large that even the designers of IFSMGR, with its many small bugs and incompatibilities that seem to have been overlooked, did not miss the need to guard against conflicts arising if the 16-bit file system already has files open when the 32-bit file system is installed).

My personal view is that we have (more or less) a No-Go theorem on file access between a non-Windows app's int 2Fh functions 1605h and 1606h — and this is deduced from a reaction that we know about. If you were planning to issue these int 2Fh functions yourself in a general environment, you would also have to contend with reactions that we can't predict.

Now, you might think that FAKEWIN doesn't "do anything with external consequences between the two calls" to functions 1605h and 1606h. However, notice in Listing 3-1 that FAKEWIN calls printf after calling win_init_notify (1605h) and before calling win_term_notify (1606h). If FAKEWIN's output is redirected to a file (which happened countless times while I was writing this chapter), there's a genuine potential problem.

On the other hand, the *Microsoft Systems Journal* has recommended that programs other than Windows issue Windows INT 2Fh broadcasts, both to detect Windows 3.0 (*Microsoft Systems Journal*, May-June 1992) and to reconfigure the SmartDrive 4.0 disk cache (*Microsoft Systems Journal*, September 1992). It's difficult to tell if this is our assurance that the technique of issuing phony Windows INT 2Fh broadcasts is really okay, or if it just never occurred to Microsoft that faking the Windows broadcast might have unexpected effects on programs (including DOS itself) that hook the broadcast.

Besides telling software that Windows has started when it actually hasn't, there's another potential danger associated with FAKEWIN: It might tell software that Windows has exited when in fact it's still running. This is exactly what would happen if you ran FAKEWIN inside a Windows DOS box. FAKEWIN.C uses the is_win function from ISWIN .C to detect whether Windows is running. (ISWIN.C isn't shown here, but is included on the *Unauthorized Windows 95* disk.) FAKEWIN will refuse to run under Windows; you must first exit back to DOS. (In Windows 95, where you normally can't exit from Windows back to DOS, you can run FAKEWIN in Single Application Mode.)

Finally, FAKEWIN shows only a few aspects of the DOS-Windows connection. For example, function 1605h isn't the only mechanism for declaring instance data. SYSTEM.INI has a LOCALTSRS= statement that turns entire TSRs into instance data items, and a LOCAL= statement that does the same for DOS device drivers. (SYSTEM.INI comes preloaded with local=CON and localtsrs=DOSEDIT,CED.) And the Windows VMM provides an _AddInstanceItem service that VxDs can directly use to declare instance data. In fact, all the other instance data methods eventually turn into _AddInstanceItem calls, so if you wanted a complete picture of instance data, you'd have to hook _AddInstanceItem.

Inside FAKEWIN

In spite of the issues discussed in the previous section, the FAKEWIN program helps show how Windows 3.*x* interacted with software loaded before it. The salient point about FAKEWIN is that it helps you understand the Windows 3.*x*-DOS connection — and unless you understand that, it's difficult to appreciate the changes that are occurring in Windows 95.

The C source code for FAKEWIN is shown in Listing 3-1. This module must be linked with several others (TEST1684.C, FAKEVXD.C, and FAKETSR.C in Chapter 4, and with ISWIN.C, DUMP.C, and MAP.C on the *Unauthorized Windows 95* disk) to create FAKEWIN.EXE.

Listing 3-1: FAKEWIN.C

```
/*
FAKEWIN.C
Andrew Schulman, 1994

bcc fakewin.c fakevxd.c faketsr.c dump.c iswin.c map.c
bcc -DTEST_1684 -- also need test1684.c

Using INT 2Fh broadcasts, FAKEWIN pretends to be Windows. It
simulates Windows initializing and terminating in order to find
out how DOS and various device drivers and TSRs want to affect
Windows startup. For each Win386_Startup_Info_Struc, FAKEWIN
prints out the name of any Windows virtual device driver (VxD)
that has been asked to be loaded, plus the addresses and sizes
of any instance data items.

Options:
    -WIN30 fakes Windows 3.0
    -VERS xxx fakes version xxx (such as -VERS 400 for 4.0)
    -STANDARD fakes Standard mode (default: Enhanced mode)
    -DUMP does hex dump of instanced data areas
*/

#include <stdlib.h>
#include <stdio.h>
#include <string.h>
#include <dos.h>
#include <io.h>
#include <fcntl.h>

typedef unsigned char BYTE;
```

```
typedef unsigned short WORD;
typedef unsigned long DWORD;
typedef void far *FP;

#pragma pack(1)

typedef struct {
    FP IIS_Ptr;
    WORD IIS_Size;
    } Instance_Item_Struc;

// the Task Switcher Identify Instance Data (2F/4B05)
// function uses the same structure
typedef struct _WINFO {
    WORD SIS_Version;       // should be 3
    struct _WINFO far *SIS_Next_Dev_Ptr;
    DWORD SIS_Virt_Dev_File_Ptr;
    DWORD SIS_Reference_Data;
    Instance_Item_Struc far *SIS_Instance_Data_Ptr;
    } Win386_Startup_Info_Struc, far *FPWININFO;

#pragma pack()

static FPWININFO fpinfo;
static void (far *switch_func)(void);

#define ENHANCED_MODE       0
#define STANDARD_MODE       1

#define WIN30               0x0300
#define WIN31               0x030A

extern void fake_dosmgr_callouts(void); // in FAKEVXD.C

extern void tsr_identify(void); // in FAKETSR.C

extern void dump(unsigned char far *fp, unsigned bytes,
    char *mask, unsigned long addr, int width); // in DUMP.C

extern int is_win(int *pmaj, int *pmin, int *pmode); // in ISWIN.C

extern char *find_owner(DWORD lin_addr); // in MAP.C

#define MK_LIN(fp)      ((((DWORD) FP_SEG(fp)) << 4) + FP_OFF(fp))

char *owner(FP fp)
{
    static char buf[32];
    char *s = find_owner(MK_LIN(fp));
    if (s) sprintf(buf, "(%s)", s);
    else buf[0] = '\0';
    return buf;
}

WORD win_init_notify(WORD vers, WORD mode)
```

```
{
    WORD retval;
    WORD handler_ds;
    _asm push si
    _asm push di
    _asm push ds
    _asm xor bx, bx
    _asm mov es, bx
    _asm mov cx, bx
    _asm mov dx, mode
    _asm mov di, vers
    _asm xor si, si
    _asm mov ds, si
    _asm mov ax, 1605h
    _asm int 2fh
    _asm mov retval, cx
    _asm mov handler_ds, ds
    _asm pop ds
    _asm cmp cx, 0
    _asm jne no_init
init:
    _asm mov word ptr fpinfo+2, es
    _asm mov word ptr fpinfo, bx
    _asm mov bx, handler_ds
    _asm mov word ptr switch_func+2, bx
    _asm mov word ptr switch_func, si
done:
    _asm pop di
    _asm pop si
    return retval;
no_init:
    goto done;
}

void win_term_notify(WORD mode)
{
    _asm mov dx, mode
    _asm mov ax, 1606h
    _asm int 2fh
}

void win_init_complete_notify(void)
{
    _asm mov ax, 1608h
    _asm int 2fh
}

void win_begin_exit_notify(void)
{
    _asm mov ax, 1609h
    _asm int 2fh
}

static int do_hex_dump = 0;
```

```
void print_startup_info(FPWININFO winfo)
{
    Instance_Item_Struc far *inst;
    if (winfo->SIS_Version >= 3)    // try to be forward compatible
    {
        printf("\nWin386_Startup_Info_Struc at %Fp %s\n",
            winfo, owner(winfo));
        if (winfo->SIS_Virt_Dev_File_Ptr != 0)
        {
            printf("VxD name: %Fs   ", winfo->SIS_Virt_Dev_File_Ptr);
            printf("(Reference data: %08lX)\n", winfo->SIS_Reference_Data);
        }
        if ((inst = winfo->SIS_Instance_Data_Ptr) != 0)
        {
            printf("Instance_Item_Struc at %Fp %s\n",
                inst, owner(inst));
            while (inst->IIS_Ptr)
            {
                printf("   %Fp   %04X %s\n",
                    inst->IIS_Ptr, inst->IIS_Size,
                    owner(inst->IIS_Ptr));
                if (do_hex_dump)
                    dump((unsigned char far *) inst->IIS_Ptr,
                         (unsigned) inst->IIS_Size, "%Fp",
                         (unsigned long) inst->IIS_Ptr, 16);
                inst++;
            }
        }
        else
            printf("No instance data\n");

        // recursively walk chain of startup info blocks
        if (winfo->SIS_Next_Dev_Ptr != 0)
            print_startup_info((FPWININFO) winfo->SIS_Next_Dev_Ptr);
    }
    else
        printf("%Fp not a valid Win386 startup info structure!\n", winfo);
}

#pragma pack(1)
typedef struct {
    DWORD addr;
    BYTE maj, min;
    } EMM_IMPORT;
#pragma pack()

void check_emm_import(void)
{
    static EMM_IMPORT emm_import;
    int emm = open("EMMXXXX0", O_RDWR | O_BINARY);
    if (emm == -1) emm = open("$MMXXXX0", O_RDWR | O_BINARY);
    if (emm == -1) emm = open("EMMQXXX0", O_RDWR | O_BINARY);
    if (emm == -1) return;  // no EMM
    emm_import.addr = 1;    // set first byte to 1
    emm_import.maj = emm_import.min = 0;
```

```
    #define IOCTLREAD 2
    if (ioctl(emm, IOCTLREAD, &emm_import, sizeof(emm_import)) != 0)
        printf("Global EMM Import @ %081Xh (version %d.%02d)\n",
            emm_import.addr, emm_import.maj, emm_import.min);
    close(emm);
}

void fail(const char *s, ...) { puts(s); exit(1); }

static char *usage_msg =
    "usage: fakewin [-standard] [-win30 | -vers xxxx] [-dump]";

void usage(void) { fail(usage_msg); }

main(int argc, char *argv[])
{
    WORD mode = ENHANCED_MODE;  // default
    WORD vers = WIN31;          // default
    char *s;
    int dummy;
    int i;

fputs("FAKEWIN 1.0 -- Simulate Windows Initialization\n", stderr);
fputs("Displays instance data, VxD startup, DOSMGR interface\n", stderr);
fputs("From \"Unauthorized Windows\" (IDG Books, 1994)\n", stderr);
fputs("Copyright (c) Andrew Schulman 1994.  All rights reserved\n\n", stderr);

    for (i=1; i<argc; i++)
        if ((argv[i][0] == '-') || (argv[i][0] == '/'))
        {
            s = strupr(argv[i]) + 1;
            if (strcmp(s, "STANDARD") == 0)   mode = STANDARD_MODE;
            else if (strcmp(s, "WIN30") == 0) vers = WIN30;
            else if (strcmp(s, "VERS") == 0) sscanf(argv[++i], "%04X", &vers);
            else if (strcmp(s, "DUMP") == 0)  do_hex_dump++;
            else                              usage();
        }
        else
            usage();

    if (is_win(&dummy, &dummy, &dummy))
        fail("Already running under Windows\n"
             "Exit back to DOS before running FAKEWIN");

    printf("FAKEWIN pretending to be Windows %u.%02u %s mode\n\n",
        (vers >> 8), (vers & 0xFF),
        (mode == ENHANCED_MODE) ? "Enhanced" : "Standard");

    // tell DOS/whoever that Windows is starting up
    if (win_init_notify(vers, mode) == 0)
    {
        // start recursive walk of info chain
        if (fpinfo == 0)
            printf("No Windows startup info\n");
        else
```

```
            print_startup_info(fpinfo);

        if (switch_func)
        {
            printf("\nV86 Enable/Disable function: %Fp %s\n",
                switch_func, owner(switch_func));

            check_emm_import();
        }
    }
    else    // someone refused the 2F/1605 call (CX != 0)
        fail("Not allowed to start Windows");

    // do device callouts -- VxD init order defined in VMM.INC
    fake_dosmgr_callouts();

    // do TSR identify call (2F/160B)
    tsr_identify();

    // tell DOS/whoever that Windows is done initializing
    win_init_complete_notify();

#ifdef TEST_1684
{
    extern void test_1684(void);    // in TEST1684.C
    test_1684();
}
#endif

    // tell DOS/whoever that Windows is beginning termination
    win_begin_exit_notify();

    // tell DOS/whoever that Windows is terminating
    win_term_notify(mode);

    return 0;
}
```


After reading any command-line options, the main routine in FAKE-WIN.C calls win_init_notify to generate the INT 2Fh function 1605h broadcast, which is normally made by the real-mode portion of WIN386. EXE. The win_init_notify function saves the addresses of the returned startup info structure and V86 enable/disable functions. Assuming that no one has refused the Windows startup broadcast by setting CX to a nonzero value, FAKEWIN then calls print_startup_info, which (not surprisingly) prints the startup info structure. If there's a Next pointer in the structure (winfo->SIS_Next_Dev_Ptr != 0), print_startup_info recursively calls itself. In this way, the function displays the linked list of startup info structures.

Displaying the startup info involves little more than some calls to printf. For the name of the startup info's owner (such as 386MAX$$,

DOSKEY, SMARTDRV, and DBLSYSH$ in the examples given earlier), print_startup_info calls the owner function, which is provided by MAP.C (MAP.C isn't shown here, but is included on the disk).

If the -DUMP option has been specified on the command line, print_startup_info calls the hex dump function provided by DUMP.C, which, again, is included on the disk.

After displaying the startup info, FAKEWIN prints the V86 enable/disable function, if a 386 memory manager has supplied one, and calls check_emm_import to see if the memory manager provides a Global EMM Import structure (see Chapter 4).

Next, FAKEWIN calls the fake_dosmgr_callouts function in FAKE-VXD.C and the tsr_identify function in FAKETSR.C. Chapter 4 discusses these functions.

Finally, because FAKEWIN has pretended to everyone that Windows is starting, FAKEWIN must now pretend several more things: that Windows has finished initializing (INT 2Fh function 1608h), that it is starting to exit (function 1609h), and that it is finally going to exit for good (function 1606h).

Chapter 4

A Marriage Made in Redmond

The previous chapter introduced the FAKEWIN program and discussed in general terms some aspects of the DOS-Windows connection, such as instance data and embedded VxDs. In this chapter, we'll take a closer look at FAKEWIN's output and focus on some of the ways that DOS and Windows work together.

Figure 4-1 shows the complete sample output from FAKEWIN. This output happened to be produced when running in the DOS 7.0 component of Chicago, with a large number of TSRs loaded. Obviously, your mileage may vary: in a different configuration FAKEWIN would produce different results. Nonetheless Figure 4-1 shows how some common DOS utilities, and DOS itself, react to the news that Windows is starting up.

```
FAKEWIN pretending to be Windows 3.10 Enhanced mode

Win386_Startup_Info_Struc at 08F4:125F (SMARTDRV)
VxD name: C:\WINDOWS\SMARTDRV.EXE   (Reference data: 08F41271)
No instance data

Win386_Startup_Info_Struc at 08C5:0107 (TSRLDR)
VxD name: C:\UNAUTHW\PIPE\PIPE.386   (Reference data: 00000000)
No instance data

Win386_Startup_Info_Struc at 085E:000A (COUNTDOS)
Instance_Item_Struc at 085E:001C (COUNTDOS)
   085E:00DD   0404 (COUNTDOS)

Win386_Startup_Info_Struc at E9F7:024B (DOSKEY)
Instance_Item_Struc at E9F7:025D (DOSKEY)
   E9F7:0000   0288 (DOSKEY)
   E9F7:0F23   0200 (DOSKEY)

Win386_Startup_Info_Struc at 0329:01EE (386MAX$$)
```

```
VxD name: C:\386MAX\386MAX.VxD   (Reference data: 00BCE3C8)
Instance_Item_Struc at C001:0440
   C001:0183   0001

Win386_Startup_Info_Struc at C0FD:3F10 (DBLSYSH$)
VxD name: H:\DBLSPACE.BIN   (Reference data: C0FD3F32)
No instance data

Win386_Startup_Info_Struc at FFFF:1D0F (HMA)
Instance_Item_Struc at FFFF:1D25 (HMA)
   0050:0000   0001
   0050:0004   0001
   0050:000E   0014
   0050:0030   0004
   0070:0012   0004 (IO)
   0070:0266   0001 (IO)
   E833:0000   0948 (DBLSYSH$)
   E808:0010   0002 (DBLSYSH$)

Win386_Startup_Info_Struc at 00A0:0EE1 (DOS)
Instance_Item_Struc at 00A0:0EF7 (DOS)
   00A0:0022   0002 (DOS)
   00A0:0032   0004 (DOS)
   00A0:01F9   0106 (DOS)
   00A0:0300   0001 (DOS)
   00A0:0EBF   0022 (DOS)
   00A0:0089   0001 (DOS)
   00A0:008C   0002 (DOS)
   00A0:0086   0001 (DOS)
   00A0:12B8   0001 (DOS)
   00A0:12B9   0001 (DOS)

V86 Enable/Disable function: 0329:03D4 (386MAX$$)
Global EMM Import @ phys 00BD9EACh (version 1.11)

DOSMGR instance interface ON
Segment of DOS drivers: 0005
Patch table: 00A0:0F47
DOS version 5.00
   05EC (SAVEDS)
   05EA (SAVEBX)
   0321 (INDOS)
   033E (USER_ID)
   0315 (CRITPATCH)
   008C (UMB_HEAD)
Current Directory Structure = 88 bytes
No DOS data structures instanced via DOSMGR API

TSR_Info_Struc at 085E:0026 (PSP 084Eh) (COUNTDOS)
TSR_WINEXEC SW_SHOWNOACTIVATE
"C:\UNAUTHW\FAKEWIN\COUNTDOS.EXE /085E:00DD"
TSR_ID_Block: "Sample TSR / Windows App"
TSR_Data_Block: 085E:00DD
```

Figure 4-1: Running FAKEWIN with a large number of TSRs loaded further illustrates the DOS-Windows connection: Some utilities are making requests of Windows, and we see DOS itself communicating with Windows.

Let's see what we have in Figure 4-1. To start with, the first Windows startup info structure in the chain belongs to SMARTDRV.EXE, the DOS portion of which, as noted in Chapter 3, asks Windows to load its VxD portion.

Next, something called TSRLDR asks Windows to load PIPE.386 (a DOS-Windows communication pipe written by Thomas Olsen). TSRLDR.ASM, which you can see in Listing 4-1, is a small DOS program illustrating how DOS software can hook function 1605h to request Windows load to a VxD.

Listing 4-1: TSRLDR.ASM

```
; TSRLDR.ASM
; by Thomas Olsen
; masm tsrldr
; link tsrldr
; exe2bin tsrldr.exe tsrldr.com

CODE    segment para public 'CODE'
        assume cs:CODE

        org 100h

EntryPoint:
        jmp       Setup

        oldInt2fOffset          dw  ?
        oldInt2fSegment         dw  ?

Win386_Startup_Info_Begin label byte
        SIS_Version                     db  3,0
        SIS_Next_Dev_Ptr_Offset         dw  ?
        SIS_Next_Dev_Ptr_Segment        dw  ?
        SIS_Virt_Dev_File_Ptr_Offset    dw  ?
        SIS_Virt_Dev_File_Ptr_Segment   dw  ?
        SIS_Reference_Data              dd  0
        SIS_Instance_Data_Ptr_Offset    dw  0
        SIS_Instance_Data_Ptr_Segment   dw  0
Win386_Startup_Info_End label byte

                                        db 'PATH='
        vxdName                         db 'C:\UNAUTHW\PIPE.386',0
                                        db  128 dup(0)
Int2fHandler proc far
        public  Int2fHandler

        cmp     ax, 1605h
        je      i2f
        jmp     dword ptr cs:oldInt2fOffset
i2f:
        ; first call previous INT 2Fh, before returning our info!
        pushf
```

```
        call    dword ptr cs:oldInt2fOffset

        ; now we have pointer to previous handler's info struct
        mov     cs:SIS_Next_Dev_Ptr_Segment, es
        mov     cs:SIS_Next_Dev_Ptr_Offset, bx

        mov     cs:SIS_Virt_Dev_File_Ptr_Segment, cs
        mov     cs:SIS_Virt_Dev_File_Ptr_Offset, offset vxdName

        mov     bx, cs
        mov     es, bx
        mov     bx, offset Win386_Startup_Info_Begin
        iret
Int2fHandler endp

Setup   proc    near
        public  Setup

        mov     bx, ds
        mov     es, bx
        mov     bx, es:[2Ch]
        mov     ah, 49h
        mov     es, bx
        int     21h                     ; Free environment

        push    cs
        pop     ds

        mov     ax,352Fh
        int     21h
        mov     cs:oldInt2fSegment,es
        mov     cs:oldInt2fOffset,bx
        mov     ax,252Fh
        lea     dx, Int2fHandler
        int     21h                     ; Hook INT 2Fh

        mov     dx,offset Setup
        mov     cl,4
        shr     dx,cl
        inc     dx
        mov     ah,31h
        int     21h
Setup   endp

CODE    ends
        end EntryPoint
```

By the way, in the event of an error in your function 1605h handling, the real-mode portion of WIN386 uses some rather poorly chosen error messages. If a TSR tells Windows to load a file that isn't actually a VxD (for example, an interoffice memo that for some reason you've renamed PIPE.386), you get the message: "A device file that is specified in the SYSTEM.INI file is damaged. It may be needed to run Windows."

The whole point of function 1605h is that the VxD hasn't been specified in SYSTEM.INI. Without a program like FAKEWIN, a system administrator might have a hard time tracking down the cause of this error message! Likewise, if the TSR has specified a VxD that can't be found at all, Windows displays this message:

```
Cannot find a device file that may be needed to run Windows.
Make sure that the PATH line in your AUTOEXEC.BAT file points to
the directory that contains the file and that it exists on your
hard disk. If the file does not exist, try running Setup to
install it or remove any references to it from your SYSTEM.INI
file.
C:\MISTAKE\PIPE.386
Press a key to continue
```


Again, the reference to SYSTEM.INI is less than helpful, as is the advice about the PATH. If PIPE.386 is actually in C:\PIPE, and C:\PIPE is on the PATH, Windows still can't find it.

DOS Instance Data and the SDA

As you continue examining Figure 4-1, you'll notice two Windows startup info structures created not by a TSR or DOS device driver but by MS-DOS itself. The first structure, located in the high memory area (HMA), with instance data items at addresses such as 0050:0000 and 0070:0012, belongs to the IO component of WINBOOT.SYS in Windows 95 (equivalent to IO.SYS in earlier versions of DOS). The second structure, with instance data items in segment 00A0h, belongs to the MSDOS component of WINBOOT.SYS (equivalent to MSDOS.SYS in earlier versions).

Of the variables typically included by DOS in its function 1605h instance data list, Geoff Chappell has noted, "Almost all the kernel variables that are instanced by Windows are related to console operation. Most notably, the buffer at DOS:01F9h serves DOS function 3Fh as the system equivalent to the buffer an application supplies when using DOS function 0Ah to read from a console device." In the second Win386_Startup_Info_Struct in Figure 4-1, you can also see DOS telling Windows about this 106-byte buffer at 00A0:01F9.

Many DOS internal variables and structures that you know Windows must instance don't show up in DOS's instance data list. (A good example is DOS's Current Directory Structure (CDS), since different DOS boxes can have different drive mappings.) That's because, as noted in Chapter 3, function 1605h is just one of several techniques for allocating instance data.

The IO and MSDOS instance items that *do* show up in Figure 4-1 are mostly the ones that DOS knows Windows can't figure out for itself using undocumented DOS calls. The DOSMGR VxD relies heavily on undocumented DOS calls to find key DOS internal variables and structures that must be instanced; it then passes the addresses and sizes of these structures to the VMM _AddInstanceItem service. A key example is the Swappable Data Area (SDA) in DOS. DOSMGR can call the undocumented INT 21h function 5D06h (Get SDA), which returns the address of a key region in DOS that must be swapped out and restored by a task switcher. The function also returns the number of SDA bytes that a task switcher must swap if the InDOS flag is set, and the number of SDA bytes that it must *always* swap, whether InDOS is set or not.

Instance data is in many ways just an extension of the SDA. The SDA unfortunately doesn't include the full DOS "state." And it can't include areas belonging to third-party TSRs. Thus, there needs to be some way to declare areas outside the SDA that must also be swapped. Instance data is basically a technique for supplementing the SDA. In fact, just as DOS function 5D06h returns both the Swap_In_DOS and Swap_Always sizes of the SDA, likewise the InstDataStruc used by _AddInstanceItem has an InstType field with the values INDOS_Field and ALWAYS_Field. VMM currently happens to ignore these particular instance data types, but in any case there's a clear connection between the DOS SDA and Windows instance data (which is hardly surprising since the same Microsoft programmer, Aaron Reynolds, is probably responsible for both pieces of code). Figure 4-2 provides the code example, and Figure 4-3 illustrates how the DOSMGR VxD instances the DOS SDA.

```
            ; First, call DOS 21/5D06 to get SDA in DS:SI
05DBB       mov [ebp.Client_AX],5D06h
05DC1       mov eax,21h
05DC6       VMMCall Exec_Int

            ; Now, form linear address to SDA
05DCC       movzx   eax, [ebp.Client_DS]
05DD0       shl eax,4
05DD3       movzx   ebx, [ebp.Client_SI]
05DD7       add eax,ebx      ; eax = (DS << 4) + SI

            ; Save away SDA-related variables
05DD9       movzx   edx,[ebp.Client_DX] ; SWAP_ALWAYS
05DDD       movzx   ecx,[ebp.Client_CX] ; SWAP_IN_DOS
05DE1       mov DOS_SDA,eax
05DE6       mov dword ptr SWAP_ALWAYS,edx
```

```
05DEC       mov dword ptr SWAP_IN_DOS,ecx

            ; Later on, instance swap-always part
            ; ESI points to an InstDataStruc
060FB       mov edi,dword ptr DOS_SDA
06101       mov ecx,dword ptr SWAP_ALWAYS
06107       mov dword ptr [esi.InstLinAddr],edi ; DOS_SDA
0610A       mov dword ptr [esi.InstSize],ecx    ; SWAP_ALWAYS
0610D       mov dword ptr [esi.InstType], ALWAYS_Field
06114       push    0
06116       push    esi
06117       VMMCall _AddInstanceItem

            ; Instance swap-InDOS part
06133       mov edi,dword ptr DOS_SDA
06139       add edi,dword ptr SWAP_ALWAYS
0613F       mov ecx,dword ptr SWAP_IN_DOS
06145       sub ecx,dword ptr SWAP_ALWAYS
0614B       mov dword ptr [esi.InstLinAddr],edi ; SDA+ALWAYS
0614E       mov dword ptr [esi.InstSize],ecx    ; IN_DOS-ALWAYS
06151       mov dword ptr [esi.InstType], INDOS_Field
06158       push    0
0615A       push    esi
0615D       VMMCall _AddInstanceItem
```

Figure 4-2: This code example shows how the DOSMGR VxD instances the SDA. There's a clear connection between the DOS SDA and Windows instance data.

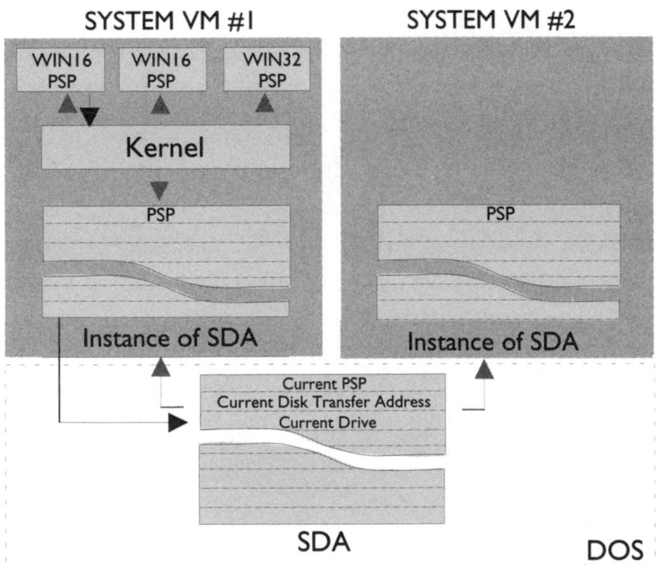

Figure 4-3. DOSMGR instances the SDA in each VM. Thus, each VM gets its own instance of DOS variables such as the current PSP. This process becomes more complicated when one of the multiple tasks in the System VM is executed and the Win16 Kernel asks DOS to create a PSP for that task. (See Chapters 12 and 13.)

Once DOSMGR has instanced the SDA, whenever VMM switches from one virtual machine to another, it switches SDAs too, even though MS-DOS started out with only one SDA. Through the miracle of instancing, Windows effectively gives DOS multiple SDAs. This is a good example of how DOS and Windows work together to form a single multitasking operating system. DOS is frequently described as if it were inhospitable to multitasking, but the SDA shows that DOS does make some accommodation for multitasking.

Earlier I noted that the SDA unfortunately does not hold the entire DOS state. This is an important point, because some programmers followed the advice in *Undocumented DOS* about using the SDA to write TSRs, and then found that certain key DOS variables aren't included in the SDA. A good example is UMBHEAD, which holds the location of the first Upper Memory Block (UMB). Interestingly, this shows up in Figure 4-1 at 00A0:008C. That is, UMBHEAD, which isn't in the SDA, *is* one of the variables that DOS declares as instance data.

This is no accident. As noted earlier, the instance data lists returned from INT 2Fh function 1605h are a kind of supplement to the SDA. This suggests a possible technique for those DOS programmers who *still* want to write TSRs using the SDA technique. Although the SDA doesn't contain the entire DOS state, it seems like it should be possible for TSRs to use the function 1605h instance data lists as a guide to what data — besides the SDA — the TSRs must save and restore. The idea is that what is important to Windows is probably important to any swappable TSR.

Unfortunately, this excellent idea has two problems, both of which I've already alluded to. First, it isn't clear how safe it is for programs other than Windows to issue the 1605h broadcast. Second, the instance data lists returned from 1605h are far from complete. Although it certainly would be better to swap these regions than not to swap them, there are still many swap-susceptible areas that would be missed. As one example, consider the local=CON statement in SYSTEM.INI; ANSI.SYS doesn't hook the function 1605h broadcast.

What was WINA20.386?

The FAKEWIN utility by default pretends to be Windows 3.1 Enhanced mode. However, a -WIN30 switch can be used to turn it into a phony Windows 3.0. When FAKEWIN -WIN30 is run on top of DOS 5.0 and later, DOS asks Windows to load the WINA20.386 VxD:

```
C:\UNAUTHW\FAKEWIN>fakewin -win30
...
Win386_Startup_Info_Struc at 0116:0FE2
VxD name: C:\wina20.386   (Reference data: 00000000)
...
```

Remember WINA20.386? Perhaps you still have it sitting in the root directory of your hard disk. WINA20.386 isn't required for Windows 3.1 (this is why it doesn't show up in Figure 4-1). DOS wants it to be loaded only when it's told that Windows 3.0 is starting up. DOS wanted it in the root directory because this made it easier for DOS to tell Windows 3.0 what to load. The SWITCHES=/W setting in CONFIG.SYS disabled this use of function 1605h: you had to explicitly put WINA20.386 in the Windows SYSTEM.INI file, but you were free to move WINA20.386 out of the root directory.

WINA20.386 is interesting as another example of how MS-DOS is "Windows aware": Windows isn't just another program that happens to run on top of MS-DOS. If you disassemble MS-DOS 5 or 6, you'll see where MSDOS.SYS handles the INT 2Fh function 1605h broadcast and, among everything else FAKEWIN reveals, tells Windows 3.0 to load WINA20.386. The specific details of WINA20.386 need not concern us here (it fixed a bug in Windows 3.0); the important thing is that DOS knows about Windows, enough to load VxDs that *patch* it. The fact that DOS's WINA20.386 patches Windows must have been what prompted a Microsoft Knowledge-Base article on WINA20.386 to oddly claim that "VxDs could be called 'structured' patches for Windows."

DOS's IN_WIN3E Flag

The FAKEWIN output doesn't show what is perhaps the best example of DOS-Windows integration: When DOS 5.0 and later see the function 1605h broadcast, it not only returns the DOS instance data list (and, if Windows 3.0 is starting up, requests that it load WINA20.386), but also uses the 1605h broadcast from Enhanced mode as a signal to turn on an IN_WIN3E flag inside DOS. Function 1606h is the signal to turn this flag off.

As discussed in more detail in *Undocumented DOS* (2d ed.), MS-DOS 5 and 6 don't care one way or the other about Windows Standard mode. But while Windows Enhanced mode (or some program, like FAKEWIN, that also issues the Windows INT 2Fh broadcasts) is running, MS-DOS wants to behave as though a *network* were running. If you think about it, multiple DOS boxes in Enhanced mode are very much like multiple machines on a network. When Enhanced mode is running, the file I/O code in DOS tests file owners using both the DOS PSP and the virtual machine ID. As you'll see shortly, the DOSMGR VxD patches this VM ID number right into DOS, which then copies it into every open-file entry.

This doesn't matter very much in Windows 95 or in WfW 3.11 with 32-bit file access enabled because these versions of Windows can do file I/O without consulting DOS. But the point remains that, even when Windows did use DOS for file I/O, it was a DOS that knew about — and contained special provision for — Windows.

IO.SYS also tests the IN_WIN3E flag, and if Windows Enhanced mode is running, IO.SYS will, under certain circumstances, call the DOSMGR VxD. VxDs can provide APIs to DOS and Windows applications; calling INT 2Fh function 1684h retrieves an API entry point for the VxD whose ID (such as 15h for DOSMGR) is given in BX.

As usual, the Windows DDK documents this INT 2Fh mechanism, but not the actual APIs provided by DOSMGR and the other VxDs built into Windows.

These VxD APIs are available even to software that, like DOS, was loaded before Windows. Yes, MS-DOS really does contain calls to INT 2Fh function 1684h. If compiled with the TEST_1684 switch, FAKEWIN lets you test this DOS behavior by calling test_1684 (shown in Listing 4-2) to hook INT 2Fh and then shelling out to a DOS prompt.

Listing 4-2: TEST1684.C

```
/*
TEST1684.C
Just a quick hack to test DOS interaction with FAKEWIN
Andrew Schulman, 1994
*/

#include <stdlib.h>
#include <stdio.h>
#include <dos.h>

typedef unsigned short WORD;

typedef struct {
#ifdef __TURBOC__
    WORD bp,di,si,ds,es,dx,cx,bx,ax;
#else
    WORD es,ds,di,si,bp,sp,bx,dx,cx,ax;     /* same as PUSHA */
#endif
    WORD ip,cs,flags;
    } REG_PARAMS;

static WORD vxd_calls = 0;
static WORD vxd = 0;
static void far *requ = (void far *) 0;
```

```
static void (interrupt far *old_2f)();

void interrupt far int2f(REG_PARAMS r)
{
    if (r.ax == 0x1684)
    {
        vxd_calls++;
        requ = MK_FP(r.cs, r.ip);
        vxd = r.bx;
    }
    _chain_intr(old_2f);
}

void test_1684(void)
{
    void interrupt far int2f(REG_PARAMS r);
    old_2f = _dos_getvect(0x2F);
    _dos_setvect(0x2f, int2f);
    // should be hooking INT 24h, and so on
    system(getenv("COMSPEC"));
    _dos_setvect(0x2F, old_2f);
    if (vxd_calls)
    {
        printf("\nReceived %d calls to 2F/1684 (Get VxD API)\n", vxd_calls);
        printf("Request VxD #%04Xh from %Fp\n", vxd, requ);
    }
}
```


The DOS prompt provided by FAKEWIN lets you see for yourself that DOS calls DOSMGR. To try this out, access the floppy drive as shown in Figure 4-4. This triggers DOS's drive-swapping logic. As you can see when you exit back to FAKEWIN, the program reports that INT 2Fh function 1684h was indeed called. This, incidentally, is a good example of why issuing phony Windows INT 2Fh broadcasts is a risky proposition. As seen in the disassembly at the bottom of Figure 4-4, DOS calls any nonzero function pointer returned from the INT 2Fh function 1684h call.

```
Microsoft(R) MS-DOS(R) Version 5.00
             (C)Copyright Microsoft Corp 1981-1991.

C:\UNAUTHW>dir b:foo.*

Insert diskette for drive B: and press any key when ready

 Volume in drive B is FAKEWIN
 Volume Serial Number is 3239-1303
 Directory of B:\
File not found
                         328,192 bytes free

C:\UNAUTHW>dir a:foo.*
```

```
Insert diskette for drive A: and press any key when ready

 Volume in drive A is FAKEWIN
 Volume Serial Number is 3239-1303
 Directory of A:\
File not found
                          328,192 bytes free
C:\UNAUTHW>exit

Received 2 calls to 2F/1684 (Get VxD API)
Request VxD #0015h from 0070:08E1

C:\UNAUTHW>debug
-u 70:8d1 8f6
0070:08D1 57            PUSH    DI
0070:08D2 06            PUSH    ES
0070:08D3 53            PUSH    BX
0070:08D4 50            PUSH    AX
0070:08D5 33FF          XOR DI,DI
0070:08D7 8EC7          MOV ES,DI
0070:08D9 BB1500        MOV BX,0015
0070:08DC B88416        MOV AX,1684
0070:08DF CD2F          INT 2F
0070:08E1 8CC0          MOV AX,ES
0070:08E3 0BC7          OR  AX,DI
0070:08E5 740B          JZ  08F2
0070:08E7 0E            PUSH    CS
0070:08E8 B8F208        MOV AX,08F2
0070:08EB 50            PUSH    AX        ; push return address
0070:08EC 06            PUSH    ES
0070:08ED 57            PUSH    DI        ; push DOSMGR API address
0070:08EE B80100        MOV AX,0001       ; SetFocus call
0070:08F1 CB            RETF              ; call DOSMGR API
0070:08F2 58            POP AX            ; this is return address
0070:08F3 5B            POP BX
0070:08F4 07            POP ES
0070:08F5 5F            POP DI
0070:08F6 CB            RETF
```

Figure 4-4: FAKEWIN output for TEST_1684 and DEBUG disassembly show that DOS calls DOSMGR.

Before displaying the "Insert diskette for drive *x*:" message seen in Figure 4-4, IO.SYS (or the IO component of WINBOOT.SYS) first checks the internal IN_WIN3E flag. If Windows Enhanced Mode is running, the DOS code at the bottom of Figure 4-4 calls a DOSMGR API to set the VM focus to ensure that the user sees the message, even if the DOS box was running invisibly in the background.

While at first it might be strange to see DOS calling Windows, this is just another example of how the old "Windows runs on top of DOS" description wasn't very accurate, even for the configuration of Windows

Enhanced mode with DOS 5 or 6. You'll see in Chapters 9 and 10 that in this configuration, DOS doesn't even run in real mode. And in Chapter 8 we'll use V86 breakpoints to show that DOS in fact makes frequent calls to Windows VxDs. In some ways, it would be just as accurate to say that DOS runs on top of Windows!

V86 Mode

Returning again to the FAKEWIN output in Figure 4-1, you can see that a 386 memory manager (in this case, 386MAX) has provided Windows (rather, FAKEWIN, which 386MAX *thinks* is Windows!) with a pointer to a V86 Enable/Disable function:

```
V86 Enable/Disable function: 0329:03D4 (386MAX$$)
```

Whenever you're running an expanded memory manager such as 386MAX, QEMM, or EMM386, your machine is in V86 mode rather than in real mode. V86 mode is actually a 1MB form of protected mode, controlled by a V86 monitor (also called a VMM), that can run real-mode software. Just as Windows Enhanced mode has VMM to control V86 DOS boxes, likewise 386 expanded memory managers are really VMMs that run a single V86 DOS box. (VMM is a generic Intel term for a V86 control program.) Because 386 expanded memory managers are so widely used, real mode is finally dying out. (I'm referring here to Intel 80x86 real mode; Windows 3.0 Real mode died out long ago.) If you run the PE program in Chapter 9 from your normal DOS prompt, the chances are good that it will report that the machine's protect-enable (PE) bit is set. It might look like real mode, but you're really in V86 mode, which, to make the point again, is really a form of protected mode.

Unfortunately, Enhanced mode won't start up when another VMM has the machine in V86 mode. (It could, if Microsoft had somehow made WIN386 comply with the Virtual Control Program Interface [VCPI] standard. In Standard mode, Windows 3.1 does comply with VCPI, but then Standard mode and Enhanced mode are different animals.) Windows wants to be king of the heap. Thus, the 386 memory manager must either switch V86 mode off itself when Windows starts or pass WIN386 a V86 enable/disable function pointer. The real-mode portion of WIN386 (or in Windows 95, of WMM32) calls the function to switch V86 mode off before jumping into protected mode.

Global EMM Import

There's just one problem with the scheme in which 386 memory managers allow themselves to be switched off by Windows. If any memory has been allocated from the memory manager, it suddenly becomes inaccessible when Windows starts. In particular, if any DOS device drivers or TSRs are loaded into upper memory blocks (UMBs), they would suddenly become invisible. This would probably result in a system crash. Thus, 386 memory managers need a way to hand off control of their page tables to Windows. This is the purpose of the Global EMM Import mentioned in Figure 4-1:

```
Global EMM Import @ phys 00BD9EACh (version 1.11)
```

The term *global* refers to the fact that the EMM is present *before* Windows has started. Global EMM Import (also called V86MMGR Paging Import) is an undocumented interface, though Microsoft briefly alludes to it in the DDK documentation for the _AddFreePhysPage and V86MMGR_GetPgStatus, and makes a document available to some memory-manager vendors. According to this document:

> Windows/386 supports importing the current EMM handle state from a 386 LIMulator [that is, an emulator for the Lotus-Intel-Microsoft expanded memory specification] which is operating when Windows/386 is loaded. This allows the current set of EMM users to continue to operate using their previously allocated EMM handles. There is also provision for importation of Upper Memory Blocks and xMS handle information from a currently operating xMS driver. NOTE that there is only one source for the import. Even though the states of two different drivers are involved (xMS and EMM), the import does not have to be separated because there is only one body of code which is doing paging, not two. The import is basically just importing a "paging state" from the currently running paging driver.
>
> The IOCTL DOS call that the V86MMGR device makes to obtain the pointer to the import information data structure is made with interrupts enabled. After this call it is quite possible that a current EMM/xMS user will "wake up" and change the EMM mapping, and/or manipulate one of the EMM or xMS handles. For this reason the contents of the import information data structure cannot be set at the time of the IOCTL because the state that it describes (of the EMS and xMS drivers) is subject to change before Windows/386 gets to the point of transition into protected mode. For this reason the "trigger" for setting the import information data structure content is not the IOCTL call used to obtain its address, but rather it is the Virtual Mode Disable call.
>
> When WIN386 is running, all EMM activity is LOCAL to the current VM, not GLOBAL. A global EMM user may have to modify his behavior to cope with this situation. In particular any mapping calls and context save calls operate relative to the currently running VM and have no meaning in other VMs. A global EMM user who ALLOCATES

> a handle while WIN386 is up will very likely malfunction because that handle will be LOCAL to the VM it is allocated in. For this reason Global EMM users need to ALLOCATE ALL their handles with the correct size at initialization.

The check_emm_import function in FAKEWIN (see Listing 3-1) simulates only the most superficial part of the EMM Import; it does this by opening the EMMXXXX0 device and issuing an I/O control (IOCTL) read. Reading the structure would require calling the V86 switch_func to turn the memory manager off and on, and calling INT 15h function 87h (Block Move) to copy the structure to conventional memory. (For sample code and a full explanation of Global EMM Import, see the article by Taku Okazaki cited in the "For Further Reading" section.)

The DOSMGR Broadcast API

Next up in Figure 4-1, you can see that FAKEWIN produced a block of output relating to an interface provided by the DOSMGR VxD. Just as Windows has its INT 2Fh function 1605h startup broadcast, VxDs can have their own individual INT 2Fh function 1607h broadcasts. This is an interface that VxDs use to call software loaded before Windows, and it should not be confused with the INT 2Fh function 1684h interface that DOS and Windows programs use to call into VxDs.

As usual, the mechanics are shown in the DDK — the VxD calls INT 2Fh with AX set to 1607h, BX set to a VxD ID (such as 15h for DOSMGR), and other registers used as the particular VxD sees fit — but nothing is said about the actual broadcast interfaces provided in Windows. This is a serious omission because some of these VxD broadcast APIs, such as the one WSHELL provides to WinOldAp, are important.

As shown in Listing 4-3, FAKEWIN emulates part of the DOSMGR broadcast API to see whether any software loaded before Windows hooks the INT 2Fh AX set to 1607h BX=15h call to communicate with DOSMGR. The FAKEWIN output back in Figure 4-1 shows that, not surprisingly, MS-DOS itself hooks this call. DOS uses the interface to provide DOSMGR with the addresses of several DOS variables, not for instance data this time but for patching. Most importantly, DOS gives DOSMGR the address of the USER_ID variable in DOS (located in Figure 4-1 at 00A0:033E), so that DOSMGR can patch in the VM ID. As noted earlier, DOS uses this VM ID for file I/O.

The DOSMGR broadcast API is described in an unpublished Microsoft document, "API to Identify MS-DOS Instance Data." Even without this document, it's fairly easy to figure out the interface by disassembling both sides of the conversation: the function 1607h calls in DOSMGR, and the function 1607h hook in MS-DOS.

Listing 4-3: FAKEVXD.C

```
/*
FAKEVXD.C
Fake DOSMGR VxD callout used with FAKEWIN.C
Andrew Schulman

For more details, see Chappell, DOS Internals, pp. 118-122;
and Schulman et al., Undocumented DOS (2d ed., pp. 24-30).
*/

#include <stdlib.h>
#include <stdio.h>

typedef unsigned short WORD;

#define VXD_CALLOUT(vxd_id) \
{ \
    _asm { mov bx, vxd_id } ; \
    _asm { mov ax, 1607h; } ; \
    _asm { int 2fh; } ; \
}

#define DOSMGR_CALLOUT(func) \
{ \
    _asm { mov cx, func } ; \
    VXD_CALLOUT(0x15); \
}

#define NUM_PATCH   6

// names from Microsoft document "API to Identify MS-DOS Instance Data"
char *patch_str[] = {
    "SAVEDS", "SAVEBX", "INDOS", "USER_ID", "CRITPATCH", "UMB_HEAD",
    } ;

void fake_dosmgr_callouts(void)
{
    WORD w, w2, w3;
    WORD far *patchtab;
    WORD far *patch;
    int i;

    DOSMGR_CALLOUT(0);      // query instance processing
    _asm mov w, cx
    if (w != 0)
    {
        _asm mov w, dx
        _asm mov word ptr patchtab+2, es
        _asm mov word ptr patchtab, bx
```

```
        printf("\nDOSMGR instance interface ON\n");

        if (w != 0)
            printf("Segment of DOS drivers: %04X\n", w);

        printf("Patch table: %Fp\n", patchtab);
        printf("DOS version %u.%02u\n",
            (patchtab[0] & 0xFF), (patchtab[0] >> 8));

        for (i=0, patch = &patchtab[1]; i<NUM_PATCH; i++, patch++)
            printf("   %04X (%s)\n", *patch, patch_str[i]);

        // probably not safe to try DOSMGR_CALLOUT(1), except
        // perhaps if immediately followed by DOSMGR_CALLOUT(2)

        #define WEIRD_MAGIC_1   0xB97C
        #define WEIRD_MAGIC_2   0xA2AB

        _asm mov dx, 1
        DOSMGR_CALLOUT(3);      // get size of DOS data structure
        _asm mov w, ax
        _asm mov w2, cx
        _asm mov w3, dx
        if ((w != WEIRD_MAGIC_1) && (w3 != WEIRD_MAGIC_2))
            printf("DOSMGR callout 3 failed: signature wrong!\n"); // AX:DX
        else
            printf("Current Directory Structure = %u bytes\n", w2); // CX

        DOSMGR_CALLOUT(4);  // determine instanced data structures
        _asm mov w, ax
        _asm mov w2, bx
        _asm mov w3, dx
        if ((w3 == 0) || (w2 == 0))
            printf("No DOS data structures instanced via DOSMGR API\n");
        else if ((w != WEIRD_MAGIC_1) && (w3 != WEIRD_MAGIC_2))
            printf("DOSMGR callout 4 failed: signature wrong!\n"); // AX:DX
        else
        {
            printf("DOS data structures instanced: %04X\n", w2);
            if (w2 & 1)     printf("   CDS\n");
            if (w2 & 2)     printf("   SFT\n");
            if (w2 & 4)     printf("   Device chain\n");
            if (w2 & 8)     printf("   SDA\n");
        }
    }
    else
        printf("\nNo DOSMGR instance interface\n");
}
```

The DOSMGR interface seems to have been designed so that DOSMGR would require less hard-wired knowledge about DOS internals; its broadcast API could ask the underlying DOS to provide it with the necessary information. However, the interface is incomplete and doesn't really decouple DOS and Windows. In fact, since the interface is unpublished, it serves only as one more piece of insider trading between DOS and Windows. In any case, the interface is another illustration of how MS-DOS and Windows form a single unit.

Interestingly, although DR DOS 6.0 didn't support the DOSMGR API (FAKEWIN prints "No DOSMGR instance interface"), Novell DOS 7.0 does at least provide the DOSMGR patch table.

TSR Identify Function

At the end of Figure 4-1, FAKEWIN detects something called a TSR_Info_Struc, belonging to COUNTDOS. FAKEWIN detected this structure by faking a call to INT 2Fh AX=160Bh, the Windows TSR Identify function. Listing 4-4 shows the FAKETSR.C module.

Listing 4-4: FAKETSR.C

```
/*
FAKETSR.C
Andrew Schulman

Refer to the David Long article on the Microsoft Developer Network
(MSDN) CD for 2F/160B doc.
*/

#include <stdlib.h>
#include <stdio.h>
#include <dos.h>

typedef unsigned char BYTE;
typedef unsigned short WORD;
typedef unsigned long DWORD;
typedef void far *FP;

#pragma pack(1)

typedef struct {
    WORD size;
    BYTE str[1];
    } TSR_ID_Block_Struc;

typedef struct _TSRINFO {
    struct _TSRINFO far *TSR_Next;
    WORD TSR_PSP_Segment;
    WORD TSR_API_Ver_ID;     /* 0x100 */
    WORD TSR_Exec_Flags;
    WORD TSR_Exec_Cmd_Show;
    char far *TSR_Exec_Cmd;
```

```
    DWORD TSR_Reserved;
    TSR_ID_Block_Struc far *TSR_ID_Block;
    FP TSR_Data_Block;
} TSR_Info_Struc;

#pragma pack()

// TSR_Exec_Flag equates
#define TSR_WINEXEC         1
#define TSR_LOADLIBRARY     2
#define TSR_OPENDRIVER      4

// TSR_Exec_Cmd_Show equates
#define SW_HIDE             0
#define SW_SHOWNORMAL       1
#define SW_SHOWMINIMIZED    2
#define SW_SHOWMAXIMIZED    3
#define SW_SHOWNOACTIVATE   4
#define SW_SHOW             5
#define SW_MINIMIZE         6
#define SW_SHOWMINNOACTIVE  7
#define SW_SHOWNA           8
#define SW_RESTORE          9

char *sw_str[SW_RESTORE+1] = {
    "SW_HIDE", "SW_SHOWNORMAL", "SW_SHOWMINIMIZED", "SW_SHOWMAXIMIZED",
    "SW_SHOWNOACTIVATE", "SW_SHOW", "SW_MINIMIZE", "SW_SHOWMINNOACTIVE",
    "SW_SHOWNA", "SW_RESTORE"
    } ;

// in FAKEWIN.C
extern char *owner(FP fp);

void print_tsr_info(TSR_Info_Struc far *tsr_info)
{
    if (tsr_info->TSR_API_Ver_ID < 0x100)
        printf("%Fp not a valid TSR structure!\n", tsr_info);
    printf("\nTSR_Info_Struc at %Fp (PSP %04Xh) %s\n",
        tsr_info, tsr_info->TSR_PSP_Segment, owner(tsr_info));
    if (tsr_info->TSR_Exec_Cmd)
    {
        switch (tsr_info->TSR_Exec_Flags)
        {
            case TSR_WINEXEC:
                printf("TSR_WINEXEC ");
                // Exec_Cmd_Show only used for TSR_WINEXEC
                if (tsr_info->TSR_Exec_Cmd_Show <= SW_RESTORE)
                    printf("%s ", sw_str[tsr_info->TSR_Exec_Cmd_Show]);
                else
                    printf("TSR_Exec_Cmd_Show: %04Xh ",
                        tsr_info->TSR_Exec_Cmd_Show);
                break;
            case TSR_LOADLIBRARY:   printf("TSR_LOADLIBRARY "); break;
            case TSR_OPENDRIVER:    printf("TSR_OPENDRIVER "); break;
            default:                printf("TSR_Exec_Flags %04Xh ",
```

```
                    tsr_info->TSR_Exec_Flags); break;
            }
            printf("\n\"%Fs\"\n", tsr_info->TSR_Exec_Cmd);
        }
        if (tsr_info->TSR_ID_Block)
            printf("TSR_ID_Block: \"%Fs\"\n", tsr_info->TSR_ID_Block->str);
        if (tsr_info->TSR_Data_Block)
            printf("TSR_Data_Block: %Fp\n", tsr_info->TSR_Data_Block);
}

void tsr_identify(void)
{
    TSR_Info_Struc far *tsr_info;
    _asm push di
    _asm xor cx, cx
    _asm mov es, cx
    _asm mov di, cx
    _asm mov ax, 160bh
    _asm int 2Fh
    _asm mov word ptr tsr_info+2, es
    _asm mov word ptr tsr_info, di
    _asm pop di
    if (tsr_info != 0)
    {
        do {
            print_tsr_info(tsr_info);
            tsr_info = tsr_info->TSR_Next;
        } while (tsr_info != 0);
    }
}
```


Just as DOS programs can hook function 1605h to ask Windows to load a VxD, they can also use hook 160Bh to ask the Windows USER module to load a Windows executable, a dynamic link library (DLL), or a Win16 driver. USER issues this call during InitApp (see Matt Pietrek, *Windows Internals*, pp. 279-281); depending on the request, USER calls the WinExec, LoadLibrary, or OpenDriver API function.

TSR Identify is documented in David Long's article "TSR Support in Microsoft Windows Version 3.1" on the Microsoft Developer Network (MSDN) CD-ROM. This documentation is accompanied by a sample program called COUNTDOS. The results of COUNTDOS's function 160Bh hook can be seen in the FAKEWIN output in Figure 4-1. According to the Microsoft documentation, function 160Bh is also used by fax software and the Windows network popup utility.

COUNTDOS is an interesting example in its own right of DOS-Windows interaction. COUNTDOS.EXE is a Windows executable, with an embedded DOS program that loads before Windows. The DOS program hooks INT 21h and keeps a log of all DOS calls; it optionally can require the user to verify file deletes. As seen at the end of Figure 4-1, the DOS portion of COUNTDOS.EXE hooks function 160Bh, so that when Windows starts, USER performs the following:

```
WinExec("C:\UNAUTHW\FAKEWIN\COUNTDOS.EXE /085E:00DD", SW_SHOWNOACTIVATE):
```

The Windows portion of COUNTDOS uses DPMI calls to talk to its DOS portion, which is loaded before Windows. Somewhat like the V86TEST program in Chapter 10, COUNTDOS displays the number of INT 21h calls; this information is quite useful for seeing the extent to which Windows has or has not cut itself off from real-mode DOS.

It's instructive to run Microsoft's COUNTDOS example, with and without 32-bit file access enabled. Figure 4-5 shows COUNTDOS in WfW 3.11, with 32-bit file access disabled (WIN /D:C). With COUNT-DOS loaded, I started Microsoft Office, ran Microsoft Word, and did a few other things. Note the calls to DOS functions 3Dh (File Open), 3Eh (File Close), 3Fh (File Read), and 40h (File Write): Windows uses DOS for file I/O.

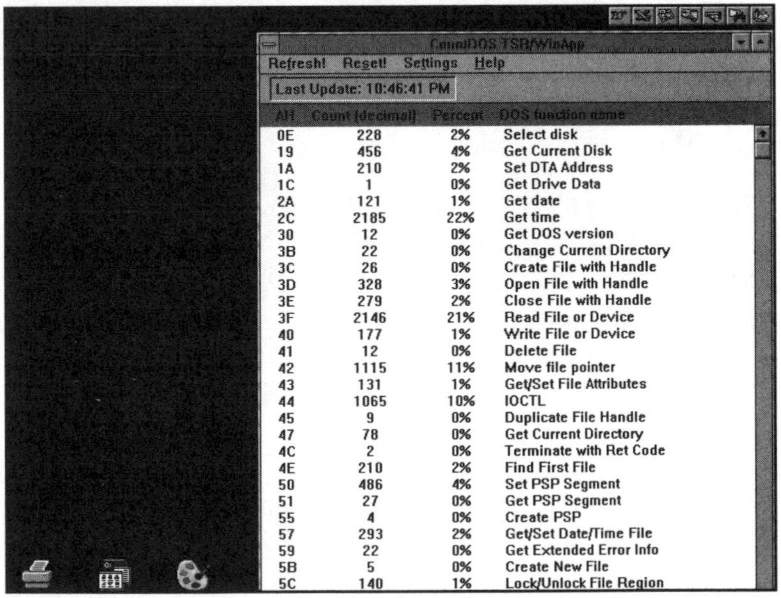

CountDOS TSR/WinApp

Refresh! Reset! Settings Help

Last Update: 10:46:41 PM

AH	Count (decimal)	Percent	DOS function name
0E	228	2%	Select disk
19	456	4%	Get Current Disk
1A	210	2%	Set DTA Address
1C	1	0%	Get Drive Data
2A	121	1%	Get date
2C	2185	22%	Get time
30	12	0%	Get DOS version
3B	22	0%	Change Current Directory
3C	26	0%	Create File with Handle
3D	328	3%	Open File with Handle
3E	279	2%	Close File with Handle
3F	2146	21%	Read File or Device
40	177	1%	Write File or Device
41	12	0%	Delete File
42	1115	11%	Move file pointer
43	131	1%	Get/Set File Attributes
44	1065	10%	IOCTL
45	9	0%	Duplicate File Handle
47	78	0%	Get Current Directory
4C	2	0%	Terminate with Ret Code
4E	210	2%	Find First File
50	486	4%	Set PSP Segment
51	27	0%	Get PSP Segment
55	4	0%	Create PSP
57	293	2%	Get/Set Date/Time File
59	22	0%	Get Extended Error Info
5B	5	0%	Create New File
5C	140	1%	Lock/Unlock File Region

Figure 4-5: Running COUNTDOS *without* enabling 32-bit file access reveals Windows' reliance on DOS.

Next, I restarted WfW 3.11 with 32-bit file access, and performed roughly the same set of operations as in Figure 4-5. Figure 4-6 shows how this looked to COUNTDOS. Notice that, while there are still plenty of DOS calls, there are none to the standard File Open, Close, Read, and Write calls, and just a few to calls such as IOCTL and Get/Set File Date/Time.

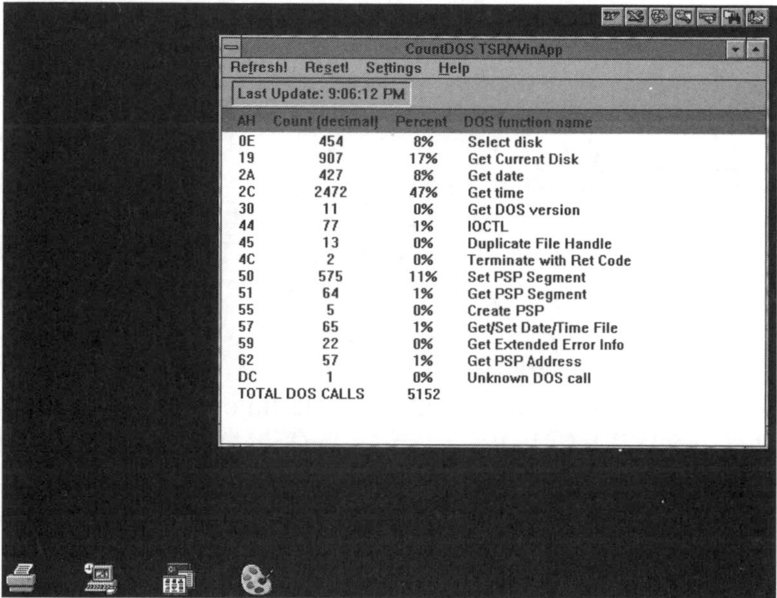

Figure 4-6: Running COUNTDOS *with* 32-bit file access reveals how WfW 3.11 could bypass DOS for most operations.

Finally, I tried COUNTDOS in Windows 95. I put INSTALL= COUNTDOS.EXE in CONFIG.SYS so that I wouldn't need an AUTO-EXEC.BAT file. When Windows 95 came up, I reset the COUNTDOS statistics so it wouldn't show the DOS calls that occurred while Windows was booting up. (I did the same reset with the WfW 3.11 tests, too.) If Windows 95 does not rely on DOS, COUNTDOS shouldn't show any DOS calls. As Figure 4-7 shows, the results are impressive (very few INT 21h calls are being sent down to DOS), but they're not *that* impressive. Especially because, aside from COUNTDOS itself, I was running only Win32 applications here: the Windows 95 shell, the Win32 version of Clock, and WinBezMT. COUNTDOS shows that even Win32 applications in Windows 95 still use real-mode DOS for some operations, such as getting the date and time and creating and setting PSPs.

Figure 4-7 is practically an icon for this book. Here we see a number of Win32 applications running (WinBezMT has a few bezier threads going), and popped up in front of them is a little program — from Microsoft, no less — reminding us that DOS is not dead.

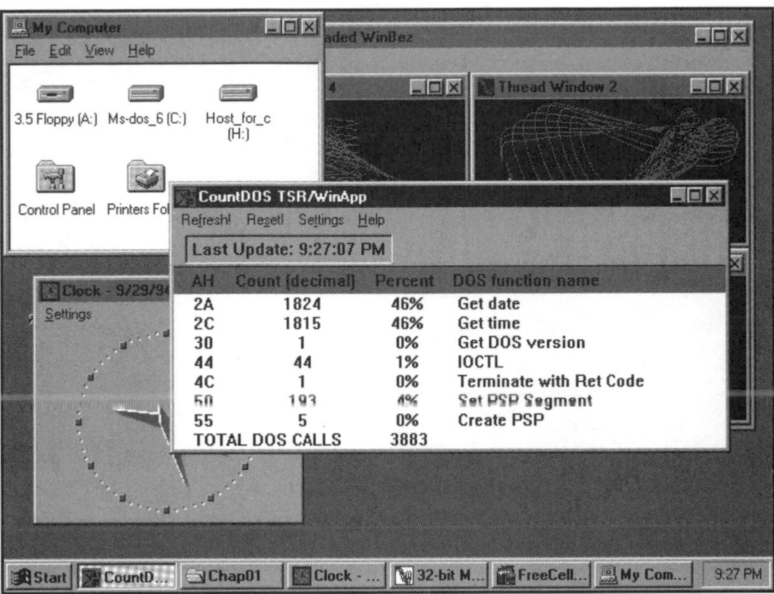

Figure 4-7: COUNTDOS running in Windows 95 shows that even Win32 applications still need DOS for some operations, such as getting the date and time, and creating and setting PSPs.

There's one final interesting point about COUNTDOS. This Microsoft sample program has a cute Confirm Deletes option. When selected, COUNTDOS's INT 21h handler looks for function 41h (File Delete) calls, and tells the Windows part of the program to pop up a dialog box asking you to confirm that you really want to delete the specified file. This works nicely in Windows 3.1, and is a good example of how a DOS program and a Windows program (embedded in a single executable file) can work together.

When 32-bit file access is enabled in WfW 3.11 or Windows 95, however, the COUNTDOS Confirm Deletes option has no effect. It's obvious why: When 32-bit file access is enabled, COUNTDOS won't see any function 41h (File Delete) calls because they are all being handled by Windows VxDs in 32-bit protected mode. COUNTDOS has no opportunity to confirm deletes because, as far as it can tell, there aren't any!

This is a good example of how bypassing DOS, which sounds so good, can have serious negative side effects. A legal DOS-Windows program — in fact, one intended to teach programmers how to use Microsoft's operating-system interfaces — has been *broken* by 32-bit file access.

Well, there's no such thing as a free lunch. But it would be nice if Microsoft from time to time told us the price of the meal.

Chapter 5

The Two Faces of Windows

"What will happen to the MS-DOS product line?" This was a question posed in Microsoft's "Chicago Questions and Answers" white paper (January, 1994). The answer seems to suggest a radical overhaul for this nearly ancient real-mode operating system:

> Microsoft will continue to enhance MS-DOS as long as customers require it. Future versions will be derived from the protected-mode technology developed in the Chicago project.

What does this mean? How can future versions of DOS be derived from protected-mode software? Will this protected-mode DOS still be recognizable as DOS? Is a protected-mode MS-DOS (or a version of DOS "derived" from protected-mode technology, whatever that means) even possible?

In this chapter, you'll see that this protected-mode DOS already exists (and in essence has existed for years) as part of Windows.

The Inner Core of Windows

If you asked a typical Windows programmer to list the core components of Windows, chances are the programmer would rattle off "KERNEL, USER, and GDI." These are the names of the Windows dynamic link libraries (DLLs) that contain the bulk of the Windows APIs used to write Windows applications. Windows APIs such as GlobalAlloc, CreateWindow, and TextOut live inside these DLLs.

These DLLs are important, but they don't constitute the core of Windows. As you'll see in the course of this chapter, the visible GUI porof Windows — the part that nearly everyone thinks of as Windows itself — is little more than an application that happens to run on top of the actual Windows operating system.

This Windows operating system doesn't reside in KERNEL, USER, or GDI. Instead, it's found largely in a file called WIN386.EXE or, in Windows 95, VMM32.VXD. At one point, Microsoft called this file DOS386.EXE, which indicates that it's difficult to say whether this program is part of Windows or part of DOS. By the end of this chapter, you might come to view WIN386.EXE as part of a future version of DOS — or perhaps as an Enhanced mode of MS-DOS — that more or less was accidentally shipped with Windows for several years.

To start Windows, you run the program WIN.COM which, as Chapter 2 showed, in turn launches another program:

- In Standard mode (WIN /S), WIN.COM runs WSWAP.EXE, which runs DOSX.EXE, which in turn runs either KRNL286.EXE (on 80286 processors) or KRNL386.EXE (on 80386 and later processors).
- In Enhanced mode (WIN /3), WIN.COM runs WIN386.EXE, which is a collection of VxDs. The WSHELL VxD inside WIN386 runs KRNL386.EXE.
- In Windows 95, WIN.COM runs VMM32.VXD (a collection of VxDs), whose WSHELL VxD runs the Win16 kernel, KRNL386.EXE.

So what sort of programs are DOSX, WIN386, and VMM32? How do they relate to the more visible aspects of Windows? In this chapter and the two that follow it, we'll run DOSX, WIN386, and VMM32 in an unusual way to see what these programs do for Windows.

DOS Extenders and the Future of DOS

Although this book focuses on WIN386.EXE and VMM32.VXD, the easiest way to understand these two programs is to look first at DOSX .EXE, which is the basis for Windows 3.*x* 286 Standard mode. (Standard mode disappeared in Windows for Workgroups 3.11, just as Windows real mode disappeared in Windows 3.1.)

WIN /S looks for DOSX.EXE and WSWAP.EXE and then executes WSWAP.EXE. WSWAP and another executable, DSWAP, are just the task-switching code from DOSSHELL.EXE, the DOS 5 task switcher. In turn, DOSSHELL.EXE was the Windows 3.0 Standard mode task switcher; it was basically lifted out "as a lump and plopped into the DOS 5.0 product" (Ray Duncan, "Programming Considerations for MS-DOS 5.0," *PC Magazine*, November 12, 1991). WSWAP runs DOSX, and DSWAP runs other DOS programs.

DOSX.EXE, as its name implies, is a *DOS extender*. This means that DOSX provides a protected-mode DOS interface: Thanks to DOSX, protected-mode Windows applications running in Standard mode can make DOS INT 21h calls to access files, allocate memory, set interrupt vectors, and so on, even though we normally think of DOS as a real-mode operating system. This is illustrated in Figure 5-1. In Enhanced mode, the Windows DOS extender resides in the DOSMGR VxD located inside WIN-386.EXE; when 32-bit file access is enabled in WfW 3.11 and Windows 95, the IFSMGR.386 VxD should probably be considered part of the DOS extender, too.

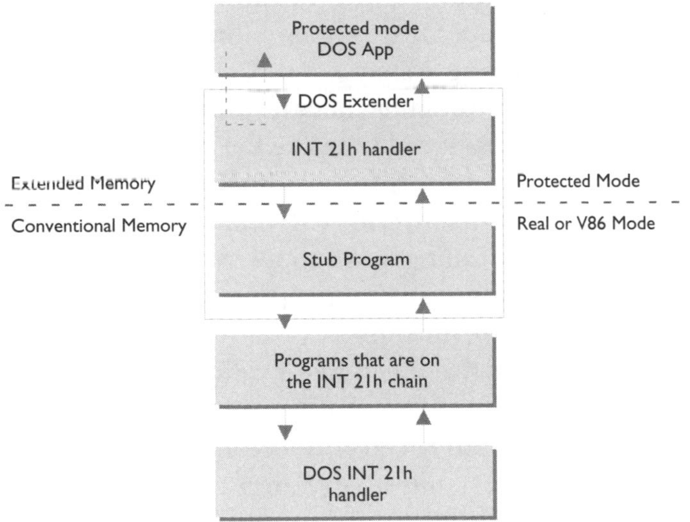

Figure 5-1: A DOS extender lets protected-mode applications (such as Windows programs) make INT 21h calls, even though MS-DOS is not a protected-mode operating system. The DOS extender often (but not always) does this by translating the protected-mode INT 21h call into real-mode terms, and then reissuing (or reflecting) it in real or V86 mode.

What does a DOS extender do? As an example, consider a program that calls DOS function 3Dh to open a file, passing a far pointer to the filename in the DS:DX registers. In a real-mode program, DS:DX is a real-mode pointer, which DOS can readily understand. But if a protected-mode program, such as a Windows application, calls INT 21h function 3Dh (either directly or via a Windows API function such as OpenFile or DOS3Call), the far pointer in DS:DX will naturally enough be a protected-mode pointer: DS holds a selector, not a paragraph address. Furthermore, this selector will most likely have a base address located in extended memory, above 1MB.

The file-open code in real-mode DOS cannot correctly interpret protected-mode pointers, nor can it see extended memory. If a Windows application or other protected-mode program passed DOS a protected-mode filename pointer, DOS would just get it wrong.

This is where a DOS extender such as DOSX.EXE comes in. A DOS extender hooks INT 21h in protected mode and provides protected-mode equivalents for all the familiar DOS functions. A DOS extender's implementation of function 3Dh, naturally, would expect a protected-mode pointer in DS:DX and would do whatever is necessary to open the file and return a DOS file handle to the protected-mode application. In essence, the DOS extender makes it appear as though DOS were a protected-mode operating system.

The DOS extender can implement its protected-mode INT 21h functions any way it chooses. It can translate the call to something that makes sense in real mode and *reflect* this translated call to DOS, or (and this is a crucial point that is often overlooked) *it can service the call entirely in protected mode*, without calling down to DOS.

As an example of this second option to bypass DOS, consider the DOS memory allocation function (INT 21h function 48h). Protected-mode programs calling this function (or calling something such as malloc in C or the *new* operator in C++ that in turn eventually relies on function 48h) will naturally want to have DOS (or whatever is providing the protected-mode INT 21h interface) return them a protected-mode selector to a block of memory. To provide a true DOS protected-mode interface, the function would have to keep the old DOS "semantics": the returned selector would have to be immediately usable in a far pointer, without requiring any sort of new "lock" function:

```
unsigned short para, sel;
char far *fp;
// ...
_asm mov ah, 48h          ; Allocate Memory function
_asm mov bx, [para]       ; number of paragraphs
_asm int 21h              ; call DOS
_asm jc error
_asm mov [sel], ax        ; save away selector
fp = MK_FP(sel, 0);       // create far pointer from selector
*fp = 'x';                // use it
```

The DOS extender *could* implement function 48h by passing the call down to real-mode DOS and then translating the real-mode paragraph address returned by DOS into a protected-mode selector. But the protected-mode caller almost never wants a protected-mode selector pointing to conventional memory below 1MB. The protected-mode program wants to get at the vast stretches of extended memory above the 1MB DOS boundary; this after all is the key reason to move to protected mode in the first place. Thus, a DOS extender that gives protected-mode applications a DOS memory allocation function would *not* pass this call down to DOS; it would service the call entirely in protected mode so that the function became a DOS interface to extended memory.

Now, if a DOS extender did this all across the board, for every INT 21h function, you'd have an entirely new protected-mode operating system, albeit with the familiar INT 21h interface. This would constitute a full-blown protected-mode DOS. In fact, a DOS extender doesn't necessarily require any underlying copy of DOS, except perhaps as a convenient bootstrap loader.

The DOS extender could even extend the INT 21h interfaces to 32 bits (for example, function 48h would expect the number of paragraphs in the 32-bit EBX register rather than in the 16-bit BX register, and function 3Dh would take a filename in EDX). It could also provide new INT 21h services (to support long filenames, for instance) that real-mode DOS doesn't supply. This, in essence, in what Microsoft is doing to DOS in Windows 95.

Notice that, even if the DOS extender doesn't carry out the "do it all in protected mode" policy — that is, even if the DOS extender does continue to pass some calls down to real-mode DOS — this doesn't really change the essence of the DOS extender as a protected-mode operating system. The decision about whether or not the protected-mode INT 21h is passed down to real-mode DOS is made entirely by the DOS extender. DOS is in a subordinate position, doing only what the DOS extender doesn't feel like doing itself. Instead of viewing the DOS extender as something that "runs on top of DOS," it's more accurate to view DOS as little more than a 16-bit real-mode driver for use by the DOS extender.

This is particularly true when the DOS extender runs DOS in V86 mode because, as you'll see in Chapters 9 and 10, the DOS extender can then exercise control over what happens inside DOS and inside DOS device drivers and TSRs. This means that the V86 DOS extender can provide INT 21h to real-mode programs, too. The DOS code called by these real-mode programs would then effectively run in protected mode. But I'm getting ahead of myself a little.

With this background on the possibilities of DOS extender technology, and a suggestion of the future of the DOS interface, let's go back in time to look at the history behind DOSX.EXE.

The DOS extender in Windows Standard mode was based on one that Microsoft used earlier in its CodeView debugger; this DOS extender in turn was based on the SST debugger written by Murray Sargent. *Gates*, the excellent biography of Bill Gates by Stephen Manes and Paul Andrews, has a good description of how Murray Sargent and David Weise used Murray's DOS extender to port Windows to protected mode; much of this work lives on in DOSX.EXE:

> In 1988 the Windows group had become a skeleton crew once Mad Dog [Steve] Ballmer began dragging people out the door to work on OS/2. Version 2 of Windows had been a death march of its own, but the Windows gang was still plugging away. Slowly but surely, a collection of Windows apps was beginning to turn up. Still, exactly what the next version of Windows should be, or even *if* it should be, remained unclear.
>
> Then in June David Weise, one of the Smart Guys from the Dynamical Systems Research acquisition, ran into an old friend..., Murray Sargent, "a world-renowned laser jock who happens to like to grope around computers." A physics professor from the University of Arizona, Sargent was up for the summer to adapt Microsoft's CodeView debugger to a kludge known as "DOS extension" that allowed specially written programs to use extended memory on 286 and 386 machines. He had recently added Windows support and a DOS extender to his own debugger, a program called SST that happened to be Weise's personal favorite.
>
> In Weise's view, the three big problems with Windows were "memory, memory, memory." You were always bumping up against the memory limits one way or another, and it compromised every aspect of the program....
>
> So Weise brought Sargent back to his office, fired up the new debugger, and starting with line one began stepping through Windows to make it run under protected mode, thereby accessing extended memory. "We're not gonna ask anybody, and then if we're done and they shoot it down, they shoot it down." Weise began working on it at home, then moved it to the office for three months of night and weekend work. The good news: "It turned out Steve Wood who I'd inherited the kernel from had structured the whole thing to wanna be" in protected mode....
>
> "There are all these little gotchas throughout [the process of bringing up Windows in protected mode], but basically you just work through the gotchas one at a time, you just close your eyes, and you just charge ahead. You don't think of the problems, or you're not gonna do it.... Piece by piece, it's coming. Okay, here comes the keyboard drivers, here come the display drivers, here comes GDI — Oh, oh, look, here's USER!
>
> "Without that debugger running in protected mode with the DOS extender I could not have done it."

A few weeks before a scheduled design review with the whole staff, including Bill [Gates], Weise let Ballmer know how close he was to getting Windows to run in protected mode. "This is interesting," Ballmer said.

Weise upped the ante at a group retreat in the basement of the nondecadent La Quinta motel in Kirkland. Product manager Russ Werner had been given his mission for Windows 3 by none other than Bill Gates: "Just make it great." What, Werner kept asking his troops, would make it great? An interface that could be custom-configured by the user, said some. A cleaner look, said another. "Using protected mode," said David Weise.

"How would that help?" Werner asked.

Without revealing how far along he was already, Weise rattled off a couple of dozen reasons. Werner told him to go ahead and give it a try.

The night before the design review, Weise told Ballmer to meet him in his office the next morning at eight. Weise stayed up until 3:00 AM getting the Windows desktop programs to run in protected mode and left the machine on when he walked out the door. When he came in to work a few minutes late, his machine had crashed. He knew who had to have done it. He ran down to Ballmer's office and asked, "Did you see it?"

"Yes," Ballmer told him. "Where do we go from here?"

"Steve, it's totally up to you."

"Let's go for it," Ballmer said.

Going into the meeting, Weise was ecstatic. "It's like [George] Gamow," he recalled, referring to the Russian-born physicist who had developed theories of stellar evolution. "His girlfriend says 'What are you thinking?' and he goes, 'I'm the only person in the world right now who knows how the sunshine works.'"

And what Weise was about to reveal might well be some sunshine in the middle of the [OS/2] Presentation Manager gloom. In a fashion, he was about to vindicate Steve Ballmer's pledge of 1985: Write your app for Windows and you'll be able to run it in protected mode without any trouble at all.

Others gave their presentations, and then Weise dropped his bombshell. Everything that had been discussed suddenly changed.... A little side bet against IBM might well be in order. "Okay, let's do it," Gates said.

Ballmer turned to Bill, "What do we tell IBM?"

A smile spread across the face of Bill Gates. "That's your problem, Steve."

And a problem it was. IBM had seen Windows as an intermediate step between DOS and PM, and not much of one at that. Now, by overcoming the inbuilt limitations of DOS, Windows was positioning itself to undercut OS/2 and Presentation Manager. The only thing it was missing was ship dates.

— Stephen Manes and Paul Andrews, *Gates*, 1993, pp. 380-382.

DOSX: A General-Purpose DOS Extender and DPMI Server

That DOSX.EXE in Windows Standard mode is based on earlier debugger technology indicates either that Windows is a debugger in disguise or that DOSX is not very Windows-specific.

Indeed, DOSX is a quite general-purpose piece of software. Besides its role as a DOS extender, this small (32,000 bytes) program is also a DPMI server (or DPMI host). DPMI stands for DOS Protected Mode Interface; DOSX supports DPMI version 0.9. Despite the name, DPMI isn't the same thing as a protected-mode INT 21h interface; that is, DPMI isn't the same thing as a DOS extender. Instead, DPMI is a set of INT 2Fh and INT 31h services you can use to write a DOS extender that's compatible with Windows or 386 memory managers such as QEMM or 386MAX.

For example, one of the services provided by DPMI servers such as DOSX.EXE is INT 2Fh function 1687h, documented in the DPMI specification (available from Intel) as "Obtain Real-to-Protected Mode Switch Entry Point." When a real-mode program calls this service, DPMI returns a far pointer to a DPMI function which, when called, switches the calling program into protected mode.

Listing 5-1 (USEDPMI.C) is a very simple example of how a real-mode DOS program can use DPMI to switch itself into protected mode. If DPMI isn't available, USEDPMI fails with the message "This program requires DPMI," but if DPMI is available (for example, when running under 386MAX or QEMM), the program prints "Greetings from protected mode!" and then exits. The key is the dpmi_init function, which first calls INT 2Fh function 1687h to obtain the DPMI switch_proc and then calls the switch_proc.

The DPMI specification states that DPMI clients must exit using INT 21h function 4Ch. Rather than rely on the C run-time library's exit procedure, USEDPMI calls a _dos_exit function. But since it's bypassing the C run-time exit, USEDPMI explicitly calls the flushall function to clean up file I/O. Otherwise, redirected output won't get written out properly.

Listing 5-1: USEDPMI.C

```
/*
USEDPMI.C -- very simple DPMI client
```

```
bcc usedpmi.c
Andrew Schulman 1994
This program *MUST* be compiled in small model because, once in
protected mode, it calls printf from the real-mode C run-time
library. In the large model, the C run-time would use far
pointers, but USEDPMI's segment registers are going to change
out from under it when it switches to protected mode.
*/

#include <stdlib.h>
#include <stdio.h>
#include <dos.h>

void _dos_exit(int retval)
{
    _asm mov ah, 04ch
    _asm mov al, byte ptr retval
    _asm int 21h
}

void fail(const char *s) { puts(s); exit(1); }

// Call the DPMI "Obtain Real to Protected Mode Switch Entry
// Point" function (INT 2Fh AX=1687h)
int dpmi_init(void)
{
    void (far *switch_proc)();
    unsigned hostdata_seg, hostdata_para, dpmi_flags;
    _asm push si
    _asm push di
    _asm mov ax, 1687h          /* test for DPMI presence */
    _asm int 2Fh
    _asm and ax, ax
    _asm jz got_dpmi            /* if (AX == 0) DPMI is present */
    _asm jmp no_dpmi
got_dpmi:
    _asm mov dpmi_flags, bx
    _asm mov hostdata_para, si   /* paras for DPMI host private data */
    _asm mov word ptr switch_proc, di
    _asm mov word ptr switch_proc+2, es
    _asm pop di
    _asm pop si

    if (_dos_allocmem(hostdata_para, &hostdata_seg) != 0)
        fail("can't allocate memory");

    dpmi_flags &= ~1;   /* this is a 16-bit protected-mode program */

    /* enter protected mode */
    _asm mov ax, hostdata_seg
    _asm mov es, ax
    _asm mov ax, dpmi_flags
    (*switch_proc)();
    /* I don't think we're in Kansas anymore, Toto! */
    return 1;
```

```
no_dpmi:
    _asm pop di
    _asm pop si
    return 0;
}

void print_regs(void)
{
    unsigned short ds_reg, cs_reg;
    _asm mov cs_reg, cs
    _asm mov ds_reg, ds
    printf("CS=%04Xh DS=%04Xh\n", cs_reg, ds_reg);
}

main(int argc, char *argv[])
{
    print_regs();
    if (! dpmi_init())      // switch into protected mode, via DPMI
        fail("This program requires DPMI");

    print_regs();
    printf("Greetings from protected mode!\n");

    // to exit from protected mode, must use 21/4C!
    // and since bypassing C exit cleanup, must do flushall ourselves
    flushall();
    _dos_exit(0);
}
```


Notice that, once in protected mode, USEDPMI calls the printf function from the C run-time library to display the "Greetings from protected mode!" message. But USEDPMI starts off as a real-mode program, and is linked with a real-mode C run-time library. Using the real-mode C run-time library in protected mode requires that this real-mode code be "protected-mode clean"; this in turn requires that USEDPMI be compiled in small model, for reasons that should be fairly evident from looking at the program's output when run under a DPMI server:

```
CS=215Ah DS=22C9h
CS=02E7h DS=027Fh
Greetings from protected mode!
```

The DPMI server changed USEDPMI's segment registers right out from under it! The DPMI server has given USEDPMI protected-mode selectors that have the same linear base address as USEDPMI's previous real-mode segment registers.

Besides requiring small model, there's another, even more fundamental assumption implicit in USEDPMI's cavalier use in protected mode of a real-mode printf function: USEDPMI is assuming not only the presence of a DPMI server but also the presence of a DOS extender providing protected-mode INT 21h services. The real-mode printf that USEDPMI calls in protected mode will almost certainly result in an INT 21h DOS call eventually, so someone had better be providing INT 21h in protected mode.

DPMI servers do almost always come with DOS extenders, but the DPMI specification says nothing one way or the other about this. Thus, you shouldn't assume that you have protected-mode INT 21h services just because you have DPMI services. The DPMI server in OS/2, a virtual device driver called VDPX.SYS, has a DPMI_DOS_API setting that can control whether or not it should provide protected-mode INT 21h. It's not clear why you would ever want DPMI_DOS_API turned off, but if it is, USEDPMI (along with many other programs that assume that DPMI servers always provide DOS extender services) will behave improperly.

At any rate, DPMI and protected-mode INT 21h are logically separate services. As I said just before Listing 5-1, one of the things you can do with DPMI is write a DOS extender. You can see how helpful the DPMI switch-to-protected-mode service would be to someone writing a DOS extender. A DOS extender starts out in real (or V86) mode and switches the machine into protected mode to run protected-mode programs under DOS. The DPMI server takes care of a lot of the messy work for the DOS extender, and makes it easier to write portable DOS extenders that can run in environments such as Windows, OS/2, and under 386 memory managers like QEMM and 386MAX.

Once running in protected mode, a DPMI client can call DPMI INT 31h services, such as function 0 to allocate protected-mode selectors, function 0501h to allocate memory, function 0600h to lock down an area of pageable memory, or function 0205h to install protected-mode interrupt handlers. This last function is quite important to DOS extenders, which need to hook protected-mode INT 21h to provide services to their clients.

To clarify, there are three levels of software here:

- The DPMI server provides INT 2Fh and INT 31h DPMI services.
- The DPMI client calls INT 2Fh and INT 31h DPMI services; in many cases, this DPMI client is a DOS extender that provides protected-mode INT 21h services. On the other hand, some DPMI clients (like USEDPMI) just assume that a DOS extender is also present.
- The DOS-extended application calls protected-mode INT 21h provided by the DOS extender. It can also call DPMI services.

In the case of DOSX.EXE, the DOS extender (a DPMI client) happens to reside in the same program as the DPMI server. As we know, DOSX.EXE runs KRNL286.EXE or KRNL386.EXE. In other words, KRNL286 and KRNL386 are DOS-extended programs. True, these are also Windows DLLs, containing the Windows KERNEL API, but these two files also contain real-mode initialization portions that call INT 2Fh function 1687h to switch into protected mode (see the description of the BootStrap routine in Chapter 1 of Matt Pietrek's book *Windows Internals*).

DPMI was initially intended to help implement portable, compatible DOS extenders. According to Ray Duncan, "It's highly unlikely that you will ever need to call DPMI functions directly in a program of your own" (*Extending DOS*, 2d ed.). However, DPMI has turned out to be useful not only to the handful of DOS extender vendors but also to developers of more typical programs, such as Windows applications, when the normal API doesn't provide everything these applications need. For example, many Windows applications call DPMI function 0300h (Simulate Real-Mode Interrupt; see WV86TEST.C in Chapter 12 for an example).

According to Duncan's excellent chapter on DPMI in the book *Extending DOS* (2d ed.), Microsoft's original intent for DPMI was that the specification would include protected-mode INT 21h; as the name DOS Protected Mode Interface still suggests, INT 21h in protected mode was originally intended as a key part of the DPMI:

> I will never forget how startled I was when I encountered the DOS Protected-Mode Interface (DPMI) in its primordial form for the first time. I was sitting in a Microsoft OS/2 2.0 ISV seminar in the Fall of 1989, with my mind only about half-engaged during an uninspiring session about OS/2 2.0's Multiple Virtual DOS Machines (MVDMs), when the speaker mentioned in passing that OS/2 2.0 would support a new interface for the execution of DOS Extender applications. This casual remark focused my mind remarkably....
>
> After the speaker finished, I went up to him and asked for more information, explaining that his mystery interface was about to have a severe impact on a book project near and dear to my heart. In a couple of hours, the Microsoftie returned with a thick document entitled "DOS Protected Mode Interface Specification, Revision Prerelease 0.04" still warm from the Xerox machine and generously garnished with "CONFIDENTIAL" warning messages. I suspect I made a most amusing spectacle, as I flipped through the pages with my eyes bulging out and my jaw dropping to the floor. The document I had been handed was nothing less than the functional specification of a protected-mode version of DOS!
>
> In retrospect, the fact that Microsoft was cooking up something like DPMI should have been obvious. Every computer journalist in America, not to mention thousands of beta testers, was well aware that the as-yet-unannounced Windows 3.0 was somehow able to take advantage of extended memory by executing applications in protected mode, even though it ran on top of DOS and used the DOS file system....

> But I never saw a word of speculation in print on how this was accomplished, and I must confess that for my own part, I never gave it a second thought....
>
> Microsoft originally defined the DPMI in two layers: a set of low-level functions for interrupt management, mode switching, and extended memory management; and a higher-level interface that provided access to MS-DOS, ROM BIOS, and mouse driver functionality via protected-mode execution of Int 21H, Int 10H, Int 33H, and so on. The higher-level DPMI functions were implemented, of course, in terms of the low-level DPMI functions and the extant real-mode DOS and ROM BIOS interface....
>
> When details of Microsoft's DPMI began to leak out to the general community of MS-DOS developers, the rumors provoked more than a few hard feelings and harsh words for two very good reasons. First, the vendors of other DOS Extenders suspected that Microsoft, having realized that OS/2 was not going to replace DOS any time soon, had decided to barge into the market niche they had established so painfully and elbow them out through the sheer weight of its development resources and marketing power. Second, Microsoft had designed the DPMI with total disregard for compatibility with the existing industry standard for DOS-based protected-mode software — the Virtual Control Program Interface (VCPI)....
>
> For a few months, it appeared that the fledgling DOS Extender market was going to fragment in two mutually-exclusive directions, resulting in additional headaches for software developers, hassles for end-users, and juicy fees for lawyers. Luckily, cooler heads prevailed. Microsoft turned control of the DPMI specification over to an industry committee with open membership, and the previous backers of the XVCPI [Extended VCPI] effort decided to join forces behind the DPMI. Intel, with its understandable enthusiasm for *anything* which might sell more 80386 chips, was instrumental in bringing about this reconciliation, and also took on the responsibility of publishing and distributing the DPMI Specification.
>
> As part of this process of accommodation, Microsoft agreed to the deletion of the portions of the DPMI which cross into DOS Extender territory, specifically, direct support of the DOS and ROM BIOS interrupts in protected mode. Consequently, DPMI version 0.9, the first public version of the specification which was released by the DPMI Committee in May 1990, defines only the "low-level" or "building block" functions.... Naturally, the higher-level or DOS Extender interface of Windows 3 still exists, but it has receded back into the twilight zone of semi-support and semi-documentation. The only Microsoft documentation on the Windows 3 DOS Extender is a five-page technical note, entitled "Windows Int 21H and NetBIOS Support for DPMI," that is mainly remarkable for what it *doesn't* say."
>
> — Ray Duncan, *Extending DOS*, 2d ed., 1992, pp. 433-438.

Indeed, the INT 21h interfaces provided by DOSX in Standard mode and by DOSMGR and IFSMGR in Enhanced mode are practically undocumented, though from Duncan's account it appears that this — at least in part — is an accommodation Microsoft made to DOS extender vendors such as Phar Lap, Rational Systems, and Ergo.

Microsoft has an internal document ("MS-DOS API Extensions for DPMI Hosts," October 31, 1990) that devotes about 30 pages to the Windows 3.0 DOS extenders. Microsoft's five-page note that Duncan mentions appears to have been boiled down from this more extensive document. For example, the 1990 document discusses the 32-bit DOS extender provided by DOSMGR. The DOS file read and write calls (INT 21h functions 3Fh and 40h) have the count register (ECX) extended to 32 bits, allowing 32-bit programs to perform DOS file I/O of more than 64K at a time.

Although DPMI itself is hardly undocumented (the DPMI specification is readily available at no charge from Intel and has been reprinted in countless books), Microsoft barely documents the presence of DPMI (version 0.9) within Windows. The Windows 3.1 SDK contains a total of four pages on both the DOS extender and DPMI ("Windows Applications with MS-DOS Functions," *Programmer's Reference*, Volume 1: *Overview*, Chapter 20). This scant chapter lists a mere seven DPMI functions that Microsoft approves for use by Windows applications. On the other hand, the same document also claims that Windows supports version 1.0 of DPMI. Windows 3.*x* Standard and Enhanced modes, as well as Windows 95, actually support DPMI 0.9.

RUNDOSX

I've stated that the DOSX.EXE portion of Windows Standard mode is a general-purpose DPMI server and DOS extender. But how general purpose is it really? After all, DOSX might have started out as code belonging to a debugger, but now it's part of Windows and doesn't seem like something you could just tear out of Windows to use for other purposes.

Indeed, DOSX will run only KRNL286.EXE or KRNL386.EXE, no matter what you specify on its command line. If DOSX can't find either of these files, it fails with the message "Cannot find files needed to run Windows in standard mode." Worse, DOSX grabs the largest available block of XMS memory and (when exiting because it can't find KRNL286 or KRNL386) neglects to deallocate this XMS memory. So when you try to rerun DOSX with KRNL286.EXE or KRNL386.EXE, DOSX fails with a "Cannot start Windows in Standard Mode" message and you have to reboot to get back the XMS memory. This doesn't seem very general purpose at all. DOSX sounds hopelessly attached to the files KRNL286 .EXE and KRNL386.EXE.

Although DOSX can run only KRNL286.EXE or KRNL386.EXE, on the other hand it will run *any* file with one of those names! If some other file calling itself KRNL286 were to request DPMI services, use

DPMI to switch itself into protected mode, and issue INT 21h calls in protected mode, DOSX would run it, just as it runs the KRNL286.EXE and KRNL386.EXE files that happen to come with Windows. For example, Figure 5-2 shows the USEDPMI example from Listing 5-1, running under DOSX.


```
C:\WINDOWS\SYSTEM>copy \unauthw\usedpmi.exe

C:\WINDOWS\SYSTEM>usedpmi
This program requires DPMI

C:\WINDOWS\SYSTEM>ren krnl386.exe krnl386.sav

C:\WINDOWS\SYSTEM>ren usedpmi.exe krnl386.exe

C:\WINDOWS\SYSTEM>dosx
CS=215Ah DS=22C9h
CS=02E7h DS=027Fh
Greetings from protected mode!

C:\WINDOWS\SYSTEM>ren krnl386.sav krnl386.exe
```

Figure 5-2: Renaming USEDPMI.EXE to KRNL386.EXE and executing it using DOSX demonstrates that DOSX is a general-purpose DPMI server and DOS extender.

See? DOSX.EXE really is something that (if it didn't constitute copyright infringement!) you could just tear out of Windows to use for other purposes.

The example given in Figure 5-2 relies on three assumptions:

- First, this example works only on a 386 or later machine. On 286 machines, you would have to change USEDPMI.EXE's name to KRNL286.EXE, since DOSX will want to run that program rather than KRNL386.EXE.
- Second, the original "This program requires DPMI" message will not occur if you're running under a memory manager that already provides DPMI, such as QEMM (with QDPMI) or 386MAX. If you are, you don't need DOSX to run USEDPMI. However, this is still a good example of the point that the small DOSX.EXE file is a general-purpose DPMI server and DOS extender. There's also some interesting history behind the capability of DOSX to run under a 386 memory manager, but unfortunately there isn't time to go into it here; for the juicy details, see Geoff Chappell's *DOS Internals* (pp. 559-569).
- Third, this example assumes you're not already running Windows. You can start DOSX only outside Windows. If you try running DOSX

from within Windows Enhanced mode, you'll get the interesting message "Cannot start Windows in Standard mode. You are using an expanded memory manager which is not compatible with Microsoft Windows 3.1, or which is configured incorrectly. Try removing or reconfiguring your memory manager, or using the copy of EMM386.EXE supplied with Microsoft Windows 3.1." DOSX thinks that Windows Enhanced mode is a 386 memory manager like EMM386. Well, in many ways it is.

Since it's a pain to rename files as shown in Figure 5-2, I've written a small DOS batch file to take care of this. This batch file, called RUNDOSX, is shown in Listing 5-2. It runs any program named on its command line under DOSX by temporarily renaming the program to KRNL286.EXE. (If a file named KRNL386.EXE is not present, DOSX will run a file named KRNL286.EXE both on 286 and 386 or later processors.)

Listing 5-2: RUNDOSX.BAT

```
@echo off
rem RUNDOSX.BAT
rem Requires modification to redirect output
if (%1)==() goto usage
if exist krnl286.exe ren krnl286.exe krnl286.zzz
if exist krnl386.exe ren krnl386.exe krnl386.zzz
if not exist %1 goto no_exe
if exist dosx.exe goto have_dosx
:
copy \windows\system\dosx.exe >nul
if not exist dosx.exe goto no_dosx
:
:have_dosx
copy %1 krnl286.exe >nul
dosx krnl286 %2 %3 %4 %5 %6 %7 %8 %9
del krnl286.exe
if exist krnl386.zzz ren krnl386.zzz krnl386.exe
if exist krnl286.zzz ren krnl286.zzz krnl286.exe
goto end
:
:usage
echo RUNDOSX runs a DPMI client (a real-mode DOS program that uses DPMI to
echo switch into protected mode) under the Windows Standard mode DOS extender
echo (DOSX.EXE), by temporarily renaming the DPMI client to KRNL286.EXE.
echo DPMI clients can be created with the DPMISH library.
echo.
echo Usage: rundosx [name of DPMI client] [args...]
goto end
:
:no_exe
echo Can't find %1
```

```
goto end
:
:no_dosx
echo Can't find \WINDOWS\SYSTEM\DOSX.EXE
:
:end
echo.
```

Although you can launch any program (even COMMAND.COM) with RUNDOSX, it makes most sense to launch DPMI clients that rely on the Windows DOS extender, such as USEDPMI:

```
C:\UNAUTHW>rundosx usedpmi.exe
CS=215Ah DS=22C9h
CS=02E7h DS=027Fh
Greetings from protected mode!
```


Incidentally, RUNDOSX \COMMAND.COM doesn't work like you might want it to work. Sure, it gives you a C:\> prompt with DOSX loaded in memory (which effectively turns DOSX into a TSR). And sure, you can run a DPMI client from this C:\> prompt:

```
C:\UNAUTHW>rundosx \command.com

C:\UNAUTHW>usedpmi
CS=1B6Ah DS=1CC7h
CS=02E7h DS=027Fh
Greetings from protected mode!

C:\UNAUTHW>exit
```

But unfortunately, you can run a DPMI client from this C:\> prompt only once:

```
C:\UNAUTHW>rundosx \command.com
C:\UNAUTHW>usedpmi
CS=1B6Ah DS=1CC7h
CS=02E7h DS=027Fh
Greetings from protected mode!
C:\UNAUTHW>usedpmi
CS=1B6Ah DS=1CC7h
This program requires DPMI
```

Huh?! This is one place where DOSX isn't so general purpose after all. DOSX assumes there is only one DPMI client per DOSX session. After switching a program into protected mode, DOSX unhooks itself from real-mode INT 2Fh. The next program to call INT 2Fh function 1687h will believe that DPMI is not present, unless some other DPMI server such as QEMM or 386MAX also happens to be running; in this case the DPMI client will get *that* DPMI server instead of the one in DOSX.

This, by the way, is why DOS programs running under Windows Standard mode cannot use the Windows DPMI server or DOS extender; only Windows programs can. After DOSX sees KRNL286.EXE or KRNL386.EXE switch into protected mode, it unhooks itself from INT 2Fh, so no other program can call DPMI to switch into protected mode. Windows applications can use DPMI INT 31h functions, and the INT 2Fh functions that DPMI supports in protected mode, because these programs *start off* in protected mode; they don't have to call the DPMI switch procedure.

To run multiple programs under DOSX, then, just use RUNDOSX each time.

Using the DPMI Shell Library

USEDPMI showed the basics of writing a DPMI client. The DPMI Shell (DPMISH) library on the *Unauthorized Windows 95* disk is a big improvement. For example, Listing 5-3 (USEDPMI2.C) shows USEDPMI rewritten to use DPMISH.

Listing 5-3: USEDPMI2.C

```
/*
USEDPMI2.C -- very simple DPMI client
bcc usedpmi2.c dpmish.c ctrl_c.asm
Andrew Schulman, 1994
*/
#include <stdlib.h>
#include <stdio.h>
#include <dos.h>
#include "dpmish.h"

void fail(const char *s, ...) { puts(s); _dos_exit(1); }

void print_regs(void)
{
    unsigned short ds_reg, cs_reg;
    _asm mov cs_reg, cs
    _asm mov ds_reg, ds
    printf("CS=%04Xh DS=%04Xh\n", cs_reg, ds_reg);
}

int real_main(int argc, char *argv[])
{
    print_regs();
    return 0;
}

int pmode_main(int argc, char *argv[])
```

```
{
    print_regs();
    printf("Greetings from protected mode!\n");
}
```

As you can see, a DPMISH program includes DPMISH.H and provides two functions, real_main and pmode_main. DPMISH calls the program's real_main function in real (or V86) mode. If real_main returns 0, DPMISH switches to protected mode and calls the program's pmode _main function. DPMISH takes care of everything else for you.

MEMLOOP

USEDPMI and USEDPMI2 are unexciting programs. For a more dramatic example of what a DOS extender is good for, consider MEMLOOP.C in Listing 5-4. MEMLOOP calls the DOS memory allocation function (INT 21h function 48h) in a loop, via the _dos_allocmem function provided by C compilers for DOS, allocating memory until it (memory, not the program) is exhausted. MEMLOOP uses _fmemset to touch each byte in each allocated block, both to show that this really is immediately usable memory (no lock or copy function required) and to make the results more realistic on systems that provide virtual memory. Each time _dos_allocmem fails, MEMLOOP chops its allocation request in half in an attempt to soak up every last drop of memory. When there's really no more memory left, MEMLOOP prints the total amount allocated and exits, leaving DOS to free all the memory.

If compiled for DPMI (#ifdef DPMI_APP), MEMLOOP.C includes real_main and pmode_main. Otherwise, it uses plain old main.

Listing 5-4: MEMLOOP.C

```
/*
MEMLOOP.C
How much memory can be allocated through DOS (INT 21h AH=48h)?
Can be compiled for real mode or protected mode (DPMI).
real mode: bcc memloop.c
prot mode: bcc -2 -DDPMI_APP memloop.c dpmish.c ctrl_c.asm
On machine with 12 megabytes:
Real mode:                 536 Kb
DPMI app, under 386MAX     10764 Kb (18916 Kb with DPMI swap file)
DPMI app, under DOSX       10894 Kb (18916 Kb with 386MAX DPMI swap file)
DPMI app, under WIN386     38096 Kb (without permanent swap file)
*/
#include <stdlib.h>
#include <stdio.h>
#include <string.h>
```

```
#include <dos.h>
#ifdef DPMI_APP
#include "dpmish.h"     // includes _dos_allocmem redefinition
#endif

void mem_loop(void)
{
    unsigned long kb = 0;
    unsigned blocks = 0;
    unsigned blocksize = 2048;
    unsigned kbytes = 32;
    unsigned segsel;
    while (kbytes)
    {
        while (_dos_allocmem(blocksize, &segsel) == 0)  // INT 21h AH=48h
        {
            // touch every byte!
            _fmemset(MK_FP(segsel, 0), 'x', blocksize * 16);
            kb += kbytes;
            blocks++;
            printf("%04Xh\t%d\t%lu\t\t\r", segsel, blocks, kb);
            #ifdef DPMI_APP
                if (ctrl_c_hit)
                    fail("\nCtrl-C detected");
            #endif
        }
        blocksize >>= 1;
        kbytes >>= 1;
    }
    printf("\nAllocated %lu Kb in %u blocks\n", kb, blocks);
}

#ifdef DPMI_APP

void fail(const char *s, ...) { puts(s); _dos_exit(1); }

int real_main(int argc, char *argv[])
{
    return 0;   // okay to switch to protected mode
}

int pmode_main(int argc, char *argv[])
#else
int main()
#endif
{
    mem_loop();
    return 0;
}
```

If we build MEMLOOP as a real-mode program, it not surprisingly allocates some amount of memory less than 640K, even on a machine with, say, 12MB of memory:

```
C:\UNAUTHW>bcc memloop.c
C:\UNAUTHW>memloop
Allocated 536 Kb in 17 blocks
```

Here's what happens if we rebuild MEMLOOP as a DPMI program and run it under DOSX.EXE on the same 12MB machine:

```
C:\UNAUTHW>bcc -DDPMI_APP -I..\dpmish memloop.c ..\dpmish\dpmish.c
..\dpmish\ctrl_c.asm
C:\UNAUTHW>rundosx memloop.exe
Allocated 10894 Kb
```


Amazing! Simply by using DOSX.EXE, the DPMI version of MEMLOOP allocated 10MB of memory, even though the almost identical non-DPMI version allocates less than 640K on the same system. Yet, all we did was type RUNDOSX MEMLOOP.EXE from the DOS command prompt, without having to switch to a new operating system. This DOS extender stuff is pretty great, eh?

Well, DOS extender technology is the foundation for Windows 3.*x* and for Windows 95. It was because Windows 1.*x* and 2.*x* were missing this technology — just a tiny program like DOSX.EXE — that they could get so little memory, and consequently were so worthless and performed so relatively poorly in the marketplace. This little DOSX.EXE program is worth a heck of a lot! I hope Murray Sargent and David Weise got a lot of stock.

RUNDOSX MEMLOOP.EXE dramatically illustrates what DPMI is and what a DOS extender is. It demonstrates that DPMI lets a real-mode program jump into protected mode with a simple function call, and that a DOS extender lets this program continue to use familiar DOS calls while in protected mode but to do things (like allocate 10MB of immediately usable memory) that aren't possible under plain-vanilla DOS.

RUNDOSX MEMLOOP.EXE also shows that there are really two parts to Windows, and that those two parts are *semi-independent* of each other. The lower-level part includes the DPMI server and DOS extender; the upper-level part includes Windows DLLs such as KRNL286 and KRNL386, USER, and GDI. MEMLOOP could just as well be the KRNL286.EXE or KRNL386.EXE files from Windows. And KRNL286 and KRNL386 could, presumably, run under some DPMI server and DOS extender other than DOSX; you'll meet one such DOS extender in the next chapter when we discuss Windows Enhanced mode.

The two parts of Windows are only semi-independent because, as is well known, the upper part of Windows is not a pure DPMI client. Matt Pietrek discusses this in his book *Windows Internals*:

> The low level KERNEL routines are not shy about considering the LDT [Local Descriptor Table] to be their own little playpen.... Why does KERNEL bypass DPMI? Wasn't DPMI created to prevent this kind of mucking with sensitive system resources? The answer is yes. However, there often comes a point where proper code and performance clash head to head. The KERNEL developers built and tested a version of KERNEL that allocated each and every selector from DPMI. The developers saw enough of a performance hit with this KERNEL that they felt hacking the code to access the LDT directly was worth it. The code is compatible with DOSX and WIN386, in that it still allows other programs to allocate selectors from the DPMI server. Unfortunately, this version of KERNEL creates a hidden assumption about the way the DPMI host manages the LDT. If another DPMI host wishes to replace WIN386 or DOSX, it must organize the LDT in the same manner. However, the DPMI specification doesn't tell a DPMI host to manage the LDT in a particular manner, which creates ambiguity between the written and real DPMI specifications.
>
> — Matt Pietrek, *Windows Internals*, 1993, p. 90.

As IBM discovered while working on its OS/2 for Windows product, KRNL386.EXE requires some serious patching to make it run under OS/2's DPMI server. On the other hand, an engineer at Qualitas says that company uses KRNL386 .EXE internally as *the* test program for the DPMI server in its 386MAX memory manager, and adds that Qualitas had more problems with Borland's DPMI software than it had with KRNL386! Although there are no VxDs in this setup, running KRNL-386.EXE under 386MAX without benefit of one of the Windows DOS extenders does work well enough to run Solitaire. Well, heck, that's what we all use Windows for anyhow.

Chapter 6

Protected-Mode DOS: WIN386 and MSDPMI

Now that the experiments with DOSX in the previous chapter have provided a solid grounding in DPMI and DOS extender technology, we can take a close look at WIN386.EXE. As noted in the previous chapter, WIN386 is a collection of VxDs. The key component of WIN386 is the Virtual Machine Manager (VMM), VxD ID #1, which is the true core of the Windows operating system. The file VMM32.VXD serves the same purpose in Windows 95 that WIN386.EXE does in Windows 3.*x*.

It's common to read statements asserting that "WIN386.EXE is the DPMI server." This is sort of like claiming that "KERNEL is the GlobalAlloc function." Although VMM does contain the DPMI server, this is just one small part of VMM. And VMM in turn is just one (albeit the most fundamental) part of WIN386 (in 3.*x* Enhanced mode) and VMM32.VxD (in Windows 95). VMM has many other responsibilities, such as preemptive multitasking of virtual machines and threads, interrupt handling, and memory management. DPMI is a layer on top of this and appears to be little more than a way for "normal" (that is, non-VxD) applications to call some VMM services.

In Enhanced mode, the Windows DOS extender resides in the DOSMGR VxD, also located inside WIN386.EXE; when 32-bit file access is enabled in WfW 3.11 and Windows 95, the IFSMGR.386 VxD should probably be considered part of the DOS extender, too.

Writing in *Windows Tech Journal* (March 1992), David Thielen, then a Microsoft employee, noted:

Win386 isn't really even part of Windows. It's a preemptive multitasking kernel that controls multiple virtual machines. Once Win386 has initialized itself, it loads Windows in the system VM (the main virtual machine that always exists). However, it could just as easily load COMMAND.COM instead, resulting in a multitasking DOS. (No, I won't tell you how to do this.)

Well, after Chapter 5's discussion of how to make DOSX.EXE load something other than the Windows kernel, it should be fairly apparent how to do the same thing with WIN386.EXE. Just as DOSX.EXE insists on running KRNL286.EXE or KRNL386.EXE, WIN386.EXE (actually, the SHELL VxD within WIN386) insists on running KRNL386.EXE. But just as with DOSX, WIN386 will run *any* file called KRNL386.EXE: even COMMAND.COM, if you rename it! For testing out the DPMI server and DOS extender in WIN386, we can construct the same sort of batch file we used for DOSX.

However, there's one difference: in addition to WIN386.EXE and a file named KRNL386.EXE, we also need a SYSTEM.INI file and (in some cases) a virtual display driver. SYSTEM.INI usually requires only an [Enh386] section, listing VxDs to be loaded. Our first version will just list the VxDs that come built into WIN386.EXE. Listing 6-1 shows GOWIN386.INI, which our batch file will copy over to SYSTEM.INI.

Listing 6-1: GOWIN386.INI

```
; gowin386.ini -- minimal system.ini for gowin386.bat
[386Enh]
display=*vddvga
device=*vpicd
device=*int13
device=*wdctrl
mouse=*vmd
network=*dosnet,*vnetbios
ebios=*ebios
keyboard=*vkd
device=*vtd
device=*reboot
device=*vdmad
device=*vsd
device=*v86mmgr
device=*pageswap
device=*dosmgr
device=*vmpoll
device=*wshell
device=*blockdev
device=*pagefile
device=*vfd
device=*parity
device=*biosxlat
device=*vcd
```

```
device=*vmcpd
device=*combuff
device=*cdpscsi
```

By examining Listing 6-1, you can already see one way Enhanced mode is different from Standard mode: it not only provides a DOS extender and DPMI server but also a VxD loader. Depending on your configuration, you might need to add other lines to SYSTEM.INI, such as SystemROMBreakPoint=false if you're running with QEMM. Or, you might need to add additional device= lines for other VxDs you need to use or want to experiment with. Listing 6-2 shows a simple DOS batch file called GOWIN386.BAT, which runs any program under WIN386.EXE.

Listing 6-2: GOWIN386.BAT

```
@echo off
rem GOWIN386.BAT
if (%1)==() goto usage
if exist krnl386.exe ren krnl386.exe krnl386.zzz
if not exist %1 goto no_exe
if exist win386.exe goto have_win386
copy \windows\system\win386.exe >nul
if not exist win386.exe goto no_win386
:
:have_win386
if exist system.ini goto have_sysini
if not exist gowin386.ini goto no_sysini copy gowin386.ini system.ini >nul
:
:have_sysini
cls
echo Loading win386 %1...
copy %1 krnl386.exe >nul
win386 %2 %3 %4 %5 %6 %7 %8 %9
del krnl386.exe
if exist krnl386.zzz ren krnl386.zzz krnl386.exe
goto end
:
:usage
echo GOWIN386 runs a DPMI client (a real-mode DOS program that uses DPMI to
echo switch into protected mode) under the Windows Enhanced mode WIN386.EXE,
echo by temporarily renaming the DPMI client to KRNL386.EXE.
echo DPMI clients can be created with the DPMISH library.
echo.
echo Usage: gowin386 [name of DPMI client]
goto end
:
:no_exe
echo Can't find %1
goto end
:
:no_sysini
```

```
echo This program requires GOWIN386.INI
goto end
:
:no_win386
echo Can't find WIN386.EXE
:
:end
echo.
```

First, let's try USEDPMI (from Chapter 5) to see if GOWIN386 works. The results aren't really very exciting, but they do show that GOWIN386 works about the same as RUNDOSX:


```
C:\UNAUTHW>gowin386 usedpmi.exe
CS=246Eh DS=25CBh
CS=0097h DS=008Fh
Greetings from protected mode!
```

Now let's try MEMLOOP (again, from Chapter 5). If you'll recall, under DOSX, MEMLOOP on my 12MB machine could allocate 10MB of memory via the DOS INT 21h function 48h interface. This is about what you'd hope for on a machine with 12MB of memory, but it seemed pretty impressive because we're normally limited to less than 640K under DOS.

However, the results of running MEMLOOP on the same 12MB machine under WIN386 are quite different from what we saw under DOSX. At first, it looks like the program isn't working, because it grinds away with the hard-disk drive light on for several seconds. Then it announces:

```
C:\UNAUTHW>gowin386 memloop.exe
Allocated 38096 Kb
```

Your mileage may vary depending on how much free disk space you have, how much physical memory you have (four times physical memory is the maximum virtual memory WIN386 will allocate), and whether there's a permanent swap file visible when running GOWIN386 (for example, if you copy the Windows SPART.PAR pointer file into the directory from which you run GOWIN386).

But in this configuration, we've allocated 37MB of memory: Welcome to the world of virtual memory!

Remeber that this is an unchanged binary copy of MEMLOOP .EXE, and that MEMLOOP is allocating memory not via some special Windows API but by using the venerable DOS memory allocation function. So this is not only virtual memory, but virtual memory with a DOS interface.

In a world where relatively minor improvements are often touted as revolutionary advances, virtual memory with a DOS interface is a refreshing change. Here's something fairly new and exciting, masquerading as something old and boring. The phrase "underpromise, overdeliver" comes to mind. Of course, this isn't Microsoft's usual approach to packaging. It would have been more typical for Microsoft to have packaged what are fundamentally V86-mode *DOS* services as Windows (WIN386.EXE), then realized that these services should be part of DOS (witness the name DOS386.EXE in pre-beta versions of Chicago), and then finally reconsidered the issue and settled on the uninteresting name VMM32.VXD.

At any rate, WIN386, DOS386, or VMM32 — whatever you want to call it (we'll see later in this chapter that Microsoft once called it MSDPMI, too) — is really a V86-mode version of MS-DOS that supports virtual memory, device virtualization, and a host of other features, some of which (like 32-bit disk and file access) even provide better performance. Figure 6-1 shows that the lower level of Windows is really an enhanced mode of MS-DOS; once we've typed GOWIN386 \COMMAND.COM on the command line, we enter a world that looks exactly like a V86-mode version of MS-DOS, complete with DPMI services and a whole host of VxDs. In fact, this is the multitasking DOS that the *Windows Tech Journal* article quoted earlier was talking about. True, we have only one virtual machine here, but you could write a VxD that let the user launch additional VMs and switch between them. Note that in contrast to the situation with DOSX, we can run more than one DPMI application from the C:\> prompt under WIN386.

```
C:\UNAUTHW>gowin386 \command.com

C:\UNAUTHW>usedpmi
CS=714Eh DS=72ABh
CS=0097h DS=008Fh
Greetings from protected mode!

C:\UNAUTHW>usedpmi2
CS=714Eh DS=72C7h
CS=0097h DS=008Fh
Greetings from protected mode!

C:\UNAUTHW>memloop
Allocated 38096 Kb

C:\UNAUTHW>..\vxdlist\vxdlist
```

```
Name      Vers  ID     DDB       Control   V86 API    PM API    #Srvc
--------  ----  -----  --------  --------  --------   --------  -----
VMM       3.11  0001h  80011A88  8000AE14                       242
VPICD     3.10  0003h  8001CB78  8001BAE4  8001C2A0   8001C2A0  21
VTD       3.10  0005h  800225C0  80021B52  80021AE7   80021AE7  8
PageFile  2.00  0021h  800366DC  80036080             800365A7  7
PageSwap  2.10  0007h  8002D1EC  8002C894                       7
PARITY    1.00  0008h  80036AF4  80036A4C                       0
Reboot    2.00  0009h  80023274  800226B8             800229E1  0
EBIOS     1.00  0012h  8001F7E0  8001F770                       2
VDD       2.00  000Ah  8001A75C  80014058             80017FDB  14
VSD       2.00  000Bh  80025238  800250C4                       2
VCD       3.10  000Eh  80037D80  8003722D             80037275  9
VMD       3.00  000Ch  8001E514  8001E2D0  8001E45D   8001E45D  3
VKD       2.00  000Dh  800216B4  8001FD90             800202C6  15
BLOCKDEV  3.10  0010h  80036038  80035D80                       7
INT13     3.11  0020h  8001D700  8001D458                       5
VFD       2.00  001Bh  800369E0  80036890                       0
VMCPD     1.02  0011h  80038258  800380BC                       3
BIOSXLAT  1.00  0013h  80036F48  80036B88                       0
VNETBIOS  3.00  0014h  8001F62C  8001E748                       4
DOSMGR    1.00  0015h  80031034  8002ECF7  8002EB3B*            12
VMPOLL    3.10  0018h  80031848  800315FB                       3
DSVXD     3.00  003Bh  80013FF8  80013E28  80013E7F             0
COMBUFF   1.00         80038650  800382A8                       0
VDMAD     2.00  0004h  80024D48  800233F8                       24
V86MMGR   1.00  0006h  8002C840  8002AED7                       21
SHELL     3.00  0017h  80035B50  80034466             80032E50  6
```

Figure 6-1: Running COMMAND.COM under WIN386.EXE switches you into V86 mode, complete with virtual memory, DPMI services, VxD services, and so on.

What good is this V86-mode version of DOS?

Well, even though it looks like you're in real-mode MS-DOS, you're actually in V86 mode now: DPMI is resident, you've got a resident DOS extender that supports both 16- and 32-bit programs, and you've got virtual memory and a whole assortment of VxDs — you just don't have any of the GUI Windows feeling. From this perspective, the Windows GUI (KERNEL, USER, GDI, and so on) is just another program like MEMLOOP or USEDPMI.

Running GOWIN386 \COMMAND.COM isn't much different from a Windows DOS box; after all, you can run DPMI clients and DOS extended applications in a Windows DOS box, too. But this DOS box is not particularly tied to Windows. WIN386 is quite separate from the rest of Windows, and as we've seen, it feels much more like part of DOS. At one point in the Chicago beta, WIN386 was renamed DOS386; that was a more accurate name than WIN386.

What mode is KRNL386 loaded in?

We've seen that WIN386.EXE will load KRNL386.EXE — *any* file we call KRNL386.EXE. WIN386 successfully loads USEDPMI, USEDPMI2, and MEMLOOP when these masquerade as KRNL386. We know that these are normal real-mode DOS executables that use DPMI to switch themselves into protected mode. But hold on a minute! We also know that WIN386.EXE consists mostly of VxDs, which run in 32-bit protected mode (look at the addresses VXDLIST spits out in Figure 6-1). If WIN386 is already running in 32-bit protected mode, how do the programs named KRNL386.EXE manage to start up in real mode?

The answer is that they don't: They start up in V86 mode. Recall that V86 mode is a simulated real mode controlled by what Intel's documentation calls a VMM. WIN386 *does* put the machine into 32-bit protected mode. But when it starts the first Windows virtual machine (VM) — the System VM — it switches the VM to V86 mode to start KRNL386.EXE. WIN386 runs KRNL386 in the System VM. KRNL386 (whether the one that comes with Windows or one of our DPMISH pretenders) uses the function pointer returned from INT 2Fh function 1687h to switch into 16-bit protected mode. Function 1687h is handled by VMM, which contains the Enhanced mode DPMI server.

Any DOS boxes the user starts in Windows become additional VMs that can be used to run real-mode DOS software, DPMI clients, and/or DOS-extended applications. This isn't very different from what happens in the System VM: KRNL386.EXE is just like a DPMI client that the user might start in a DOS box. Furthermore, you can run real-mode software in the System VM by listing it in WINSTART.BAT. There's a lot of symmetry between DOS boxes and the System VM.

For what it's worth, Windows 3.0 was different. DPMISH calls INT 2Fh function 1686h to see if it's *already* running in protected mode. If so, DPMISH doesn't call dpmi_init. That's because, in Windows 3.0, KRNL386.EXE expected WIN386.EXE to have already put the System VM into protected mode; KRNL286.EXE also expected to be launched in protected mode by DOSX.EXE. This means that, if you took a real-mode program like COMMAND.COM, renamed it KRNL386.EXE, and ran it under the Windows 3.0 version of WIN386, WIN386 would try to run COMMAND.COM in protected mode. Not a pretty sight.

DPMIINFO

RUNDOSX is a cute example, but GOWIN386 \COMMAND.COM is the genuine article: an Enhanced mode of MS-DOS. But what exactly *are* the differences between DOSX and WIN386? One clear difference is the size of the files:

```
DOSX.EXE        32682   11-01-93    3:11a
WIN386.EXE     577557   11-01-93    3:11a
```

What does WIN386 do that DOSX doesn't that would account for an extra 540,000 bytes of code? We already know that WIN386, unlike DOSX, supports more than one DPMI client, provides virtual memory, and loads VxDs. The VxDs listed in Figure 6-1 account for most of WIN386.EXE's bulk.

To get a more systematic look at the differences between WIN386 and DOSX, you can use the sample program DPMIINFO, shown in Listing 6-3. This small program (which again uses the DPMISH library) calls INT 31h function 0400h to retrieve information about the installed DPMI server, such as whether it supports 32-bit programs and whether it reflects interrupts to real mode or V86 mode.

Listing 6-3: DPMIINFO.C

```
/*
DPMIINFO.C -- display information about DPMI server
Andrew Schulman, 1994
*/

#include <stdlib.h>
#include <stdio.h>
#include <dos.h>
#include "dpmish.h"

void fail(const char *s, ...) { puts(s); exit(1); }

unsigned _dpmi_flags(void)
{
    _asm mov ax, 0400h
    _asm int 31h
    _asm mov ax, bx
    // retval in AX
}

unsigned _dpmi_version(void)
{
    _asm mov ax, 0400h
    _asm int 31h
    // retval in AX
}

unsigned long _dpmi_mem(void)
{
    unsigned long buf[12], far *fp = buf;
```

```
    _asm push di
    _asm mov ax, 0500h
    _asm les di, fp
    _asm int 31h
    _asm pop di
    return buf[0];
}

static unsigned dpmi_32_flag = -1;

int real_main(int argc, char *argv[])
{
    // Should only get this flag from real/V86 mode, so call in
    // real_main, but let DPMISH tell us if DPMI is really present
    // before actually using the flag.
    _asm push si
    _asm push di
    _asm mov ax, 1687h
    _asm int 2Fh
    _asm pop di
    _asm pop si
    _asm mov dpmi_32_flag, bx
    return 0;
}

int pmode_main(int argc, char *argv[])
{
    unsigned flags = _dpmi_flags();
    unsigned vers = _dpmi_version();

    unsigned char maj = vers >> 8;
    unsigned char min = vers & 0xFF;
    if ((maj == 0) && (min == 0x90)) min = 90;  // silly Std mode bug
    printf("DPMI version %d.%02d\n", maj, min);

    printf("%s programs supported\n",
        (flags & 1) ? "32-bit" : "Only 16-bit");
    printf("%d-based DPMI host\n",
        (flags & 1) ? 386 : 286);
    printf("Interrupts reflected to %s mode\n",
        (flags & 2) ? "real" : "V86");
    printf("%s virtual memory\n",
        (flags & 4) ? "Supports" : "No");
    printf("%lu bytes available in largest block\n",
        _dpmi_mem());
}
```

Figure 6-2 shows DPMIINFO output for both DOSX and WIN386. As you can see, both DPMI servers support DPMI version 0.90. But WIN386 is far more capable than DOSX: It supports 32-bit programs, reflects interrupts to V86 mode rather than to real mode (see Chapters 9 and 10 for the, like, totally awesome significance of this), and supports virtual memory.

```
C:\UNAUTHW>rundosx dpmiinfo.exe
DPMI version 0.90
Only 16-bit programs supported
286-based DPMI host
Interrupts reflected to real mode
No virtual memory
11104192 bytes available in largest block

C:\UNAUTHW>gowin386 dpmiinfo.exe
DPMI version 0.90
32-bit programs supported
386-based DPMI host
Interrupts reflected to V86 mode
Supports virtual memory
43909120 bytes available in largest block

C:\UNAUTHW>dpmiinfo
DPMI version 0.90
32-bit programs supported
386-based DPMI host
Interrupts reflected to V86 mode Supports virtual memory
21508096 bytes available in largest block
```

Figure 6-2: Running DPMIINFO under DOSX, WIN386, and QEMM highlights the differences between these environments.

Notice that, in addition to RUNDOSX and GOWIN386, Figure 6-2 also shows DPMIINFO run straight from the DOS command prompt. QEMM 7.03 was loaded for this test; as you can see, the DPMI server in QEMM looks much like the one in WIN386. It even (via the DPMI.SWP file) supports virtual memory, which happened to be set to 10MB:

```
DEVICE=C:\QEMM\QDPMI.SYS SWAPFILE=DPMI.SWP SWAPSIZE=10240
```

QEMM also includes a DOS extender from Ergo Computing. 386MAX supports similar features (and also implements DPMI 1.0).

WIN386 really, really is a memory manager

The fact that 386 memory managers support many of the same features as WIN386 can be turned around to point out that WIN386, in many ways, resembles a 386 memory manager that you can start up from the DOS command prompt. The V86MMGR (V86 memory manager) VxD inside

WIN386 provides its own Expanded Memory Specification (EMS) and Extended Memory Specification (XMS) drivers — even if you already had an EMS provider before starting WIN386, and even though an XMS driver is *required* before starting WIN386.

You can see this if you run a diagnostics program such as Quarterdeck's Manifest, once before running WIN386 and again from inside WIN386. In one configuration, running HIMEM.SYS 3.09 and EMM386.EXE 4.44, you get the results shown in this table:

	Before WIN386	**Inside WIN386**
With EMM386 OFF:		
EMS version	None	4.00
XMS version	3.00	2.00
XMS driver	3.09	2.05
With EMM386 ON:		
EMS version	4.00	4.00
VCPI version	1.00	None
XMS/EMS sharing	Yes	No

Microsoft seems confused on this point, because a KnowledgeBase article, "XMS Version Information in MS-DOS Window Incorrect" (Q83455, September 1992), maintains that the behavior we've just seen is some sort of error:

> *The application retrieves the version number of the XMS driver in enhanced mode Windows, not the version number of the "real" XMS driver (which was present before Windows startup).*

But this is the way it *should* work. The V86MMGR VxD inside WIN386 really is a V86 memory manager; it really does supplant preexisting XMS and EMM drivers. As far as applications running under Windows are concerned, V86MMGR is the "real" memory manager. For example, even if an XMS 3.0 server is present before Windows started, once Windows is running you can use only XMS 2.0 functions.

The fact that V86MMGR takes over EMS and XMS from any memory managers loaded before it has important implications for software loaded before Windows. Chapter 3 discussed the Global EMM Import specification for memory managers, but V86MMGR's assumption of all EMS and XMS responsibilities also has serious implications for run-of-the-mill DOS TSRs that use EMS or XMS and that expect to continue working while WIN386 is running. V86MMGR is the "real" EMS and XMS memory manager, not only for programs running under Windows but even for TSRs loaded *before* Windows. This is just one of the many remarkable effects that Windows has on software loaded before it. As Chapters 9 and 10 will show, Windows can be said to rest on top of DOS only in the sense that an elephant might be said to ride on top of a mouse.

> Microsoft does get this right on the MSDN CD-ROM. David Long's excellent article on "TSR Support in Microsoft Windows Version 3.1" has a lengthy appendix, "How to Be a Good EMS/XMS Client," that provides guidance for global (that is, loaded before Windows) TSRs and device drivers that use EMS or XMS. For example:
>
> *Be aware of XMS version number anomalies. The WIN386 XMS version number is 2.00. If the running XMS driver at WIN386 startup time is an XMS version 3.0 driver, the XMS version number will change across the startup and exit boundaries. The WIN386 XMS driver* really *is a 2.00 driver. Any XMS 3.0 calls made while WIN386 is running will fail.*
>
> Okay, now that we've got that straight...

Given that 386 memory managers provide a similar environment to WIN386 (and vice-versa), what's the big fuss about running GOWIN386 \COMMAND.COM? How can this be viewed as some kind of sneak preview for the future of DOS when it doesn't appear substantially different from what's provided by commonly available third-party managers? As you've seen, if the 386MAX or QEMM DPMI server is loaded, you can run USEDPMI, USEDPMI2, and MEMLOOP, just as you can from within GOWIN386 \COMMAND.COM. Indeed, these memory managers do change the operating system in a far more dramatic way than many programmers realize. (See the article by Ralf Brown cited in the "For Further Reading" section at the back of this book.)

However, there's one crucial thing these memory managers don't provide: VxDs. It's not apparent now, but as you'll see during the course of this book, the VxDs shown in Figure 6-1, particularly VMM, constitute a complete new operating system. Memory managers don't have VxDs, though Helix Software's Cloaking API provides something somewhat analogous. Cloaking is a method for moving BIOS and DOS system software into protected mode. For example, Helix provides protected-mode versions of the system BIOS and video BIOS, the Microsoft CD-ROM Extensions (MSCDEX), the Logitech mouse driver, a disk/CD-ROM cache, and a RAM driver. This cloaked protected-mode software can run under Helix's NetRoom memory manager or, using Helix's generic Cloaking driver, under any 386 memory manager. Another API for moving DOS system software into protected mode is Novell's DOS Protected Mode Services (DPMS), used in Novell DOS 7 for Stacker disk compression, NWCACHE, DELWATCH, and the Personal NetWare server.

But whereas APIs such as Cloaking and DPMS are (so far) being used only to move selected system services into protected mode, with VxDs

Microsoft is much closer to moving the entire PC/BIOS/DOS substrate into protected mode. However, it's important to realize that, even in Windows 95, Microsoft has a long way to go before it can truthfully claim that the entire core of standard PC system services has been moved into protected mode. Besides, it's not entirely clear that having 100% new protected-mode code is even *desirable* as an ultimate goal. MS-DOS has its share of known problems, but at least they are *known* problems. And as we'll see in Chapter 9, Windows is in any case able to run the old real-mode DOS code in a fairly controlled V86 environment.

If I seem to be waffling here — maintaining that VxDs are exciting because they will eventually give us a fully protected-mode PC architecture, but that Microsoft is a long way from this goal, and that it's not necessarily even a totally desirable goal, and that even short of that not-necessarily-desirable goal Windows is still able to fundamentally alter the underlying PC architecture — well, that's because things are in flux right now. The important thing now is to realize the direction in which VxDs are moving the PC architecture.

MSDPMI

Yanking WIN386.EXE out of Windows and using it to run COMMAND.COM provides an excellent picture of the future of DOS and helps explain what Microsoft means when it says that future versions of DOS will be derived from protected-mode technology. In fact, this GOWIN386 \COMMAND.COM thing we've cobbled together is nearly identical to something that Microsoft itself did a few years ago, called MSDPMI.

Never heard of MSDPMI? Well, try running Windows from within GOWIN386 \COMMAND.COM:

```
C:\UNAUTHW>gowin386 \command.com
C:\UNAUTHW>win
The MS-DOS Protected Mode Interface (MSDPMI) is running on this
computer. You cannot start Windows when it is running. To quit
the MSDPMI, type exit and then press Enter.
```

MSDPMI was a short-lived Microsoft DPMI server and DOS extender from the early days of the Microsoft C/C++ 7.0 (MSC7) beta test. Basically, it was WIN386.EXE, renamed MSDPMI.EXE and slightly altered to run COMMAND.COM instead of KRNL386.EXE. Microsoft intended this to host MSC7, which required DPMI and a DOS extender. Many beta sites protested at the inanity of having to load over 500K of system software just to run a compiler, so Microsoft junked MSDPMI and instead bundled a copy of 386MAX from Qualitas with each copy of MSC7.

It's rather odd to see the retail WIN.COM (both in Windows 3.1 and Windows 95) referring to this beta software that never shipped. However, the documentation for the MSC7 run-time library made frequent reference to "the Microsoft DOS extender," so perhaps Microsoft really did plan to release MSDPMI as a product.

In a way, Microsoft *did* release MSDPMI: That's what Windows is! Indeed, there might be little reason for Microsoft to put out this technology under the boring name MS-DOS, when it can — and already has — put out the same thing under the more exciting name Windows. Either way, it's the same software, though perhaps Microsoft can earn more money by packaging this technology under the Windows moniker than by describing it as a new version of DOS.

How does WIN decide that GOWIN386 \COMMAND.COM is actually MSDPMI? Disassembly of the WIN.CNF file used to build WIN.COM reveals the following code:

```
4534:2002        db      'The MS-DOS Protected Mode Interface (MSDPMI) is
                          running on this computer.  You cannot start Windows
                          when it is running.', 0

4534:341C  B8 1683       mov ax,1683h
4534:341F  33 DB         xor bx,bx
4534:3421  CD 2F         int 2Fh          ; Get current virtual machine ID
4534:3423  8D 16 1FDF    lea dx,cs:[1FDFh] ; 'You are already running Win...'
4534:3427  83 FB 01      cmp bx,1         ; System VM
4534:342A  75 2D         jne short loc_ret_365
4534:342C  8D 16 2002    lea dx,cs:[2002h] ; 'The MS-DOS Protected Mode...'
4534:3430  EB 27         jmp short loc_ret_365
```

WIN calls INT 2Fh function 1683h (documented in the Windows DDK), a service provided by VMM that returns the current VM ID in BX. (Note, by the way, how close this non-DPMI function number is to function 1687h, which is used by DPMI. VMM doesn't distinguish between DPMI and non-DPMI INT 2Fh functions, which suggests that DPMI might be little more than a specification-after-the-fact codification of what already existed in VMM, similar to the way the XMS specification emerged from the HIMEM.SYS implementation.) If function 1683h returns nonzero in BX, WIN knows that Windows is already running and that, if the function returns with BX=1, WIN is being run from the System VM. WIN decides that this means MSDPMI is running.

As shown in Figure 6-3, I've incorporated this same test into ISWIN.C, which is available on the *Unauthorized Windows 95* disk.

```
define SYSTEM_VM 1
#//...
unsigned short vm;
/* call 2F/1683 to see if DOS app running in System VM; if so,
   this must be some hacked version of Windows like MSDPMI,
   or we must be running inside WINSTART.BAT */
_asm mov ax, 1683h
_asm int 2fh
_asm mov vm, bx
if (vm == SYSTEM_VM)
    printf("Running DOS app in System VM: "
           "Must be WINSTART.BAT or hacked Windows!\n");
else
    printf("VM #%u\n", vm);
```

Figure 6-3: ISWIN.C, a DOS program that tests for the presence of Windows, also includes tests for MSDPMI.

Running ISWIN under GOWIN386 \COMMAND.COM prints the following message:

```
C:\UNAUTHW>gowin386 \command.com
C:\UNAUTHW>iswin

Running Windows 3.10 (or higher) Enhanced mode
Running DOS app in System VM: Must be WINSTART.BAT or hacked Windows!
```

Note the reference to "hacked Windows": That's certainly what we have here! But also notice that ISWIN, unlike WIN, refers to WINSTART.BAT. After starting the System VM and before starting the Windows kernel, Windows Enhanced mode (specifically, the DOSMGR VxD) looks along the path for WINSTART.BAT. This is an optional ordinary DOS batch file that you can create to run DOS software in the System VM. WINSTART.BAT is typically used to load TSRs that are needed by Windows applications; rather than loading the TSR globally before Windows, which would occupy memory in every VM, WINSTART.BAT allows the TSR to be loaded solely in the System VM.

If you're perverse enough to run WIN from WINSTART.BAT under GOWIN386 \COMMAND.COM, WIN will think you've got MSDPMI:

```
C:\UNAUTHW>type winstart.bat
echo %0
win
iswin
```

```
C:\UNAUTHW>gowin386 \command.com
C:\UNAUTHW>echo C:\UNAUTHW\EXPERM\WINSTART
C:\UNAUTHW\WINSTART

C:\UNAUTHW>win

The MS-DOS Protected Mode Interface (MSDPMI) is running on this
computer. You cannot start Windows when it is running. To quit
the MSDPMI, type exit and then press Enter.
■ Type Exit and press Enter to quit this MS-DOS prompt and
  return to Windows.
■ Press ALT+TAB to switch to Windows or another application

C:\UNAUTHW>iswin

Running Windows 3.11 (or higher) Enhanced mode
Running DOS app in System VM: Must be WINSTART.BAT or hacked Windows!
```

Running WIN from WINSTART.BAT produces this MSDPMI message only if you've run WIN386.EXE without first running WIN. If you start Windows the normal way with WIN.COM, the second instance of WIN (the one launched from WINSTART.BAT) detects the first instance by calling INT 2Fh function 160Ah and issues a more sensible "You are already running Enhanced mode Windows" message.

But in a way, WIN is correct even when it confuses WINSTART.BAT and MSDPMI. After all, if you put COMMAND.COM in WINSTART and never type exit, you've essentially got MSDPMI, which in turn is the same thing as renaming COMMAND.COM to KRNL386.EXE. These are all just different ways of having Windows Enhanced mode (the low-level WIN386 operating system), but without Windows. In truth, what we have here is V86 DOS. It just sounds better to call it Windows.

Using WIN386 as GOWIN386 or MSDPMI, or running COMMAND.COM from WINSTART.BAT is no more than an experiment; this would be no way to deliver protected-mode DOS to customers. But using WIN386 as MSDPMI does emphasize how separate WIN386 is from the rest of Windows. All the functionality you see in MSDPMI — V86 mode, device virtualization, virtual memory, DPMI services, a 16- and 32-bit DOS extender, and so on — belongs in DOS. WIN386 really is part of MS-DOS, except that right now it ships with Windows, and Microsoft has decided for sound marketing and packaging reasons to call it Windows 95.

Chapter 7

Where Do 32BFA and LFN Come From?

Taking WIN386.EXE from Windows Enhanced mode and using it to run a copy of COMMAND.COM (masquerading under the name KRNL386.EXE) creates a new Enhanced mode of MS-DOS. But this may not be completely clear from the experiment in the previous chapter. After all, most of the special functionality available under GOWIN386 is also available to anyone who uses a 386 memory manager. The point should perhaps be made again that these 386 memory managers represent more of a departure from standard DOS than most programmers seem to realize. But still, providing DPMI, protected-mode INT 21h, and even a DOS INT 21h interface to virtual memory is fairly common these days and doesn't seem to justify characterizing Windows' DOS box as the future of DOS. Other than providing its own (possibly less capable) version of XMS, this setup doesn't seem to do much for regular DOS programs.

In this chapter, we'll be experimenting with a WIN386 configuration that in some ways isn't significantly different from the configuration we tried in the previous chapter but whose departure from plain-vanilla DOS is much more apparent.

This time we'll take the 32-bit file access (32BFA) functionality from WfW 3.11 and use it to further enhance DOS. We'll use GOWIN386 .BAT again, but now we'll copy the WIN386.EXE from WfW 3.11 instead of from Windows 3.1, change the SYSTEM.INI file slightly to replace BLOCKDEV with IOS.386, and add several additional VxDs:

```
;;; device=*BLOCKDEV
device=ios.386
device=ifsmgr.386
```

```
device=vfat.386
device=vcache.386
device=vxdldr.386
device=vshare.386
```

These are the new VxDs:

- *IOS.386*: I/O Supervisor, an enhanced version of Windows 3.1's BLOCKDEV, which in turn was an enhanced version of the Windows 3.0 Virtual Hard Disk (VHD) VxD.
- *IFSMGR.386*: Installable File System (IFS) Manager.
- *VFAT.386*: Virtual FAT File System (oddly, VFAT.386 contains the description string "Win386 HPFS Driver (Prototype)"; HPFS normally refers to the OS/2 High Performance File System).
- *VCACHE.386*: Virtual File Cache (replaces SMARTDRV.EXE).
- *VXDLDR.386*: VxD Loader (for dynamic loading and unloading of run-time VxDs, such as the real-mode mapper, RMM.D32).
- *VSHARE.386*: Virtual SHARE (replaces SHARE.EXE).

These VxDs must be copied over from the same WfW 3.11 directory as WIN386.EXE. (These VxDs won't load under the 3.1 version of WIN386.EXE; if you try, you'll get the message "A device file specified in the SYSTEM.INI file is corrupted.")

You also need to copy over the real-mode mapper, RMM.D32, and a copy of SPART.PAR, which contains a pointer to the permanent swap file.

Finally, 32BFA requires a DOS device driver, IFSHLP.SYS, which is included with WfW 3.11; your CONFIG.SYS will need a line such as:

```
device=c:\wfw311\ifshlp.sys
```

Note that if the IFSMgr (Installable File System Manager) VxD can't find IFSHLP (device name IFSHLP), it silently disables 32BFA. Why is there no error message? IFSMGR.386 does contain code to pass the message "The Microsoft Installable File System Manager (IFSMGR) cannot find the helper driver. Please ensure that IFSHLP.SYS has been installed." to VMM's Fatal_Error_Handler service. Unfortunately, IFSMGR has a bug and gets confused by an intervening call to a different VMM service; rather than do a fatal exit, IFSMGR ends up with a null function pointer to IFSHLP. Fortunately, however, the VFAT VxD also tests for IFSHLP.SYS — and this time does it properly, telling WIN386 that it can't load (though no message is produced).

With IFSHLP.SYS installed, with WfW 3.11's WIN386.EXE, VxDs, and RMM.D32, and with the modified SYSTEM.INI, run GOWIN386 \COMMAND.COM. The environment this command produces looks just like GOWIN386 based on Windows 3.1, and for the most part it is the same. But those extra VxDs we added have a significant impact: Until you exit from GOWIN386, they effectively replace key parts of real-mode MS-DOS with 32-bit protected-mode code.

How can you tell? Well, for one thing, your hard disk should seem significantly faster than it did before. But that proves nothing: maybe this VCACHE.386 is simply an aggressive disk cache like SMARTDRV.EXE, or maybe you already had SMARTDRV loaded.

No, the best way to understand what this 32-bit file access is all about is to see how file access under WIN386 translates into file I/O calls that are seen by real-mode MS-DOS.

Let's back up a moment then and see how Windows and DOS interact when 32BFA is turned off. Exit from GOWIN386 back to the real-mode DOS prompt. (You can tell the difference because WIN386 flickers the screen in a gross way when it exits.) From the DOS prompt, load a utility that logs INT 21h file I/O calls. For example, I used the INTRSPY utility from *Undocumented DOS*, along with the INTRSPY script FOPEN.SCR:

```
C:\UNDOCDOS>intrspy
C:\UNDOCDOS>cmdspy compile fopen
```

This logs all calls to the following INT 21h functions:

- 0Fh (Open File with FCB)
- 3Ch (Create File)
- 3Dh (Open File)
- 4Bh (EXEC)
- 4Eh (Find First File)
- 6Ch (Extended Open/Create)

Next, start GOWIN386 with 32BFA disabled. You can do this either by running the GOWIN386 configuration based on Windows 3.1 or by temporarily disabling 32BFA in the WfW 3.11 configuration. You can disable 32BFA either by putting the statement 32BitFileAccess=FALSE in SYSTEM.INI or by running WIN /D:C. (Similarly, you can turn off 32-bit disk access with 32BitDiskAccess=FALSE or with WIN /D:F.) We're not using WIN.COM here, so the /D:C switch needs to be passed directly to WIN386.EXE. Do this with GOWIN386 by putting the /D:C switch after the name of the program to run:

```
C:\UNAUTHW>gowin386 \command.com /D:C
```

(Yes, I know this is stupid, because WIN386.EXE, not COMMAND .COM, uses the /D:C switch. But this is just a toy batch file and doesn't merit more work.)

Next, from within the GOWIN386 DOS prompt, flush the INTRSPY buffer so you don't see the files that WIN386.EXE opened during startup:

```
C:\UNAUTHW>cmdspy flush
```

Finally, do something to generate a lot of file open activity, such as:

```
C:\UNAUTHW>copy con foo.bar
This is foo.bar
^Z
C:\UNAUTHW>copy con foo.bat
type foo.bar
foo
^Z
C:\UNAUTHW>foo
```

Let this silly recursive batch file run for a few seconds, and then press Ctrl-C. Next, generate an INTRSPY report:

```
C:\UNAUTHW>cmdspy report
XOPEN con
FIND  con
XOPEN CON
XOPEN foo.bar
XOPEN foo.bar
XOPEN con
FIND  con
XOPEN CON
XOPEN foo.bat
XOPEN foo.bat
FIND  foo.???
FIND  C:\UNAUTHW\FOO.BAT
OPEN  C:\UNAUTHW\FOO.BAT
XOPEN foo.bar
OPEN  C:\UNAUTHW\FOO.BAT
FIND  foo.???
FIND  C:\UNAUTHW\FOO.BAT
OPEN  C:\UNAUTHW\FOO.BAT
XOPEN foo.bar
OPEN  C:\UNAUTHW\FOO.BAT
; ...
```

Recall that we loaded INTRSPY before starting Windows, so INTRSPY is seeing whatever calls Windows sends down to DOS. INT 21h file access in the DOS box is being serviced by real-mode DOS. But what did you expect: that Windows would somehow handle INT 21h file access without calling down to DOS?

Well, crazy as that might seem, that's exactly what happens when 32BFA is enabled. Exit from GOWIN386 back to real-mode DOS, then start up GOWIN386 again, but this time get rid of whatever you did to disable 32BFA. For example, restart GOWIN386 \COMMAND.COM, but this time without the /D:C switch. Then flush the INTRSPY buffer, repeat the FOO.BAR/FOO.BAT test, and generate an INTRSPY report:


```
C:\UNAUTHW>exit
C:\UNAUTHW>gowin386 \command.com
C:\UNAUTHW>cmdspy flush
C:\UNAUTHW>copy con foo.bar
; ...
C:\UNAUTHW>foo
; ... let the batch file run for a few seconds, like before ...
C:\UNAUTHW>cmdspy report
XOPEN con
FIND  con
XOPEN CON
XOPEN con
FIND  con
XOPEN CON
EXEC  C:\UNAUTHW\CMDSPY.EXE report
```

Holy Toledo! All INTRSPY could see were the file opens from the COPY CON commands and from CMDSPY REPORT. If INTRSPY didn't see them, DOS (which of course is loaded before INTRSPY) certainly didn't see them. None of that FOO.BAR/FOO.BAT activity went down to DOS! It was all handled in 32-bit protected-mode VxD-land.

That's right, even though this isn't significantly different from the version of GOWIN386 created with Windows 3.1, we've got something very close to a 32-bit protected-mode operating system here.

It would be nice to have a test for 32BFA that was less empirical than seeing if INT 21h calls make it down to real-mode DOS. Testing for the presence of IFSMGR, VFAT, and VCACHE (perhaps using their V86 APIs, accessible via INT 2Fh function 1684h) sounds like it would be a good idea, but turning off 32BFA does *not* prevent these VxDs from loading. Thus, although the absence of these VxDs would tell you that 32BFA is definitely disabled, the presence of these VxDs doesn't guarantee that 32BFA *is* enabled.

Aside from using a program like INTRSPY, how else can you tell that the 32BFA VxDs replace much of MS-DOS? Well, you can use the TEST21 program from Chapter 8. In the following output from TEST21, we see that File Open (function 3Dh), File Close (3Eh), and File Read (3Fh) were handled without calling DOS. The minus sign (–) at the end of three of the lines indicates that fewer calls were received than generated. This in turn means (as TEST21 notes in its last line of output) that "Some INT 21h are handled without calling DOS!" This test is explained in more detail in Chapter 8.

```
C:\UNAUTHW>test21
Generated 301 calls    Received 1 calls
21/25    1 called      1 received
21/3D    100 called    0 received      -
21/3E    100 called    0 received      -
21/3F    100 called    0 received      -

Some INT 21h are handled without calling DOS!
```


By adding a few VxDs to our GOWIN386 setup, then, we get a brand new 32-bit protected-mode DOS. And we didn't need any Windows GUI components: this GOWIN386 trick is accomplished entirely with VxDs. (Well, okay, we also needed the IFSHLP.SYS DOS device driver.)

It's amazing that Microsoft released 32BFA as a minor upgrade (WfW 3.11) because it represents a far more significant change than many of the features for which Microsoft has seen fit to increment the DOS major version number (such as DOS=HIGH in DOS 5.0 and DoubleSpace in DOS 6.0). This is the first unmistakable sign of DOS's evolution into a 32-bit protected-mode operating system. It's another rare case in which Microsoft has underpromised and overdelivered.

Onward to Windows 95: VMM32

We've seen a gradual evolution of functionality from DOSX in Chapter 5 to WIN386 in Chapter 6 to WIN386 with 32-bit file access earlier in this chapter. Our final stop is VMM32.VXD, which is the operating system in Windows 95 (just as WIN386.EXE is the operating system in Windows 3.*x*). Let's first take a look inside VMM32.VXD using the W3MAP utility on the *Unauthorized Windows 95* disk. The results are shown in Figure 7-1.

```
C:\UNAUTHW>w3map \windows\system\vmm32.vxd
W3          00010000
VMM         00011000
VDD         00058000
VFLATD      00063000
ENABLE      00065000
```

```
VSHARE      0006d000
VWIN32      00071000
VFBACKUP    0007c000
VCOMM       00080000
COMBUFF     00089000
VCD         0008c000
IFSMGR      00091000
IOS         000b0000
SPOOLER     000be000
VFAT        000c5000
VCACHE      000d1000
VCOND       000d4000
VCDFSD      000dd000
INT13       000e2000
VXDLDR      000e5000
VDEF        000ec000
DYNAPAGE    000ef000
CONFIGMG    000f4000
EBIOS       00104000
VMD         00109000
DOSNET      0010d000
VPICD       00111000
VTD         0011c000
REBOOT      00124000
VDMAD       00129000
VSD         00132000
V86MMGR     00134000
PAGESWAP    0014b000
DOSMGR      0014f000
VMPOLL      00163000
SHELL       0016b000
PARITY      0017a000
BIOSXLAT    0017d000
VMCPD       00182000
VTDAPI      00185000
PERF        0018a000
VMOUSE      0018f000
VPD         00197000
VKD         0019c000
VPOWERD     001a8000
```

Figure 7-1: This W3MAP utility displays information about Virtual Device Drivers inside a W3 file. Using this utility to examine VMM32.VXD reveals that VMM32 is an anthology of over 40 VxDs.

Some of these VxDs are new to Windows 95. For example, VWIN32 provides services to Win32 applications, and VCOND is the Virtual CON Device.

W3MAP has several command-line options that can provide more information about individual VxDs built into an executable that uses Microsoft's W3 file format, such as VMM32.VXD or WIN386.EXE. Figure 7-2 shows one example, taken more or less at random.

```
C:\UNAUTHW\W3MAP>w3map -vxd vxdldr \windows\system\vmm32.vxd
Module name: VXDLDR
VXDLDR_DDB @ 00000068
Real-mode Init @ 0000:00000000
Device # 0027
Dynamic VxD Loader
Version 3.00
Init order: 16000000
DDB_Control_Proc @ 00000000
DDB_V86_API_Proc @ 000021c9
DDB_PM_API_Proc  @ 000021c9
DDB_Service_Table @ 0000002c (0f services)
    270000 @ 0000001d   VXDLDR_Get_Version
    270001 @ 00000000   VXDLDR_LoadDevice
    270002 @ 000000b1   VXDLDR_UnloadDevice
    270003 @ 000000b7   VXDLDR_DevInitSucceeded
    270004 @ 00001137   VXDLDR_DevInitFailed
    270005 @ 00000024   VXDLDR_GetDeviceList
    270006 @ 0000219c   VXDLDR_UnloadMe
    270007 @ 00002220   PELDR_LoadModule
    270008 @ 00002860   PELDR_GetModuleHandle
    270009 @ 000028b0   PELDR_GetModuleUsage
    27000a @ 000028e0   PELDR_GetEntryPoint
    27000b @ 00002910   PELDR_GetProcAddress
    27000c @ 000029f0   PELDR_AddExportTable
    27000d @ 00002ad0   PELDR_RemoveExportTable
    27000e @ 00002b90   PELDR_FreeModule
```

Figure 7-2: To get more information on a particular VxD in a W3 file, use W3MAP's -VXD option as shown here. To get detailed information on all the VxDs in a file, use the -VERBOSE option.

The VXDLDR_LoadDevice and VXDLDR_UnloadDevice services are used as part of Windows 32-bit disk access. In addition, according to a Microsoft document, "the Plug and Play architecture is dependent on dynamically loadable VxDs. When the system starts, it determines what devices are present, then uses the VxD loader to load VxDs for those devices." From the W3MAP output, we can see that VXDLDR also provides a set of PELDR services that allow VxDs to dynamically link to Win32 Portable Executable (PE) files.

Just as with the earlier environments, we can take VMM32.VXD and run it without the Windows GUI. In fact, this is precisely the setup I used for months during the early part of the Chicago test period. The pre-beta version of Chicago from late 1993 wouldn't run on my machine, but it did appear to get pretty far along in its initialization. This perhaps meant that the lower VMM/VxD layer of Windows might be able to run, even though the upper graphical layer didn't. Being able to test the

VMM and VxD components of Chicago seemed better than nothing, so I renamed KRNL386.EXE to KRNL386.SAV and then copied COMMAND.COM to KRNL386.EXE. With COMMAND.COM passing itself off as KRNL386.EXE, I could type WIN, and DOS386 (as the VMM/VxD portion of Chicago was then called) would run COMMAND.COM. This gave me a V86 version of DOS 7 that worked exactly as you would expect from our earlier GOWIN386 experiments.

But Windows 95 looks so seamless, so integrated! How could the VMM/VxD portion of Windows 95 be ripped out and used to run something other than the GUI portion of Windows 95?

To the casual user of Windows 95, Windows appears to boot as soon as you turn on the machine. Instead of the "Starting MS-DOS..." message that MS-DOS 5 and 6 display when booting, the same point in the Windows 95 boot sequence displays a "Starting Windows..." message. This small change has a subtle but important effect. It makes the average user feel as if Windows has replaced MS-DOS and that there is no longer anything sitting between Windows and the machine itself.

Yes, when you turn on a Windows 95 machine, it says "Starting Windows...," but as we saw in Chapter 1, it's still more or less the same old real-mode DOS code that's running at this point. This portion of Windows 95 is really just MS-DOS 90: MS-DOS in drag, as it were. Chicago's seemingly seamless loading of Windows is pretty seamy, really.

Whether autoloaded by WINBOOT.SYS or by COMMAND.COM, or started in the old-fashioned way by typing WIN at the C:\> prompt, WIN.COM will spawn VMM32.VXD, just as WIN.COM in Windows 3.*x* would spawn DOSX or WIN386. There's no magic here. None, that is, except the magic of repackaging. By taking something that has always been considered part of MS-DOS — the real-mode code located in IO.SYS and MSDOS.SYS — and repositioning it under the more exciting, less generic, less technoid brand name Windows (and Windows 95, at that), Microsoft has cleverly capitalized on what has for years been an unclear division of labor between DOS and Windows. Where exactly did DOS end and Windows begin? Microsoft is now taking all its PC system software and calling it Windows. New Package! Same Great Taste!

Although Windows 95 at least superficially appears seamless, and although Microsoft now appears to regard real-mode DOS as part of Windows (as best illustrated, again, by the "Starting Windows..." message that Windows 95 displays when you're starting what would up until now have been called MS-DOS), the fact remains that Windows 95 consists of several separate, semi-independent pieces that fit together in roughly the same way that the pieces of Windows have always fit together.

This means that, even in Windows 95, it's possible to take the VMM/VxD layer from Windows 95 and use it to create a small, self-contained V86 mode version of DOS. If it's okay for Microsoft to declare pieces of real-mode MS-DOS as part of Windows, then surely it makes as much sense for us to say certain pieces of Windows are really a part of DOS. Recall from the preceding chapter this statement from a former employee of Microsoft: "Win386 isn't really even part of Windows." The same is true of VMM32.VXD. So let's use VMM32.VXD to create a version of DOS that supports 32-bit file access and long filenames.

On my hardware, the Chicago setup created a directory tree containing over 1,000 files. In this Land of a Thousand Files, I wanted to find the minimal set of Chicago files for a non-GUI DOS386/VMM32 setup. At the time of DOS386, it turned out that I needed only about 50 files to get something working. With VMM32, even fewer files are needed.

Although a full-blown Windows 95 setup is a lot more useful than the minimal setup I'm describing here, going through the exercise of locating the minimum number of files needed to provide 32-bit file access, long filenames, or some other Windows 95 feature is quite instructive because you get a real sense of what constitutes the core of Windows 95.

Here's what it takes to create a small, self-contained VMM32 setup:

- VMM32 requires DOS 7.0 or higher. Running VMM32 on DOS 5 or 6 generates the message "Cannot run Windows with the installed version of MS-DOS. Upgrade MS-DOS to a version that is at least 7.0." Trying to fake this with SETVER VMM32.VXD 7.0 doesn't appear to work.
- Just as with WfW 3.11, you must have DEVICE=IFSHLP.SYS in CONFIG.SYS. But when running Windows 95 (even the scaled-down VMM32.VXD hack we're putting together here), make sure you use the version of IFSHLP.SYS that comes with Windows 95. The WfW 3.11 version doesn't know about the new INT 21h Long Filename (LFN) functions.
- The registry file SYSTEM.DAT should be in the root directory. If VMM32 can't find SYSTEM.DAT, it still runs, but it displays the warning "Registry File was not found. Registry services may be inoperative for this session."

- You need VMM32.VXD, of course. The Windows 95 setup program builds this file by packing together all the VxDs (including one called VMM32.VXD) needed for your particular configuration into a single file (also called VMM32.VXD). This omnibus file is generally about 1700K, considerably larger than WIN386.EXE, and contains among other things a VMM that provides many more services than the VMM in WIN386. (See Chapter 2.)
- You need a program to play the part of KRNL386.EXE, such as COMMAND.COM.

You'll encounter a few other requirements as you work through the rest of this chapter, but this is enough to get you started.

I created a VMM32 subdirectory and copied two files into it:

```
C:\>md vmm32
C:\>cd vmm32
C:\VMM32>copy \windows\system\vmm32.vxd vmm32.exe
C:\VMM32>copy \command.com krnl386.exe
C:\VMM32>vmm32
```

With just these two files, typing the command VMM32 worked, at least in the sense that I got a DOS prompt from which I could run DPMI programs. There were no loose VxDs (setup bound all the ones required for this configuration into VMM32.VXD). There wasn't even a SYSTEM.INI file.

Oops, my genuine Chicago directory was still on the path, and so VMM32 picked up its SYSTEM.INI from there. This pulled in who knows what. It turned out that VMM32 really did want a SYSTEM.INI file after all.

However, there is a way to make this minimal setup work: Run VMM32 in *fail-safe mode*. This is a useful feature that lets you boot Windows 95 even if your configuration files are hopelessly screwed up. You can trigger fail-safe mode by pressing F5 when your machine boots; you can also enable fail-safe mode by running WIN /D:M. WIN.COM passes the /D:M switch to VMM32, so you can just run VMM32 /D:M.

This works! With just VMM32.VXD (renamed to VMM32.EXE so I could start it from the DOS command line) and COMMAND.COM masquerading as KRNL386.EXE, I could run the lower layer of Windows 95. No GUI, no .INI files, no nuthin' except VMM32 and COMMAND.COM. In this hacked Windows 95 environment, I could run the usual DPMI test programs:

```
C:\VMM32>vmm32 /D:M
C:\VMM32>dpmitest
CS=21AAh DS=237Bh
CS=0097h DS=008Fh
CS base=00021AA0 limit=0000FFFF
DS base=000237B0 limit=0000FFFF

C:\VMM32>dpmiinfo
DPMI version 0.90
32-bit programs supported
386-based DPMI host
Interrupts reflected to V86 mode
Supports virtual memory
4014080 kbytes available in largest block
```


Again, this isn't a particularly useful configuration compared to full-blown Windows 95, but you can learn a lot about Windows 95 by experimenting with this and other scaled-down versions.

For example, I was quite surprised to discover that when I was finished running these VMM32 experiments I could exit back to real-mode DOS. The capability to exit from Windows back to DOS seems like an obvious and uninteresting feature. However, when you start Windows 95 in the normal way, typing WIN rather than VMM32, exiting Windows doesn't return you to the DOS prompt from whence you came. Instead, your choices are to restart Windows, shut off the machine, or press Ctrl-Alt-Del. Starting VMM32 lets us exit back to the real-mode DOS component of Windows 95, so it must be WIN.COM that normally prevents this.

Given that some Windows 95 VxDs might rely on the supposed impossibility of ever exiting back to DOS — perhaps some VxD patches DOS and, starting in Windows 95, doesn't bother to put back the original patched code when Windows exits — you might think that this exit-prevention would have been a bit more tightly integrated into Windows. On the other hand, perhaps the presence of Single Application Mode in Windows 95 means that all VxDs must be ready to properly restore clobbered data anyway. But if that's the case, there's no good technical reason for WIN.COM in Windows 95 to prevent you from exiting back to DOS. It's just Microsoft trying to make Windows 95 appear to be "at one" with the PC.

To make it a bit easier to test this minimal VMM32 environment, I cobbled together another batch file, RUNVMM32, shown in Listing 7-1.

Listing 7-1: RUNVMM32.BAT

```
@echo off
rem runvmm32.bat
set path=\dos;\bin;\eps;\borlandc\bin
```

```
if (%1)==() goto usage
if exist vmm32.exe goto have_vmm32
copy \windows\system\vmm32.vxd vmm32.exe >nul
if not exist vmm32.exe goto cant_get
:
:have_vmm32
copy %1 krnl386.exe >nul
vmm32 %2 %3 %4 %5
cls
echo Back in DOS
goto done
:
:cant_get
echo Can't find \WINDOWS\SYSTEM\VMM32.VXD
goto done
:
:usage
echo usage: RUNVMM32 [program] [args to VMM32]
:done
echo.
```


For example, to create the minimal VMM32 environment I've been describing, just type:

```
C:\VMM32>runvmm32 \command.com /D:M
```

This grinds away on your hard disk for a few seconds, and then you're presented with a C:\> prompt, from which you can run a variety of programs that would not otherwise be supported under DOS. We already saw that DPMITEST and DPMIINFO do the right thing in this environment. Another good test is the MEMLOOP program:

```
C:\VMM32>memloop
Allocated 8178 Kb in 257 blocks
```

Hmm, this doesn't look very good at all! Recall from Chapter 6 that MEMLOOP, running under WIN386.EXE from WfW 3.11, could allocate 37MB on this same machine. Why only 8MB with the presumably more advanced VMM32 from Windows 95?

Actually, this looks like a feature (and a sensible one, at that) of fail-safe mode, in which VMM32 will use a paging file (386SPART.PAR) located on the first hard disk, but it won't grow the paging file beyond its current size.

So let's stop using fail-safe mode. We'll need a SYSTEM.INI file to do this. Figure 7-3 shows the SYSTEM.INI file I threw together.

```
[386Enh]
PagingFile=H:\386SPART.PAR
MinPagingFileSize=4075
32BitDiskAccess=on
```

```
32BitFileAccess=on
OverlappedIO=on
VirtualHDIRQ=true
FileSysChange=off
maxbps=512
mouse=*vmouse
ebios=*ebios
display=*vdd
keyboard=*vkd
device=vfd.vxd
device=c:\unauthw\generic\vxd.386
device=*int13
device=*vpicd
device=*reboot
device=*vdmad
device=*vsd
device=*v86mmgr
device=*pageswap
device=*dosmgr
device=*vmpoll
device=*parity
device=*biosxlat
device=*vcd
device=*vmcpd
device=*combuff
device=*enable
device=*vshare
device=*vwin32
device=*vfbackup
device=*vcomm
device=*ifsmgr
device=*ios
device=*spooler
device=*vfat
device=*vcache
device=*vcond
device=*vcdfsd
device=*vxdldr
device=*vdef
device=*dynapage
device=*vtd
device=*shell
device=*vtdapi
device=*perf
device=*vpd
device=*vpowerd
```


Figure 7-3: A SYSTEM.INI file customized for testing a minimal VMM32 environment.

In addition to the VxDs embedded in VMM32.VXD, I'm also loading two loose VxDs here: VFD.VXD, because VBACKUP said it wanted it, and VXD.386, which is my generic VxD that will come in handy when experimenting with VMM32. Note that the SYSTEM.INI also explicitly points to the paging file.

With this SYSTEM.INI file, the amount of memory allocated by MEMLOOP is determined by the available disk space on the drive with the paging file. Unfortunately, I no longer had as much space available as when I ran the test with WfW 3.11, but you can still see that MEMLOOP, on my 12MB machine, is definitely using virtual memory from the paging file:

```
C:\VMM32>memloop
Allocated 16866 Kb in 528 blocks
```

As shown in Figure 7-4, running the VXDLIST program from the *Unauthorized Windows 95* disk revealed that 43 VxDs comprised this minimal configuration. Incidentally, under VMM32, VXDLIST uses a new VMM service (VMM_GetDDBList) to find the root of the VxD chain; it also could have used the VXDLDR_GetDeviceList service whose name appeared in the W3MAP -VXD VXDLDR output shown back in Figure 7-2.


```
VXDLIST version 1.20
Displays Windows Enhanced mode Virtual Device Driver (VxD) Chain
Copyright (c) 1994 Andrew Schulman. All rights reserved.

Using VMM function #1013F

Name      Vers   ID     DDB       Control   V86 API   PM API    #Srvc
--------  ----   -----  --------  --------  --------  --------  -----
VMM       4.00   0001h  C000EC28  C00023DE  C0002A11  C0002A11  377 ! 39
VCACHE    3.01   048Bh  C0032F6C  C0032A8D  C0032ED9  C0032ED9  15
VPOWERD   4.00   0026h  C0035CAC  C0035984  C0265B6C  C0265B6C  14
VPICD     3.10   0003h  C001A9F8  C0019480  C001A064  C001A064  22
VTD       4.00   0005h  C0033FE4  C0033DC6  C0262114  C0262114  9
VXDLDR    3.00   0027h  C00336C0  C0033658  C0261289  C0261289  15
CONFIGMG  4.00   0033h  C0036038  C0035D48  C02663CC  C02663CC  81
VCDFSD    3.00   0041h  C0033534  C0033428                      5
IOS       3.10   0010h  C00298F0  C0027E74  C0257EA4  C0256710  17
PAGEFILE  4.00   0021h  C0033C6C  C0033BE8            C0262068  10
PAGESWAP  2.10   0007h  C001E958  C001E854                      10
PARITY    1.00   0008h  C001EF0C  C001EE4C                      0
REBOOT    2.00   0009h  C001B3AC  C001B27C            C0233B50  0 ! 2
EBIOS     1.00   0012h  C0011B50  C0011B28                      2
VDD       2.00   000Ah  C0016658  C0011BA0  C0014944  C0014944  20
VSD       2.00   000Bh  C001D4F4  C001D32C                      4
VCD       3.10   000Eh  C001F360  C001F014            C023D3E9  11
VMOUSE    4.00   000Ch  C00118C8  C00112F8  C022F204  C022F204  10
VKD       2.10   000Dh  C0018350  C00172D8            C02334B0  21
ENABLE    0.128  0037h  C001FDE8  C001FACF  C023E298  C023E241  10
VPD       3.00   000Fh  C00357C0  C0034FA0            C003521A  0
INT13     3.10   0020h  C0018F9C  C00188F6                      5
VFD       2.00   001Bh  C001883C  C00186D4                      0
VMCPD     1.02   0011h  C001F7C8  C001F428                      8
BIOSXLAT  1.00   0013h  C001EFAC  C001EF64                      0
DOSMGR    4.00   0015h  C001EB60  C001E9B4  C023C5A8            16
```

```
VSHARE    1.00  0483h  C0020244  C002011F  C00200F4  C00200F4   1
VMPOLL    4.00  0018h  C001EDE0  C001ECD4                        4
DSVXD     3.00  003Bh  C0010F1C  C0010D4C  C0010DA3              0
VXD       2.00  28C0h  C0011280  C0010F7C  C0010FA6  C0010FA6*  0
COMBUFF   1.00         C001F9A8  C001F830                        0
VWIN32    1.02  002Ah  C0022670  C00216C8            C023FD78   21 ! 65
VCOMM     1.00  002Bh  C0023180  C0022ED0  C0243350  C0243350   35 ! 27
VCOND     1.00  0038h  C003315C  C0033118  C025B4D8  C025B5E2   2 ! 52
VTDAPI    4.00  0442h  C0034EAC  C0034E83            C0265330   0
VDMAD     2.00  0004h  C001D08C  C001B5CC                        28
V86MMGR   1.00  0006h  C001E6CC  C001DAAF                        25
SPOOLER   1.00  002Ch  C0029CF8  C0029C10                        18
VFAT      3.00  0486h  C003285C  C0030CDC                        0
VDEF      3.00         C0033B98  C0033964                        0
IFSMGR    3.00  0040h  C0025EB0  C0023380  C0246B33              103
VFBACKUP  4.00  0036h  C0022E60  C002281A  C0022847  C0022848   5
SHELL     4.00  0017h  C0034A70  C003476E  C02624E5  C02624E5   26
```

Figure 7-4: VXDLIST displays the VxDs currently in memory. Here, VXDLIST displays the 43 VxDs that make up a minimal VMM32 environment.

If you look back at the VXDLIST output in the preceding chapter (Figure 6-1), you'll see that, in contrast to Figure 7-4, Windows 3.1 (which doesn't provide 32-bit file access) used only about half as many VxDs as Chicago. We saw at the beginning of this chapter that WfW 3.11 32-bit file access requires about five additional VxDs. Although these are rough figures — a lot depends on your individual configuration, including whether you're on a network and which graphics accelerator card you use — it seems clear that Windows 95 relies far more heavily on VxDs than earlier versions of Windows did.

In the VXDLIST output in Figure 7-4, those numbers on the right (following the exclamation marks) indicate the number of special services a given VxD provides for Win32 applications; many advanced Win32 API functions available in Windows 95, but not in Win32s, are implemented using these VxD Win32 services. For example, the CreateThread API provided by KERNEL32 is based on the VMMCreateThread function; KERNEL32 calls this VMM function via one of the Win32 services provided by VWIN32. The undocumented VXDCall0 function in KERNEL32, which is used later in this book, lets Win32 applications call these VxD-provided Win32 services.

Well, we see that Windows 95 has tons of VxDs, and it makes sense that these would help implement many of the new features of Windows 95, but so far we haven't really seen any Windows 95 behavior that differs from WfW 3.11 with 32BFA. In the next section we'll look at an aspect of Windows 95 that's a real departure from previous versions of Windows: long filenames.

Long Filename Support in Windows 95

Since its inception, MS-DOS has been plagued by the so-called 8.3 filename convention. Instead of sensible filenames such as "3rd quarter 1994 report from Cleveland" or "Piano Concerto No. 20 in D minor," users have to create and remember names such as CLEV3Q94.WKS and PI20DMIN.SCR. In Windows 95, you can have long filenames and directory names (up to 255 characters), with a maximum path length of 260 characters. The following is output from the DIR command in Windows 95:

```
3RDQUART          36,517  09-13-94  8:43p 3rd quarter 1994 report from Cleveland
PIANOCON 20I     126,455  09-13-94  8:44p Piano Concerto No. 20 in D minor
```

Every long filename in Windows 95 has a unique short alias automatically generated by the operating system. In the DIR output, 3RDQUART is the alias for "3rd quarter 1994 report from Cleveland". Windows 95 is case-preserving (though case-insensitive), so essentially all files and directories created under Windows 95 have two forms. For example,

```
copy foo.bar foobarsk.doc
```

would create both a standard FOOBARSK.DOC directory entry and, even though FOOBARSK.DOC fits within the standard 8.3 filename confines, a second, case-preserving foobarsk.doc entry.

Of course, Microsoft had to implement these long filenames in a way that didn't break existing applications. Also, media written under Windows 95 must still be usable under older versions of DOS and Windows.

Let's say a DOS program calls INT 21h function 47h to get the current directory. According to Microsoft's *DOS 6.0 Programmer's Reference*, a program calling this function needs a buffer of at least 64 bytes, which is large enough to contain the largest possible path. The program now finds itself running under Windows 95, where a single directory name, not to mention the entire path, can be larger than 64 bytes. What happens?

The program gets the short form, of course. Otherwise, Windows 95 would break every DOS program that had obeyed the rules and allocated as few as 64 bytes in which to receive the current directory string. This means that developers don't have to worry about long filenames breaking old programs.

However, many programs will need to work with the full filenames. Getting the long filename instead of the short alias requires a new set of functions. Windows programs will use Win32 API functions such as GetCurrentDirectory and CreateFile. A DOS program will be able to use a new set of subfunctions under INT 21h function 71h, where the subfunction in AL is the same as the old DOS AH function number. For example, because the old DOS Get Current Directory function is INT 21h function 47h, the new one that knows about long pathnames is INT 21h function 7147h; although the other registers are identical to the old call, the buffers pointed to by DS:SI must be large enough to receive the maximum-allowed path. As you'll see in the LFN.C example later in this chapter, programs can call the new Get Volume Information function (INT 21h function 71A0h) to get the length of the maximum-allowed path.

Long filenames aren't supported in the real-mode WINBOOT.SYS portion of Windows 95, which runs before VMM32.VXD. This means that real-mode programs such as TSRs and device drivers can't call the new long filename APIs if they run at system startup. Similarly, the few programs run in so-called Single Application Mode also won't be able to call the long filename APIs. To determine if the new APIs are available, a program can use INT 21h function 71A0h.

If these new DOS INT 21h functions aren't available in real-mode DOS 7, who provides them? A VxD, of course: IFSMgr. Since long filenames aren't provided in the real-mode portion of DOS 7, and since they don't require any Win16 or Win32 code, we can look at them from our cobbled-together VMM32 environment.

But there's a slight problem. Trying to create a long filename in the tiny VMM32 environment doesn't yield the expected results:

```
C:\VMM32>copy data.1 "3rd quarter 1994 report from Cleveland"
        1 file(s) copied

C:\VMM32>copy data.2 "Piano Concerto No. 20 in D minor"
        1 file(s) copied

C:\VMM32>dir
...
3RD QUAR                2,481  09-13-94  9:01p
PIANO CO  20            2,526  09-13-94  9:01p
```

Not only that, but it also just doesn't feel as though 32-bit file access is enabled: the disk is too slow. If LFN support is clearly absent, it makes sense that 32-bit file access would be absent as well, since both are provided by IFSMgr. Yet, in the VXDLIST output shown earlier, IFSMgr is clearly loaded, as are the other main components of 32-bit file and disk access:

```
Name      Vers   ID      DDB        Control    V86 API    PM API      #Srvc
--------  ----   -----   --------   --------   --------   -------     -----
IFSMGR    3.00   0040h   C0025EB0   C0023380   C0246B33               103
VCACHE    3.01   048Bh   C0032F6C   C0032A8D   C0032ED9   C0032ED9    15
VFAT      3.00   0486h   C003285C   C0030CDC                          0
VSHARE    1.00   0483h   C0020244   C002011F   C00200F4   C00200F4    1
IOS       3.10   0010h   C00298F0   C0027E74   C0257EA4   C0256710    17
INT13     3.10   0020h   C0018F9C   C00188F6                          5
```

What gives? We must be missing one or more files — probably VxDs — that VMM32 needs to enable 32BFA and LFN support. To see what VMM32 apparently wants in order to enable 32BFA and LFN, we can take David Maxey's INTRSPY utility from *Undocumented DOS*, load the utility before starting the RUNVMM32 batch file, and have INTRSPY log all File Open, Find First, and EXEC calls. After starting and exiting VMM32, INTRSPY produced the report (which I've trimmed a little) shown in Figure 7-5.

```
EXEC  C:\VMM32\VMM32.EXE
OPEN  QEMM386$ [FAIL 2]
OPEN  386MAX$$ [FAIL 2]
XOPEN C:\WINDOWS\EMM386.EXE
OPEN  SMARTAAR [FAIL 2]
OPEN  C:\SYSTEM.DAT
OPEN  C:\VMM32\VMM32.EXE
OPEN  $DebugDD [FAIL 2]
OPEN  NDISHLP$ [FAIL 2]
OPEN  C:\VMM32\SYSTEM.INI
FIND   [FAIL 3]
OPEN  H:\DBLSPACE.BIN
OPEN  c:\vmm32\vfd.vxd
OPEN  EMMXXXX0
OPEN  SMARTAAR [FAIL 2]
OPEN  IFS$HLP$
OPEN  CONFIG$
OPEN  SCSIMGR$ [FAIL 2]
OPEN  C:\VMM32\IOS.INI [FAIL 2]
OPEN  C:\VMM32\IOS.INI [FAIL 2]
OPEN  C:\VMM32\IOS.INI [FAIL 2]
FIND  C:\VMM32\IOSUBSYS\*.vxd [FAIL 3]
OPEN  C:\VMM32\IOSUBSYS\rmm.pdr [FAIL 3]
OPEN  C:\VMM32\WINSTART.BAT [FAIL 2]
OPEN  \dos\WINSTART.BAT [FAIL 2]
OPEN  \bin\WINSTART.BAT [FAIL 2]
OPEN  C:\VMM32\UNICODE.BIN [FAIL 2]
OPEN  IFS$HLP$
OPEN  C:\VMM32\VFD.VXD
OPEN  C:\VMM32\KRNL386.EXE
OPEN  C:\VMM32\USER.DAT
OPEN  C:\VMM32\USER.DAT
OPEN  C:\VMM32\KERNEL32.DLL [FAIL 2]
OPEN  C:\VMM32\KERNEL32.DLL [FAIL 2]
```

```
OPEN  \dos\KERNEL32.DLL [FAIL 2]
OPEN  \bin\KERNEL32.DLL
EXEC  C:\VMM32\KRNL386.EXE
OPEN  C:\VMM32\KRNL386.EXE
OPEN  C:\VMM32\KRNL386.EXE
OPEN  C:\COMMAND.COM
OPEN  C:\SYSTEM.DAT
XOPEN C:\SYSTEM.~~~
OPEN  C:\VMM32\RUNVMM32.BAT
```

Figure 7-5: INTRSPY lists the files requested by a minimal VMM32 environment.

There's a bunch of interesting stuff in Figure 7-5: We can see Windows looking for various DOS device drivers such as QEMM386$, 386MAX$$, SMARTAAR, $DebugDD, NDISHLP$, EMMXXXX0, IFSHLP, CONFIG$, and SCSIMGR$; we can see Windows looking along the path for a WINSTART.BAT file; and so on. But the key lines that command attention are:

```
OPEN  C:\VMM32\IOS.INI [FAIL 2]
FIND  C:\VMM32\IOSUBSYS\*.vxd [FAIL 3]
OPEN  C:\VMM32\IOSUBSYS\rmm.pdr [FAIL 3]
```

For 32BFA and LFN support, VMM32 must require IOS.INI (the safe driver list used by the I/O Supervisor, IOS.VXD), and/or an IOSUBSYS subdirectory, and/or the real-mode mapper, RMM.PDR.

Our next move is clear: Create a \VMM32\IOSUBSYS subdirectory and copy the contents of Windows 95's \WINDOWS\SYSTEM\IOSUBSYS subdirectory into it. (Significantly, IOSUBSYS can contain a DBLSPACE VxD, but we'll get into that later.) It probably wouldn't hurt to copy over IOS.INI, too.

With the IOSUBSYS directory in place, restart VMM32. If you run VXDLIST again, you'll see that three new VxDs have shown up; IOS dynamically loads these VxDs with the VXDLDR_LoadDevice service:

```
Name      Vers  ID     DDB       Control   V86 API   PM API   #Srvc
--------  ----  -----  --------  --------  --------  -------  -----
DiskTSD   3.10         C0FD23CC  C0FD21A8                     0
voltrack  3.10  0090h  C0FD54D8  C0FD5000                     0
RMM       3.10         C0FD6224  C0FD5850                     0
```

DISKTSD is a fixed-disk type-specific driver, VOLTRACK.VXD is a volume tracker, and RMM.PDR is a real-mode mapper. There are almost a dozen layers to the Windows file/disk architecture. I know I can never keep all this file/disk driver stuff straight. If you have as much trouble as I do remembering what the heck port drivers and miniport drivers are, see "The eleven kinds of windows disk/file drivers."

The eleven kinds of Windows disk/file drivers

The following glossary of Windows file/disk driver terminology is a handy cheat sheet that I've cribbed almost word-for-word from a Microsoft document on "Layered Block Device Drivers." As you'll see, the word *layered* is a mild understatement for this veritable tower of drivers.

- *File system driver (FSD)*: Manages the high-level I/O requests from applications. The FSD processes requests from applications and initiates low-level I/O requests through the I/O supervisor. VFAT is an FSD; FSDs are installable file system drivers, and are managed by IFSMgr. There are also FSD extensions such as the DBLSPACE VxD.
- *I/O supervisor (IOS)*: Provides various services to FSDs and other drivers in the system. The IOS registers drivers, routes and queues I/O requests, sends asynchronous notifications to the drivers as needed, and provides services that drivers can use to allocate memory and complete I/O requests. The IOS also provides BlockDev services to support compatibility with BlockDev clients.
- *Volume tracker*: Works with a group of devices that share removability rules. The volume tracker ensures that the correct media is in the device and detects and reports improper media removal or insertion.
- *Type-specific driver (TSD)*: Works with all devices of a specific type, such as all CD-ROM devices. The TSD validates incoming I/O requests, converts logical requests to physical requests, and notifies the requestor when the request is complete. The TSD can also initiate logical error recovery as needed for certain types of devices, principally disks.
- *SCSI'izer*: Works with all SCSI devices of a given type, such as all SCSI disks. The SCSI'izer constructs SCSI Command Descriptor Blocks (CDBs) for a specific class and carries out device-level error recovery and logging.
- *Vendor-supplied driver (VSD)*: Intercepts and processes I/O requests for a given block device. The VSD gives a vendor an efficient way to either incorporate enhancements into an existing layered block device driver or extend the capabilities of the driver to new but similar hardware.
- *SCSI port driver (SCSI manager)*: Manages the interaction between the SCSI'izer and a Windows NT SCSI miniport driver. The SCSI port driver initializes the miniport driver, converts the I/O request format, and carries out all interactions with the miniport driver.
- *NT SCSI miniport driver (MPD)*: Works with a specific set of SCSI adapters. The miniport driver detects and initializes the adapter, handles interrupts, transmits I/O requests to the device, and carries out adapter-level error recovery and logging.

- *Port driver (PDR)*: Works with a specific adapter, usually proprietary. For example, there are port drivers for IDE/ESDI and NEC floppy drivers. A port driver provides the same functionality as a combination of SCSI manager and miniport driver. The port driver detects and initializes the adapter, handles interrupts, transmits I/O requests to the device, and carries out adapter-level error recovery and logging.
- *Real-mode mapper (RMM)*: Provides the interface between a file system and a DOS real-mode driver such as DBLSPACE.BIN, making the real-mode driver appear to upper levels as though it were a protected-mode driver.
- *Real-mode driver*: An existing DOS device driver, such as DBLSPACE .BIN, that Windows executes in V86 mode.

All these layers of port drivers and miniport drivers make my head hurt. One of the foundations of user-interface design is psychologist George Miller's "seven plus or minus two" rule (that is, the average human mind can retain between five and nine things in short-term memory). Surely this rule applies to programming interfaces too.

With DISKTSD, VOLTRACK, and RMM loaded, we now have 32BFA and LFN support. Why is that? These are all part of 32-bit *disk* access (32BDA), and we're talking about 32-bit *file* access here. However, 32BFA requires 32BDA, *or something that looks just like it.* That's the role of the real-mode mapper.

My hard disk is compressed with DblSpace. (This, combined with the fact that I'm using 32-bit file access, in a beta version no less, shows that I like to live, or at least compute, on the edge. I have lost a frightening amount of work in the course of this book.) Without a DblSpace VxD (discussed in a moment), all disk access must go through the 16-bit real-mode DblSpace driver. True, this driver will in turn access the DblSpace Compressed Volume File (CVF) on the host drive, and *those* accesses will be 32-bit. But in the absence of a DblSpace VxD, calling the real-mode DblSpace driver is unavoidable. But as just noted, 32BFA requires 32BDA. The real-mode mapper, then, will make a 16-bit real-mode compression driver such as DblSpace look to 32BFA as though it were a 32-bit protected-mode driver.

Indeed, it's RMM that did the trick here. With a IOSUBSYS directory containing only the single RMM.PDR file, we still get 32BFA and LFN support.

To demonstrate 32BFA, we can use the V86TEST program from Chapter 10. Loading V86TEST before VMM32, we can use it to see how many INT 21h calls VMM32 is sending down to DOS. By running V86TEST -QUERY before and after performing an operation and then subtracting the before statistics from the after statistics, we can measure the DOS "cost" of the operation.

Before creating the IOSUBSYS directory, one test (searching for the string "foobish" in the 3210K comprising Ralf Brown's Interrupt List) under VMM32 took 19 seconds and generated 367 INT 21h calls (73 of them to Read function 3Fh). Immediately running the test again (to try to measure any caching) took 14 seconds.

By comparison, the same test in plain-vanilla real-mode DOS used the same number of INT 21h calls but required only 11 seconds each time. Clearly, without something like 32-bit file access, a V86 mode DOS like VMM32 can hurt rather than help performance.

After creating the IOSUBSYS directory and restarting VMM32 under V86TEST, the same test took 13 seconds and generated only 218 INT 21h calls, none of them to the Read function. Immediately running the test again took only 4 seconds. Yes, the first test still took longer than in plain old DOS, but we picked up the benefits of 32BFA in the second test. Notice that the combined times for the two tests under 32BFA (13 + 4 = 17 seconds) are shorter than the combined times for plain DOS (11 + 11 = 22 seconds), though not spectacularly so.

Because 32BFA required two passes through the data before it demonstrated any benefits, it can appear as though 32BFA is nothing more than a cache. Certainly VCACHE is a crucial part of 32BFA. Perhaps we would do just as well using SmartDrv? This subject is taken up in more detail in Chapter 8, in the sidebar titled,"32BFA versus disk cache performance."

For now, I'll just note that, contrary to what is often claimed, size is important (cache size, that is). A lot depends on the cache size you specify for SmartDrv. Whereas VCACHE grows and shrinks as needed, the maximum SmartDrv cache size is fixed once you start it. If the cache size isn't sufficient for your data "working set," SmartDrv will do little good. In this example, a 2048K SmartDrv cache provided little benefit in reading 3210K of data: combined time for the two passes was 12 + 11 = 23 seconds. By comparison, a 4096K cache cut the time down to 11 + 6 = 17 seconds. Note that this is similar to the time taken by 32BFA.

At any rate, we definitely do have 32BFA now. As noted earlier, 32BFA and LFN support go hand-in-hand in Windows 95; both are provided by IFSMgr. To ensure that we now also have LFN support, we should repeat the experiment that failed earlier:

```
C:\VMM32>copy data.1 "3rd quarter 1994 report from Cleveland"
        1 file(s) copied

C:\VMM32>copy data.2 "Piano Concerto No. 20 in D minor"
        1 file(s) copied

C:\VMM32>dir
...
3RDQUART         36,517  09-13-94  8:43p 3rd quarter 1994 report from Cleveland
PIANOCON 20I    126,455  09-13-94  8:44p Piano Concerto No. 20 in D minor
```

You can also have long directory names. Figure 7-6 shows some examples; I've deleted uninteresting portions of the DIR output.


```
C:\VMM32>md "this is a long directory name"

C:\VMM32>dir /a:d

IOSUBSYS      <DIR>         06-13-94  4:25p IOSUBSYS
THISIS~1      <DIR>         06-13-94 10:49p this is a long directory name

C:\VMM32>cd "this is a long directory name"
C:\VMM32\THIS IS A LONG DIRECTORY NAME>ver > "a long filename with a.big exten-
sion"

C:\VMM32\THIS IS A LONG DIRECTORY NAME>dir

 Directory of C:\VMM32\THIS IS A LONG DIRECTORY NAME

ALONGFIL BIG          30  06-13-94 10:50p "a long filename with a.big extension"

C:\VMM32\THIS IS A LONG DIRECTORY NAME>dir *."big extension"

ALONGFIL BIG          30  06-13-94 10:50p "a long filename with a.big extension"
```

Figure 7-6: Directory listings will look very different once users start creating long filenames and directory names.

Notice that file extensions are no longer limited to three characters: A file extension consists of anything following the final dot in a filename. Notice too that you can do wildcard searches on these large extensions (DIR *."big extension").

All this is an important step up from WIN386, even from WIN386 with 32BFA. 32BFA in WfW 3.11 provided a 32-bit protected-mode implementation of the INT 21h file I/O API but didn't change the API itself, at least not in such a visible way. On the other hand, you could argue that, in bypassing the DOS INT 21h chain as we saw in the TEST21 example, WfW 3.11 *did* change the DOS API. In any case, Windows 95 is obviously providing a new DOS API, yet this API isn't available in real-mode DOS 7. To underline the point one last time: *you get this new DOS API only if VxDs are loaded.* That is an excellent illustration of the point that VxDs represent the future of DOS (albeit repackaged under the name Windows).

As an example of how to test for the presence of this new DOS API, LFN.C, shown in Listing 7-2, is a real-mode DOS program that calls INT 21h function 71A0h (Get Volume Information) and displays some information about the file system.

Listing 7-2: LFN.C

```
/* LFN.C -- test presence of long filename functions */

#include <stdlib.h>
#include <stdio.h>
#include <string.h>
#include <dos.h>

#define GET_VOLUME_INFORMATION          0x71A0
#define OLD_GET_VOLUME_INFORMATION      0x4302

#define FS_CASE_SENSITIVE               1
#define FS_CASE_IS_PRESERVED            2
#define FS_UNICODE_ON_DISK              4
#define FS_LFN_APIS                     0x4000
#define FS_VOLUME_COMPRESSED            0x8000

int GetVolumeInformation(char far *RootName,
    char far *Buffer, unsigned BufSize,
    unsigned *pFlags, unsigned *pMaxFilename, unsigned *pMaxPath)
{
    unsigned rbx, rcx, rdx;
    _asm {
         push ds
         push di
         les di, dword ptr Buffer
         lds dx, dword ptr RootName
         mov cx, BufSize
         mov ax, GET_VOLUME_INFORMATION
         int 21h
         pop di
         pop ds
         jc no_71A0
         mov rbx, bx
         mov rcx, cx
         mov rdx, dx
     }
    *pFlags = rbx;
    *pMaxFilename = rcx;
    *pMaxPath = rdx;
    return 0;
no_71A0:
    _asm xor ah, ah
```

```
    // error code in AL
}

main(int argc, char *argv[])
{
    char *RootName = (argc < 2) ? "C:\\" : argv[1];
    char Buffer[128];
    char *name;
    unsigned Flags, MaxFilename, MaxPath;
    int ret;

    if ((ret = GetVolumeInformation(RootName,
        Buffer, sizeof(Buffer),
        &Flags, &MaxFilename, &MaxPath)) != 0)
    {
        printf("%s -- No long filename (LFN) support\n", RootName);
        printf("error code: %d (%02Xh)\n", ret, ret);
        return 1;
    }

    printf("%s -- Long filename (LFN) support\n", RootName);
    printf("File system name: \"%s\"\n", Buffer);
    printf("MaxFilename: %d\n", MaxFilename);
    printf("MaxPath: %d\n", MaxPath);

    #define PRINT_FLAG(fl, s1, s2) \
        printf("%s\n", (Flags & (fl)) ? (s1) : (s2))

    PRINT_FLAG(FS_CASE_SENSITIVE,
        "Searches are case sensitive",
        "Searches are NOT case sensitive");
    PRINT_FLAG(FS_CASE_IS_PRESERVED,
        "Preserves case in directory entries",
        "Does NOT preserve case in directory entries");
    PRINT_FLAG(FS_LFN_APIS,
        "Supports DOS long filename functions",
        "Does NOT support DOS long filename functions");
    PRINT_FLAG(FS_VOLUME_COMPRESSED,
        "Volume is compressed",
        "Volume is NOT compressed");
    PRINT_FLAG(FS_UNICODE_ON_DISK,
        "Uses Unicode characters in file and directory names",
        "Does NOT use Unicode for file/directory names");

    return 0;
}
```

Figure 7-7 is the output from LFN, under real-mode DOS 7 and then in our minimal VMM32 setup. The "Uses Unicode" message *is* correct: Windows 95 stores file and directory names using two-byte characters.

```
C:\UNAUTHW>lfn
C: -- No long filename (LFN) support
```

```
C:\VMM32>runvmm32 \command.com

C:\VMM32>lfn
C:\ -- Long filename (LFN) support
File system name: "FAT"
MaxFilename: 255
MaxPath: 260
Searches are NOT case sensitive
Preserves case in directory entries
Supports DOS long filename functions
Volume is compressed
Uses Unicode characters in file and directory names

C:\VMM32>ren lfn.exe "Long Filename Test Program.exe"

C:\VMM32>"Long Filename Test Program"
m -- Long filename (LFN) support
File system name: "FAT"
MaxFilename: 255
MaxPath: 260
Searches are NOT case sensitive
Preserves case in directory entries
Supports DOS long filename functions
Volume is compressed
Uses Unicode characters in file and directory names
```

Figure 7-7: LFN reports that the maximum filename length is 255 characters, and that the maximum total path length is 260 characters.

Probably the most interesting thing in Figure 7-7 is its use of a long filename for an executable. It seemed appropriate that LFN.EXE should have a long filename, so I gave it the name "Long Filename Test Program.exe". This could be successfully launched from the VMM32 DOS prompt. However, there was one small problem (this *is* beta software, after all). Notice in Figure 7-7 that, when the program was executed using its long filename, the program received a command-line argument consisting of the final character of the long executable name.

Long filenames are a great addition to DOS, Windows, or whatever you want to call it. They are provided not by some amorphous mass called Windows 95, but specifically by the IFSMgr VxD in Windows. A version of IFSMgr without LFN support also existed in WfW 3.11. It seems clear that, from a purely technical standpoint, WfW 3.11 could have provided LFN support too. In one way LFN support is an enormous change, but in other ways it's just a logical use of the VxD capabilities that have resided in Windows for years.

The DblSpace VxD Saga

I noted a few moments ago that on machines running DblSpace or some other disk-compression software such as Stacker, 32BFA requires RMM to make the 16-bit real-mode compression software appear as though it were a 32-bit protected-mode disk driver.

Another solution, however, is to put disk compression into a genuine 32-bit protected-mode driver.

The Chicago pre-beta release from late 1993, distributed at Microsoft's Professional Developer's Conference in Anaheim, CA, came with VxDs for both DblSpace (DBLSPACE.386) and for the Microsoft Real-Time Compression Interface (MRCI32.386), which is the compression/decompression engine used by DblSpace and by other Microsoft utilities, such as BACKUP.

Neither DBLSPACE.386 nor MRCI32.386 appeared in the next major release of Chicago (the May 1994 beta), undoubtedly because in February 1994, a jury in federal district court in Los Angeles turned in its verdict in the *Stac v. Microsoft* case, finding that Microsoft's DblSpace infringed two disk-compression patents owned by Stac (US Patent No. 5,016,009, Doug Whiting et al., "Data Compression Apparatus and Method," May 14, 1991; US Patent No. 4,701,745, John Waterworth (Ferranti plc), "Data Compression System," October 20, 1987). The jury awarded Stac $120 million in damages.

Microsoft won a second part of the case, with $13.6 million damages, in which Microsoft argued that Stac's reverse engineering and use of the undocumented preload interface in MS-DOS 6 constituted a trade-secrets violation (see "LA Law," *Dr. Dobb's Journal*, May 1994).

On June 8, 1994, Federal District Judge Edward Rafeedie issued a permanent injunction that ordered Microsoft (and Vertisoft, whose DoubleDisk Microsoft licensed to create DblSpace) to "recall, erase or have destroyed," worldwide, all copies of MS-DOS 6.0, MS-DOS 6.2, Microsoft's Flash File System, Microsoft's Windows NT Remote Access Server, Vertisoft's DoubleDisk Gold, and "Any Microsoft product that contains the DoubleSpace compression technology contained in the commercial version of MS-DOS 6." Although not issued until June, an oral ruling had been issued several weeks earlier. So by the time Microsoft was ready to ship the May 1994 Chicago beta, it was clear that the judge was likely to issue an injunction against Microsoft's disk compression.

A few weeks after the injunction, there was an interesting twist. On June 21, Microsoft and Stac reached an out-of-court settlement, agreeing to drop all damages, payments, and appeals. Microsoft agreed to pay Stac $1 million per month for 43 months and to buy $39.9 million in Stac stock (representing about a 15% stake in the company). The two companies signed a patent cross-licensing agreement, so Microsoft is now free to use DblSpace, which the jury had found incorporated technology covered by Stac's patents. Stac, conversely, is now free to use the undocumented preload interface. Although Microsoft has licensed Stac's patents, not its products, there's always the possibility that future Microsoft operating systems might borrow something from Stac's superior disk-compression technology.

As a sneak preview for 32-bit protected-mode disk-compression software, I thought it would be useful to take the DBLSPACE.386 and MRCI32.386 VxDs from the December pre-beta release and drop them into the VMM32 setup:

```
copy \oldchic\dblspace.386 iosubsys
copy \oldchic\mrci32.386
```

After adding the lines:

```
DEVICE=C:\VMM32\IOSUBSYS\DBLSPACE.386
DEVICE=C:\VMM32\MRCI32.386
```

to SYSTEM.INI and restarting VMM32, the VXDLIST program shows that, indeed, the VxDs are loaded:

```
Name      Vers   ID     DDB       Control   V86 API   PM API    #Srvc
--------  ----   -----  --------  --------  --------  --------  -----
MRCI32    3.10   0042h  C0FD16D4  C0FD167C                      5
DBLSPACE  3.10          C001AC30  C00186D0                      0
```

Now, what effect does this have? Unfortunately, these VxDs don't appear to be drop-in replacements for the real-mode DblSpace and MRCI code. Performance is not greatly improved when these VxDs are loaded, and the real-mode code doesn't appear to be bypassed. For instance, by running the INTCHAIN utility (included on the *Unauthorized Windows 95* disk), we can see that both the DblSpace and MRCI Get Version functions are handled by the real-mode code:

```
C:\VMM32>intchain 2f/4a11/0

Tracing INT 2F AX=4A11
109 instructions

1D77:0F27   WINICE
1892:0EF2   DOSKEY
12EA:01C8   COMMAND
12E9:0154   COMMAND
FFFF:F94F   HMA
```

```
0385:0017   DBLSYSH$
0313:006C   XMSXXXX0
0215:0808   IFS$HLP$
01F6:002D   D:
03BC:41A3   DBLSYSH$
01F6:0028   D:
03BC:1478   DBLSYSH$

C:\VMM32>intchain 2f/4a12/0/4d52/4349

Tracing INT 2F AX=4A12
74 instructions

1D77:0F27   WINICE
1892:0EF2   DOSKEY
12EA:01C8   COMMAND
12E9:0154   COMMAND
FFFF:F94F   HMA
0385:0017   DBLSYSH$
```

Among the data returned by the MRCI Get Version function is a callable far function pointer to the MRCI server. MRCI clients call this entry point with requests to compress and decompress blocks of in-memory data. (DblSpace takes care of moving data to and from the disk, and MRCI does the actual compression/decompression of the data.)

Normally the server entry point will have some address such as 0385:001E. However, when MRCI32 is loaded, it changes this to an odd-looking address such as FBA1:2632. Furthermore, disassembling this address reveals that it starts off with an illegal instruction, ARPL, which causes a GP fault if issued from V86 mode. This ARPL instruction represents a *V86 callback*. When a DOS program executes the illegal instruction, this causes a trap into VMM, which can then see where the fault came from (in this case FBA1:2632) and use that address to locate a piece of VxD code intended to handle this fault. VxDs such as MRCI32 allocate these odd V86 callbacks by using (naturally enough) the Allocate_V86_Call_Back routine supplied by VMM. Here, MRCI32 is obviously intercepting all calls to the MRCI server.

For its part, the DBLSPACE VxD appears to interact closely with VCACHE, presumably with the intention of caching *compressed* rather than uncompressed file data. This would nearly double the effective size of the cache.

What all this means is that we're definitely going to be seeing disk-compression VxDs in Windows 95, even though the May 1994 beta couldn't provide any such support because of the then-impending injunction against DblSpace and even though the drivers in the December 1993 pre-beta appeared to have fairly limited goals.

Four Steps Toward DOS Nirvana

Probably the most significant feature we've seen here is the support for long filenames and directory names in Windows 95. This new DOS interface, provided by a VxD and implemented in 32-bit protected mode, shows the next step in the evolution of DOS. This new DOS interface is available only when running under VxDs; real-mode DOS doesn't include code to support long filenames.

How did we reach this point where new DOS interfaces are being made available only via 32-bit protected mode? Quite gradually. In the past few chapters, we've seen slow but steady movement, all under the guise of Windows, towards a protected-mode DOS:

- DOSX (like any DPMI server or DOS extender) showed that protected-mode services can be retrofitted onto DOS.
- WIN386 provided all the basic functionality for a V86 DOS, including VMM and VxD services with which more interesting functionality can be produced.
- 32BFA took advantage of VMM and VxD services to reimplement file access, which is the most important part of DOS in 32-bit protected mode. (We didn't get into this much, but in Windows 3.1, 32-bit disk access did the same thing for a key part of the ROM BIOS.)
- VMM32 adds new VMM and VxD services, and creates an entirely new DOS interface that isn't available under real-mode DOS.

It seems likely that all future additions to the foundations of DOS and Windows will be made with VxDs; it's hard to imagine any substantial additions to the real-mode DOS code base. Does this mean that "DOS is dead," as so many trade publications have announced? Not quite. While the real-mode DOS code is unlikely to see much, if any, improvement, the DOS INT 21h interface seems alive and kicking. We'll see in later chapters that even the newest Win32 application, under the covers, makes massive use of the INT 21h interface.

In other words, DOS isn't dead, nor does it need to die. As our experiments with WIN386 and VMM32 have shown, DOS has basically turned into a 32-bit protected-mode operating system, organized around a VMM and consisting of VxDs. In the next few chapters we'll see that these VxDs continue to call down to the real-mode DOS code quite frequently. However, we'll see also that VxDs are on top and that the real-mode DOS code is playing a subservient role.

Chapter 8

The Case of the Gradually Disappearing DOS

Microsoft has been claiming — and the computer trade press has been dutifully repeating — that Windows 95 is a brand-new operating system that does not require MS-DOS. But if the truth be known, Windows 95 continues to use real-mode DOS. Frankly, there's nothing wrong with Windows 95's employment of DOS; the problem is Microsoft's unwillingness to admit it.

More important, however, is the fact that although Windows 95 bypasses DOS for most operations, the same thing is true of 32-bit file access (32BFA) in Windows for Workgroups (WfW) 3.11. In fact, WfW bypasses DOS to a greater extent than Windows 95 does. As we'll see, this is a flaw in WfW.

Perhaps most important, though, is that Windows 95's ability to bypass real-mode code has been part of Windows 3.*x* Enhanced mode from its very beginnings in 1990. Indeed, this ability goes back further still, to Windows/386 2.*x*, which Microsoft introduced in 1988.

With Windows 95, then, Microsoft is doing nothing more (or less) than making particularly extensive use of what is by now a nearly ancient Windows feature: the capability to take services normally handled in 16-bit real mode by DOS, device drivers, TSRs, or the BIOS and instead handle them in 32-bit protected mode. The fact is, even Windows 3.*x* Enhanced mode was a genuine 32-bit protected-mode operating system:

- When Windows Enhanced mode is running, MS-DOS is no longer the operating system. DOS is only an assistant to Windows. This is true in Windows 3.*x*; it hasn't changed in Windows 95.

- The operating system is actually the Windows Virtual Machine Manager (VMM), assisted by the Windows Virtual Device Drivers (VxDs). This has been true since the introduction of Windows 3.0 in 1990.
- Under Windows, INT 21h — and in fact all interrupts — are serviced first (and sometimes, only) in 32-bit protected mode. For example, there isn't much sense in calling _dos_getvect (0x21) to see where INT 21h is handled. Before (and sometimes instead of) routing interrupts through the low-memory Interrupt Vector Table (IVT), Windows first (and sometimes only) uses an entirely different 80x86 data structure, the protected-mode Interrupt Descriptor Table (IDT).
- INT 21h calls aren't necessarily serviced by DOS. DOS gets to service INT 21h only if Windows lets it. More and more, as we'll see, Windows *doesn't* let it: Since 1990, real-mode DOS has been slowly but surely disappearing.

The TEST21 and TEST2F16 programs in this chapter provide convincing proof for these outrageous-sounding claims. These programs show that DOS calls don't necessarily go to DOS but are instead sometimes handled within Windows. They also show that this gradual replacement of real-mode DOS by Windows has been going on right under our noses for at least five years, since the introduction of Enhanced mode in Windows 3.0. And finally, these programs show that this process has not been completed even in Windows 95, and has actually taken a small but necessary step *backward* from WfW 3.11.

In other words, Windows 95 is the "new" protected-mode operating system we've had all along.

Bypassing DOS

TEST21.C, shown in Listing 8-1, is a real-mode DOS program that installs an INT 21h handler and then issues some INT 21h calls. The INT 21h handler should see the program's own INT 21h calls. Even if some memory-resident DOS program (TSR) hooks INT 21h, TEST21's own INT 21h handler will have been installed more recently and should see the program's own INT 21h calls first. But, as you'll see in a minute, TEST21's behavior is sometimes not what you'd expect. And, although TEST21 is a boring-looking DOS program, you'll see that it can reveal quite a bit about the workings of the newest versions of Windows.

Listing 8-1: TEST21.C

```
/*
TEST21.C  -- See if INT 21h calls are reflected to V86 mode
Andrew Schulman, 1994
bcc -2 -P- test21.c
bcc -2 -P- -DTESTFILE="test" test21.c

test21
test21 -mysetvect
test21 > tmp.tmp
*/

#include <stdlib.h>
#include <stdio.h>
#include <string.h>
#include <time.h>
#include <dos.h>
#include <fcntl.h>

typedef unsigned short WORD;
typedef unsigned long DWORD;

#pragma pack(1)

typedef struct {
#ifdef __TURBOC__
    WORD bp,di,si,ds,es,dx,cx,bx,ax;
#else
    WORD es,ds,di,si,bp,sp,bx,dx,cx,ax;      /* same as PUSHA */
#endif
    WORD ip,cs,flags;
    } REG_PARAMS;

static void interrupt far int21(REG_PARAMS r);
static void interrupt far ctrl_c(REG_PARAMS r);
static void interrupt far crit_err(REG_PARAMS r);
static int failed = 0;

typedef void (interrupt far *INTPROC)();
static INTPROC old_21 = (INTPROC) 0;

static void (*setv)(unsigned intno, INTPROC proc) = _dos_setvect;
static INTPROC (*getv)(unsigned intno) = _dos_getvect;

static DWORD total_called = 0;
static DWORD called[0x100] = {0};
static DWORD total_received = 0;
static DWORD received[0x100] = {0};

void fail(const char *s) { puts(s); exit(1); }

void my_setvect(unsigned intno, INTPROC proc)
{
    INTPROC far *ivt = (INTPROC far *) 0L;
```

```
    ivt[intno] = proc;
}

INTPROC my_getvect(unsigned intno)
{
    INTPROC far *ivt = (INTPROC far *) 0L;
    return ivt[intno];
}

main(int argc, char *argv[])
{
    char *filename = argv[0];
    time_t t1, t2;
    WORD num_iter = 100;
    WORD i;
    int use_my_setvect = 0;
    int received_less = 0, received_more = 0;

    for (i=1; i<argc; i++)
        if (argv[i][0] == '-' || argv[i][0] == '/')
        {
            char *s = strupr(&argv[i][1]);
            if ((strncmp(s, "MYSETVECT", 2)) == 0)
            {
                use_my_setvect++;
                setv = my_setvect;
                getv = my_getvect;
                printf("Using my_setvect\n");
            }
            else
                fail("usage: test21 [-mysetvect] [num_iter] [filename]");
        }
        else if (atoi(argv[i]))
            num_iter = atoi(argv[i]);
        else
            filename = argv[i];

    time(&t1);

    /* hook INT INT 21h, and prepare to restore upon Ctrl-C, Crit Err */
    old_21 = (*getv)(0x21);
    (*setv)(0x23, ctrl_c);
    (*setv)(0x24, crit_err);
    (*setv)(0x21, int21);

    /* issue INT 21h calls */
    for (i=0; i<num_iter; i++)
    {
    #ifdef   TESTFILE
    #include TESTFILE
    #else
        unsigned n;
        char buf;
        int f;

        // we don't care if these calls succeed or fail
```

```
        _dos_open(filename, O_RDWR, &f); called[0x3d]++;  // or 0x6c
        _dos_read(f, &buf, 1, &n); called[0x3f]++;
        _dos_close(f); called[0x3e]++;
        _dos_open(filename, O_RDWR, &f); called[0x3d]++;  // or 0x6c
        _dos_write(f, &buf, 1, &n); called[0x40]++;
        buf = '.';
        #define STDOUT 1
        _dos_write(STDOUT, &buf, 1, &n); called[0x40]++;
        _dos_close(f); called[0x3e]++;
        total_called += 7;
    #endif
        if (failed)
        {
            (*setv)(0x21, old_21);
            fail("\nCritical error!");
        }
        // See if anyone is playing the old SideKick trick
        if (my_getvect(0x21) != int21)
            fail("\nSomeone grabbed my INT 21h!");
    }

    /* unhook INT 21h: don't forget to include this call too
       (unless if using my_setvect rather than _dos_setvect)! */
    (*setv)(0x21, old_21);
    if (! use_my_setvect) { called[0x25]++; total_called++; }
    // INT 23h and 24h automatically restored on exit

    time(&t2);

    /* display results */
    printf("\n%lu seconds elapsed\n\n", t2 - t1);
    printf("Generated %lu calls\tReceived %lu calls\n",
        total_called, total_received);
    for (i=0; i<0x100; i++)
        if (called[i] || received[i])
        {
            printf("21/%02X\t%lu called\t%lu received\t\t",
                i, called[i], received[i]);
            if (received[i] < called[i])
            {
                received_less++; printf("-");
            }
            else if (received[i] > called[i])
            {
                received_more++; printf("+");
            }
            printf("\n");
        }

    printf("\n");
    if (received_less)
        printf("Some INT 21h are handled without calling DOS!\n");
    if (received_more)
        printf("Some extra INT 21h calls are occurring!\n");
    if (! (received_less || received_more))
```

```
        printf("INT 21h appears to be handled in the normal way\n");

    return 0;
}

void interrupt far int21(REG_PARAMS r)
{
    total_received++;
    received[r.ax >> 8]++;
    _chain_intr(old_21);
}

void interrupt far ctrl_c(REG_PARAMS r)
{
    (*setv)(0x21, old_21);
    fail("Ctrl-C detected!");
}

void interrupt far crit_err(REG_PARAMS r)
{
    failed++;
    r.ax = 3;    // fail the operation
}
```


The code for TEST21 is fairly straightforward. The main function calls the _dos_setvect C library function (or, if -MYSETVECT is specified on the command line, the my_setvect function discussed later in this chapter) to install a handler for INT 21h. This handler, at the very bottom of TEST21.C, has the highly original name of int21. Each time int21 is called, it uses the incoming DOS function number in AH to index into an array of counters. After incrementing the appropriate counter, int21 uses the _chain_intr function to pass the interrupt to the previously installed handler, whose address was retrieved earlier when TEST21 called _dos_getvect or my_getvect.

After installing the int21 handler (and hooking Ctrl-C and Critical Error to unhook INT 21h if the program terminates unexpectedly), TEST21 then runs a loop issuing some DOS calls. Notice the #ifdef TESTFILE. Later, we'll define TESTFILE on the compiler command line so we can use TEST21 as a generic test rig. By default, however, each time through the loop TEST21 opens a file, reads a byte, closes the file, opens the file again, writes a byte, writes . (a period) to stdout (which can be redirected to a disk file with a command such as TEST21 > FOO.BAR), and closes the file. For each DOS call, TEST21 increments a counter.

If you don't specify a different filename on the command line, the file that TEST21 reads each time through the loop happens to be the program itself, that is, TEST21.EXE. (TEST21 learns its own filename from the C expression argv[0].) At least for an initial test, we don't care *what* TEST21 reads or even if it succeeds — we just want to generate some INT 21h calls and see them show up at TEST21's own INT 21h handler.

After the DOS-call loop is complete, TEST21 unhooks its int21 handler by restoring the previous handler and then displays the test results. For each possible INT 21h function number 0 through FFh, TEST21 sees how many calls to that function were issued and how many calls its INT 21h handler received. Obviously, these two numbers should match.

When TEST21 is running under plain-vanilla DOS, the numbers *do* match. Given how the program is structured, this is hardly surprising. Figure 8-1 shows the rather boring results.


```
C:\UNAUTHW>test21
21 seconds elapsed

Generated 701 calls      Received 701 calls
21/25    1 called        1 received
21/3D    200 called      200 received
21/3E    200 called      200 received
21/3F    100 called      100 received
21/40    200 called      200 received

INT 21h appears to be handled in the normal way
```

Figure 8-1: When TEST21 runs under a plain-vanilla DOS configuration, DOS receives all the INT 21h calls made by the program.

Aside from the "INT 21h appears to be handled in the normal way" message, indicating that — of course — DOS INT 21h handlers handle INT 21h calls, the only marginally interesting item in Figure 8-1 is the "21 seconds elapsed" output.

The time will differ from one configuration to the next. If you redirect TEST21's output to a file, the time goes up quite a bit (in the configuration I used here, to 29 seconds), because DOS must write each period to a file on disk rather than to the screen.

If you run TEST21 under a disk cache such as Microsoft's SmartDrv, the elapsed time drops radically (not surprising given that TEST21 does unbuffered reads and writes of only one byte at a time). In this same configuration, running TEST21 under SmartDrv cut the time to about 4 seconds, (or 5 seconds when redirecting TEST21's output to a disk file).

The test in Figure 8-1 was run on a compressed DoubleSpace drive. If run instead on a non-DoubleSpace drive without a disk cache, the elapsed time again drops dramatically, as shown in Table 8-1.

Table 8-1: Elapsed time (in seconds) for TEST21

	DblSpace drive	**Host (non-DblSpace) drive**
TEST21		
No cache	21	7
Cache	4	< 1
TEST21 > FOO.BAR		
No cache	29	10
Cache	5	1

Now let's take TEST21 and run it in a DOS box under WfW 3.11, with 32-bit file access (32BFA) enabled. To enable 32BFA, Microsoft makes you tunnel through a series of several dialog boxes: run Control Panel, select the 386 Enhanced icon, select Virtual Memory (yes, Virtual Memory, even though it's unclear what this has to do with 32-bit *file* access, as opposed to disk access), select Change, and then check the Use 32-Bit File Access box. You must restart Windows for 32BFA to take effect.

Figure 8-2 shows the results from running TEST21 under 32BFA. These results are quite surprising, especially since we only checked one box buried in an obscure Control Panel dialog box.

```
C:\UNAUTHW>test21
0 seconds elapsed

Generated 701 calls     Received 101 calls
21/25   1 called        1 received
21/3D   200 called      0 received      -
21/3E   200 called      0 received      -
21/3F   100 called      0 received      -
21/40   200 called      100 received    -

Some INT 21h are handled without calling DOS!
```

Figure 8-2: When TEST21 runs under WfW 3.11 with 32BFA enabled, most of the INT 21h calls generated by the program bypass DOS.

First, note that TEST21 took less than one second to run. I didn't have SmartDrv (or any other disk cache) loaded here. If I had, the results would have been the same anyway, because 32BFA supplies its own built-in, dynamically sized file cache (the VCACHE VxD). On a DblSpace drive, TEST21 runs faster with 32BFA but without SmartDrv than it does with SmartDrv but without 32BFA. (Yes, I know that's a mouthful. See the "32BFA versus disk cache performance" sidebar later in this chapter.)

Second, notice the "Some INT 21h are handled without calling DOS!" message. Even if you assumed that 32BFA means that Windows somehow "bypasses" DOS (whatever that means), these results are still pretty amazing: TEST21's INT 21h handler doesn't see most of the program's own INT 21h file I/O calls!

One important note: If you've run TEST21 from a floppy disk, your results will look like Figure 8-1 rather than Figure 8-2. This indicates that WfW 3.11 does not provide 32BFA for floppies. We'll see later that this has been corrected in Windows 95.

The minus sign (-) indicates that TEST21 saw fewer calls than it expected from a given DOS function. TEST21 puts up a plus sign (+) if it sees *more* INT 21h calls than it expected, which, believe it or not, can also happen.

TEST21 *did* see its own call to INT 21h function 25h (Set Interrupt Vector), which unhooked the INT 21h handler. But while TEST21 issued 200 calls to INT 21h function 3Dh (File Open), its INT 21h handler saw *zero* calls to that function. Ditto for function 3Eh (File Close) and function 3Fh (File Read).

TEST21 issued 200 calls to function 40h (File Write), but it saw only 100 calls to that function. If you redirect TEST21's output to a file (for example, TEST21 > FOO.BAR), TEST21 no longer sees any calls to function 40h either. Empirically, 32BFA must send function 40h writes to the screen down the INT 21h chain, but it must intercept and block writes to disk files.

But given that the int21 function in Listing 8-1 is the most recently installed INT 21h handler, this interception of INT 21h calls seems impossible. In Listing 8-1 there is practically nothing coming between the call to _dos_setvect (or my_setvect) and the call to dos_open. How could someone have slipped another INT 21h handler in there ahead of TEST21?! Furthermore, if TEST21 isn't going to see this INT 21h call, how is DOS (which is installed much earlier in the INT 21h chain) ever going to see it?

The answer to the second question is that DOS *isn't* going to see these INT 21h calls. Using the V86TEST program from Chapter 10, I've confirmed that the INT 21h calls issued by TEST21, when running under WfW 3.11 with 32BFA, really and truly are not sent down to any software that is loaded before Windows, including DOS itself. While TEST21 was running, V86TEST saw the following INT 21h calls:

```
INT 21h calls:
02: 8   08: 7   0B: 2433        19: 2   1A: 11  25: 10  29: 4
```

```
2A: 3   2C: 3   30: 1   35: 5   38: 1   3E: 15  40: 121 44: 2
48: 2   49: 1   4A: 1   4B: 1   4C: 1   4D: 1   5D: 2   71: 2
```

Without getting into the other INT 21h calls seen by V86TEST, we can see that this matches pretty well with what TEST21 itself shows: No calls to function 3Fh were detected, but over 100 calls to function 40h were. If TEST21's output is redirected to a file, the V86TEST log of function 40h calls also drops, just as you'd expect:

```
02: 18  08: 13  0B: 2915        19: 3   1A: 11  25: 10  29: 4
2A: 3   2C: 3   30: 1   35: 5   38: 1   3E: 15  40: 3   44: 1
48: 2   49: 1   4A: 1   4B: 1   4C: 1   4D: 1   5D: 2   71: 3
```


So 32BFA somehow does keep most file I/O DOS calls away from DOS and, in WfW, away from even the most recently installed INT 21h hooker in a DOS box. Well, this is pretty much what Microsoft says 32BFA does, so it shouldn't come as much of a surprise.

But consider the mechanism involved: TEST21 has hooked INT 21h *just before* issuing these INT 21h calls. Yet Windows has somehow grabbed INT 21h away from TEST21. You might think that perhaps Windows is playing the same trick for which SideKick was notorious in the bad old days of DOS TSRs: SideKick would hook the timer interrupt and ensure upon each timer tick that its other interrupt handlers were still in place. However, TEST21 checks for this possibility by verifying each time through its DOS-call loop that my_getvect(0x21) = int21. The only time I've seen TEST21 display its "Someone grabbed my INT 21h!" message was while running within an EMACS process buffer in the Epsilon text editor.

Clearly, 32BFA does not hook INT 21h in any simple-minded way. Indeed, Microsoft's excellent WfW 3.11 *Resource Kit* (pp. 1-20) notes that 32BFA works "by intercepting the MS-DOS Int 21H services in protected mode." TEST21 shows that this is true: 32BFA is somehow *intercepting* (as opposed to merely hooking) INT 21h.

I keep saying "somehow." You might be wondering, How *does* Windows intercept INT 21h? I'm going to explain this in more detail in the "Interrupts 101: The IDT versus the IVT" section at the end of this chapter, but the basic idea is that Windows uses the protected-mode Interrupt Descriptor Table (IDT) to intercept interrupts coming from real-mode programs running in V86 mode. As the IDTMAP program on the *Unauthorized Windows 95* disk helps show, these interrupts go to the Windows VMM and to other VxDs.

This is true not only of INT 21h but of *all* interrupts coming from V86 mode. Nor is this just a feature of 32BFA. Windows in 386

Enhanced mode has always intercepted all interrupts coming from V86 mode, because that is how V86 mode works. All V86 environments behave the same way: When a DOS user is running a 386 memory manager such as EMM386, QEMM, 386MAX, or NetRoom, interrupts are handled first in protected mode, before DOS or any DOS TSRs or device drivers ever see them.

Yet, if you run TEST21 with a 386 memory manager but without 32BFA, TEST21 claims that "INT 21h appears to be handled in the normal way." If 386 memory managers behave essentially the same as 32BFA, why doesn't TEST21 reveal this?

The answer is simple: When a 386 memory manager (or Windows Enhanced mode without 32BFA) intercepts an INT from V86 mode, it sends (or *reflects*) this call back down to V86 mode. What makes 32BFA different is that it often doesn't bother to do this: It handles many INT 21h calls entirely in protected mode, without reflecting the call down to V86 mode. The calls that TEST21 *does* see when running under Windows are simply those that VMM or other VxDs have chosen to reflect. In the case of 32BFA, the key VxD is the Installable File System Manager, IFSMgr. Later in this chapter, we'll examine some of the IFSMgr code that produces the behavior we're seeing with TEST21.

The important point is that in 386 Enhanced mode, V86 interrupts under Windows have *always* passed through the IDT. In Enhanced mode, the DOS Get Interrupt Vector function (_dos_getvect, INT 21h function 35h) has never correctly determined who will first see an interrupt; VMM and other VxDs have always seen the interrupt first. Figure 8-3 shows that they have complete discretion over how to handle the interrupt. They might very well decide not to pass the interrupt down to real-mode programs. Back in Figure 8-2, for example, they did pass down the _dos_setvect (function 25h) call and the _dos_write (function 40h) calls involving stdout, but they didn't pass down any I/O calls involving disk files.

Putting it in the strongest terms, what Figure 8-2 shows is that Windows is the operating system and DOS is a subservient subsystem that Windows can use to handle whatever calls it doesn't feel like bothering with. And although the TEST21 results are admittedly unusual, this behavior is implicit both in Intel's documentation for V86 mode and in Microsoft's documentation for VxDs. In particular, see the Windows Device Driver Kit (DDK) documentation for the Hook_V86_Int_Chain service.

Like Mr. Jourdain in Moliere's play *Le Bourgeois gentilhomme*, who one day is delighted to discover that he's been speaking prose all his life, it has taken 32BFA to make us realize that we've had a 32-bit protected-mode operating system, called the Windows VMM, sitting right in front of us *all along*. 32BFA makes it impossible to continue ignoring this "new" old operating system.

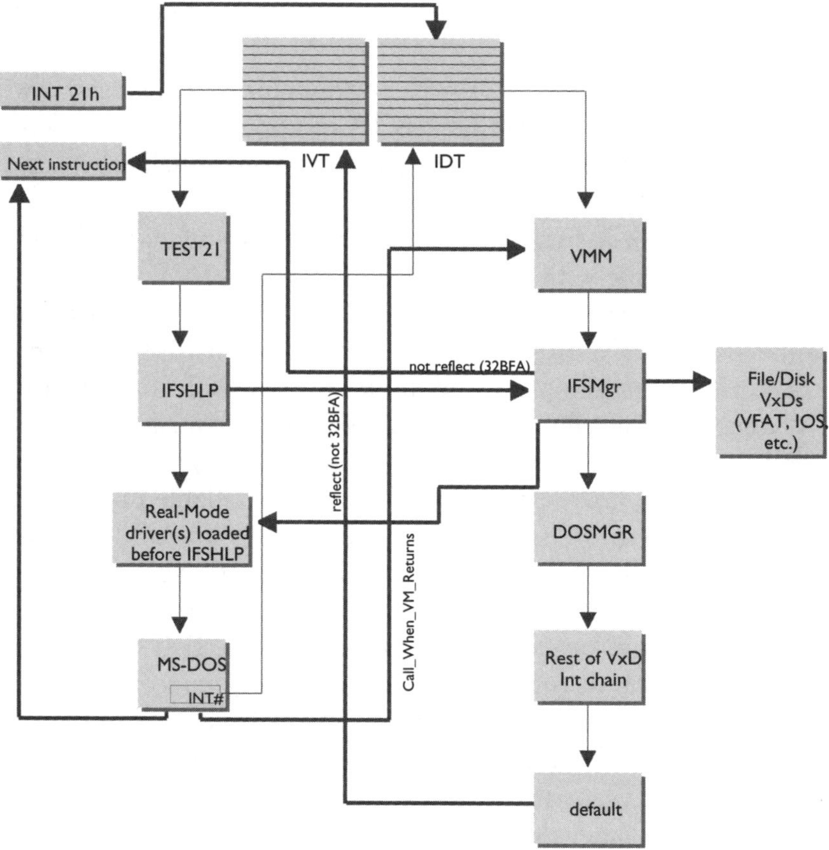

Figure 8-3: Depending on the function, a software interrupt can take several paths. If 32-BFA handles the call in protected mode, it follows the path from the program calling INT 21h to the protected mode IDT, VMM, ISFMgr, and back to the program. If the call is reflected to DOS, however, the path continues through the VxD chain to the real-mode IVT, then down the DOS interrupt chain. The real-mode IFSHLP driver can send the call back to IFSMgr. Once inside MS-DOS, if there's another interrupt, the path repeats recursively.

All the same, it can be surprising to discover how few people have checked the appropriate box in the Control Panel to enable 32BFA. And as we'll see later, 32BFA *can* cause such problems. But even with these problems, when you consider the PC industry's complaints about MS-DOS and how much it's supposedly holding back Windows, it is odd that most power users and developers tend to ignore what is essentially a 32-bit protected-mode version of DOS.

32BFA versus disk cache performance

It's not clear why more users and developers didn't jump up and down about 32BFA in WfW 3.11. Certainly 32BFA has some problems. The biggest one is that if Windows crashes, you lose all the data in 32BFA's file cache. But that's the same risk taken by anyone using a write-behind disk cache. (In fact, 32BFA can be safer than SmartDrv, because there's no write-behind cache in WfW 3.11.)

Another possible explanation is that the performance benefits of 32BFA are somewhat confusing. A *Byte* (February 1994) review of WfW 3.11 by Jon Udell noted the following performance characteristics of 32BFA:

> *The results can be impressive. An Advanced Logic Research Flyer 32LCT 4DX2/66 with an IDE controller more than doubled its sequential file I/O throughput using the VFAT/VCACHE combo, while bettering its random file I/O throughput by about a third. But, on an Everex Step 486DX2/50 with an Adaptec AHA-1742 controller and an IBM PS/2 Model 90 XP 486 with an IBM SCSI-2 controller, the story was quite different. Here, random file I/O throughput improved by 73 percent and 83 percent, respectively. These marks were close to (for the Everex) or better than (for the PS/2) those posted by Windows NT on the same two machines. But in both cases, 32-bit file access hurt sequential file I/O performance. The PS/2 lost a fifth of its 16-bit throughput; the Everex lost a fourth. This degradation made application load times noticeably slower on the two SCSI machines.*

How does 32BFA differ from a disk cache? I've received reports saying things like "Surprisingly, with a reasonably sized SmartDrv cache (which is otherwise disabled by default by WFW), 16-bit mode is faster for most operations." In my admittedly limited testing with SmartDrv 5.0 on about half a dozen machines, TEST21 doesn't confirm these reports. For example, in a DOS box under WfW 3.11, on both a compressed DblSpace drive and its non-DblSpace host drive, I ran TEST21 3000 > FOO.BAR on a 486SL with an IDE hard-disk controller and collected the following results:

Configuration	Host drive*	DblSpace drive*
32BFA, no SmartDrv	5	8
SmartDrv, no 32BFA	15	171
No 32BFA, no SmartDrv	251	800

* *Elapsed time in seconds*

In addition to SmartDrv, I also tried Helix Software's protected-mode CacheClk. Although it was certainly faster than SmartDrv, it too did not even approach the 32BFA times. In this test, 32BFA is a clear winner over a disk cache, not to mention over raw DOS, on both DblSpace drives and non-DblSpace drives.

Of course, TEST21 is somewhat contrived. I also tried a more realistic example using grep to search for a non-present string ("foobish") in 3210K of data from Ralf Brown's interrupt list (\UNDOCDOS\INTRLIST\INTERRUP.*). I performed the search twice so that a cache would optimize the second search if the data were already in memory. In the results listed here, 1 and 2 indicate the first and second searches. I performed the searches both on a compressed DblSpace drive and on its non-DblSpace host drive.

Configuration	Host drive*	DblSpace drive*
(A) Real-mode DOS, no cache		
Search 1	15.4	16.9
Search 2	15.4	16.8
(B) 32BFA, no disk cache		
Search 1	12.6	17.5
Search 2	10.1	10.4
(C) CACHECLK 3400		
Search 1	16.0	16.7
Search 2	10.1	13.0
(D) CACHECLK 3287		
Search 1	16.1	16.9
Search 2	16.0	13.0
(E) CACHECLK 1800		
Search 1	16.1	16.8
Search 2	16.1	13.0
(F) CACHECLK 1750		
Search 1	16.1	16.8
Search 2	16.0	16.8

* *Elapsed time in seconds.*

These results give a better picture of one 32BFA benefit: It dynamically resizes its file cache, based on available memory and the user's needs. In test B, 32BFA was able to optimize search 2 on both the DblSpace and non-DblSpace drives without any end-user fine-tuning of the cache size. Notice also that, whereas search 1 took a good deal longer on the DblSpace drive, in search 2 32BFA largely erased the usual performance hit from DblSpace: The data came out of the 32BFA file cache, so DblSpace basically dropped out of the picture. At the same time, also note that 32BFA made search 1 take slightly longer on the DblSpace drive.

In test C, I used Helix Software's CACHECLK with CACHESIZE=3400. Since DIR reported 3210K of data, it isn't surprising that the disk cache could optimize search 2 on both the DblSpace and non-DblSpace drives. Note that CACHECLK turned in the same time as 32BFA for search 2 on the non-DblSpace drive. On the other hand, 32BFA appears to solidly outperform disk caches (even a good one like CACHECLK) on DblSpace drives.

Next, in test D, since DIR reported 3,287,421 bytes of data, I naively set CACHESIZE=3287. As you can see, for the non-DblSpace drive this cache size was too small: search 2 took as long as search 1. This points to a major benefit of 32BFA over disk caches: Whereas a disk cache will be worthless if its size is even slightly smaller than the user's file I/O "working set," 32BFA *adapts* itself to the user's file I/O patterns.

But why, with an apparently insufficient cache size for the non-DblSpace drive in test D, was CACHECLK still able to shave 3.7 seconds off search 2 on the DblSpace drive? Because CACHECLK was caching the *compressed* data, which fit into the same 3287K cache in which the noncompressed data wouldn't go.

Test C showed that CACHESIZE=3400 was sufficient for the noncompressed data, and DIR /CH reported a 2.0:1.0 compression ratio. Nonetheless, when I tried CACHESIZE=1700, it was too small to have any effect on search 2. Tests E and F reflect a *binary search* that I did to find the proper cache size for the compressed data; it turned out that CACHESIZE=1750 was too small and that CACHESIZE=1800 was sufficient. By playing around with cache sizes in this way, you can see that the true compression ratio must be about 1.8:1.0 (3400/1800).

Anyway, the point is that 32BFA seems to eliminate the need to manually fine-tune cache sizes. Besides, 32BFA provides nonperformance benefits. For example, long filename (LFN) support in Windows 95 is really a by-product of IFSMgr's capability to bypass the old DOS file system code.

At the same time, 32BFA's performance resembles the performance of a fancy cache. The cache aspect of 32BFA is managed by a VxD called VCACHE. Although VCACHE (like all the other 32BFA components, including IFSMgr and VFAT) is undocumented in WfW 3.11, both IFSMgr and VCACHE are supposed to be documented in Microsoft's Device Driver Kit (DDK) for Windows 95. This might provide some interesting opportunities for third-party developers to improve on VCACHE, in the same way that they improved on SmartDrv.

Getting and Setting the Current Drive

As an alternative to the open/read/close/open/write/close sequence of INT 21h calls we've been using, TEST21's DOS-call loop can instead include a file designated on the compiler's command line with -DTESTFILE ="filename" (see Listing 8-1). This allows TEST21 to be used as a rig for other INT 21h tests.

As just one example, which we'll examine in considerable detail, the little test in Listing 8-2 is a standard piece of DOS code to get the LASTDRIVE= setting. It does this by calling INT 21h function 19h to get the current drive and by passing this value to function 0Eh (Set Current Drive), which also happens to return the value of LASTDRIVE (see *Undocumented DOS*, 2d ed., pp. 68-69).

Listing 8-2: TEST_1

```
/* TEST_1 for TEST21.C:
   21/19 (Get Current Drive) and 21/0E (Set Current Drive) */

_asm mov ah, 19h
_asm int 21h
_asm mov dl, al
_asm mov ah, 0Eh
_asm int 21h
/* LASTDRIVE now in AL */

called[0x19]++;
called[0x0e]++;
total_called += 2;
```

If you recompile TEST21 with -DTESTFILE="test_1" and run the new TEST21 under 32BFA, you don't get the "Some INT 21h are handled without calling DOS!" message. Windows doesn't bypass DOS for these Get/Set current-drive calls. Yet the results are distinctly odd, as you can see in Figure 8-4.

```
Generated 201 calls       Received 301 calls
21/0E    100 called       100 received
21/19    100 called       200 received        +
21/25    1 called         1 received

Some extra INT 21h calls are occurring!
```

Figure 8-4: In this example from WfW 3.11 with 32BFA, DOS has received more calls than TEST21 generated.

Someone, somehow, is generating *extra* calls to function 19h. But who? How? Why? This provides us with a good excuse to sneak a peak at the code in the Installable File System Manager VxD, IFSMgr. We'll see that even when Windows does let DOS do its thing, it keeps DOS on a short leash.

During its device initialization, IFSMgr uses VMM services to install handlers for all INT 21h calls that occur in either V86 or protected mode (PM). Figure 8-5 shows a fragment of the IFSMgr initialization code.

```
;;; Install V86 INT 21h handler
0CFA0       mov eax,21h
0CFA5       mov esi,offset V86_INT21_PROC
```

```
0CFAA       VMMcall Hook_v86_Int_Chain

;;; Get previous PM INT 21h handler
0CFB0       mov eax,21h
0CFB5       VMMcall Get_PM_Int_Vector
0CFBB       mov dword ptr PREV_INT21_PM_VECT_SEG,ecx
0CFC1       mov dword ptr PREV_INT21_PM_VECT_OFS,edx

;;; Install new PM INT 21h handler
0CFC7       mov esi,offset PM_INT21_PROC
0CFCC       VMMcall Allocate_PM_Call_Back
0CFD2       movzx   edx,ax
0CFD5       mov ecx,eax
0CFD7       shr ecx,10h
0CFDA       mov eax,21h
0CFDF       VMMcall Set_PM_Int_Vector
```

Figure 8-5: IFSMgr code for installing V86 and protected mode INT 21h handlers.

The V86_INT21_PROC and PM_INT21_PROC routines in IFS-Mgr are nearly identical. Simplifying slightly, the IFSMgr V86 and PM INT 21h handlers take the DOS function number from the caller's AH register (which is available to VxDs inside a Client Register Structure pointed to by the EBP register) and, as shown in Figure 8-6, use it to index into a table of IFSMgr handlers that provide preliminary handling of the INT 21h functions.

```
01947       movzx   ecx,byte ptr [ebp.Client_AH]
01950       cmp cl,6Dh          ;; in Windows 95, 72h functions
01953       jae short elsewhere
01955       call    dword ptr INT21_TAB[ecx*4]  ;;; table @ IFSMgr+1700h
0195C       jnc short elsewhere2
0195E       retn
        elsewhere:
            ; ...
```

Figure 8-6: This fragment shows the start of the IFSMgr INT 21h handler.

The table called INT21_TAB in Figure 8-6 is quite important for understanding how IFSMgr handles INT 21h. In one WfW 3.11 configuration, this table happened to be at linear address 800A5600h (which is IFS-Mgr+1700h); I used the PROTTAB program from the *Unauthorized Windows 95* disk to dump this table, filtering out all the default entries. The resulting output, sorted by address, gives a good initial picture of the INT 21h calls that IFSMgr takes some interest in. In Figure 8-7, I've rearranged the output slightly to point out IFSMgr functions that handle multiple DOS functions. (For example, the function at IFSMgr+1AFFh handles INT 21h functions 1Ch, 32h, 36h, and 47h, all of which expect a drive number in the DL register.)

```
C:\UNAUTHW>prottab 800a5600 6d 4 int21 800a589c IFSMgr=800a3f00 | sort
; Table at 800A5600h
; Filter all out entries = 800A589Ch
; IFSMgr=800A3F00
800A58A0    int21_004D  ; IFSMgr+19A0
800A58D0    int21_004B  ; IFSMgr+19D0
800A58E4    int21_005F  ; IFSMgr+19E4
800A5948    int21_005E  ; IFSMgr+1A48
800A5958    int21_001A  ; IFSMgr+1A58
800A5976    int21_000E  ; IFSMgr+1A76
800A59D4    int21_0044  ; IFSMgr+1AD4
800A59FB    int21_001F  ; IFSMgr+1AFB
800A59FF    int21_001C  ; IFSMgr+1AFF       1C  32  36  47
800A5A25    int21_004F  ; IFSMgr+1B25
800A5A7E    int21_0045  ; IFSMgr+1B7E       45  46
800A5A8C    int21_003E  ; IFSMgr+1B8C       3E-40  42  57  5C  68
800A5AD1    int21_0011  ; IFSMgr+1BD1       11-13  17
800A5B5C    int21_006C  ; IFSMgr+1C5C
800A5B63    int21_0039  ; IFSMgr+1C63       39-3D  41  43  4E  56  5B
800A5D04    int21_005D  ; IFSMgr+1E04
800A5E60    int21_000D  ; IFSMgr+1F60
800A5E80    int21_000B  ; IFSMgr+1F80
```

Figure 8-7: This IFSMgr INT 21h handler table from WfW 3.11 is a good indication of the INT 21h calls IFSMgr is interested in.

Figure 8-7 hardly presents a complete picture of IFSMgr's INT 21h handling, but it's a good first approximation of the DOS calls that WfW 3.11 can handle in 32-bit protected mode.

Now, we were wondering why TEST_1 makes 100 calls each to INT 21h functions 0Eh and 19h and yet receives 100 additional calls to function 19h. From inspecting Figure 8-7, it seems that IFSMgr doesn't do anything special with function 19h; it has a default handler that PROTTAB has filtered out. However, there is a handler for function 0Eh, located at IFSMgr+1A76h. Figure 8-8 shows what we find when we disassemble the code at that address.

```
    i21_000E    proc    near        ;;; Set Current Drive
01A76       test    dword ptr [ebx.CB_VM_Status], VMSTAT_PM_EXEC
01A7C       jnz short i210e_done
        i210e_v86:
01A7E       sub eax,eax
01A80       mov esi,offset32 I21_0E_CALL_WHEN_RET
01A85       VMMcall Call_When_VM_Returns
01A8B   i210e_done:
01A8B       stc     ;; carry set -- pass to next handler
```

```
01A8C        retn
    i21_000E    endp
```

Figure 8-8: A disassembly of IFSMgr's INT 21h function 0Eh (Set Current Drive) handler.

In the code in Figure 8-8, IFSMgr is checking whether the function 0Eh call came from protected mode (for example, from a Windows application). If it did (the VMSTAT_PM_EXEC bit is set in the current virtual machine's status flags), IFSMgr doesn't do anything special: it sets the carry flag, indicating that the call should be passed to the next protected-mode INT 21h handler. If the function 0Eh call came from V86 mode, IFSMgr also passes the call along to the next handler — and, eventually, all the way down to DOS — but first it calls a VMM service, Call_When_VM_Returns, passing it the address of another function in IFSMgr.

Call_When_VM_Returns, as its name implies, installs a handler that VMM calls when the current virtual machine (VM) returns from an interrupt handler. This service, documented in the DDK, forces an IRET to return not to the instruction after the INT but to VMM. Even though TEST21 seems to indicate that function 0Eh "appears to be handled in the normal way" (TEST21 sees all its own calls to function 0Eh), the IFSMgr code shows that something odd is nonetheless happening. IFS-Mgr will intercept function 0Eh *after* passing it down to DOS and to DOS programs such as TEST21. This is known as a *post-reflection hook.*

This brings up an important point. Although TEST21's "Some INT 21h are handled without calling DOS" message is reliable, the example of function 0Eh shows that the "INT 21h appears to be handled in normal way" message means little more than that: To TEST21, INT 21h handling appears normal. DOS is still possibly being subjected to strange VxD practices like post-reflection hooks. That IFSMgr uses a post-reflection hook to handle function 0Eh — that IFSMgr even *can* intercept in such a way — is a good indication that the Windows-DOS relationship is not at all the simple, straightforward "Windows runs on top of DOS" situation that many users and developers seem to expect.

So what does IFSMgr do when it receives control after DOS has returned from handling INT 21h function 0Eh? You can see what it does by examining Figure 8-9, which shows the callback function that IFSMgr installed with Call_When_VM_Returns.

```
    I21_0E_CALL_WHEN_RET    proc    near
01A8D       Push_Client_State
```

```
01A9C       VMMcall Begin_Nest_V86_Exec
01AA2       mov byte ptr [ebp.Client_AH],19h    ;; Get Current Drive
01AA6       mov eax,21h
01AAB       VMMcall Exec_Int                     ;; issue INT 21h AH=19h
01AB1       mov dl,byte ptr [ebp.Client_AX]      ;; AL = current drive
01AB4       mov ecx,dword ptr DEVICE_CB_AREA     ;; per-VM data
01ABA       mov byte ptr [ebx+0Ah][ecx],dl       ;; save new current drive
01ABE       VMMcall End_Nest_Exec
01AC4       Pop_Client_State
01AD3       retn
    I21_0E_CALL_WHEN_RET    endp
```

Figure 8-9: IFSMgr's Call_When_VM_Returns handler for INT 21h function 0Eh.

We were wondering why TEST_1 receives extra calls to INT 21h function 19h. Well, Figure 8-9 shows exactly why. After a V86 mode application calls function 0Eh to set the current drive, and after DOS handles the call, IFSMgr gets control, issues a function 19h to *get* the current drive, and stores this value in a data structure it keeps on a per-VM basis in the VM Control Block (VMCB; VxDs use the VMM_Allocate_Device_CB_Area service to allocate memory in the VMCB).

To issue the INT 21h function 19h, IFSMgr uses the standard set of VMM services shown in Figure 8-9: Begin_Nest_V86_Exec, Exec_Int, and so on. The phrases I've been using in this chapter such as "Windows calls down to DOS" and "Windows reflects the interrupt to V86 mode" are really just nebulous-sounding descriptions for this sequence of calls involving Begin_Nest_V86_Exec and Exec_Int.

In fact, when running under Windows Enhanced mode with or without 32BFA, any and all INT 21h calls seen by TEST21's INT 21h handler — in fact, any and all interrupts seen by any real-mode program's interrupt handler — got there only because VMM or some VxD called Begin_Nest_V86_Exec and Exec_Int. Notice that this means there is no necessary correlation between the INT 21h calls issued under Windows and those seen by DOS.

Incidentally, IFSMgr should have been able to use a single service, Exec_VxD_Int, instead of the longer sequence of calls just shown. Unfortunately, though, Exec_VxD_Int is nearly unusable due to a bug in another service, Begin_Nest_Exec. (Geoff Chappell has discovered the simple coding error underlying this persistent bug and has posted a correction called NESTFIX.ASM in the CompuServe WINSDK forum.)

Okay, so we see that whenever a V86 mode program calls INT 21h function 0Eh, IFSMgr follows it with a Begin_Nest_V86_Exec and Exec_Int of INT 21h function 19h. We can also see that IFSMgr takes the value returned from function 19h and stores it in its DEVICE_CB_AREA+0Ah.

But why? If IFSMgr wants to store the current drive on a per-VM basis (which is sensible enough), why can't it just take the intended new current-directory value the user passes in DL to function 0Eh? Instead of the i21_000E function shown, with its roundabout scheduling of another function to be called later on, it seems as if IFSMgr could have simply performed the following:

```
wrong_i21_000E proc near
    mov dl,byte ptr [ebp.Client_DL]      ;; DL = new current drive
    mov ecx,dword ptr DEVICE_CB_AREA     ;; per-VM data
    mov byte ptr [ebx+0Ah][ecx],dl       ;; save new current drive
    stc                                  ;; carry set -- pass to next handler
    retn
wrong_i21_000E endp
```

What's wrong with this picture?

What's wrong is that there's no guarantee that the value the user passed to function 0Eh is valid! Unfortunately, function 0Eh doesn't have an error return (instead, it rather irrelevantly returns LASTDRIVE in AL). Thus, the only way to tell if a call to function 0Eh succeeded is to call function 19h. And that is precisely what IFSMgr is doing.

Why doesn't IFSMgr do this when a VM is running in protected mode (VMSTAT_PM_EXEC)? Without any special protected-mode handling for function 0Eh, VMM automatically sends the call to the V86 interrupt hook chain. Thus, IFSMgr sees the function 0Eh call a second time, and at that time it can call function 19h and save the current-drive value.

In other words, for every PM call to function 0Eh, there's an additional V86 mode call to function 19h. The WLOG212F program on the *Unauthorized Windows 95* disk confirms this. As we saw in Chapter 1, WLOG212F is a protected-mode Windows application that hooks INT 21h in three places: twice in protected mode and once (using DPMI callbacks) in V86 mode. WLOG212F can then compare the interrupts issued in protected mode with those seen down to V86 mode. After running several Windows applications, WLOG212F reported the following results for INT 21h functions 0Eh and 19h:

```
Func        KernelDOSProc (Prot mode)      V86 mode
0Eh               688                        688          Passed down
19h               674                       1362          Passed down
```

WLOG212F detected 1362 V86 calls to function 19h. But only 674 of these calls were issued in protected mode. Where did the extra function

19h calls come from? Well, 1362 – 674 = 688, which is the number of protected-mode calls to function 0Eh. Just as you'd expect from the IFS-Mgr code, there's an extra V86 call to function 19h for every PM call to function 0Eh.

The point that emerges from this close look at function 0Eh is this: Even for a simple INT 21h call that Windows passes down to DOS, it's really Windows' VMM/VxD layer that is in control. The IFSMgr VxD saw the call before DOS, and it saw the call again when DOS was finished with it. The only reason DOS saw the call at all was that IFSMgr let it see the call. IFSMgr can even take one INT 21h call (function 0Eh) and generate another (function 19h). To make the point one more time, there is no necessary correlation between the INT 21h calls issued under Windows — even by DOS programs such as TEST21 — and the INT 21h calls that eventually wend their way down to real-mode DOS.

It's also important to realize that the calls that are passed down to DOS depend on what VxDs happen to be loaded. Although IFSMgr comes built-in to WfW 3.11 and Windows 95, the capability to write VxDs that bypass DOS is a standard part of the VMM programming interface and is documented in the DDK.

Take function 19h, for example. As noted in *Undocumented DOS* (2d ed., p. 69), real-mode DOS's implementation of this function is trivial. It just moves the contents of DOS's CURR_DRIV variable, located at offset 336h in the DOS data segment (offset 16h in the Swappable Data Area [SDA]), into the AL register:

```
-u fdc9:4c64
FDC9:4C64 A03603    MOV    AL,[0336]   ; DOS_DS:0336 = CURR_DRIV
FDC9:4C67 C3        RET
```

Thus, a VxD that handles this function entirely in 32-bit protected mode is a piece of cake. CURRDRIV.ASM, shown in Listing 8-3, is a VxD that does just this. We've talked a lot about how VxDs have become the operating system and how they can handle DOS calls in protected mode, so it would be useful to examine one small VxD to see how all this works.

Listing 8-3: CURRDRIV.ASM

```
comment %
CURRDRIV.ASM
Sample VxD that handles one INT 21h function entirely in protected mode
INT 21h Function 19h (Get Current Drive)

masm5 -p -w2 currdriv.asm
```

```
link386 currdriv.obj,currdriv.386,,,currdriv.def
addhdr currdriv.386

put device=\unauthw\currdriv\currdriv.386 into system.ini [386Enh]

currdriv.def:

LIBRARY  CURRDRIV
DESCRIPTION 'INT 21h Function 19h Handler'
EXETYPE  DEV386
SEGMENTS
    _LTEXT PRELOAD NONDISCARDABLE
    _LDATA PRELOAD NONDISCARDABLE
    _ITEXT CLASS 'ICODE' DISCARDABLE
    _IDATA CLASS 'ICODE' DISCARDABLE
    _TEXT  CLASS 'PCODE' NONDISCARDABLE
    _DATA  CLASS 'PCODE' NONDISCARDABLE
EXPORTS     CURRDRIV_DDB  @1
%

.386p

INCLUDE VMM.INC
INCLUDE V86MMGR.INC

;;; This will become CURRDRIV_DDB
Declare_Virtual_Device CURRDRIV, 1, 0, \
    Control_Proc, \
    Undefined_Device_ID, \
    Undefined_Init_Order, , ,\

VxD_DATA_SEG

;;; need to add in linear DOS data segment
Lin_CurDrv          dd  0336h

VxD_DATA_ENDS

VxD_CODE_SEG

BeginProc   Int21V86
    movzx   eax, [ebp.Client_AH]
    cmp     al, 19h
    je      short Do_GetCurDrv
    stc     ; keep looking for someone to handle this
    ret

Do_GetCurDrv:
    mov     eax, [Lin_CurDrv]
;;  add     eax, [ebx.CB_High_Linear]
    mov     al, byte ptr [eax]
    mov     byte ptr [ebp.Client_AL], al
    clc     ; done, I've handled this
    ret
EndProc     Int21V86
```

```
VxD_CODE_ENDS

VxD_LOCKED_CODE_SEG

BeginProc   Control_Proc
    Control_Dispatch Device_Init, Do_Device_Init
    clc
    ret
EndProc     Control_Proc

VxD_LOCKED_CODE_ENDS

VxD_ICODE_SEG

BeginProc   Do_Device_Init
    Push_Client_State
    VMMcall Begin_Nest_V86_Exec
    mov     [ebp.Client_AH], 52h     ; get SysVars
    mov     eax, 21h
    VMMcall Exec_Int
    movzx   eax, [ebp.Client_ES]     ; but just use DOS data seg
    shl     eax, 4
    add     Lin_CurDrv, eax          ; add linear DOS
    VMMcall End_Nest_Exec
    Pop_Client_State

    mov     eax, 21h
    mov     esi, offset32 Int21V86
    VMMcall Hook_V86_Int_Chain

    ret
EndProc     Do_Device_Init

VxD_ICODE_ENDS

VXD_REAL_INIT_SEG

real_init proc near
    xor ax, ax
    xor bx, bx
    xor si, si
    xor edx, edx
    ret
real_init endp

VXD_REAL_INIT_ENDS

    END
```

Like all VxDs, CURRDRIV.ASM has a Declare_Virtual_Device statement, which will eventually become the VxD's Device Descriptor Block (DDB). This includes a pointer to CURRDRIV's Control_Proc routine. VMM calls each Control_Proc in each VxD for a variety of events, such as the creation or termination of a VM or thread.

The only event CURRDRIV cares about is Device_Init. CURRDRIV's Do_Device_Init routine first uses the standard Begin_Nest_V86_Exec/Exec_Int block of code to issue an INT 21h function 52h call in V86 mode. This DOS function returns with ES:BX pointing to the undocumented DOS SysVars structure (the List of Lists). However, CURRDRIV ignores BX and uses ES as the DOS data segment. It shifts ES left by 4 to form a linear address and adds it onto CURRDRIV's Lin_CurDrv variable, which is predefined as 0336h. Lin_CurDrv now contains the linear address of DOS's current-drive variable.

Once Lin_CurDrv is properly set up, CURRDRIV uses VMM's Hook_V86_Int_Chain service to install the Int21V86 routine as a handler for INT 21h. At this point, CURRDRIV is dormant until an INT 21h call comes in. Note that CURRDRIV's INT 21h handler will be called not only for INT 21h calls coming from V86 mode but also for any Exec_Int 21h calls made by VxDs in a nested V86 Exec block, such as that shown back in Figure 8-9.

The Int21V86 routine uses [ebp.Client_AH] to see which INT 21h function is being called. For any DOS function other than 19h, CURRDRIV sets the carry flag. This is a signal to VMM to pass the call to the next VxD in the V86 hook chain.

When an INT 21h function 19h call comes in, CURRDRIV jumps to the Do_GetCurDrv routine. This reads the current drive out of Lin_CurDrv, moves it into the caller's AL register (ebp.Client_AL), and returns with the carry flag clear. This is a signal to VMM that the interrupt has been serviced and should neither be passed on to any other VxD (such as IFSMgr) in the V86 hook chain nor passed down to the DOS interrupt chain in V86 mode. (It's crucial to understand the difference between these two chains: the first is maintained by the Hook_V86_Int_Chain service and consists of 32-bit protected-mode VxD code, and the second chain is the familiar one from DOS programming.)

That's it: INT 21h function 19h is now being handled entirely in 32-bit protected mode, bypassing DOS and any other VxDs that might have been interested in seeing calls to this function. After using the DDK tools to build CURRDRIV.386 (see the instructions at the top of Listing 8-3) and putting device=currdriv.386 in the [386Enh] section of your SYSTEM.INI, you can run the TEST_1 version of TEST21 again to see that, indeed, CURRDRIV is bypassing DOS:

```
Generated 201 calls      Received 101 calls
21/0E    100 called      100 received
```

```
21/19   100 called        0 received
21/25   1 called          1 received

Some INT 21h are handled without calling DOS!
```

Note the change from Figure 8-4: Instead of getting the message "Some extra INT 21h calls are occurring!" we now get the message "Some INT 21h are handled without calling DOS!" — all because of the simple code in CURRDRIV.ASM.

CURRDRIV.ASM doesn't use any features of 32BFA. The VMM services it uses, especially Hook_V86_Int_Chain, have all been around since 1990. Yet CURRDRIV is doing basically the same thing as 32BFA, although on a much smaller scale. All the resources necessary to make DOS disappear have been quietly sitting in VMM, just waiting to be used.

Windows 95: Still Bypassing DOS, but Supporting TSRs

So far, we've used TEST21 only to experiment with 32BFA in WfW 3.11. Now we need to run TEST21 under Chicago, which of course also supports 32BFA. Figure 8-10 shows the results of that test.

```
0 seconds elapsed

Generated 701 calls       Received 701 calls
21/25   1 called          1 received
21/3D   200 called        200 received
21/3E   200 called        200 received
21/3F   100 called        100 received
21/40   200 called        200 received

INT 21h appears to be handled in the normal way
```

Figure 8-10: Running TEST21 under Chicago.

What?! The "INT 21h appears to be handled in the normal way" message in Figure 8-10 is unexpected under Windows 95, given that 32BFA in WfW 3.11 (which Microsoft's own advertisements said was "powered by 32-bit technology from our 'Chicago' project") triggers TEST21's "Some INT 21h are handled without calling DOS!" message.

Furthermore, the V86TEST program from Chapter 10, which loads before Windows, shows that when running TEST21 (or any other program that hooks INT 21h) in a DOS box, Windows is sending these calls down to DOS or at least to global (that is, loaded before Windows) DOS programs such as V86TEST. While running TEST21 locally (that is, in a DOS box), V86TEST detected the following INT 21h calls:

```
02: 42  08: 5   0B: 1846        19: 3   1A: 1   25: 12  29: 4   2A: 3
2C: 3   30: 1   35: 5   38: 1   3D: 200 3E: 215 3F: 100
40: 203 44: 1   48: 2   49: 1   4A: 1   4B: 1   4C: 1   4D: 1   5D: 2
```

Note that the calls to functions 3Dh–40h (File Open, Close, Read, and Write) match up reasonably well with the calls made by TEST21. Recall from earlier in this chapter that in 32BFA under WfW 3.11, V86TEST only saw TEST21's function 40h writes to stdout.

At least in terms of its apparent reliance on DOS, these TEST21 results make Windows 95 appear to be a step *backward* from WfW 3.11!

Hold on a moment: Although TEST21's INT 21h did see all the program's INT 21h calls, the "0 seconds elapsed" message in Figure 8-10 calls into question whether MS-DOS itself really could have seen these calls, no matter what TEST21 and V86TEST seem to indicate. Back in Figure 8-1, TEST21 on the same machine took 21 seconds without 32BFA. If TEST21 takes roughly the same amount of time — which was no time at all — under Chicago as it did under WfW 3.11 with 32BFA, it's a good indication that the "INT 21h appears to be handled in the normal way" message is in some way misleading.

Also, if you install the CURRDRIV VxD from Listing 8-3 under Windows 95 and then run the TEST_1 version of TEST21 (Listing 8-2), you'll see the "Some INT 21h are handled without calling DOS!" message that CURRDRIV has successfully trapped and emulated INT 21h function 19h, just as under WfW 3.11. Clearly there's nothing wrong with the fundamental Hook_V86_Int_Chain mechanism for emulating INT calls in 32-bit protected mode, so there must just be something different about Windows 95's implementation of 32BFA.

We need the TEST21 -MYSETVECT option to see Windows 95's true colors. With -MYSETVECT, TEST21 will get and set its interrupt vectors not with INT 21h functions 25h and 35h (_dos_ setvect and _dos_ getvect) but instead with my_setvect and my_getvect, two functions that directly poke and peek the low-memory IVT. (See Listing 8-1 and the "Interrupts 101: IDT versus the IVT" section later in this chapter.)

Guess what? As Figure 8-11 shows, running TEST21 -MYSETVECT under Chicago produces the same "Some INT 21h are handled without calling DOS!" results as running TEST21 under WfW 3.11 32BFA.

```
C:\THIS IS A LONG WINDOWS 95 DIRECTORY NAME>test21 -mysetvect > test21.log

C:\THIS IS A LONG WINDOWS 95 DIRECTORY NAME>type test21.log
Using my_setvect
1 seconds elapsed

Generated 700 calls      Received 0 calls
21/3D   200 called       0 received      -
21/3E   200 called       0 received      -
21/3F   100 called       0 received      -
21/40   200 called       0 received      -

Some INT 21h are handled without calling DOS!
```

Figure 8-11: Running TEST21 -MYSETVECT under Chicago produces these results.

Once again, V86TEST confirms that these INT 21h function 3Dh-40h calls are not sent down to DOS:

```
02: 12   08: 11   0B: 2608         19: 3    1A: 1    25: 8    29: 4    2A: 3
2C: 3    30: 1    35: 4    38: 1    3E: 15
40: 3    44: 1    48: 2    49: 1    4A: 1    4B: 1    4C: 1    4D: 1    5D: 2
```

Why did using my_setvect rather than _dos_setvect to install TEST21's INT 21h handler make such a difference?

Empirically, the Chicago version of IFSMgr must be hooking INT 21h function 25h (Set Interrupt Vector) and using it to set some sort of flag, indicating that DOS calls must be sent down the INT 21h chain for a given VM.

Indeed, using the PROTTAB program to generate an IFSMgr table for Chicago, similar to the one for WfW 3.11 back in Figure 8-7, shows that the IFSMgr INT 21h table in Chicago *does* contain a handler for function 25h. Without boring you with the entire new table, here are the differences between the Chicago and WfW 3.11 IFSMgr INT 21h tables:

- Four FCB-related functions are handled in WfW but not in Windows 95: 11h, 12h, 13h, and 17h.
- Five functions are handled in Windows 95 but not in WfW: 1Bh, 25h, 60h, 69h, and 71h. Function 1Bh gets allocation information for the current drive. Function 60h is the undocumented TRUENAME function (see *Undocumented DOS*, 2d ed., pp. 148-151, 428-430). Function 69h is an undocumented call to get and set the disk serial number. Function 71h is new; it provides long filename (LFN) support in Windows 95. For example, since function 60h is TRUENAME, function 7160h is the LFN version.

Anyway, we're interested in function 25h. Just as we'd expect from the different results we got from running TEST21 and TEST21 -MYSETVECT, inspection of the IFSMgr code for function 25h shows that if the caller is setting the INT 21h vector, the handler for function 25h sets or clears a flag in IFSMgr's DEVICE_CB_AREA. As noted earlier, the DEVICE_CB_AREA is part of the VMCB, so there is a separate flag for each VM.

IFSMgr's INT 21h handlers in Windows 95 are somewhat different from the ones in WfW 3.11 (see Figure 8-6). For one thing, the INT 21h handlers in Windows 95 check the flag that function 25h sets. If the flag is set, indicating that the VM has hooked INT 21h, IFSMgr passes down the INT 21h call.

This is evidently Microsoft's response to widespread complaints about the failure of 32BFA in WfW 3.11 to pass down INT 21h. For example, the same bypass-DOS 32BFA behavior we saw in TEST21 *broke* Stacker disk compression in WfW 3.11! According to *PC Week* ("Stacker clashes with WFW's file access; Stac working on fix," March 7, 1994), "VCache blocks certain DOS calls to the Stacker driver." It's not clear why VCache is singled out as the culprit — it's IFSMgr, not VCache, that handles INT 21h — but the phrase "blocks certain DOS calls" certainly has a familiar ring to it from the output shown by TEST21 and V86TEST under WfW 3.11.

Microsoft has a dilemma here: 32BFA entails bypassing MS-DOS, but bypassing DOS means that key DOS utilities such as Stacker won't see the stream of INT 21h calls that they expect. Were TEST21 a genuinely useful program that did more than simply log INT 21h calls and whose functionality actually depended on seeing INT 21h calls, we wouldn't be so sanguine about its capability to detect the presence of 32BFA in WfW 3.11. We would instead say that Windows had broken TEST21.

The trade press likes to beat up on Microsoft for what seems like its failure to move more rapidly away from real-mode DOS. Yet when Windows *does* take giant steps away from real-mode DOS, as in 32BFA, the trade press again beats up on Microsoft, or the vendor of the broken DOS utility, or both — only this time, they view such movement away from DOS compatibility as a bug! What everyone wants, apparently, is DOS compatibility but not DOS.

Well, that's reasonable enough. Sort of. Microsoft must bypass DOS yet support DOS programs (such as Stacker) that need to see DOS calls.

We'll see later that 32-bit disk access (32BDA, also known as FastDisk), introduced in Windows 3.10, had a clean solution to a similar problem.

In Windows 95, 32BFA uses a not-so-clean solution. Note how easy it was for TEST21 -MYSETVECT to trick Windows 95 into thinking that we hadn't hooked INT 21h. Although the my_setvect code might seem contrived, it's not uncommon for DOS programs to directly manipulate the low-memory IVT rather than call functions 25h and 35h. As only one example, Windows itself does this.

As I write this, Chicago is still in beta. It's possible that Microsoft will correct the my_setvect loophole by the time of Windows 95's commercial release. If so, the time elapsed while running TEST21 will be the only indication of 32BFA, and TEST21 -MYSETVECT will falsely declare that "INT 21h appears to be handled in the normal way."

Frankly, TEST21 *should* make this false declaration. TEST21 demonstrates 32BFA so nicely under WfW 3.11 only because of a *flaw* in 32BFA. This flaw remains in Windows 95 but is not as big. Apart from the elapsed time to perform file I/O, 32BFA is supposed to be "transparent" (that is, invisible to applications), yet we've detected the presence of 32BFA with TEST21, a perfectly "legal" DOS program that doesn't use any undocumented or underhanded tricks.

INTVECT: Another Sample VxD INT 21h Hooker

As another example of how easy it is to defeat IFSMgr's test that a VM is hooking INT 21h, consider a VxD that grabs function 25h calls before IFSMgr gets to see them. In addition to beating the -MYSETVECT horse just a little more thoroughly, a VxD that hooks function 25h (and 35h too, while we're at it) is even more important as an additional demonstration of how VxDs can handle DOS in protected mode.

The CURRDRIV VxD (Listing 8-3) showed how easy it is, at least for simple INT 21h calls, to bypass DOS. INTVECT.ASM in Listing 8-4 is another VxD like this.

INTVECT.ASM hooks INT 21h functions 25h (Set Interrupt Vector) and 35h (Get Interrupt Vector), handling these two calls entirely in 32-bit protected mode. INTVECT basically uses the my_setvect and my_getvect code from Listing 8-1, translated into 32-bit assembler.

Listing 8-4: INTVECT.ASM

```
comment %
INTVECT.ASM
Sample VxD that handles two INT 21h functions entirely in protected mode
INT 21h function 25h: Set Interrupt Vector
INT 21h function 35h: Get Interrupt Vector

(Same basic instructions, .def file as CURRDRIV.ASM)
%

.386p

INCLUDE VMM.INC
INCLUDE V86MMGR.INC

IFSMgr_Init_Order   EQU 0A0011000h  ;; found by running VXDSHOW IFSMGR.386

;;; this will become INTVECT_DDB
Declare_Virtual_Device INTVECT, 1, 0, \
    Control_Proc, \
    Undefined_Device_ID, \
    IFSMgr_Init_Order+10000H, , ,\

VxD_CODE_SEG

BeginProc   Int21V86
    movzx   eax, [ebp.Client_AH]
    cmp     al, 25h
    je      short Do_SetVect
    cmp     al, 35h
    je      short Do_GetVect
    stc                                     ;; chain to previous handler
    ret

Do_SetVect:
    movzx   eax, [ebp.Client_AL]            ;; interrupt number
    movzx   edx, [ebp.Client_DS]            ;; get interrupt handler
    shl     edx, 16                         ;; from caller's DS:DX
    mov     dx, [ebp.Client_DX]
    mov     ecx, [ebx.CB_High_Linear]
    mov     dword ptr [ecx + (eax * 4)], edx  ;; shove into IVT[eax]
    clc                                     ;; done -- don't chain!
    ret

Do_GetVect:
    movzx   eax, [ebp.Client_AL]            ;; interrupt number
    mov     ecx, [ebx.CB_High_Linear]
    mov     edx, dword ptr [ecx + (eax * 4)]  ;; get handler from IVT[eax]
    mov     [ebp.Client_BX], dx             ;; put into caller's ES:BX
    shr     edx, 16
    mov     [ebp.Client_ES], dx
    clc                                     ;; done -- don't chain!
    ret
EndProc     Int21V86
```

```
VxD_CODE_ENDS

VxD_LOCKED_CODE_SEG

BeginProc   Control_Proc
    Control_Dispatch Device_Init, Do_Device_Init
    clc
    ret
EndProc     Control_Proc

VxD_LOCKED_CODE_ENDS

VxD_ICODE_SEG

BeginProc   Do_Device_Init
    mov     eax, 21h
    mov     esi, offset32 Int21V86
    VMMcall Hook_V86_Int_Chain
    ret
EndProc     Do_Device_Init

VxD_ICODE_ENDS

VXD_REAL_INIT_SEG

real_init proc near
    xor ax, ax
    xor bx, bx
    xor si, si
    xor edx, edx
    ret
real_init endp

VXD_REAL_INIT_ENDS

    END
```

As with the earlier CURRDRIV example (to which INTVECT has a more than passing resemblance), INTVECT's Do_Device_Init routine uses the VMM Hook_V86_Int_Chain service to install Int21V86 as a handler for V86 INT 21h. Unlike CURRDRIV, though, INTVECT has to worry about its order in the V86 INT 21h hook chain. We know that IFSMgr in Windows 95 hooks function 25h; that's the reason I've chosen this example. For reasons that will soon become clear, I want INTVECT to see (and deal with) function 25h before IFSMgr gets a chance to. A VxD's location in the V86 INT 21h hook chain depends on when the VxD called Hook_V86_Int_Chain. This in turn depends in part on the VxD's initialization order, so I've given CURRDRIV an initialization order slightly higher than IFSMgr's. Many aspects of 32BFA depend on VxD initialization order. Gosh, this VxD programming is just like working with TSRs, except that VxD writers get to play "load me last" games instead of requiring that users do so.

When INTVECT receives a call to function 25h, it jumps to the Do_SetVect routine. This routine takes the interrupt number from [ebp.Client_AL] and the new handler from [ebp.Client_DS] and [ebp.Client_DX]. INTVECT is going to shove the new handler right into the low-memory IVT, just as the my_setvect function back in Listing 8-1 did. VxDs have a 4GB flat address space representing the entire machine, and the current VM's address space is mapped in at linear address 0, so INTVECT could access the IVT with an expression as simple as DWORD PTR [intno * 4]. However, the current VM's address space is also available via the [ebx.CB_High_Linear] field in the VMCB, and INTVECT adds this in.

In the event of a function 35h call, INTVECT goes to Do_GetVect, which pulls the handler address out of the IVT and returns it in [ebp .Client_ES] and [ebp.Client_BX]. This is similar to the my_getvect code in TEST21.C.

After building and installing INTVECT.386, it's time to see if it works. Recall that TEST21 has always seen its own call to function 25h. With INTVECT.386 installed, you can run TEST21 and — voilà! — TEST21 no longer sees function 25h calls. See how easy it is to bypass DOS?

As a more interesting test, install INTVECT.386 in Windows 95's SYSTEM.INI and run TEST21 again, this time *without the -MYSETVECT switch*. Now TEST21 outputs its "Some INT 21h are handled without calling DOS!" message, indicating the presence of 32BFA.

What's happening is that INTVECT grabbed function 25h ahead of IFSMgr, serviced the function by poking the IVT, and cleared the carry flag so that VMM wouldn't pass the call to anyone else. This capability of VxD V86 INT handlers to bypass not only DOS and TSRs but also other VxDs is powerful but distressing. It shows that VxDs play the same role in Windows that TSRs played in DOS: You have the same kind of power but also the same kind of confusing interactions that should be fully expected when thousands of third-party developers have been given free reign to hack the operating system.

VxDs become a true part of the Windows operating system. This is both a blessing and a curse. The blessing is that at the VxD layer, Windows is a relatively open system. The curse is that at the VxD layer Windows is a relatively open system! A crucial system component such as IFSMgr can make certain assumptions (such as that local INT 21h hookers can be detected by hooking INT 21h function 25h), and some third-party VxD such as INTVECT can come along and, in a perfectly legal fashion (according to the laws laid down in the Windows DDK), undermine its assumptions.

Thus, bypassing DOS isn't really all that difficult. We did it for two key (albeit simple) DOS functions in about 100 lines of code. But we've also interfered with IFSMgr's rather simple-minded test for local INT 21h hookers. Bypassing DOS might be easy, but supporting other software (including other VxDs) that expects to see a stream of INT 21h calls is a difficult and — given the thousands of developers writing VxDs — unbounded problem.

Global and Local INT 21h Hookers

Far more important than the my_setvect loophole, IFSMgr's function 25h handler can't do anything about programs such as Stacker that hook INT 21h before Windows starts. IFSMgr detects the presence of an INT 21h hooker solely by monitoring calls to function 25h. Because IFSMgr begins its monitoring long after programs such as Stacker have called function 25h, it concludes that INT 21h need not be passed down.

Indeed, this policy is deliberate. A Microsoft white paper by Russ Arun, "Chicago File System Features — Tips & Issues" (April 22, 1994) contains the following explanation:

> On default all INT 21 interrupts, except file API INT 21s, are passed down to any hooker present in the system. The file API INT 21s are just passed to VM (local) hookers, but not to global (AUTOEXEC.BAT) type hookers. This is done because there are new file APIs (new INT 21s) that support long file names for delete, rename and so on that an older hooker won't understand anyway. Furthermore not all file API calls are INT 21 calls. Specifically server calls and swapper calls to the file system are not INT 21 calls.

Although this statement explains much of the behavior we've seen in Windows 95 with TEST21, it raises more questions than it answers (it also raises some eyebrows regarding the "global hooker," "local hooker," and "older hooker" phrases, but we won't get into that):

- "*On default all INT 21h interrupts, except file API INT 21s, are passed down to any hooker present in the system.*" Since MS-DOS itself (WINBOOT.SYS) is an INT 21h hooker, doesn't this mean that all DOS functions not related to file I/O are passed down to and handled by DOS? Doesn't this contradict Microsoft's frequent claims that

Windows 95 doesn't require DOS? (Indeed, to anticipate the point of Chapter 10, the V86TEST output shown earlier certainly seems to confirm that Windows does use DOS for a wide variety of INT 21h calls, including functions 2Ah and 2Ch to get the date and time.)

- "*The file API INT 21s are just passed to VM (local) hookers, but not to global (AUTOEXEC.BAT) type hookers.*" Isn't it precisely *global* hookers such as Stacker that would *most* need to see file-related INT 21h calls? Why the special treatment for these so-called local hookers?
- "*This is done because there are new file APIs (new INT 21s) that support long file names for delete, rename and so on that an older hooker won't understand anyway.*" But if that's true for global hookers, isn't it equally true for local hookers? Why are global hookers presumed to be older?
- "*Furthermore not all file API calls are INT 21 calls. Specifically server calls and swapper calls to the file system are not INT 21 calls.*" This refers to the fact that some VxDs in Windows 95, such as the DynaPage replacement for PageFile, make direct calls to IFSMgr. But as Geoff Chappell has noted, "if there are non-trivial DOS hookers in global memory, they will be as [expletive deleted] about not seeing VxDs' file activity as they would be about not seeing int 21h." How would a global INT 21h hooker know or care about a file I/O call originated from within Windows? To a global INT 21h hooker, all of Windows, and all programs running under Windows look like one big DOS program.

These major questions aside, we can at least see that Windows 95 intends to support global INT 21h hookers for non-file calls and local INT 21h hookers for all calls. IFSMgr uses function 25h to check for local INT 21h hookers. Microsoft doesn't intend to send file-related calls to global INT 21h hookers.

But wait a minute! Although V86TEST didn't see file calls from TEST21 -MYSETVECT, it did see all file calls from TEST21 (that is, without the -MYSETVECT option). Yet V86TEST is a *global* INT 21h hooker, loaded before Windows, to which, so says Microsoft, file INT 21h's won't — and shouldn't! — be delivered. So why did V86TEST see file I/O calls from TEST21?

Because TEST21, like any reasonable hooker, chains to the previous handler (see Listing 8-1). Any calls sent to TEST21 will eventually be sent to V86TEST as well. Thus, when IFSMgr lets a local hooker like TEST21 see a call, global hookers such as V86TEST will also see it. This means that, although Windows 95 doesn't intend to send file

INT 21h calls to global hookers, this will nonetheless happen if there are any local hookers. It would be simple to write a DOS TSR that does nothing but hook INT 21h and chain to the previous handler. Running this TSR in each VM would force Windows 95 to deliver all INT 21h, including file calls, to global hookers.

The Role of IFSHLP.SYS and V86 Callbacks

But there's a remaining mystery here: Although running a local hooker such as TEST21 entails the delivery of INT 21h calls to global hookers such as V86TEST, and although MS-DOS itself clearly qualifies as a global INT 21h hooker, nonetheless Windows 95 *can't* let MS-DOS see file-related INT 21h calls. Allowing DOS to handle these calls would not only cause tremendous confusion, but also wipe out all the performance improvements from 32BFA.

The TEST21 "0 seconds elapsed" message back in Figure 8-10 shows that, indeed, Windows 95 *doesn't* let these calls go all the way down to DOS. Yet, the V86TEST TSR sees these calls, and (as you can see from V86TEST.C in Chapter 10) this reasonable hooker chains these calls to the previous handler. How can TSRs such as V86TEST see file INT 21h calls and chain them on to the previous handler — and yet MS-DOS itself doesn't see them?

IFSHLP.SYS, a DOS device driver supplied both with Windows 95 and with WfW 3.11, is the answer. 32BFA *requires* IFSHLP.SYS, and will not load without it. If it fails to find IFSHLP (whose device name is IFSHLP) IFSMgr displays the message: "The Microsoft Installable File System Manager (IFSMgr) cannot find the helper driver. Please ensure that IFSHLP.SYS has been installed."

Running the INTCHAIN program from *Undocumented DOS* (2d ed., pp. 302-308) shows that IFSHLP sits between MS-DOS (including the DblSpace driver) on the one side and TSRs such as V86TEST on the other:

```
C:\UNDOCDOS>intchain 21/3000

Tracing INT 21 AX=3000
242 instructions
Skipped over 1 INT

2032:09B1   V86TEST
020E:04A8   IFS$HLP$
```

```
01EF:0023   D:
0A29:1956   DBLSYSH$
00A0:0FAC   DOS
FE9E:4249   HMA
```

Now, what does IFSHLP do when it receives a DOS call that's been passed on from a hooker such as TEST21 or V86TEST? Knowing from INTCHAIN that IFSHLP's INT 21h handler in this configuration happens to be located at real-mode address 0215:04A8, we can use a debugger such as Soft-ICE/Windows to place a breakpoint on this address. The next time someone generates an INT 21h call that for whatever reason is sent down to the V86 interrupt chain, the breakpoint on IFSHLP is triggered, and we can trace through the code.

I generated the log in Figure 8-12 by continally pressing F8 (trace) in Soft-ICE, using WLOG to save the results to a file, running the file through the VXDNAME utility from thc *Unauthorized Windows 95* disk, and then adding comments. This trace of about 100 instructions is a remarkable example of how Windows VxDs insinuate themselves into DOS, and of how even the lowliest DOS call — one which Windows reflects down to DOS — ain't what it used to be.

```
0215:04A8   CMP    AH,72                 ;;; inside IFSHLP INT 21h handler
0215:04AB   JAE    04EB                  ;;; in this particular case, AH = 0Bh
0215:04AD   TEST   BYTE PTR CS:[0035],02
0215:04B3   JZ     04D5                    (NO JUMP)
0215:04B5   TEST   BYTE PTR CS:[0035],0C
0215:04BB   JZ     04D5                    (JUMP)
0215:04D5   PUSH   AX
0215:04D6   PUSH   BX
0215:04D7   MOV    BL,AH
0215:04D9   MOV    BH,00
0215:04DB   MOV    AL,CS:[BX+042A]       ;;; table of INT 21h handlers
0215:04E0   MOV    AH,00                 ;;; AX = 2Bh
0215:04E2   POP    BX
0215:04E3   ADD    AX,04FC
0215:04E6   CALL   AX                    ;;; call handler (04FCh + 2Bh = 0527h)

0215:0527   TEST   BYTE PTR CS:[0035],02 ;;; handler for 0B,0D,0E,71
0215:052D   JNZ    0531                    (JUMP)
0215:0531   RET

0215:04E8   JAE    04F0                    (JUMP)
0215:04F0   POP    AX
0215:04F1   PUSH   BX
0215:04F2   MOV    BL,AH                 ;;; put INT 21h func number in BX
0215:04F4   SUB    BH,BH
0215:04F6   JMP    FAR CS:[0012]         ;;; jump to V86 callback

FBCA:23A2   ARPL   [BX+SI+6E],BP         ;;; V86 callback at FBCA:23A2
```

```
VMM+240   SUB     ESP,+04                 ;;; IDT INT 06h handler (illegal opcode)
VMM+243   PUSHAD
VMM+244   MOV     ESI,00000018            ;;; 18h = 6 * 4
VMM+249   JMP     VMM+2B0
VMM+2B0   CLD                             ;;; VMM generic INT handler
VMM+2B1   MOV     EBP,ESP
VMM+2B3   MOV     DI,0030
VMM+2B7   TEST    BYTE PTR [EBP.Client_EFLAGS+2],02
VMM+2BB   JZ      VMM+320                     (NO JUMP)
VMM+2BD   MOV     DS,DI
VMM+2BF   MOV     EBX,[VMM+F6E4]          ;;; current VM handle
VMM+2C5   MOV     ES,DI
VMM+2C7   MOV     EDI,[VMM+F670]          ;;; current thread handle
VMM+2CD   XCHG    ESP,[EDI+48]            ;;; switch stacks
VMM+2D0   PUSH    VMM+2E0                 ;;; return address (see below)
VMM+2D5   JMP     [ESI+VMM+E410]          ;;; goto INT 06h handler

VMM+928   STI                            ;;; INT 6: invalid opcode
VMM+929   MOVZX   EAX,WORD PTR [EBP.Client_CS]      ;;; FBCAh
VMM+92D   MOV     ECX,EAX
VMM+92F   MOV     EDX,[EBP.Client_EIP]              ;;; 23A2h
VMM+932   SHL     EAX,04
VMM+935   ADD     EAX,EDX                 ;;; FBCA0h + 23A2h = FE042h

VMM+937   CMP     EAX,000FE042            ;;; all V86 callbacks == FE042h
VMM+93C   JNZ     VMM+952                   (NO JUMP)
VMM+93E   SUB     ECX,0000FB04            ;;; FBCAh - FB04h (base) = 0C6h
VMM+944   MOV     EDX,[C41DB004+8*ECX]    ;;; table of V86 CB ref data
VMM+94B   JMP     [C41DB000+8*ECX]        ;;; goto handler for this V86 CB

IFSMgr+4B0   CALL    [Simulate_Pop]
IFSMgr+4B6   CALL    [Simulate_Iret]
IFSMgr+4BC   MOVZX   ECX,WORD PTR [EBP.Client_BX] ;;; IFSHLP put func in BX
IFSMgr+4C0   MOV     [EBP.Client_BX],AX
IFSMgr+4C4   CMP     CL,72
IFSMgr+4C7   JAE     IFSMgr+4E1               (NO JUMP)
IFSMgr+4C9   MOV     EDX,00000002
IFSMgr+4CE   MOV     ESI,FFFFFFFF
IFSMgr+4D3   MOV     EAX,00000021
IFSMgr+4D8   CALL    [IFSMgr+C78+4*ECX] ;;; call handler for INT 21h func

IFSMgr+F6C   TEST    DWORD PTR [EBX],00000020    ;;; inside 21/0B handler
IFSMgr+F72   JNZ     IFSMgr+FB6               (NO JUMP)
IFSMgr+F74   TEST    EDX,00000001
IFSMgr+F7A   JNZ     IFSMgr+FB6               (NO JUMP)
IFSMgr+F7C   MOV     EAX,[IFSMgr+39D8]
IFSMgr+F81   MOVZX   EAX,WORD PTR [EAX+10]
IFSMgr+F85   SHL     EAX,04
IFSMgr+F88   MOVZX   EDX,WORD PTR [EAX+36]
IFSMgr+F8C   SHL     EDX,04
IFSMgr+F8F   MOVZX   EAX,WORD PTR [EAX+34]
IFSMgr+F93   LEA     EDX,[EAX+EDX]
IFSMgr+F96   MOVZX   EDX,BYTE PTR [EDX]
IFSMgr+F99   MOV     EDI,[IFSMgr+2EB0]
IFSMgr+F9F   ADD     EDI,[EBX+04]
IFSMgr+FA2   TEST    BYTE PTR [EDX+EDI+2E],04
```

```
IFSMgr+FA7    JZ      IFSMgr+FB6                (JUMP)
IFSMgr+FB6    STC
IFSMgr+FB7    RET

IFSMgr+4DF    JB      IFSMgr+507                (JUMP)
IFSMgr+507    MOV     EDX,[IFSMgr+2EB0]  ;;; 2174 -- IFSHLP table
IFSMgr+50D    MOV     CX,[EDX+01CE]      ;;; 01F6h -- prev INT 21h
IFSMgr+514    MOVZX   EDX,[EDX+01CC]     ;;; 0023h
IFSMgr+51B    CALL    [Build_Int_Stack_Frame]    ;;; not shown
IFSMgr+521    RET

VMM+2E0    MOV     EBX,[VMM+F6E4]  ;;; back in VMM, at pushed ret addr
VMM+2E6    MOV     EDI,[VMM+F670]
VMM+2EC    CLI
VMM+2ED    XOR     EAX,EAX
VMM+2EF    CMP     EAX,[VMM+DC88]
VMM+2F5    JNZ     VMM+304               (NO JUMP)
VMM+2F7    TEST    BYTE PTR [EBX],20
VMM+2FA    JNZ     VMM+358               (NO JUMP)
VMM+2FC    XCHG    ESP,[EDI+48]
VMM+2FF    POPAD
VMM+300    ADD     ESP,+04
VMM+303    IRETD

01F6:0023   JMP    03BC:1956
03BC:1956   PUSHF
03BC:1957   STI
; ...
```

Figure 8-12: This output from Soft-ICE demonstrates that IFSHLP can send INT 21h calls back to IFSMgr.

Without trying to understand every line in Figure 8-12, here's the basic idea: In the first block of code, for example, IFSHLP.SYS is examining a call to INT 21h function 0Bh (Get Keyboard Status). As we have seen in some of the sample output from V86TEST, when COMMAND .COM is running in a Windows DOS box, it calls function 0Bh often. IFSHLP uses the INT 21h function number (0Bh in this case) as an index into a table of bytes, located in Figure 8-12 at 0215:042A. For INT 21h function n, table[n] + 4FCh is the address of a small piece of code that tells IFSHLP how to handle the INT 21h function. It's helpful to dump out this table and sort it by address:

```
C:\UNAUTHW>ftab 215:42a 72 i21 1 | sort | massage
table[n] + 4FC      INT 21h function n
--------------      ------------------
4FC                 5F
510                 5E
520                 00-0A, 0C, 0F-3D, 41, 43, 45, 46, 48-56, 58-5B,
                    5D, 60-67, 69-70
527                 0B, 0D, 0E, 71
532                 44
```

```
550                 47
570                 3E, 3F, 40, 42, 57, 5C, 68
```

As you can see, IFSHLP uses the code at offset 520h to deal with most INT 21h functions:

```
-u 215:520
0215:0520 58            POP    AX
0215:0521 58            POP    AX
0215:0522 2EFF2EEC04    JMP    FAR CS:[04EC]

-dd 215:4ec
0215:04EC  01F6:0023
```

In the INTCHAIN output shown earlier, 01F6:0023 belonged to a block device driver controlled by DblSpace, which was loaded before IFSHLP. In other words, for the majority of INT 21h function calls that for whatever reason find their way to IFSHLP, IFSHLP simply chains the call to the previous INT 21h handler. The call eventually makes its way to the real-mode DOS code.

The remaining INT 21h functions (0B, 0D, 0E, 3E, 3F, 40, 42, 44, 47, 52, 57, 5C, 5E, 5F, 68, and 71) are possible candidates for IFSHLP to send to IFSMgr.

In our case, IFSHLP sends the function 0Bh call to IFSMgr. How IFSHLP, which is 16-bit real-mode code (running in V86 mode), calls IFSMgr, which is 32-bit protected-mode code, is pretty interesting and merits the following extremely long digression on V86 callbacks and breakpoints.

At the end of the first block of code in Figure 8-12, there's a JMP FAR CS:[0012], which takes us to the odd-looking address FBCA:23A2. This is an odd address because it's in the ROM BIOS; why would IFSHLP be jumping into the ROM BIOS? Furthermore, on most machines, the address IFSHLP jumps to is not only in the ROM BIOS — it's in the middle of the ROM copyright message!

```
C:\UNAUTHW>debug
-d fbca:23a2
FBCA:23A0        63 68 6E 6F 6C 6F-67 69 65 73 20 4C 74 64     chnologies Ltd
FBCA:23B0  2E 00 FF FF FF FF FF FF-FF FF FF E9 3B 20 4E 45   ............; NE
FBCA:23C0  43 20 43 6F 72 70 6F 72-61 74 69 6F 6E 0D 0A 55   C Corporation..U
FBCA:23D0  6C 74 72 61 4C 69 74 65-20 56 65 72 73 61 00 00   ltraLite Versa..
```

What the...? Well, if you look at the Soft-ICE trace in Figure 8-12, you'll see that the data at FBCA:23A2 *can*, like all data, be interpreted (or misinterpreted) as code:

```
FBCA:23A2   63686E      ARPL    [BX+SI+6E],BP
```

It so happens that the letter *c*, ASCII code 63h, corresponds to an ARPL instruction. It's not necessary to get into what this instruction is supposed to do. The important thing is that this instruction in *illegal* in V86 mode.

So what happens when a program running in a DOS box under Windows executes this illegal instruction? Windows must display a dialog box saying "The application has committed a heinous crime and by the will of the people will be terminated," right?

No. Illegal instructions, GP faults, page faults, and the like, aren't necessarily crimes against humanity. They are merely triggers for interrupts. In our case, executing the illegal 'c'/ARPL/63h instruction generates an INT 6, which is the illegal opcode fault. If someone has hooked INT 6 and chooses to interpret the fault as a crime, then they can certainly put up a frightening-looking dialog and proceed to annihilate the DOS box (perhaps using a VMM service called — I'm not making this up — Nuke_VM). But another, more sanguine INT 6 hooker might take a more relaxed view of the matter.

In the code in Figure 8-12, the INT 6 handler lives in VMM, which as you know by now, is 32-bit protec....

Notice what's just happened. Recall that there was some question about how IFSHLP, which is 16-bit real-mode code (running in V86 mode), could manage to hoist itself into 32-bit protected mode in order to call IFSMgr. Well, IFSHLP just did it. Merely by executing an illegal instruction, IFSHLP has switched itself out of 16-bit V86 mode into 32-bit protected mode.

Pretty clever, eh? So clever, in fact, that a number of top programmers at Microsoft, including Phil Barrett, Ralph Lipe (RAL), and Aaron Reynolds (AAR), managed to secure a patent on it:

> U.S. Patent 4,974,159
>
> Control transferring method for multitasking computer system - writing virtual machine break point instruction into executable code of selected disk operating system (DOS) routines.
>
> Patent Assignee: MICROSOFT CORP
>
> Author (Inventor): HARGROVE R R; BARRETT P R; LIPE R A; REYNOLDS A R; WILSON M D
>
> The method provides for the insertion of a virtual machine break point (VMBP) instruction into the DOS code at a point where DOS will be executing in such a state, referred to a Break Point Locations (BPL). When the VMBP instruction is executed, the 80386 transfers control from the DOS to Virtual machine control (VMM). When the VMM receives control, it determines that the transfer was caused by the execution of a VMBP instruction. The VMM is then free to start another task or perform other functions without corrupting the DOS data structures. A VMM that modifies a DOS is referred to a virtual DOS monitor machine (VDMM).

> Pref., the VDMM uses a copy of the contents of a selected routine where a break point is to be stored to locate the selected routine within DOS. Alternatively, the VDMM could load from a file the BPL addresses for a particular version of DOS under which the application programs are to execute. Alternatively, the BPL addresses could be hard coded into the VDMM.
>
> ADVANTAGE - Avoids inefficiency caused by calls of indefinite duration.

Cleverness is not by itself a valid basis for securing a patent, however. Another criteria is originality. Microsoft's use of an illegal instruction to make the hyperspace jump from 16-bit real mode to 32-bit protected mode is remarkably similar to a well-known technique dating back over twenty years to IBM's VM operating system, which used an illegal instruction as a supervisor call. A nonexistent instruction, often referred to as DIAGNOSE, forced an exception within a virtual machine so that the exception could be caught by the VM kernel and interpreted as a service request. Sound familiar? (For more information on the history of this great hack, see the letters to the editor in *Windows/DOS Developer's Journal*, July 1993, pp. 99-100).

At any rate, this ARPL trick is one of the underpinnings of Windows, including Windows 95. VxDs such as IFSMgr can call a VMM service, Allocate_V86_Call_Back, passing in ESI the address of a 32-bit protected-mode callback procedure (such as offset 4B0h in IFSMgr). Allocate_V86 _Call_Back returns with EAX holding a V86 mode segment:offset address, such as FBCA:23A2. This address points to the ARPL instruction. The VxD can then pass the segment:offset address to any V86 mode clients, such as IFSHLP, that might want to call in to the VxD. The ARPL is what Microsoft sometimes (not quite accurately) calls a *thunk*, in this case a thunk from 16-bit V86 mode to 32-bit protected mode.

In the IFSHLP/IFSMgr example, IFSMgr during its initialization called Allocate_V86_Call_Back, passing it the address IFSMgr+4B0h. Allocate_V86_Call_Back returned the address FBCA:23A2. IFSMgr then passed this address to IFSHLP. IFSHLP now knows that FBCA:23A2 is a stand-in or thunk for IFSMgr+4B0h.

That phrase "passed this address to IFSHLP" is rather vague. *How* does IFSMgr pass the V86 callback's address to IFSHLP? By using an important but unfortunately undocumented backdoor IOCTL interface. Geoff Chappell (as usual!) has written a thorough description of this interface for WfW 3.11. Geoff's document needs to be brought up to date for Windows 95 and published in full, but in the meantime here's a portion that explains how IFSMgr passes the V86 callback address to IFSHLP:

```
INT 21 - IFSHLP.SYS - GET API ENTRY POINT
        AX = 4402h
        BX = file handle for device "IFS$HLP$"
        CX = 0008h
        DS:DX -> buffer for entry point record
Return: CF clear if successful
            AX = number of bytes actually read (should be 0008h) CF set on error
            AX = error code

Format of entry point record on return:
Offset  Size    Description
 00h    DWORD   EF703734h
 04h    DWORD   address of entry point

Note:  This structure can be obtained by an IOCTL READ, IOCTL WRITE or a normal
READ. In the IOCTL cases, the first dword of buffer must be 3734E970h on entry.

Call IFSHLP entry point with:
        STACK:  WORD    function number (0000h-000Ch)
        Some functions have an additional DWORD argument
        pushed before the mandatory WORD argument.
Return: STACK unchanged
        si,di,bp,ds preserved
        bx corrupt

// ... IFSHLP function 00h ...

Call IFSHLP function 01h with:
        STACK:  DWORD   address of trap
                WORD    0001h (function "Set Trap")
Return: dx:ax = 0000:0000 success
                0000:0001 failure (trap already set)
        bx,cx,es corrupt

Notes:

The trap routine supplied by the IOCTL caller will receive control when interrupts
08h, 17h, 21h, 2Ah and 2Fh occur in circumstances that IFSHLP considers interesting.

Ints 21h and 2Fh are hooked trivially (a simple far jump to the previous handler
replaces the first five bytes of the full handler) when IFSHLP.SYS is installed.
This call non-trivialises those handlers by restoring the first five bytes.

Ints 08h, 17h and 2Ah are hooked when this IOCTL call is made.

Int 08h is not hooked if the byte at offset 11h in the table given by IOCTL
function 00h has bit 0 set.

When the trap routine is called, all registers are as they would be had the routine
got control directly, except for bx, whose original value is on the stack, underneath
the interrupt return ddress: a default trap would therefore be to POP BX then IRET.

At least, that's the general principle (there are some exceptions, but this is
complicated enough already). This list is not meant to suggest that IFSHLP traps
```

```
all conditions of the type given, just that if the trap is called with a particular
value in register BX, then the reason is described as follows:

bx < 0069h              corresponding int 21h function
0076h <= bx < 00A6h     int 2Fh function 11h subfunction bx-0076h
00A6h <= bx < 00B7h     int 2Fh function 11h subfunction bx-0026h
bx = 00C7h              int 2Fh function 16h subfunction != 80h
bx = 00C9h              int 2Ah function 84h
                        or int 2Fh function 1680h
bx = 00CAh or 00CBh     various int 08h conditions not yet studied
bx = 00CCh              various int 17h conditions not yet studied
bx = 00CDh              int 2Fh function 02h or function BFh
bx = 00CEh              int 2Fh function 1606h
bx = 00D2h              int 2Fh function 05h subfunction != 00h

One further consequence of this function is to adjust the word a 0040:0010 to
indicate the presence of four parallel ports. This does not seem to be undone (is
this word instanced beforeIOCTL function 01h is ever called?).
```

Notice in particular that the function at IFSMgr+4B0, an ARPL thunk which IFSMgr passes down to IFSHLP using function 1 (Set Trap) of this IOCTL interface, is not just for INT 21h.

Besides IFSHLP/IFSMgr communications, there are many more situations in which Windows uses these ARPL thunk V86 callback thingies. For example, consider INT 2Fh function 1684h (Get Device Entry Point Address), which returns a far function pointer that DOS or Windows applications can call to communicate with a VxD. In the section titled "DOS's IN_WIN3E Flag" in Chapter 4, we saw that MS-DOS in certain situations uses function 1684h to call into DOSMGR. You might have wondered how 16-bit code manages to leap from V86 mode to 32-bit protected mode, merely by calling the pointer returned by function 1684h.

The answer, you won't be surprised to hear, is ARPL. This is nicely illustrated (at least I think so) with a little program called VXD86API, which locates all V86-mode VxD APIs by calling INT 2Fh function 1684h in a loop for every possible VxD ID (0 through 0FFFFh). If function 1684h (via a GetDeviceAPI routine) returns nonzero, VXD86API prints the VxD ID, the segment:offset address of the VxD's V86 entry point, the same address expressed in linear form (segment << 4 + offset), and finally the first byte at the entry-point address. Listing 8-5 shows VXD86API.C, which is a plain DOS real-mode program.

Listing 8-5: VXD86API.C

```
/* VXD86API.C */

#include <stdlib.h>
#include <stdio.h>
```

```
#include <dos.h>

typedef unsigned char BYTE;
typedef unsigned short WORD;
typedef unsigned long DWORD;

typedef DWORD (far *FUNCPTR)(void);

// call the Windows "Get Device Entry Point Address" function
// Interrupt 2Fh Function 1684h
FUNCPTR GetDeviceAPI(WORD vxd_id)
{
    _asm {
        push di
        push es
        xor di, di
        mov es, di
        mov ax, 1684h
        mov bx, vxd_id
        int 2fh
        mov ax, di
        mov dx, es
        pop es
        pop di
        }
    // return value in DX:AX
}

int IsEnhancedMode(void)
{
    _asm {
        mov ax, 1600h
        int 2fh
        test al, 7fh
        jz no
        }
    return 1;
no: return 0;
}

void fail(const char *s, ...) { puts(s); exit(1); }

int main()
{
    WORD i;
    FUNCPTR fp;

    if (! IsEnhancedMode())
        fail("This program requires Windows Enhanced mode");

    puts("V86 VxD APIs:");
    puts("VxD   V86 entry   Linear  Byte");
    puts("----  ---------   ------  ----");
    // for each possible device id, see if there's an API
    for (i=0; i<0xffff; i++)
```

```
        if (fp = GetDeviceAPI(i))
            printf("%04Xh   %Fp   %01X   %02X\n",
                i,                                  // VxD ID
                fp,                                 // V86 entry point
                ((DWORD) FP_SEG(fp)<<4)+FP_OFF(fp), // linear addr
                *((BYTE far *) fp));                // byte (ARPL)
    return 0;
}
```


VXD86API looks only for V86 VxD APIs; it could easily be modified to use the DPMISH library and look for PM VxD APIs as well. If function 1684h is called from protected mode rather than V86 mode, it returns a protected-mode selector:offset address that a Win16 or protected-mode DOS application in Ring 3 can call to communicate with the VxD in Ring 0. The returned address points to an INT 30h instruction. Whereas ARPL is a V86 callback, INT 30h is a protected-mode callback. In Windows 3.0, protected-mode callbacks instead involved the HLT instruction. It's sort of amusing that fundamental mode-switching code in Windows pretended to be halting the processor because Microsoft once used a mode-switching technique — described by Gordon Letwin in U.S. Patent 4,825,358 ("Method and Operating System for Executing Programs in a Multi-Mode Microprocessor," April 25, 1989) — that *did* shut down the processor.

The output from our simple VXD86API program looks rather boring at first glance. If you stare at it long enough, however it's quite interesting. Well, I suppose that's true of anything, but you really *can* learn a lot about Windows 95 by pondering the output from VXD86API:

```
Virtual-8086 (V86) VxD APIs:
VxD     V86 entry   Linear  Byte
-----   ---------   ------  ----
0001h   FBE9:21B2   FE042   63
0003h   FBEA:21A2   FE042   63
0005h   FBEB:2192   FE042   63
000Ah   FBEC:2182   FE042   63
000Ch   FBED:2172   FE042   63
0010h   FBEE:2162   FE042   63
0015h   FBEF:2152   FE042   63
0017h   FBF0:2142   FE042   63
0026h   FBF1:2132   FE042   63
0027h   FBF2:2122   FE042   63
002Bh   FBF3:2112   FE042   63
0033h   FBF4:2102   FE042   63
0037h   FBF5:20F2   FE042   63
0038h   FBF6:20E2   FE042   63
003Bh   FBF7:20D2   FE042   63
0040h   FBF8:20C2   FE042   63
0202h   FBF9:20B2   FE042   63
0483h   FBFA:20A2   FE042   63
```

```
048Bh    FBFB:2092    FE042    63
2200h    FBFC:2082    FE042    63
28C0h    FBFD:2072    FE042    63
28C2h    FBFE:2062    FE042    63
296Eh    FBFF:2052    FE042    63
```

In this example, over 20 different VxDs provide some form of API to real-mode software running in V86 mode under Windows 95. For instance, VxD 0015h is DOSMGR; Chapter 4 showed that MS-DOS sometimes calls the DOSMGR API. VxD 0027h is VXDLDR; real-mode DOS programs can call the VXDLDR API to dynamically load and unload VxDs (function 1 calls VXDLDR_LoadDevice, and function 2 calls VXDLDR_UnloadDevice). VxD 0001h is the VMM, and its V86 API provides real-mode DOS programs with access to the Windows 95 registry (function 0100h is RegOpenKey, 0102h is RegCloseKey, 0105h is RegQueryValue, 0106h is RegEnumKey, and so on). In other words, one INT 2Fh function 1684h call can open up vast new worlds of services to DOS programs running under Windows.

More directly relevant to the topic of V86 callbacks and how IFSHLP calls into IFSMgr (which you may dimly recall was the original point here), is the fact that all the V86 VxD APIs point to an ARPL instruction (63h) and that all have the same linear address (FE042h). It looks like every V86 VxD API is the same!

We'll see in a few moments how VMM, when given a single ARPL located at a single linear address, figures out which VxD API the caller wanted. For now, just remember that every single V86 callback points to the same byte 63h, merely represented in different ways (FBE9:21B2 is the same real-mode address as FBEA:21A2, and as FBEB:2192, and so on).

Generally, this single byte 63h is located in the copyright message in the system ROM. During initialization, VMM finds the 'c'/ARPL/63h using an otherwise pointless-sounding VMM service called Locate_Byte_In_ROM. Why in ROM? Because that way, VMM knows there's no danger of someone accidentally or maliciously changing the byte to something other than 63h. This won't work if you're using a 386 memory manager that remaps ROM BIOS memory, however, so Windows provides a System-ROMBreakPoint=off setting. If SystemROMBreakPoint= off, all V86 call-backs will still point to a single byte 63h, but it will be located in potentially alterable low memory (specifically, in the Global V86 Data Area, visible at all times in all virtual machines) rather than in ROM.

So far, we've seen some situations in which one of these crazy ARPL addresses can be *passed* to an application that has asked for it. However, Windows also uses the ARPL scheme for one more situation. Suppose that an existing piece of real-mode code must be intercepted by VMM or a VxD. If the code starts off with an INT instruction or something else that's readily trappable in V86 mode, everything's cool. But there are situations in which Windows might want to intercept some code that doesn't use any of the instructions that are normally trappable in V86 mode.

You can probably see what's coming: VMM has the capability to take an arbitrary address in V86 mode, save away the byte at that address, and replace it with a new byte that will allow all calls to this address to be intercepted by VMM or a VxD. The new byte is an ARPL. The Install_V86_Break_Point service takes a V86 mode address on which to place the ARPL, and the 32-bit protected-mode address of a VxD routine to callback whenever the breakpoint is triggered.

Programmers newly exploring the underside of Windows are often confused about V86 breakpoints, thinking they must have something to do with debugging or error handling. Despite the term breakpoint, V86 breakpoints have nothing to do with debugging or error handling. Instead, like V86 and PM callbacks, they play an important role in the normal everyday operation of Windows, allowing execution of real-mode code to trigger calls into 32-bit protected-mode code. The DDK documentation for Install_V86_Break_Point provides a good example: "For example, the XMS driver in the virtual V86MMGR device inserts a breakpoint in the real-mode XMS driver during device initialization. Thereafter, all calls to the real-mode XMS driver are intercepted by the virtual XMS driver." (We'll look into this XMS example a little more in a few moments.)

As already noted, all V86 callbacks in Windows point to the same ARPL byte in memory. A debugger breakpoint placed on this byte will be triggered constantly. Significantly, even in a pure Win32 Windows 95 system, with no DOS or Win16 applications running, the V86 callback is used so heavily that even a Soft-ICE BPX C=50 (break every 50 hits) placed on the ARPL location is triggered so frequently that you can't accomplish any work in Windows.

These ARPL V86 breakpoints are at the very foundation of Windows, even on a pure Win32 Windows 95 version. But if you don't believe me, here's an experiment you can try: Set SystemROMBreakPoint=off in SYSTEM.INI, restart Windows 95, figure out where in low memory Windows has located the crucial 'c'/ARPL/63h byte (you can run the WINBP program discussed next to find it), close down everything that's not a Win32 application, use Soft-ICE to change the byte to something other than 'c'/ARPL/63h, and see Windows immediately blow up. Yes, even the purest Win32 Windows 95 system depends on V86 breakpoints. (And yes, you're much better off with SystemROMBreakPoint=on.)

Now, don't all you OS/2 fans out there start snickering about how ridiculous Windows is because it's built using illegal instructions. OS/2 2.*x* uses the same scheme, and you can look it up:

> *VDM breakpoints* are used by the 8086 emulation component to control execution flow when in v86 mode. The ARPL instruction is inserted into the VDM's interrupt vector table and interrupt stack frame when VDM breakpoints are set. Execution of the ARPL instruction in v86 mode causes a general protection fault [actually, an illegal opcode fault], and the system ultimately vectors to the 8086 emulation component. VDM breakpoints are used to transition from v86 mode in a VDM to the MVDM kernel running in kernel mode.
>
> — Harvey Deitel and Michael Kogan, *The Design of OS/2*, p. 297.

The word *ultimately* in the quote is quite appropriate. Much like the path from one topic to the next in this book, the path from an ARPL instruction to the appropriate 32-bit callback is anything but direct. For example, when a DOS application calls an entry point returned from INT 2Fh function 1684h, it executes the ARPL, which causes an INT 6, which lands in VMM, which passes the call off to the appropriate VxD V86 API handler. Those readers who played the Milton-Bradley game Mousetrap! in their youths or who have examined the cartoons of Rube Goldberg will be well equipped to understand this flow of control.

Let's see how all this helps us understand what's going on when IFSHLP calls into IFSMgr back (way back) in Figure 8-12. There is a single-instruction transition from the ARPL at FBCA:23A2 to the INT 06h illegal-opcode handler at VMM+240h. VMM must now figure out that it's dealing with a V86 callback and not with a genuine illegal opcode. It does this by taking the address at which the fault occurred (Client_CS << 4 + Client_EIP) and comparing this with (in this case) the number FE042h. Any illegal-opcode fault coming from this address is deemed a V86 callback.

Now VMM must figure out which 32-bit protected-mode callback goes with this V86 callback. This at first glance seems impossible, as we've just seen, all V86 callbacks point to the same byte. Only the superficial segment:offset form of their address differs. However, this superficial segment:offset form is sufficient. In Figure 8-12, we can see VMM take the faulting Client_CS (FBCAh in this example) and subtract a number (here, FB04h) that is the base segment for all V86 callbacks. VMM patches this number into its own code (see the SUB ECX, 0FB04h at

VMM+93E in Figure 8-12) during initialization, after it's figured out where the V86 callback's ARPL will be located. It also patches in the linear address of the callback (see the CMP EAX, 0FE042 at VMM+937 in Figure 8-12).

In the IFSHLP/IFSMgr example in Figure 8-12, the superficial address of the ARPL was FBCA:23A2. VMM verifies that FBCAh << 4 + 23A2h = FE042h, and then it subtracts FB04h from FBCAh, leaving 0C6h. This is the number of the V86 callback. VMM next uses this number to index into a table of V86 callbacks. In Figure 8-12, this table is located at C41DB000h. Each entry is eight bytes: four bytes for the address of the V86 callback and four bytes for optional reference data that VMM will pass to the callback.

```
VMM+929   MOVZX   EAX,WORD PTR [EBP.Client_CS]      ;;; FBCAh
VMM+92D   MOV     ECX,EAX
VMM+92F   MOV     EDX,[EBP.Client_EIP]              ;;; 23A2h
VMM+932   SHL     EAX,04
VMM+935   ADD     EAX,EDX                 ;;; FBCA0h + 23A2h = FE042h
VMM+937   CMP     EAX,000FE042            ;;; all V86 callbacks == FE042h
VMM+93C   JNZ     VMM+952                   (NO JUMP)
VMM+93E   SUB     ECX,0000FB04            ;;; FBCAh - FB04h (base) = 0C6h
VMM+944   MOV     EDX,[C41DB004+8*ECX] ;;; table of V86 CB ref data
VMM+94B   JMP     [C41DB000+8*ECX]        ;;; goto handler for this V86 CB
```

We can examine this table with the PROTDUMP utility from the *Unauthorized Windows 95* disk:

```
C:\UNAUTHW\PROTDUMP>protdump c41db000 -dword
C41DB000 | C022C708 C4520298 C0003244 0010B210
C41DB010 | C0003268 0010B210 C02200B8 0010B210
C41DB020 | C0004184 0000005E C0227BBF 00000208
C41DB030 | C0226A1C 00000208 C0227348 00000208
C41DB040 | C0228CE8 0010B210 C0229764 00000000
C41DB050 | C0229798 00000000 C022973C 00000000
C41DB060 | C022973C 00000000 C00026FC 00000000
C41DB070 | C00699AC C006A774 C00699A8 C006A774
```

For example, Callback 0 is handled at C022C708h; the handler is passed the reference data C4520298h. Given the callback number and the V86 address of the first callback, we could figure out the V86 address corresponding to any other callback. However, this is sufficiently tedious — and Windows breakpoints are sufficiently important — that it's worth having a dedicated program to dump out the callback tables.

WINBP.C in Listing 8-6 is a protected-mode DOS program that shows all V86 breakpoints, V86 callbacks, and PM callbacks. WINBP is able to figure out both the size of the breakpoint table (this corresponds to the MaxBPs= SYSTEM.INI setting, immortalized by Brian Livingston in his January 24, 1994 *InfoWorld* column, "Correct most Windows instability with just a single command") and its location given nothing more than one V86 callback and one PM callback, which WINBP can easily get by calling INT 2Fh function 1684h for any arbitrary VxD known to provide both a V86 and PM API.

Listing 8-6: WINBP.C

```
/*
WINBP.C -- Display Windows Breakpoints
Andrew Schulman, 1994
*/

#include <stdlib.h>
#include <stdio.h>
#include <ctype.h>
#include <dos.h>
#include "dpmish.h"
#include "prot.h"

typedef void far *FP;

FP GetVxDAPI(WORD vxd_id);
DWORD GetGDTSelectorBase(WORD seg);
DWORD GetGDTSelectorLimit(WORD seg);

#define PUT(s)              { fputs(s, stderr); fputs("\n", stderr); }

void fail(const char *s, ...) { PUT(s); _dos_exit(1); }

static DWORD v86bp_lin, pmbp_base, bp_tab_lin;
static WORD pmbp_size, max_bps;
static int win_ver = 0;

#pragma pack(1)

typedef struct {    // V86/PM callback/breakpoint
    union {
        struct {
            DWORD callback, refdata;
            } CALLBACK;
        struct {
            DWORD brk_addr;
            union {
                struct {    // better packing in Windows 95
                    WORD bp_num;
                    BYTE replaced;
                    } WIN4;
                struct {
                    BYTE replaced;
                    WORD bp_num;
                    } WIN3;
                } REPLBP;
```

```
            BYTE ff;
            } V86;
        } u;
        // extra DWORD in debug?
    } CB;

#define ARPL        0x63
#define INT30       0x30CD

int real_main(int argc, char *argv[])
{
    FP v86_api;
    BYTE far *fp;

    PUT("WINBP -- Examine Windows Breakpoints and Callbacks");
    PUT("Copyright (c) 1994 Andrew Schulman. All rights reserved.");
    PUT("From \"Unauthorized Windows\" (IDG Books, 1994)\n");

    if (! (v86_api = GetVxDAPI(5))) // get any V86 callback
        fail("This program requires Windows Enhanced mode");
    fp = (BYTE far *) v86_api;
    if (*fp != ARPL)
        fail("Something wrong! 2F/1684/5 V86 should return ptr to ARPL");

    v86bp_lin = MK_LIN(v86_api);
    printf("V86 breakpoints @ %08lXh ('", v86bp_lin);
    while (isprint(*fp)) { putchar(*fp); fp++; }
    printf("')\n");

    _asm mov ax, 1600h
    _asm int 2fh
    _asm mov byte ptr win_ver+1, al

    return 0;
}

int pmode_main(int argc, char *argv[])
{
    CB far *cb_tab, far *cb;
    FP pm_api;
    DWORD api_cb_addr;
    WORD avail_bps;
    WORD v86_seg, v86_ofs, pm_seg, pm_ofs;
    WORD first_v86_bp_seg, first_v86_bp_ofs;
    WORD last_v86_bp_seg, last_v86_bp_ofs;
    int verbose = 0;
    int i;

    char *s = argv[1];
    if ((argc > 1) &&
        ((s[0] == '-') || (s[0] == '/')) &&
        ((s[1] == 'v') || (s[1] == 'V')))
        verbose++;

    if (! (pm_api = GetVxDAPI(5)))      // get any PM callback
```

```
        fail("This program requires Windows Enhanced mode");
    if (*((WORD far *) pm_api) != INT30)
        fail("Something wrong! 2F/1684/5 PM should return ptr to INT 30h");

    pm_seg = FP_SEG(pm_api);
    pmbp_base = GetGDTSelectorBase(pm_seg);
    printf("PM breakpoints @ %08lXh\n", pmbp_base);

    pmbp_size = GetGDTSelectorLimit(pm_seg) + 1;
    max_bps = (pmbp_size >> 1) - 0x100;
    printf("MaxBPs = %u (%04Xh)\n", max_bps, max_bps);

    last_v86_bp_seg = v86bp_lin >> 4;
    last_v86_bp_ofs = v86bp_lin & 0x0F;
    first_v86_bp_seg = (v86bp_lin >> 4) - max_bps;
    first_v86_bp_ofs = v86bp_lin - ((DWORD) first_v86_bp_seg << 4);
    printf("First V86 BP = %04X:%04X\n", first_v86_bp_seg, first_v86_bp_ofs);
    printf("Last  V86 BP = %04X:%04X\n", last_v86_bp_seg, last_v86_bp_ofs);

    bp_tab_lin = pmbp_base - (max_bps << 3);
    if (bp_tab_lin & 0xFFF) // not on page boundary!
        fail( (bp_tab_lin & 0xFFF) == (max_bps * 4) ?
            "Looks like Debug Windows has larger BPs?" :
            "Can't get BP table address!"),

    printf("BP table @ %08lXh\n", bp_tab_lin);

    if (! verbose)
        fail("\nRun WINBP -VERBOSE to list all breakpoints and callbacks");

    cb_tab = (CB far *) map_linear(bp_tab_lin, max_bps * sizeof(CB));
    if (! cb_tab) fail("Couldn't map callback table!");

    printf("\nV86 Breakpoints:\n");
    printf("BP #    V86 addr   Repl   CB #    Callback    Ref Data\n");
    printf("----    --------   ----   ----    --------    --------\n");

    for (i=0, cb=cb_tab; i<max_bps; i++, cb++)
    {
        if (cb->u.V86.ff == 0xff)
        {
            WORD bp_num;
            BYTE replaced;
            if (cb->u.V86.brk_addr > 0x1010FFEFL)   // only V86 mode mem
                continue;   // skip bogus entries
            if (win_ver < 4)
            {
                bp_num = cb->u.V86.REPLBP.WIN3.bp_num;
                replaced = cb->u.V86.REPLBP.WIN3.replaced;
            }
            else
            {
                bp_num = cb->u.V86.REPLBP.WIN4.bp_num;
                replaced = cb->u.V86.REPLBP.WIN4.replaced;
            }
```

```
            printf("%04X    %08lX    %02X    %04X    ",
                i,
                cb->u.V86.brk_addr,
                replaced,
                bp_num);
            if (bp_num <= max_bps)
                printf("%08lX    %08lX",
                    cb_tab[bp_num].u.CALLBACK.callback,
                    cb_tab[bp_num].u.CALLBACK.refdata);
            printf("\n");

#ifdef  SANITY_CHECK
            {
                BYTE far *fp = (BYTE far *) map_linear(cb->u.V86.brk_addr, 1);
                if (! fp) fail("Couldn't map breakpoint");
                if (*fp != ARPL)
                    printf("Something wrong!!\n");
                free_mapped_linear(fp);
            }
#endif
        }
        if (ctrl_c_hit)
            goto done;
    }

    /* locate V86, PM API 2f/1684 callbacks */
    api_cb_addr =
        cb_tab[((FP_OFF(pm_api) << 2) - 0x800) >> 3].u.CALLBACK.callback;

    printf("\nV86 and PM callbacks:\n");
    printf("BP #    Callback    Ref Data      V86          PM    \n");
    printf("----    --------    --------    ---------    ---------\n");

    v86_seg = first_v86_bp_seg;
    v86_ofs = first_v86_bp_ofs;
    pm_ofs = 0x200;

    for (i=0, cb=cb_tab;
         i<max_bps;
         i++, cb++, v86_seg++, v86_ofs -= 0x10, pm_ofs += 2)
    {
        if (cb->u.V86.ff != 0xff)
        {
            if (cb->u.CALLBACK.callback == 0)
                continue;   // skip blanks
            printf("%04X    %08lX    %08lX    %04X:%04X    %04X:%04X",
                i,
                cb->u.CALLBACK.callback,
                cb->u.CALLBACK.refdata,
                v86_seg, v86_ofs,
                pm_seg, pm_ofs);
            if (cb->u.CALLBACK.callback == api_cb_addr)
            {
                DWORD far *fp = (DWORD far *)
                    map_linear(cb->u.CALLBACK.refdata, sizeof(DWORD));
```

```
                if (! fp) fail("Couldn't map API callback addr");
                printf("  ->  %08lX", *fp); // show actual API callback addr
                free_mapped_linear(fp);
            }
            printf("\n");
        }
        if (ctrl_c_hit)
            goto done;
    }

done:
    free_mapped_linear(cb_tab);

    return 0;
}

/**********************************************************************/

// call the Windows "Get Device Entry Point Address" function
// Interrupt 2Fh Function 1684h
FP GetVxDAPI(WORD vxd_id)
{
    _asm {
        push di
        push es
        xor di, di
        mov es, di
        mov ax, 1684h
        mov bx, vxd_id
        int 2fh
        mov ax, di
        mov dx, es
        pop es
        pop di
        }
    // return value in DX:AX
}

/**********************************************************************/

#pragma pack(1)

typedef struct {
    WORD rpl : 2;
    WORD ti : 1;
    WORD index : 13;
    } SELECTOR;

typedef struct {
    WORD limit_lo, base_lo;
    BYTE base_hi, rts_lo, limitrts_hi, base_xhi;
    } DESCRIPTOR;

// Global Descriptor Table (GDT) register
typedef struct { WORD limit; DWORD base; } GDTR;
```

```
DESCRIPTOR far *get_gdt(WORD *plimit);
void sgdt(GDTR far *pgdtr);
static DWORD get_desc_base(DESCRIPTOR far *desc);
static DWORD get_desc_limit(DESCRIPTOR far *desc);

DWORD GetGDTSelectorBase(WORD seg)
{
    SELECTOR sel = *((SELECTOR *) &seg);
    DWORD base;
    if (sel.ti == 0)    // GDT
    {
        WORD gdt_limit;
        DESCRIPTOR far *gdt = get_gdt(&gdt_limit);
        if ((seg & ~8) > gdt_limit)
            fail("Invalid GDT selector");
        base = get_desc_base(&gdt[sel.index]);
        free_mapped_linear(gdt);
    }
    else                // LDT: oh what the heck, get it for them
        base = GetSelectorBase(seg);
    return base;
}

DWORD GetGDTSelectorLimit(WORD seg)
{
    SELECTOR sel = *((SELECTOR *) &seg);
    DWORD limit;
    if (sel.ti == 0)    // GDT
    {
        WORD gdt_limit;
        DESCRIPTOR far *gdt = get_gdt(&gdt_limit);
        if ((seg & ~8) > gdt_limit)
            fail("Invalid GDT selector");
        limit = get_desc_limit(&gdt[sel.index]);
        free_mapped_linear(gdt);
    }
    else                // LDT: oh what the heck, get it for them
        limit = GetSelectorLimit(seg);
    return limit;
}

// when done, free with free_mapped_linear
DESCRIPTOR far *get_gdt(WORD *plimit)
{
    DESCRIPTOR far *gdt;
    GDTR gdtr;
    WORD sel;

    /* get the linear base address and size (limit) of the Global
       Descriptor Table (GDT), using the Intel SGDT instruction */
    sgdt(&gdtr);
    gdt = (DESCRIPTOR far *) map_linear(gdtr.base, gdtr.limit + 1);
    if (! gdt) fail("Couldn't map GDT!");
    *plimit = gdtr.limit;
    return gdt;
```

```
}

void sgdt(GDTR far *pgdtr)
{
    _asm les bx, pgdtr
    _asm sgdt fword ptr es:[bx]
}

DWORD get_desc_base(DESCRIPTOR far *desc)
{
    return ((DWORD) desc->base_xhi << 24L) +
       ((DWORD) desc->base_hi << 16L) +  desc->base_lo;
}

DWORD get_desc_limit(DESCRIPTOR far *desc)
{
    DWORD limit = ((DWORD) (desc->limitrts_hi & 0x0F) << 16L) +
        (DWORD) desc->limit_lo;
    if (desc->limitrts_hi & 0x80)   // page granularity
        limit *= 4096;
    return limit;
}
```


I wish I had time to explain exactly how WINBP works, such as how it calculates the MaxBPs= value and how it relates V86 breakpoints to V86 callbacks, but this would take many pages. Well okay, let me just give you the formula used to calculate MaxBPs:

```
pm_api = GetVxDAPI(5);                         // get any PM callback
pm_seg = FP_SEG(pm_api);                       // get its segment (3Bh)
pmbp_size = GetGDTSelectorLimit(pm_seg) + 1;   // get segment size
max_bps = (pmbp_size / 2) - 0x100;             // get MaxBPs=
```

Calling INT 2Fh function 1684h (GetVxDAPI) in protected mode will return a PM callback. All we're interested in is the segment. All PM callbacks come out of the same segment, and the size of this segment is directly related to the MaxBPs value. It would be nice to get the size of this segment with the GetSelectorLimit Windows API (or its DPMI equivalent, INT 31h function 8). However, these work only with the Local Descriptor Table (LDT), and this segment's selector is in the Global Descriptor Table (GDT), so WINBP.C supplies its own Get-GDTSelectorLimit and GetGDTSelectorBase routines (WINBP uses the non-privileged SGDT instruction to access the GDT). Each PM callback is two bytes (an INT 30h instruction is CDh 30h), so WINBP divides the segment size by two. It then subtracts 0x100, because VMM always reserves that amount (see Chapell, *DOS Internals*, p. 71).

If you run WINBP, it spits out a few statistics:

```
V86 breakpoints @ 000FE042h ('chnologies Ltd.')
PM breakpoints @ C41DC0800h
```

```
MaxBPs = 768 (0300h)
First V86 BP = FB04:3002
Last  V86 BP = FE04:0002
BP table @ C41DB000h
```

It's also useful to run WINBP when SystemROMBreakPoint=off:

```
V86 breakpoints @ 0001D6C0h ('c')
PM breakpoints @ C41DC800h
MaxBPs = 768 (0300h)
First V86 BP = 1A6C:3000
Last  V86 BP = 1D6C:0000
BP table @ C41DB000h
```


If you run WINBP -VERBOSE, it prints out all V86 breakpoints and all V86 and PM callbacks. It's useful to run the output through the VXDNAME utility so that instead of addresses such as C00735ACh, you can deal with addresses such as IFSMgr+4B0h. For example:

```
V86 Breakpoints:
BP #     V86 addr    Repl    CB #     Callback            Ref Data
----     --------    ----    ----     --------            --------
02F1     000C0525     90     00CA     SHELL.10+01C        C0500003
02F2     0001D73A     90     00C2     V86MMGR.9+000       00000000
02F3     0001D731     90     00C1     V86MMGR.3+131A      00000000
02F4     0001D72D     FF     00C0     V86MMGR.3+2777      00000000
02F5     0001D733     90     00BF     V86MMGR.3+12F5      00000000
02F6     0001D72B     90     00BE     V86MMGR.3+12E0      00000000
02F7     0001D729     90     00BD     V86MMGR.3+12C4      00000000
02F8     00000953     90     00A5     VKD.2+3B8           00000A17
02F9     0001DAFC     90     00A4     VMOUSE.2+1154       00000000
02FA     0001DAF5     90     00A3     VMOUSE.2+112E       00000000
02FB     0001DADD     90     00A0     VDD+21B6            00000000
02FC     0001DAD6     90     009F     VDD+2114            00000000
02FF     0001D6DC     00     008F     VMOUSE.2+118        00000000

V86 and PM callbacks:
BP #     Callback     Ref Data       V86          PM
----     --------     --------      ---------    ---------
0000     VMM.9+264    C4520298      FB04:3002    003B:0200
0001     VMM+2244     0010B210      FB05:2FF2    003B:0202
0002     VMM+2268     0010B210      FB06:2FE2    003B:0204
0003     VMM.2+0B8    0010B210      FB07:2FD2    003B:0206
; ...
00C6     IFSMgr+4B0   00000007      FBCA:23A2    003B:038C
; ...
00E5     VMM+32E4     VMM+DC44      FBE9:21B2    003B:03CA  ->  VMM+1A11
00E6     VMM+32E4     VPICD+1938    FBEA:21A2    003B:03CC  ->  VPICD+F88
00E7     VMM+32E4     VTD+33C       FBEB:2192    003B:03CE  ->  VTD.3+000
00E8     VMM+32E4     VDD+4AD4      FBEC:2182    003B:03D0  ->  VDD+2DA4
00E9     VMM+32E4     VMOUSE+5EC    FBED:2172    003B:03D2  ->  VMOUSE.2+78C
00EA     VMM+32E4     IOS+1A98      FBEE:2162    003B:03D4  ->  IOS.2+1864
00EB     VMM+32E4     DOSMGR+1C8    FBEF:2152    003B:03D6  ->  DOSMGR.12+000
00EC     VMM+32E4     SHELL+9E8     FBF0:2142    003B:03D8  ->  SHELL.2+0C5
```

```
00ED    VMM+32E4    VPOWERD+344 FBF1:2132    003B:03DA  ->  VPOWERD.2+000
00EE    VMM+32E4    VXDLDR+084  FBF2:2122    003B:03DC  ->  VXDLDR.3+1C9
00EF    VMM+32E4    VCOMM+2CC   FBF3:2112    003B:03DE  ->  VCOMM.2+1A8
00F0    VMM+32E4   CONFIGMG+30C FBF4:2102    003B:03E0  ->  CONFIGMG.3+000
00F1    VMM+32E4    ENABLE+39C  FBF5:20F2    003B:03E2  ->  ENABLE.2+2C4
00F2    VMM+32E4    VCOND+060   FBF6:20E2    003B:03E4  ->  VCOND.2+000
00F3    VMM+32E4    DSVXD+1EC   FBF7:20D2    003B:03E6  ->  DSVXD+057
00F4    VMM+32E4    IFSMgr+2C18 FBF8:20C2    003B:03E8  ->  IFSMgr.2+1CA7
00F5    VMM+32E4   WINICE+24F28 FBF9:20B2    003B:03EA  ->  WINICE+7AC
00F6    VMM+32E4    VSHARE+3FC  FBFA:20A2    003B:03EC  ->  VSHARE+290
00F7    VMM+32E4    VCACHE+5DC  FBFB:2092    003B:03EE  ->  VCACHE+52D
00F8    VMM+32E4    VFINTD+25C  FBFC:2082    003B:03F0  ->  VFINTD+022
00F9    VMM+32E4    VXD+320     FBFD:2072    003B:03F2  ->  VXD+02A
00FA    VMM+32E4    CR3+050     FBFE:2062    003B:03F4  ->  CR3+002
00FB    VMM+32E4    PSVXD+8DC   FBFF:2052    003B:03F6  ->  PSVXD+0E3
00FC    VMM+32E4    VTD+340     FC00:2042    003B:03F8  ->  VTD.3+000
```

The first section shows V86 breakpoints. For example, recall the earlier quotation from the DDK documentation about how the V86-MMGR VxD uses a V86 breakpoint to take over XMS. Now that we have WINBP, it's easy to see how this works. First, use a debugger to call INT 2Fh function 4310h (Get XMS Driver Address) and walk the XMS handler chain (see Chappell, *DOS Internals*, pp. 505-512, for a good explanation of this little-known aspect of XMS):

```
C:\>symdeb
-a
7C0D:0100 mov ax, 4310
7C0D:0103 int 2f
7C0D:0105
-p
AX=4310  BX=0000  CX=0000  DX=0000  SP=82E2  BP=0000  SI=0000  DI=0000
DS=7C0D  ES=7C0D  SS=7C0D  CS=7C0D  IP=0103   NV UP EI PL NZ NA PO NC
7C0D:0103 CD2F          INT    2F
-p
AX=4310  BX=00CF  CX=0000  DX=0000  SP=82E2  BP=0000  SI=0000  DI=0000
DS=7C0D  ES=0313  SS=7C0D  CS=7C0D  IP=0105   NV UP EI PL NZ NA PO NC
7C0D:0105 0000          ADD    [BX+SI],AL         DS:00CF=00
-u es:bx
0313:00CF EA45006F1D    JMP    1D6F:0045

-u 1d6f:45
1D6F:0045 EB03          JMP    004A
1D6F:0047 90            NOP
1D6F:0048 90            NOP
1D6F:0049 90            NOP
1D6F:004A 63            DB 63
```

There's ARPL (which SYMDEB outputs as DB 63) at 1D6F:004A. 1D6F0h + 4Ah = 1D73Ah. Sure enough, WINBP can tell us about this V86 breakpoint at linear address 1D73Ah:

```
C:\UNAUTHW\WINBP>winbp -verbose | grep 1D73A
02F2    0001D73A    90    00C2    C0239EBC    00000000

C:\UNAUTHW\WINBP>winbp -verbose | grep 1D73A | vxdname
02F2    0001D73A    90    00C2    V86MMGR.9+000    00000000
```

What all this means is that there's a V86 breakpoint on 1D73Ah (we knew that!) corresponding to V86 callback 90h, that ARPL replaced the byte C2h, and that C0239EBCh (or offset 0 in segment 9 of V86-MMGR) is the XMS handler.

Now we can put a breakpoint (a debugger breakpoint, I mean) on C0239EBCh, do something that uses XMS, and see if the breakpoint is triggered. I ran the DOS MEM utility, which among other things reports the amount of available XMS memory. Sure enough, the breakpoint in V86MMGR was triggered, and I could see a variety of XMS calls coming into V86MMGR.

For example, there was a call to XMS function 6 (Local Disable A20), followed by one to XMS function 5 (Local Enable A20). On receipt of these XMS calls, V86MMGR turned around and called the VMM_MMGR_Toggle_HMA service. Actually, these two calls have nothing in particular to do with the DOS MEM utility; for reasons we don't have time to get into here (but see Chappell, *DOS Internals*, pp. 207-209), DOS calls these functions whenever it loads an executable. These calls, from deep inside the DOS kernel, end up being serviced in 32-bit protected mode by _MMGR_Toggle_HMA.

MEM itself called XMS function 8 (Query Free Extended Memory). To service this call, V86MMGR in turn called PageSwap_Get_Version, PageSwap_Test_IO_Valid, and _PageGetAllocInfo. *Once again, DOS ends up calling Windows.*

Next, let's look at the V86 and PM callbacks section of the WINBP output. Much earlier in this long digression on V86 callbacks, the VXD86API program revealed the presence of some V86 VxD APIs:

```
0001h   FBE9:21B2   FE042   63      ;;; VMM
0015h   FBEF:2152   FE042   63      ;;; DOSMGR
0027h   FBF2:2122   FE042   63      ;;; VXDLDR
```

We know that addresses such as FBE9:21B2 don't contain the actual code that services the V86 VxD API request. Instead, there's nothing at these addresses but ARPLs. (In fact, as we saw, it's all the same ARPL at the same linear address.) So where is the actual code that provides VMM's or DOSMGR's or VXDLDR's V86 API? Just search through WINBP's output for an address such as FBE9:21B2 or FBEF:2152, and you'll find the location where the 32-bit protected-mode code resides:

```
00E5    VMM+32E4    VMM+DC44     FBE9:21B2    003B:03CA  ->  VMM+1A11
00EB    VMM+32E4    DOSMGR+1C8   FBEF:2152    003B:03D6  ->  DOSMGR.12+000
00EE    VMM+32E4    VXDLDR+084   FBF2:2122    003B:03DC  ->  VXDLDR.3+1C9
```

Let's look briefly at DOSMGR. In Chapter 4, we saw that DOS in certain situations will call function 1 (Set Focus) of DOSMGR's V86 API. Examining the code at DOSMGR.12+0 (here located at C023DAD0h), we see DOSMGR taking the function number specified in AX, and using it to index into a table of function pointers:

```
:u c023dad0
0028:C023DAD0    MOVZX    EAX,WORD PTR [EBP.Client_AX]
0028:C023DAD4    CMP      EAX,06
0028:C023DAD9    JAE      C023DAE3
0028:C023DADB    CALL     [C02C380C+4*EAX]
0028:C023DAE2    RET
```


We can use the PROTDUMP utility to examine this table; the CMP EAX,06 tells us that DOSMGR's V86 API supports six functions:

```
C:\UNAUTHW\PROTDUMP>protdump c02c380c -dword
C02C380C | C023DAEE C023DAFD C023DB07 C023DB24
C02C381C | C023DB3D C023DB42
```

The code that DOS sometimes calls for function 1 is quite simple; it basically just calls the VMM System_Control service with AX=0Fh:

```
:u c023dafd
0028:C023DAFD    CALL     C023B524
0028:C023DB02    AND      BYTE PTR [EBP+2C],FE
0028:C023DB06    RET

:u c023b524
0028:C023B524    MOV      EAX,0000000F
0028:C023B529    XOR      EDX,EDX
0028:C023B52B    XOR      ESI,ESI
0028:C023B52D    INT      20 VXDCall System_Control
```

System_Control sends a control message to every VxD in the system. Message 0Fh is Set_Device_Focus. If EDX is zero (as it is here), *all* VxDs receive the focus. Incidentally, there's a nearly identical function, INT 2Fh function 168Bh, that uses System_Control Set_Device_Focus to set the input focus to a specified VM. David Long discusses this function in detail in an excellent article, "TSR Support in Microsoft Windows Version 3.1," on the MSDN CD-ROM. According to Long, "This service has some inherent risks" when setting the focus to a windowed DOS box because the keyboard and execution focus are set to the specified VM, but (because the DOS box is windowed) the display and mouse focus are set to the System VM. Long's article includes "some rainy-day experiments you can perform with SetFocus in the privacy of your own home."

At any rate, MS-DOS's call to DOSMGR, made via an ARPL instruction, ends up calling System_Control Set_Device_Focus. Repeating the point made in Chapter 4, the fact that DOS can call Windows is an excellent example of how the old "Windows runs on top of DOS" description was never very useful.

Popping back to our IFSHLP example, after this long but necessary digression about Windows breakpoints and callbacks, let's see what WINBP can tell us about that ARPL located at FBCA:23A2 way back in Figure 8-12:

```
; from trace in Figure 8-12
FBCA:23A2   ARPL    [BX+SI+6E],BP       ;;; V86 callback at FBCA:23A2

; from WINBP | VXDNAME
00C6    IFSMgr+4B0    00000007    FBCA:23A2    003B:038C
```

Sure enough, WINBP tells us that when IFSHLP executes the ARPL at FBCA:23A2, it will call into IFSMgr+4B0, just as we saw in Figure 8-12. Ta-da!

Now that IFSHLP has passed the INT 21h function 0Bh call up to IFSMgr, IFSMgr deals with the upward-reflected INT 21h call in whatever way it sees fit. In some cases, IFSMgr will absorb the call in 32-bit protected mode. In other cases, IFSMgr will want to reflect the call back down to the DOS interrupt chain in V86 mode. Of course, it does no good to send it back down to the head of the INT 21h chain, because then IFSHLP will see it again. IFSMgr needs to send the call to the INT 21h handler that was installed *before* IFSHLP. In Figure 8-12, you can see IFSMgr getting ready to do this by passing the previous handler's segment:offset address to the Build_Int_Stack_Frame service. IFSMgr knows the address of the INT 21h handler installed before IFSHLP because IFSHLP keeps this address in a table; it gives IFSMgr a pointer to this table.

IFSMgr now returns to VMM, which eventually does an IRETD. But instead of returning to whatever V86 code originally issued the INT 21h that got us started on this whole mess, the IRETD instead "returns" to the address that IFSMgr passed to Build_Int_Stack_Frame. This takes us to the INT 21h handler installed before IFSHLP. Even when an INT 21h call is sent down to DOS (as happens with the DOS box's frequent calls to function 0Bh), the call often bops back into VxD-land for some handling.

To make a ridiculously long story short, one role for IFSHLP.SYS is to prevent certain reflected INT 21h file calls from reaching DOS. As Geoff Chappell has put it:

> Int 21h etc. can be reflected into the VM, knowing that IFSHLP is there to wrest control back to ring 0 before it reaches the nasty, ugly, old DOS kernel. IFSHLP is the cut-off: everything that hooks int 21h after it gets supported, everything that hooked before IFSHLP gets replaced.

IFSHLP.SYS wears several other hats, including keeping simulated INTs (see the "Replacing Real-Mode Code: It's Not New" section later in this chapter) from reaching DOS. IFSHLP.SYS also hooks several other interrupts besides INT 21h, including INT 08h, 17h, 2Ah, and 2Fh.

Figure 8-13 presents a schematic view of the path taken by a V86 INT 21h call in Chicago.


```
INT 21h in DOS program
    -> VMM
    -> V86 hook int chain
    -> ... (other VxD INT 21h hooks, like VMPoll and SHELL) ...
    -> IFSMgr
       if (VM hooked INT 21h via 21/25)*
       -> local INT 21h hookers (such as TEST21)
       -> global INT 21h hookers (such as V86TEST)
       -> IFSHLP.SYS
          -> (via ARPL) VMM
          -> IFSMgr
             if (file function that IFSMgr emulates)
                emulate it
             else
                pass to V86 handler underneath IFSHLP

*This is the test IFSMgr uses, but it probably ought to instead be:
    if (INT 21h vector != original IFSHLP.SYS INT 21h vector)
```

Figure 8-13: The path of a V86 INT 21h call in Chicago.

One important point: The TEST21 results back in Figure 8-10 showed that even with INT 21h calls reflected to INT 21h hookers, 32BFA is still significantly faster than letting DOS handle the file I/O. In addition, whereas TEST21 -MYSETVECT 3000 > FOO.BAR took 12 seconds in one test under Chicago, TEST21 3000 > FOO.BAR (without -MYSETVECT) took only 3 seconds longer. I was quite surprised by this, and I asked Geoff Chappell what he made of the fact that reflected INT 21h calls, blocked and rerouted by IFSHLP, were nearly as fast as absorbed INT 21h calls. Here's his explanation:

> Well, yes, I expect it to run nearly as fast. The reflection of interrupts into VMs is not likely to be a serious delay in the overall context of DOS operations. 32BFA picks up its performance gain by replacing the DOS kernel, which as we know executes large tracts of code in critical sections and, worse, sees to its device driver calls one at a time, always waiting for completion. True, write-behind disk caches help out with this last matter by making it seem like the device driver has completed quickly — but

> this works only for write operations, which are relatively infrequent compared to reads (for which waiting is inescapable).

By now, you no doubt feel that Windows 95's solution to the "support DOS TSRs without calling DOS" problem is far from ideal. Why all this complexity? It's interesting to contrast how Microsoft handled the equivalent problem in 32-bit disk access (32BDA).

Just as 32BFA bypasses DOS for file-related INT 21h calls, 32BDA bypasses the BIOS for INT 13h direct disk access. And, just as with 32BFA, Windows must somehow try to support INT 13h hookers and yet still keep INT 13h calls away from the BIOS. But, in contrast to INT 21h and the situation with 32BFA, there is a simple solution for INT 13h: The I/O Supervisor (IOS) VxD, previously known as BLOCKDEV, uses an undocumented call, INT 2Fh function 13h, which manipulates the INT 13h chain underneath IO.SYS's handler. This function is described in great detail in Geoff Chappell, *DOS Internals*, pp. 57-95 (also see the DDK documentation for the Int13_Hooking_BIOS_Int and Int13_Unhooking_BIOS_Int services, which IOS/BLOCKDEV calls when manipulating the INT 13h chain). Figure 8-14 shows the route taken by an INT 13h call under 32BDA.

```
INT 13h in DOS program
    -> VMM
    -> VFD (Virtual Floppy Device sees if it's INT 13h for a floppy)
    -> BLOCKDEV/IOS
    -> any INT 13h hook in DOS -> ...
    -> Handler installed with INT 2Fh function 13h
    -> BLOCKDEV/IOS
```

Figure 8-14: The path of an INT 13h with 32-bit disk access.

Incidentally, this form of INT 13h handling means that if we wanted to write a TEST13 program to show off 32BDA, similar to TEST21 for 32BFA, we couldn't just hook INT 13h. We would have to use INT 2Fh function 13h. Unfortunately, MS-DOS does not instance (see Chapter 4 on instance data) the INT 13h hook function pointer it keeps at 0070:00B4, and so calling INT 2Fh function 13h under Windows makes it blow up. Once again, I asked Geoff Chappell about this. Here's his response:

> Yes, it is as simple as having Windows instance the pointers in IO.SYS. Really, I think IO/MSDOS should do this via 2F/1605.... If you want to write a VxD to support 2F/13 being used by a VM to install local code as an int 13h handler under IO.SYS, then you must either know/determine the addresses of the relevant pointers (see

> IOS.386 for an example of how to test the assumptions about 0070:00B0/0106 and 0070:00B4) or hook 2F/13 in the V86 int chain (and then confront the complicated problem of emulating the interface as if it had been local all along). I claim that doing all this is Windows' responsibility, precisely because a program using 2F/13 in a VM cannot arrange on its own for the interface to be usable.

Especially since Windows 95 sports a supposedly new version of DOS (WINBOOT.SYS), it's a shame that INT 2Fh function 13h can't be safely called within a Windows DOS box and that there is no equivalent INT 2Fh function 21h interface to manipulate the INT 21h chain. In the absence of such a function, IFSHLP.SYS acts as sort of a DOS equivalent to INT 2Fh function 13h. Here's Geoff Chappell again:

> IFSHLP's only possible claim to existence is to terminate the int 21h chain in virtual machines. 32BDA aims to replace the BIOS's int 13h handling, much as 32BFA aims to replace DOS's int 21h. The end of the int 13h chain, that is, just before it whizzes off to the BIOS, can be located easily, albeit through an undocumented interface (int 2Fh function 13h). There is no obvious way to find the end of the int 21h chain, that is, just before it reaches the DOS kernel. This is the only sensible role for IFSHLP.
>
> Some Microsoft developer offering silly excuses for WfW 3.11 claimed that the choice was to reflect always or to reflect never — and that Microsoft was indeed attending to concerns by offering the choice to enable/disable 32BFA.
>
> Instead, when they get the interrupt in ring 0, they should look at the V86 int vector: if it hasn't been hooked away from IFSHLP, then sure, it would only hit performance to reflect, but if someone has hooked it, then they can reflect into the VM and support the old software for the price of a slight hit. Instead, they've presented troubled users with a stark choice between their old driver/TSR or the wonderful new 32BFA.
>
> I wouldn't put it past some people in Microsoft to have thought that the presumably short-lived WfW 3.11 could not only keep the market interested while Chicago was being developed but could also accelerate the death of these awkward DOS drivers/TSRs and thereby give the Chicago developers less to worry about. You know something, I think they've very nearly gotten away with it, too.

Certainly, Microsoft does want to move developers away from TSRs and towards VxDs. For applications that need to track file access in Windows 95, IFSMgr provides a new FileHook API, which can only be called (directly, at any rate) from a VxD.

In truth, 32BFA in WfW 3.11 appears more and more to be a pre-beta test for Windows 95. Microsoft's ads for WfW 3.11 said that the product was "powered by 32-bit technology from our 'Chicago' project." Given that Chicago was not even in alpha testing at the time, this should have produced at least some concern about the state of the 32BFA code in WfW 3.11, as should the description string "Win386 HPFS Driver (Prototype)" in the WfW 3.11 commercial release of VFAT.386. Prototype?!

Now, putting pre-alpha Chicago 32BFA code into WfW 3.11 *was* a great way to get millions of users banging on the Chicago code. But it's not clear that these users should have had to pay for Microsoft's prototype code, especially when the standard Microsoft response to any complaints about 32BFA in WfW 3.11 was that the user should disable it. As one Microsoft representative put it in the WINSDK forum on CompuServe, 32BFA is "a nice feature, IMHO [in my humble opinion], but it is kind of a case of 'if it interferes with your life, disable it.'" This was Microsoft's major shipping version of Windows at the time. In fact, as I write this, WfW 3.11 with its prototype version of 32BFA is *still* Microsoft's major shipping version of Windows.

32BFA and Networks, CD-ROM, and Floppies

You may by now, have a nagging feeling about the TEST21 results we've spent so long poring over. Although we've run TEST21 in a number of environments — plain-vanilla DOS, DOS with a disk cache, WfW 3.11 with 32BFA, and Windows 95 — all of our file access has involved a hard disk. Earlier, we did compare 32BFA on a DblSpace and non-DblSpace (host) drive, but we haven't said anything about other media, such as floppy disks, CD-ROM, RAM disks, and most important of all, networks.

First, 32-bit network file access bypasses DOS in the same way that 32-bit disk file access bypasses DOS. Under WfW 3.11, the message "Some INT 21h are handled without calling DOS!" is produced both by TEST21 running on a network server that's running Windows NT Advanced Server and by TEST21 running via peer-to-peer access on another WfW 3.11 machine.

Should this come as any surprise? On the most prevalent networks for the PC, NetWare 2.*x* and 3.*x*, workstations run the NetWare shell, NETX, which hooks INT 21h and largely replaces large chunks of DOS (see *Undocumented DOS*, 2d ed., pp. 195-205). You would *expect* network file access to bypass DOS.

But the NETX approach of hooking INT 21h ahead of DOS, while typical in the sense that NetWare is the dominant PC network, isn't typical when you look at the whole range of PC networking software, including NetWare 4.*x*. Rather than hooking INT 21h, workstation shells for DOS are supposed to use the undocumented but well-known Network Redirector interface (see *Undocumented DOS*, 2d ed., pp. 494-540, 769-783).

The redirector operates *underneath* DOS: programs make INT 21h file I/O calls to MS-DOS, and if the call is intended for a network drive, DOS generates an INT 2Fh function 11h. Redirectors hook INT 2Fh, look for calls to function 11h, and handle various subfunctions, such as 1108h (Read from Remote File), 1109h (Write to Remote File), 111Bh (Find First Remote File), and 111Ch (Find Next Remote File). The redirector generally sends this request over the network to another machine, waits for the response, and returns from the INT 2Fh. DOS then passes the information back to whoever made the original INT 21h call.

So, with 32BFA on network drives, we might have expected to see INT 21h calls passed down to DOS, with network 32BFA possibly implemented at the INT 2Fh function 11h level. Well, TEST21 shows that's not how it works, at least for network drives.

Microsoft's CD-ROM Extensions (MSCDEX) also use the redirector interface, and if MSCDEX is loaded before WfW 3.11, IFSMgr passes down all INT 21h calls (except attempted function 40h writes) involving the CD-ROM drive. The INT 2Fh function 11h calls that DOS generates when it receives an INT 21h for a CD-ROM drive (or any redirector drive, for that matter) are also passed down.

Curiously, in 32BFA under WfW 3.11 (but not in Windows 95), hard disks are marked as network redirector drives. IFSHLP.SYS has an INT 2Fh handler and can ship redirector calls over to IFSMgr, which also has an INT 2Fh handler. This should all change in Windows 95, which has a CD-ROM VxD driver that is supposed to replace MSCDEX by providing 32-bit protected-mode CD-ROM access. (Actually, you can get that today without Windows 95 by using the Cloaked version of MSCDEX that comes with Helix Software's Multimedia Cloaking product.

Returning to 32BFA on a true network drive (as opposed to CD-ROM drives, which MSCDEX pretends are network drives), it's important to understand that applications still use INT 21h calls. Windows and Win32 applications — both in Windows 3.*x* and in Windows 95 — use the INT 21h interface either directly with an INT 21h or a DOS3Call or indirectly with a Windows API function that in turn uses DOS (such as the CommDlg functions GetOpenFileName and GetSaveFileName). Anticipating somewhat the WV86TEST and WSPY21 programs discussed in Chapters 12 and 13, note that Windows applications accessing files, including files on the network, *think* they're calling DOS. For example, while using WinWord to access a file on another machine, WISPY logged a vast number of INT 21h calls, including the following:

```
<WINWORD> (51) GET PSP
<WINWORD> (2f) GET DTA
<WINWORD> (1a) SET DTA 4CCF:79DA
<WINWORD> (50) SET PSP 00a7
<WINWORD> (4e) FIND FIRST \\T_NEUHAUS\TRUDY\MSS\ANDREW\DIRTYWIN\JUNK.DOC
<WINWORD> (3d) OPEN E:\MSS\ANDREW\DIRTYWIN\JUNK.DOC
```

Similarly, MS Mail uses INT 21h to access post-office files on the server (which here happened to be running Windows NT):

```
<MSMAIL> (3d) OPEN \\progpress1\WGPO\nme\gal.nme
<MSMAIL> (3d) OPEN \\progpress1\WGPO\nme\admin.nme
<MAILSPL> (3d) OPEN \\progpress1\WGPO\glb\master.glb
```


However, the WLOG212F program from the *Unauthorized Windows 95* disk shows that calls to functions such as 3Dh and 4Eh are handled inside Windows and aren't sent down to DOS. Functions 1Ah and 2Fh for getting and setting the Disk Transfer Address (DTA) are also handled inside Windows. But, WLOG212F does show that functions 50h and 51h for getting and setting the current PSP *are* passed down to DOS.

Since IFSMgr isn't sending network file INT 21h calls down to DOS, it's not surprising that almost no INT 2Fh function 11h redirector calls are generated, either.

So who handles 32BFA over the network? INT 21h calls that target network drives go to IFSMgr, as do all INT 21h calls. IFSMgr, as its name implies, isn't tied to hard-disk access: it is an Installable File System (IFS) Manager. Interestingly, the old network redirector interface was once called IFS too, so IFSMGR is really the successor to the network redirector, except that now all file-system access, including seemingly built-in access like that involving hard disks, requires an installable file-system driver.

VFAT, the VxD that handles 32BFA to hard disks using the old DOS File Allocation Table (FAT) file system, is just one driver that plugs into IFSMgr. There are others, including VREDIR, which is the Virtual Redirector device, and VSERVER, which acts as a peer server, managing file I/O requests from other machines on the network.

How about 32BFA and floppy disks? In WfW 3.11, 32BFA isn't supported for floppies. If TEST21 is run off a floppy disk, it takes seemingly forever to run. But it eventually finishes and produces the message: "INT 21h appears to be handled in the normal way."

Windows 95 does support 32BFA for floppies. Running TEST21 off a floppy under Windows 95 takes about half the time as under WfW 3.11, and TEST21 -MYSETVECT produces the same "Some INT 21h are handled without calling DOS!" message as seen when running TEST21 on a hard disk.

Replacing Real-Mode Code: It's Not New

The two sample VxDs in this chapter, CURRDRIV (Listing 8-3) and INTVECT (Listing 8-4), which handle certain DOS calls entirely in 32-bit protected mode and which induce TEST21 to output "Some INT 21h are handled without calling DOS!", could have been written and run under Windows 3.0 Enhanced mode. VMM and any VxD — whether one supplied by Microsoft or written by a third-party developer — have always had full discretion over whether interrupts should be reflected to V86 mode (*back* to V86 mode in the case of INTs originating there) or consumed in 32-bit protected mode.

So why do WfW 3.11 and Windows 95 seem so new and different from previous versions of Windows? Largely because 32BFA finally makes extensive use of this capability to consume or absorb interrupts rather than pass them down to V86 mode. The capability is nothing new; what's new is nothing more (but also nothing less) than the extent to which WfW 3.11 and Windows 95 employ it.

The point has been made several times that 32BFA's ability to bypass DOS isn't based on any new technology; it represents nothing more (but also nothing less) than the exploitation of a long-hidden capability. Still, you might wonder why so little fuss was made about Windows' capability to bypass the DOS interrupt chain. Surely we would have heard about this!

Well, actually, it was fairly well-known that Windows would sometimes refuse to let DOS software see an interrupt. But instead of being viewed as the first sign that Windows was becoming a genuine operating system, this behavior was viewed as ... a bug! Every now and then, someone with a DOS TSR would complain about some of the INT 2Fh function 16h services provided by Windows — namely, how come their DOS TSR didn't see them?

For example, when I was at Phar Lap Software in March 1990, some of us sent Microsoft a list of bugs and problems we ran into while bringing up 286|DOS-Extender under Windows 3.0 enhanced mode. Bug #4 on this list was:

> Windows hooks interrupt 2Fh through the IDT rather than through the real mode interrupt vector. This means that INT 2Fh must be called through an INT instruction and not by simulating an INT instruction with a PUSHF followed by a far call. This bug also breaks trace packages which monitor INT calls like the INTRSPY utility found in *Undocumented DOS*.

In a way, this "bug," when applied to INT 21h file I/O calls, is called 32BFA. Vendors frequently claim that what users call bugs are actually features. In this case, the claim would have been somewhat accurate! Whether or not it's a bug (as we've seen with IFSHLP.SYS, Windows *can* bypass DOS and still reflect interrupts to TSRs that need to see them), this INT 2Fh behavior did reflect an inherent feature of Windows Enhanced mode. It was our first glimpse at how Windows could pull away from its DOS moorings.

But the bug report nonetheless raises an interesting point: In V86 mode, since interrupts are hooked via the IDT, an INT instruction can behave quite differently from a PUSHF followed by a far CALL. For a variety of reasons, DOS software sometimes uses the PUSHF/CALLF combination instead of INT, and many DOS programmers are accustomed to thinking of an INT as nothing more than a fancy way of doing a PUSHF/CALLF. But in V86 mode, where the INT instruction vectors through the IDT, this equivalence no longer holds: the processor doesn't know that your PUSHF/CALLF is really an INT in disguise.

Furthermore, if the INT handler installed in the IDT doesn't reflect interrupts back to V86 mode, the two methods of calling the interrupt can get different results!

As an example, consider one of the Windows INT 2Fh services that we at Phar Lap were complaining about. Function 1600h indicates whether Windows Enhanced mode is running. A return value of 0 or 80h in AL indicates that Enhanced mode isn't running; any other return value indicates the Windows version number. For example, Windows 95 (also known as Windows 4.0) returns AX=0004h.

To demonstrate, TEST1600.C (Listing 8-7) calls INT 2Fh function 1600h, both with an INT and with the C expression (*intfunc)(), where intfunc is declared with the _interrupt keyword, so the compiler automatically generates the PUSHF/CALLF (unfortunately, it forgets to also generate the CLI instruction, which I've added by hand). TEST1600 also uses the once-popular int86 function, because some compiler run-time libraries in the past implemented this with a PUSHF/CALLF.

Listing 8-7: TEST1600.C

```
/*
TEST1600.C  --  Show that under Windows, PUSHF/CALLF != INT
Andrew Schulman, 1994
bcc test1600.c
*/
```

```
#include <stdlib.h>
#include <stdio.h>
#include <dos.h>

main()
{
    union REGS r;
    void (interrupt far *int2f)(void);  // will do pushf
    unsigned char retval, retval2;

    _asm mov ax, 1600h
    _asm int 2fh
    _asm mov retval, al
    printf("Via INT,   2F/1600 returns %02Xh\n", retval);

    // sometimes int86() is implemented with a far call!
    r.x.ax = 0x1600;
    int86(0x2f, &r, &r);
    printf("Via int86, 2F/1600 returns %02Xh\n", r.h.al);

    int2f = (void (interrupt far *)(void)) _dos_getvect(0x2f);
    _asm mov ax, 1600h
    _asm cli             // Borland forgets this for (*intfunc)()
    (*int2f)();          // equivalent to pushf, far call
    _asm mov retval2, al
    printf("Via CALL,  2F/1600 returns %02Xh\n", retval2);

    printf("\nPUSHF/FAR CALL %s INT\n",
        (retval2 == retval) ? "same as" : "different from");

    return 0;
}
```


This is a straightforward, if slightly contrived-looking, program. If Windows Enhanced mode isn't running, the three different ways of calling INT 2Fh function 1600h all produce the same result: AL=0, indicating that, indeed, Windows Enhanced mode is not running.

When Windows Enhanced mode is running, you would hope that all three methods of calling the function would reflect this fact. But that's not what happens:

```
C:\UNAUTHW>test1600
Via INT,   2F/1600 returns 03h
Via int86, 2F/1600 returns 03h
Via CALL,  2F/1600 returns 00h

PUSHF/FAR CALL different from INT
```

When the Get Enhanced Mode Windows Installed State function is called with PUSHF/CALLF, the return value is 0, indicating that Windows isn't present! What's happening is that, although every interrupt goes into VMM, CALLF does not. VMM contains the handler for these

Windows INT 2Fh services. VMM never sees the CALLF and never services the request, so it appears as if Windows is not present. Windows relies on the V86 IDT mechanism to handle its INT 2Fh calls.

It might seem contrived to simulate an interrupt with (*intfunc)() instead of just using a genuine interrupt. However, there are sound reasons why DOS software sometimes simulates interrupts. After all, Windows itself provides a Simulate_Int service; to implement this service in V86 mode, Windows basically grabs function pointers right out of the IVT.

For an example of why DOS software sometimes simulates interrupts, look at the INTCHAIN utility in *Undocumented DOS* (2d ed., Chapter 6). INTCHAIN uses single-step debugging mode to trace through and display interrupt chains. The code contains the comment, "single-step doesn't go through INT, so turn the INT into a PUSHF and far CALL" (p. 305). Not so fast! This can produce misleading results when running under Windows because INT vectors through the IDT and PUSHF/CALLF does not. (Perhaps even more misleading, though, is the real-mode INTCHAIN program's failure to show the interrupt's trip through 32-bit protected mode.)

Debuggers commonly use simulated INTs to achieve the effect of tracing through an INT instruction. Under Windows Enhanced mode, however, this can produce incorrect results. Using DEBUG to trace through a call to INT 2Fh function 1600h, for example, produces AX=1600h instead of something like AX=0B03h (Windows 3.11) or AX=0004h (Windows 4.0):

```
C:\UNAUTHW>debug

;;; Assemble an INT 2Fh function 1600h call
-a
77B1:0100 mov ax, 1600
77B1:0103 int 2f
77B1:0105

;;; Step (proceed)
-p

AX=1600  BX=0000  CX=0000  DX=0000  SP=FFEE  BP=0000  SI=0000  DI=0000
DS=77B1  ES=77B1  SS=77B1  CS=77B1  IP=0103   NV UP EI PL NZ NA PO NC
77B1:0103 CD2F          INT 2F
-p

AX=0004  BX=0000  CX=0000  DX=0000  SP=FFEE  BP=0000  SI=0000  DI=0000
DS=77B1  ES=77B1  SS=77B1  CS=77B1  IP=0105   NV UP EI PL NZ NA PO NC
```

```
;;; Correct result came back:  AX=0004
;;; Now reset instruction pointer, and *TRACE* instead of step
-rip
IP 0105
:0100
-t

AX=1600  BX=0000  CX=0000  DX=0000  SP=FFEE  BP=0000  SI=0000  DI=0000
DS=77B1  ES=77B1  SS=77B1  CS=77B1  IP=0103   NV UP EI PL NZ NA PO NC
77B1:0103 CD2F          INT 2F
-t

;;; Don't need to see any more here, so go to other side of INT 2Fh

-g 77b1:0105

AX=1600  BX=0000  CX=0000  DX=0000  SP=FFEE  BP=0000  SI=0000  DI=0000
DS=77B1  ES=77B1  SS=77B1  CS=77B1  IP=0105   NV UP EI PL NZ NA PO NC
77B1:0105 CD21          INT 21

;;; Yikes!  Came back with wrong answer:  AX=1600 instead of AX=0004,
;;; even though all we did was T instead of P in DEBUG!
```

Also, we noted earlier that some compiler run-time libraries implement the int86 function using a simulated INT. This is because the interrupt number for the Intel INT instruction must be included as part of the instruction itself; for example, INT AX is not a valid instruction. Thus, functions that take the interrupt number as a parameter (such as int86) must either use self-modifying code to smack the interrupt number into the instruction or use PUSHF/CALLF to simulate the INT. Today, most versions of int86 use self-modifying code. Perhaps the vendors discovered the hard way that, under Windows, PUSHF/CALLF != INT.

How does 32BFA cope with DOS programs that use PUSHF/CALLF to make file I/O calls? Again, IFSHLP.SYS comes to the rescue: It is sitting in the appropriate place to deliver these calls to IFSMgr.

Another Old Example: TEST1600

The V86TEST program in Chapter 10 has an INT 2Fh handler. While Windows is running, V86TEST calls INT 2Fh function 1683h (Get Current Virtual Machine ID) — from inside the INT 2Fh handler! I've seen commercial code that does the same thing, blithely calling Windows INT 2Fh function 16h services from inside an INT 2Fh handler, apparently without any awareness that this is a bizarre thing to do. How come this doesn't cause an endless loop?

Because, if Windows is running, the INT 2Fh vectors through the IDT to VMM, and for most INT 2Fh function 16h requests, VMM immediately services the request and doesn't bother to reflect the call back down to a caller such as V86TEST. The program's INT 2Fh handler never sees its own call to function 1683h.

To demonstrate this long-standing Windows behavior, TEST2F16.C (Listing 8-8) both generates and intercepts INT 2Fh function 16h calls, similar to what TEST21 does with INT 21h calls.

Listing 8-8: TEST2F16.C

```
/*
TEST2F16.C  --  Show that Windows doesn't reflect INT 2Fh func 16h
    to V86 mode
Andrew Schulman, 1994
bcc -2 -P- test2f16.c
*/

#include <stdlib.h>
#include <stdio.h>
#include <dos.h>

typedef unsigned short WORD;
typedef unsigned long DWORD;

#pragma pack(1)

typedef struct {
#ifdef __TURBOC__
    WORD bp,di,si,ds,es,dx,cx,bx,ax;
#else
    WORD es,ds,di,si,bp,sp,bx,dx,cx,ax;     /* same as PUSHA */
#endif
    WORD ip,cs,flags;
    } REG_PARAMS;

void interrupt far int2f(REG_PARAMS r);
void (interrupt far *old_2F)();

static DWORD int2f16_calls[0x100] = {0};
static DWORD total_int2f16_calls = 0;
static DWORD int2f_calls = 0;
static DWORD int2f1200_calls = 0;

void fail(const char *s) { puts(s); exit(1); }

main(int argc, char *argv[])
{
    DWORD i;
    DWORD num_iter = (argc < 2) ? 100 : atol(argv[1]);

    /* hook INT INT 2Fh */
```

```
    old_2F = _dos_getvect(0x2F);
    _dos_setvect(0x2f, int2f);

    /* issue lots of 2F/168x calls */
    for (i=0; i<num_iter; i++)
    {
        _asm mov ax, 1200h      // sanity check
        _asm int 2fh
        _asm mov ax, 1680h
        _asm int 2fh
        _asm mov ax, 1681h
        _asm int 2fh
        _asm mov ax, 1682h
        _asm int 2fh
        _asm mov ax, 1683h
        _asm int 2fh
    }

    /* unhook INT 2Fh */
    _dos_setvect(0x2F, old_2F);

    /* sanity check */
    if (int2f1200_calls < num_iter)
        fail("Something wrong? Not seeing 2F/12 calls!");

    /* display results */
    printf("TEST2F16 issued %lu calls to 2F/1200\n", num_iter);
    printf("TEST2F16 issued %lu calls each to 2F/1680-2F/1683\n",
        num_iter);
    printf("TEST2F16 detected %lu INT 2Fh calls\n", int2f_calls);
    if (total_int2f16_calls)
    {
        printf("TEST2F16 detected the following 2F/16 calls:\n");
        for (i=0; i<0x100; i++)
            if (int2f16_calls[i])
                printf("%02lX:%lu\t", i, int2f16_calls[i]);
        printf("\n");
    }
    else
        printf("TEST2F16 detected 0 calls to INT 2Fh function 16h!\n");

    if (total_int2f16_calls < num_iter)
        printf("\nINT 2Fh function 16h isn't reflected to V86 mode!\n");

    return 0;
}

void interrupt far int2f(REG_PARAMS r)
{
    int2f_calls++;
    if (r.ax == 0x1200)
        int2f1200_calls++;
    if ((r.ax >> 8) == 0x16)
    {
        total_int2f16_calls++;
```

```
        int2f16_calls[r.ax & 0xff]++;
    }
    _chain_intr(old_2F);
}
```

TEST2F16 issues the following Windows INT 2Fh calls, which are documented in the Windows DDK:

```
1680h       Release Current VM Time-Slice
1681h       Begin Critical Section
1682h       End Critical Section
1683h       Get Current Virtual Machine ID
```


When run under Windows Enhanced mode (any version, including Windows 3.0 from 1990), TEST2F16 doesn't see these calls:

```
TEST2F16 issued 100 calls to 2F/1200
TEST2F16 issued 100 calls each to 2F/1680-2F/1683
TEST2F16 detected 100 INT 2Fh calls
TEST2F16 detected 0 calls to INT 2Fh function 16h!

INT 2Fh function 16h isn't reflected to V86 mode!
```

That "INT 2Fh function 16h isn't reflected to V86 mode!" message shows that VMM handles the Windows INT 2Fh services and, seeing no need to let anyone else see them, returns from its Hook_V86_Int_Chain handler with carry clear. Microsoft didn't anticipate that some DOS TSRs might want to *see* these calls, even if Windows is expected to *service* them.

A major problem with many INT-based services is that the interface is "overloaded": aside from handling interrupts to service requests, a lot of DOS software also handles interrupts to discover when some event has occurred. It's difficult to implement new, more efficient servicing for interrupts and yet continue to let other programs receive the events they expect to see.

This "INT 2Fh function 16h isn't reflected to V86 mode!" message was really just an early indication that, even when we're running real-mode DOS programs under Windows, things are not what they seem. We're not in Kansas anymore. So where are we? We're in V86 mode.

Interrupts 101: IDT versus the IVT

"Everything you know is wrong."
— *Firesign Theatre*

At a number of places in this chapter, I've mentioned without really explaining that interrupts in V86 vector through a data structure called the IDT rather than through the low-memory IVT. Given the unusual things we've seen, such as Windows somehow invisibly grabbing control of INT 21h away from the most recently loaded INT 21h handler, I'd like to explain this in more detail. Some of this will seem like old, familiar material to seasoned DOS programmers, but please bear with me. You need to understand this stuff. Here goes:

Most operating systems use some form of interrupt or trap to provide services to applications. MS-DOS provides its programming interface via software interrupts, primarily INT 21h. For example, when a DOS application opens a file, it either directly or indirectly executes code such as the following:


```
mov ah, 3Dh                 ; 3Dh = Open File function number
mov al, 0                   ; read-only access
lds dx, dword ptr _name     ; filename to open goes in DX:DS
int 21h                     ; call DOS!
```

When a Windows program opens a file, the program itself probably doesn't contain code like this, but it will call some Windows API function that calls some function that eventually calls code like this. This is true even of Win32 applications running in Windows 95 or Win32s.

Now, the "call DOS!" comment next to the INT 21h instruction ain't necessarily so. One of the points of this chapter has been that an INT 21h doesn't necessarily mean "call DOS!" More and more, it really means "call some VxD!" But let's return for a moment to the old days of real mode. Not V86 mode, but genuine real mode.

In real mode, an INT instruction consults an Interrupt Vector Table (IVT) located at address 0 in the first 400h bytes of memory. This table has 100h entries, one entry for each interrupt (INT 0 through INT FFh). Each entry can contain a four-byte far pointer to a piece of code that handles an interrupt. In real mode, the INT instruction pulls the far pointer out of the IVT and calls it:

```
; code for INT n
pushf                      ; push flags
cli                        ; don't forget to turn off interrupts!
xor ax, ax
mov es, ax                 ; es = 0
mov bx, _n
shl bx, 2                  ; bx = intnum * 4
call far ptr es:[bx]       ; call [0000:intnum*4]
```

This level of indirection — INT n calls the function pointer at IVT[n] — is what makes this instruction so useful for operating system services. Applications can call the operating system without knowing its location in memory; all they need is a magic number like 21h or 2Fh.

Furthermore, this level of indirection makes it easy for third-party software to extend the operating system. They merely change IVT entries to point to their own code. Consider the MS-DOS Set Interrupt Vector function (INT 21h function 25h): As we saw earlier in the my_setvect function in Listing 8-1 and in Do_SetVect in Listing 8-4, establishing the function pointer fp as the new handler for INT n involves little more than setting IVT[n] = fp. Likewise, Get Interrupt Vector (INT 21h function 35h), which returns the current handler for INT n, need only return IVT[n] (see my_getvect in Listing 8-1 and Do_GetVect in Listing 8-4).

Using these together lets programs create entire *chains* of interrupt handlers:

```
previous_handler = get_vector(n);
set_vector(n, my_handler);

my_handler:
    // do something with interrupt
    if (previous_handler != 0)
        call previous_handler
```

These interrupt chains let third-party software easily extend the operating system and are largely responsible for the longevity of MS-DOS.

Undocumented DOS (2d ed., Chapter 6) includes a program called INTVECT that displays the IVT. Here's some output from INTVECT when it's run under WfW 3.11:

```
C:\UNDOCDOS\CHAP6>intvect
INT 00h   2315:094E   INTVECT
INT 01h   0070:026D   IO          iret -- NOP function
INT 02h   120A:0016   DBLSYSH$
INT 03h   0070:026D   IO          iret -- NOP function
INT 04h   0070:026D   IO          iret -- NOP function
INT 05h   E000:27C4
INT 06h   F000:B6DD
INT 07h   F000:B6DD
INT 08h   1C55:0000   win386
INT 09h   1208:0028   DBLSYSH$    jmp 1208:002C
INT 0Ah   1208:003A   DBLSYSH$    jmp 1208:004C
... etc. ...
INT 21h   020E:0498   IFS$HLP$
INT 22h   1E11:020B   COMMAND
INT 23h   1E11:0168   COMMAND
INT 24h   1E11:0173   COMMAND
INT 25h   00A0:0FB6   DOS
INT 26h   01EF:0037   D:          jmp 03A4:1B60
INT 27h   00A0:0FCA   DOS
INT 28h   00A0:1069   DOS         iret -- NOP function
INT 29h   0070:026E   IO
```

```
INT 2Ah   020E:059C   IFS$HLP$
INT 2Bh   00A0:1069   DOS        iret -- NOP function
INT 2Ch   00A0:1069   DOS        iret -- NOP function
INT 2Dh   00A0:1069   DOS        iret -- NOP function
INT 2Eh   12D1:015D   COMMAND
INT 2Fh   1B8E:0424   win
... and so on ...
```

Unfortunately, the INTVECT output under Windows can be deceptive. INTVECT would have you believe, for example, that INT 2Fh is handled by the WIN program at 1B8E:0424 and that the primary handler for INT 21h is the IFSHLP device driver at 020E:0498.

The TEST21 and TEST2F16 results in this chapter have shown that this *can't* be true. If the TEST21 and TEST2F16 handlers don't see certain calls, the WIN and IFSHLP handlers loaded earlier certainly won't. After all, interrupts are handled on a last-in/first-out basis. All INTVECT under Windows shows is where an interrupt *would* go, *if* VMM or a VxD decides to reflect it to V86 mode. Well, in *Undocumented DOS*, I did warn in a vague sort of way that "a more sophisticated version" of INTVECT would be needed to deal with Windows Enhanced mode.

Now, by this I didn't mean putting a Windows interface on INTVECT. Sometimes vendors try to make old DOS utilities and diagnostics packages "Windows aware" by putting fancy user interfaces on them, and so there are a number of nice-looking Windows diagnostics tools that dutifully display the real-mode interrupt vector table. Unfortunately, displaying this old real-mode structure inside a Windows list box is *not* what it takes to be truly Windows aware. As with INTVECT, the results are largely meaningless because the real-mode interrupt vector table, no matter how nicely displayed, doesn't show where the interrupts are really going.

In Windows, INT n is no longer just a fancy way of calling the function located at IVT[n]. All INTs in V86 mode are instead vectored through a completely different data structure called the Interrupt Descriptor Table (IDT). The Intel microprocessor defines the format of the IDT; an operating system such as Windows is responsible for setting up the structure and telling the processor its address. A crummy-looking character-mode program that displays the IDT, such as the crummy-looking IDTMAP program on the disk, is more of a Windows program than a nice-looking GUI diagnostics program that continues to display the IVT.

The IDT is similar in structure to the Local Descriptor Table (LDT) and Global Descriptor Table (GDT). The IDT can be located anywhere in memory. An Intel-based protected-mode operating system such as

Windows sets the IDT's address with the LIDT instruction; the IDT's address can be retrieved with the SIDT instruction. SIDT isn't privileged, so any program can get the address of the IDT. The nonprivileged SIDT instruction is used in the IDTMAP program, which prints the IDT under Windows (or under any other operating system that provides DPMI services).

By the way, that last parenthetical point is actually quite important: 386 memory managers such as QEMM, 386MAX, or NetRoom are really 32-bit protected-mode operating systems. When a user is running one of the memory managers, INT 21h is handled first in protected mode, just as with Windows Enhanced mode.

This isn't usually apparent because these memory managers generally pass the calls down to DOS. But they don't have to. For example, consider the Cloaking API provided by Helix Software, which works both with its own NetRoom memory manager and with others such as QEMM and 386MAX. Similar to VxDs in Windows, Cloaking is an interface for writing 32-bit protected-mode PC system software: DOS software continues to make the usual INT calls, and these are trapped, as always, by the 386 memory manager. But instead of blindly sending the call back down to V86 mode, Cloaking allows the call to be handled in 32-bit protected mode. Helix has worked with Award Software to create a Cloaked BIOS, has licensed Microsoft's CD-ROM Extensions to create a Cloaked MSCDEX, has written a Cloaked version of Logitech's mouse driver, and so on.

So, the capability to bypass real-mode code is really a feature of V86 mode rather than of Windows Enhanced mode, and is potentially available with any 386 memory manager. Well, what is Windows Enhanced mode anyway but a sophisticated 386 memory manager?

Returning to the IDT, each entry in the IDT is an eight-byte gate descriptor containing the selector:offset address of an interrupt handler, plus some flags indicating the gate type. The IDT can contain Trap Gates, Task Gates, or Interrupt Gates. There are also Call Gates, but these don't go into the IDT. (And no, the IDT can't contain Bill Gates. Not even the Antitrust Division of the U.S. Department of Justice was able to do that.)

In Windows, the most prevalent gates are 32-bit Interrupt Gates. Windows also uses 16-bit Trap Gates to trap interrupts generated by protected-mode programs, such as Windows applications. Windows doesn't use many of the more esoteric features of the IDT such as Task Gates, to which the Intel 386 programmer's manual devotes so much attention. In fact, most operating systems use only a handful of these fancy transistor-consuming features (which is something that RISC advocates are only too happy to point out). Because Windows relies so heavily on the IDT, the Intel documentation is an essential supplement to the Windows programming documentation. Just don't get too caught up in all the various bells and whistles that Intel provides.

When the processor sees an INT n in V86 mode or protected mode, it consults the gate at IDT[n] and calls the address contained there. Thus, an innocent-looking INT 21h or INT 2Fh in a DOS program or even — and this is quite amazing and important — in DOS software loaded *before* Windows won't call the real-mode procedure whose address is located at IVT[21h] or IVT[2Fh]. Instead, it calls the 32-bit protected-mode Ring 0 code located at IDT[21h] or IDT[2Fh]. These are 48-bit far pointers: 16 bits for the protected-mode selector and 32 bits for the offset. Hence, as you can see if you run the IDTMAP program, this 32-bit PM code will be located at some weird-looking address in VMM such as 0028:80006FAA or 0028:8000701A. This is not your father's Oldsmobile!

Like the IVT, the IDT can contain up to 256 (100h) entries, one for each interrupt (0 through FFh). In Windows, however, the IDT contains only 60h entries, for INT 0 through 5Fh. An INT 60h or higher — such as INT 67h for expanded memory services (EMS) — causes a GP fault, which reappears right back at the IDT as an INT 0Dh, with an error code containing the original faulting INT number.

You read right: Every EMS call under Windows causes a GP fault. You might be accustomed to thinking of GP faults as nothing more than what Microsoft once called UAEs, but GP faults and other types of faults (such as INT 6 for Invalid Opcodes) aren't just for errors. Windows uses GP faults and Invalid Opcode faults as some of its most basic mechanisms for accomplishing real work.

Windows has separate IDTs for V86 and protected modes. In many cases the corresponding V86-mode and protected-mode entries in each LDT point to the same interrupt handler inside VMM. In other cases, the corresponding entries point to different handlers. For example, Windows handles protected-mode INT 21h differently from V86-mode INT 21h.

What does VMM do with these interrupts? In some cases, it handles them itself. DPMI INT 31h services are an important example: The DPMI server is located right inside VMM, so any INT 31h calls from protected-mode applications are also serviced directly by VMM. Similarly, many of the Windows INT 2Fh services are provided by VMM.

In other cases, however, VMM doesn't handle the interrupts itself; instead it passes them along to any VxDs that have asked for them by calling Hook_V86_Int_Chain. Similarly, VMM passes faults along to any VxD that has requested them by calling a VMM function such as Hook_VMM_Fault or Hook_V86_Fault.

The key point is that the IDT gives VMM control over what goes on in Windows by routing all key interrupts and faults into VMM. The VMM then handles these events, or dispatches them to one or more VxDs for further processing, or both.

So does Windows totally ignore the low-memory IVT? Not at all. Windows uses the IVT to provide interrupt *reflection* which, as we saw, is the capability for a protected-mode interrupt handler to issue an interrupt in V86 mode: The machine switches to V86 mode and the interrupt vectors through the IVT to the chain of real-mode (at least they think they're in real mode) interrupt handlers.

Windows uses interrupt reflection to handle some interrupts coming from V86 mode: the interrupt goes first to 32-bit protected mode, but is then reflected back into V86 mode. The DOS extender in Windows also uses interrupt reflection, for example, to handle some INT 21h calls coming from protected-mode applications. When a Windows application makes an INT 21h call, the DOS extender can get help from DOS in servicing the call. The key words in the previous two sentences are *some* and *can*: as we've seen in this chapter, Windows VxDs have no obligation to reflect INT 21h calls down to DOS. On the other hand, Windows will no doubt continue to reflect some calls to DOS until Microsoft (or some enterprising third-party vendor) decides to rewrite all of MS-DOS and the BIOS as a VxD.

We've seen how INT n vectors through a gate at IDT[n], but what function do these gates serve? Gates provide protection for transferring control among code segments executing at different privilege levels. For example, because an interrupt in V86 mode goes through the IDT and can thus use an Interrupt Gate, a user-level program such as a DOS TSR, which knows nothing about Windows, can call privileged code inside VMM.

In other words, Interrupt Gates are what make VMM the operating system. Because interrupts go through an IDT Interrupt Gate to VMM, DOS isn't the operating system any more. VMM is. Again, real-mode DOS receives an INT 21h call only if VMM or a VxD makes a conscious effort to send DOS the call. Taking this one step further, since VxDs can ask VMM to call them upon receipt of an interrupt, the Windows operating system is actually the combination of VMM and VxDs. And this has been true ever since VMM was introduced in Windows 3.0 Enhanced mode! Innovations such as Windows for Workgroups (WfW) 3.11's 32-bit file access, and Windows 95 are really just (a lot) more of the same. The underpinning of the new Windows 95 technology dates back to the very beginnings of Windows Enhanced mode. Windows 95 is the not-so-new 32-bit protected-mode version of DOS. We've had it all along but we just didn't notice.

Chapter 9

Who's in Charge: Windows or DOS?

In earlier chapters I claimed that Windows — not just Windows 95, but also Windows 3.*x* Enhanced mode — is a genuine 32-bit protected-mode operating system that uses real-mode DOS as a mere assistant. In Chapter 4 I even maintained that, rather than Windows running on top of DOS, in many ways DOS runs on top of Windows.

This claim might have been hard to swallow. After all, when you get right down to it, Windows starts up from a DOS C:\> prompt or AUTOEXEC.BAT file or, at best, from the real-mode DOS code that calls itself WINBOOT.SYS in Windows 95. Real-mode DOS is still there. Windows starts up from it. That's all there is to it, right?

Not quite. In fact, you'll see that Windows runs DOS in Virtual-8086 (V86) mode. I don't just mean that the DOS programs you start in a DOS box use V86 mode. I mean that, once Windows starts up, software that was loaded before it — DOS device drivers, TSRs, and even DOS itself — runs in V86 mode. As you'll see, this in turn means that Windows can control DOS.

"A Thing on a Thing"?

Partisans of larger operating systems such as OS/2, Windows NT, and UNIX frequently consider the combination of Windows and MS-DOS as amounting to something less than a genuine operating system. After all, they reason, Windows wasn't designed from the ground up, and it isn't a self-contained whole. For several years, in fact, Microsoft itself referred to Windows as an operating environment rather than as a complete operating system. As WordPerfect once put it in its ads for the now-moribund OS/2 version of its product, Windows is just "a thing on a thing."

Although the advocates of OS/2, Windows NT, and UNIX often deride Windows for depending on DOS, at the same time they all agree that these operating systems must be able to run old DOS programs. And they all agree that these operating systems can control real-mode DOS programs inside a Virtual DOS Machine (VDM), or DOS box. The VDM protects the rest of the system from any low-level crimes (such as writing directly to memory or banging on I/O ports) that the DOS program might want to commit.

So how can old real-mode code do all the grungy stuff that real-mode code likes to do — such as direct screen writes and port I/O — when it's under another program's control? Well, it can do these things because on Intel 80386 and later microprocessors, V86 mode allows a protected-mode operating system to simulate one or more 1MB real-mode 8086 machines. These simulated machines can be multitasked, paged to disk (under some circumstances), and prevented from interfering with other applications or with the operating system. As shown in Figure 9-1, operating systems that run DOS programs in V86 mode can intercept the DOS programs' memory accesses, interrupts, I/O port access, and so on. The operating systems can then simulate, refuse, or ignore the actions of the DOS programs, or they can allow them to take place, as they see fit.

Confidence in this VDM scheme based on V86 mode is so high that IBM has even claimed that its OS/2 2.*x* provides a "better DOS than DOS."

Of course, Windows 3.*x* also provides a V86 environment for DOS programs, using a scheme similar to that used by OS/2 and by Intel-based versions of Windows NT or UNIX. But there is one fundamental difference between the VDM schemes used by Windows and by these other operating systems. The OS/2, Windows NT, and UNIX operating systems take the INT 21h or INT 2Fh calls coming from a DOS program and turn them into calls to the operating system's own API (see *Undocumented DOS*, 2d ed., Chapter 4). These operating systems can't pass an INT 21h call onto DOS because DOS isn't there.

In contrast, when a DOS program running under Windows makes a DOS call, DOS is *still running* and can therefore handle INT 21h or INT 2Fh calls. In addition, some Windows API calls from protected mode can get turned into real-mode INT 21h calls. Thus, although running a real-mode program in a DOS box under OS/2, NT, or UNIX is nice and protected, Windows itself runs under DOS so its whole foundation is shaky, right?

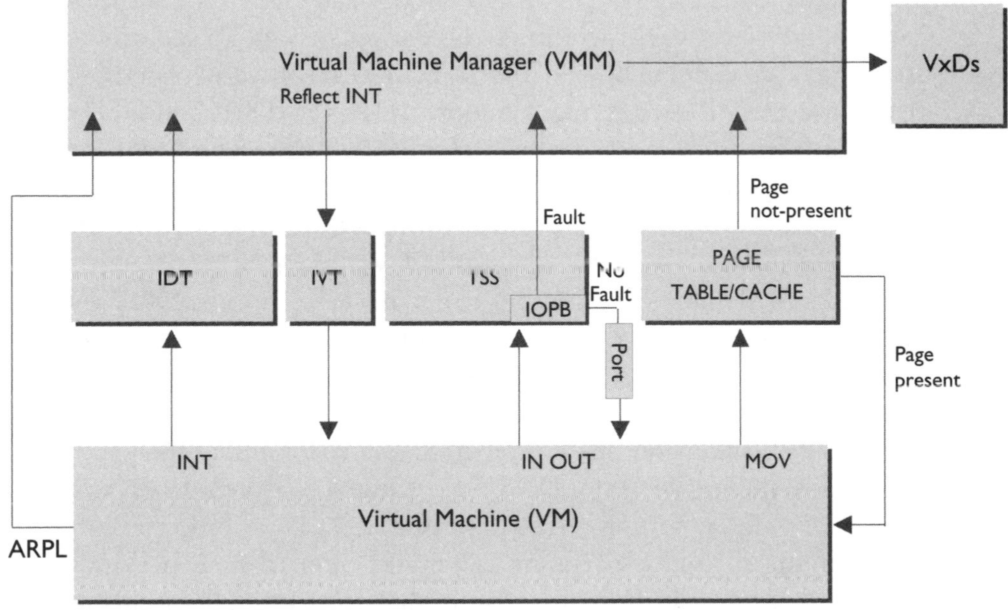

Figure 9-1: In real-mode, all interrupts vector through the IVT, I/O is sent directly to the ports, and all memory reads and writes directly access MOVs memory. When running in V86 mode, under VMM, all these common actions take a different path: All interrupts and illegal instructions (such as ARPL, used for V86 breakpoints) trap into VMM; all I/Os from V86 mode consult the I/O permission bitmap (IPOB); and, all memory access consults the page table (actually the cached page-access entries).

Before we jump to any conclusions, let's step back a minute and ask a question that might sound naive at first: Is an operating environment that sits on top of DOS, such as Windows, really all that different from a DOS box? In other words, is there a fundamental difference between the way Windows or OS/2 or NT or UNIX handles programs running in a DOS box and the way Windows handles software (including DOS itself) that was loaded before it?

Surprisingly, the answer is no — there's no fundamental difference between a DOS box and an operating environment that sits on top of DOS. (Chapter 4 did discuss one difference, having to do with instance data.) When Windows runs on top of DOS, it has the same options for controlling DOS that OS/2, Windows NT, and UNIX have for controlling DOS programs running in a VDM. That's right: the "thing on a thing" turns out to be fundamentally the same as the "better DOS than DOS"!

Running DOS in Protected Mode

Running an operating system on top of DOS isn't much different from running DOS in a VDM within the operating system. To see why this is so, we need to examine how Windows relates to software loaded *before* it; that is, we need to look at how Windows relates to TSRs and DOS device drivers, to DOS itself, and to the ROM BIOS. The FAKEWIN program in Chapters 3 and 4 showed some of the interaction between Windows and DOS. But there's another aspect to this that FAKEWIN didn't reveal: exactly *how* Windows calls down to DOS.

Although Windows applications run in protected mode, DOS is a real-mode operating system. DOS doesn't know anything about protected-mode selectors and it can't access extended memory. For Windows to call down to DOS, therefore, Windows must switch back to real mode, right? And this is the ultimate source of Windows's instability, right?

No. Recall our friend the DOS box. When OS/2, Windows NT, UNIX, or Windows run real-mode software in a DOS box, the software is *not* run in real mode; it's run in V86 mode. Similarly, when Windows Enhanced Mode calls down to software that was loaded before it, such as DOS, it does so not in real mode but in V86 mode.

Let me repeat that: *Windows calls down to DOS in V86 mode.* Please don't dismiss this point as mere semantic hairsplitting or as the remark of a pedant. (A pedant is someone who, when you refer to the State of Massachusetts, tells you that Massachusetts is actually a Commonwealth.) It's important to note the difference between the two statements "Windows switches to real mode to call down to DOS" and "Windows calls DOS in V86 mode," because there's an enormous difference between real mode and V86 mode.

When real-mode software — such as a DOS program or (more relevant here) MS-DOS itself — runs in V86 mode, it "thinks" it's running in real mode. However, as described in the Intel documentation, V86 mode "operates similarly to protected mode." Note that Intel *doesn't* say that V86 mode operates similarly to real mode. Intel says that V86 mode operates similarly to protected mode.

V86 mode is an amazing thing, really: a form of protected mode that runs real-mode software. V86 mode is similar to real mode in one sense only: both modes use the same mechanism for accessing memory addresses. For example, when a DOS program refers to ES:[BX], V86 mode and real mode use the same formula — they take the value in ES, multiply it by 16, and add the value of BX — to find the location in memory that the DOS program wants to access. The similarity between V86 mode and real mode ends there.

Here are some of the differences between V86 mode and real mode:

- In V86 mode, the resulting (ES*16)+BX address isn't necessarily a physical address, as it would be in real mode. Instead, it's a linear address that the processor uses as an index into a page table. The page table in turn contains what might be a physical address that equals the (ES*16)+BX linear address (linear == physical), or a physical address that differs from the linear address (linear != physical), or even an indication that the associated data is not currently present in memory and has to be swapped in from disk. Thus, parts of the DOS box might be located anywhere in memory — or not in memory at all. If the DOS box accesses memory whose page-table entry is marked "not present," the processor automatically calls a protected-mode page-fault handler, which can swap the memory in from disk.
- If a DOS program running in V86 mode issues an INT instruction (for example, an INT 21h to call DOS), the INT isn't vectored through the low-memory interrupt vector table as it would be in real mode. Instead, the INT vectors through the Interrupt Descriptor Table (IDT), just as it would if the INT instruction were contained in a protected-mode program. In Windows, all interrupts coming from V86 mode are first handled in 32-bit protected mode.
- If real-mode software running in V86 mode issues an IN or OUT instruction (for example, if the ROM BIOS needs to access an I/O port), the processor first looks up the port number in the I/O Permission Bitmap (IOPB). This bitmap can tell the processor to make the I/O illegal, thereby causing a trap into the protected-mode operating system.
- If the protected-mode operating system so chooses, it can specify that certain instructions (such as CLI, STI, PUSHF, POPF, and IRET) will trap into the operating system. These instructions manipulate the interrupt flag (IF). CLI and STI clear and set IF; in the course of pushing or popping the entire flags register, PUSHF, POPF, and IRET affect IF, too. All other things being equal — which, we'll see later, they often aren't — it's a bad idea for protected-mode operating systems to let a V86 process turn off the processor's actual IF, because doing so disables interrupts for *all* processes. The operating system

can instead choose to let real-mode software manipulate only a virtual IF. For example, CLI would clear the virtual IF, disabling interrupts only for the current process. The operating system maintains this virtual IF by telling the processor that instructions that affect IF are, in effect, illegal. Thus, an innocent-looking CLI or IRET inside MS-DOS might cause a jump to somewhere deep inside Windows.

- Some instructions are always illegal in V86 mode and automatically cause an exception, which can be caught and handled in 32-bit protected mode. A good example is ARPL. As already discussed in Chapter 8, Windows relies heavily on the ARPL instruction to control the execution of programs running in V86 mode.

In all these cases, real-mode code running in V86 mode might cause a *trap*, *fault*, or *exception* (the differences between traps, faults, and exceptions really don't matter right at this moment).

The Virtual Machine Monitor (VMM)

So where do these traps, faults, and exceptions *go*? They are intercepted and handled by a privileged 32-bit protected-mode program that is sometimes called a V86 monitor or a virtual machine monitor (VMM). All hardware interrupts go to the VMM, too. According to Intel's *80386 System Software Writer's Guide*,

> It is convenient to package the code that responds specially to V86 exceptions in a procedure (or collection of procedures) called a virtual machine monitor (VMM). A VMM simulates the 8086 instructions that the 80386 will not execute in V86 mode.

As noted in previous chapters, the key component of WIN386.EXE in Windows Enhanced mode and of VMM32.VXD in Windows 95 is called VMM. (Back in 1988, in Windows/386 2.*x*, it was called VDMM or Virtual DOS Machine Manager.) According to the *Virtual Device Adaptation Guide* included with Microsoft's Windows Device Driver Kit (DDK):

> The VMM is a 32-bit protected-mode operating system. Its primary responsibility is to create, run, monitor, and terminate virtual machines. The VMM provides services that manage memory, tasks, interrupts, and protection faults. The VMM works with virtual devices — 32-bit protected-mode dynamic-link libraries — to allow the virtual devices to intercept interrupts and faults in order to control the access an application has to hardware devices and installed software.

The term VMM originated in work performed at IBM's Scientific Research Center in Cambridge, MA, in the late 1960s and early 1970s;

this research was written up in several key articles on the Virtual Machine concept in the *IBM Systems Journal* in the 1970s and culminated in IBM's VM/370 operating system, announced in 1972. Whether directly or indirectly, the Windows operating system is heavily based on this work.

The VMM is an operating system that runs virtual machines (VMs). In the case of VM/370, the VMM (known as Control Program or CP) runs on top of IBM's System/370 and creates and manages virtual 370s. In each virtual 370, VM/370 can run *another* operating system, including even another copy of VM/370. This other operating system thinks it's running on bare 370 hardware, even though it's actually running in a VM. In fact, there should be no way (apart from timing) to determine whether it's running in a VM or on the bare hardware.

Under this scheme, users can run applications for dissimilar operating systems at the same time. The VMs are relatively isolated from each other: An application running in one VM can't accidentally trash an application running in another VM. But this scheme can still offer some interesting options for inter-VM communications.

A major benefit of the VM scheme to the developer of the operating system is that the operating system is logically separated into two parts: The VMM handles multitasking and provides services required by operating systems, and these operating systems in turn provide services to applications. This is quite similar to the *microkernel* concept used in operating systems such as Mach and Windows NT, in which many of the tasks typically associated with the operating system are pushed off onto user-level subsystems.

In a VMM-based operating system, applications call into the operating system in the normal way (such as a SVC or INT instruction). The operating system call itself can trap into the VMM, or it can continue to go to the operating system (now running essentially as a user-level application under the VMM). The operating system, in the course of carrying out the request, will generate instructions that trap into the VMM.

For the sake of robustness, it's important that every *sensitive* instruction (that is, every instruction that affects or examines the VM's state) also be a *privileged* instruction (that is, it should cause a trap into the VMM). At the same time, for the sake of performance, it's equally important that as few instructions as possible do trap. This sets a VMM apart from a CPU emulator (such as the Insignia Soft PC software used in Windows NT to run 80x86 software on non-Intel hardware). In general, the virtual machine should be quite close to the underlying machine, if performance is to be acceptable. The VMM creates the illusion of *multiple* copies of the underlying machine.

Because some instructions trap into the VMM, running in a VM should be slower than running on the bare hardware. However, there is sometimes a "virtual machine performance anomaly," in which software runs *faster* in the VM than on the bare hardware because device virtualization allows caching, reordering of requests, and so on that might be more efficient than the actual device. An excellent example is 32-bit disk access in Windows.

Speaking of device virtualization, this idea (and the need for virtual device drivers) also comes out of IBM's research on virtual machine operating systems in the late 1960s and early 1970s. To create the illusion that each VM is a complete, separate machine, each VM must think it has its own disk, display, printer, and so on. Rather than build this into the VMM itself, a virtual device driver is written to manage each device. The driver can arbitrate requests from multiple VMs, refuse requests, pass them directly through to the device, or simulate them completely.

In Windows, VMM *is* the operating system. In Chapters 6 and 7 you saw that the Windows kernel, KRNL386.EXE, is essentially an application for which you could substitute any other application that happened to have the same name (COPY \COMMAND.COM KRNL386.EXE). Of course, the Windows kernel is, in its own right, almost an operating system. But it runs under VMM, just as operating systems like CMS or MVS can run under VM/370.

It should be clear from Chapters 6 and 7 that you could potentially run different operating environments under VMM. Or that, potentially, you could run multiple copies of KRNL386.EXE, each in its own VM. Windows won't let you do this, but there's no *inherent* reason why not. In fact, if you typed WIN from a DOS box within Windows 3.0, you *would* get another copy of Windows (running in real mode) in that VM. This undoubtedly confused many users, so starting in Windows 3.1, WIN .COM checks to see if Windows is already running. In any case, VMM could host multiple operating environments in somewhat the same way that the Windows NT microkernel can host multiple subsystems.

I noted earlier that VM/370 was even able to run another copy of VM/370 in a VM. A number of operating system textbooks note that such "recursive" VMs could be exploited for debugging, testing new versions of VM/370, collecting experimental data about program behavior, and so on. VMM, however, is not recursive. For one thing, although it contains a DPMI server, VMM is not a DPMI client. This is one reason why the VMM/VxD portion of Windows can't run under OS/2 (and, as noted in Chapter 5, even the higher-level KRNL386 portion must be heavily patched to make it run under OS/2).

This background on the VMM concept might suggest something about how Windows interacts with software loaded before it, such as MS-DOS. A VMM is an operating system for running other operating systems. MS-DOS is an operating system (and, aside from the implications of its enormous customer base and the huge number of applications written for it, not a very complex one at that). VMM can run MS-DOS. VMM *does* run MS-DOS!

At first it seems that Windows, perched atop a real-mode operating system like MS-DOS, is built on shaky ground. But, as noted countless times already, when Windows (VMM, specifically) calls down to DOS, it does so in V86 mode. And, as also noted, the Windows VMM has the option to make a wide variety of real-mode activities generate V86 exceptions, which VMM and VxDs can catch and handle in any way they see fit. In essence, therefore, VMM runs all software that was loaded before it in protected mode. For performance or other reasons, it doesn't always take full advantage of this protection, but it's there.

The key point to understand is that when VMM runs on top of DOS, VMM is running DOS and not the other way around. Although Windows loads *after* DOS and (with the important exceptions noted in Chapters 3 and 4) looks to DOS like just another application, VMM is the boss when Enhanced mode is running. Real-mode DOS is under the control of Windows.

Yet another way to put this is that Windows runs DOS itself *in a DOS box*, just as though DOS were some application that the user started under Windows. When a DOS TSR issues an INT 21h call, the call goes to VMM, which decides what to do with it. When a DOS device driver issues an IN or OUT instruction, VMM or a VxD can catch the I/O and do whatever is appropriate.

The claim that Windows can run DOS in protected mode sounds so outlandish that we need to write a test program to see if it's true. We'll do just that in the next chapter. This real-mode DOS memory-resident program, called V86TEST, will load before Windows and hook INT 21h and INT 2Fh. Each time V86TEST is invoked, it will check to see if the processor is in V86 mode.

V86 Mode and the PE Bit

But how can a program determine whether the processor is in V86 mode? The Set_V86_Exec_Mode and Set_PM_Exec_Mode services provided by VMM set and clear V86 mode by manipulating bit 17 (the VM flag) of the EFLAGS register. VMM checks for V86 mode by testing bit 17. EFLAGS is the 32-bit flags register, of which the 16-bit FLAGS register known to most PC programmers is just a truncated view.

Since the VM flag is located at bit 17, it's out of reach from 16-bit code. And even by using 32-bit code in a 16-bit program, you *still* can't get to bit 17 because the PUSHF instruction is hard-wired to clear the VM flag before pushing it on the stack. This is shown in the pseudocode for PUSHF provided in Rakesh Agarwal's excellent *80x86 Architecture and Programming:*

```
/* == Push [E]FLAGS image. == */
if (os == 32)
{   eflg = EFLAGS;
    /* Clear VM and RF flags before pushing onto stack */
    eflg<17> = 0;
    eflg<16> = 0;
    push4(eflg);
}
else /* os == 16 : push low-order WORD of EFLAGS */
    push2(EFLAGS<15:0>);
```

In a moment, we'll get into *why* Intel hides the VM flag from applications. The point right now is that you *can't* read the VM flag.

Now, the Intel 80286 and later microprocessors do have a Machine Status Word (MSW), which in turn contains a Protect Enable (PE) bit. When the machine is in protected mode *or* V86 mode, the PE bit is set. So you can query V86 mode by reading the PE bit. This is another indication that V86 mode is actually a form of protected mode.

On the 80386 and later microprocessors, the MSW expands to become the DWORD CR0 register. PE is the bottom bit (bit 0) of both MSW and CR0. Since V86 mode isn't present on the 286, you'd think that CR0 would provide the best way to check PE:

```
mov eax, cr0
and eax, 1
// PE bit in EAX
```

However, if you try to execute this code in V86 mode under Windows, it won't produce the desired results. The MOV instruction leaves the EAX register unchanged!

The fact that MOV CR0 "doesn't work" under Windows actually provides a good example of how V86 mode is different from real mode and of how Windows uses V86 mode to control real-mode software.

MOV CR0 is privileged in V86 mode. According to the Intel documentation, this instruction (along with the other Move to/from Special Register instructions) causes a general protection (GP) fault if it's attempted in V86 mode. The GP fault is INT 0Dh; VMM installs a handler for this fault by placing a function pointer in the IDT.

Why does MOV CR0 cause a GP fault? For that matter, why does Intel deliberately hide the VM flag? Recall the point made earlier in the discussion of IBM's VM/370: There should be no way (apart from timing) for nonprivileged software to determine whether it's in a VM or on bare hardware. For this reason, MOV CR0 *should* cause a GP fault; the VMM should decide if the caller is allowed to see whether or not it's in a VM.

This is just what happens: If real-mode software running in V86 mode tries to execute this MOV EAX, CR0 instruction, the instruction causes an exception that is caught by VMM. The machine suddenly switches from user-level (Ring 3) V86 mode to privileged (Ring 0) 32-bit protected mode. VMM handles the offending code in any way it likes. It just so happens that VMM handles the MOV EAX, CR0 by skipping past the instruction without doing anything else. That's right, VMM just ignores it!

The GP fault (INT 0Dh) handler in VMM first examines the faulting instruction located at the V86 mode program's instruction pointer (CS:EIP). It does this by consulting a Client Register Structure (CRS) pointed to by the EBP register:

```
movzx esi, [ebp.Client_CS]
shl   esi, 4
add   esi, [ebp.Client_EIP]                 ; esi = (CS << 4) + IP
mov   cx, [esi]                             ; cx = *esi
movzx edi, cl                               ; cl = opcode
jmp   dword ptr ds:[OPCODE_TABLE][edi*4]    ; jump to opcode
handler
```

The MOV EAX, CR0 instruction encodes as the three bytes 0F 20 C0. VMM has a single handler for all instructions 0F 20 through 0F 23, which includes moves to and from the control and debug registers (CR2, CR3, DR0, and so on). Here's the handler:

```
add [ebp.Client_EIP], 3
ret
```

That's it! VMM just bumps the client's instruction pointer (EIP) past the offending instruction and does nothing more. This explains why

MOV EAX, CR0 in a DOS program running under Windows leaves EAX unchanged.

More importantly, seeing the actual VMM code also provides an example of how VMM (and any VxD) can exercise control over real-mode software, including DOS. VMM's capability to change the Client EIP value in the CRS shows the wide discretion VMM has over the behavior of anything running in V86 mode. This includes software loaded *before* Windows as well as software running under it. (You'll see in a moment that the before/under distinction is rather meaningless.)

Clearly, MOV CR0 isn't going to help read the PE bit. Now, VMM and VxDs are privileged-level code, so they could read the CR0 register and handle a faulting MOV EAX, CR0 instruction by moving CR0 into Client_EAX:

```
mov eax, cr0                    ; do what client wants
mov [ebp.Client_EAX], eax       ; get result into client's EAX
add [ebp.Client_EIP], 3         ; now skip past client's instruction
ret
```

Although VMM doesn't behave this way, we could easily write a VxD that did, providing transparent support for the Move to/from Special Register instructions. However, we're just interested in reading the PE bit, which, as noted earlier, is also available as part of the MSW. SMSW (Store MSW), the Intel instruction to read the MSW, is *not* privileged.

Yes, it does seem odd that SMSW isn't privileged when MOV CR0 is; but the important Store Global Descriptor Table (SGDT), Store Interrupt Descriptor Table (SIDT), Store Local Descriptor Table (SLDT), and Store Task Register (STR) instructions aren't privileged, either. Given what was said earlier about the need for VMs to appear identical to bare machines, it is clearly a *flaw* that the SMSW instruction lets us read the PE bit.

This flaw (which Intel probably cannot eliminate) does make it easy to see if you're in V86 mode. Assuming your compiler provides inline assembly language and allows 286-style instructions such as SMSW (use the Borland -2 switch or the Microsoft -G2 switch), the following simple function retrieves the current value of the PE bit:

```
int pe(void)
{
    _asm smsw ax
    _asm and ax, 1
    // retval in AX
}
```

If this function is incorporated in a protected-mode program (such as a Windows application), it naturally returns 1 to indicate that the PE bit is on. As you'd expect, PE is always on in a protected-mode program.

Conversely, if this function is incorporated in a real-mode DOS program, you'd expect it to always return 0 to indicate that the PE bit is off. After all, PE is always off in a real-mode program, right?

Not! That's the whole point about V86 mode. Even when you're running a real-mode program, if you're running it in a V86-mode environment, the PE bit will be on. You really are in protected mode; it just dresses down to *look* like real mode. For example, if you compile PE.C as shown in Listing 9-1 and run it under a 386 memory manager (such as EMM386, QEMM, or 386MAX) or in a DOS box under Windows, OS/2, or Windows NT, PE displays the message "PE (protect enable) bit SET."

Listing 9-1: PE.C

```
/*
bcc -2 pe.c
cl -G2 pe.c
*/

#include <stdio.h>

int get_pe(void)
{
    _asm smsw ax
    _asm and ax, 1
    // return value in AX
}

main()
{
    int pe = get_pe();
    printf("PE (protect enable) bit %s\n", pe? "SET" : "NOT set");
    return pe;
}
```

That's right. When you're running one of these memory managers, what looks like an ordinary real-mode DOS prompt is in fact running in V86 mode, under the control of a VMM provided by the 386 memory manager. The fact that the PE bit is set indicates that you're in protected mode: You have a real-mode program, but each execution of an INT instruction vectors through the IDT, each execution of an IN or OUT instruction must consult the IOPB, and so on. Welcome to V86 mode, in which nothing is quite what it seems, and upon which Microsoft builds Windows Enhanced mode and Windows 95.

Now, what would happen if DOS itself contained this code to test the PE bit? Although it's easy to accept the fact that the PE bit will be set in software running under Windows in a DOS box, it's not so easy to believe that it will also be set in software that was loaded *before* Windows. Can Windows really control software loaded before it? In the next chapter you'll see that it can.

Chapter 10

How Windows Runs DOS

In the previous chapter, I stated that Windows uses V86 mode not only to run software in a DOS box but also to run software — including DOS itself — that the user loaded before starting Windows. The implications of this statement are far-reaching. You saw in the last chapter that V86 mode is really a form of protected mode. Therefore, if Windows really does call down to DOS in V86 mode rather than in real mode, Windows can potentially control DOS in the same way that it can control protected-mode Windows programs or programs running in a DOS box.

The tiny PE program in the previous chapter (Listing 9-1) showed how to use the processor's PE bit to test for V86 mode. Now, to ensure that the test for V86 mode is invoked whenever Windows calls down to DOS, you just have to put this test for V86 mode inside some code that loads before Windows.

This chapter presents a memory-resident program, V86TEST, that performs this test. V86TEST can readily prove that Windows calls down to DOS in V86 mode rather than in real mode, and therefore that Windows can control DOS.

V86TEST

V86TEST isn't a TSR; it's a *wrapper* program that hooks INT 21h and INT 2Fh and then spawns whatever program is named on its command line. Generally, you would run V86TEST WIN so that V86TEST spawns Windows. When Windows calls down to DOS, it will also call

V86TEST. V86TEST's interrupt handlers chain all calls onto the previous handler, but first they call a check_state function to keep statistics about how many times they've been called, how many times the PE bit was set, and so on. When Windows exits, V86TEST unhooks its interrupt handlers and displays the statistics.

V86TEST also provides a little INT 2Fh API so you can display the statistics with V86TEST -QUERY while Windows is still running, or with a Windows version of V86TEST. A -VERBOSE switch provides a function-by-function census of which INT 21h and INT 2Fh calls were made. The next chapter discusses this census of DOS calls in detail and uses a Windows version of V86TEST that calls down to the resident DOS version.

Figure 10-1 provides a pseudocode summary of how V86TEST works.

```
main:
    process command-line
    if (-QUERY or -CLEAR)
        invoke already-installed copy of V86TEST, and exit
    if already running under Windows or already in V86 mode
        fail
    hook INT 21h -> int21 function
    hook INT 2Fh -> int2f function
    spawn command (usually Windows)
    unhook INT 21h and INT 2Fh
    display results

int21:
    call check_state
    chain to previous INT 21h

int2f:
    look for Windows startup/exit broadcasts, to set Windows "state"
    look for function FFh, to return statistics
    call check_state
    chain to previous INT 2Fh

check_state:
    increment number of calls for current Windows state
    if PE bit is set
        increment number of V86 calls for current Windows state
    if Windows running
        see which VM we're running in
    see what current IOPL is
    increment int 21h and int 2Fh statistics
```

Figure 10-1: V86TEST operation.

V86TEST keeps separate counters for five different Windows states:

Windows State	**Description**
Before Windows started	Haven't yet received INT 2Fh AX=1605h
During Windows init	Received INT 2Fh AX=1605h (Win Init Notify)
While Windows running	Received INT 2Fh AX=1608h (Win Init Complete)
During Windows exit	Received INT 2Fh AX=1609h (Win Exit Begin)
After Windows exited	Received INT 2Fh AX=1606h (Win Exit Notify)

V86TEST knows which state Windows is in because its INT 2Fh handler looks for the function 16h broadcasts from Windows Enhanced mode. For more information on these broadcasts, see the FAKEWIN program in Chapters 3 and 4. (Incidentally, FAKEWIN and V86TEST are dance partners, and I've used "V86TEST FAKEWIN" to test both programs.)

The While Windows running state is what we'll focus on to determine how Windows calls down to DOS. This is the period after Windows has issued a Win Init Complete broadcast and before it has issued Win Exit Begin: during this time, Windows is truly up and running. When V86TEST receives the Win Init Complete and Win Exit Begin broadcasts, it calls the C time function. This helps V86TEST determine how long Windows was running.

Although the operation of V86TEST is quite simple — it points INT 21h and INT 2Fh at interrupt handlers that maintain statistics, spawns a command, unhooks INT 21h and INT 2Fh, and displays the statistics — the code is a little more complicated than that. Listing 10-1 shows the source code for V86TEST.

Listing 10-1: V86TEST.C

```
/*
V86TEST.C -- take over INT 21h and INT 2Fh, count calls in V86 mode
Andrew Schulman, 1994

Some of the complexity here is artificial, so that V86TEST could be
tested with programs other than Windows, such as FAKEWIN.

bcc -2 -P- v86test.c
*/

#include <stdlib.h>
#include <stddef.h>
#include <stdio.h>
#include <string.h>
#include <ctype.h>
```

```
#include <process.h>
#include <time.h>
#include <dos.h>

typedef unsigned short WORD;
typedef unsigned long DWORD;

#define VM_MAX      8
#define VM_OTHER    VM_MAX

#define GET_STATS   0xFFFF
#define SIGNATURE   "V86TEST"

#define VXD_MAX     0x100
#define VXD_OTHER   VXD_MAX

#if 0
struct {
    WORD vxd_id;
    DWORD num_calls;
    } VXDCALLS;

VXDCALLS vxdcalls[100] = {0};
int num_vxds = 0;
#endif

#pragma pack(1)

typedef struct {
#ifdef __TURBOC__
    WORD bp,di,si,ds,es,dx,cx,bx,ax;
#else
    WORD es,ds,di,si,bp,sp,bx,dx,cx,ax;     /* same as PUSHA */
#endif
    WORD ip,cs,flags;
    } REG_PARAMS;

void interrupt far int21(REG_PARAMS r);
void interrupt far int2f(REG_PARAMS r);

void (interrupt far *old)();
void (interrupt far *old_2F)();

#define WIN_INIT_NOTIFY     0x1605
#define WIN_INIT_COMPLETE   0x1608
#define WIN_EXIT_BEGIN      0x1609
#define WIN_EXIT_NOTIFY     0x1606

typedef enum {
    NO_WIN,
    WIN_INIT_BEGIN,             // got WIN_INIT_NOTIFY
    WIN_INIT_DONE,              // got WIN_INIT_COMPLETE
    WIN_FINI_BEGIN,             // got WIN_EXIT_BEGIN
    WIN_FINI_DONE,              // got WIN_EXIT_NOTIFY
    NUM_STATES } STATE;
```

```
static char *state_str[NUM_STATES] = {
    "Before Windows started",
    "During Windows init",      // got WIN_INIT_NOTIFY
    "While Windows running",    // got WIN_INIT_COMPLETE
    "During Windows exit",      // got WIN_EXIT_BEGIN
    "After Windows exited",     // got WIN_EXIT_NOTIFY
    } ;

typedef struct {
    char signature[8];
    DWORD calls[NUM_STATES], v86_calls[NUM_STATES];
    DWORD iopl_count[4];
    DWORD vm[VM_MAX+1];
    DWORD int21[0x100];
    DWORD int2f[0x100], int2f16[0x100], int2f1607[VXD_OTHER+1];
    time_t start, end;
    } STATS;

static STATE state = NO_WIN;
static STATS *stats;
static STATS far *fpstats;
static int not_verbose = 1;
static int not_filter = 1;
static int v86_okay = 0;

char *usage = "usage: v86test [-okv86] [-filter | -verbose]"
    " [-query | -clear | win] <args...>";

#define PUT(s)  { fputs(s, stderr); fputs("\n", stderr); }
#define FAIL(s) { PUT(s); exit(1); }

/**********************************************************************/

int win3e(void) // is Windows Enhanced mode running?
{
    int maj = 0;
    _asm mov ax, 1600h
    _asm int 2fh
    _asm mov byte ptr maj, al
    return (maj && (maj != 0x80));
}

int pe(void)    // is processor Protect Enable bit set?
{
    _asm smsw ax
    _asm and ax, 1
    // retval in AX
}

int iopl(void)  // get I/O Privilege Level from flags
{
    _asm pushf
    _asm pop ax
    _asm shr ax, 12
```

```
    _asm and ax, 3
    // retval in AX
}

int vmid(void)  // Get Windows Virtual Machine ID. If Windows Enh mode
{               // is running, V86TEST will never see this 2f/1683 call!
                // And if we tried calling it with PUSHF/CALLF rather
                // than with INT, it would get the wrong results!
    _asm mov ax, 1683h
    _asm int 2fh
    _asm mov ax, bx
    // retval in AX
}

/**********************************************************************/

void display_results(STATS far *fp2)
{
    STATS *fp;
    DWORD elapsed;
    time_t start, end;
    int i;

    if (! (fp = malloc(sizeof(STATS))))
        FAIL("Insufficient memory");
    // copy over so stats don't change while reading them
    _fmemcpy(fp, fp2, sizeof(STATS));

    printf("\n");
    for (i=NO_WIN; i<NUM_STATES; i++)
        printf("%s:\t%lu INT 21/2F calls, %lu in V86 mode\n",
            state_str[i], fp->calls[i], fp->v86_calls[i]);

    printf("\nWhile Windows running:\n");
    if (fp->end) end = fp->end; else time(&end);
    if (fp->start) start = fp->start; else time(&start);
    if ((elapsed = end - start) != 0)
    {
        printf("Windows active for %lu seconds\n", elapsed);
        printf("%lu INT 21/2F calls/second\n",
            fp->calls[WIN_INIT_DONE] / elapsed);
    }

    for (i=0; i<4; i++)
        if (fp->iopl_count[i])
            printf("IOPL=%d - %lu calls\n", i, fp->iopl_count[i]);

    for (i=0; i<VM_MAX; i++)
        if (fp->vm[i])
            printf("VM #%d - %lu calls\n", i, fp->vm[i]);
    if (fp->vm[VM_OTHER])
        printf("VM > #%d - %lu calls\n", VM_MAX, fp->vm[VM_OTHER]);

    // put before verbose check: always show 2f/16 calls
    printf("\nINT 2Fh AH=16h calls seen by V86TEST:\n");
```

```
    for (i=0; i<0x100; i++)
        if (fp->int2f16[i])
            printf("%02X: %lu\t", i, fp->int2f16[i]);
    printf("\n");

    if (not_verbose)
        return;

    // get following by running V86TEST -VERBOSE
    printf("\nINT 21h calls:\n");
    for (i=0; i<0x100; i++)
        if (fp->int21[i])
            printf("%02X: %lu\t", i, fp->int21[i]);

    printf("\n\nINT 2Fh calls:\n");
    for (i=0; i<0x100; i++)
        if (fp->int2f[i])
            printf("%02X: %lu\t", i, fp->int2f[i]);

    printf("\n\nINT 2Fh AX=1607h calls:\n");
    for (i=0; i<VXD_MAX; i++)
        if (fp->int2f1607[i])
            printf("%02X: %lu\t", i, fp->int2f1607[i]);
    if (fp->int2f1607[VXD_OTHER])
        printf("VxD>#%04X: %lu\n", VXD_MAX, fp->int2f1607[VXD_OTHER]);
    printf("\n\n");

    free(fp);
}

STATS far *get_stats(void)  // call resident copy of V86TEST
{
    STATS far *fp;
    _asm mov ax, GET_STATS
    _asm int 2fh
    _asm mov word ptr fp+2, es
    _asm mov word ptr fp, bx
    return (_fstrcmp(fp->signature, SIGNATURE) == 0) ? fp : 0;
}

main(int argc, char *argv[])
{
    int i;

    PUT("V86TEST — Test effect of Windows on software loaded before it");
    PUT("From \"Unauthorized Windows\" (IDG Books, 1994)");
    PUT("Copyright (c) 1994 Andrew Schulman.  All rights reserved.\n");

    /* look for command-line switches */
    while (argv[1][0] == '-')
    {
        STATS far *fp;
        switch (toupper(argv[1][1]))
        {
            case 'F' :  // filter
```

```
                not_filter = 0;
                break;
            case 'O' :  // okv86
                v86_okay = 1;
                break;
            case 'V' :  // verbose
                not_verbose = 0;
                break;
            case 'Q' :  // query
                if (! (fp = get_stats()))
                    FAIL("Can't get V86TEST statistics");
                display_results(fp);
                exit(0);
            case 'C' :  // clear
                if (! (fp = get_stats()))
                    FAIL("Can't clear V86TEST statistics");
                _fmemset(&fp->calls, 0,
                    sizeof(STATS) - offsetof(STATS, calls));
                exit(0);
            default:
                FAIL(usage);
        }
        argv++; argc—;
    }

ok:
    if (argc < 2) FAIL(usage);

    if (win3e()) FAIL("Already running under Windows Enhanced mode\n"
                      "Exit Windows and try again");

    if (! v86_okay)
    if (pe()) FAIL("Already in V86 mode — test would be pointless\n"
                   "Remove 386 memory manager from CONFIG.SYS and reboot");

    if ((stats = calloc(1, sizeof(STATS))) == 0)
        FAIL("Insufficient memory");
    fpstats = (STATS far *) stats;
    strcpy(stats->signature, SIGNATURE);

    /* hook INT 21h and INT 2Fh */
    old = _dos_getvect(0x21);
    _dos_setvect(0x21, int21);
    old_2F = _dos_getvect(0x2F);
    _dos_setvect(0x2f, int2f);

    /* run command */
    spawnvp(P_WAIT, argv[1], &argv[1]);

    /* unhook INT 21h, 2Fh */
    _dos_setvect(0x2F, old_2F);
    _dos_setvect(0x21, old);

    display_results(fpstats);
    return 0;
```

```
}

/************************************************************************/

void check_state(int intno, int ah, int al, int bx)
{
    stats->calls[state]++;

    if (pe())
        stats->v86_calls[state]++;

    if (state == WIN_INIT_DONE)
    {
        /* The following is a little confusing. V86TEST is normally able
           to make Windows INT 2Fh calls (such as vmid()) from inside an
           INT 2Fh handler, without causing an endless loop, because VMM
           gets these INT 2Fh calls and doesn't reflect them back to V86
           mode. Thus, V86TEST mode's INT 2Fh handler never sees
           calls such as 2F/1680 and 2F/1683. However, it's useful to
           test V86TEST with programs other than Windows, such as FAKEWIN.
           In this case, the 2F/168x calls would wind up right back at
           V86TEST, causing an endless loop if called from inside the
           INT 2Fh handler. So if genuine Windows VMM isn't running (as
           determined by the 2F/1680 call), V86TEST doesn't call 2F/1683.
           2F/1680 is called just once; logging is turned off for that one
           call to prevent an endless loop if something other than Windows
           VMM is running. */

        int cur_vm;

        static int logging = 1;
        static int is_win = 0xff;
        if (logging == 0) return;
        else if (is_win == 0xff) // one-time init
        {
            logging = 0;
            is_win = win3e();
            logging = 1;
        }

        cur_vm = (is_win) ? vmid() : 0;

        stats->vm[(cur_vm < VM_MAX) ? cur_vm : VM_OTHER]++;

        // only collect this while Windows running!!
        stats->iopl_count[iopl()]++;
    }

    if (intno == 0x21)
        stats->int21[ah]++;
    else if (intno == 0x2f)
    {
        stats->int2f[ah]++;
        if (ah == 0x16)
        {
```

```
                stats->int2f16[al]++;
                if (al == 7)    // 2f/1607/18 is most popular (VMPOLL)
                    stats->int2f1607[(bx < 0x100) ? bx : VXD_OTHER]++;
            }
        }
}

void interrupt far int21(REG_PARAMS r)
{
    check_state(0x21, r.ax >> 8, r.ax & 0xff, r.bx);
    _chain_intr(old);
}

void interrupt far int2f(REG_PARAMS r)
{
    switch (r.ax)
    {
        case WIN_INIT_NOTIFY:    state = WIN_INIT_BEGIN;
                                 break;
        case WIN_INIT_COMPLETE: state = WIN_INIT_DONE;
                                 time(&stats->start);
                                 break;
        case WIN_EXIT_BEGIN:     state = WIN_FINI_BEGIN;
                                 time(&stats->end);
                                 break;
        case WIN_EXIT_NOTIFY:    state = WIN_FINI_DONE;
                                 break;
        case GET_STATS:          r.es = FP_SEG(fpstats);
                                 r.bx = FP_OFF(fpstats);
                                 break;
    }
    // -FILTER option ignores 2f/1607/18 (VMPOLL)
    if (not_filter || (r.ax != 0x1607 && r.bx != 0x18))
        check_state(0x2f, r.ax >> 8, r.ax & 0xff, r.bx);
    _chain_intr(old_2F);
}
```


Since the goal of V86TEST is to demonstrate that Windows calls DOS in V86 mode, it doesn't make sense to run V86TEST if the machine is *already* in V86 mode. All interrupt calls would be in V86 mode anyway, whether or not you ran Windows, so V86TEST would reveal little about the Windows-DOS interface.

Therefore, V86TEST checks the PE bit at startup. If the PE bit is already set (probably because you're running under a 386 memory manager such as EMM386, QEMM, or 386MAX), V86TEST displays an error message and exits. Except when handling the -VERBOSE and -CLEAR command-line options discussed in the next chapter, V86TEST also fails with an error message if you're already running under Windows. An interesting alternative might be for V86TEST to force the machine from V86 mode to real mode and then spawn Windows, but this is more complicated than it sounds (see the "Switching from V86 mode to real mode" sidebar).

Because the next chapter uses V86TEST for a somewhat different purpose than detecting the mode in which Windows calls down to DOS, V86TEST also provides an -OKV86 switch that forces the program to run even if the processor is already in V86 mode.

Switching from V86 mode to real mode

If the machine is in V86 mode when V86TEST starts up and if the user hasn't specified -OKV86, the program fails with this error message:

```
Already in V86 mode -- test would be pointless
Remove 386 memory manager from CONFIG.SYS and reboot
```

An interesting alternative would be for V86TEST to force the machine out of V86 mode and back to real mode before spawning Windows. Memory managers such as EMM386 and QEMM generally provide an OFF command-line option to disable the memory manager, so it seems like V86TEST should be able to call some function in the memory manager to deactivate the memory manager and return to real mode. Indeed, Windows itself must call such a function when it starts up. Windows Enhanced mode can't switch to protected mode if the machine is *already* in protected mode (that is, V86 mode). As seen in FAKEWIN in Chapters 3 and 4, the INT 2Fh function 1605h broadcast allows an installed memory manager to give Windows the address of a V86 switch function.

Like FAKEWIN, V86TEST could pretend to be Windows and issue an INT 2Fh function 1605h to get the address of the switch function. It could then call this function to switch from V86 mode back to real mode before spawning Windows. If the memory manager has already been turned OFF, or if the switch function has already been called to disable V86 mode, the memory manager should return NULL for the switch function address.

However, the V86 switch function that memory managers return via INT 2Fh function 1605h isn't exactly like EMM386 OFF or QEMM OFF. Whereas those command-line options fail if the memory manager is currently providing UMBs (Upper Memory Blocks) or EMS, the V86 switch function just does what it's told and disables V86 mode. What this means, unfortunately, is that some key device driver or TSR that has been loaded high will suddenly become invisible — and this is likely to result in a crash.

What does Windows itself do in this situation? As shown in Chapters 3 and 4, the V86MMGR VxD in Windows uses a Global EMM Import interface to take over the memory manager's page tables. Rather than get into the Global EMM Import business, it makes more sense for V86TEST — which, after all, is just a test program — to simply fail if it detects that the machine is already in V86 mode.

As noted earlier, V86TEST keeps statistics that indicate how many calls it has seen and how many of these calls occurred in V86 mode rather than in real mode. Figure 10-2 shows some sample output from V86TEST; to increase the number of DOS calls, I temporarily disabled 32-bit file access. (Actually, the /D:C switch to disable 32-bit file access was unnecessary here, since redirecting Windows' stdout to a file will do that anyhow.)

```
C:\>v86test /D:C > v86test.log
C:\>type v86test.log
Before Windows started: 109 INT 21/2F calls, 0 in V86 mode
During Windows init:     5216 INT 21/2F calls, 354 in V86 mode
While Windows running:  174712 INT 21/2F calls, 174712 in V86 mode
During Windows exit:     13 INT 21/2F calls, 10 in V86 mode
After Windows exited:    12 INT 21/2F calls, 0 in V86 mode

While Windows running:
Windows active for 256 seconds
682 INT 21/2F calls/second
IOPL=0 -- 2929 calls
IOPL=3 -- 171783 calls
VM #1 -- 135326 calls
VM #2 --  39386 calls

INT 2Fh AH=16h calls seen by V86TEST:
00: 2   05: 1   06: 1   07: 125887  08: 1   09: 1   0A: 2   0B: 2   8A: 1
```

Figure 10-2: Sample output from V86TEST, a program that shows Windows calls DOS in V86 mode.

The third line of the output in Figure 10-2 tells us that every one of the 174,712 INT 21h and INT 2Fh calls made while Windows was running occurred in V86 mode. No DOS calls occurred in V86 mode either before Windows started or after Windows completed its exit procedure. It's apparent from this figure that the switch from real mode to V86 mode occurs sometime during Windows init and that the switch back to real mode occurs sometime during Windows exit. Well, that's sensible enough.

While Windows is running, V86TEST, in addition to testing the PE bit, also checks the processor flags to get the I/O privilege level (IOPL) and calls INT 2Fh function 1683h (Get Current Virtual Machine ID) to get the current Virtual Machine ID number (VMID).

You might be asking, nay, demanding: How can V86TEST make an INT 2Fh call from *inside* an INT 2Fh handler? This is an excellent question, and the answer gets to very heart of how Windows exercises control over programs running in V86 mode. Stay tuned for the exciting explanation.

But first, to understand the next part of the V86TEST output in Figure 10-2 (the two lines showing numbers for IOPL=0 and IOPL=3), we need to take what will at first appear to be a detour to look at the I/O Privilege Level on the Intel 80386 and later microprocessors. It's not a pretty sight, but here goes.

IOPL and the Interrupt Flag

The Intel 80x86 architecture has a dizzying array of protection and privilege mechanisms. Books on the subject typically bombard the reader with terms like Requestor Privilege Level (RPL), Descriptor Privilege Level (DPL), Current Privilege Level (CPL), and I/O Privilege Level (IOPL). One of the most intelligent books on microprocessors, after the obligatory section on Intel 80386 privilege levels, presents a section titled "Is All This Worthwhile?" The authors observe,

> The previous section is virtually incomprehensible. You probably have to read it several times to understand it, and it is still easy to get the DPLs, CPLs, and RPLs hopelessly mixed up. No other commonly used microprocessors have anything like this protection complexity, and we can legitimately raise the question of whether these features are useful and worthwhile (the Intel position) or represent design gone berserk (the position of many others).
>
> — Robert B.K. Dewar and Matthew Smosna, *Microprocessors: A Programmer's View,* pp. 95-96.

I'm not going to bore you with yet another discussion of the baroque privilege-level mechanism on Intel's 80386, 80486, and Pentium microprocessors. If you want, you can read about this in the Intel manuals (or in many widely available books that have been cribbed from the Intel manuals) or in some of the few genuinely good books on the subject, which I've listed in "For Further Reading."

But we do need to look at one aspect of this mess: the IOPL. To simplify matters somewhat (which I must do to avoid dragging in a discussion of the CPL), the IOPL determines which instructions a program running in V86 mode can execute. If the I/O Privilege Level is less than 3 (such as IOPL=0), programs running in a DOS box cannot execute the following instructions:

Instruction	Description
PUSHF	Push flags
POPF	Pop flags

INT n	Software interrupt
IRET	Interrupt return
CLI	Clear interrupt flag (disable interrupts)
STI	Set interrupt flag (enable interrupts)

You might wonder what these six instructions have to do with each other or with an I/O privilege level. Furthermore, since these instructions are all commonly used in real-mode software, you might wonder what possible use there could be in a V86 mode configuration that runs real-mode software but doesn't allow execution of these instructions.

To deal with these points in reverse order (popping the stack, as it were), let's first dismiss any "cannot execute" concerns you might have. Whenever discussions of the Intel processors say that something "can't happen," it just means that an exception is generated. In the case of these can't-execute instructions, all that happens is that a General Protection (GP) fault is triggered. In other words, if a real-mode program running in V86 mode with IOPL=0 generates, say, an INT 21h to call MS-DOS, this triggers a GP fault.

A GP fault?! That doesn't sound very good. GP faults are what make Windows display its ominous-looking "Unrecoverable Application Error! Do Not Pass Go! Do Not Collect $200!" message boxes. How is generating a GP fault any different from saying that the instruction can't execute?

Relax: don't get your knickers in a twist over GP faults. The GP fault is really just an INT 0Dh. The protected-mode operating system (such as VMM in Windows) will have an INT 0Dh handler that will catch this GP fault and do with it what it wants. VMM could terminate the offending application, ignore the instruction, emulate the instruction, whatever. So a real-mode program running in a Windows DOS box with IOPL=0 that generates, say, an INT 21h to call MS-DOS will trap into VMM's GP fault handler.

This GP fault handler doesn't necessarily display an error message and terminate the application. In fact, Windows' GP fault handlers almost never respond this way to GP faults. That's because GP faults, along with Invalid Opcode exceptions, are a normal and crucial part of the underlying system architecture of Windows, and VMM's GP fault handler silently deals with many GP faults per second.

Let's return to what the six illegal instructions — PUSHF, POPF, INT n, IRET, CLI, and STI — have to do with each other. Why are these instructions different from all other instructions? Because they all affect the Interrupt Flag (IF). CLI and STI of course clear and set IF, but so can POPF and IRET in the course of popping the top of the stack into the flags register. The PUSHF and INT (which does an implicit PUSHF) instructions don't directly affect the flags register, but they are symmetrical to POPF and IRET. (That's not quite the real reason for their inclusion, but the real reason won't make sense for a few moments.)

Okay, then what's so important about IF that Intel would go to all this trouble? As already noted at the end of Chapter 9, all other things being equal, it's a bad idea for protected-mode operating systems to let a V86 process turn off the processor's actual IF, because doing so disables interrupts for *all* processes. If a program running in a DOS box could freely execute CLI or use POPF or IRET to disable interrupts, it could disable interrupts for every other program too, including Windows applications and other DOS boxes.

This would not be good. So Intel gives protected-mode operating systems the option of trapping these instructions. If IOPL<3 (such as IOPL=0), then every time a DOS program — or a program loaded before Windows, such as DOS itself — generates one of these instructions, VMM could take over. VMM could maintain a "virtual" IF for each VM. (Interestingly, the Pentium processor has some undocumented V86 extensions that provide a Virtual IF in hardware.) The processor needs to trap PUSHF and INT, even though these don't affect the IF, so that a V86 monitor like VMM can maintain this virtual IF. (This is the *real* reason I alluded to a moment ago.)

This is a good example of how V86 mode lets a protected-mode operating system have its way with real-mode software. But why is IOPL<3 just an option? Why would you ever want to give some crummy DOS program the freedom to turn off interrupts for everyone else? Because, if every PUSHF, POPF, INT, IRET, CLI, and STI caused a GP fault that VMM had to handle, performance would probably stink (see CLISTI.C in Listing 10-4). When IOPL=3, these instructions don't fault; they execute just as they would in real mode.

Actually, that's not quite true. The Intel manual says that "If the IOPL is less than 3, INT n instructions are intercepted by the virtual-8086 monitor," which seems to imply that if IOPL *isn't* less than 3, then INT n instructions aren't intercepted by the V86 monitor. In fact, they are. As Intel explains elsewhere in the manual, *all* INT instructions from V86 mode, regardless of IOPL, are vectored through the protected-mode Interrupt Descriptor Table (IDT). So, whatever the IOPL, all INT 21h, INT 2Fh, and so on from DOS programs — and, once again, from programs loaded before Windows, including DOS itself — will be handled initially (and sometimes exclusively) by VMM or a VxD. This is an important point, and I'll return to it many times.

At any rate, if IOPL=3, none of the instructions that affect IF will generate a fault. A DOS program running in V86 mode with IOPL=3 will actually turn off the machine's IF if it executes a CLI. Thus, IOPL=0 gives you a more robust operating system under which DOS programs may take a hefty performance hit, and IOPL=3 gives you a less-robust operating system with better performance. Again, Intel's Pentium processor has some currently undocumented V86 extensions that, sometime in the future, might make this robustness versus performance tradeoff unnecessary.

What does Windows do about this robustness versus performance dilemma? The output from V86TEST (Figure 10-2) shows what it does:

```
IOPL=0 -- 2929 calls
IOPL=3 -- 171783 calls
```

Although occasionally IOPL=0,the vast majority of the time IOPL=3. This has tremendous implications for Windows's performance and robustness. A setting of IOPL=3 means that CLI/STI, PUSHF/POPF, and IRET will *not* trap into the Windows VMM. This results in far better performance than a setting of IOPL=0 (which causes each such instruction to trap into VMM); it also means that DOS software can freely manipulate the interrupt flag.

Geoff Chappell has suggested a nice demonstration that illustrates both this point and the point that Windows provides preemptive multitasking of VMs. Inside a Windows DOS box, run DEBUG and assemble a tight loop that enables interrupts:

```
C:\>debug
-a
7713:0100 sti
7713:0101 jmp 100    ; or jmp 101
7713:0103
-g
```

This is a *dynamic halt*: the processor is executing instructions, but you can't do anything in the DOS box. Pressing Ctrl-C or Ctrl-Break has no effect. If you were in DOS, you'd have no choice but to reboot the machine.

However, this is a Windows DOS box, so you can run other programs in the background and switch to other programs. You can even make the DOS box windowed or full screen, cut data from the hung DOS box into the Clipboard, and so on. These virtual machines are better than genuine machines! You can press Ctrl-Alt-Del to do a "local reboot" of the DOS box and then start another DOS box. This capability to throw away a hung DOS machine and get another one makes Windows (or any preemptive multitasking environment) great for software development.

Now, use DEBUG to assemble a tight loop that *disables* interrupts:

```
C:\>debug
-a
7713:0100 cli
7713:0101 jmp 100    ; or jmp 101
7713:0103
-g
```


Once again, the DOS box is hung: Ctrl-C and other keys have no effect. But this time, because we've used CLI (clear interrupt flag) rather than STI (set interrupt flag) and because Windows almost always uses IOPL=3, the programs running in the background halt; you can't switch to other programs and you can't even press Ctrl-Alt-Del (well, you can press Ctrl-Alt-Del all you want, but nothing will happen). There's nothing to do but power the machine off and on again. (By the way, don't try this experiment with 32-bit file access enabled because you could lose any file data held in memory by the VCACHE VxD.)

This shows that any DOS program can turn off interrupts for all of Windows. Although this is a massive security breach, you can also see that it isn't an inherent property of running protected-mode Windows on top of real-mode DOS. Instead, setting the IOPL level involves a tradeoff that *all* operating systems must consider: Robustness versus performance.

V86TEST shows, however, that Windows occasionally sets IOPL=0. Why? The answer appears in a book on the design of OS/2. It shouldn't be surprising that OS/2 provides clues about the inner workings of Windows Enhanced mode, since Microsoft largely designed OS/2 2.0 before its divorce from IBM. It turns out that, just like Windows, OS/2's Virtual DOS Machines (VDMs) use IOPL=3 most of the time but do every now and then need IOPL=0:

> IOPL is set to 0 for a single VDM only when that VDM needs to have the interrupt flag virtualized. For example, when some VDD [an OS/2 virtual device driver] needs to simulate an interrupt into a VDM, it must be able to detect when the VDM can be interrupted. Therefore, IOPL is decreased to less than 3, so that the interrupt flag can be virtualized for a VDM, and the system can detect when the interrupts are enabled in that VDM. IOPL is increased back to 3 when the simulated interrupt is delivered to the VDM.
>
> — H.M. Deitel and M.S. Kogan, *The Design of OS/2,* p. 296.

This sounds like a description of the VDHArmSTIHook service in OS/2, which allows OS/2 virtual device drivers to install ("arm" in IBM-speak) a handler that receives control when interrupts are enabled (STI) in a DOS box. The equivalent function in Windows is Call_When_VM_Ints_Enabled. Sure enough, inspection of the code in VMM shows that Call_When_VM_Ints_Enabled sets IOPL=0. And the Windows VPICD device, which simulates hardware interrupts into VMs, uses Call_When_VM_Ints_Enabled, just as you'd gather from the description of OS/2. When V86TEST detects IOPL=0, it's generally because VPICD wants to simulate a hardware interrupt (usually a timer tick) into a VM.

Despite the similarity here between OS/2 and Windows (which really is remarkable when you consider the bad blood between Microsoft and IBM's PSP division, which markets OS/2), there is an interesting difference. According to Deitel and Kogan:

> To make sure that a DOS application does not disable interrupts and go into a spin loop and hang the system, OS/2 uses a *watchdog timer.* A watchdog timer is set with a duration interval; as long as the timer is primed before that interval expires, the timer does not interrupt. If the watchdog timer interrupts, the system terminates the DOS application. Therefore, setting IOPL to 3 allows the system to achieve maximum performance, and using the watchdog timer prevents DOS applications from taking down the system or disrupting protected-mode applications.
>
> — *The Design of OS/2,* p. 296.

Even here, though, the difference between OS/2 and Windows turns out not to be very large. The "watchdog timer" that OS/2 uses is available only on PS/2 and EISA machines, which provide an extra timer that can trigger a nonmaskable interrupt (NMI) if interrupts have been disabled for too long. On machines with the watchdog timer, OS/2 responds to the CLI loop with an error message and allows you to terminate the VDM. On standard ISA machines missing this nice feature, however, a CLI loop in a DOS box hangs OS/2, exactly as happens under Windows. So much for "Crash Protection."

Executing a CLI loop in a DOS box under Windows NT, however, will *not* hang the machine. NT runs DOS programs with IOPL=0, and every single CLI will trap into a part of NT called NTVDM; NTVDM can maintain a virtual interrupt flag for each VDM. With IOPL=0, every PUSHF, POPF, INT, IRET, and STI will also trap into NTVDM, so the downside is that performance isn't very good.

Note that there's nothing inherent in NT's status as a full-blown operating system that prevents DOS applications from hanging the machine: NT has just chosen to run DOS applications with IOPL=0.

Similarly, there's nothing inherent in Windows's status as a seeming extension to real-mode DOS —by now, the extension is wagging the operating system — that makes it vulnerable to DOS applications. Windows has simply chosen (most of the time) to run DOS applications with IOPL=3. These are just examples of engineering decisions and tradeoffs; there's no magic.

With all this talk of the interrupt flag, I neglected to answer one question: What does the interrupt flag have to do with the I/O privilege level? In V86 mode, IOPL has very little to do with I/O per se. In protected mode, IOPL (together with the I/O permission bitmap) determines whether an application can issue the Intel I/O instructions — IN, INS, OUT, and OUTS — without generating a GP fault. But in V86 mode, the four I/O instructions consult the I/O permission bitmap regardless of the IOPL, and IOPL is *reused* for interrupt-flag management. IOPL just has different meanings in protected mode and V86 mode, and the name in V86 mode doesn't make a whole lot of sense.

Speaking of protected mode, it's worth repeating the earlier STI and CLI loop tests that used DEBUG in V86 mode, but this time using a small protected-mode Windows application. Listing 10-2 does just that.

Listing 10-2: CLITEST.C (Windows version)

```
/* bcc -WS clitest.c */
#include "windows.h"

int PASCAL WinMain(HANDLE hInstance, HANDLE hPrevInstance,
    LPSTR lpszCmdLine, int nCmdShow)
{
    #define YN (MB_YESNO | MB_ICONQUESTION)
    if (MessageBox(0, "Would you like a STI loop?", "CLITEST", YN) == IDYES)
    {
        for (;;)
            _asm sti
    }
    if (MessageBox(0, "How about a CLI loop?", "CLITEST", YN) == IDYES)
    {
        for (;;)
            _asm cli
    }
    return 0;
}
```

When you run CLITEST, the STI loop behaves pretty much like the V86 mode DOS version: the machine seems hung, but you can do a local reboot (Ctrl-Alt-Del) to terminate the CLITEST application. Rather than terminating the System VM, just the application is terminated. On the other hand, while CLITEST is running, you can't switch to other Win16 applications because CLITEST isn't reading the message queue. Unfortunately, in the May 1994 Chicago beta, the STI loop in CLITEST seemed to prevent all Win32 threads (such as those belonging to Clock and WinBezMT) from running, and Windows 95's "Close Hung Application" feature seemed confused because CLITEST doesn't have a window.

What's more interesting is that this Windows CLITEST behaves the same way in its CLI loop! Recall that when a DOS program went into a CLI loop, the machine was truly locked up. But you can just use Ctrl-Alt-Del to terminate the Windows program and go on to something else.

So what magical qualities do Windows applications have that DOS applications don't have? None, actually. The difference is that we tried the CLI loop from a real-mode program (DEBUG) running in V86 mode; the Windows program, on the other hand, was running in protected mode. It's not a Windows versus DOS difference, but a protected mode versus V86 mode difference. So, in Listing 10-3, let's use the DPMISH library on the *Unauthorized Windows 95* disk to try a protected-mode DOS version of CLITEST.

Listing 10-3: CLITEST2.C (DPMI version)

```
/* bcc clitest2.c dpmish.c ctrl_c.asm */
#include <stdio.h>
#include "dpmish.h"

void fail(const char *s, ...)         { puts(s); _dos_exit(1); }
int real_main(int argc, char *argv[])  { return 0; }
int pmode_main(int argc, char *argv[])
{
    if (argc < 2)
    {
        puts("STI loop");
        for (;;)
            _asm sti
    }
    else
    {
        puts("CLI loop");
        for (;;)
            _asm cli
    }
}
```

Sure enough, with the protected-mode DOS version of the CLI loop, you can still do a local reboot to throw away the application without resetting the machine. This demonstrates the symmetry between the System VM and DOS boxes: protected-mode DOS programs behave much like Windows applications. Actually, in this case the DOS program is a little better than a Win16 program. Since the DOS program doesn't have to poll the message queue, it doesn't hold up other programs, Clock continues to run, you can switch away to other programs, and so on.

Okay, so a CLI loop from a protected-mode DOS or Windows program won't hang the machine. But why not?

For one thing, the REBOOT VxD in Windows, which installs a handler for the Ctrl-Alt-Del hot key and manages the local-reboot facility, contains code that, on receipt of a Ctrl-Alt-Del from a protected-mode program, checks to see if the interrupt flag is disabled; if it is, it enables it!

But the more fundamental reason is that, under protected mode in Windows, IOPL=0. (You can see this if you call the iopl function in Listing 10-1 from a Windows application; see Listing 10-4.) This means that CLI and STI instructions from protected-mode DOS and Windows programs *always* generate a GP fault that is handled by VMM.

So what does VMM do when its GP fault handler is called on account of a CLI? When IOPL=0 (either in protected mode or in V86 mode), a CLI instruction will wind up invoking the following piece of code in VMM:

```
CLI_HANDLER:
    inc [ebp.Client_EIP]
    and byte ptr [ebp.Client_FLAGS+1], 0FDh
    retn
```

This code skips past the 1-byte CLI instruction, clears the interrupt flags in a virtualized copy of the flags register, and then returns. The STI handler is a bit more complicated because it has to work with the Call_When_VM_Ints_Enabled service mentioned earlier:

```
STI_HANDLER:
    inc [ebp.Client_EIP]
    bts [ebp.Client_Flags], 9    ;; bit to carry, reset
    jnc ENABLED_INTS             ;; if went from disabled to enabled
    retn

ENABLED_INTS:
    ;;; See if anyone is waiting for VM_Ints_Enabled:
    ;;; If so, schedule their CallWhen routine to get called.
    ;;; (There's a good bit of code here.)
```

But even STI_HANDLER looks so simple that you must be wondering why VMM doesn't just provide interrupt-flag virtualization all the time. Unfortunately, whenever a GP fault occurs, VMM has to execute a lot of code before it can do something useful (in this case, calling CLI_HANDLER or STI_HANDLER). This isn't something you want happening a lot. Even by avoiding IOPL=0 most of the time in V86 mode, Windows *still* suffers from far too many internal GP faults.

Without looking at all the VMM GP fault handling code, it's still easy to see that interrupt-flag virtualization comes at a very high price. The DPMI 1.0 specification warns that in protected mode, the CLI and STI instructions "should be assumed to be very slow." An earlier version of the specification specifically mentioned that virtualized CLI and STI can take 300 clocks each! The Intel 80x86 manuals say CLI and STI take 3-5 clocks each. It's easy to determine whether IOPL=0 (whether in protected or V86 mode) really does take such a terrible toll, by seeing how many seconds it takes to execute a large number of CLIs and STIs in protected mode (where under Windows IOPL=0). In protected mode IOPL=0 so a protected-mode test program gives us an idea how V86 must behave when IOPL=0.

CLISTI in Listing 10-4 is a DPMI program that executes a CLI/STI loop first in V86 or real mode and then switches to protected mode to run the CLI/STI loop again. It prints out the elapsed time in each mode.

Listing 10-4: CLISTI.C

```
/* clisti.c */
#include <stdlib.h>
#include <stdio.h>
#include <time.h>
#include "dpmish.h"

void fail(const char *s, ...)           { puts(s); _dos_exit(1); }

#define ITER    1000000L

int pe(void)    // is processor Protect Enable bit set?
{
    _asm smsw ax
    _asm and ax, 1
    // retval in AX
}

int iopl(void)  // get I/O Privilege Level from flags
{
    _asm pushf
    _asm pop ax
    _asm shr ax, 12
    _asm and ax, 3
    // retval in AX
}

int cpl(void)   // get pmode Ring X from bottom two bits of CS
{
```

```
    _asm mov ax, cs
    _asm and ax, 3
    // retval in AX
}

void clisti_loop(int pmode)
{
    time_t t1, t2;
    unsigned long i;
    printf("\n%s mode ", pmode? "Prot" : pe() ? "V86" : "Real");
    printf("IOPL=%d", iopl());
    if (pmode) printf(" CPL=%d", cpl());
    printf("\n");
    time(&t1);
    for (i=0; i<ITER; i++)
    {
        _asm cli
        _asm sti
    }
    time(&t2);
    printf("%lu CLI/STI in %lu seconds\n", ITER, t2-t1);
}

int real main(int argc, char *argv[])   { clisti_loop(0); return 0; }
int pmode_main(int argc, char *argv[])  { clisti_loop(1); return 0; }
```

Here are the results from running CLISTI in various modes on one machine:

```
In real-mode MS-DOS:
    Real mode IOPL=3          1000000 CLI/STI in 1 second

In a WfW 3.11 DOS box:
    V86 mode IOPL=3           1000000 CLI/STI in 1 second

    Prot mode IOPL=0 CPL=3    1000000 CLI/STI in 70 second

In a Windows 3.0 DOS box:
    V86 mode IOPL=3           1000000 CLI/STI in 1 second

    Prot mode IOPL=0 CPL=1    1000000 CLI/STI in 24 second
```

With CLI/STI taking about seventy times longer in Windows 3.1 with IOPL=0 than with IOPL=3, the DPMI specification's estimate of about 300 clocks sounds just about right for the VMM implementation. Interestingly, the Windows 3.0 implementation was a good bit faster in this area. Although the CLI and STI handlers themselves don't do much (well, the STI handler does do a fair amount for Call_When_VM_Ints_Enabled), just getting in and out of VMM is quite expensive.

It's important to remember that this is not a distinction between V86 mode and protected mode per se. Whether CLI and STI cause these expensive GP faults or not has to do entirely with the IOPL. When IOPL=0 in a DOS box, any CLI or STI — even one located inside DOS or the BIOS — will execute the VMM code shown earlier. Judging from Figure 10-2, IOPL=0 about ten times per second, probably when VPICD wants to send hardware interrupts such as timer ticks into the VM.

I ought to confess now that the absolute value of IOPL isn't really what matters. What the processor cares about is whether IOPL is less than CPL; for example, if IOPL<CPL, a CLI or STI will generate a GP fault. CPL is what is sometimes called the privilege "ring," as in Ring 0 or Ring 3. V86 mode is effectively always in Ring 3, so any IOPL<3 will turn PUSHF, POPF, INT, IRET, CLI, and STI into a GP fault. Still, IOPL=0 and IOPL=3 are convenient shorthand.

In protected mode, the CPL is determined from the bottom two bits of the CS register (see the cpl function in Listing 10-4). In Windows 3.0, protected-mode programs ran in Ring (CPL) 1; in Windows 3.1 and higher, they run in Ring 3. In both cases, IOPL=0, so CLI, STI, IN, INS, OUT, and OUTS all cause GP faults from Windows applications and from protected-mode DOS applications running under Windows.

In VMM and VxDs, there is a single flat 4GB code segment whose value is 0028h. Although the value itself is not that important, and may change, note that the bottom two bits of 0028h are clear: VMM and VxDs run in Ring 0, so when they issue a CLI, STI, IN, OUT, INT, IRET, or whatever, no GP fault occurs. VMM and VxDs can do whatever they want. VMM and VxDs are in charge of virtualization and can't themselves be virtualized; this makes VxDs perfect for low-level Windows systems programming, but it also makes life difficult for environments such as OS/2 that want to run Windows as a subtask. The Windows virtualizer can't itself easily be virtualized. Windows is not a recursive VMM.

One last point about IOPL. In the iopl function in Listings 10-1 and 10-4, note that the first instruction is a PUSHF: the function pushes the flags on the stack so it can extract the IOPL bits. There's one problem here: in V86 mode, if IOPL=0 then PUSHF causes a GP fault, which the operating system can handle any way it likes. It's conceivable that an operating system's PUSHF handler could change the IOPL bits in the emulated flags register so that it *appeared* as if IOPL=3; the V86-mode program would have no way of knowing.

Thus, if the iopl function comes back with IOPL=0, you know that IOPL=0, but if it comes back with anything else, you can't be sure: perhaps IOPL=0 and the operating system has emulated PUSHF in a way that makes it appear as if IOPL=3. It's a weird world, this V86 mode, when you can't even completely trust a PUSHF to do what it appears to do. There are really only two ways to find out what PUSHF is doing: generate a lot of CLIs and STIs and see how long they take (as in Listing 10-4) or examine the operating system's PUSHF handler. Well, let's see what the PUSHF handler in VMM looks like:

```
PUSHF_HANDLER:
    test     byte ptr [ebx.CB_VM_Status], VMStat_PM_Exec_Bit  ;; prot mode?
    jnz STD_OPCODE_HANDLER          ;; this for V86 mode only
    inc [ebp.Client_EIP]            ;; skip past PUSHF
    mov cx,2                        ;; assume 16-bit PUSHF
    test     edi,20000h             ;; has 32 bit override (66h) ?
    jz  short ADJUST_STACK
    mov cx,4                        ;; 32-bit PUSHF
ADJUST_STACK:
    sub word ptr [ebp.Client_SP],cx
    movzx    esi,word ptr [ebp.Client_SS]
    shl esi,4
    add esi,dword ptr [ebp.Client_ESP]
MUCK_WITH_FLAGS:
    mov ecx,[ebp.Client_EFLAGS]
    and ecx,0FFFCFFFFh              ;; clear VM/V86 bit and Resume flag
    test     edi,20000h             ;; 32-bit override (66h) ?
    jnz short PUSHF32
PUSHF16:
    mov [esi],cx                    ;; 16-bit PUSHF
    retn
PUSHF32:
    mov [esi],ecx                   ;; 32-bit PUSHF
    retn
```

Windows doesn't mess with the IOPL bits, so (at least in the current implementation) PUSHF can be relied on by the iopl function. On the other hand, you can see that VMM does clear out the VM and RF bits; this matches what the processor itself does with a PUSHF from V86 mode (see the Chapter 9 section on "V86 Mode and the PE Bit").

You might recall that this discussion of IOPL, the interrupt flag, instructions that trap or don't trap into VMM, and so on was inspired by two lines of output from V86TEST. If we're to get anywhere before sundown, we'd better move on to the next two lines of V86TEST output.

Running DOS in a Virtual Machine

Chapter 9 claimed that Windows runs DOS itself in a DOS box and promised that V86TEST would prove this. Well, the VMID statistics from Figure 10-2 provide the proof:

```
While Windows running:
VM #1 -- 135326 calls
VM #2 --  39386 calls
        ------------
        174712 calls, 174712 in V86 mode
```

In other words, every DOS call made while Windows is running *occurs in the context of a specific VM*, just as if DOS had been started from inside a DOS box.

If no DOS boxes are opened, V86TEST shows all DOS calls coming from VM #1; this is the System VM in which Windows applications run. The System VM, which is used to run Windows applications, is really just another DOS box, running a DPMI client called KRNL386.EXE. DOS boxes (and hidden VMs such as that created by the VSERVER VxD for peer-to-peer networking) start with VM #2.

While running V86TEST to produce the output shown in Figure 10-2, I opened a DOS box, searched through my entire hard disk ("grep -di foo .c"), and then closed the DOS box. All other DOS calls came from Windows applications, such as WinWord, Clock, Control Panel, and Program Manager.

The fact that every DOS call made while Windows is running occurs in the context of a specific VM shows that Chapter 9 was correct: Running Windows on top of DOS isn't much different from running programs inside a DOS box. The before/under distinction is almost meaningless, and the "better DOS than DOS" turns out to be essentially the same as the "thing on a thing." So much for marketing slogans.

But why hedge this statement with the words *almost* and *essentially*? Because there's one crucial difference between software loaded *before* Windows starts (which, as we've just seen, Windows will run in the context of a specific VM) and software loaded in a DOS box *after* Windows starts. What we've been referring to as "software loaded before Windows" is what Microsoft calls Global V86 Code (see the Windows 3.1 DDK reference for the Install _V86_Break_Point service). Generally, memory allocated before Windows starts is called Global V86 Memory. The term *global* is what sets software loaded before Windows apart from software running in a VM. As Microsoft explains in the DDK documentation for _TestGlobalV86Mem:

> Global V86 memory has addresses that are valid and identical in all virtual machines. Local memory has addresses that are only valid in one virtual machine. Instanced memory has addresses that are valid in all virtual machines, but the content of the memory varies with each virtual machine.

Therefore, the before versus under distinction is actually a global versus local versus instance distinction. Any shakiness in the foundation of

Windows has little to do with DOS being a real-mode operating system. That's because, as we've seen, Windows can control DOS by running it in V86 mode, which is really a form of protected mode. Instead, any possible instability stems from the fact that software loaded before Windows, unless it's specifically declared as instance data, is *global*; that is, it is visible in all VMs. Changes made to global data in one VM will leak across to all other VMs. This isn't true for software started from a DOS box; such software is *local*. See the "Instance Data" section in Chapter 3 for a discussion of the global-data problem and its instance-data solution.

Simulating versus Reflecting Interrupts

Besides showing that VMM runs DOS in a VM, there's something else interesting about the VM detection code in V86TEST. V86TEST is loaded before Windows; yet, to get the VMID, the vmid function in Listing 10-1 calls a service provided by Windows, INT 2Fh function 1683h. I've already noted that V86 mode causes many real-mode instructions to transparently trap into VMM. By calling INT 2Fh function 1683h, V86TEST is *deliberately* trapping into VMM. You already saw in Chapter 4 (TEST1684.C) that DOS itself on occasion traps into Windows by issuing a INT 2Fh function 1684h and calling the returned API pointer.

Trap is the correct term here. Observe in Listing 10-1 that V86TEST.C calls INT 2Fh function 1683h — from inside its own INT 2Fh handler! Why doesn't the INT 2Fh call go to V86TEST's own INT 2Fh handler, which calls INT 2Fh, which calls INT 2Fh, which...?

Why doesn't this result in an endless loop? Because if Windows Enhanced mode is running, V86TEST *never sees* its own calls to this function. Likewise for most other Windows INT 2Fh AH=16h calls. Recall from Figure 10-2 that, while V86TEST lists the INT 2Fh function 16h calls it received, no calls to function 1683h are shown:

```
INT 2Fh AH=16h calls seen by V86TEST:
00: 2   05: 1   06: 1   07: 125887  08: 1   09: 1   0A: 2   0B: 2   8A: 1
```

(Yes, the most noticeable thing here is the huge number of calls to INT 2Fh function 1607h. We'll get to those in the next chapter.)

As with all system calls in V86 mode, the INT 2Fh made by V86-TEST's vmid function goes through the protected-mode Interrupt Descriptor Table (IDT; see Chapter 12) and is handled initially by VMM. The difference here is that Windows never sends the INT 2Fh back to

V86 mode. The call is handled entirely in VMM/VxD-land. The fact that VMM and VxDs can absorb (or consume, which is the term Microsoft uses, or simulate, which is the term Intel uses) INT calls in this way is important. Carried to its logical conclusion, VMM and VxDs could absorb/consume/simulate all INT calls, without ever calling down to DOS.

Guess what? If Windows 95 actually did that, Microsoft could claim that Windows no longer requires DOS and have it mean something other than that the Windows 95 product will bundle DOS and Windows in the same box. VMM and VxDs could potentially handle all INT calls in 32-bit protected mode, without reflecting them to V86 mode. This capability is already present in the 32-bit file access provided by WfW 3.11. This capability has been present in Windows from the moment it started hooking interrupts via the protected-mode IDT.

The point is that there's no hard line between a Windows resting on DOS and a Windows that doesn't require DOS. As shown in Figure 10-3, this seemingly far-reaching architectural decision is actually made piecemeal, on a function-by-function basis. The choice about whether to consume a particular call in 32-bit protected mode or to reflect it down to V86 mode is a choice that Windows Enhanced mode has been making for years. Consume or reflect a particular INT 21h call: That's what the issue of Windows running on DOS comes down to.

Furthermore, we saw in the previous section that even when Windows does reflect a call down to DOS, it does so in V86 mode. This means that Windows can exercise control over what DOS does in the same way that it can exercise control over Windows applications.

The underlying technology for the Windows 95 operating system is old hat. Windows has had the consume-or-reflect capability since 1988, when Microsoft introduced WIN386.EXE and VxDs in Windows/386 2.*x*. (See the article by Ray Duncan cited in "For Further Reading" for an idea of the similarities between Windows/386 on the one hand and Enhanced mode, WfW 3.11, and Windows 95 on the other.) Similarly, the consume-or-reflect capability was all laid out years ago in the Intel manuals; we're only now really starting to take advantage of this capability on the bulk of 80x86 machines. Intel talks about *simulating* system calls; this is the same as what we've called consuming or absorbing a system call:

> Many 8086 operating systems use an INT n instruction for a system call.... The VMM can handle the 8086 system call in one of two ways: it can simulate the call by making an equivalent call on the 80386 operating system, or it can reflect the call to a copy of the 8086 operating system loaded into the V86 task's address space.
>
> To simulate an 8086 system call, the VMM must decode the call, transform the call and the parameters to 80386 operating system equivalents, and call the 80386 oper-

ating system. When the 80386 operating system returns to the VMM, the VMM must transform the results into the format expected by the V86 task, advance the V86 task's saved EIP, and return to the V86 task with an IRET instruction.

— *80386 System Software Writer's Guide*, 1987.

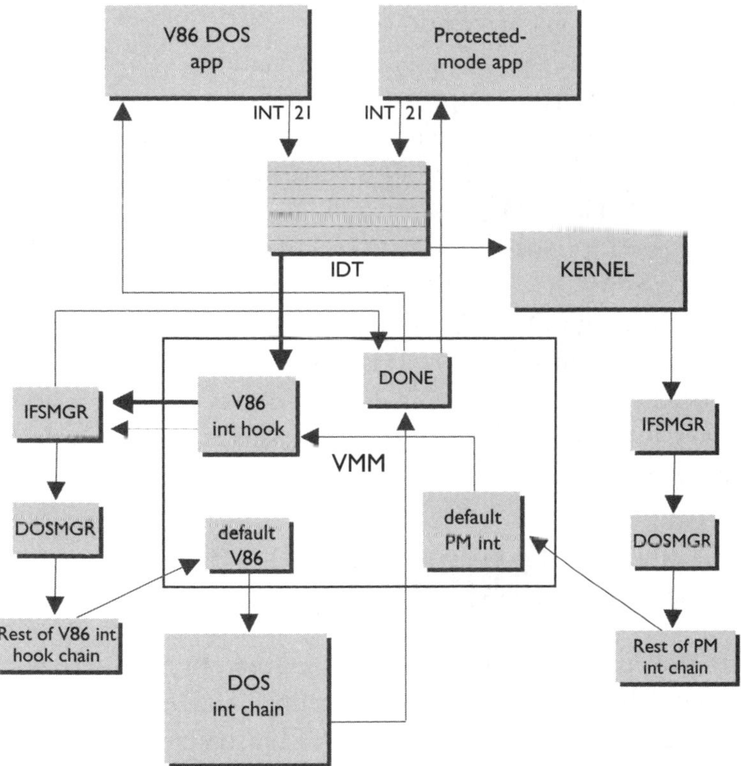

Figure 10-3: Windows handles DOS calls on a function-by-function basis. Depending on the VxDs installed, some DOS calls are handled in protected mode, and some are sent down to DOS in V86 mode. Note that this has no relation to the mode of the program that issued the original INT 21h calls. An INT 21h from a DOS app running in V86 mode (thick arrow) might be serviced entirely in Windows, whereas a different INT 21h from a protected-mode Win16 or Win32 program (thin arrow) might be sent down to DOS.

Recall from Chapter 9 that a VMM runs an operating system in a VM. That's all that's happening in Windows, except that the operating system (DOS) happened to have been started before VMM. Windows, Windows applications, and DOS applications all think they're calling DOS. But every INT system call goes to VMM, which distributes the INT to VxDs. VxDs can pass the system call down to DOS by calling VMM's Begin_ Exec_V86_Mode and Exec_Int services, but increasingly they don't. Instead, many system calls are processed entirely in 32-bit protected mode by VxDs such as IFSMgr, with the results passed back to the calling application, just as Intel described back in 1987.

Windows Enhanced mode has *always* been able to choose between simulating or reflecting a DOS call. Hence, Windows 95's capability to handle operating system calls, without bothering to call down to DOS (even a DOS that Windows runs in V86 mode), isn't a radical departure from past versions of Windows.

Although the operating system in Windows 95 does incorporate numerous important improvements, this supposedly "new" operating system merely takes many of the features of Windows Enhanced mode to their logical conclusion. This is particularly true when you consider WfW 3.11. Here, Microsoft could take 32-bit file access from Windows 95 and graft it onto an otherwise-unchanged Windows 3.1 Enhanced mode base. With 32-bit file access enabled, Windows avoids much of its interaction with DOS. Yet this was possible without adopting any of the other features of Windows 95! This is a good indication that Windows 95 does not relate to DOS in a quantitatively different way from previous versions of Windows. By the way, this is a good thing (unless you like novelty just for the sake of novelty).

Options for Controlling DOS

In this chapter, I've repeatedly asserted that, by the mere fact that it runs DOS in V86 mode, Windows can control DOS. However, except for showing what happens to CLI and STI instructions that DOS might issue on the rare occasions (about ten times per second) when IOPL=0, I've said little about how Windows *exercises* this control. Basically, whereas in real mode certain instructions are handled by the processor, in protected mode these same instructions are handled by VMM. VMM can do what it wants with these instructions. Here are some of the ways VMM can gain control from DOS running in V86 mode:

- Just as in protected mode, all interrupt calls from V86 mode are vectored through the IDT. The IDT entry can contain an interrupt gate that points to Ring 0 code in VMM. The interrupt handler in VMM can absorb or reflect the interrupt, as it sees fit. The real-mode interrupt vector table at address 0 is consulted only for interrupt reflection. This reflection, as noted for the example of INT 2Fh function 1683h, is entirely optional.
- All I/O access (IN, OUT, INS, and OUTS) consults the I/O Permission Bitmap (IOPB, not to be confused with IOPL). If the specified

port is being trapped, the IN/OUT triggers a GP fault (INT 0Dh). The GP fault handler in VMM determines that an IN/OUT has attempted to access a hooked port and calls handlers that VxDs have installed with the Install_IO_Handler service. The I/O handler can simulate the IN/OUT, refuse it, ignore it, ask the user about it, and so on.

- As you saw earlier, when IOPL=0 in V86 mode, all execution of the instructions PUSHF/POPF, INT/IRET, and CLI/STI causes a GP fault that is caught by VMM. Note that if IOPL=0, any interrupt will appear at VMM's door as an INT 0Dh rather than as an INT n. VMM's INT 0Dh handler must decode the faulting opcode and pass control to the appropriate opcode handler. In this chapter we looked at VMM's handlers for CLI, STI, and PUSHF.
- Any 4K page of V86 memory can be marked "not present," so that reading or writing the page causes a page fault (INT 0Eh) that is handled by VMM. VxDs can hook this event with the Hook_V86_Page service provided by VMM.
- Many instructions are illegal in V86 mode; executing one of these instructions generates an Invalid Opcode exception (INT 6) or a GP fault (INT 0Dh) that VMM catches. VMM can handle the exception any way it wants. For example, Chapter 9 showed how VMM deals with the GP fault generated when a program in V86 mode issues a MOV to/from a special register such as CR0: by manipulating Client_EIP, it effectively makes the instruction NOP. (Actually, if VMM wanted to, it could even *patch* the MOV instruction in memory to make it NOP, thus preventing further exceptions.) As another example, the ARPL instruction generates an INT 6 fault into VMM; Windows deliberately uses this illegal instruction to implement V86 breakpoints. (I put the cart before the horse and spent a lot of time talking about ARPL back in Chapter 8.)

Notice that, in each of these cases, VMM grabs control from DOS software because an interrupt, an exception, a fault, or a trap has occurred. Programmers are accustomed to viewing software interrupts as a way to call the operating system, and if you've done any Motorola 680x0 systems programming, the term *trap* should hold no terrors for you. But programmers typically view exceptions and faults as signs of a buggy program. How could these possibly help give Windows control over DOS?

You have to look at exceptions and faults in a new way. Rather than viewing them as something bad, erroneous, or unintended, you can instead view them as providing an opportunity for VMM and VxDs to take control. They're really just another form of interrupt that VMM and VxDs can hook.

VMM and VxDs can hook almost anything and everything happening down in DOS; to get an idea of their flexibility in this respect, look at the DDK documentation for some of the services provided by VMM. Each of the following services installs a handler for an event:

```
Allocate_V86_Call_Back
Call_When_Idle
Call_When_VM_Ints_Enabled
Call_When_VM_Returns
Hook_Device_V86_API
Hook_V86_Fault
Hook_V86_Int_Chain
Hook_V86_Page
Install_IO_Handler
Install_Mult_IO_Handlers
Install_V86_Break_Point
Set_V86_Int_Vector
```

This range of options is quite a contrast to plain-vanilla DOS, which merely provides a function to set an interrupt vector (INT 21h function 25h). On the other hand, if Windows used all these options all the time, performance would suffer. For example, as you saw in the earlier discussion, Windows makes sparing use of IOPL=0.

This chapter has emphasized that the capability of Windows to run on top of real-mode DOS doesn't diminish its status as a genuine protected-mode operating system. Because Windows runs DOS in V86 mode, inside a VM, it can control DOS. For performance reasons, Windows doesn't exercise all the control available to it, but the capability is there.

Chapter 11

Who Needs DOS?

The previous chapter showed that when Windows calls down to DOS, it does so in V86 mode, thereby using DOS as a subservient subsystem. This chapter explains *why* Windows needs to call down to DOS in the first place. Why, and when, does Windows use — and just as important, *not* use — DOS? The V86TEST program introduced in the preceding chapter will help us answer this question.

Using the V86TEST -VERBOSE option, we'll see that Windows bypasses most DOS services and that there isn't a qualitative difference in this respect between Windows 95 and previous versions of Windows. In a way, this isn't surprising: for years nearly all commercial DOS applications bypassed DOS — refusing, for example, to use its supposed services for screen output and keyboard input. From its very beginnings, Windows, like most DOS applications, has avoided this aspect of DOS; it also long ago provided its own memory-management services to replace the rudimentary ones DOS provides.

But almost all DOS and Windows applications have relied on DOS for at least one thing: file I/O. With 32-bit file access (32BFA), Windows avoids even this.

So what are we left with? Windows still consistently relies on a few DOS calls, even with 32BFA, even in Windows 95. Thus, statements such as "In Chicago, once VMM32.VXD is up and running, calls to MS-DOS functions are handled entirely in VMM32 with all new 32-bit code" (*Microsoft Systems Journal*, August 1994, p. 29) are not quite true.

Here's why. First, the "all new 32-bit code" that *Microsoft Systems Journal* refers to isn't all new — essentially the same code appeared in WfW 3.11. Second, DOS functions aren't handled "entirely" in 32-bit protected mode; we'll see that some are still passed down to real-mode DOS. As V86TEST will show, these include the DOS functions that get and set the current PSP, the date and time, and the default drive. Windows 95 relies on DOS to maintain certain data structures, such as the Current Directory Structure (CDS) and System File Table (SFT). We'll also see that Windows calls down to DOS when it has nothing better to do, that is, when it's idle. Of course, we know from the preceding chapter that even when Windows does issue these DOS calls, it does so in V86 mode. All in all, as Chapter 10 noted, there isn't a qualitative difference between a Windows that calls down to DOS and one that doesn't.

It's important that I clarify what I mean by "DOS calls." If you were to look through the code for the Windows kernel or for an application like Word for Windows, you would see many INT 21h calls. To read and write files, Word uses INT 21h functions 3Fh and 40h. To launch programs, the Windows kernel uses INT 21h function 4Bh. But these aren't necessarily DOS calls. If the INT 21h call is handled somewhere in Windows, it merely has the convenient and recognizable *form* of a DOS call. This applies even to INT 21h calls issued by DOS programs running under Windows. If real-mode DOS doesn't see it, it's not a DOS call for the purposes of this discussion.

Conversely, even if something doesn't look at first like a DOS call, it might still be one. For example, the Win32 API provides functions such as CopyFile, CreateFile, GetFileSize, LockFile, MoveFile, and ReadFile. When a Win32 application calls one of these services, if real-mode DOS eventually "sees" an equivalent INT 21h call, we'll consider this a DOS call. What matters is whether the copy of DOS (possibly called WINBOOT.SYS) loaded before Windows receives the call. Later, we'll look at a concrete example in which the GetSystemTime and GetLocalTime functions in Windows 95 end up calling the MS-DOS INT 21h functions 2Ah and 2Ch to get the date and time.

What Does V86TEST Actually Show?

Recall that the purpose of the V86TEST program is to show that Windows calls down to DOS in V86 mode. However, the reason that running DOS in V86 mode matters in the first place is that this gives Windows control over DOS. For example, in V86 mode all interrupts vector to the VMM via the IDT, so that even INTs coming from software loaded before Windows are handled first (and sometimes, only) in 32-bit protected mode.

But V86TEST doesn't literally show that all INTs under Windows are handled first in 32-bit protected mode. We simply infer this from what V86TEST *does* show, which is that Windows runs DOS in V86 mode rather than in real mode. Chapter 10 mentioned that V86TEST never sees its own calls to INT 2Fh function 1683h because these are handled entirely in VMM. These calls that V86TEST *doesn't* see are the best examples of how interrupts coming from software loaded before Windows are handled first in 32-bit protected mode.

All V86TEST will ever see are the INT 21h and INT 2Fh calls that Windows happens to reflect down to DOS. Thus, while one goal of V86TEST was to demonstrate that VMM runs DOS in V86 mode, and therefore that VMM intercepts and monitors INTs coming from MS-DOS, in one sense the program demonstrates only the opposite point: VMM and VxDs still happen to send some INTs back to V86 mode, even though they don't have to. Well, that's a useful piece of information too, and we'll squeeze whatever we can out of it in this chapter and the next.

In a way, we didn't need V86TEST to establish that Windows uses V86 mode to call down to DOS. The DPMI specification contains a function (INT 31h function 0400h) that returns information about the current DPMI implementation. This information includes a flag indicating whether interrupts are reflected in real mode or in V86 mode. Calling this DPMI function under Windows Enhanced mode returns the V86 mode flag (see Listing 6-3 and Figure 6-2). But this possibly could just refer to how Windows handles DOS boxes; we still need V86TEST to load *before* Windows and establish that the Windows-to-DOS relationship is nearly the same as the Windows-to-DOS-box relationship.

It's important to realize that V86TEST stands in for real-mode DOS: If V86TEST sees a call, it passes the call down the interrupt chain to DOS. And if V86TEST doesn't see a call, DOS won't either, except perhaps through some non-interrupt-based backdoor interface (such as the IOCTL interface IFSHLP.SYS uses to communicate with the IFSMgr VxD). Thus, V86TEST should tell us what calls will be seen by DOS.

Remember that V86TEST is trapping only INT 21h and INT 2Fh; if it intercepted additional interrupts, such as INT 13h BIOS disk services, INT 15h system services, or the INT 28h idle broadcast, V86TEST would pick up even more calls made by Windows to software that's loaded before it. (For a brief discussion of interrupts other than INT 21h and INT 2Fh, see the "What About BIOS Calls?" section at the end of this chapter.)

Windows at Work?

Back in Figure 10-1, Windows ran for a little over four minutes, yet it made over 170,000 calls to INT 21h and INT 2Fh:


```
While Windows running:  174712 INT 21/2F calls, 174712 in V86 mode
Windows active for 256 seconds
682 INT 21/2F calls/second
```

The most noticeable feature of the V86TEST output in Chapter 10 is probably the huge number of calls that Windows makes to software loaded before it. The following two lines from Figure 10-1 show that almost three-quarters (125887 / 174712 = 72%) of the calls detected by V86TEST were VxD callouts (INT 2Fh function 1607h):

```
INT 2Fh AH=16h calls seen by V86TEST:
00: 2   05: 1   06: 1   07: 125887  08: 1   09: 1   0A: 2   0B: 2   8A: 1
```

And, as shown in the last line of Figure 11-1, almost all callouts (or broadcasts as we referred to them in earlier chapters) in turn came from a single VxD, VMPoll, which is responsible for idle detection, of all things. It looks like Windows spends most of its time spinning its wheels!

Besides the VxD callout, the other INT 2Fh function 16h calls seen by V86TEST include the four Windows initialization and termination broadcasts discussed in the preceding chapter; functions 1600h and 160Ah, which check if Windows is running; function 160Bh, which is the Windows Identify TSR callout discussed in Chapter 4; and function 168Ah, which is the DPMI Get Vendor-Specific API call (if someone asks for a vendor-specific API using any vendor name other than "MS-DOS", VMM passes this call down to V86 mode).

If you run V86TEST with the -VERBOSE switch, the program displays a census of all INT 21h and INT 2Fh calls, broken out by AH function number. (This is similar to the census of INT 21h calls provided by the COUNTDOS program discussed in Chapter 4, though COUNT-DOS has a better user interface than V86TEST.) To demonstrate this V86TEST option, I ran V86TEST -VERBOSE with WfW 3.11, using WIN /D:C to temporarily disable 32BFA. For about four minutes, I ran Clock and used WinWord to search through four large documents; no DOS box was started. This test produced the results shown in Figure 11-1.

```
C:\>v86test -verbose /D:C > v86test.log
C:\>type v86test.log
Before Windows started: 91 INT 21/2F calls, 0 in V86 mode
During Windows init:    5214 INT 21/2F calls, 352 in V86 mode
While Windows running:  400183 INT 21/2F calls, 400183 in V86 mode
During Windows exit:    13 INT 21/2F calls, 10 in V86 mode
After Windows exited:   12 INT 21/2F calls, 0 in V86 mode

While Windows running:
Windows active for 275 seconds
1455 INT 21/2F calls/second
IOPL=0 -- 4384 calls
IOPL=3 -- 395799 calls
VM #1 -- 400183 calls

INT 2Fh AH=16h calls seen by V86TEST:
00: 2   05: 1   06: 1   07: 391147  08: 1   09: 1   0A: 2   0B: 2   8A: 1

INT 21h calls:
06: 153 09: 1   0C: 2   0D: 256 0E: 288 19: 81  1A: 409
1C: 1   25: 12  29: 4   2A: 492 2C: 2760    2F: 9   30: 22  32: 2   33: 6
34: 5   35: 12  3B: 26  3C: 6   3D: 344 3E: 245 3F: 1906    40: 3449
41: 6   42: 1530    43: 29  44: 282 47: 86  48: 8   4A: 3   4B: 3
4C: 7   4D: 3   4E: 85  4F: 316 50: 440 51: 4   52: 10  55: 4   57: 125
58: 7   59: 3   5B: 1   5D: 1   5E: 1   5F: 3   62: 99  65: 3
6C: 1   DC: 5

INT 2Fh calls:
08: 1   11: 774 13: 4   16: 391158  43: 7   46: 1   4A: 7   7A: 2   FE: 2

INT 2Fh AX=1607h calls:
06: 1   0C: 2   10: 2   14: 1   15: 5   18: 391133  21: 2   VxD>#0100: 1
```

Figure 11-1: Taking a census of INT 21h and 2Fh calls from Windows; no DOS box is running.

Notice that although Windows made plenty of calls to INT 21h functions 40h (Write File), 2Ch (Get Time), and 42h (Move File Pointer), the overwhelming majority of its calls were to INT 2Fh function 1607h, with BX=18h. Function 1607h is documented in the DDK as Device Call Out. VxDs can issue this call to communicate with software loaded before Windows; since V86TEST is loaded before Windows and has caught these calls, we can see that this works. The BX register holds the ID number of the VxD issuing the broadcast. The VMM.INC file included with the Windows DDK lists many VxD IDs; it turns out that 18h is VMPoll.

According to VMPOLL.INC (also included with the DDK), this VxD issues the INT 2Fh function 1607h callout when Windows has nothing better to do:

```
;
;    Int 2Fh call-out API when system is idle
;    AX = 1607h
;    BX = VMPoll_Device_ID
;    CX = VMPoll_Call_Out_Sys_Idle
;
;    If TSR or device driver wants to "eat" the idle call, they should
;    set AX = 0 and not chain to other Int 2Fh hooks. Otherwise, chain.
;
VMPoll_Call_Out_Sys_Idle     EQU     0        ; CX = 0
```


TSRs or device drivers can hook this call to receive notification that Windows is idle and perhaps use this opportunity to do some background processing. VMPoll takes the function that makes this callout and registers it with the VMM Call_When_Idle service:

```
    DO_2F_1607_18:
00246       Push_Client_State
00255       VMMcall Begin_Nest_V86_Exec             ;; set up VM for V86 mode call
0025B       mov word ptr [ebp.Client_EAX],1607h
00261       mov word ptr [ebp.Client_EBX],18h       ;; VMPoll_Device_ID
00267       mov word ptr [ebp.Client_ECX],0         ;; VMPoll_Call_Out_Sys_Idle
0026D       mov eax,2Fh
00272       VMMcall Exec_Int                        ;; uses Simulate_Int
00278       movzx   ecx,word ptr [ebp.Client_EAX]   ;; "eat" idle call?
0027C       VMMcall End_Nest_Exec
00282       Pop_Client_State
00291       jecxz   short IDLE_EATEN
00293       stc     ;; VMM will call next idle callback
00294       retn
00295    IDLE_EATEN:
00295       clc     ;; VMM won't call other idle callbacks
00296       retn

        DO_DEVICE_INIT:
            ;; ...
01103       mov esi,offset DO_2F_1607_18
01108       VMMcall Call_When_Idle
```

When it decides that the system is idle, VMM calls the functions in its call-when-idle list, such as the function installed by VMPoll, and the function the PageSwap VxD installs to asynchronously write changed virtual-memory pages to disk (_PageOutDirtyPages). VMM decides the system is idle based on calls it receives to INT 2Fh function 1689h (Windows KERNEL idle). As Matt Pietrek explains in Chapter 6 of *Windows Internals*, the idle loop in the KERNEL scheduler calls INT 2Fh function 1689h, thus setting off the chain of events that eventually results in a VMPoll callout. KERNEL also calls INT 28h, the DOS idle broadcast and, as one would expect, software loaded before Windows sees about as many INT 28h calls as VMPoll calls (see Figure 11-9 later in this chapter).

As seen in the disassembly of VMPoll, the VxD makes this broadcast using the Begin_Nest_V86_Exec and Exec_Int services provided by VMM. Exec_Int in turn uses the Simulate_Int call, which consults the low-memory Interrupt Vector Table (IVT) — assuming no VxD intercepts the interrupt first via Hook_V86_Int_Chain. This is how Windows makes *all* its calls down to DOS. Thus, although V86TEST set out to show the possibility for VMM interrupt *interception* via the IDT, what it really shows is VMM interrupt *reflection* via the IVT.

Oddly, even though the test in Figure 11-1 seemed to be exercising Windows (the Clock was running, and WinWord was asked to crank through four large documents), VMPoll generated over 1000 idle broadcasts per second! These V86TEST results make it seem as if Windows spends most of its time twiddling its thumbs. But that's not true: Sometimes people use Windows to play Solitaire.

On a more serious note, these figures probably do make some sense. During the same period, even though Windows appeared to be furiously busy, Microsoft's power-management driver, POWER.EXE, reported that the CPU was idle more than 25% of the time.

Now let's run the test again, this time opening a DOS box. There's no need to actually *do* anything in the DOS box (which is a good thing, since it's difficult to do anything in the DOS box when its output is redirected to V86TEST.LOG). Figure 11-2 shows the result.

```
C:\>v86test -verbose /D:C > v86test.log

C:\>type v86test.log
Before Windows started: 91 INT 21/2F calls, 0 in V86 mode
During Windows init:    5214 INT 21/2F calls, 352 in V86 mode
While Windows running:  207174 INT 21/2F calls, 207174 in V86 mode
During Windows exit:    13 INT 21/2F calls, 10 in V86 mode
After Windows exited:   12 INT 21/2F calls, 0 in V86 mode

While Windows running:
Windows active for 187 seconds
1107 INT 21/2F calls/second
IOPL=0 -- 2403 calls
IOPL=3 -- 204771 calls
VM #1 -- 197551 calls
VM #2 -- 9623 calls

INT 2Fh AH=16h calls seen by V86TEST:
```

```
00: 2    05: 1    06: 1    07: 190292  08: 1    09: 1    0A: 2    0B: 2    8A: 1

INT 21h calls:
02: 93   06: 153  09: 1    0B: 9424    0C: 3    0D: 256  0E: 289  19: 84   1A: 102
1C: 1    25: 18   29: 8    2A: 430     2C: 1742 2F: 9    30: 23   32: 2    33: 6
34: 5    35: 12   38: 2    3B: 20      3C: 6    3D: 365  3E: 268  3F: 1907     40: 3454
41: 6    42: 1515     43:  28  44: 319 47: 92   48: 13   49: 1    4A: 6    4B: 4
4C: 7    4D: 3    4E: 93   4F: 1       50: 355  51: 7    52: 10   55: 4    57: 139
58: 9    59: 3    5B: 1    5D: 3       5E: 1    5F: 3    62: 48   63: 1    65: 4
6C: 1    71: 1    DC: 5

INT 2Fh calls:
08: 1    11: 799  12: 6    13: 4    16: 190303  43: 9    46: 1    48: 1    4A: 7
55: 1    7A: 2    B7: 2    FE: 2

INT 2Fh AX=1607h calls:
06: 1    0C: 2    10: 2    14: 1    15: 5    18: 190278  21: 2    VxD>#0100: 1
```

Figure 11-2: A census of INT 21h and 2Fh calls from Windows, with one DOS box running.

Notice that there now are a large number of calls to INT 21h function 0Bh (Check Keyboard Status). Furthermore, this number roughly corresponds to the number of calls in VM #2. COMMAND.COM uses function 0Bh to poll the keyboard; V86TEST shows that Windows passes these calls down to DOS. One way that VMPoll detects idle VMs is to hook INT 21h and look for calls to function 0Bh. VMPoll and other VxDs will see the function 0Bh call long before V86TEST or DOS sees it.

Since these idle broadcasts occur so much more frequently than any other interrupt call, V86TEST provides a -FILTER option to ignore them. The calls still occur at the same tremendous rate, but at least they don't clutter the V86TEST results. As for actually eliminating the calls, I've used WINICE to assemble NOPs over the Exec_Int 2Fh call from VMPoll (see VMPoll+272h in the code fragment shown earlier) and commented-out the device=*vmpoll statement in SYSTEM.INI, both without ill effect. Although power management on a laptop could rely on the VMPoll callout as a signal to issue a HLT to power-down the processor, in practice the VMPoll callout seems to go to waste. For example, Microsoft's POWER.EXE doesn't know about the VMPoll broadcast, and instead looks for idle calls such as INT 28h and INT 2Fh function 1680h.

One way of turning off these VMPoll callouts definitely *can* have a deleterious effect on the health of Windows. If you use a standard PeekMessage loop in your Win16 application (as many Windows programming books recommend if you need to do background processing), you'll prevent KERNEL from issuing its INT 2Fh function 1689h call:

```
for (;;)
    while (PeekMessage(&msg, NULL, NULL, NULL, PM_REMOVE))

        TranslateMessage(&msg);
        DispatchMessage(&msg);
```

In *Windows Internals*, Matt Pietrek shows that PeekMessage prevents the Windows scheduler from falling into its idle loop. The scheduler's idle loop is responsible for both the KERNEL idle call and INT 28h so PeekMessage prevents KERNEL from issuing these idle calls.

But who cares? Several discussions of this subject (see "For Further Reading") have noted that PeekMessage can disable power management on battery-powered laptops. Although Microsoft's POWER.EXE doesn't know about VMPoll broadcasts, the interesting POWER.ASM code included with the MS-DOS OEM Adaptation Kit (OAK) does hook INT 28h as one part of idle detection. Also, some TSRs rely on INT 28h calls (see *Undocumented DOS*, 2d ed., pp. 564-565).

But there's another issue here that's more important than power management or TSR friendliness. As noted, VMM receives the INT 2Fh function 1689h calls and uses them as a trigger to walk the Call_When_Idle list. Consequently, whenever a Windows application is in a PeekMessage loop, thereby preventing the KERNEL scheduler from issuing the INT 2Fh function 1689h "heartbeat," all VMM Call_When_Idle processing is suspended. In one standard configuration, four VxDs had established Call_When_Idle handlers: IFSMGR, VMPoll, PageSwap, and VTD. As noted earlier, for example, PageSwap uses its idle handler to do a _PageOutDirtyPages operation. This useful background processing will never occur while a Win16 application is in a PeekMessage loop.

VxD callouts

We've seen that a lot of the interaction that Windows has with software loaded before it involves little more than a "not much going on" callout made by the VMPoll VxD. How about those other VxD callouts shown in the last line of Figures 11-1 and 11-2?

```
INT 2Fh AX=1607h calls:
06: 1   0C: 2   10: 2   14: 1   15: 5   18: 190278  21: 2   VxD>#0100: 1
```

In Windows 95, V86TEST sees a slightly different set of VxD callouts:

```
INT 2Fh AX=1607h calls:
06: 1   0D: 1   10: 1   14: 1   15: 3   18: 156133    21: 1   40: 1
```

These calls that VxDs make to software loaded before Windows are important to understanding DOS-Windows interaction.

Besides, examining these VxD callouts provides a good opportunity to look over the Windows source code provided with the DDK. Although the DDK doesn't provide source for such core components as VMM, IFSMGR, DOSMGR, VFAT, VPICD, or V86MMGR, it does provide source code for the virtual display (VDD), keyboard (VKD), and mouse (VMD) devices and for VxDs such as PageFile, PageSwap, INT13, and VDMAD. Even the vast majority of Windows programmers who have no intention of writing a replacement VDD or VKD (or, indeed, of ever writing any VxD) would benefit from studying this code. There's no better way to get a feel for how the Windows operating system operates.

First, what are these other VxDs (besides VMPoll) whose callouts V86TEST detected? Let's match up the VxD ID numbers shown by V86TEST with the names of these VxDs provided in the DDK:

VxD ID	Name
0006h	V86MMGR — V86 Memory Manager
000Ch	VMD — Virtual Mouse Device
000Dh	VKD — Virtual Keyboard Device
0010h	BLOCKDEV in 3.1; IOS (I/O Supervisor) in WfW 3.11 and Windows 95
0014h	VNETBIOS — Virtual NetBIOS Device
0015h	DOSMGR — DOS Manager
0018h	VMPoll — Idle detection
0021h	PageFile — Demand Paging File
0040h	IFSMGR (Installable File System Manager) in Windows 95
>100h	IFSMGR in WfW 3.11 (0484h)

Additional VxDs besides these probably also issue INT 2Fh function 1607h, but these are the ones detected by running V86TEST in fairly standard WfW 3.11 and Chicago configurations.

We just covered VMPoll, and Chapters 3 and 4 discussed the DOSMGR callout API. Let's take a quick look at the other callouts detected by V86TEST.

The V86MMGR callout is named V86CallOut_LclA20forGlblHMA in the V86MMGR.INC file included with the DDK. What this long name means is that the state of the A20 address line should be local to each VM even if the High Memory Area (HMA) is global (that is, shared by all VMs). This is distinct from (but possibly related to) the odd XMS calls for local and global A20 enable and disable. If any software loaded before Windows responds to this call, it has the same effect as if a VxD called the V86MMGR_SetLocalA20 service, which is documented in the DDK:

> *When there is a global HMA user, the A20 state associated with the HMA is also global. Changing A20 in a virtual machine changes it in all virtual machines simultaneously. Some global A20 users (such as MS-DOS 5.0) desire that the A20 state be local even though the HMA is global.*

If DOS=HIGH (as determined by calling INT 21h function 3306h), DOSMGR in Windows 3.1 and later will automatically call V86MMGR_SetLocalA20.

The VMD (Virtual Mouse Device) has two callouts that are defined in VMD.INC as VMD_CO_API_Test_Inst and VMD_CO_API_Get_Call_Back. Although these descriptions aren't terribly helpful, the DDK also comes with the source code to VMD; the source file, INT33.ASM, shows exactly what these callouts do. A comment in the Get_Mouse_Instance routine in INT33.ASM notes that the Test_Inst callout allows a DOS mouse device driver to declare its own instance data (using the INT 2Fh function 1605h interface described in Chapter 3), rather than have VMD instance the entire mouse driver. The Int33_Init routine in INT33.ASM issues the Get_Call_Back callout to give a DOS mouse driver the chance to provide mouse support in a windowed DOS box.

The VKD (Virtual Keyboard Device) callout seen in Chicago isn't currently documented, but a brief examination of MS-DOS 7.0 shows that WINBOOT.SYS looks for this callout and returns a pointer to a keyboard buffer in ES:DI.

The BLOCKDEV VxD was introduced in Windows 3.1 as a replacement for the VHD (Virtual Hard Disk Device) and was in turn replaced in WfW 3.11 and Windows 95 by IOS (the I/O Supervisor). The BLOCKDEV callouts, which are also used by IOS, are described in the DDK documentation and in Chapter 2 of Geoff Chappell's *DOS Internals* (pp. 76-77). BlockDev_API_Hw_Detect_Start informs DOS TSRs and device drivers that a FastDisk device such as WDCTRL is performing hardware detection (the TSR or driver could use this as an opportunity to disable a write-behind cache, for example); BlockDev_API_Hw_Detect_End indicates that hardware detection has been completed.

More interesting than these text descriptions, though, is the source code included with the DDK. Although the DDK doesn't include the BLOCKDEV source, it does provide the source for the WDCTRL FastDisk device, which uses BLOCKDEV services and which issues the BLOCKDEV callout. The WDCtrl_Real_Mode_Init routine in WDRMINIT.ASM attempts to detect the presence of a standard AT-type Western Digital hard-disk controller by monitoring changes to the cylinder register after various reads. A comment to this routine reads:

```
;   Now do lots of party stuff to make sure cache programs flush or at least
;   don't try to lazy-write any data while we do this test. To make sure
;   of this we will do the following:
;   Broadcast the BlockDev hardware detection API Int 2Fh
```

```
;    Do an Int 13h read of sector 0 on both drives
;    Do a DOS disk reset on drives C-Z (may flush)
;    Set the InDOS flag
```

(The word "party" seems to be standard Microsoft lingo for any low-level activity.)

Although there is scant documentation for the VNETBIOS VxD, once again the DDK provides source code, and this clearly makes up for any lack of documentation. A comment in VNETBIOS.ASM says "This virtual device serves two purposes: It buffers asynchronous network requests and translates netbios calls for protected mode apps." VNETBIOS.ASM issues the VxD callout to "request information about network extensions." A NetBIOS driver can return the address in ES:DI of an "extended NETBIOS table," which tells VNETBIOS how to handle each NetBIOS INT 2Ah or INT 5Ch call.

When reading VNETBIOS.ASM, it's particularly interesting to see how it uses V86 breakpoints to handle the post routine for NoWait NetBIOS calls. There is also an (apparently otherwise undocumented) NoWaitNetIO=true setting, which converts all NetBIOS commands to NoWait. As with all the DDK source code, the change log at the top of the file (almost always by RAL, Ralph Lipe) also makes interesting reading:

```
;    25-Apr-1988 RAL Complete rewrite of network (used to be VND)
;    27-Oct-1988 RAL Updated to use new Get_Crit_Section_Status
;    06-Nov-1988 RAL Redesigned to use remap instead of buffering
;    09-Mar-1989 RAL Real mode stub to not load if no redirector
;    05-Apr-1989 RAL This sucker actually works!
;    07-Apr-1989 RAL Added Int 2Fh API to get extended NETBIOS table
;    04-May-1989 RAL Works with 32-bit Build_Int_Stack_Frame
;    24-May-1989 RAL Test for NETBIOS instead of redir when loading
;    12-Jun-1989 RAL Fixed horrible page fault of doom bug
;    01-Sep-1989 RAL Make POSTS go to the RIGHT VM!!!
;    08-Oct-1989 RAL Fixed horrible InDOS assumption bug
;    29-Oct-1989 RAL Finished exit cancel code and documentation
;    04-Dec-1989 RAL Fixed critical section bug for non-hooked NCBs
```

Next up in the V86TEST log of VxD callouts is PAGEFILE, which manages the virtual-memory swap file (in Windows 95, there is another pagefile device, called DYNAPAGE). Once again, the DDK includes source code for this VxD.

```
;    No other PageFile is loaded. Get Bimbo info about cache lock pointer.
     mov ax, (W386_Int_Multiplex SHL 8) OR W386_Device_Broadcast
     mov bx, PageFile_Device_ID
     xor cx, cx
     int 2Fh
     or  ax, ax                     ; if ax not 0, then...
     jnz SHORT PF_RI_No_Bimbo       ; ...Bimbo did not respond

; Bimbo responded to int2Fh - pointer to cache lock byte is in es:di.
     mov dx, es
     shl edx, 16
     mov dx, di
```

```
    jmp SHORT PageFile_RI_Exit

PF_RI_No_Bimbo:
;   Bimbo not around, get SmartDrv info about cache lock pointer
```

The PageFile_Real_Init routine in PAGEFILE.ASM tries to make an IOCTL call to SmartDrv to retrieve a pointer to a disk cache lock pointer. However, in case SmartDrv isn't loaded, PAGEFILE makes the VxD callout to allow a disk cache other than SmartDrv to return a cache lock pointer in ES:DI. (By the way, it seems that "Bimbo" is Microsoft's name for any non-SmartDrv disk cache. This is mildly amusing in a nerdy kind of way, since for years the general industry name for SmartDrv has been DumbDrv.

In WfW 3.11, V86TEST sees *two* PAGEFILE callouts because the VMPoll VxD (which, as noted earlier, does a _PageOutDirtyPages operation when the system is idle) also tries to retrieve a disk cache lock pointer.

Finally, we come to the callout issued by IFSMGR, the Installable File System manager, which is the foundation for 32BFA and long filenames. Although IFSMGR played a key role in WfW 3.11, it is documented only in Chicago, and even there only with an incomplete (at least at the time of this writing) IFSMGR.INC file. Even without proper documentation or source code for IFSMGR, a disassembly of IFSMGR shows that its VxD callout retrieves the size of the DOS Current Directory Structure (CDS); this is immediately obvious from the numbers 51h in DOS 3 and 58h in DOS 4 and later:

```
0C0AC       Push_Client_State
0C0BB       VMMcall Begin_Nest_V86_Exec
; ...
0C1A6       mov word ptr [ebp.Client_AX],1607h
0C1AC       mov word ptr [ebp.Client_BX],484h       ;; 40h in Windows 95
0C1B2       mov word ptr [ebp.Client_CX],3
0C1B8       mov word ptr [ebp.Client_DX],1
0C1BE       mov eax,2Fh
0C1C3       VMMcall Exec_Int
0C1C9       cmp word ptr [ebp.Client_AX],0B97Ch     ;; DOSMGR magic
0C1CF       jne short NO_API_RESPONSE
0C1D1       cmp word ptr [ebp.Client_DX],0A2ABh     ;; DOSMGR magic
0C1D7       jne short NO_API_RESPONSE
0C1D9       movzx   ecx,word ptr [ebp.Client_CX]
0C1DD       jmp short GOT_CDS_SIZE
0C1DF   NO_API_RESPONSE:
0C1DF       push    ebx
0C1E0       VMMcall Get_Machine_Info    ;; returns DOS major version in AH
0C1E6       pop ebx
0C1E7       mov ecx,58h                 ;; 58h = CDS size in DOS 4+
0C1EC       cmp ah,3                    ;; DOS version > 3??
0C1EF       ja  short GOT_CDS_SIZE
0C1F1       sub ecx,7                   ;; 58h-7=51h = CDS size in DOS 3
0C1F4   GOT_CDS_SIZE:
0C1F4       mov dword ptr CDS_SIZE,ecx
; ...
0C262       VMMcall End_Nest_Exec
0C268       Pop_Client_State
```

> What makes this otherwise pedestrian code interesting is that, even in Windows 95, IFSMGR cares about a DOS internal structure like the CDS. This makes perfect sense (and in any case IFSMGR.INC mentions a different service which "Updates the CDSs in all the VMs" when a new volume appears in the system), but it isn't what you'd expect after hearing the claim "Windows no longer uses DOS."

The Top Windows INT 21h Calls

Now that we've examined the VxD callouts that Windows makes to software loaded before it, let's focus on the DOS INT 21h calls that Windows sends down to software loaded before it.

Back in Figure 11-1, V86TEST provided a census of INT 21h calls made by Windows while I ran Clock and used WinWord to search through four large documents (1.7MB of data, containing the text for *DOS Internals*). Figure 11-2 showed the same thing, except that I also opened a DOS box. In both cases, 32BFA was disabled (in a few moments, we'll repeat the same test, with 32BFA enabled). In Figure 11-3, I've taken the INT 21h census from Figures 11-1 and 11-2 and compared them using a *diff* utility. The similarities between the two tests give us some confidence that the results aren't random; the differences hopefully show the impact of running a DOS box.

```
<         06: 153 09: 1             0C: 2   0D: 256 0E: 288 19: 81  1A: 409
> 02: 93  06: 153 09: 1   0B: 9424  0C: 3   0D: 256 0E: 289 19: 84  1A: 102

< 1C: 1   25: 12  29: 4   2A: 492 2C: 2760  2F: 9   30: 22  32: 2   33: 6
> 1C: 1   25: 18  29: 8   2A: 430 2C: 1742  2F: 9   30: 23  32: 2   33: 6

< 34: 5   35: 12          3B: 26  3C: 6   3D: 344 3E: 245 3F: 1906    40: 3449
> 34: 5   35: 12  38: 2   3B: 20  3C: 6   3D: 365 3E: 268 3F: 1907    40: 3454

< 41: 6   42: 1530    43: 29  44: 282 47: 86  48: 8           4A: 3   4B: 3
> 41: 6   42: 1515    43: 28  44: 319 47: 92  48: 13  49: 1   4A: 6   4B: 4

< 4C: 7   4D: 3   4E: 85  4F: 316 50: 440 51: 4   52: 10  55: 4   57: 125
> 4C: 7   4D: 3   4E: 93  4F: 1   50: 355 51: 7   52: 10  55: 4   57: 139

< 58: 7   59: 3   5B: 1   5D: 1   5E: 1   5F: 3   62: 99          65: 3
> 58: 9   59: 3   5B: 1   5D: 3   5E: 1   5F: 3   62: 48  63: 1   65: 4

< 6C: 1           DC: 5                              < means no DOS box
> 6C: 1   71: 1   DC: 5                              > means with a DOS box
```

Figure 11-3: Comparing the results of the INT 21h tests presented earlier.

In Figure 11-4, I've sorted these INT 21h calls, starting with the most frequent, to show the top DOS calls made by Windows in this standard non-network configuration when 32BFA is disabled. Where opening a DOS box seems to make a significant difference, I've noted this.

```
40h         Write File or Device
2Ch         Get Time
3Fh         Read File
42h         Move File Pointer (lseek)
2Ah         Get Date
50h         Set PSP                       Task switch: Fewer with DOS box
1Ah         Set DTA                       Fewer with DOS box
3Dh         Open File
44h         I/O Control (IOCTL)           More with DOS box
4Fh         Find Next File                Almost none with DOS box???
0Eh         Set Default Drive
3Eh         Close File
0Dh         Reset Drive
06h         Direct Console I/O
57h         Get File Date and Time
62h         Get PSP                       Task switch: Fewer with DOS box
02h         Display Character             Used for DOS box only
4Eh         Find First File
47h         Get Current Directory
19h         Get Default Drive
43h         Get/Set File Attributes
3Bh         Change Current Directory
30h         Get DOS Version
```

Figure 11-4: The top Windows INT 21h calls without 32BFA.

What does all this mean? To answer that question, let's first look at the functions in which opening a DOS box clearly doesn't make a significant difference:

- Without 32BFA, Windows uses DOS for file I/O. Naturally!
- Without 32BFA, Windows uses DOS to Get and Set the current drive and directory.
- Windows (particularly the Windows Clock application, or *applet*, as Microsoft refers to little applications) uses DOS to get the current date and time. Windows asks DOS what day it is, almost as frequently as it asks DOS for the time: whenever Clock receives a WM_TIMER message, it calls INT 21h functions 2Ah and 2Ch. (This is also true for the Win32 version of Clock, but it calls the DOS functions in a more roundabout fashion; we'll get to this later on.)

Opening a DOS box affects only a few DOS functions. This is an important point, because you sometimes hear assertions that Windows relies on DOS in order to run DOS programs. Figures 11-3 and 11-4 show that running DOS programs has little to do with the Windows-DOS relationship. Windows relies on DOS for certain services required by both DOS programs and Windows applications. Conversely, if Windows can bypass DOS while providing services to Windows applications, it can do the same thing for DOS programs: just because a real-mode DOS program running in V86 mode makes an INT 21h doesn't mean that Windows has to pass that INT 21h call down to real-mode DOS running in V86 mode. When we discuss 32BFA in more detail, we'll see that, in protected mode, Windows can service many INT 21h calls coming from DOS programs.

The few differences that do occur when a DOS box is opened (see Figure 11-4) mostly turn out to reveal things about the Windows-DOS relationship in general, rather than about DOS boxes in particular:

- When a DOS box is open, Windows passes the Check Keyboard Status call (INT 21h function 0Bh) down to DOS. But this doesn't mean that Windows absorbs function 0Bh when it comes from a Windows application! The fact is, no normal Windows application calls function 0Bh; this is the only reason it didn't show up in Figure 11-1. COMMAND.COM calls function 0Bh to poll the keyboard; this is why it showed up in Figure 11-2. If a Windows application happened to call function 0Bh, Windows would pass the call down to DOS, just as it does when a DOS program such as COMMAND.COM calls this function. (Yes, I've tried this.) A DOS program could similarly bypass the DOS input services, and many do. Windows is a fairly typical DOS program in this regard.

  Windows applications don't call INT 21h function 0Bh because they get keyboard input via the Windows keyboard driver, whose INT 9 handler calls the Keybd_Event function in USER, which in turn places keystrokes in the Windows hardware event queue, eventually to end up at a Windows application's WndProc as a message like WM_KEYDOWN, WM_KEYUP, or WM_CHAR. (See the description of Keybd_Event and the System Message Queue in *Undocumented Windows*, Chapter 6.) This is a good example of how, from the very beginning, Windows has bypassed many DOS "services" (if you want to call them that).
- The same story applies to function 02h (Display Character). If a Windows application used this call, Windows would pass the call down to DOS, just as occurs when COMMAND.COM uses this call in a DOS

box. Windows applications use a different mechanism — the Windows Graphics Device Interface (GDI) — for displaying output; they have bypassed DOS's feeble assistance ever since Windows 1.0. A DOS program could similarly bypass the DOS output services, and many do.

- With INT 21h functions 50h (Set PSP) and 62h (Get PSP), it's first of all quite significant that Windows makes these calls, whether or not a DOS box is running. The Windows kernel uses the DOS Program Segment Prefix (PSP) to task switch between Windows applications (though, as noted in Chapter 5 of *Undocumented Windows*, KERNEL postpones making the Set PSP call until the Windows application has made an INT 21h call). In Figures 11-1 and 11-2, the kernel was switching between WinWord and Clock. Win32 applications, even in Windows 95, have DOS PSPs (see the WINPSP program in Chapter 13). Examples like the PSP show that Windows 95 requires DOS — and bypasses DOS — to just about the same extent as did previous versions of Windows. Microsoft has simply chosen for the first time to make a big deal about a capability that Windows has had ever since Windows 3.0 Enhanced mode.

  Oddly, starting a DOS box in Figure 11-2 caused *fewer* Set and Get PSP calls than we saw in Figure 11-1, in which we performed the same operations but without starting a DOS box. This is surprising at first: you'd expect more PSP calls, since the DOS box is an additional task.

  However, KERNEL uses DOS PSPs for switching between tasks in the System VM, that is, for Win16 and Win32 applications. A DOS box is a separate VM, and VMM task switching is different than kernel task switching. When VMM switches between VMs, PSPs must also get switched, but to do this VMM uses instance data. (The "DOS Instance Data and the SDA" section in Chapter 4 noted that Windows instances the DOS Swappable Data Area [SDA]; which includes DOS's current-PSP variable.)

  Okay, so VMM uses a different mechanism for keeping PSPs straight from what KERNEL uses. But why does DOS see *fewer* Get and Set PSP calls when we start a DOS box? Simply because, with the extra VM, the System VM wasn't scheduled as often, so the sub-scheduler within KERNEL didn't have to switch between WinWord and Clock as often.

- When a DOS box is running, DOS also sees fewer calls to function 1Ah, Set Disk Transfer Address (DTA), for the same reason that it sees fewer Get and Set PSP calls. The KERNEL sub-scheduler has to switch DTAs when it switches PSPs. On the other hand, the VMM scheduler relies on instance data to keep DTAs, like PSPs, in sync with VMs. When multiple VMs are running, the System VM naturally doesn't run as often, so the KERNEL sub-scheduler doesn't kick in as often either. The one significant difference between the DTA and PSP calls is that with 32BFA, Windows handles Set DTA without calling down to DOS. In contrast, as we'll see, Windows (even with 32BFA and even in Windows 95) still passes Get and Set PSP calls down to DOS.

- In comparing Figure 11-2 to Figure 11-1, we can see that Windows seems to send more I/O Control (IOCTL; INT 21h function 44h) calls down to DOS when a DOS box is running. However, this is just a testing "artifact"; I unintentionally allowed Windows to run for a little longer in Figure 11-2 than in Figure 11-1. More careful examination shows that Windows passes the same IOCTL calls down to DOS, whether they come from a Windows application or a DOS application. Without 32BFA, the two major IOCTL calls Windows sends down to DOS are 4408h (Does Device Use Removeable Media?) and 4409h (Is Drive Remote?).
- The only truly surprising result in comparing Figures 11-1 and 11-2 is that with the DOS box running in Figure 11-2, Windows sent almost no Find Next File (function 4Fh) calls down to DOS, whereas there were over 300 when performing roughly the same operation *without* a DOS box! Fortunately, there's a simple explanation: when I brought WinWord up the second time, the full pathnames of the four files I wanted to open (Parts 1-4 of *DOS Internals*) were already showing in the File menu, left over from the first test. Rather than use the File Open dialog again, I just selected the four files straight from the menu. It all makes sense. Whew! I was worried there for a minute.

Bouncing Back into Windows

One last point before we move on to see the effect of 32BFA: Remember that, even when Windows does call down to DOS, it does so in V86 mode. This means that even these INT 21h calls that are sent down to DOS aren't at all like the good old INT 21h calls you're used to:

- Before the call shows up at the DOS interrupt chain, the call will already have been preprocessed by any VxDs that have used VMM's Hook_V86_Int_Chain service (see Chapter 8).
- When the call returns, it will be postprocessed by any VxDs that have used VMM's Call_When_VM_Returns service.
- Any further interrupts made inside DOS or a TSR or a device driver will vector through the IDT to VMM, which will send the interrupt on to any VxDs that have called Hook_V86_Int_Chain.
- One or more Windows VxDs might have placed V86 breakpoints on the code. As discussed in Chapter 8, VMM's Install_V86_Break_Point service patches a specified segment:offset address with an ARPL instruction, which causes a GP fault into VMM, which then calls a handler associated with the V86 breakpoint. VxDs can use this service to control real-mode code in whatever way they want.
- If DOS makes a device-driver call, the device driver's Strategy and Interrupt routines might have been V86 breakpointed. For example, in WfW 3.11 RMM.D32, the real-mode mapper VxD that provides a 32-bit disk access (32BDA) interface on non-FastDisk devices places a V86 breakpoint on the Strategy routine for every built-in device driver.
- If DOS or a TSR or a device driver performs an IN or OUT to an I/O port, you might once again bop into VMM- and VxD-land. VxDs can hook I/O port access, using the Install_IO_Handler and Install_ Mult_IO_Handlers services provided by VMM.
- Windows installs some handlers in the DOS interrupt chain; these handlers can use various backdoor protocols to pass calls back up to Windows. For example, we saw in Chapter 8 (in "The Role of IFSHLP.SYS and V86 callbacks"section) that IFSHLP.SYS uses a V86 callback to pass some DOS calls up to the IFSMGR VxD.

Thus, while you're in the middle of some INT 21h call that Windows has passed down to DOS, you're likely to bounce back several times into Windows VMM- and VxD-land before the call returns.

To take just one example, we've seen that Windows passed INT 21h function 19h (Get Default Drive) down to DOS; we'll soon see that 32BFA doesn't change this behavior. But following the DOS INT 21h chain with a utility such as INTCHAIN (provide on the disk) shows that even once "inside" DOS, the call can bounce back into Windows multiple times.

```
C:\UNAUTHW>intchain -a20off 21/1900 > tmp.tmp

C:\UNAUTHW>type tmp.tmp
049E:0498    IFS$HLP$          ;; IFSHLP doesn't send 21/19 to IFSMGR
01EF:0023    D:
0594:1956    SETVERXX
00A0:0FAC    DOS                ;; low-memory stub checks A20
020E:00C9    XMSXXXX0          ;; I forced A20 off, so DOS calls XMS
0314:1338    $MMXXXX0          ;; disabled EMMXXXX0
3053:0045    win386
3053:004A    win386  ARPL     ;; V86 breakpoint -> V86MMGR XMS handler
00A0:10BE    DOS
FE9E:4249    HMA                ;; DOS INT 21h handler in HMA
2900:000A    win386            ;; INT 2Ah AH=82h ->
FE9E:433B    HMA
2900:0094    win386            ;; -> V86 BP -> DOSMGR V86 API -> Begin_Crit
FE9E:5356    HMA
0070:0166    IO   ARPL         ;; RMM.D32 V86 breakpoint on IO Strategy
FCA1:1632         ARPL         ;; VMM V86 breakpoint
FE9E:897C    HMA
0070:0171    IO   ARPL         ;; V86 breakpoint (on CON Interrupt routine??)
FFFF:0040    HMA
```

Here, I forced A20 off before calling function 19h in order to demonstrate one of these V86 breakpoints. MS-DOS's INT 21h handler checks whether DOS=HIGH but A20 is off; in this situation, DOS calls XMS function 5 (Local Enable A20). This code lives inside MS-DOS (see *Undocumented DOS*, 2d ed., Figure 6-6), so if you get here, it certainly seems like you're "in DOS." However, as noted in Chapter 8, the V86MMGR VxD provides its own XMS services, regardless of the XMS server you had loaded under DOS, and it uses Install_V86_Break_Point to patch the XMS function whose address is returned by INT 2Fh function 4310h. Thus, when MS-DOS's INT 21h handler calls the XMS function, it winds up executing 32-bit protected-mode code inside V86MMGR.

Windows called down to DOS to handle this trivial function 19h call, but DOS called back into Windows several times. This is one reason why the distinction between DOS and Windows seems so fluid and why the "Does Windows call down to DOS?" question can seem so meaningless. Even when Windows does call down to DOS, it's a DOS over which Windows has pretty tight control.

All the same, it's easier to see the true Windows-DOS relationship when Windows bypasses DOS than when Windows calls down to DOS and then DOS bops back into Windows several times. So let's now look at 32BFA, where according to Microsoft, Windows bypasses DOS. V86TEST helps us substantiate this claim, while also pointing to the places where Windows still relies on DOS (albeit, as we've just seen, a heavily V86-breakpointed DOS).

The Effect of 32-Bit File Access

I took several false steps before I came up with a reasonable way to use V86TEST to show off 32BFA. First, I repeated the test in Figures 11-1 and 11-2, but this time without the /D:C command-line switch that disables 32BFA:

```
C:\UNAUTHW\V86TEST>v86test -verbose win > v86test.log
```

However, I found that the V86TEST results were nearly identical to those produced when using the /D:C switch!

No, 32BFA is *not* a crock. Instead, redirecting Windows' stdout turns off 32BFA, so that leaving off the /D:C had no effect.

Since I wouldn't be able to start V86TEST before Windows and redirect stdout, and I was too lazy to change V86TEST to write out a log file, I next tried running V86TEST -QUERY from within a DOS box. Sure enough, there were significant differences between WIN /D:C and Windows with 32BFA. But the difference was that 32BFA generated *more* DOS calls than WIN /D:C!

It turns out that the system goes idle more often with 32BFA, and VMPoll thus issues more VxD broadcasts. So I ran the test again using V86TEST -FILTER, and this time got some reasonable-looking results. Under WfW 3.11 with and without 32BFA, I used WinWord to open and save a 340K document, and ran V86TEST -QUERY from a DOS box, redirecting its output to a file. I used a *diff* utility to compare the V86TEST results with and without 32BFA; the results are shown in Figure 11-6, to which I've added a large number of comments.

```
< v86test -filter win /D:C (no 32BFA)        < means no DOS box
> v86test -filter win (32BFA)                > means with a DOS box

< During Windows init:    5203 INT 21/2F calls, 344 in V86 mode
> During Windows init:    5198 INT 21/2F calls, 339 in V86 mode

< While Windows running:  25574 INT 21/2F calls, 25574 in V86 mode
> While Windows running:  17146 INT 21/2F calls, 17146 in V86 mode

Once filter out VMPoll, a third fewer calls in 32BFA:
25574 - 17146 = 8428 (8428 / 25574 = 32%)

< Windows active for 101 seconds
> Windows active for 77 seconds

Same operation took 101 - 77 = 24 seconds less with 32BFA (24/101 = 23%)

< 253 INT 21/2F calls/second
```

```
> 222 INT 21/2F calls/second
```

If VMPoll were counted, 32BFA would show more 21/2F per second

```
< VM #1 -- 4007 calls
> VM #1 -- 438 calls
```

Aside from VMPoll, almost no DOS calls from System VM with 32BFA!

Would be good to know what those few remaining calls are. Unfortunately, in the INT 21h census below, they are combined with DOS calls from the DOS box (VM #2). However, most DOS box calls are to 21/0B. See WV86TEST in Chapter 12 for a census that doesn't include DOS box.

```
< VM #2 -- 21569 calls
> VM #2 -- 16708 calls
```

With 32BFA, a lot fewer DOS calls from DOS box too: whatever 32BFA can do for Windows applications, it can do for DOS boxes.

```
INT 2Fh AH=16h calls seen by V86TEST:
< 00: 2   05: 1   08: 1   0A: 2   0B: 2   8A: 1
> 00: 2   05: 1   08: 1   0A: 2   0B: 2   8A: 1

INT 21h calls:
< 02: 149 06: 154 08: 55  09: 1   0B: 21159   0C: 2   0D: 255 0E: 289 19: 87
> 02: 151 06: 150 08: 57  09: 1   0B: 16359   0C: 2   0D: 257 0E: 289 19: 87
```

Figure 11-3 demonstrated that 21/0B (Check Keyboard Status) is used by the DOS box only. With 32BFA, almost all calls from the DOS box (VM #2) were 21/0B:

16708 - 16359 = only 349 other DOS calls from DOS box under 32BFA.

```
< 1A: 79  25: 17  29: 16  2A: 15  2C: 17  2F: 9   30: 24  32: 2   33: 4  34: 5
> 1A: 19  25: 17  29: 16  2A: 15  2C: 17  2F: 9   30: 24  32: 2   33: 4  34: 5
```

With 32BFA, a lot fewer calls to 21/1A (Set DTA).

```
< 35: 14  38: 3   3B: 18  3C: 4   3D: 307 3E: 221 3F: 1614    40: 3480   41: 3
> 35: 14  38: 3   3B: 1   3C: 1   3D: 110 3E: 90  3F: 266     40: 3416
```

With 32BFA, a lot fewer calls to:
21/3B (Change Current Directory)
21/3D (Open File)
21/3E (Close File)
21/3F (Read File)

In 32BFA, most 21/40 (Write File) appear to be passed through.
But wait a minute: the numbers don't add up:
16359 (21/0B) + 3416 (21/40) = 19775 calls to these two functions alone.
Yet summary above says only 17146 calls under 32BFA.
There's a simple explanation:
I generated this log under an older version of V86TEST that didn't "freeze" the stats before printing them out.
So almost all these 21/40 calls reflect V86TEST's own printf to stdout. In 32BFA,

```
writes to stdout are passed down to DOS. But wait again: V86TEST output was redi-
rected to a file. No, I lied: it wasn't! I captured V86TEST output in an Epsilon
process buffer. So it was a write to stdout, which 32BFA passed down. We'll confirm
later that in 32BFA, most 21/40 are not passed down.

< 42: 1238   43: 19  44: 244 45: 1   47: 86  48: 13  49: 2   4A: 7   4B: 5
> 42: 226    43: 1   44: 35  45: 1   47: 9   48: 13  49: 2   4A: 7   4B: 5

With 32BFA, a lot fewer calls to:
21/42 (LSEEK)
21/43 (Get/Set File Attributes)
21/44 (IOCTL)
21/47 (Get Current Directory)

< 4E: 70  4F: 23  50: 197 51: 7   52: 10  55: 3   56: 2   57: 114 58: 8   59: 2
> 4E: 9   4F: 1   50: 196 51: 7   52: 10  55: 3           57: 1   58: 8   59: 2

With 32BFA, a lot fewer calls to:
21/4E (Find First File)
21/4F (Find Next File)
21/57 (Get/Set File Date/Time)

< 5B: 3   5D: 5   5E: 1   5F: 3   62: 48  63: 1   65: 4   6C: 2   71: 4   DC: 5
>         5D: 5   5E: 1   5F: 3   62: 48  63: 1   65: 4   6C: 1   71: 4   DC: 5

INT 2Fh calls:
< 08: 1   11: 692 12: 11  13: 4   16: 9   43: 8   46: 1   48: 2   4A: 6
> 08: 1   11: 392 12: 11  13: 4   16: 9   43: 8   46: 1   48: 2   4A: 6

With 32BFA, a lot fewer calls to 2F/11 (Network Redirector)

< 55: 1 7A: 2   AE: 3   B7: 2   FE: 2   FF: 1
> 55: 1 7A: 2   AE: 3   B7: 2   FE: 2   FF: 1

The call to 2F/FF is V86TEST's call to V86TEST stats from resident copy.
```

Figure 11-6: Running V86TEST in WfW 3.11, with and without 32BFA.

Figure 11-6 is a dramatic demonstration of how Windows and DOS truly relate under 32BFA. It provides most of the answers to this chapter's question; Why does Windows need DOS?

- Aside from VMPoll broadcasts (and the INT 28h idle calls that we know go along with them), the most frequent DOS call for which Windows uses DOS is function 0Bh (Check Keyboard Status). This call is used only to poll the keyboard in a DOS box.
- Aside from function 0Bh, a fairly I/O-intensive operation (opening and saving a document with WinWord) generated only a few hundred DOS calls. Without 32BFA, the same operation generates several thousand DOS calls.

- Aside from function 40h Write File calls to stdout (which would only occur in a DOS box), almost all DOS file I/O calls are handled in 32-bit protected mode without calling down to DOS. Figure 11-7 shows some INT 21h calls that 32BFA generally absorbs; this list is not complete and just reflects what we've seen using V86TEST.
- Even with 32BFA, a scattering of INT 21h calls are still sent down to DOS. These are shown in Figure 11-8; compare this with Figure 11-4, which showed the top INT 21h calls without 32BFA.

```
1Ah         Set DTA
3Bh         Change Current Directory
3Ch         Create File
3Dh         Open File
3Eh         Close File
3Fh         Read File
40h         Write File
41h         Delete File
42h         LSEEK
43h         Get/Set File Attributes
44h         IOCTL
47h         Get Current Directory
4Eh         Find First File
4Fh         Find Next File
57h         Set/Set File Date/Time
71h         Long Filename functions
```

Figure 11-7: Some major INT 21h calls that 32BFA handles in protected mode, without calling DOS.

```
0Bh         Check Keyboard Status
0Dh         Reset Drive
0Eh         Set Default Drive
19h         Get Default Drive
2Ah         Get Date
2Ch         Get Time
50h         Set PSP
51h, 62h   Get PSP
52h         Get SysVars (undoc)
55h         Create PSP
```

Figure 11-8: The top INT 21h calls that 32BFA sends down to DOS.

Now, there's nothing particularly magical about 32BFA: it's just a collection of VxDs such as IFSMGR.386, VCACHE.386, VSHARE, and VFAT.386. In WfW 3.11, Microsoft was able to plop these VxDs on top of an essentially unchanged VMM. These VxDs could have been written by an enterprising third-party developer. All the capabilities for bypassing

DOS have been present all along in VMM, most notably in its Hook_V86_Int_Chain and Set_PM_Int_Vector services. 32BFA just makes more extensive use of these services. The entire Windows-DOS relationship is quite fluid, and really comes down to how the VMMservices are employed. This is just another way of saying that VMM is the operating system.

What about BIOS Calls?

With all this talk about the relationship between Windows and MS-DOS, it's natural to wonder how Windows relates to the ROM BIOS.

HOOKINT.C in Listing 11-1 is a simple program that reports on any program's usage of the BIOS software interrupts. I also included the DOS INT 25h and 26h disk read and write calls and the INT 28h idle call; it's easy to add additional entries to HOOKINT.

Listing 11-1: HOOKINT.C

```
/*
HOOKINT.C
bcc hookint.c
hookint [program name]
hookint -win [program name]
Creates HOOKINT.LOG
*/

#include <stdlib.h>
#include <stdio.h>
#include <string.h>
#include <process.h>
#include <dos.h>
#include <bios.h>

typedef unsigned short WORD;
typedef unsigned long DWORD;

#pragma pack(1)

typedef struct {
#ifdef __TURBOC__
    WORD bp,di,si,ds,es,dx,cx,bx,ax;
#else
    WORD es,ds,di,si,bp,sp,bx,dx,cx,ax;     /* same as PUSHA */
#endif
    WORD ip,cs,flags;
    } REG_PARAMS;

typedef void (interrupt far *FUNCPTR)(REG_PARAMS);
```

```
typedef struct {
    FUNCPTR old, new;
    DWORD count, *func;
    int intno, has_func;
    char *str;
    } INT_DATA;

extern INT_DATA int_data[];

int check_windows = 0, in_windows = 0;
int int_ndx[0x100] = {0} ;

#define INT_HANDLER(rax, intno) { \
    INT_DATA *pid = &int_data[int_ndx[intno]]; \
    if (in_windows || (! check_windows)) { \
        if (pid->has_func) \
            pid->func[rax >> 8]++; \
        pid->count++; \
        } \
    _chain_intr(pid->old); \
    }

void interrupt far int10(REG_PARAMS r) { INT_HANDLER(r.ax,0x10); }
void interrupt far int11(REG_PARAMS r) { INT_HANDLER(r.ax,0x11); }
void interrupt far int12(REG_PARAMS r) { INT_HANDLER(r.ax,0x12); }
void interrupt far int13(REG_PARAMS r) { INT_HANDLER(r.ax,0x13); }
void interrupt far int14(REG_PARAMS r) { INT_HANDLER(r.ax,0x14); }
void interrupt far int15(REG_PARAMS r) { INT_HANDLER(r.ax,0x15); }
void interrupt far int16(REG_PARAMS r) { INT_HANDLER(r.ax,0x16); }
void interrupt far int17(REG_PARAMS r) { INT_HANDLER(r.ax,0x17); }
void interrupt far int1A(REG_PARAMS r) { INT_HANDLER(r.ax,0x1A); }
void interrupt far int25(REG_PARAMS r) { INT_HANDLER(r.ax,0x25); }
void interrupt far int26(REG_PARAMS r) { INT_HANDLER(r.ax,0x26); }
void interrupt far int28(REG_PARAMS r) { INT_HANDLER(r.ax,0x28); }
void interrupt far int33(REG_PARAMS r) { INT_HANDLER(r.ax,0x33); }

INT_DATA int_data[] = {
//  old,    new,    count, func,    intno,  has_func,   str
    0,      int10,  0, 0,           0x10,   1,          "Video",
    0,      int11,  0, 0,           0x11,   0,          "Equipment List",
    0,      int12,  0, 0,           0x12,   0,          "Memory Size",
    0,      int13,  0, 0,           0x13,   1,          "Disk",
    0,      int14,  0, 0,           0x14,   1,          "Serial",
    0,      int15,  0, 0,           0x15,   1,          "System Services",
    0,      int16,  0, 0,           0x16,   1,          "Keyboard",
    0,      int17,  0, 0,           0x17,   1,          "Printer",
    0,      int1A,  0, 0,           0x1A,   1,          "Time",
    0,      int25,  0, 0,           0x25,   0,          "DOS Disk Read",
    0,      int26,  0, 0,           0x26,   0,          "DOS Disk Write",
    0,      int28,  0, 0,           0x28,   0,          "Idle",
    0,      int33,  0, 0,           0x33,   1,          "Mouse",
    } ;

#define NUM_INT     (sizeof(int_data) / sizeof(INT_DATA))

FUNCPTR GetSetInt(int intno, FUNCPTR new)
```

```
{
    FUNCPTR old = _dos_getvect(intno);
    _dos_setvect(intno, new);
    return old;
}

FUNCPTR prev_2f = (FUNCPTR) 0;

#define WIN_INIT_COMPLETE   0x1608
#define WIN_EXIT_BEGIN      0x1609

void interrupt far int2f(REG_PARAMS r)
{
    if (r.ax == WIN_INIT_COMPLETE)
        in_windows++;
    else if (r.ax == WIN_EXIT_BEGIN)
        in_windows--;
    _chain_intr(prev_2f);
}

void fail(const char *s) { puts(s); exit(1); }

main(int argc, char *argv[])
{
    int i, j;
    INT_DATA *pint;
    FILE *f;

    if (strncmp(strupr(argv[1]), "-WIN", 3) == 0)
    {
        check_windows++;
        argv++; argc--;
    }

    /* set up func counters */
    for (i=0, pint=int_data; i<NUM_INT; i++, pint++)
        if (pint->has_func)
            if ((pint->func = (DWORD *) calloc(0x100, sizeof(DWORD))) == 0)
                fail("Insufficient memory");

    /* initialize int_ndx */
    for (i=0, pint=int_data; i<NUM_INT; i++, pint++)
        int_ndx[pint->intno] = i;

    /* install handlers */
    for (i=0, pint=int_data; i<NUM_INT; i++, pint++)
        pint->old = GetSetInt(pint->intno, pint->new);
    if (check_windows)
        prev_2f = GetSetInt(0x2f, int2f);

    /* run the command */
    if (argc < 2)
        system(getenv("COMSPEC"));
    else
        spawnvp(P_WAIT, argv[1], &argv[1]);
```

```
    /* restore previous handlers */
    if (check_windows)
        (void) GetSetInt(0x2f, prev_2f);
    for (i=0, pint=int_data; i<NUM_INT; i++, pint++)
        (void) GetSetInt(pint->intno, pint->old);

    /* open log file to display results */
    if (f = fopen("HOOKINT.LOG", "w"))
        printf("Creating HOOKINT.LOG\n");
    else
        f = stdout;

    /* show command line */
    for (i=1; i<argc; i++)
        fprintf(f, "%s ", argv[i]);
    fprintf(f, "\n");

    if (check_windows)
        fprintf(f, "While Windows running:\n");

    /* show grand totals for each INT */
    for (i=0, pint=int_data; i<NUM_INT; i++, pint++)
        if (pint->count)
            fprintf(f, "INT %02Xh\t\t%-8lu\t\t%s\n",
                pint->intno, pint->count, pint->str);
    fprintf(f,"\n");

    /* if INT has functions, show individual function counts */
    for (i=0, pint=int_data; i<NUM_INT; i++, pint++)
        if (pint->has_func && pint->count)
        {
            for (j=0; j<0x100; j++)
                if (pint->func[j])
                    fprintf(f,"%02X/%02X: %lu\t",
                        pint->intno, j, pint->func[j]);
            fprintf(f,"\n");
        }

    fclose(f);
    return 0;
}
```


If you run HOOKINT without any command-line parameters, it spawns a command shell; when you exit from the shell, HOOKINT reports the usage of the hooked interrupts. Rather than send its output to stdout, which would then have to be redirected to a file with the possibly disruptive results we saw earlier in V86TEST, HOOKINT instead writes out a file, HOOKINT.LOG.

You can also specify a program for HOOKINT to run, such as WIN or WIN /D:C. Finally, an optional -WIN command-line switch tells HOOKINT to only track interrupts while Windows is running (or at least in between calls to INT 2Fh functions 1608h and 1609h). Figure 11-9 shows a typical HOOKINT.LOG file after using WfW 3.11 for a while. In this configuration, 32-bit disk access (32BDA) was enabled; I ran a large number of Windows applications (including WinWord, Solitaire, the Win32 version of FreeCell, Control Panel, Print Manager, and File Manager), but I didn't open a DOS box. I didn't use the HOOKINT -WIN switch, so this log includes calls Windows made during initialization and termination.

```
INT 10h      160             Video
INT 11h      6               Equipment List
INT 12h      1               Memory Size
INT 13h      2501            Disk
INT 15h      28173           System Services
INT 16h      195             Keyboard
INT 1Ah      12              Time
INT 25h      4               DOS Disk Read
INT 28h      499260          Idle
INT 33h      3               Mouse

10/00: 7     10/01: 1     10/0E: 100  10/0F: 4     10/10: 4     10/11: 6
10/12: 10    10/1A: 1     10/6F: 2    10/F0: 4     10/F1: 6     10/F2: 3
10/F3: 12
13/02: 2307 13/03: 191  13/08: 3
15/53: 17968     15/87: 2050 15/90: 4067 15/91: 4085 15/C0: 2    15/C1: 1
16/01: 98    16/11: 97
1A/00: 9     1A/02: 1     1A/03: 1    1A/05: 1
33/00: 3
```

Figure 11-9: Sample HOOKINT results generated under WfW 3.11.

There are a few noticeable features in Figure 11-9. First, there are many INT 28h idle calls; this matches what we saw earlier in the VMPoll broadcasts. The "Reschedule" function in KRNL386 makes these INT 28h calls.

Second, there are a hefty number of INT 15h calls, but these don't necessarily come from Windows. INT 15h function 53h belongs to the Advanced Power Management (APM) specification; I had Microsoft's POWER.EXE loaded here. Functions 90h and 91h are the BIOS Device Busy and Device Post operating system hooks. The BIOS calls these functions, and an operating system such as Windows can intercept them; the IOS VxD can use INT 15h function 90h as a signal to call the Enable_VM_Ints service. INT 15h function 87h is the Copy Extended Memory service; Windows uses this during initialization.

Other calls, such as INT 10h video, INT 16h keyboard, and INT 33h mouse services, are called far less often than is typical in a full-screen DOS application (which, in a way, is what Windows is). In one completely unscientific comparison, I ran a full-screen DOS program (the Borland C++ integrated development environment) very briefly under HOOK-INT — certainly for a much shorter period than I had run Windows — and there were almost 200,000 calls each to INT 16h functions 11h and 12h to poll the keyboard, over 11,000 calls to INT 33h to get the mouse status, and over 1000 calls to INT 10h function 2 to set the cursor position. This is quite different from what happens in Windows.

Third, and last, we come to INT 13h disk reads and writes. Here there's actually something important to say. Starting in Windows 3.10, Microsoft provided 32-bit disk access (32BDA), often referred to as Fast-Disk. This is frequently confused with 32-bit *file* access, but is quite separate: 32BFA handles DOS file I/O calls in 32-bit protected mode, whereas 32BDA handles INT 13h disk reads and writes in 32-bit protected mode.

So how can we summarize Windows' relation to the BIOS? First, Windows applications have long bypassed the BIOS services for video, keyboard, printing, and so on; as noted earlier, the Windows API provides its own services. Of course, the occasional Windows program does uses BIOS services; a good example is Microsoft's CodeView debugger. The source code for the Windows DISPLAY driver included with the DDK (DDK\286\DISPLAY\8PLANE\V7VGA\SRC\VGA.ASM) contains the following note:

```
; why would a windows app do a INT 10h you ask? CodeView does so we need
; to trap INT 10h
```

Second, examining the source code included with the DDK shows that Windows device drivers such as DISPLAY and KEYBOARD (these are Win16 DRV files, not to be confused with 32-bit VxDs) make occasional use of BIOS calls, for example, INT 10h and INT 16h.

And third, an examination of the VxD source code included with the DDK shows that a number of VxDs hook the BIOS interrupts in V86 and protected mode. The VDD (Virtual Display Device) hooks INT 10h; the IOS (I/O Supervisor; called BLOCKDEV in Windows 3.1) hooks INT 13h; VKD (Virtual Keyboard Device) hooks INT 16h; VPD (Virtual Printer Device) hooks INT 17h; VTD (Virtual Timer Device) hooks INT 1Ah; and VMD (Virtual Mouse Device) hooks INT 33h.

For example, VKD uses Hook_V86_Int_Chain to hook INT 16h in V86 mode. VKD will thus see INT 16h before any real-mode software does. VKD also uses Call_When_VM_Returns to install a "post-reflection hook" that will be called when the real-mode BIOS attempts to IRET back to what it thinks is its caller. Why does VKD hook INT 16h? The INT 16h handler in VKD.ASM explains why:

```
;   DESCRIPTION:    This software interrupt handler will convert blocking
;           int 16s into polling int 16s. If no key is ready then
;           the current VMs time slice will be given up.

;;; ...
    Push_Client_State
    VMMcall Begin_Nest_Exec         ; Nest execution level

    mov dh, [ebp.Client_AH]
    inc dh                  ; Polling int 16  (0 - 1)
                            ; extended polling (10h - 11h)
I16_Poll_Loop:
    mov [ebp.Client_AH], dh
    mov eax, 16h
    VMMcall Exec_Int
    TestMem [ebp.Client_Flags], ZF_Mask ; Q: Key ready?
    jz  SHORT I16_Key_Ready     ;     Y: Done
    VMMCall Release_Time_Slice
    jmp I16_Poll_Loop

I16_Key_Ready:
    VMMcall End_Nest_Exec           ; Pop off execution level
    Pop_Client_State
    stc                     ; Reflect blocking int 16 now
    ret
```

As another example, VDDINT.ASM attempts to emulate (rather than reflect) a number of INT 10h video calls, including functions 2 and 3 (get and set cursor position), functions 6 and 7 (scroll up and down), function 9 (write character and attribute at cursor position), and function 0Eh (write TTY). It's well worth reading this code (DDK\386\VDDVGA\VDDINT.ASM) to see how Windows VxDs can take over not only from DOS but also from the BIOS. For example:

```
; Emulate this Get Cursor Position call, if possible
;
VI10GetCurs:
    call    VDD_Int_Can_Emulate      ;Q: can emulate INT 10?
    jnz VI10_Reflect                 ;   N:
    movzx   ecx,[ebp.Client_BH]      ; ECX = output page
    BEGIN_Touch_1st_Meg
    mov ax, WORD PTR DS:[460h]       ; get top & bottom lines of cursor
    mov [ebp.Client_CX],ax           ; Client CH,CL = cursor type
    mov ax, WORD PTR DS:[450h+ecx*2] ; get row/column
    END_Touch_1st_Meg
    mov [ebp.Client_DX],ax           ; Client DH,DL = cursor posn
    jmp VI10ExitEmYes                ; Call emulated, exit
```

As a final example, VFD.ASM hooks INT 13h:

```
; This Device hooks INT 13's and checks for the high bit to be clear in the
; drive specification (DL). If the bit is clear, then Begin_Critical_Section
; is called and timer port trapping is disabled. When the bios INT 13 handler
; IRET's, then timer port trapping is reenabled and End_Critical_Section
; is called. INT 13's that do have the high bit of DL set are simply
; reflected so that VHD can handle them.
;
; Also if the INT 13 is a format command (AL=5), then VDMAD is called to
; disable DMA channel #3. This is done, because the BIOS programmes the
; DMA channel for a large random DMA transfer that never occurs (the
; disk controller never actually performs DMA during a format track operation)
; By ignoring this random programming of the DMA channel, VDMAD is able to
; work with allocating a smaller (more realistic) DMA buffer.
```


What this all means is that even BIOS interrupts coming from DOS applications and from DOS software loaded before Windows will be handled in 32-bit protected mode by some VxD. In most cases the VxD does some preprocessing, reflects the interrupt to V86 mode, and then possibly does some postprocessing (via Call_When_VM_Returns).

In other words, Microsoft is effectively moving large parts of the BIOS into 32-bit protected mode VxDs. In fact, this movement has been going on for some time, probably with little realization outside the relatively small circle of VxD writers. For example, the VDD code to emulate rather than reflect some INT 10h calls appears to have been written in 1988, presumably for the Windows/386 3.*x* project. The more things change, the more they stay the same.

Chapter 12

Exploring with WV86TEST

The V86TEST program used in the previous chapter helped illustrate the situations under which Windows does and does not need DOS. In this chapter we're going to further explore the Windows-DOS relationship by enhancing V86TEST in several ways.

- Using V86TEST requires either redirecting Windows' output to a file, which silently disables 32BFA, or running V86TEST -QUERY, which pollutes the V86TEST results with INT 21h calls coming from the DOS box. It's true that Windows doesn't treat DOS boxes in a substantially different way than does the System VM in which Windows applications run, but DOS programs do tend to make calls — such as function 0Bh to poll the keyboard — that Windows applications don't. These calls clutter up the V86TEST results.

  The first issue — having to redirect V86TEST's output to a file — could be easily addressed by changing V86TEST to write out a log file, as I did with the HOOKINT program back in Listing 10-1.

  The second issue — having to open a DOS box in order to run V86TEST -QUERY — has a solution which, in a book ostensibly about Windows programming, should be obvious: write a Windows version of V86TEST (WV86TEST). This isn't really a matter of putting a graphical user interface on V86TEST. Instead, WV86TEST increases the accuracy of V86TEST's INT 21h log.

- V86TEST lumps together DOS calls coming from Windows applications, from DOS applications running under Windows, and from Windows itself. Every time we run V86TEST, we see the entire history of DOS calls, including those that Windows made during its initialization.

  Although this problem could be partially fixed by making V86TEST collect only INT 21h statistics during the period that Windows is truly up and running — V86TEST.C (Listing 10-1) could check if (state == WIN_INIT_DONE) before logging INT 21h calls — WV86TEST has a better solution: a Show Changes menu item that will let us focus on the DOS calls made by particular Win16 and Win32 applications.

- Recall my complaint from the preceding chapter that, by definition, V86TEST knows nothing about INT 21h calls that are *not* passed down to DOS. Just because V86TEST doesn't see some INT 21h call, it doesn't mean that Windows emulates this call in 32-bit protected mode. It's equally possible that no one is making the INT 21h call in the first place. V86TEST can't tell the difference between calls that Windows emulates and calls that no one makes.

To solve this last problem, the next two chapters will use WSPY21, a Windows program that hooks INT 21h and displays the DOS calls that a Windows application thinks it's making or that some DLL is making on the application's behalf. Using WSPY21, we'll examine the DOS activity generated by some common Windows applications.

This chapter presents the code for WV86TEST and shows some sample sessions with the program. The next two chapters will then spend a lot of time looking at the Clock applet in both Windows 3.1 and Windows 95. Comparing the output generated by WSPY21 with that generated by WV86TEST will give us a much better idea of the DOS calls that Windows handles — and does not handle — in protected mode.

The next two chapters also take several lengthy side trips to examine some fascinating sights in Windows 95, including memory-mapped files, thunking between 16- and 32-bit code, and demand-paged virtual memory. These side trips are all inspired by some odd-looking results displayed by WV86TEST and WSPY21.

Breaking All Ties with DOS?

WV86TEST, as shown in Figure 12-1, is a Windows application that communicates with the DOS version of V86TEST (see Listing 10-1) loaded before Windows.

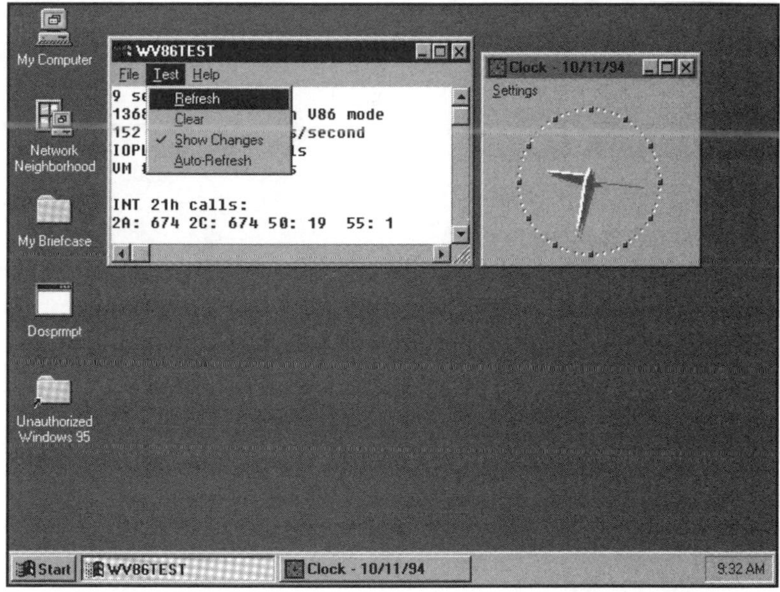

Figure 12-1: WV86TEST, running under Windows 95 alongside the Win32 clock, shows the INT 21h calls from Clock that Windows 95 sends down to V86-mode DOS.

For example, after starting WV86TEST under Windows 95 and selecting the Show Changes and Refresh options, I used the WordPad application that comes with Windows 95 to read in a 78K WinWord .DOC file and save it out as a plain-ASCII .TXT file. WV86TEST shows how this looked to real-mode DOS:

```
141 seconds elapsed
542 calls, 542 in V86 mode
3 INT 21/2F calls/second
IOPL=3 -- 542 calls
VM #1 -- 542 calls

INT 21h calls:
ØE: 138 2A: 25  2C: 16  3Ø: 6   45: 2   5Ø: 348 55: 1   57: 4   5A: 1

INT 2Fh calls:
11: 1
```

Notice that there are *no* calls to the INT 21h functions that open, close, read, or write files. At the same time, there are plenty of calls to INT 21h functions 0Eh, 2Ah, 2Ch, and 50h.

In another test, I started Calc, Microsoft's calculator applet, did a few calculations, browsed Calc's on-line help (this starts the WinHelp program), exited Calc, and did a WV86TEST Refresh. Here's how the slightly more than two minutes of CALC.EXE and WINHELP.EXE activity looked to DOS under Windows 95, as logged by V86TEST and reported by WV86TEST:


```
138 seconds elapsed
200 calls, 200 in V86 mode
1 INT 21/2F calls/second
IOPL=3 -- 200 calls
VM #1 -- 200 calls

INT 21h calls:
0E: 44  2A: 3   2C: 14  30: 2   4C: 2   50: 129 55: 2

INT 2Fh calls:
11: 4
```

I happened to still have my CURRDRIV.386 from Chapter 7 loaded here, so function 19h (Get Current Drive) calls that normally would have been sent down to DOS were instead consumed by the VxD in 32-bit protected mode. Even so, this isn't much DOS activity to show for running two Windows applications. DOS has seen two PSPs created with undocumented function 55h (Create PSP), lots of function 50h (Set PSP) activity, two programs exiting with function 4Ch, and so on. But there's no file I/O, aside perhaps from four network redirector calls (INT 2Fh function 11h).

Windows 95 is evidently bypassing DOS for most services. But there's nothing brand new or Windows 95-specific about this. WfW 3.11, with 32BFA enabled, shows just as little DOS activity for roughly the same level of Calc and WinHelp activity:

```
185 seconds elapsed
59 calls, 59 in V86 mode
0 INT 21/2F calls/second
IOPL=3 -- 59 calls
VM #1 -- 59 calls

INT 21h calls:
2A: 2   2C: 2   30: 2   4C: 2   50: 43  55: 2   59: 2

INT 2Fh calls:
11: 4
```

Not only is Windows 95's capability to bypass DOS nothing new, but in this admittedly unscientific test, WfW 3.11 bypassed DOS to a *greater* extent than Windows 95. Note that, even though the WfW test ran for a little longer than the Windows 95 test, there were somewhat fewer Set PSP calls than in Windows 95 and no function 0Eh (Set Disk) calls.

But which DOS calls — regardless of whether DOS or Windows eventually handles them — are Calc and WinHelp generating in the first place? Running WfW 3.11 *without* 32BFA provides one way to see the DOS activity that 32BFA evidently absorbs. Here's the same Calc/WinHelp test, this time under WfW 3.11 with 32BFA disabled (WIN /D:C):


```
223 seconds elapsed

INT 21h calls:
1A: 7    2A: 3    2C: 3    30: 2    3B: 3    3D: 20   3E: 13   3F: 165 42: 131
43: 8    44: 21   47: 10   4C: 2    4E: 7    50: 39   55: 2    57: 12   59: 3

INT 2Fh calls:
11: 42
```

Here we see the DOS file I/O calls — such as function 3Dh to open files, 3Eh to close them, 3Fh to read from a file, and 42h to move the file pointer — that Calc and WinHelp must still be making when 32BFA is enabled, but that DOS won't see because IFSMgr has usurped its role.

Table 12-1 presents the three sets of WV86TEST results for Calc.

Table 12-1: WV86TEST results for Calc/WinHelp

Function	Windows 95	WfW with 32BFA	WfW without 32BFA
0Eh	44	–	–
1Ah	–	–	7
2Ah	3	1	3
2Ch	14	1	3
30h	2	2	2
3Bh	–	–	3
3Dh	–	–	20
3Eh	–	–	13
3Fh	–	–	165
42h	–	–	131
43h	–	–	8
44h	–	–	21
47h	–	–	10
4Ch	2	2	2

4Eh	–	–	7
50h	129	35	39
55h	2	2	2
57h	–	–	12
59h	–	2	3

All three environments pass function 55h (Create PSP) and function 4Ch (Exit Program) down to DOS. Windows 95 is generating a lot of calls to function 0Eh (Set Disk) and to function 2Ch (Get Time). And of the three environments, Windows 95 appears to be making the *heaviest* use of function 50h to set the current PSP.

This is all very strange in light of Microsoft's claims regarding Windows 95's relationship to MS-DOS. For example:

> Chicago is a 32-bit operating system. Windows no longer can be likened to a fancy paint job on an old MS-DOS Yugo. Because the entire operating system is freshly designed from the ground up, you now have killer features such as threads, memory-mapped files, and asynch I/O.
>
> — Dave Edson, "Seventeen Techniques for Preparing Your 16-bit Applications for Chicago," *Microsoft Systems Journal*, February 1994, p. 15.

One of the cardinal rules of marketing is to push what you have to sell today rather than what you'll have tomorrow. Given that this statement was written at least a year before the general availability of Windows 95, it's odd to see Microsoft not only selling what it won't have until tomorrow but positively *trashing* (unless you think the Yugo is a good car) what it has for sale today. Yes, we have no bananas!

The key assertion here is that Windows 95 is "freshly designed from the ground up." In fact, Windows 95 is built on the foundation of the VMM code written by Ralph Lipe, Aaron Reynolds, and others in early 1988. For example, the VPICD.H header file included with the DDK is dated "13-Apr-1988 RAL," VMDA.H is dated "05-May-1988 ARR," and the all-important VMM.INC is dated "05-May 1988 RAL." The core code in Windows 95's VMM is anything but fresh. But this is a good thing, because the devil you know is preferable to the devil you don't know.

However, we shouldn't make too big a deal out of this "freshly designed" claim from February 1994. The article carries a prominent disclaimer that "The information presented here is based on an early prerelease of Chicago. Anything and everything is subject to change." Furthermore, one of the C files included with the article contains a truly wonderful 20-line disclaimer:

> Consult your physician before using this program. Batteries not included. May cause drowsiness. Not available in all states.... Keep this and all software out of the reach of children. Parental guidance suggested. The buyer assumes all risks associated with using this product. [Actually, that one is very close to the true state of affairs in software.] In case of irritation, flush eyes with cold water and consult your physician. Not insured by the Federal Deposit Insurance Corporation.... PLEASE NOTE: Some quantum physics theories suggest that when the consumer is not directly observing this product, it may cease to exist or will exist only in a vague and undetermined state.

Well, we've been warned. Let's then turn to another *Microsoft Systems Journal* article that isn't so hedged with warnings:

> The big difference in Chicago's relationship with MS-DOS from that of Windows 3.1 is that if you only run Windows-based applications, you'll never execute any MS-DOS code.
>
> — Adrian King, "Windows, the Next Generation: An Advance Look at the Architecture of Chicago," *Microsoft Systems Journal*, January 1994, p. 18.

In the Calc/WinHelp test, we're only running Windows-based applications (this was why we needed WV86TEST in the first place), yet Table 12-1 shows that Windows 95 is quite clearly still calling down to DOS to roughly the same extent that WfW 3.11 did.

At this point, you might be very concerned about what are sometimes called (as we'll get into later) "Heisenberg" effects. WV86TEST talks to V86TEST, which is a real-mode DOS program. *Microsoft Systems Journal* quite specifically said "if you only run Windows-based applications, you'll never execute any MS-DOS code." Perhaps V86TEST, although it loads *before* Windows, violates this condition. More generally, perhaps the DOS activity that these programs reveal wouldn't occur in the first place if these programs weren't running.

I address these concerns in detail in Chapter 14, where we'll see conclusively that Windows 95 calls down to DOS to the same extent whether or not V86TEST is loaded. For now, though, let me show the "steady state" when only WV86TEST and V86TEST are running so that I can try to assure you that WV86TEST has little effect on the Windows-DOS relationship:

```
1 seconds elapsed
2 calls, 2 in V86 mode
2 INT 21/2F calls/second
IOPL=3 -- 2 calls
VM #1 -- 2 calls

INT 21h calls:
2A: 1   2C: 1
```

These two DOS calls, which get the date and time, appear whenever you select Refresh from the WV86TEST menu. The display_results function in WV86TEST.C later in this chapter (Listing 12-2) calls the C time function, which in turn calls INT 21h functions 2Ah and 2Ch. These two calls need to be subtracted from any WV86TEST results. But in the Calc/WinHelp test, this still leaves us (both in WfW 3.11 and in Windows 95) with calls to Create PSP, Set PSP, DOS exit, and a few others.

So what's the "big difference in Chicago's relationship with MS-DOS"? Adrian King's *Microsoft Systems Journal* article cited previously does address this issue:

> As successive versions of Windows have appeared, each has supported more and more of the MS-DOS INT-based software services, and Windows-based applications have had an ever-lessening need to switch in and out of virtual-86 mode to execute MS-DOS code. The big exception to this (until Windows for Workgroups version 3.11) was the support for the file system services.

This is certainly an accurate history of Windows' relationship with MS-DOS. But in the next sentence, the article says:

> Chicago finally breaks all ties with the real-mode MS-DOS code and, with few exceptions, even existing 16-bit Windows-based applications will follow a protected-mode path through the new File Management Subsystem to the disk and back.

WV86TEST shows that this sentence is almost exactly wrong:

- The mere fact that Windows 95 sends Set PSP calls involving Windows applications down to MS-DOS indicates that Windows 95 hasn't broken all ties with real-mode DOS. I don't see any good reason why Windows 95 should break all ties with real-mode DOS, but Microsoft ought to stop claiming that it has.
- The "new File Management Subsystem" isn't new. IFSMgr, VFAT, VCACHE, and so on in Windows 95 are largely the same as IFSMgr, VFAT, VCACHE, and so on in WfW 3.11. This should come as no surprise, since Microsoft's ads for WfW 3.11 explicitly said that its 32-bit file access came from Chicago: "Using the 32-bit file system from our Chicago project, Windows for Workgroups performs 50% faster on disk-intensive tasks" (Microsoft advertisement, *InfoWorld*, January 10, 1994, p. 55).

  Now, 32BFA in Windows 95 *should* be an improvement over that in WfW 3.11. After all, the flip-side to Microsoft's boast that WfW 3.11 in January 1994 included 32-bit code from Windows 95 (a product that wouldn't be ready for at least another year) is that WfW 3.11

contained *pre-beta* code. And, as a result of the way it used the WfW 3.11 commercial release as a widespread test for its pre-beta code, Microsoft has improved 32BFA in Windows 95.

But some of these improvements entail the re-knotting of some ties to DOS that were too hastily broken in WfW 3.11: Windows 95 is a little *more* tied to DOS than was WfW 3.11. For example, recall from Chapter 8 (the "Global and Local INT 21h Hookers" section) that WfW 3.11 wouldn't reflect file INT 21h calls to local hookers, but that Windows 95 will.

- Having just told us that "Chicago finally breaks all ties with the real-mode MS-DOS code," it's hard to know what to make of the next phrase: "with few exceptions, even existing 16-bit Windows-based applications will follow a protected-mode path." Perhaps I'm looking too carefully at some hastily chosen wording, but there is a direct contradiction between "all" and "with few exceptions, even." Either Windows 95 breaks all ties with the real-mode MS-DOS code or it doesn't. WV86TEST has already shown us that it doesn't.

  The extent of Windows 95's separation from real-mode DOS is already quite impressive, and Microsoft doesn't need to exaggerate it. Nor, having already advertised that WfW 3.11 contained a significant chunk of the Windows 95 project, should Microsoft now turn around and claim that Windows 95's relationship to DOS marks a significant departure from WfW 3.11. Besides, the experience of WfW 3.11 shows that breaking too many ties with real-mode DOS can produce compatibility problems.

Perhaps all *Microsoft Systems Journal* was trying to say was that Windows 95 keeps some ties to DOS for the sake of old DOS and Win16 software, but DOS is gone if the user runs only Win32 applications. The phrase, "with few exceptions, even existing 16-bit Windows-based applications will follow a protected-mode path" seems to imply that *without* exception Win32 applications will never leave the 32-bit protected-mode path.

However, we'll see shortly (in "The Windows 95 Explorer and DOS" section) that this isn't really true, either. Although Win32 applications *can* bypass DOS to a greater extent than Win16 applications can, the ties are still there. Win32 applications rely on essentially the same small but significant core of real-mode DOS calls that Win16 applications require. There's absolutely nothing wrong with this reliance on a code base that has proven itself on something like 100 million machines, and Microsoft should stop pandering to operating-system purists by claiming that real-mode DOS is gone.

WinWord and DOS

In Figure 12-2, I used WinWord to open and save a large document in WfW 3.11, both with and without 32BFA. I then saved WV86TEST's output to a file and compared the results with *diff*. Unfortunately, I neglected to use V86TEST -FILTER, so those pesky VMPoll broadcasts discussed in Chapter 11 (in the "Windows at Work?" section) show up in the results. However, since we're focusing on INT 21h calls here, it doesn't really matter.


```
< win /D:C (32BFA disabled)
> win (32BFA enabled)

< 62 seconds elapsed
> 42 seconds elapsed

< 41076 calls, 41076 in V86 mode
> 47318 calls, 47318 in V86 mode

< 662 INT 21/2F calls/second
> 1126 INT 21/2F calls/second

< IOPL=0 -- 339 calls
> IOPL=0 -- 403 calls

< IOPL=3 -- 40737 calls
> IOPL=3 -- 46915 calls

< VM #1 -- 41076 calls
> VM #1 -- 47318 calls

INT 21h calls:

< 1A: 28  2A: 14  2C: 16  30: 1   3B: 8   3C: 3   3D: 28  3E: 25  3F: 708
>         2A: 13  2C: 15  30: 1

< 40: 60  41: 2   42: 596 43: 5   44: 42  45: 1   47: 13
>                                         45: 1   47: 3

< 4E: 28  50: 150 55: 1   56: 2   57: 14  59: 1   5B: 2   62: 41  DC: 1
>         50: 150 55: 1           57: 1   59: 1           62: 41  DC: 1

INT 2Fh calls:
< 11: 80  16: 39206
>         16: 47090
```

```
< means without 32BFA
> means with 32BFA
```

```
INT 2Fh AH=16h calls:
< 07: 39206
> 07: 47090

INT 2Fh AX=1607h calls:
< 18: 39206
> 18: 47090
```

Figure 12-2: WinWord File Open/Save, with and without 32BFA.

In Figure 12-2, notice that the same operation took twenty seconds less with 32BFA enabled:

```
< 62 seconds elapsed
> 42 seconds elapsed
```

This 32 percent (20 out of 62) performance improvement is consistent with *InfoWorld*'s findings (August 1994, 1994, p. 66) in an extensive review of peer-to-peer network operating systems: With 32-bit file (32BFA) and disk (32BDA) access enabled, *InfoWorld* saw an improvement of between 30 and 33 percent over WfW 3.11 without 32-bit access. With 32BFA and 32BDA enabled, WfW 3.11 gave better performance than any other peer-to-peer network tested, including Artisoft's LANtastic. (Novell's Personal NetWare came in dead last, taking 2:29 hours to complete a task that WfW 3.11 completed in 1:48 without 32-bit access and 1:23 with 32-bit access; LANtastic took 1:43.)

Figure 12-2 indicates that Windows generated *more* calls to V86 mode with 32BFA enabled, but this is entirely due to the VMPoll VxD broadcasts. With 32BFA, the system evidently goes idle more often. Notice that all calls came from VM #1, indicating that no DOS box was open.

I won't say much about the IOPL=0 counts shown by WV86TEST, since this topic was discussed in Chapter 10 (in the "IOPL and the Interrupt Flag" section). As mentioned there, VMM employs IOPL=0 in V86 mode as part of the Call_When_VM_Ints_Enabled service. This VMM service is used primarily by VPICD to simulate hardware interrupts, such as the timer tick, into a VM. To behave like a genuine hardware PIC and to make VMs look like genuine machines, VPICD must not send an interrupt to a VM that has disabled interrupts. It's easy for VPICD to tell when a VM has disabled interrupts (just check [ebp.Client_FLAGS]), but how can it gain control when the VM decides to reenable interrupts? With Call_When_VM_Ints_Enabled, naturally. By setting IOPL=0, this service causes the CLI instruction to generate a GP fault. When VMM catches this GP fault, it calls VPICD's handler and resets IOPL=3.

By comparing the INT 21h calls logged with and without 32BFA, we can draw up a list of some INT 21h calls that can bypass DOS when 32BFA is enabled:

Function Number	Function
1Ah	Set Disk Transfer Address (DTA)
3Bh	Set Current Directory
3Ch	Create File
3Dh	Open File
3Eh	Close File
3Fh	Read File
40h	Write File
41h	Delete File
42h	Move File Pointer (Lseek)
43h	Get/Set File Attributes
44h	IOCTL
4Eh	Find First File
56h	Rename File
57h	Get/Set File Date/Time
5Bh	Create New File

Notice that these are merely calls for which Windows *can* bypass DOS. The absence of a call from the 32BFA portion of Figure 12-2 is no proof that 32BFA *always* bypasses DOS for that call. For example, if WinWord here had been reading and/or writing to a floppy disk, under WfW 3.11 — which, unlike Windows 95, does not provide 32BFA for floppies — WV86TEST would have shown Windows passing many of the INT 21h file I/O calls down to DOS.

As another example, consider INT 21h function 44h (IOCTL). Although some IOCTL calls such as 4408h (Does Device Use Removable Media?) and 4409h (Is Drive Remote?) can be handled by 32BFA, it seems obvious that there must be *some* driver-specific I/O control calls that Windows passes down to DOS device drivers.

In other words, WV86TEST's output by itself means little. WV86TEST needs to be used in conjunction with some other program, such as WSPY21, that indicates which INT 21h calls have been generated on the Windows side of the fence.

Returning to Figure 12-2, we can see that the following INT 21h calls are at least sometimes passed down to DOS, even with 32BFA:

Function Number	Function
2Ah	Get Date
2Ch	Get Time
30h	Get DOS Version
45h	Duplicate File Handle
47h	Get Current Directory
50h	Set PSP
55h	Create PSP
59h	Get Extended Error Information
62h	Get PSP
DCh	Novell NetWare: Get Connection Number

Figure 12-2 makes an extremely misleading suggestion about the handling of network redirector (INT 2Fh function 11h) calls. Note that WV86TEST shows 80 such calls without 32BFA and no calls with 32BFA. This seems to suggest that 32BFA doesn't pass network redirector calls down to V86 mode. But this is false. Instead, in this particular test, when 32BFA was enabled, no INT 2Fh function 11h calls were generated in the first place. DOS itself usually issues these calls; when 32BFA bypasses DOS, the network redirector calls are also bypassed.

But when 32BFA can't bypass DOS (for example, if you're using a CD-ROM drive managed by MSCDEX under WfW 3.11), Windows will see the network redirector calls generated by MS-DOS and pass them back down to V86 mode.

The Windows 95 Explorer and DOS

Calc, WinHelp, WordPad, and WinWord are all 16-bit Windows (Win16) applications. Because Microsoft seems to imply that Win32 applications *really and truly* break all ties to the real-mode MS-DOS code, I also used WV86TEST with the excellent Find File feature of the Windows 95 Explorer, which is a Win32 application (CAB32.EXE). I shut down every other program except WV86TEST. The Soft-ICE/Windows (WINICE) TASK command confirmed that nothing was running besides WV86-TEST and the standard tasks that are *always* present in Windows 95:

```
:task
TaskName   SS:SP      StackTop  StackBot  StackLow  TaskDB  hQueue  Events
BATMETER   0000:0000  00737000  00740000            1EEE    1EFF    0000
```

```
CAB32     * 0000:0000  00756000  00760000            1296   207F   0000
TIMER       1307:1F88  00B2      201C      201C      132F   12EF   0000
MSGSRV32    13EF:327E  00E2      3314      3078      140F   16AF   0000
WV86TEST    27EF:40F8  222E      4198      360A      0A87   1E6F   0000
KERNEL32    012F:1218  0004FD50  0005FD4F            009F   16AF   0000
```

Of these, BATMETER, CAB32, and KERNEL32 are Win32 tasks, and MSGSRV32 and TIMER are hidden (windowless) Win16 tasks that Windows 95 loads automatically. MSGSRV32 is described in the file MSGSRV32.EXE as the "Windows 32-bit VxD Message Server" and "Microsoft Windows DOS386 WShell Server." TIMER comes from MMTASK.TSK ("Multimedia background task support module").

With V86TEST and WV86TEST loaded, I used the Explorer's file finder (located on the Tools menu) to locate the *.C files on my hard disk that contain the string "foo".

There are 20 such files on my hard disk; to find them, the Explorer must look through about 500 directories and read 840 .C files. WV86-TEST showed how this furious level of activity looked to the real-mode DOS component of Windows 95:

```
136 seconds elapsed
36 calls, 36 in V86 mode
0 INT 21/2F calls/second
IOPL=3 -- 36 calls
VM #1 -- 36 calls

INT 21h calls:
1A: 2   2A: 3   2C: 3   44: 24  4E: 1   50: 1

INT 2Fh calls:
11: 2
```

Before we get upset that a Win32 application under Windows 95 is *still* calling the ostensibly defunct real-mode DOS code ("I'm not dead yet!"), let's first take a moment to note that, in fact, the results shown by WV86TEST are excellent: for a massively disk-intensive operation, real-mode DOS saw almost nothing. This is quite amazing.

Still, despite Microsoft's propaganda, we can see that Chicago (at least in this beta release) continues to use DOS to get the date and time, to manipulate the PSP, and so on.

But there's something interesting here: When the search is completed, if you keep the file finder open on the desktop, do a WV86TEST refresh, and then perform the search again, WV86TEST sees almost no DOS activity:

```
INT 21h calls:
2A: 2   2C: 2   50: 1
```

Wow! And remember that one pair of function 2Ah and 2Ch calls belongs to WV86TEST. Thus, once Explorer had loaded the file finder, it took only three calls to real-mode DOS to look through 500 directories and open 840 files; all the other calls detected by WV86TEST must have occurred when Explorer was loading the file finder.

Furthermore, it turns out that the function 2Ah and 2Ch calls have nothing to do with finding files. If you turn on the CAB32 Show Clock option, when CAB32's TrayClockWClass window receives a WM_TIMER message (which occurs once a minute), CAB32 calls GetLocalTime. As we'll see in Chapter 13 when we examine the Win32 version of Clock, GetLocalTime generates function 2Ah and 2Ch calls that are sent down to real-mode DOS.

What's left, then, is a single function 50h (Set PSP) call while the Explorer plowed through the *.C files on my hard disk.

This is just one single measly DOS call, but trying to uphold Microsoft's "you'll never execute any MS-DOS code" claim in the face of this call is like saying someone is "just a little bit pregnant." In Windows 95, you *will* execute some real-mode MS-DOS code even if you stick to Win32 applications.

PSPs and Other DOS Data in Windows 95

Set PSP is about as close to DOS as you can get. As I probably should have explained earlier, the Program Segment Prefix (PSP) is a DOS data structure whose handle serves as the DOS process ID (PID). The PSP itself is a 100h-byte structure (120h bytes in Windows 95) containing per-application "state" such as the open file handle table and environment segment. Most file I/O operations in DOS must be performed in the context of a particular PSP. MS-DOS has only one current PSP at any given time; programs change it by calling INT 21h function 50h. For example, a DOS TSR that pops up while another program is running must call function 50h to change DOS's PSP before performing any file I/O (see *Undocumented DOS*, 2d ed., pp. 560-561).

It's significant that each Win32 application running in Windows 95 has not only a process ID, one or more thread IDs, and a surrogate Win16 task ID but also a PSP. This is a genuine DOS PSP located in conventional memory (though offset 2Ch does contain a protected-mode selector to the environment segment).

You can see this if you run the WINPSP program from Chapter 13 under Windows 95. There's something a little unusual about that one function 50h (Set PSP) call that V86TEST detected, though. To skip ahead a bit, even though V86TEST sees this call being sent down to real-mode DOS, the WSPY21 program, which hooks INT 21h on the Windows side of the fence, doesn't see anyone generating this call! Figure 12-3 shows what WSPY21 saw from CAB32, in its entirety, during the two minutes it was grinding through my hard disk.

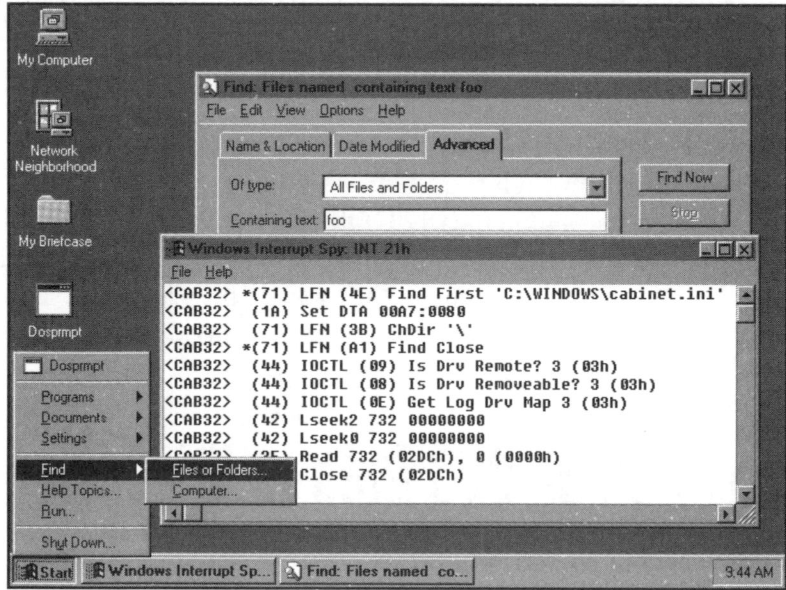

Figure 12-3: WSPY21 shows the INT 21h calls from the Chicago shell that are passed through the Win16 KERNEL.

WSPY21 sees INT 21h calls generated only in a Windows executable or by a Windows DLL on behalf of a Win16 or Win32 executable. If a VxD generates an INT 21h on behalf of a Win16 or Win32 executable, WSPY21 won't see it. This is what happened with the function 50h (Set PSP) call.

The DOSMGR VxD is generating the Set PSP call on CAB32's behalf. Some background information is required to understand why.

Windows Enhanced mode has always given each VM its own separate instance data copy of the DOS Swappable Data Area (SDA), which among other things contains DOS's current PSP variable. (See "DOS Instance Data and the SDA" in Chapter 4.) Thus, even though real-mode DOS is a single-tasking operating system with the notion of only a single current PSP, the miracle of instance data gives each VM its own version of the current PSP.

However, multiple Windows applications, each with their own PSP, all run within the single System VM, and thus all share the single instance data copy of the DOS current PSP variable in the SDA. The single current PSP variable in the System VM is multiplexed among all Win16 and Win32 tasks. Instance data works only on a per-VM basis and so provides no assistance to the multitasking that goes on *within* the System VM. This is typical of the separation between Windows' upper API layer and its lower VxD layer.

In Windows 95, the DOSMGR VxD's handler for protected-mode INT 21h calls does something new: If a protected-mode program is calling INT 21h from the System VM, DOSMGR checks if the caller has a different PSP from the previous caller. If it does, DOSMGR takes whatever INT 21h call the Windows application wanted to make and temporarily turns it into a function 50h Set PSP call! When this returns, DOSMGR switches back to the original INT 21h call and lets it go through. In this way, DOSMGR ensures that the INT 21h call is lined up with the correct PSP. The code is fairly interesting:

```
    CALL    [Simulate_Iret]
    MOVZX   EAX,BYTE PTR [EBP.Client_AH]
    CMP     EAX,+71                        ; max INT 21h function number
    JA      Too_High
    MOVZX   EDX,[Xlat_Script_Type+EAX]
    MOV     EDX,[Xlat_Script_Tab+4*EDX]
    CMP     EBX,[Sys_VM_Handle]      ; INT 21h coming from System VM?
    JNZ     Do_Xlat      ; No: nothing special for prot-mode apps in DOS box
    XOR     ECX,ECX
    CALL    [Begin_Critical_Section]
    PUSH    EAX
    PUSH    ECX
    PUSH    EDX
    MOVZX   ECX,WORD PTR [Prev_PSP]
    JECXZ   PSP_Okay          ; first time through: don't have to switch
    MOV     EDX,[Ptr_This_PSP]
    MOV     DX,[EDX]
    CMP     CX,DX             ; same PSP as last time?
    JZ      PSP_Okay

;;; Previous PM INT 21h caller in System VM (Win app) had
;;; different PSP. So have to switch PSPs.

Switch_PSPs:
    MOV     EAX,00005000         ; Set PSP (21/50)
    XCHG    EAX,[EBP.Client_AX]  ; temp change call into 21/50
    XCHG    EDX,[EBP.Client_BX]  ; put new PSP into BX
    CALL    Nested_V86_INT21     ; call DOS! (see below)
```

```
   XCHG    EDX,[EBP.Client_BX]  ; get back original EBX
   MOV     [Prev_PSP],DX        ; for next time
   MOV     [EBP.Client_EAX],EAX ; restore original 21/XX call

PSP_Okay:                       ; at this point, PSP is okay
   ; ...
   CALL    [V86MMGR_Xlat_API]
   ; ...
   JMP     [End_Critical_Section]

Do_Xlat:
   JMP     [V86MMGR_Xlat_API]

Too_High:
   MOV     EDX,C02C0F70
   JMP     C022016D

Nested_V86_INT21:
   PUSH    EAX
   CALL    [Begin_Nest_V86_Exec]
   MOV     EAX,00000021
   CALL    [Exec_Int]
   CALL    [End_Nest_Exec]
   POP     EAX
   RET
```


In Windows 3.*x*, the KRNL386 Win16 DLL had to do something similar to keep INT 21h calls from Win16 applications from accidentally misusing the PSP of other Win16 applications. KERNEL has its own protected-mode INT 21h handler, which issues a NoHookDOSCall of function 50h during the first INT 21h call following a task switch (see *Undocumented Windows*, pp. 346-347). Why doesn't KERNEL just switch PSPs whenever it switches tasks? Matt Pietrek has a good explanation in *Windows Internals* (p. 422):

> Reschedule() now turns to the task of waking up the incoming task.... Note however that INT 21h function 50h is not invoked to switch what DOS thinks is the current PSP.... Since Windows relies so heavily on the PSP and DOS for file I/O [this was written before WfW 3.11], you might think that it would call DOS to change the current PSP each time a task switch happens. As it turns out, KERNEL delays switching the PSP until it absolutely has to, such as during a file I/O operation. Switching the PSP requires a transition to DOS, a relatively slow process. If the only reason for a particular task switch is to deal with an intertask SendMessage(), it would get expensive. Thus, KERNEL holds out switching the current PSP until it's unavoidable. This causes problems on occasion, as the current PSP in DOS may not match the current TDB in Windows.

So this mechanism has been in place for years as part of KERNEL. Why then does Windows 95 include PSP tracking in DOSMGR instead of just continuing to use the KERNEL code? Because Win32 programs in Windows 95 don't go through KERNEL's INT 21h handler. Win32 applications can't issue direct INT 21h calls and must instead ask the VWIN32 VxD to issue INT 21h for them (see "Win32 File Handles and Thunking" and the WIN32PSP.C example in Chapter 14). Thus the PSP tracking must be located in a VxD.

This PSP-tracking code inside DOSMGR probably explains why WV86TEST sees Windows 95 making heavier use than WfW 3.11 of the Set PSP call. On the other hand, it's important to realize that DOS-MGR does *not* switch PSPs for every single INT 21h call. It does this only for those INT 21h calls that will be sent down to real-mode DOS. That is not a deliberate decision that DOSMGR makes, however. By the time DOSMGR sees an INT 21h call, that call *will* be sent down to real-mode DOS. The reason for this is simple: IFSMgr hooks the V86 INT 21h hook chain *after* DOSMGR, and therefore sees INT 21h calls *before* DOSMGR. When IFSMgr decides to handle a call in protected mode, its INT 21h handler clears the carry flag (CLC) before returning to VMM. As explained in the DDK documentation for Hook_V86_Int_Chain, when a VxD's V86 interrupt hook clears the carry flag, VMM won't pass the interrupt to any other VxDs:

> If the hook procedure services the interrupt, it must clear the carry flag to prevent the system from passing the interrupt to the next hook procedure.

Thus, when IFSMgr decides to handle a call in protected mode, it not only keeps the call away from real-mode DOS but also keeps the call away from any VxDs that installed INT 21h handlers before IFSMgr did. In fact, 32BFA's consumption of INT 21h calls in protected mode and its failure to reflect INT 21h calls to real-mode DOS are really just incidental by-products of IFSMgr's decision not to pass these INT 21h calls onto previously loaded VxDs, such as DOSMGR and VMM, that would reflect the call to real-mode DOS.

Because IFSMgr will have already picked off all INT 21h calls that it intends to service in protected mode, DOSMGR will only do its Set PSP switcheroo for those INT 21h calls that are going down to DOS. In this case, IFSMgr's blockage of INT 21h calls from other VxDs works out well. In other cases, it has produced unintended consequences.

For example, DOSMGR's INT 21h hook also tracks DOS file I/O calls to support the FileSysChange feature in Windows. If FileSys-Change=ON in SYSTEM.INI, DOSMGR broadcasts notifications of file and directory creation, deletion, and so on to the Windows File Manager, or to any other program that has called the FileCdr function (see *Undocumented Windows*, Chapter 4, and WM_FILESYSCHANGE in Chapter 6).

But there's one problem: If 32BFA is enabled, the FileSysChange=ON setting *has no effect* because IFSMgr doesn't pass the relevant INT 21h calls along to the VxDs (such as DOSMGR) that called Hook_V86_Int_Chain before it. The order of VxDs in the V86 interrupt hook chain can make an enormous difference. (It's just like the load-order dependency of DOS TSRs in the early 1980s.) IFSMgr's preemption of FileSysChange is just one of the unintended effects of 32BFA. And 32BFA in turn really is just a side-effect of the ability Hook_V86_Int_Chain functions have to refuse previously-loaded VxDs the right to see interrupts.

But back to the topic of PSPs. Windows 95 has additional mechanisms for manipulating the PSP. Since DOS's implementation of the Get and Set PSP functions are so simple (see *Undocumented DOS*, 2d ed., pp. 287-288), and since it's easy to manipulate DOS variables from a VxD (see CURRDRIV.386 in Chapter 8), it isn't surprising that VMM in Windows 95 provides a Get_Set_Real_DOS_PSP service:

```
Input:
    AX  = PSP (if setting)
    ECX = Ø (Get PSP), 1 (Set PSP)
    EBX = VM handle
VMMcall Get_Set_Real_DOS_PSP
Output:
    (EDX destroyed)
    AX  = PSP (if getting)
```

Although undocumented, this service is heavily used by the VWIN32 VxD. VWIN32 calls VMM's Call_When_Task_Switched service, passing it the address of a function. Whenever VMM switches tasks, it then calls this VWIN32 function, which switches PSPs:

```
CALL_WHEN_TASK_SWITCHED_PROC:           ;; VWIN32+936
    xor ecx, ecx
    VMMcall Get_Sys_VM_Handle  ;; loader turns into mov ebx, [SysVMHandle]!
    VMMcall Get_Set_Real_DOS_PSP
    mov [esi+56h], ax
    mov ax, word ptr [edx+56h]
    mov ecx, 1
    VMMcall Get_Sys_VM_Handle  ;; loader turns into mov ebx, [SysVMHandle]!
    VMMcall Get_Set_Real_DOS_PSP
    ; ...
    VMMcall ContextSwitch       ;; loads CR3 (Page Directory Base register)
```

Get_Set_Real_DOS_PSP doesn't directly manipulate DOS's current-PSP variable, which is located at offset 10h in the SDA. Instead, it manipulates the VM's instance data copy of the SDA. When the VM is next switched in, VMM's page-fault handler copies this instance data — including the current-PSP variable — into low DOS memory. When

Windows 95 swaps contexts, it must keep DOS informed. The DOS SDA was designed for just this sort of thing: building a multitasking operating system on top of a thin layer of single-tasking DOS. As explained in the "DOS Instance Data and the SDA" section of Chapter 4, the DOS SDA and Windows instance data go hand-in-hand.

With Get_Set_Real_DOS_PSP, VMM is supplying 32-bit protected-mode code to indirectly manipulate DOS data. Such manipulation of real-mode DOS data from 32-bit VxD code is a frequent occurrence in Windows 95. For example, during initialization, the Windows 95 IFS-Mgr creates protected-mode pointers to several key DOS internal data structures, including the SDA and SysVars (also known as the "List of Lists"). It is worth examining this grungy undocumented DOS code:

```
        ;;; fragment of Windows 95 IFSMgr initialization

        ;;; Use INT 21h func 34h (Get InDOS flag) to get linear address
        ;;; of DOS SDA. LIN_SDA used all over IFSMgr!
50436       mov byte ptr [ebp.Client_AH],34h
5043A       mov eax,21h
5043F       VMMcall Exec_Int     ;; Call INT 21h func 24h (Get InDOS Flag)
50445       movzx   ecx,word ptr [ebp.Client_ES]
50449       movzx   eax,word ptr [ebp.Client_BX]
5044D       dec eax              ;; InDOS ptr - 1 = SDA ptr!
5044E       shl ecx,4            ;; ECX = InDOS seg << 4 = linear addr DOS data
50451       add eax,ecx          ;; linear addr = (seg << 4) + ofs
50453       mov LIN_SDA,eax      ;; linear SDA (at IFSMgr 39D8h)

        ;;; Now add linear addr DOS data onto some hard-wired offsets
        ;;; (See Undocumented DOS, 2d ed., pp. 730-733)
        ;;; Note that SDA is at DOS+320h
50458       add dword ptr CURR_SFT_PTR,ecx  ; (39DCh = 59Eh)         SDA+27E
5045E       add dword ptr SHARE_NET_PSP_PTR,ecx ; (39E0h = 33Ch)     SDA+1C
50464       add dword ptr FFIRST_SEARCH_ATTR_PTR,ecx ; (39E4 = 56Bh) SDA+24B

        ;;; Get pointer to DOS SysVars ("List of Lists") using
        ;;; undocumented INT 21h function 52h
5046A       mov byte ptr [ebp.Client_AH],52h
5046E       mov eax,21h
50473       VMMcall Exec_Int
50479       movzx   ecx,word ptr [ebp.Client_ES]
5047D       movzx   eax,word ptr [ebp.Client_BX]
50481       shl ecx,4
50484       add eax,ecx      ;; linear addr = (seg << 4) + ofs
50486       mov LIN_SYSVARS,eax

        ;;; Get pointer to DOS's counter for number of System FCBs
5048B       movzx   ecx,word ptr [eax+1Ah]  ;; SYSVARS+1Ah = FCB table seg
5048F       cmp cx,0FFFFh
50493       je  short NO_FCB_TAB
50495       movzx   eax,word ptr [eax+1Ch]  ;; SYSVARS+1Ch = FCB table ofs
50499       shl eax,4
```

```
5049C        add eax,ecx      ;; EAX = linear addr DOS System FCB table
5049E        movzx   eax,word ptr [eax+4]    ;; FCB table + 4 = # files
504A2        mov DOS_FCB_COUNT,eax
```

IFSMgr is using the VMM Exec_Int service to issue an INT 21h function 34h, which returns a pointer to the InDOS flag. This function, crucial for TSR programming, was undocumented until DOS 5.0. Here, IFSMgr is not especially interested in the InDOS flag. Instead, it's relying on the fact that the InDOS flag is located at offset 1 in the SDA. This is an undocumented way to use a documented function (Get InDOS Pointer) to access the SDA, rather than to use the undocumented function 5D06 (Get SDA), which was designed for this purpose. As seen in the preceding code, IFSMgr gets a real-mode pointer to the InDOS flag, backs up one byte, and then, using the standard formula (linear address = (segment * 16) + offset), converts this into a flat, linear, 32-bit, protected-mode pointer to the SDA.

IFSMgr also takes the segment that function 34h returns in ES, multiplies this by 16, and adds the resulting linear address onto a number of variables. These variables already contain hard-wired offsets into the DOS data segment. For example, IFSMgr relies on the fact that SHARE_NET_PSP is at offset 33Ch in the DOS data segment and doesn't care that this is offset 1Ch in the SDA (which starts at offset 320h in the DOS data segment). Because the InDOS flag is located in the DOS data segment, adding the linear address onto these hard-wired offsets produces protected-mode pointers to yet more DOS internal data.

Next, IFSMgr gets a linear pointer to both the SysVars internal DOS data structure and to DOS's count of System FCBs.

Having set up LIN_SDA and the other 32-bit protected-mode pointers to the real-mode DOS data, IFSMgr is now ready to access the DOS data segment whenever it feels like it. These variables are used constantly throughout IFSMgr.

It's easy to see this with the WINICE debugger. WINICE lets you set breakpoints on code execution (using the BPX command), interrupts (BPINT command), I/O port access (BPIO command), and Windows WM_XXX message traffic (BMSG command). It also lets you set a breakpoint that will be triggered just after a memory location or range of memory locations is read or written to (BPM and BPR commands). WINICE uses the 386 debug registers, so these data breakpoints don't slow down the system (much).

In Windows 95 on my machine, INT 21h function 34h returns 00A0:0321, so the SDA is located at 00A0:0320, and IFSMgr's LIN_SDA variable therefore has the value (00A0h * 10h) + (321h - 1) = A00h + 320h = D20h. To set a breakpoint on any access to the first 20h bytes of the SDA, I used the following WINICE command:

```
BPR D20 D40 RW
```

This breakpoint is hit constantly in Windows 95, even when running only Win32 applications such as the Explorer and not running any DOS boxes or Win16 tasks (other than the built-in TIMER and MSGSRV32 Win16 tasks, that is). For example:

```
Break Due to BPR #0030:00000D22 #0030:00000D28 RW C=01
:? ecx
00000D20
: u C025B09C
0028:C025B09C   MOV     BYTE PTR [ECX+03],00
0028:C025B0A0   MOV     WORD PTR [ECX+04],0000
0028:C025B0A6   MOV     BYTE PTR [ECX+07],00
0028:C025B0AA   MOV     BYTE PTR [ECX+06],00
0028:C025B0AE   MOVSX   EAX,WORD PTR [EAX+1A]
```

A few instructions before the breakpoint was hit, IFSMgr had loaded ECX with DWORD PTR [LIN_SDA]. If you consult a listing of the SDA's contents (such as *Undocumented DOS*, 2d ed., pp. 730-733), you'll see that SDA offset 1Ah in the last line of the WINICE disassembly holds the value of AX on a call to INT 21h, and that offsets 3, 4, 6, and 7 in the previous lines all hold DOS error information. In its capacity as protected-mode DOS, IFSMgr is setting these values to 0 to indicate that no error has occurred:

SDA+3	BYTE	Locus of last error
SDA+4	WORD	Extended error code of last error
SDA+6	BYTE	Suggested action for last error
SDA+7	BYTE	Class of last error

Elsewhere in IFSMgr there is code to fill these SDA values with error information:

```
:u c025b07c
0028:C025B07C   MOV     WORD PTR [ECX+04],00EA  ;; extended error
0028:C025B082   MOV     BYTE PTR [ECX+03],03    ;; locus
0028:C025B086   MOV     BYTE PTR [ECX+07],02    ;; class
0028:C025B08A   MOV     BYTE PTR [ECX+06],01    ;; suggested action
```

As another example, IFSMgr also uses LIN_SDA to set and clear the InDOS flag:

```
;;; IFSMgr+5E0
0028:C007363C   MOV     EAX, [C0076A34]     ;; LIN_SDA
```

```
0028:C0073641   INC     BYTE PTR [EAX+01]   ;; InDOS++

;;; IFSMgr+7F0
0028:C007384C   MOV     EAX,[C0076A34]          ;;; LIN_SDA
0028:C0073851   SUB     BYTE PTR [EAX+01],01    ;;; InDOS--
0028:C0073855   ADC     BYTE PTR [EAX+01],00
```

Well, Microsoft said "you'll never execute any MS-DOS code" in Windows 95; it didn't say anything about never touching any DOS *data*. We've just seen that you'll do that too.

CAB32's single Set PSP call revealed that even Win32 applications in Windows 95 end up partying with DOS. Nonetheless, I hope that you're impressed with CAB32's capability to scrounge through my entire hard disk while sending only a single INT 21h call down to real-mode DOS.

Once again, it's also important to see that this capability isn't new. CAB32 won't run under WfW 3.11, but File Manager has a somewhat similar File Search feature. It won't search for the string "foo" but it will find all 840 C files among the 500 directories on my hard disk. When I did this under WfW 3.11 with 32BFA enabled, WV86TEST logged the following results:

```
35 seconds elapsed

INT 21h calls:
2A: 2   2C: 2   50:2
```

By performing the same operation under WfW 3.11 without 32BFA (WIN /D:C), we can see which DOS calls 32BFA must be handling entirely in protected mode. Not surprisingly, File Search consists mostly of calls to functions 1Ah (Set Disk Transfer Area [DTA]), 4Eh (Find First), and 4Fh (Find Next):

```
55 seconds elapsed

11: 1       1A: 1317    2A: 2   2C: 2   3F: 5   42: 4   47: 1
4E: 988     4F: 12590   50:2
```

The difference between 35 and 55 seconds, with and without 32BFA, shows that 32BFA can make it practical to frequently use a feature such as File Search. Even with a 2MB SmartDrv installed but no 32BFA, the same operation took 43 seconds (your mileage will vary). Handling all those DOS calls in protected mode improves performance enormously.

Still, this isn't a fair comparison with CAB32 under Windows 95, since File Manager won't search for strings in files. However, WinWord has a Find File feature that can be used in WfW 3.11 to find all C files with the string "foo", just as I did with CAB32 under Windows 95.

Here's how this looked to WV86TEST:

```
141 seconds

INT 21h calls:
2A: 857      2C: 857      50: 1    57: 160
```

See? There's nothing special about Windows 95's capability to bypass DOS for most operations. That's just standard fare when you have VxDs handling INT 21h calls. True, a lot of WinWord's Get date/time calls to functions 2Ah and 2Ch and Get file date/time/attributes calls to function 57h are being sent down to real-mode DOS. But this is still remarkably little contact with DOS; as usual, we can see just how remarkably little by performing the same operation under WfW 3.11 without 32BFA (WIN/D:C):


```
208 seconds elapsed

INT 21h calls:
1A: 14427   2A: 858      2C: 858      3D: 1689    3E: 1689     3F: 2013
40: 10      42: 4221     44: 6402     47: 160     4E: 2123     4F: 12304
50: 1       57: 1849
```

With 32BFA enabled, almost all of these thousands of INT 21h calls bypassed real-mode DOS, thereby reducing the running time by 32 percent (208 - 141 = 67 / 208 = 32).

To finish up this experiment, we can now take these Win16 applications and run them under Windows 95. Frankly, the results are positively bizarre, and I hope they are just an aberration of the beta version of Chicago I'm using.

Recall that WinFile's File Search took 35 seconds to locate all the C files on my hard disk and used only a few calls to functions 2Ah, 2Ch, and 50h. In contrast, here's what happened when I did same thing with WinFile under Chicago:

```
60 seconds elapsed

INT 21h calls:
2A: 2   2C: 2   4F: 12591      50: 4
```

Weird! We saw that 32BFA in WfW 3.11 could handle function 4Fh in protected mode. Why is Chicago passing all those Find Next (function 4Fh) calls down to real-mode DOS? Whatever the reason, the end result is that the elapsed time is nearly identical to that for WfW 3.11 *without 32BFA*.

Using WinWord's file finder produces similar results in Chicago. Although locating all the C files with the string "foo" took 141 seconds in

WfW 3.11 with 32BFA (and 136 seconds when using CAB32 in Chicago), the time needed to perform this same WinWord operation under Chicago was almost as bad as under WfW 3.11 *without 32BFA*:

```
180 seconds elapsed

1A: 12306    2A: 860     2C: 860    4F: 12306   50: 9   57: 160
```

There's definitely something very odd in how this beta version of Chicago (May 1994) handles functions 1Ah (Set DTA) and 4Fh (Find Next). Nor is this confined to Win16 applications. Using V86TEST -VERBOSE -QUERY, I checked on how DIR *.C /S behaves under Chicago. On my hard disk, it took 66 seconds and sent 39,323 function 4Fh calls down to DOS. In contrast, the same operation under WfW 3.11 with 32BFA took only 38 seconds and sent *no* function 4Fh calls down to DOS.

Even with our earlier knowledge that Windows 95 passes some INT 21h calls down to DOS, there's something wrong here. Certainly, function 4Fh is an odd call because the DTA is an implicit parameter and because until Windows 95 there wasn't a Find Close function. (In Windows 95, it's INT 21h function 71A1h.) But 32BFA in WfW 3.11 managed to avoid passing function 4Fh calls down to DOS. In Windows 95, passing all these calls down to DOS significantly hurts performance.

Win32 FindNextFile Is INT 21h Function 714Fh

No doubt this Find Next performance problem will be fixed by the time you read this. But it still raises an interesting question: Why didn't we see this same performance problem when digging through the hard disk from a Win32 application? Recall that CAB32 performed the same operation (find *.C with "foo") in 136 seconds with no Find Next calls sent down to real-mode DOS; it took 16-bit WinWord running under Windows 95 180 seconds with a whopping 12,306 real-mode Find Next calls and an equal number of Set DTA calls.

That's the magic of 32-bit code, right? Not! The performance difference here has little or nothing to do with the bit orientation of the application. It has to do with the API.

The CAB32 file finder's main loop calls the FindFirstFileA, FindNextFileA, and FindClose Win32 API functions; the trailing *A* indicates that these functions work with ASCII (that is, non-Unicode) strings:

```
#define MAX_PATH        260

typedef struct _WIN32_FIND_DATAA {
    DWORD    dwFileAttributes;
    FILETIME ftCreationTime, ftLastAccessTime, ftLastWriteTime;
    DWORD    nFileSizeHigh, nFileSizeLow;
    DWORD    dwReserved0, dwReserved1;
    CHAR     cFileName[MAX_PATH], cAlternateFileName[14];
} WIN32_FIND_DATAA, *PWIN32_FIND_DATAA, *LPWIN32_FIND_DATAA;

HANDLE WINAPI FindFirstFileA(LPCSTR lpFileName,
    LPWIN32_FIND_DATAA lpFindFileData);
BOOL WINAPI FindNextFileA(HANDLE hFindFile,
    LPWIN32_FIND_DATAA lpFindFileData);
BOOL WINAPI FindClose(HANDLE hFindFile);
```


If you use a debugger such as Soft-ICE/Windows to place a breakpoint on FindNextFileA, you can confirm that the file finder is constantly hitting this function. (Actually, CAB32 is calling the SHELL32 DLL, which in turn is calling the FindNextFileA function in KERNEL32.)

If you peer inside FindNextFileA, you'll see that it consists of some parameter validation and a jump to an internal FindNextFileA function:

```
KERNEL32!FindNextFileA
; ... parameter validation ...
0137:BFF82CE9   JMP     BFF93D23        ; nonvalidation FindNextFileA

:u bff93d23
0137:BFF93D23   PUSH    EBP
0137:BFF93D24   MOV     EBP,ESP
0137:BFF93D26   PUSH    EBX
0137:BFF93D27   PUSH    ESI
0137:BFF93D28   PUSH    EDI
0137:BFF93D29   MOV     EAX,0000714F    ; 714Fh sound familiar?
0137:BFF93D2E   MOV     EBX,[EBP+08]
0137:BFF93D31   MOV     EDI,[EBP+0C]
0137:BFF93D34   XOR     ESI,ESI
0137:BFF93D36   CALL    BFF71E5F        ; where the action is
0137:BFF93D3B   JB      BFF93D4D        ; on error (not shown)
0137:BFF93D3D   MOV     EAX,00000001
0137:BFF93D42   POP     EDI
0137:BFF93D43   POP     ESI
0137:BFF93D44   POP     EBX
0137:BFF93D45   LEAVE
0137:BFF93D46   RET     08
```

Now, obviously the function at BFF71E5Fh must do all the actual work of FindNextFileA. But this function is nothing more than

```
:u bff71e5f
0137:BFF71E5F   PUSH    ECX
0137:BFF71E60   PUSH    EAX
0137:BFF71E61   PUSH    002A0010
```

```
0137:BFF71E66    CALL    KERNEL32!VxDCall0
0137:BFF71E6B    RET
```

I don't want to jump the gun on this VxDCall0 2A0010h code, which is quite important and will be discussed in detail in Chapter 14. However, if you look back at the code for FindNextFileA, you'll notice that just before it calls this VxDCall 2A0010h function, FindNextFileA does a MOV EAX, 714Fh. This number ought to ring a bell.

As noted in Chapter 7, Windows 95 provides INT 21h long filename (LFN) functions. These new functions use AH=71h, with AL equal to the old short-filename INT 21h function number, if there is one. For example, INT 21h function 39h is Create Directory, so INT 21h function 7139h is the new LFN Create Directory function. Likewise, function 4Fh is Find Next File, so 714Fh (the number we see KERNEL32!FindNextFileA moving into AX) is the LFN Find Next File function.

There are also some entirely new functions, such as 71A1h (Find Close) and 71A6h (Get File Info By Handle), and documented equivalents (function 7160h, Get Full Path, and Get Short Path) for a previously undocumented DOS function (function 60h, TRUENAME). For a good description of the INT 21h function 71h interface, see Walter Oney, "Unconstrained Filenames on the PC! Introducing Chicago's Protected Mode Fat File System" (*Microsoft Systems Journal*, August 1994).

On learning of INT 21h function 71h, most programmers assume that these must be DOS wrappers that Microsoft retrofitted around the Win32 API functions. Microsoft's MSDOS.DOC says that the INT 21h functions "match the operations provided by the Win32 file management functions." It's probably a small point, but the relationship between INT 21h function 71h and the Win32 API file-management functions works the other way around: The Win32 functions are wrappers around INT 21h function 71h.

We saw a moment ago that FindNextFileA is nothing more than some parameter validation, some error-handling code, and a VxDCall0 2A0010h with AX=714Fh. We'll see in Chapter 14 that VxDCall0 2A0010h, via a long, circuitous route, eventually ends up at the following code in the VWIN32 VxD:

```
C025250B   MOV     [EDX+1C], EAX        ;; 1Ch = Client_EAX
; ...
C0252515   MOV     EAX,00000021
C025251A   CALL    [Exec_PM_Int]
```

As you might have guessed, VMM's Exec_PM_Int service simulates a protected-mode INT 21h. Thus, FindNextFileA is actually a protected-mode INT 21h function 714Fh call.

I hope I've explained that well enough that you can now see why CAB32's file finder doesn't go down to the real-mode DOS Find Next code: Even though the Win32 file-management APIs are just fancy wrappers around INT 21h calls, real-mode DOS — even DOS 7 in Windows 95 — *doesn't know how to handle function 71h.*

When CAB32 and SHELL32 call FindNextFileA, and FindNextFileA calls VxDCall0, and VxDCall0 eventually calls some code in VWIN32 that calls Exec_PM_Int in VMM, VMM sends an INT 21h to the protected-mode INT 21h chain and, if no one there fully handles the call, to the V86 INT 21h hook chain. The IFSMgr VxD installs INT 21h handlers on both these chains and will see the function 71h call. IFSMgr is the provider of the LFN services in Windows 95 and handles function 71h in protected mode. It wouldn't do IFSMgr any good to pass function 71h down to the real-mode DOS code, which doesn't know anything about long filenames.

The Win32 file-management APIs, then, are just wrappers around IFSMgr services. To access these IFSMgr services, the KERNEL32 DLL in Windows 95 issues (or, rather, uses VxDCall0 to ask VWIN32 and VMM to issue) INT 21h function 71h calls. These might be new DOS functions, but they aren't handled by real-mode DOS. IFSMgr not only provides DOS file I/O in protected mode, but also *extends* the DOS interface with new services.

This explains why neither DOS nor WV86TEST saw CAB32's INT 21h calls: IFSMgr is a protected-mode extension to DOS that takes care of these calls.

We can also now understand why WSPY21 doesn't see CAB32 issuing INT 21h function 714Fh on the Windows side of the fence: CAB32 calls KERNEL32, which uses VxDCall0 to issue the INT 21h. To see these calls, WSPY21 would need to hook VxDCall0. Although this would make an interesting project (an exercise left for you to do in your abundant spare time), it's a lot easier to use the Soft-ICE/Windows debugger to place a breakpoint on VxDCall0.

However, VxDCall0 isn't just for making INT 21h calls. As Chapter 14 explains, 2A0010h is just one service that VxDs provide to Win32 applications. A breakpoint on VxDCall0 will see all sorts of other Win32 service calls (for example, 2A002Eh, 2A0030h, 10011h, and 10013h) that we're not interested in right now.

A better solution is to put a breakpoint on the VWIN32 code shown earlier:

```
C025250B    MOV     [EDX+1C], EAX         ;; good place for breakpoint
; ...
C0252515    MOV     EAX,00000021
C025251A    CALL    [Exec_PM_Int]
```

A debugger breakpoint placed here will see all sorts of INT 21h activity that's hidden both from WSPY21 (because the INT 21h has been issued from a VxD, *below* WSPY21, albeit on behalf of a Win32 application running at more or less the same level as WSPY21) and from WV86TEST (because the call isn't sent down to real-mode DOS but is instead consumed in IFSMgr, which we might as well realize is protected-mode DOS).

For example, while the Explorer file finder is looking for C files containing the string "foo", here are some of the INT 21h calls that show up at C025250Bh in VWIN32. As shown in the table, you can trace backwards to see where these INT 21h calls are coming from.

INT 21h Function	Called from KERNEL323
3Eh (Close File)	CloseHandle, _lclose
3Fh (Read File)	_hread
714Eh (LFN Find First File)	FindFirstFileA
714Fh (LFN Find Next File)	FindNextFileA
716Ch (LFN Create/Open File)	_lopen
71A1h (Find Close)	FindClose
71A7h (DOS Time To File Time)	DosDateTimeToFileTime

I'm a little surprised that when Explorer locates a C file, it doesn't use memory-mapped file I/O to look for the string "foo" (see Chapter 14).

It's also helpful to put a breakpoint on IFSMgr's handler for INT 21h function 71h because this lets us check not only Win32 programs but also any Win16 or DOS programs that are using the new LFN functions.

In the "Getting and Setting the Current Drive" section in Chapter 8, I showed how to examine the INT 21h function tables in the WfW 3.11 version of IFSMgr. The same examination can be done on the Windows 95 version:

```
0028:C0073E9C   MOVZX   ECX,BYTE PTR [EBP+1D]
0028:C0073EA0   CMP     CL,72
; ...
0028:C0073ECF   CALL    [C0073CD4+4*ECX]


C:\UNAUTHW\PROTTAB>prottab c0073cd4 72 4 i21
; ...
C0257E3F    i21_004F
```

```
; ...
C0258164    i21_0071
```

To track all function 71h calls, then, we could put a breakpoint on C0258164h. But the best place to put the breakpoint is a few instructions later, right after the following instruction, where the function 71h handler is examining the subfunction number in the client's AL register:

```
C025816B        MOVZX EAX, BYTE PTR [EBP+1C]        ;; Client_AL
```

Interestingly, IFSMgr turns all 21/71*xx* calls into 21/*xx* calls, with the LFN bit enabled:

```
    C025817A   MOVZX    EDI,AL
    ; ...
    C025818B   MOV      [EBP.Client_AH],AL        ; 21/71XX/BL = 21/XXBL
    C025818E   MOV      AH,[EBP.Client_BL]
    C0258191   MOV      [EBP.Client_AL],AH
    C0258194   MOV      CL,AL
    ; ..
    C0258197   OR       ECX,40000000              ; turn on LFN bit
    ; ...
    C02581B8   CMP      EDI,000000A0
    C02581BE   JB       low_func
high_func:
    C02581C0   CALL     [C0257EC3+4*EDI]          ; table for func >= A0h
    C02581C7   JMP      done
low_func:
    C02581C9   MOVZX    EDI,CL
    C02581CC   CALL     [C0073CD4+4*EDI]          ; back through table again
done:
    C02581D3   RET
```

Thus, IFSMgr will turn a function 714Fh call from CAB32 into a function 4Fh call with the LFN bit set. IFSMgr's function 4Fh handler checks this bit. If this bit is set, IFSMgr handles the call in protected mode, and — in the current implementation — if the bit isn't set, IFSMgr sends the call down to real-mode DOS.

As noted earlier, a breakpoint on IFSMgr's function 71h handler lets us see who, besides Win32 applications, is calling the new LFN functions. For example, the Win16 _lopen function in KERNEL does the following:

```
KERNEL!_lopen:
0117:000093E9   MOV     AX,716C
0117:000093EC   PUSHF
0117:000093ED   PUSH    CS
0117:000093EE   CALL    7F38
```

The function at 0117:7F38 that _lopen is calling is the basis for the old Dos3Call API:

```
:u dos3call
KERNEL!DOS3CALL
0117:000081C3    PUSHF
0117:000081C4    PUSH     CS
0117:000081C5    CALL     7F38
0117:000081C8    RETF
```

When we examine the WSPY21 code later in this chapter, we'll see that the program not only hooks INT 21h in protected mode but also uses an undocumented function, GetSetKernelDOSProc (see *Undocu-mented Windows*, pp. 271-273), to hook this internal function used by Dos3Call. Thus, WSPY21 will see LFN INT 21h calls that come from Win16 KERNEL functions such as _lopen.

However, some of the Win16 function 71h calls seen by the breakpoint at IFSMgr's handler *still* aren't visible to WSPY21. For example:

```
KERNEL!FINDNEXTFILE
0127:00003276    MOV      CX,000C
0127:00003279    JMP      33D4
KERNEL!FINDFIRSTFILE
0127:0000327C    MOV      CX,0010
0127:0000327F    JMP      33D4
```

These are Win16 thunks to the Win32 file-management API and are used, for example, by the Win16 common dialogs (COMMDLG). Chapter 14 discusses these Win16 thunks in detail, but to finish our investigation of Find Next in Windows 95, we need to sneak a brief look here.

As we see, the Win16 versions of FindNextFile and FindFirstFile just move a magic number into CX and then jump to 0127:33D4. When examining the code starting at 0127:33D4, there's a chunk that Soft-ICE/Windows doesn't unassemble properly:

```
0127:000033E6 66EA7E21F7BF        JMP      BFF7:217E
0127:000033EC 37                   AAA
0127:000033ED 0100                 ADD      [BX+SI],AX
```

This 66 EA is 32-bit code on the Win16 side of a thunk; EAh is the opcode for JMP, and 66h is an override that turns it into a 48-bit far jump. Executing this one instruction thunks up from the Win16 KERNEL to Win32 KERNEL32:

```
0127:000033E6 66EA7E21F7BF3701  JMP      0137:BFF7217E

0137:BFF7217E 1E                   PUSH     DS
0137:BFF7217F 57                   PUSH     EDI
; ...
; Use CX to index into table, etc.
; ...
0137:BFF9118A E88F12FEFF          CALL     KERNEL32!MapSLFix
; ...
```

```
0137:BFF9118F 50              PUSH    EAX
0137:BFF91190 FF731A          PUSH    DWORD PTR [EBX+1A]
0137:BFF91193 E88B2B0000      CALL    BFF93D23
; ...
0137:BFF911A1 E89B12FEFF      CALL    KERNEL32!UnMapSLFixArray
```

That function BFF93D23h is the workhorse here. You might recall that earlier we saw that FindNextFileA consisted of

```
KERNEL32!FindNextFileA
; ... parameter validation ...
0137:BFF82CE9   JMP     BFF93D23
```


Thus, KERNEL!FindNextFile thunks up to KERNEL32!FindNextFileA, which, as we saw, in turn does an INT 21h function 714Fh via VxDCall0.

So, Explorer's FindNextFileA calls don't end up at real-mode DOS because FindNextFileA calls function 714Fh, not function 4Fh. It's not clear why IFSMgr in Windows 95 is currently passing function 4Fh down to real-mode DOS, but at any rate if a DOS or Win16 program called function 714Fh, either directly or via the FindNextFile thunk in KERNEL, this wouldn't turn into a real-mode DOS call.

There are several reasons why DOS or Win16 applications might use the LFN functions. One reason is to access files and directories with long names. Another reason is that the new function 71h calls are often cleaner than their predecessors. For example, calling the LFN find first/next functions no longer requires getting and setting the DTA. As we saw earlier, IFSMgr internally accesses the DTA, along with all the other real-mode DOS data structures that it accesses, but at least this DTA usage is no longer in your face.

Performance is another reason to consider using the LFN functions. I hope the poor performance we've seen with INT 21h function 4Fh is just a pre-release aberration, but in general the LFN functions are attractive because they *can't* be passed down to real-mode DOS. (Unless some third-party vendor decides to do an LFN TSR for DOS 7.)

To measure the performance of an LFN Find First/Next, in contrast to an old-style Find First/Next, I've written a small DOS program that can be compiled to use either the new or old functions. MYDIR.C (Listing 12-1) simply walks the entire disk with Find First/Next calls. If compiled with -DLFN, the program (which is then called LFNDIR) uses functions 714Eh, 714Fh, and 71A1h. If compiled without the -DLFN option, the program (which is then called DOSDIR) uses the C run-time functions _dos_findfirst and _dos_findnext, which in turn generally call functions 1Ah (Set DTA), 2Fh (Get DTA), 4Eh (Find First), and 4Fh (Find Next).

Listing 12-1: MYDIR.C

```
/*
MYDIR.C
bcc -edosdir.exe mydir.c
bcc -DLFN -elfndir.exe mydir.c
*/

#include <stdlib.h>
#include <stdio.h>
#include <string.h>
#include <ctype.h>
#include <io.h>
#include <fcntl.h>
#include <share.h>
#include <dos.h>
#include <time.h>

typedef unsigned char BYTE;
typedef unsigned short WORD;
typedef unsigned long DWORD;
typedef unsigned short HANDLE;
typedef int BOOL;

#ifdef LFN
#define MAX_PATH        260

typedef struct {
    DWORD dwLowDateTime, dwHighDateTime;
} FILETIME;

// changed some field names so can use WIN32_FIND_DATA instead of find_t,
// without ifdef LFN all over the place

typedef struct {
    DWORD    attrib;
    FILETIME ftCreationTime, ftLastAccessTime, ftLastWriteTime;
    DWORD    nFileSizeHigh, nFileSizeLow;
    DWORD    dwReserved0, dwReserved1;
    BYTE     name[MAX_PATH], cAlternateFileName[14];
} WIN32_FIND_DATA;

#define DATETIME_DOS             1

HANDLE FindFirstFile(char far *Name, WIN32_FIND_DATA far *Result,
    WORD Attributes, WORD DateTimeFormat)
{
    HANDLE Handle;
    WORD ConversionCode;            // not used
    _asm {
        push si
        push di
        push ds
        mov ax, 714Eh               // Find First File
```

```
        mov cx, Attributes        // file attributes
        lds dx, dword ptr Name
        les di, dword ptr Result
        mov si, DateTimeFormat    // format for returned date and time
        int 21h
        pop ds
        pop di
        pop si
        jc  error
        mov [Handle], ax          // search handle for Find Next, Close
        mov [ConversionCode], cx  // UNICODE to OEM/ANSI conversion ok?
    }
    return Handle;
error:
    return 0;
}

BOOL FindNextFile(HANDLE Handle, WIN32_FIND_DATA far *Result,
    WORD DateTimeFormat)
{
    WORD ConversionCode;          // not used
    _asm {
        push si
        push di
        push ds
        mov ax, 714Fh             // Find Next File
        mov bx, Handle            // search handle from Find First
        les di, dword ptr Result
        mov si, DateTimeFormat    // format for returned date and time
        int 21h
        pop ds
        pop di
        pop si
        jc error
        mov [ConversionCode], cx  // UNICODE to OEM/ANSI conversion ok?
        }
    return 1;
error:
    return 0;
}

BOOL FindClose(HANDLE Handle)
{
    _asm {
        mov ax, 71A1h   // Find Close
        mov bx, Handle  // search handle from Find First
        int 21h
        jc  error
        }
    return 1;
error:
    return 0;
}
#endif
```

```
#ifdef LFN
#define FIND_DATA   WIN32_FIND_DATA
#else
#define FIND_DATA   struct find_t
#endif


void fail(const char *s) { puts(s); exit(1); }

void do_filename(int dirpos, const char *dir, FIND_DATA *pinfo);
void do_directory(int dirpos, const char *s);

static char dirname[2048] = {0};

static unsigned long ffirst = 0, fnext = 0;

#define PRINT_IT        0       // can turn on to print filenames

main(int argc, char *argv[])
{
    clock_t c1, c2;

    c1 = clock();
    do_directory(0, (argc < 2) ? "C:" : argv[1]);
    c2 = clock();

    printf("Find First calls: %lu\n", ffirst);
    printf("Find Next calls:  %lu\n", fnext);
    printf("Clocks:           %lu\n", c2 - c1);
    printf("Calls/Clock:      %lu\n", (ffirst + fnext) / (c2 - c1));
    return 0;
}

void do_directory(int dirpos, const char *s)
{
    struct find_t info;
    int prev_dirpos;
    char *s2 = (char *) malloc(2048);
    if (! s2) fail("Insufficient memory");

    if ((prev_dirpos = dirpos) == 0)
        strcpy(dirname, s);
    else
    {
        strcat(dirname, "\\");
        strcat(dirname, s);
    }
    dirpos = strlen(dirname);

    strcpy(s2, dirname);
    strcat(s2, "\\*.*");

    #define ATTRIB (_A_NORMAL | _A_SUBDIR | _A_RDONLY)
```

```
#ifdef LFN
{
    HANDLE h;
    FIND_DATA info;
    ffirst++;
    if ((h = FindFirstFile(s2, &info, ATTRIB, DATETIME_DOS)) == 0)
        return;
    do_filename(dirpos, dirname, &info);
    while (FindNextFile(h, &info, DATETIME_DOS))
    {
        fnext++;
        do_filename(dirpos, dirname, &info);
    }
    FindClose(h);
}
#else
    ffirst++;
    if (_dos_findfirst(s2, ATTRIB, &info) != 0)
        return;
    do_filename(dirpos, dirname, &info);
    while (_dos_findnext(&info) == 0)
    {
        fnext++;
        do_filename(dirpos, dirname, &info);
    }
#endif

    dirname[prev_dirpos] = '\0';
    free(s2);
}

void do_filename(int dirpos, const char *dir, FIND_DATA *pinfo)
{
    if (pinfo->attrib & FA_DIREC)
    {
        if (pinfo->name[0] != '.')
            do_directory(dirpos, pinfo->name);
    }
    else if (PRINT_IT)
        printf("%s\\%s\n", dir, pinfo->name);
}
```

I used DOSDIR and LFNDIR to test all the standard environments. (The functions used by LFNDIR are available only in Windows 95.) In all cases, the program logged 494 Find First Calls (I didn't create any new subdirectories while running the tests) and between 11,311 and 11,319 Find Next calls (I must have created a few new files during the test). For each environment, I ran the programs twice to include any cache effect.

Table 12-2 summarizes the results of this test. The Clocks column shows the time (in standard 55 millisecond clocks) for each run, plus the combined time for the two runs.

Table 12-2: Walking a Directory Structure

Configuration	Clocks	Calls/Clock	Seconds
Real-mode MS-DOS	659+654=1313	17	72
SmartDrv	548+513=1061	21	58
WfW 3.11 32BFA	538+82=620	36	34
Chicago DOSDIR	953+409=1362	17	74
Chicago LFNDIR	699+216=915	24	50

Just to be compulsive, I used V86TEST to see what real-mode DOS activity LFNDIR was generating in Windows 95. There was almost no such activity, showing once again that even real-mode DOS programs don't necessarily require real-mode DOS:

```
VM #2 -- 121 calls

INT 21h calls:
19: 5   1A: 2   25: 16  29: 6   2A: 1   2C: 1   30: 2   35: 8   38: 2
3E: 30  40: 10  44: 3   48: 4   49: 2   4A: 2   4B: 2   4C: 2   4D: 2
```

In contrast, DOSDIR hits DOS plenty of times under Windows 95:

```
VM #2 -- 48879 calls

INT 21h calls:
19: 5   1A: 24628   25: 16  29: 6   2A: 1   2C: 1   2F: 12313   30: 2
35: 8   38: 2   3E: 30  40: 10  44: 3   48: 4   49: 2   4A: 2   4B: 2
4C: 2   4D: 2   4F: 11819
```

Since DOSDIR and LFNDIR are essentially the same program, the difference between 74 seconds for DOSDIR and 50 seconds for LFNDIR gives some idea of the true cost of a real-mode DOS call. Or perhaps this is just Microsoft's subtle way of getting programmers to use Win32 or the new DOS LFN services.

At the same time, WfW 3.11 comes out as the clear winner here: DOSDIR ran significantly faster under WfW's 32BFA than even LFNDIR did under Chicago's. Of course, it's important to remember that Chicago is still in beta and that the final Windows 95 may well perform better than this.

Still, even this beta aberration tells us something: The idea that Windows 95 "breaks all ties with the real-mode MS-DOS code" is almost meaningless, because breaking ties with MS-DOS is done on a case-by-case, function-by-function basis. If one day the very last INT 21h call that used to be shipped down to real-mode DOS is finally handled by a protected-mode VxD, would that constitute a qualitative transformation in

Windows? No. The real transformation took place years ago, when Ralph Lipe, Aaron Reynolds, and others were writing VMM and giving it functions such as Hook_V86_Int_Chain. Everything you need to know about Windows' relationship to DOS, you can learn by reading and re-reading that one sentence quoted earlier from the DDK documentation for Hook_V86_Int_Chain: "If the hook procedure [such as IFSMgr's INT 21h handler] services the interrupt, it must clear the carry flag to prevent the system from passing the interrupt to the next hook procedure."

The WV86TEST Code

Having spent some time examining WV86TEST's output, we should now look at how the program produces this output. Listing 12-2 shows the source code for WV86TEST, which uses the WINIO library (provided on the disk). WINIO lets Windows applications use C stdio functions such as printf and provides functions such as winio_setmenufunc and wmhandler_set, which make it easy to create menus and handle messages. To retrieve statistics from the resident DOS version of V86TEST, WV86TEST uses the real_int86x and map_real functions from the PROT library (also on the disk).

WV86TEST has a .DEF file containing the following statement:

```
STUB 'v86test.exe'
```

This binds the DOS and Windows versions together in a single executable. There's a lot more that could be accomplished with this: V86-TEST could hook INT 2Fh function 160Bh (TSR Identify) and tell Windows to automatically start WV86TEST; this is what the COUNT-DOS program discussed in Chapter 3 does. Conversely, if WV86TEST finds that V86TEST isn't resident (the get_stats function fails), WV86-TEST could use the Windows API functions ExitWindows(EW_RESTARTWINDOWS) and ExitWindowsExec to give the user the option of restarting Windows under V86TEST. These exercises are left for you to pursue in your free time.

Listing 12-2: WV86TEST.C

```
/*
WV86TEST.C -- take over INT 21h and INT 2Fh, count calls in V86 mode
winiobc wv86test prot
Uses wv86test.def with STUB '\unauthw\v86test\v86test.exe'
*/

#include <stdlib.h>
```

```
#include <stddef.h>
#include <string.h>
#include <ctype.h>
#include <process.h>
#include <time.h>
#include <dos.h>
#include "windows.h"
#include "winio.h"
#include "wmhandlr.h"
#include "prot.h"

typedef unsigned short WORD;
typedef unsigned long DWORD;

#define VM_MAX      8
#define VM_OTHER    VM_MAX

#define GET_STATS   0x0FFFF
#define SIGNATURE   "V86TEST"

#define VXD_MAX     0x100
#define VXD_OTHER   VXD_MAX

typedef enum {
    NO_WIN,
    WIN_INIT_BEGIN,             // got WIN_INIT_NOTIFY
    WIN_INIT_DONE,              // got WIN_INIT_COMPLETE
    WIN_FINI_BEGIN,             // got WIN_EXIT_BEGIN
    WIN_FINI_DONE,              // got WIN_EXIT_NOTIFY
    NUM_STATES
    } STATE;

static char *state_str[NUM_STATES] = {
    "Before Windows started",
    "During Windows init",      // got WIN_INIT_NOTIFY
    "While Windows running",    // got WIN_INIT_COMPLETE
    "During Windows exit",      // got WIN_EXIT_BEGIN
    "After Windows exited",     // got WIN_EXIT_NOTIFY
    } ;

#pragma pack(1)

typedef struct {
    char signature[8];
    DWORD calls[NUM_STATES], v86_calls[NUM_STATES];
    DWORD iopl_count[4];
    DWORD vm[VM_MAX+1];
    DWORD int21[0x100];
    DWORD int2f[0x100], int2f16[0x100], int2f1607[VXD_OTHER+1];
    time_t start, end;
    } STATS;

static STATE state = NO_WIN;
static BOOL display_changes = 0;
static BOOL do_auto_refresh = 0;
```

```
static UINT htimer = 0;
static STATS far *fp;
static STATS *stats;
static HMENU gmenu;

/*********************************************************************/

void display_results(STATS far *fp2)
{
    STATS *fp = stats;
    STATS *delta;
    DWORD elapsed;
    int i;

    if (display_changes)
    {
        if (! (delta = malloc(sizeof(STATS))))
            fail("Insufficient memory");

        // Show changes: first copy the new stats over to delta
        _fmemcpy(delta, fp2, sizeof(STATS));

        // Then subtract the previous stats to get changes
        time(&delta->end);
        elapsed = delta->end - fp->end;
        delta->calls[WIN_INIT_DONE] -= fp->calls[WIN_INIT_DONE];
        delta->v86_calls[WIN_INIT_DONE] -= fp->v86_calls[WIN_INIT_DONE];
        printf("%lu seconds elapsed\n", elapsed);
        printf("%lu calls, %lu in V86 mode\n",
            delta->calls[WIN_INIT_DONE], delta->v86_calls[WIN_INIT_DONE]);
        if (elapsed)
            printf("%lu INT 21/2F calls/second\n",
                delta->calls[WIN_INIT_DONE] / elapsed);

        for (i=0; i<4; i++)
        {
            delta->iopl_count[i] -= fp->iopl_count[i];
            delta->vm[i] -= fp->vm[i];
        }
        delta->vm[VM_OTHER] -= fp->vm[VM_OTHER];
        for (i=0; i<0x100; i++)
        {
            delta->int21[i] -= fp->int21[i];
            delta->int2f[i] -= fp->int2f[i];
            delta->int2f16[i] -= fp->int2f16[i];
        }
        for (i=0; i<=VXD_MAX; i++)  // get VXD_OTHER too
            delta->int2f1607[i] -= fp->int2f1607[i];
        fp = delta; // have display_results work on delta
    }
    else
    {
        _fmemcpy(fp, fp2, sizeof(STATS));

        for (i=NO_WIN; i<NUM_STATES; i++)
```

```
            printf("%s:\t%lu INT 21/2F calls, %lu in V86 mode\n",
                state_str[i], fp->calls[i], fp->v86_calls[i]);

        printf("\nWhile Windows running:\n");
        time(&fp->end);
        if (! fp->start) time(&fp->start);
        if ((elapsed = fp->end - fp->start) != 0)
        {
            printf("Windows active for %lu seconds\n", elapsed);
            printf("%lu INT 21/2F calls/second\n",
                fp->calls[WIN_INIT_DONE] / elapsed);
        }
    }

    for (i=0; i<4; i++)
        if (fp->iopl_count[i])
            printf("IOPL=%d -- %lu calls\n", i, fp->iopl_count[i]);

    for (i=0; i<VM_MAX; i++)
        if (fp->vm[i])
            printf("VM #%d -- %lu calls\n", i, fp->vm[i]);
    if (fp->vm[VM_OTHER])
        printf("VM > #%d -- %lu calls\n", VM_MAX, fp->vm[VM_OTHER]);

    #define PRINT_CALLS(s, fp) { \
        DWORD *p; \
        printf("\n%s:\n", (s)); \
        for (i=0, p=fp; i<0x100; i++, p++) \
            if (*p) \
                printf("%02X: %lu\t", i, *p); \
        }

    PRINT_CALLS("INT 21h calls", fp->int21);
    PRINT_CALLS("\nINT 2Fh calls", fp->int2f);
    PRINT_CALLS("\nINT 2Fh AH=16h calls", fp->int2f16);
    PRINT_CALLS("\nINT 2Fh AX=1607h calls", fp->int2f1607);

    if (fp->int2f1607[VXD_OTHER])
        printf("VxD>#%04X: %lu\n", VXD_MAX, fp->int2f1607[VXD_OTHER]);

    printf("\n\n");

    _fmemcpy(stats, fp2, sizeof(STATS));
    time(&stats->end);
    if (display_changes) free(delta);
}

/***********************************************************************/

STATS far *get_stats(void)  // call resident copy of V86TEST
{
    union REGS r;
    struct SREGS s;
    STATS far *fp;
    r.x.ax = GET_STATS;
```

```
    memset(&s, 0, sizeof(s));
    real_int86x(0x2f, &r, &r, &s);      // real_int86x in PROT.C
    if (s.es == 0)
        return 0;
    fp = MK_FP(s.es, r.x.bx);
    if ((fp = map_real(fp, sizeof(STATS))) == 0)   // map_real in PROT.C
        return 0;
    return (_fstrcmp(fp->signature, SIGNATURE) == 0) ? fp : 0;
}

void free_stats(HWND hwnd) { free_mapped_linear(fp); }

/*********************************************************************/

/* MENU HANDLERS (see MK_MENU in main) */

void refresh(HWND hwnd, int wID)
{
    winio_clear(hwnd);
    display_results(fp);
}

void clear(HWND hwnd, int wID) { _fmemset(fp, 0, sizeof(STATS)); }

void show_changes(HWND hwnd, int wID)
{
    CheckMenuItem(gmenu, 3, display_changes ? MF_UNCHECKED : MF_CHECKED);
    display_changes = ! display_changes;
    refresh(hwnd, wID);
}

long on_time(HWND hwnd, unsigned message, WORD wParam, LONG lParam)
{
    winio_clear(hwnd);
    display_results(fp);
}

void auto_refresh(HWND hwnd, int wID)
{
    if (do_auto_refresh)    // on, turn off
    {
        do_auto_refresh = 0;
        KillTimer(hwnd, htimer);
        CheckMenuItem(gmenu, 4, MF_UNCHECKED);
    }
    else    // off, turn on
    {
        do_auto_refresh = 1;
        wmhandler_set(hwnd, WM_TIMER, on_time);
        if (! (htimer = SetTimer(hwnd, 1, 5000, NULL))) // every 5 seconds
            fail("Can't create timer");
        CheckMenuItem(gmenu, 4, MF_CHECKED);
    }
}

/*********************************************************************/
```

```
main(int argc, char *argv[])
{
    HWND hwnd;
    int i;

    // only one instance: should put INT handler in DLL
    if (__hPrevInst)
        fail("WV86TEST already running");

    hwnd = winio_current();
    gmenu = CreateMenu();   // global
    #define MK_MENU(id, str, func) { \
        AppendMenu(gmenu, MF_STRING | MF_ENABLED, id, str); \
        winio_setmenufunc(hwnd, id, func); \
        }
    MK_MENU(1, "&Refresh", refresh);
    MK_MENU(2, "&Clear", clear);
    MK_MENU(3, "&Show Changes", show_changes);
    MK_MENU(4, "&Auto-Refresh", auto_refresh);
    InsertMenu(winio_hmenumain(hwnd), 1,
        MF_STRING | MF_POPUP | MF_BYPOSITION, gmenu, "&Test");
    DrawMenuBar(hwnd);

    if (! (fp = get_stats()))
    {
        // Instead of failing, could do ExitWindowsExec of
        // V86TEST and then ExitWindows(EW_RESTARTWINDOWS).
        fail("Can't get V86TEST statistics");
    }
    winio_onclose(hwnd, free_stats);

    if (! (stats = malloc(sizeof(STATS))))
        fail("Insufficient memory");
    display_results(fp);

    return 0;
}
```

In WV86TEST.C, main (WINIO lets Windows programs use a standard main function rather than the odd WinMain proposed by the Windows SDK) installs some menu handlers, using a MK_MENU macro that calls AppendMenu and winio_setmenufunc. For example, MK_MENU(1, "&Refresh", refresh) means that, when a user selects Refresh from the WV86TEST menu, WINIO's WM_COMMAND handler will call a function named refresh.

As noted earlier, WV86TEST gets a protected-mode pointer to the V86TEST statistics via the real_int86x and map_real functions from the PROT library on the disk. These functions in turn rely on DPMI INT 31h function 0300h (Simulate Real-Mode Interrupt) and on the Windows API functions AllocSelector, SetSelectorBase, and SetSelectorLimit.

WV86TEST uses winio_onclose to install a handler that, just before the program exits, frees up the selector used for the mapped-in statistics.

The workhorse of WV86TEST is display_results, which is called from each of the menu-handling functions. This normally just copies the mapped-in statistics to a local buffer and displays the statistics using WINIO's printf function. WV86TEST first copies the statistics, rather than work off the mapped-in "live" ones belonging to V86TEST, so that the statistics don't change out from under the program if more DOS calls are generated in the middle of display_results.

If the user selects the Show Changes menu item, WV86TEST sets the display_changes variable. If this variable is set, the display_results function copies the statistics to a "delta" buffer, from which it subtracts the previously-refreshed statistics, and then it proceeds to display this delta buffer.

The Auto Refresh menu item installs a timer, using the Windows SetTimer function. Every five seconds (assuming no one has reprogrammed the timer), the timer goes off, and the WMHANDLER module of WINIO calls WV86TEST's on_time function, which WV86TEST installed with wmhandler_set. The on_time function simply calls winio_clear and display_results, thereby refreshing the WV86TEST display every five seconds.

Windows 95 and Protected-Mode DOS

Here's what we've learned so far:

- In Windows 95, non-file INT 21h calls from Win32, Win16, and DOS applications are sent down to real-mode DOS. Windows 95 doesn't break "all ties with the real-mode MS-DOS code."
- Windows 95 also doesn't break all (or even many) ties with the real-mode DOS data. Windows 95 relies heavily on real-mode DOS data structures such as the SDA, PSP, and DTA. However, IFSMgr does access this data directly from protected mode.
- Windows 95 relies heavily on INT 21h calls, though usually these calls are serviced by IFSMgr in 32-bit protected mode. Although it isn't true that Windows 95 "breaks all ties with the real-mode MS-DOS code," it is true that protected-mode MS-DOS is here to stay. In Windows 95, you're running a protected-mode version of MS-DOS that uses the real-mode DOS code and data as a subservient assistant.

- To the large extent that Windows 95 is *not* dependent on real-mode DOS, though, the same is true of WfW 3.11. If anything, WfW is less dependent on DOS than is Windows 95. WfW's hostility to real-mode DOS caused problems in some areas, so Windows 95 backs off a bit from this aggressive stance.
- Programs that use the Win32 API or the DOS LFN services can bypass DOS to a significantly greater extent than programs that stick to the old DOS APIs. In addition to the Win32 file-management API's bypassing of real-mode DOS code (but not, as we saw, of INT 21h services), we'll also see in "Executable Loading and Memory-Mapped Files" in Chapter 14 that Win32 applications can bypass both the real-mode DOS code and protected-mode INT 21h by using memory-mapped files. But even Win32 programs continue to implicitly use real-mode DOS data structures such as the SDA, PSP, and DTA.
- Win16 programs and DLLs that avoided direct use of INT 21h or Dos3Call and instead used Windows API functions such as _lopen or higher-level services such as the GetOpenFileName and GetSaveFileName common dialogs will end up using the new LFN services.

Notice that while we're discussing Windows-DOS relations in general, the subject of how Win32 applications relate to DOS keeps coming up. This in turn takes us into the subject of how the Win32 and Win16 components of Windows 95, particularly the Win32 and Win16 kernels (KERNEL32.DLL and KRNL386.EXE, respectively), relate to each other. This subject is discussed in detail in the next two chapters.

Chapter 13

Thunk! Kernel32 Calls KRNL386

The WV86TEST program in the previous chapter was a big improvement (if I do say so myself) over the plain real-mode DOS-based V86TEST from Chapter 10. WV86TEST provides some real insights into how Windows and Win32 applications interact with real-mode DOS.

However, as I pointed out earlier, WV86TEST by itself doesn't tell you much about those INT 21h calls that are absorbed inside protected-mode Windows rather than passed down to real-mode DOS. The problem is that WV86TEST doesn't know anything about which INT 21h calls protected-mode Windows applications and DLLs are generating in the first place.

This chapter presents WSPY21, a Windows program that hooks INT 21h inside protected-mode Windows rather than down in V86 mode DOS. For example, Figure 13-1 shows WSPY21 logging some INT 21h calls made by the Windows 95 Explorer (which here happens to launch a Windows application with a long filename, contained in a folder with a long directory name).

Because WSPY21 hooks INT 21h on the Windows side of the fence, the program can display the DOS calls that a Windows application makes, or which a DLL is making on the application's behalf. In contrast, V86TEST and WV86TEST were oblivious to any INT 21h calls that Windows didn't send down to real-mode DOS, and had no idea which part of Windows an INT 21h call was coming from.

For example, since 32-bit file access in WfW 3.11 and Windows 95 absorbs most INT 21h file calls, V86TEST and WV86TEST wouldn't see any of the following randomly selected calls logged by WSPY21:

```
<WINWORD>  (4E) Find First '\\PROGPRESS1\EDIT\IDGREPOR\PP_MTM\*.txt'
<WINWORD>  (4E) Find First '\\PROGPRESS1\EDIT\INTERNET\DUMMIES\*.txt'
<WINWORD>  (3D) Open 'C:\WINDOWS\SYSTEM\COMPOBJ.DLL'
<WINWORD>  (3D) Open 'C:\WINDOWS\SYSTEM\OLE2.DLL'
<WINWORD>  (3D) Open 'C:\WINDOWS\SYSTEM\STORAGE.DLL'
<WINWORD>  (3D) Open 'C:\WINDOWS\SYSTEM\OLE2DISP.DLL'
<PROGMAN>  (3B) ChDir '\MSOFFICE'
<PROGMAN>  (3D) Open 'C:\WINDOWS\SYSTEM\CTL3DV2.DLL'
<PROGMAN>  (3D) Open 'C:\WINDOWS\SYSTEM\MSFFILE.DLL'
<PROGMAN>  (3D) Open 'C:\WINDOWS\SYSTEM\SDM.DLL'
<PROGMAN> *(4B) Exec 'C:\MSOFFICE\MSOFFICE.EXE'
<MSOFFICE>  (3D) Open 'C:\WINDOWS\MSOFFICE.INI'
<MSOFFICE>  (43) Get/Set File Attr 'C:\WINWORD\WINWORD.EXE'
<MSOFFICE>  (43) Get/Set File Attr 'C:\EXCEL\EXCEL.EXE'
<MSOFFICE>  (43) Get/Set File Attr 'C:\POWERPNT\POWERPNT.EXE'
<MSOFFICE>  (43) Get/Set File Attr 'C:\ACCESS\msaccess.exe'
<MSOFFICE>  (43) Get/Set File Attr 'C:\WINDOWS\MSMAIL.EXE'
<MSOFFICE>  (3D) Open 'C:\WINDOWS\SYSTEM\AB.DLL'
<MSOFFICE>  (3D) Open 'C:\WINDOWS\SYSTEM\FRAMEWRK.DLL'
<MSOFFICE>  (3D) Open 'C:\WINDOWS\SYSTEM\DEMILAYR.DLL'
<MSOFFICE>  (3D) Open 'C:\WINDOWS\SYSTEM\MAILMGR.DLL'
<MSOFFICE>  (3D) Open 'C:\WINDOWS\SYSTEM\STORE.DLL'
<MSOFFICE>  (3D) Open 'C:\WINDOWS\SYSTEM\OLECLI.DLL'
<MSMAIL>  (3D) Open 'C:\WINDOWS\WGPOMGR.DLL'
<MSMAIL>  (3D) Open 'C:\WINDOWS\SYSTEM\VFORMS.DLL'
<MAILSPL> *(4E) Find First 'C:\WINDOWS\MSMAIL.INI'
<MAILSPL>  (3D) Open 'C:\WINDOWS\SYSTEM\MSSFS.DLL'
<MAILSPL>  (3D) Open 'C:\WINDOWS\SYSTEM\PABNSP.DLL'
<MSOFFICE>  (3D) Open 'C:\WINDOWS\SYSTEM\TOOLHELP.DLL'
<MSOFFICE>  (3D) Open 'C:\WINWORD\WWINTL.DLL'
<MSOFFICE>  (3D) Open 'C:\WINDOWS\SYSTEM\OLE2.DLL'
<MSOFFICE>  (3D) Open 'C:\WINDOWS\SYSTEM\OLE2NLS.DLL'
<EXCEL>  (4E) Find First '{00020841-0000-0000-C000-000000000046}'
<EXCEL>  (3D) Open 'C:\WINDOWS\SYSTEM\256_1024.DRV'
<EXCEL>  (4E) Find First '\\PROGPRESS1\EDIT\FOOBISH.XLS'
<EXCEL>  (3D) Open 'C:\WINDOWS\SYSTEM\NETAPI.DLL'
```


Using WSPY21, this chapter and the next will examine the INT 21h activity (which, as we've learned and probably all know by heart, isn't necessarily the same as real-mode DOS activity) generated by some common Windows applications. We'll pay particular attention to the way that Win32 software in Windows 95 interacts with real-mode DOS.

As will be explained when we examine WSPY21.C toward the end of this chapter, WSPY21 sees INT 21h calls coming through the 16-bit Windows kernel (KRNL386.EXE). This means that WSPY21 will *not* see INT 21h calls that Win32 applications and DLLs make via the VxDCall0 mechanism discussed in the "Win32 FindNextFile is INT 21h Function 714Fh" section in Chapter 12.

However, WSPY21's oversight is a blessing in disguise. As we'll see in a moment, WSPY21 nonetheless still detects some INT 21h calls originating in Win32 applications and DLLs. That WSPY21 sees these calls means that they don't involve VxDCall0 and instead must be passing through 16-bit KRNL386's INT 21h handler. Following up this otherwise unimportant factoid will lead us to an important conclusion about the Windows 95 architecture: namely, that the Win32 kernel (KERNEL32) calls down to the Win16 kernel (KRNL386), even though Microsoft quite strenuously claims that it doesn't. We'll examine this false claim in detail in this chapter, and look into some of the thinking that's possibly behind it.

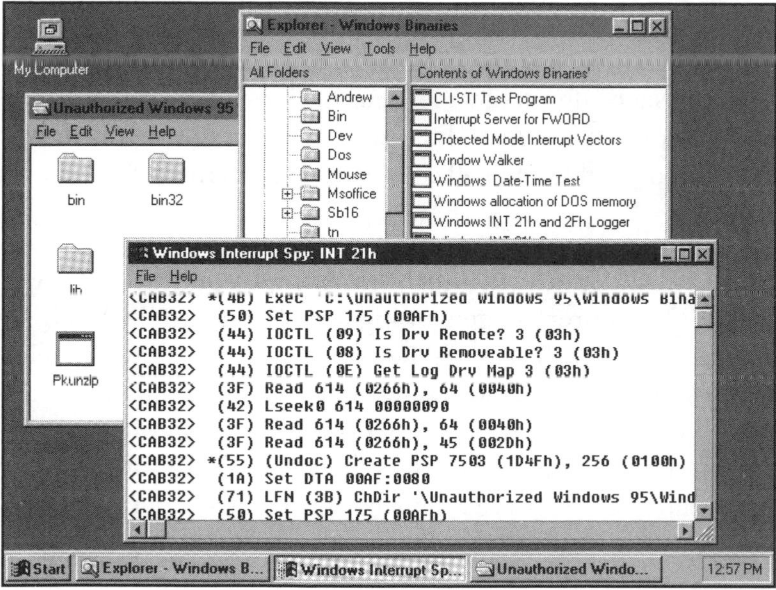

Figure 13-1: WSPY21 is a Windows program that watches INT 21h calls from other Windows programs. Here, WSPY21 is watching the Windows 95 Explorer start a Windows program with a long filename. The complete string passed to EXEC was "C:\Unauthorized Windows 95\Windows Binaries\Window Walker".

WSPY21 not only sees many protected-mode INT 21h calls that V86TEST never sees, but also provides a substantially different view of how Windows applications interact with DOS. Whereas V86TEST and WV86TEST merely accumulate running totals of the number of calls to each INT 21h function, WSPY21 displays each specific INT 21h with the name of its caller. V86TEST might show that a whole mess of function 50h (Set PSP) calls are being generated, for example, but WSPY21 would show that these calls tend to occur just before and after a task switch. (It might be helpful for some future version of WSPY21 to use the ToolHelp NotifyRegister API to display task switches and other events.) For example:

```
<WINWORD>  (42) Lseek0 17 000004f0
<WINWORD>  (3F) Read 17 (0011h), 1168 (0490h)
<PROGMAN> *(59) Get Extended Error Info
<PROGMAN>  (50) Set PSP 6039 (1797h)
<PROGMAN>  (1A) Set DTA 1797:0080
<PROGMAN>  (3B) ChDir '\WINDOWS'
<PROGMAN> *(19) Get Disk
<PROGMAN> *(47) Get Curr Dir 3 (03h)
<NETDDE>   (50) Set PSP 4495 (118Fh)
<NETDDE>   (2A) Get Date
<NETDDE>   (2C) Get Time
<NETDDE>   (2A) Get Date
<WINWORD>  (50) Set PSP 10351 (286Fh)
<WINWORD>  (2C) Get Time
```


Following up such admittedly unpromising-looking output will teach us a lot about Windows 95 internals. For example, the following line displayed by WSPY21 is remarkable and will command our attention for many pages:

```
<CAB32> *(55) (Undoc) Create PSP 7503 (1D4Fh), 256 (0100h)
```

Why is a Win32 application — nay, *the* Win32 application (CAB32 is the Windows 95 Explorer) — generating a DOS Create PSP call? And, for that matter, a DOS call that will be sent all the way down to real-mode DOS (as we saw in the preceding chapter)? Examination of this single line of WSPY21 output will cast a bright light on the larger relationship between the Win32 and Win16 kernels in Windows 95.

Likewise, understanding the following innocuous-looking line of WSPY21 output will require a lot of digging:

```
<WINHELP>  (3F) Read 750 (02EEh), 25958 (6566h)
```

How and why is WinHelp — an old-style Win16 executable, no less — reading with a file handle such as 750 instead of with a normal one like 6 or 17 or 42? In the "Win32 File Handles and Thunking" section of Chapter 14, we'll dig into this seemingly obscure point to turn up answers to much larger questions about the internal architecture of Windows 95.

Even though WSPY21 watches protected-mode INT 21h activity, we're going to use it to spy not only on the Windows-DOS relationship in Windows 95 but also on the Win32-Win16 relationship.

Launching a Win16 App from the Explorer

In the preceding chapter, we started the Win16 Calc applet from the Windows 95 Explorer, did a few calculations (an amusing one is 3.11

minus 3.10, which yields the answer 0 — incidentally, this bug has persisted since Windows 3.0, and lives on in all implementations, including Windows NT), clicked on Help, browsed Help a little, closed Help, and then closed Calc. WV86TEST, from its worm's-eye perspective, saw all this as a series of a little under 200 calls to real-mode DOS:

```
138 seconds elapsed

INT 21h calls:
0E: 44  2A: 3   2C: 14  30: 2   4C: 2   50: 129 55: 2
```


For the same set of operations, WSPY21 in Windows 95 logged over 500 INT 21h calls. Most of the INT 21h activity came from WINHELP. When I took the WSPY21 log, removed some of the detail (such as the number of bytes read and the file offset sought), sorted it, and used a throw-away AWK program to count the number of identical lines, the top INT 21h calls (with the number of calls shown on the left) were as follows:

```
43      <WINHELP> *(50) Set PSP 175 (00AFh)
42      <WINHELP> *(50) Set PSP 7391 (1CDFh)
40      <WINHELP> *(3F) Read 689
31      <WINHELP> *(42) Lseek0 5
29      <WINHELP> *(42) Lseek0 689
28      <WINHELP> *(3F) Read 5
23      <WINHELP> *(42) Lseek0 6
22      <WINHELP> *(3F) Read 6
18      <CALC> *(50) Set PSP 175 (00AFh)
16      <CALC> *(50) Set PSP 7567 (1D8Fh)
13      <CALC> *(3F) Read 686
11      <CALC> *(42) Lseek0 686
```

Most of these calls were overlooked by WV86TEST, for the simple reason that Windows didn't send them down to DOS in the first place. Here are some fragments from the WSPY21 output:

```
<CAB32> *(4B) Exec 'C:\WINDOWS\calc.exe'
<CAB32>  (50) Set PSP 167 (00A7h)
; ...
<CAB32> *(55) (Undoc) Create PSP 7503 (1D4Fh), 256 (0100h)
<CAB32>  (1A) Set DTA 00A7:0080
<CAB32>  (71) LFN (3B) ChDir '\WINDOWS'
<CAB32>  (50) Set PSP 167 (00A7h)
<CAB32> *(71) LFN (4E) Find First 'C:\WINDOWS\WIN.INI'
<CAB32> *(71) LFN (A1) Find Close
; ...
<CALC>  (30) Get DOS Vers
<CALC> *(25) Set Vect 2 (02h)
<CALC> *(25) Set Vect 117 (75h)
<CALC> *(25) Set Vect 62 (3Eh)
<CALC>  (50) Set PSP 167 (00A7h)
; ...
```

```
<CALC> *(4B) Exec 'C:\WINDOWS\WINHELP.EXE'
; ...
<CALC> *(55) (Undoc) Create PSP 7263 (1C5Fh), 256 (0100h)
<CALC>  (1A) Set DTA 1D4F:0080
<CALC>  (55) (Undoc) Create PSP 7263 (1C5Fh), 256 (0100h)
<CALC>  (50) Set PSP 167 (00A7h)
<CALC> *(71) LFN (4E) Find First 'C:\WINDOWS\WIN.INI'
<CALC> *(71) LFN (A1) Find Close
; ...
<CALC>  (50) Set PSP 7503 (1D4Fh)
<WINHELP>  (30) Get DOS Vers
<WINHELP>  (50) Set PSP 167 (00A7h)
<WINHELP>  (42) Lseek0 750 000219d0
<WINHELP>  (3F) Read 750 (02EEh), 25958 (6566h)
<WINHELP>  (3F) Read 750 (02EEh), 1120 (0460h)
; ...
<WINHELP>  (1A) Set DTA 1C5F:0080
; ...
<WINHELP>  (71) LFN (6C) Open/Create 'C:\WINDOWS\HELP\CALC.HLP'
; ...
<WINHELP>  (71) LFN (6C) Open/Create 'C:\WINDOWS\CALC.ANN'
<WINHELP>  (59) Get Extended Error Info
; ...
<WINHELP>  (71) LFN (6C) Open/Create 'C:\WINDOWS\HELP\CALC.GID'
; ...
<WINHELP>  (2F) Get DTA
<WINHELP>  (1A) Set DTA 1B07:353E
<WINHELP>  (4E) Find First 'C:\WINDOWS\HELP\CALC.CNT'
<WINHELP>  (1A) Set DTA 1C5F:0080
; ...
<WINHELP>  (71) LFN (6C) Open/Create 'C:\WINDOWS\SYSTEM\commctrl.dll'
; ...
<WINHELP>  (50) Set PSP 7263 (1C5Fh)
<WINHELP>  (42) Lseek0 5 00005619
<WINHELP>  (3F) Read 5 (0005h), 9 (0009h)
<WINHELP>  (42) Lseek0 5 00005622
<WINHELP>  (3F) Read 5 (0005h), 14 (000Eh)
; ... etc. ...
<WINHELP>  (00) Exit
<WINHELP>  (50) Set PSP 167 (00A7h)
<WINHELP>  (3E) Close 750 (02EEh)
<CALC>  (00) Exit
<CALC>  (50) Set PSP 167 (00A7h)
<CALC>  (3E) Close 747 (02EBh)
```

Before we get into the specifics of this output — in particular, why a Win32 application such as CAB32 is calling the INT 21h EXEC function, creating a real-mode DOS PSP, setting the current PSP and DTA, and generally cavorting about like a cheap DOS program — it's important to first understand a few general points about the output that WSPY21 produces.

The first point is that the name that WSPY21 shows for each INT 21h call, such as CAB32, CALC, or WINHELP, is the module name belonging to the current task at the time of the INT 21h call. WSPY21 extracts the name from offset 0F2h in the current Task Data Block (TDB; see *Undocumented Windows*, Chapter 5). WSPY21.C uses code somewhat like the following:

```
printf("<%8Fs>", MK_FP(GetCurrentTask(), 0xf2), 8);
```

But when WSPY21 calls GetCurrentTask, why doesn't this just get back WSPY21's own task handle? Because it is WSPY21's INT 21h handlers that call GetCurrentTask. When WSPY21's interrupt handlers are running, WSPY21 is *not* necessarily the current task. Like some Windows API callbacks, interrupt handlers run in the context of whatever task was current at the time of the interrupt. Since WSPY21 makes few INT 21h calls, this will usually be some task other than WSPY21.

During initialization, WSPY21 uses GetCurrentTask to get its own task ID; the interrupt handlers will filter out any INT 21h calls coming from WSPY21 itself. WSPY21 usually only calls INT 21h when you save the WSPY21 log out to a file. To digress slightly, you won't see any code for this in WSPY21.C (shown in this chapter), because WINIO automatically gives all WINIO programs a File/Save Buffer... menu item. The WINIO code to support this menu item uses the GetSaveFileName common dialog, and then saves out the WINIO buffer to disk with the _lcreat, _lwrite, and _lclose APIs. The _lcreat call turns into an INT 21h function 716Ch, so WSPY21 (or any other WINIO program) can save files with long names in Windows 95, even though this was never a consideration in the design of WINIO. This wouldn't work if WINIO had employed direct INT 21h calls or the C run-time library instead of the _lxxxx APIs (which, incidentally — how's this for a second-level digression? — were once undocumented; see the section on "Undocumented File I/O Functions" in the first [1988] edition of Charles Petzold's classic *Programming Windows*).

See? It pays to use the Windows APIs, even once-undocumented ones. However, while WINIO applications can write out a long filename in Windows 95, like other old Win16 applications they cannot read a long filename back in — darn confusing for the user!

Popping back to the task names displayed by WSPY21, all Win32 applications have a Win16 TDB surrogate, so WSPY21's technique for getting task names also works for Win32 applications, whether running in Windows 3.*x* with Win32s or in Windows 95. In a moment, we'll see why all Win32 applications come to have a Win16 TDB in the first place; the reason is significant.

When WSPY21 shows a task's module name such as CAB32 or CALC associated with an INT 21h call, it usually means not that the application itself called INT 21h but that some dynamic link library (DLL) called INT 21h on the current task's behalf. DLLs aren't tasks (though, interestingly, the KERNEL32 DLL in Windows 95 does have an associated KERNEL32 task). When an application calls a Windows API, the DLL providing that API does not temporarily become the current task (as it might in a client/server operating system). Instead, the current task just "steps around to the other side of the counter" (as Gordon Letwin nicely explains this point in his *Inside OS/2*) and runs the API code in the DLL.

One final general point about WSPY21's output: as we'll see when we examine WSPY21.C toward the end of this chapter, WSPY21 has two INT 21h handlers. One is installed with the DPMI Set Protected Mode Interrupt Vector function (INT 31h function 0205h), and the other is installed with an undocumented Windows API, GetSetKernelDosProc (*Undocumented Windows*, pp. 188, 271-273). The DPMI call lets WSPY21 stick a protected-mode INT 21h handler before the one in the Win16 KERNEL; GetSetKernelDosProc lets WSPY21 insert another handler *after* KERNEL's, but before the first VxD-based protected-mode INT 21h handler.

All this will be explained in the usual gory detail toward the end of the chapter. For now, all that matters is that an asterisk (*) in WSPY21's output means that the INT 21h call was first seen at the spot called KernelDosProc, where KERNEL is about to hand INT 21h off to the VxD protected-mode INT 21h chain. A blank indicates the call was first seen earlier (or higher, depending on how you look at it) in KERNEL's INT 21h handler. If the INT 21h handler saw a call, WSPY21 doesn't bother showing it again at KernelDosProc unless you specify the WSPY21 -SHOWALL switch.

Later, -SHOWALL will let us see that some INT 21h functions in Windows bypass real-mode DOS — and for years and years have bypassed real-mode DOS — because KERNEL (rather than a VxD such as IFSMgr) consumes them. The best example is INT 21h function 4Bh (EXEC). Neither real-mode DOS nor even a Windows VxD would know what to do with the EXEC of a Win16 executable, and so KERNEL's INT 21h handler deals with this call (decomposing it, naturally, into other DOS calls, such as File Open; see "Win32 File Handles and Thunking" in Chapter 14).

CAB32: KERNEL32 Uses the Win16 KERNEL

The WSPY21 log shown in the preceding section started out in CAB32, the Windows 95 Explorer/Cabinet. The log shows that when I clicked on the Calc icon, Explorer (or a DLL acting on its behalf) called function 4Bh to start CALC.EXE, called function 55h to give it a PSP, and so on. We know from WV86TEST that Windows will handle the function 4Bh exec call itself (for the reason just given at the end of the preceding section). On the other hand, we also know from WV86TEST that Windows will send the function 55h Create PSP call down to DOS.

Calc is a Win16 application. What happens when we use a Win32 application such as CAB32 to run another Win32 application? Although Win32 applications such as CAB32 do not use INT 21h function 4Bh to run other Win32 applications, WSPY21 *will* see a Create PSP call whenever you launch a Win32 application. This, as I've said, is significant; we'll soon see why.

The following WSPY21 log shows some of the INT 21h activity generated when I launched Clock, WinBezMT, and FreeCell from the Windows 95 Explorer, let them run for a while, and then closed them. I also used Find File and Control Panel, which are built into the Explorer.

```
<CAB32> *(50) Set PSP 167 (00A7h)
<CAB32>  (55) (Undoc) Create PSP 7431 (1D07h), 256 (0100h)
<CAB32> *(1A) Set DTA 00A7:0080
<CAB32> *(71) LFN (3B) ChDir '\WINDOWS'
<CAB32> *(50) Set PSP 4719 (126Fh)
<CLOCK> *(50) Set PSP 167 (00A7h)
<CLOCK> *(42) Lseek0 730 0000038a
<CLOCK> *(3F) Read 730 (02DAh), 217 (00D9h)
; ...
<CAB32> *(50) Set PSP 167 (00A7h)
<CAB32>  (55) (Undoc) Create PSP 7343 (1CAFh), 256 (0100h)
<CAB32> *(71) LFN (3B) ChDir '\WINDOWS'
<CAB32> *(55) (Undoc) Create PSP 7343 (1CAFh), 256 (0100h)
<CAB32> *(50) Set PSP 4719 (126Fh)
<WINBEZMT> *(50) Set PSP 167 (00A7h)
<WINBEZMT> *(42) Lseek0 570 00000631
<WINBEZMT> *(3F) Read 570 (023Ah), 1863 (0747h)
; ...
<CLOCK> *(50) Set PSP 167 (00A7h)
<CLOCK> *(42) Lseek0 730 000079e0
<CLOCK> *(3F) Read 730 (02DAh), 12205 (2FADh)
; ...
<CAB32> *(50) Set PSP 167 (00A7h)
<CAB32>  (55) (Undoc) Create PSP 7207 (1C27h), 256 (0100h)
<CAB32> *(71) LFN (3B) ChDir '\win32app\freecell'
```

```
<CAB32> *(55) (Undoc) Create PSP 7207 (1C27h), 256 (0100h)
<CAB32> *(50) Set PSP 4719 (126Fh)
<FREECELL> *(50) Set PSP 167 (00A7h)
<FREECELL> *(42) Lseek0 570 00000631
<FREECELL> *(3F) Read 570 (023Ah), 1863 (0747h)
<FREECELL> *(50) Set PSP 7207 (1C27h)
; ...
<FREECELL> *(50) Set PSP 7207 (1C27h)
<CAB32> *(44) IOCTL (09) Is Drv Remote? 3 (03h)
<CAB32> *(44) IOCTL (08) Is Drv Removeable? 3 (03h)
<CAB32> *(44) IOCTL (0E) Get Log Drv Map 3 (03h)
; ...
<CAB32> *(50) Set PSP 10415 (28AFh)
<KERNEL32> *(50) Set PSP 10415 (28AFh)
<KERNEL32> *(00) Exit
<KERNEL32> *(50) Set PSP 167 (00A7h)
<CAB32> *(50) Set PSP 167 (00A7h)
<CAB32> *(42) Lseek0 538 00052280
<CAB32> *(3F) Read 538 (021Ah), 4941 (134Dh)
<CAB32> *(3F) Read 538 (021Ah), 368 (0170h)
<CAB32> *(50) Set PSP 4719 (126Fh)
<RUNDLL32> *(50) Set PSP 167 (00A7h)
<RUNDLL32> *(42) Lseek0 570 00000631
<RUNDLL32> *(3F) Read 570 (023Ah), 1863 (0747h)
; ...
<RUNDLL32> *(71) LFN (3B) ChDir '\WINDOWS'
<RUNDLL32> *(2F) Get DTA
<RUNDLL32> *(1A) Set DTA 0BE7:856C
<RUNDLL32> *(4E) Find First 'C:\WININST0.400\*.INF'
<RUNDLL32> *(1A) Set DTA 00A7:0080
<RUNDLL32> *(2F) Get DTA
<RUNDLL32> *(1A) Set DTA 0BE7:856C
<RUNDLL32> *(4E) Find First 'C:\WININST0.400\*.MWD'
<RUNDLL32> *(1A) Set DTA 00A7:0080
<RUNDLL32> *(50) Set PSP 167 (00A7h)
<RUNDLL32> *(42) Lseek0 619 00029200
<RUNDLL32> *(3F) Read 619 (026Bh), 256 (0100h)
<RUNDLL32> *(50) Set PSP 11463 (2CC7h)
<KERNEL32> *(50) Set PSP 11463 (2CC7h)
<KERNEL32> *(00) Exit
<KERNEL32> *(50) Set PSP 167 (00A7h)
<CAB32> *(50) Set PSP 167 (00A7h)
<CAB32>  (55) (Undoc) Create PSP 11591 (2D47h), 256 (0100h)
<CAB32> *(71) LFN (3B) ChDir '\WINDOWS'
<CAB32> *(55) (Undoc) Create PSP 11591 (2D47h), 256 (0100h)
<CAB32> *(50) Set PSP 4719 (126Fh)
<RUNDLL32> *(50) Set PSP 167 (00A7h)
<RUNDLL32> *(42) Lseek0 570 00000631
<RUNDLL32> *(3F) Read 570 (023Ah), 1863 (0747h)
; ...
```

This contains only fragments — mostly the "edges" where Windows 95 switched from one task to another — from the almost 1000-line log file I generated while running this group of Win32 applications under

Windows 95. Although it would be boring to show the entire WSPY21 log, it's useful to take a look at the most frequent calls, and also to single out the Create PSP calls:

```
130     <CAB32> *(50) Set PSP 167 (00A7h)
129     <CAB32> *(50) Set PSP 4719 (126Fh)
32      <RUNDLL32> *(50) Set PSP 167 (00A7h)
28      <CAB32> *(44) IOCTL (0E) Get Log Drv Map 3 (03h)
28      <CAB32> *(44) IOCTL (09) Is Drv Remote? 3 (03h)
28      <CAB32> *(44) IOCTL (08) Is Drv Removeable? 3 (03h)
23      <RUNDLL32> *(3F) Read 619
22      <RUNDLL32> *(50) Set PSP 11463 (2CC7h)
22      <RUNDLL32> *(42) Lseek0 619
19      <CAB32> *(3F) Read 675
12      <CAB32> *(3F) Read 707
; ...
1       <CAB32>  (55) (Undoc) Create PSP 7343 (1CAFh), 256 (0100h)
1       <CAB32>  (55) (Undoc) Create PSP 7207 (1C27h), 256 (0100h)
1       <CAB32>  (55) (Undoc) Create PSP 11591 (2D47h), 256 (0100h)
1       <CAB32>  (55) (Undoc) Create PSP 11575 (2D37h), 256 (0100h)
1       <CAB32>  (55) (Undoc) Create PSP 10415 (28AFh), 256 (0100h)
1       <CAB32>  (55) (Undoc) Create PSP 7431 (1D07h), 256 (0100h)
```

Now, calls such as Read and Lseek are absorbed in IFSMgr; they look like DOS calls, and they smell like DOS calls, but they ain't real-mode DOS calls. A big chunk of DOS now resides as 32-bit protected-mode code in VxD-land. On the other hand, this big chunk of protected-mode DOS converses frequently with an assistant — known as real-mode MS-DOS — left behind in 16-bit V86 mode.

The WV86TEST program from Chapter 12 lets us listen in on these conversations between Windows and DOS. While running the same batch of Win32 applications under Windows 95, WV86TEST logged the following INT 21h calls that Windows made to its real-mode DOS assistant:

```
179 seconds elapsed

INT 21h calls:
2A: 1542    2C: 1542    30: 7    44: 22  4C: 3    50: 449 51: 1
55: 3       65: 2       EA: 1
```

Actually, this isn't exactly the same test as the one I performed with WSPY21. Although I opened the Explorer's Control Panel, I didn't click any of the Control Panel icons. As we'll see in a few moments, clicking a Control Panel icon ends up loading a Win16 DLL; I wanted to see the real-mode DOS calls coming from as pure a Win32 environment as possible (although WV86TEST, a Win16 program, was still running). Microsoft and the trade press both speak of Windows 95 as though there were a qualitative difference between a configuration running a mixture of Win32, Win16, and DOS applications and one running only Win32 applications. Throughout this chapter, I'll try to make the point that this distinction doesn't exist.

While I've been stressing the issue of whether an INT 21h call is processed by a VxD or by the real-mode DOS code, this book's technical reviewer (*Microsoft Systems Journal* contributing editor Jim Finnegan) notes that there's an additional point to be made here:

> What seems more important here, regardless of whether an INT 21h actually makes it to DOS or not, is that the Win32 API calls are turning into INTs in the first place! I care less about who processes the INTs (DOS or a VxD); the fact that Chicago at its core is still very interrupt based, rather than procedure based, is a hell of a point. You might remember that one of Microsoft's original selling points for OS/2 was that it left behind that ol' interrupt based foundation. Guess we'll never get there...

Apart from the sheer spectacle of pure Win32 applications stooping to make INT 21h calls — some of which we know from WV86TEST will be passed all the way down to real-mode DOS (albeit a real-mode DOS that Windows is controlling in V86 mode) — there are some interesting specifics worth following up in the output from WSPY21.

For example, every now and then we see KERNEL32 issue a sequence of three DOS calls:

```
<KERNEL32> *(50) Set PSP 10415 (28AFh)
<KERNEL32> *(00) Exit
<KERNEL32> *(50) Set PSP 167 (00A7h)
```

First, how can KERNEL32 perform an exit via INT 21h function 0, and then keep going to do a Set PSP call? KERNEL32 seems to say "I'm outa here!" and then stick around to talk with DOS some more.

Second, why is KERNEL32 — the most fundamental and ostensibly the purest Win32 module — mucking with the PSP and calling an ancient DOS function?

Third, isn't KERNEL32 a Win32 DLL? How did it become a task? DLLs aren't tasks; when a task calls an API located in a DLL, the code for that API runs in the context of the calling task. We'll see later (in the "Win32 and the PSP" section) that 0A7h is KERNEL32's PSP. But how did the very foundation of Windows 95's brand spankin' new Win32 API acquire a clunker of a DOS data structure like a PSP?

If you've ever done any TSR programming, answering the first question will probably be easy. KERNEL32's task keeps running after making a DOS Exit call for the simple reason that it wasn't KERNEL32 that exited. Yes, KERNEL32 called the DOS exit function, but just before that it called Set PSP, passing in the PSP (28AFh in this example) *belonging to some other task*. The DOS Exit call works off the *current* PSP; because of the Set PSP call, this is not necessarily the caller's PSP.

In other words, KERNEL32 has forced *some other task* to exit. This is a fairly standard technique in TSR programming. When a user asks to uninstall a TSR, the non-resident portion of the TSR can switch to the PSP of the resident portion and then exit. When one task foists an exit on some other task like this, DOS frees the memory allocations and closes the open file handles belonging to that other task (see *Undocumented DOS*, 2d ed., p. 603, based on material supplied for the first edition by Tim Paterson).

To put it yet another way, when a Win32 application such as RUNDLL32 exits, KERNEL32 cleans up after the application using, in part, this Set PSP/Exit/Set PSP sequence.

This answers the other questions too. This clean-up operation runs as a separate thread. KERNEL32.DLL has acquired a task handle and a PSP because these are required to own a thread. The Win-ICE debugger shows that KERNEL32 has several threads:

```
:thread kernel32
Ring0TCB  ID    Context   Ring3TCB  Process   TaskDB  PDB   SZ   Owner
C0FDE188  0005  C0FD98C0  81106804  81104250  0097    00A7  32   KERNEL32
C0FDBCDC  0003  C0FD98C0  81105FC0  81104250  0097    00A7  32   KERNEL32
C0FD12CC  0002  C0FD98C0  811052A8  81104250  0097    00A7  32   KERNEL32
C4520298  0001  C0FD98C0  81104328  81104250  0097    00A7  32   VM 01
```

But who issues the Set PSP/Exit/Set PSP sequence of calls? WSPY21 sees it, so we know that KERNEL32 isn't using VxDCall0 here. Some hunting around with Win-ICE reveals that these calls are coming from the Win16 KERNEL (KRNL386) via an internal version of the undocumented NoHookDOSCall API.

Wait a minute, though. If KERNEL32 is the current task, how did the Win16 KERNEL get into the act? This isn't supposed to happen. As we'll see later, Microsoft claims that "The KERNEL32 module is completely independent of its 16-bit version. There is some communication from the 16-bit to the 32-bit side, but the 32-bit KERNEL never calls across to the 16-bit side" (*Microsoft Systems Journal*, May 1994).

Backtracing in the debugger from the point of the Set PSP/Exit/Set PSP NoHookDOSCalls in the Win16 KERNEL shows that KERNEL32 extracts the far 16-bit selector:offset address of this Win16 KERNEL code from a table of DWORDs, and then passes the address to KERNEL32's QT_Thunk routine. We'll examine QT_Thunk and this table a little later (in the "From Explorer to Create PSP in Six Easy Steps" section). For now, it suffices to say that KERNEL32 *is* thunking down not only to a Win16 KERNEL routine but also to a Win16 KERNEL routine that calls INT 21h functions.

And, just to send more chills down the spines of operating system purists, these INT 21h functions 0 and 50h are sent down to the real-mode DOS code. The DOSMGR VxD handles Set PSP calls from protected mode by calling the VMM _SelectorMapFlat service to convert the protected-mode PSP to a real-mode paragraph address, which it then passes down to DOS via Begin_Nest_V86_Exec and an Exec_Int 21h. And DOSMGR handles a protected-mode call to function 0 (which is considered obsolete), by turning this into a new-style function 4Ch exit, which it again passes down to DOS via Begin_Nest_V86_Exec and Exec_Int 21h. Yes, KERNEL32 really does employ the real-mode MS-DOS code.

Another interesting facet of the WSPY21 log is that we sometimes see two Create PSP calls sandwich an LFN ChDir call:

```
<CAB32>  (55) (Undoc) Create PSP 7343 (1CAFh), 256 (0100h)
<CAB32> *(71) LFN (3B) ChDir '\WINDOWS'
<CAB32> *(55) (Undoc) Create PSP 7343 (1CAFh), 256 (0100h)
```

There's actually only one Create PSP call here. WSPY21 sees the call first in its INT 21h handler and then in its KernelDosProc (marked with an asterisk). But unless you use the -SHOWALL command-line option (which wasn't used here), WSPY21 is supposed to filter out a call at KernelDosProc that matches one just shown at the higher-up INT 21h handler. Why didn't that happen here? Because the second call didn't *immediately* follow on the heels of the first call; WSPY21 has no way of knowing they represent the *same* call.

Somehow, a call to LFN ChDir snuck in after the Create PSP reached the Win16 KERNEL's INT 21h handler, but before it arrived at KernelDosProc's doorstep. But how? Very simple: KERNEL's INT 21h handler insinuated the call to LFN ChDir. Why? Because just after a task switch, KERNEL's INT 21h handler often must manufacture extra INT 21h calls not only to set the current directory (ChDir) but also to set the current drive, PSP, or DTA.

The scheduler in the Win16 KERNEL is responsible for ensuring the consistency of each task's DOS "state." Let's say the scheduler lets a Win16 or Win32 task run for a while, and then switches to a second task that calls the GetOpenFileName common dialog, which in turn changes the current directory and uses Find First File and Find Next File to enumerate the *.TXT files in that directory. Because of the find first/next, this second task has undoubtedly changed the current PSP and DTA as well as the current directory. Perhaps it's switched the current drive too. When KERNEL eventually switches back to the first task, what happens when the first task makes an INT 21h call? KERNEL must ensure that the second task's DOS operations have *no effect* on the first task. This might require restoration of the first task's current drive, directory, PSP, and DTA.

Note that VMM doesn't help with any of this; as far as it's concerned, the System VM is one big task. This is an indication that the descriptions of Windows 95 as an "integrated" operating system mean very little: the lower half of Windows knows almost nothing about what goes on in the upper half. In Windows 95, VMM schedules threads as well as VMs, but things like the current drive and directory aren't maintained on a per-thread basis. Thus, the Win16 KERNEL must take the single System VM current drive, directory, PSP, DTA, and so on that VMM's instance data mechanism provides (these DOS variables are contained in the instanced SDA and CDS) and share it among all Win16 and Win32 tasks. This is a crucial role for the Win16 KERNEL, even on a pure Win32 system.

A final question about the WSPY21 log: What the heck is this RUNDLL32 thing?

```
<RUNDLL32> *(2F) Get DTA
<RUNDLL32> *(1A) Set DTA 0BE7:856C
<RUNDLL32> *(4E) Find First 'C:\WININST0.400\*.INF'
```

I didn't start any program called RUNDLL32. But I did click some icons in the Windows 95 Control Panel, and that triggered RUNDLL32. The Control Panel icons represent Control Panel applications, which reside in Win16 DLLs with the extension .CPL (see the Windows 3.1 *Programmer's Reference, Volume 1: Overview*, Chapter 15). The Control Panel is built into the Windows 95 Cabinet/Explorer, which is a Win32 executable. The Win32 Control Panel uses RUNDLL32 to load Win16 .CPL files. As in many other areas, Windows here takes a fairly Byzantine approach. However, it's worth briefly examining what happens when you click a Control Panel icon such as New Device, which launches the New Device Installation Wizard.

First, CAB32 launches RUNDLL32.EXE (which, like CAB32, is a Win32 executable), with a lengthy "command line from hell":

```
C:\WINDOWS\RUNDLL32.EXE shell32,Control_RunDLL \
C:\WINDOWS\SYSTEM\SYSDM.CPL,-602,New device
```

RUNDLL32 takes the first part of the command tail and passes the "shell32" string to the Win32 LoadLibrary API. It gets back a handle to SHELL32.DLL and passes this, along with the next part of the command tail (the "Control_RunDLL" string), to GetProcAddress, thereby dynamically linking to the Control_RunDLL routine in SHELL32. DLL. Armed with a function pointer to this routine, RUNDLL32 calls the routine, passing it the remainder of the command line. Notice that RUNDLL32 has taken two strings from its command line and transformed them into a callable function pointer; isn't run-time dynamic linking amazing?

With the portion of the command line it's been given, Control_RunDLL takes the next string, "C:\WINDOWS\SYSTEM\SYSDM.CPL", and passes it to an undocumented function in KERNEL32 called LoadLibrary16. As you might infer from the name, LoadLibrary16 is a Win32 API that loads Win16 DLLs. How it does this is quite interesting:

```
KERNEL32!LoadLibrary16
0137:BFF91D52   MOV     CL,36
0137:BFF91D54   JMP     BFF91D60
```

Later (in "From Explorer to Create PSP in Six Easy Steps"), we'll see that BFF91D60h is a generic routine that uses the value in CL as an index into a table of DWORDs such as 011F66CEh, 011F0B5Bh, and 011F00EBh. You probably won't be too surprised to hear that 011Fh happens in this configuration to be one of the Win16 KERNEL's code segments, and that entry 36h in the table of DWORDs is 011F00EBh, 011F:00EB just happening to be the address of the Win16 LoadLibrary API. In other words, the Win32 LoadLibrary16 API retrieves the 16-bit far selector:offset address of the Win16 LoadLibrary API. This address is then passed to a KERNEL32 function called QT_Thunk (discussed in detail in a moment), which lets 32-bit code call down to 16-bit code. Hmm, I thought KERNEL32 was supposed to *never* thunk down to the Win16 KERNEL.

When KERNEL32!LoadLibrary16 thunks down to KERNEL!LoadLibrary, it gets back a handle to the Win16 DLL, SYSDM.CPL. Control_RunDLL takes this handle and a string, "CplApplet" (CplApplet is the main entry point for all Control Panel applications), and passes them to another undocumented KERNEL32 API, GetProcAddress16. The implementation of this API is similar to that of LoadLibrary16, except there's a MOV CL,34 instead of a MOV CL,36.

GetProcAddress16 calls down to GetProcAddress in the Win16 KERNEL, again using QT_Thunk, and returns a 16-bit far selector:offset pointer to the Win16 function. In our current example, Control_RunDLL gets back a 16-bit far selector:offset pointer to the CplApplet routine in SYSDM.

Listing 13-1 is a throwaway Console program that demonstrates how Win32 applications can use LoadLibrary16 and GetProcAddress16:

Listing 13-1: DYNLINK32.C


```
/*
DYNLINK32.C -- Win32 Console app
Illustrates Win32 run-time dynlink to Win16
*/

#include <stdlib.h>
#include <stdio.h>
#define  WIN32_LEAN_AND_MEAN
#include "windows.h"

HINSTANCE (WINAPI *LoadLibrary16)(LPCSTR lpLibFileName);
FARPROC (WINAPI *GetProcAddress16)(HINSTANCE hModule, LPCSTR lpProcName);

void fail(const char *s) { puts(s); exit(1); }

main(int argc, char *argv[])
{
    HINSTANCE mod;
    FARPROC fp;
    DWORD arg, retval;

    if (argc < 3)
        fail("usage: dynlnk32 [module name] [function name]");

    #define GET_PROC(mod, func) \
        GetProcAddress(GetModuleHandle(mod), (func))

    #define GET(func, str) \
        if (! (func = GET_PROC("KERNEL32", str))) \
            fail("Cannot link to " str);

    GET(LoadLibrary16, "LoadLibrary16");
    GET(GetProcAddress16, "GetProcAddress16");

    if (! (mod = LoadLibrary16(argv[1])))
        fail("LoadLibrary16 failed");
    printf("LoadLibrary16(\"%s\") ==> 0x%08X\n", argv[1], mod);
    if (! (fp = GetProcAddress16(mod, argv[2])))
        fail("GetProcAddress16 failed");
    printf("GetProcAddress16(0x%08X, \"%s\") ==> 0x%08X\n",
        mod, argv[2], fp);

    // major cop-out:  I should show how to call QT_Thunk!
}
```

You can try out Win32-to-Win16 dynamic linking by typing a module name and function name on the program's command line. For example:

```
C:\UNAUTHW>dynlnk32 kernel getselectorbase
LoadLibrary16("kernel") ==> 0x0000012F
GetProcAddress16(0x0000012F, "getselectorbase") ==> 0x01174BE0

C:\UNAUTHW>dynlnk32 sysdm cplapplet
LoadLibrary16("sysdm") ==> 0x00002236
GetProcAddress16(0x00002236, "cplapplet") ==> 0x226F029C
```

It's all well and good for SHELL32!Control_RunDLL, a Win32 function, to own a selector:offset function pointer to SYSDM!CplApplet, a Win16 function. ("That's nice, dear.") But by itself, SHELL32's possession of a far 16-bit function pointer to SYSDM is like a telephone number without a telephone, or an address without a mode of transportation. How's a Win32 DLL like SHELL32 going to call down to a Win16 DLL like SYSDM? Gee, somehow this question reminds me of a foolish pop song about an "uptown girl" (Win32) and a "downtown boy" (Win16), but perhaps I'm just being fanciful.

How are these two going to get together? It's fairly simple, really. SHELL32!Control_RunDLL can call SYSDM!CplApplet in the same way that KERNEL32!LoadLibrary16 called KERNEL!LoadLibrary or that KERNEL32!GetProcAddress16 called KERNEL!GetProcAddress: via QT_Thunk (whose workings we'll examine in detail a little later). In Windows 95, thunks are what make the world go around.

In addition to telling us how the Win32 Control Panel calls the CplApplet routine in Win16 .CPL files, the very existence of the LoadLibrary16 and GetProcAddress16 functions in KERNEL32 is significant. Here we have KERNEL32 APIs (which, although undocumented, are heavily used by the rest of the system), whose entire purpose is to thunk down to their Win16 KERNEL equivalents.

In fact, KERNEL32's capability to thunk down to KERNEL is the basis for all other 32/16 thunking in Windows 95, such as communication between USER32 and USER and between GDI32 and GDI, because initialization of these thunks requires LoadLibrary16 and GetProcAddress-16. A debugger breakpoint placed on these routines during Windows 95 initialization reveals the following thunk-related dynamic links:

```
During initialization:
    LoadLibrary16 GDI.EXE
        GetProcAddress16:
            GdiThkConnectionDataLS
            FT_GdiFThkThkConnectionData
            FdThkConnectionDataSL
```

```
            IcmThkConnectionDataSL
    LoadLibrary16 USER.EXE
        GetProcAddress16:
            UsrThkConnectionDataLS
            MsgThkConnectionDataLS
            FT_UsrFThkThkConnectionData
            FT_UsrF2ThkThkConnectionData
            Usr32ThkConnectionDataSL
Start Clock:
    LoadLibrary16 COMMDLG.DLL
        GetProcAddress16 DlgThkConnectionDataLS
Start Font Manager:
    LoadLibrary16 SYSTHUNK.DLL
        GetProcAddress16 FT_LzFThkThkConnectionData
Examine File Properties:
    LoadLibrary16 VER.DLL
        GetProcAddress16 FT_VerFThkThkConnectionData
```


Besides LoadLibrary16 and GetProcAddress16, other KERNEL32 APIs based on the Win16 KERNEL include FreeLibrary16, GlobalAlloc16, and GlobalLock16. In addition, the KERNEL32 thunk table mentioned earlier contains pointers to many Win16 KERNEL (KRNL386) routines whose names don't appear in the Windows 95 binaries. To see how extensively these KERNEL32->KRNL386 thunks are used, you can place a debugger breakpoint on the code where KERNEL32 has a thunk number in the CL register and is about to index into the thunk table:

```
0137:BFFB7C44   XOR    ECX,ECX
0137:BFFB7C46   MOV    CL,[EBP-04]              ; thunk number
0137:BFFB7C49   MOV    EDX,[00030464+4*ECX]     ; thunk table
0137:BFFB7C50   MOV    EAX,BFF71247             ; offset32 QT_Thunk
0137:BFFB7C55   JMP
EAX
```

A breakpoint placed on this code is hit almost twenty times when starting up a Win32 application such as Clock and about an equal number of times when exiting the Win32 application. Mileage may vary depending on the Win32 application, of course, but for what it's worth, the following indicates the KERNEL32->KRNL386 activity generated by starting and exiting the Win32 Clock:

```
31, 32, 2E, 36, 34, 3E (x3), 1E (x6), 1C (x5),
Clock appears on display
1F,
Clock now running (no K32->K16 thunks while running)
Close Clock
1B (x3), 2F, 3D (x3), 33 (x2), 29 (x2), 30
```

Of these, thunk 30h is the Set PSP/Exit cleanup routine mentioned previously, 36h is LoadLibrary16, and 34h is GetProcAddress16.

I've been emphasizing these cases where KERNEL32 thunks down to KRNL386 mostly because Microsoft has claimed such thunks don't exist. There are also plenty of important cases where KRNL386 thunks up to KERNEL32, just as Microsoft says. For example, in the preceding chapter (in the section titled "Win32 FindNextFile is INT 21h Function 714Fh") we saw that the FindNextFile API in KERNEL thunks up to FindNextFileA in KERNEL32.

That's enough poring over this one WSPY21 log. It's clear that WSPY21 can alert us to some important places in Chicago that we probably wouldn't otherwise have seen. An operating system purist might say that WSPY21 reveals some of the seamy sides of Chicago. I wouldn't agree that WSPY21 reveals anything particularly seamy or distasteful about Chicago, but certainly the program does show *seams*: places where Win32 is stitched onto Win16 and where Win16 is stitched onto real-mode DOS.

What have we learned so far?

- The Windows 95 Explorer, a Win32 application, uses INT 21h function 4Bh (EXEC) to launch Win16 applications. This call is not passed down to real-mode DOS, but (like all calls seen by WSPY21) it does involve the Win16 KERNEL. This is significant because Win32 applications in Windows 95 are not supposed to employ the Win16 KERNEL at all.
- Win32 applications in Windows 95 rely on a variety of INT 21h calls. WSPY21 doesn't see most of these calls because they're made using VxDCall0. However, the calls that WSPY21 does see are significant because they show that even a pure Win32 Windows 95 environment relies on the Win16 kernel. It is significant that some of these calls are sent all the way down to real-mode DOS because it shows that even a pure Win32 Windows 95 environment relies on real-mode DOS (which Windows is running in V86 mode, however).
- The Windows 95 Explorer, a Win32 application, uses INT 21h function 55h (Create PSP) not only to support Win16 applications but also to support Win32 applications. We'll see that this call, too, involves the Win16 KERNEL. We've already seen from WV86TEST that the call is sent all the way down to DOS. Thus, every running Win32 application in Windows 95, like every running Win16 application, has a real-mode DOS PSP, created down in the bowels of real-mode DOS by function 55h.

Win32 and the PSP

By using a Win16 program, WINPSP.C, it's easy to see that every Win32 task in Windows 95 has a genuine real-mode DOS PSP. This program is based on, but fairly different from, the version of WINPSP that appeared in *Undocumented DOS* (2d ed., pp. 151-155). Figure 13-12 shows WINPSP under Windows 95, when running Explorer, Clock, WinBezMT, and three Control Panel windows (System, Telephony, and the New Device Installation Wizard), which show up as RUNDLL32.

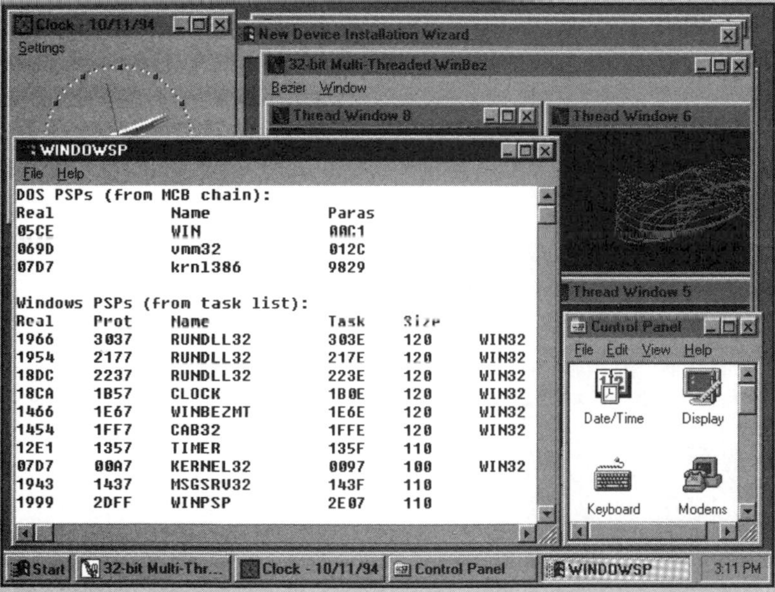

Figure 13-2: The WINPSP program shows that every task in Windows 95, including every Win32 task, comes with a real-mode DOS Program Segment Prefix (PSP).

As you can see, each Win32 task has a corresponding real-mode DOS PSP. While the PSP structure itself doesn't appear to be heavily used in Windows 95, its *address* is heavily used as the source for a DOS process ID.

In the WSPY21 logs shown earlier, you probably noticed lots of calls that set the current PSP to 0A7h, set the current DTA to 00A7:0080, and so on. Many but not all of these calls came from CAB32. From WINPSP's display of the Windows PSP chain, we can see that protected-mode selector 0A7h corresponds to real-mode address 07D7:0000, and that this PSP belongs to KERNEL32. If you look back at the DOS PSP chain in Figure 13-2, you can see that 07D7h belongs, as far as real-mode DOS is concerned, to a DOS application called KRNL386, which has allocated 9829 paragraphs (over 600K).

WINPSP.C, as shown in Listing 13-2, is a Win16 application that uses the WINIO library:

Listing 13-2: WINPSP.C

```
/*
WINPSP.C
Andrew Schulman, 1993 (Undocumented DOS, 2d ed., pp. 151-155)
Revised 1994 (Unauthorized Windows)
*/

#include <stdlib.h>
#include <stdio.h>
#include <string.h>
#include <dos.h>
#include "windows.h"
#include "prot.h"
#include "toolhelp.h"

#ifdef __cplusplus
extern "C" BOOL FAR PASCAL IsWinOldApTask(HANDLE hTask);
#else
extern BOOL FAR PASCAL IsWinOldApTask(HANDLE hTask);
#endif

#define MAP(ptr, bytes)      map_real((ptr), (bytes))
#define FREE_MAP(ptr)        free_mapped_linear(ptr)
#define GET_REAL(ptr)        get_real_addr(ptr)

#pragma pack(1)
typedef struct {
    BYTE type;
    WORD owner, size;
    BYTE unused[3], name[8];
    } MCB;
#pragma pack()

WORD get_first_mcb(void)
{
    RMODE_CALL r;
    memset(&r, 0, sizeof(r));
    r.eax = 0x5200;
    if (dpmi_rmode_intr(0x21, 0, 0, &r))
    {
        // Extract seg of first MCB from SysVars. Note that this is
        // at sysvars[-2]. You can't call map_real() on sysvars, and
        // then back up 2! You must map in sysvars-2 to begin with.
        WORD far *tmp = (WORD far *) MAP(MK_FP(r.es, (WORD) r.ebx-2), 2);
        WORD first_mcb = *tmp;
        FREE_MAP(tmp);
        return first_mcb;
    }
    else
```

```
        return 0;
}

void display_dos_psp(WORD psp_seg, BYTE far *psp, MCB far *mcb)
{
    printf("%04X\t ", psp_seg);
    if (_osmajor >= 4)
    {
        char buf[9];
        _fmemcpy(buf, mcb->name, 8);
        buf[8] = '\0';
        if (*buf) printf("\t%-8s", buf);
        else      printf("\t\t");
    }
    printf("\t%04X\n", mcb->size);
}

void display_win_psp(WORD prot_psp, char *szModule, WORD hTask)
{
    BYTE far *psp = (BYTE far *) MK_FP(prot_psp, 0);
    WORD real_psp = GetSelectorBase(prot_psp) >> 4;
    WORD flags;

    printf("%04X\t%04X\t%-8s\t%04X\t%lX\t",
        real_psp, prot_psp, szModule, hTask,
        GetSelectorLimit(prot_psp) + 1);

    // WinOldAp flag in Windows PSP
    flags = *((WORD far *) &psp[0x48]);
    if (IsWinOldApTask(hTask) && (! (flags & 1))) /* insanity check */
        fail("IsWinOldApTask flag weirdness!");
    if (flags & 1) printf("DOS ");

    // Win32 flag in TDB
    flags = *((WORD far *) MK_FP(hTask, 0x16));
    if (flags & 0x10) printf("WIN32");
    printf("\n");
}

// void fail(char *s) { printf("%s\n", s); exit(1); }

main()
{
    TASKENTRY te;
    BYTE far *maybe_psp;
    MCB far *mcb;
    WORD mcb_seg, mapped;
    BOOL ok;

    printf("DOS PSPs (from MCB chain):\n");
    printf("Real\t    \tName    \tParas\n");

    // walk DOS MCB chain, looking for PSPs
```

```
    if (! (mcb_seg = get_first_mcb()))
        fail("Can't get MCB chain!");
    for (;;)
    {
        mcb = (MCB far *) MAP(MK_FP(mcb_seg, 0), sizeof(MCB));
        maybe_psp = (BYTE far *) MAP(MK_FP(mcb_seg + 1, 0), 512);
        // does it look like a PSP?
        {
            if ((mcb_seg + 1) == mcb->owner)      // regular DOS app PSP
                display_dos_psp(mcb_seg + 1, maybe_psp, mcb);
        }
        FREE_MAP(maybe_psp);
        if (mcb->type == 'Z')
            break;                                // end of list
        mcb_seg = mcb_seg + mcb->size + 1;        // walk list
        FREE_MAP(mcb);
    }
    FREE_MAP(mcb);                                // free last one
    if ((mapped = get_mapped()) != 0)
        printf("ERROR!  %u mapped selectors remaining!\n", mapped);

    printf("\nWindows PSPs (from task list):\n");
    printf("Real\tProt\tName    \tTask\tSize\n");

    // now walk Windows task list, and extract PSPs
    te.dwSize = sizeof(te);
    ok = TaskFirst(&te);
    while (ok)
    {
        BYTE far *tdb = (BYTE far *) MK_FP(te.hTask, 0);
        WORD prot_psp = *((WORD far *) &tdb[0x60]);
        /*really a PSP? */
        if (*((WORD far *) MK_FP(prot_psp, 0)) == 0x20CD)
            display_win_psp(prot_psp, te.szModule, te.hTask);
        ok = TaskNext(&te);
    }

    return 0;
}
```

WINPSP first walks the DOS MCB chain, looking for PSPs. WINPSP employs fairly standard MCB-walking code, except that WINPSP is a protected-mode Windows program and therefore needs to map real-mode addresses into its address space. It does this using the map_real function from the PROT library on disk (also see *Undocumented DOS*, 2d ed., pp. 131-138). For each PSP encountered, WINPSP calls a routine named display_dos_ps.

Next, WINPSP uses ToolHelp to walk the Windows task list. For each task, WINPSP extracts a protected-mode selector to the PSP from offset 60h in the task database (TDB), sees if it's really a PSP by checking that the first two bytes are CDh 20h, and calls the display_win_psp routine. This in turn calls GetSelectorBase to compute a real-mode paragraph address for the PSP (all PSPs must be located in conventional memory, and therefore must have valid return values from GetSelectorBase). The module name associated with the PSP comes from information that ToolHelp supplies about the task. Finally, display_win_psp checks two flags in the TDB: the WinOldAp ("DOS") flag and the Win32 flag.

As Windows takes on more of the responsibilities once performed by real-mode DOS, more "DOS programs" will in fact be Windows programs that look something like WINPSP. Welcome once again to the not-so-new world of protected-mode DOS programming!

Who's Calling INT 21h?

We know from the preceding chapter that Win32 applications in Windows 95 rely far more on INT 21h than Microsoft would suggest happens even with Win16 applications. But does CAB32.EXE really contain INT 21h instructions? No, it doesn't. So how then is the launching of a Win16 application from the Explorer turning into a function 4Bh EXEC? And how does the launching of any application, whether Win16 or Win32, end up creating a real-mode DOS data structure like the PSP?

Significantly, these very DOS-like events do *not* occur through the VxDCall0 2A0010h 21h mechanism discussed in the preceding chapter. If someone in Win32-land *were* issuing an INT 21h function 4Bh or 55h via VxDCall0, WSPY21 wouldn't see it. As noted earlier, WSPY21 hooks INT 21h at the Win16 KERNEL level.

But wait a minute! If WSPY21 hooks INT 21h at the Win16 KERNEL level, and if WSPY21 is detecting INT 21h calls occurring while a Win32 application is the current task, this means that KERNEL32 must call over (or "thunk down" in Microsoft parlance) to KRNL386. Yet, as we've seen, Microsoft claims that KERNEL32 *never* thunks down to KRNL386.

There's more, though. Both when CAB32 starts CALC, and when CALC starts WINHELP, we saw that the parent task uses function 55h to create a PSP for the child task. It's natural enough to expect this call when CALC uses WinExec to start WINHELP, since Matt Pietrek has shown in his indispensable *Windows Internals* (pp. 229-256) that:

```
WinExec -> INT 21h function 4B00h -> LoadModule -> LMCheckHeader ->
OpenApplEnv -> CreateTask -> BuildPDB -> INT 21h function 55h
```

But in the case of CAB32, where are these Create PSP calls coming from? Pietrek is talking about the Win16 version of WinExec here.

WSPY21 is seeing CAB32 call INT 21h function 55h even when CAB32 launches a Win32 application such as Clock or WinBezMT. How the heck (and why?) is CAB32 issuing a function 55h call? Again, it can't be using VxDCall0, or WSPY21 wouldn't be seeing it in the first place.

Well, the answer is staring us right in the face. Pietrek shows that the internal CreateTask function in KRNL386 calls another internal function, BuildPDB (PDB, which stands for Process Data Block, is another name for PSP), which in turn calls function 55h.

Of course! (Sound of one hand clapping.) Some KERNEL32 code *must* be calling CreateTask in KRNL386! Later on, we'll see *how* KERNEL32 is doing this.

We already know that all Win32 applications have corresponding Win16 TDBs (WSPY21 relies on this to display a name such as CAB32). And, even if we didn't already know this, it would be easy enough to stumble upon when running any Windows diagnostic tool that displays Win16 tasks, using the ToolHelp TaskFirst and TaskNext APIs or the task-walking methods described throughout *Undocumented Windows*. For example, Matt Pietrek's WINWALK includes a TaskWalk function (*Undocumented Windows*, pp. 646-647); note that this uses the old Win16 ToolHelp APIs, and not the new ToolHelp32 API:

```
void TaskWalk(void)
{
    TASKENTRY te;
    BOOL ok;

    // using printf from WINIO library
    printf("Task list:\n");
    printf("NAME      HTASK  HMOD  HINST  PARENT\n");

    te.dwSize = sizeof(te);
    ok = TaskFirst(&te);
    while ( ok )
    {
        printf("%-8s  %04X   %04X  %04X   %s\n",
            te.szModule, te.hTask, te.hModule, te.hInst,
            GetModuleNameFromHandle(te.hTaskParent));
        // GetModuleNameFromHandle uses ModuleFindHandle, TaskFindHandle

        ok = TaskNext(&te);
    }
}
```

Running CAB32, Clock, WinBezMT, and the Win32 version of FreeCell, but no Win16 applications except for WinWalk itself, this code produces the following output in Windows 95:

```
Task list:
NAME      HTASK  HMOD  HINST  PARENT
```

```
FREECELL  1B9E   1E06  1B9E
WINBEZMT  1CA6   1CFE  1CA6
CLOCK     1E26   1E3E  1E26
BATMETER  1F1E   1F06  1F1E
CAB32     1276   125E  1276
TIMER     130F   132F  12E6   MSGSRV32
MSGSRV32  13EF   13FF  13CE   KERNEL32
KERNEL32  0097   010F  0097
WINWALK   1B87   1B67  1C66   CAB32
```

The code just walks the Win16 task list. It knows nothing about Windows 95 or about Win32 processes, yet it sees the name of each Win32 process. Thus, each Win32 process in Windows 95 has a corresponding Win16 TDB. (*Windows Internals*, p. 226, notes that a 10h flag in the WORD at offset 16h in the TDB indicates a Win32 task. WINPSP.C shown earlier relies on this, as does the WALKWIN.C program we'll examine a little later.)

On the other hand, it's also important to note that the Win16 TDB for a Win32 task differs somewhat from one that a Win16 task has (which, in turn, differs somewhat from the Windows 3.*x* TDB format; see the following section, "Where's the Windows 95 Current Directory?"). For example, the parent task handle at offset 22h is 0 in a Win32 TDB (notice that WINWALK was unable to locate any Win32 task's parent).

There's another key difference between Win32 and Win16 tasks: Although a Win32 task's TDB has a protected-mode selector to the PSP at offset 60h, just like the TDB for a Win16 task, the actual PSP (as opposed to its selector) is *not* located at offset 210h in the TDB, the way it is for Win16 tasks in Windows 95. (In Windows 3.*x*, this embedded PSP was located at offset 100h in the TDB.) Because a Win16 task's TDB includes (and acts as an extension to) a real-mode DOS PSP, the entire TDB must be located in conventional memory. Again, Pietrek shows this in *Windows Internals* (p. 254):

```
// Allocate the TDB below 1Mb, so that it can be accessed by DOS
// for file I/O
TDB = GlobalDosAlloc(tdb_alloc_size)
```

In contrast, here are typical TDB and PSP values for both a Win32 task and a Win16 task running under Windows 95:

	TDB			PSP		
	Sel	**Base**	**Size**	**Sel**	**Base**	**Size**
Win16	1BDF	00030E00	320	1AB7	00031010*	110
Win32	1BC6	800E0B20	210	1B1F	00031120	120

**Win16 PSP base = Win16 TDB base + 210h*

Although the Win32 task's TDB is not allocated in conventional memory, its associated PSP still is. This is significant. If you place a breakpoint on the GlobalDosAlloc routine in the Win16 KERNEL and start up a Win32 application under Windows 95, the breakpoint is hit. Each Win32 task's PSP is allocated with the Win16 GlobalDosAlloc API. Thus, Windows 95's Win32 kernel really does call down not only to real-mode DOS but also to the Win16 kernel.

In the Win32 API, you launch applications with CreateProcess. You can also use a Win32 version of the older WinExec call; this in turn calls an internal version of CreateProcess. When you consider that each Win32 process has a Win16 TDB, it seems plain that CreateProcess must somehow be calling down to CreateTask in KRNL386 not only for Win16 applications but even for Win32 applications.

We'll see later that the CreateProcess API in KERNEL32 *does* create a TDB by calling the internal CreateTask function in KRNL386. This makes perfect sense. It is surprising only because Microsoft claims that such things don't take place in Chicago. But really, how else would each Win32 process wind up with a Win16 TDB (albeit one that as we've seen differs a little from the TDB that Win16 tasks get and from the TDB in Windows 3.*x*)?

Where's the Windows 95 Current Directory?

Windows 95 makes another important change to the TDB layout for both Win32 and Win16 tasks.

In Windows 3.*x*, the TDB maintains the current drive and directory in a 68-byte buffer at offset 66h, and there's an embedded PSP at offset 100h (see *Undocumented Windows*, pp. 366-368).

In Windows 95, however, the current drive number continues to reside in the byte at offset 66h in the TDB but the current directory has been moved to offset 100h. As we've seen, the PSP, which formerly resided at offset 100h, has been moved out either to offset 210h (for Win16 tasks) or into an entirely separate conventional-memory segment (for Win32 tasks).

This movement of the current directory from the 67-byte buffer at offset 67h (remember, the byte at 66h is the current drive) to the 272 (110h) bytes at offset 100h has to do with long directory and file names, as you probably guessed.

The Win16 KERNEL must maintain the current drive and directory on a per-task basis. This is just another example of the problem, noted in Chapter 12 (in the "PSPs and Other DOS Data in Windows 95" section), that the upper and lower layers of Windows are remarkably separate from each other. As far as IFSMgr is concerned, there is one current directory per virtual machine (VM); DOSMGR likewise instances DOS's current-drive variable on a per-VM basis. But the System VM runs multiple tasks, each of which can have its own current drive and directory.

VxDs don't really know anything about what happens inside the System VM; all the different Win16 and Win32 applications look like one big application, called KRNL386.EXE. As we saw in Chapters 6 and 7, this separation between the upper and lower layers of Windows means, potentially at least, that the VMM/VxD layer can run something other than the Windows graphical user interface and, conversely, that the Windows GUI can run on something other than Microsoft's VMM/VxD layer. Loosely coupled systems are generally preferable to tightly coupled "integrated" ones.

However, the benefits to such modularity may be outweighed by the duplication of effort it entails. The kernel in the System VM often has to fake out the lower levels of Windows, making them believe there is only a single application running — one that just likes to switch the current PSP, DTA, drive, and directory a lot!

In time, the upper and lower levels of Windows should become more tightly integrated. VxDs will come to know more about Windows tasks and will be used for mainstream Windows programming. The Appy Time and run-time dynamic linking services — such as _SHELL_CallAtAppyTime, _SHELL_LoadLibrary, _SHELL_GetProcAddress, and_SHELL_CallDll — provided by the SHELL VxD in Windows 95 are an important step in this direction. During so-called AppyTime (application time), a VxD can make Windows API calls. The VWIN32 VxD in Windows 95 also appears to be a step toward greater integration between Windows applications and Windows VxDs.

In Windows 95, VxDs do know about threads as well as about VMs, and as we saw back in Chapter 1, VxDs can use Thread Local Storage (TLS). But the current drive and directory aren't appropriate to maintain on a per-thread basis. Therefore, the single current directory that IFSMgr provides to the System VM, and the DOS current-drive variable instanced by DOSMGR, must be multiplexed at the kernel level rather than at the VxD level among all Win16 and Win32 tasks. When there's a task switch, KERNEL might have to switch the current drive and directory too. Thus, it makes sense to keep each task's current drive and directory in its TDB.

So far, all this remains unchanged in Windows 95. Win32 tasks in part need Win16-style TDBs to store their current drive and directory. The difference in Windows 95, however, is that long filenames and directory names make it impossible to continue using the current-directory buffer at offset 67h in the TDB. Windows 95 keeps the task's possibly longer current directory at the location where Windows 3.*x* keeps a PSP. The current-drive byte is still kept at offset 66h.

Why do TDBs for Win16 tasks need the extra current directory space too? Because Win16 applications can call the INT 21h function 71h LFN functions. In addition, the Win16 kernel (KRNL386) contains functions such as SetCurrentDirectory and GetCurrentDirectory, which thunk up to the equivalent functions in KERNEL32 (which then just turn around and call INT 21h functions such as 19h and 7147h for GetCurrentDirectory and 0Eh and 713Bh for SetCurrentDirectory).

As noted earlier, the Win16 common dialogs in Windows 95 can sometimes call these LFN functions on behalf of a Win16 application without the application knowing it. (Users will just see that they can save out long filenames and directory names.) This only applies to out-bound (Set) calls. Silently replacing an application's old in-bound (Get) call with a new one that potentially returns more data (a longer file or directory name) could overrun its buffers.

The point here is that even Win32 tasks store their current drive and directory in a Win16 TDB. This can be easily demonstrated with a small Win32 Console application, CHGDIR.C, shown in Listing 13-3.

Listing 13-2: CHGDIR.C

```
// CHGDIR.C -- Win32 Console app
// Shows that Win32 tasks keep current drv/dir in Win16 TDB

#include <stdlib.h>
#include <stdio.h>
#define  WIN32_LEAN_AND_MEAN
#include "windows.h"

DWORD (WINAPI *VxDCall)(DWORD srvc, DWORD eax, DWORD ecx);

#define GET_PROC(mod, func) GetProcAddress(GetModuleHandle(mod), (func))
#define VWIN32_INT21_CALL   0x2A0010
#define VWIN32_INT31_CALL   0x2A0029
#define DosCall(eax, ecx)   VxDCall(VWIN32_INT21_CALL, (eax), (ecx))
#define DPMICall(eax, ecx)  VxDCall(VWIN32_INT31_CALL, (eax), (ecx))

char curdir[MAX_PATH], buf[MAX_PATH], bufupr[MAX_PATH];

void fail(const char *s) { puts(s); exit(1); }
```

```
main()
{
    HANDLE id;
    BYTE *tdb_drv, *tdb_curdir, *tdb_base;
    WORD tdb, psp;

    // Thread Id == Ring 3 THCB (Thread Control Block)
    id = GetCurrentThreadId();
    printf("Thread ID: %08lXh\n", id);

    // Win16 TDB is at offset 1Ch in Ring 3 THCB
    // I'm a little surprised it's so easy to get at this!
    tdb = *((WORD *) (((BYTE *) id) + 0x1c));
    printf("TDB: %04Xh\n", tdb);

    // Use run-time dynamic linking to turn strings
    // into callable function pointers
    if ((VxDCall = GET_PROC("KERNEL32", "VxDCall0")))
    {
        // Get linear base address for TDB by calling
        // DPMI INT 31h function 6 (Get Selector Base).
        // Even though we're a 32-bit app, we get the 16-bit
        // DPMI services, since we're calling DPMI indirectly
        _asm mov bx, tdb
        DPMICall(0x0006, 0);
        _asm mov word ptr tdb_base+2, cx
        _asm mov word ptr tdb_base, dx
        printf("TDB base: %08lXh\n", tdb_base);

        // Call DOS INT 21h function 62h (Get PSP)
        DosCall(0x6200, 0);
        _asm mov psp, bx
        printf("PSP: %04Xh\n\n", psp);

        // Sanity check:  is TDB[60h] == PSP?
        if (*((WORD *) (tdb_base + 0x60)) != psp)
            fail("TDB and PSP don't match!");

        // Current drv at offset 66h in TDB, curr dir at offset 100h
        // SetCurrentDirectory changes these.
        // Note: Current drv/dir on per-task basis, not per-thread.
        tdb_curdir = tdb_base + 0x100;
        tdb_drv = tdb_base + 0x66;
    }
    else
        printf("Warning: Can't access VxDCall0\n\n");

    for (;;)
    {
        if (GetCurrentDirectory(MAX_PATH, curdir) == 0)
            printf("invalid>");
        else
            printf("[%s] ", curdir);
        gets(buf);
        if ((buf[0] == '\0') || (buf[0] == '\n'))
```

```
            continue;
        strcpy(bufupr, buf);
        strupr(bufupr);
        /*NOTE! CHGDIR.C and CHGDIR.EXE on disk have a bug: instead of sizeof
              (cmd)-1, they just have size of (cmd). Need to recompile CHGDIR,
              putting in -1, for this program to work.*/
        #define MATCH(cmd)  (strncmp(bufupr, (cmd), sizeof(cmd)-1) == 0)
        if (MATCH("EXIT"))
            break;
        else if (MATCH("CD "))
        {
            if (! SetCurrentDirectory(&buf[3]))
                printf("CD failed\n");
            else if (tdb_curdir)
            {
                printf("TDB+66h:  %02Xh\n", *tdb_drv);
                printf("TDB+100h: \'%s\'\n", tdb_curdir);
            }
        }
        else if (MATCH("MD "))
        {
            if (! CreateDirectory(&buf[3], 0))
                printf("MD failed\n");
        }
        else
            WinExec(buf, SW_NORMAL);
    }
    printf("done\n");
    return 0;
}
```

As you can see, CHGDIR consists of little more than a loop that lets the user type in a few commands: MD (make directory), CD (change directory), EXIT, or a command that will be passed through to WinExec. There's a prompt that prints (within square brackets) the current drive and directory returned by the GetCurrentDirectory Win32 API.

Before entering the loop, though, the program does a few odd-looking things that you probably don't expect to see in a Win32 program.

For example, CHGDIR calls the GetCurrentThreadId Win32 API and interprets the returned thread ID as a Ring 3 Thread Control Block (THCB). At least in the beta version of Chicago this book is based on, the WORD at offset 1Ch in the Ring 3 THCB is the Win16 TDB. (Of course, any or all of this might change in the final released version of Chicago.) The Win32 application can dereference its own thread ID (a 32-bit near pointer such as 810FE91Ch) and retrieve a selector to its TDB without any problem. Notice that because CHGDIR is a 32-bit program, it doesn't need far pointers to access this external data:

```
WORD tdb = *((WORD *) (((BYTE *) GetCurrentThreadId()) + 0x1C));
```

A selector to its own TDB won't do a Win32 application much good, however. CHGDIR needs the 32-bit linear address of its own TDB. In a Win32 program, this 32-bit linear address (such as 800E0A80h) can be used as a near pointer, assuming that the linear address is mapped into your address space. The GetSelectorBase function from the Win16 API is not supported in the Win32 API, so we'll have to use something else. DPMI provides a function (INT 31h function 6, Get Segment Base Address) that, given a selector, returns its linear base address:

```
BYTE *tdb_drv, *tdb_curdir, *tdb_base;
_asm mov bx, tdb
DPMICall(0x0006, 0);     // Get Selector Base
_asm mov word ptr tdb_base+2, cx
_asm mov word ptr tdb_base, dx
```

DPMICall is just a wrapper around the undocumented VxDCall service provided by KERNEL32 (see "Win32 File Handles and Thunking" in Chapter 14). CHGDIR uses GetProcAddress to get a function pointer to VxDCall (whose actual name in KERNEL32 is VxDCall0):

```
// Use run-time dynamic linking to turn strings
// into callable function pointers
#define GET_PROC(mod, func) GetProcAddress(GetModuleHandle(mod), (func))
#define VWIN32_INT31_CALL   0x2A0029
#define DPMICall(eax, ecx)  VxDCall(VWIN32_INT31_CALL, (eax), (ecx))

DWORD (WINAPI *VxDCall)(DWORD srvc, DWORD eax, DWORD ecx);
VxDCall = GET_PROC("KERNEL32", "VxDCall0");
```

After using DPMICall, CHGDIR should have a readily usable 32-bit flat pointer to its own TDB. Just to make sure, CHGDIR calls INT 21h function 62h (again with VxDCall, this time using Win32 service 2A0010h) to get the PSP, and compares the returned selector with the WORD at offset 60h in what, we hope, is the TDB. As explained earlier, offset 60h in the TDB holds a protected-mode selector to the task's PSP. This is true for Win32 as well as Win16 tasks:

```
WORD psp;
DosCall(0x6200, 0);  // Get Current PSP
_asm mov psp, bx
assert(*((WORD *) (tdb_base + 0x60)) == psp);
```

Finally, just before entering its read-eval-print loop, CHGDIR creates pointers to offset 100h in the TDB, where the current directory is stored, and to offset 66h, where the current drive is stored:

```
tdb_curdir = tdb_base + 0x100;
tdb_drv = tdb_base + 0x66;
```

Inside the loop, whenever the user does a CD (SetCurrentDirectory), CHGDIR prints the contents of TDB+66h and TDB+100h:

```
SetCurrentDirectory(&buf[3]);
printf("TDB+66h:  %02Xh\n", *tdb_drv);
printf("TDB+100h: \'%s\'\n", tdb_curdir);
```

Here's some sample output from CHGDIR:

```
Thread ID: 810FF300h
TDB: 1CA6h
TDB base: 800E0CA0h
PSP: 1CEFh

[C:\UNAUTHW\TEST] md This is a long directory name

[C:\UNAUTHW\TEST] cd This is a long directory name
TDB+66h:  82h
TDB+100h: '\UNAUTHW\TEST\This is a long directory name'

[C:\UNAUTHW\TEST\This is a long directory name] md This is another long \
directory name

[C:\UNAUTHW\TEST\This is a long directory name] cd This is another long \
directory name
TDB+66h:  82h
TDB+100h: '\UNAUTHW\TEST\This is a long directory name\This is another \
long directory name'

[C:\UNAUTHW\TEST\This is a long directory name\This is another long \
directory name] cd \
TDB+66h:  82h
TDB+100h: '\'

[C:\] cd unauthw\test
TDB+66h:  82h
TDB+100h: '\unauthw\test'

[C:\unauthw\test] cd h:\
TDB+66h:  87h
TDB+100h: '\'

[h:\] cd c:
TDB+66h:  82h
TDB+100h: '\'
```

Indeed, TDB+66h holds the current drive (in the form described in the earlier discussion of the internal KERNEL SaveState function), and TDB+100h holds the current directory.

Note that the SetCurrentDirectory and GetCurrentDirectory APIs manipulate not only the directory but also the drive. There isn't a separate SetDrive or SetVolume function in the Win32 API. If you want to change drives, you call SetCurrentDirectory. (Note the CD H: and CD

C: in the preceding CHGDIR output; this is not legal in Windows 95's COMMAND.COM, by the way.) SetCurrentDirectory also supports \\servername\sharename (UNC) disk designators.

The absence of a separate change-drive function does have one unusual effect, which can be seen at the end of the CHGDIR output: if you're at C:\unauthw\test (note that the names are case-insensitive but case-preserving), and call SetCurrentDirectory (H:), and then SetCurrentDirectory (C:), you'll wind up not at C:\unauthw\test but at C:\. From this one example, Windows 95 appears to have no built-in notion of multiple current directories on different drives. MS-DOS in contrast gives each drive its own current directory, maintained in the internal Current Directory Structure (CDS; see *Undocumented DOS*, 2d ed., pp. 163-167, 443-449).

To see how CHGDIR looks to real-mode DOS, I ran the program with V86TEST. A wide variety of INT 21h calls appeared. To try to understand all these INT 21h calls showing up at V86TEST, I wrote a Win32 Console application, NOTHING.EXE, which consisted of nothing but

```
main() { return 0; }
```

I then ran that under V86TEST and compared the V86TEST output from CHGDIR with the V86TEST output from NOTHING. CHGDIR is responsible for only three different INT 21h calls:

```
06: 43550   40: 140     62: 1
```

The large number of calls to function 06h (Console I/O) represent time CHGDIR spends inside the C gets function, waiting for input. (Hmm, why the spin cycle? Why not block the VM until some input is ready?) The Microsoft C 32-bit run-time library implements gets with a call to ReadFile. Reading from the console generates a VxDCall to the VCOND (Virtual CON Device) VxD. The actual function 06h call is generated in V86 mode by CONAGENT.EXE which, in turn, is launched by VMM32 when you start a Win32 Console application.

The function 40h (Write) calls come from CHGDIR's printfs to stdout. And the function 62h (Set PSP) call is CHGDIR's VxDCall-(0x2A0010, 0x6200, 0).

Without dwelling on the fact that a Win32 application (albeit a character-mode one) uses real-mode DOS for input (remember, Windows 95 supposedly does away with real-mode DOS), the important point here is that V86TEST — and therefore real-mode DOS — didn't see any calls to get or set the current directory or the current drive. Although these Win32 APIs might have more involvement with the Win16 kernel than Microsoft cares to acknowledge, we can at least see that they aren't calling down to real-mode DOS, even though internally they use INT 21h function 71h.

What does WSPY21 think of this Win32 Console application? If a Win32 Console application calls FreeConsole to detach from the current console (usually a DOS box) and calls AllocConsole to create a separate one (in Windows 95, these consoles are just VMs), WSPY21 will see the Win32 application call INT 21h function 4Bh to start CONAGENT.EXE. But in the case of CHGDIR, WSPY21 sees nothing special. In fact, WSPY21 displays the same results for CHGDIR as for NOTHING:

```
<WINOLDAP> *(50) Set PSP 167 (00A7h)
<WINOLDAP>  (55) (Undoc) Create PSP 7407 (1CEFh), 256 (0100h)
<WINOLDAP> *(1A) Set DTA 1E57:0080
<WINOLDAP> *(71) LFN (3B) ChDir '\WINDOWS'
<WINOLDAP> *(50) Set PSP 7767 (1E57h)
<KERNEL32> *(50) Set PSP 7407 (1CEFh)
<KERNEL32> *(00) Exit
<KERNEL32> *(50) Set PSP 167 (00A7h)
```

Note that the PSP created by WINOLDAP (here, 1CEFh) matches the PSP that CHGDIR displays when it starts up.

But why do Win32 processes need Win16 TDBs in the first place?

For one thing, Win32 applications require Win16 TDBs to work with the existing Win16 messaging system in USER. A lot of attention has been paid to the fact that Windows 3.*x* has a single input queue shared by all tasks — so a task that doesn't yield will lock out every other task — and to the solution in Windows 95 of giving each thread its own input queue. Microsoft refers to this as input desynchronization. However, one point hasn't been stressed enough: the Windows messaging system still resides in Win16-land.

Matt Pietrek has pointed this out in *Microsoft Systems Journal* ("Investigating the Hybrid Windowing and Messaging Architecture of Chicago," September 1994, p. 17):

> Even though the window procedure for a 32-bit program window is written in 32-bit code, existing 16-bit applications ... expect any window, regardless of whether it's 16 or 32 bits, to act just like it would in Windows 3.x. Consider something like window subclassing.... If Chicago were to store a 32-bit linear address in the WND structure, things would quickly go up in smoke. To prevent such problem scenarios, Chicago goes to great lengths to make all windows behave as if they were 16-bit windows.

One of the lengths to which Windows 95 goes to make Win32 windows behave like Win16 windows is to give every Win32 task a Win16 TDB with a Win16 task queue.

Furthermore, every Win32 WndProc has a corresponding Win16 WndProc. As far as the USER windowing system is concerned, all windows are 16-bit, with 16-bit WndProcs and 16-bit message queues. You can easily see this with any Win16 program that walks the window list. For example, WALKWIN.C in Listing 13-4 is a simple WINIO application that uses the GetWindow API to walk the window list:

Listing 13-4: WALKWIN.C

```
// WALKWIN.C

#include <stdlib.h>
#include <string.h>
#include <dos.h>
#include "windows.h"
#include "toolhelp.h"
#include "winio.h"

void print_hwnd(HWND hwnd, int level)
{
    char taskname[9];
    char wndproc_owner[9];
    GLOBALENTRY *pge;
    HANDLE htask, htaskq;
    void far *wndproc;
    char *wndtext, *classname;
    int flag32, i;

    if (! (wndtext = (char *) malloc(128)))
        fail("Insufficient memory");
    if (! (classname = (char *) malloc(128)))
        fail("Insufficient memory");

    // get information about this window
    htask = GetWindowTask(hwnd);
    GetWindowText(hwnd, wndtext, 128);
    wndproc = GetClassLong(hwnd, GCL_WNDPROC);
    GetClassName(hwnd, classname, 128);
    flag32 = *((WORD far *) MK_FP(htask, 0x16)) & 0x10;
    htaskq = *((WORD far *) MK_FP(htask, 0x20));
    _fmemcpy(taskname, MK_FP(htask, 0xF2), 8);
    taskname[8] = '\0';

    // use ToolHelp to get module name of WndProc owner
    wndproc_owner[0] = '\0';
    if (! (pge = (GLOBALENTRY *) malloc(sizeof(GLOBALENTRY))))
        fail("Insufficient memory");
    pge->dwSize = sizeof(GLOBALENTRY);
    if (GlobalEntryHandle(pge, FP_SEG(wndproc)))
```

```
    {
        MODULEENTRY *pme;
        if (! (pme = (MODULEENTRY *) malloc(sizeof(MODULEENTRY))))
            fail("Insufficient memory");
        pme->dwSize = sizeof(MODULEENTRY);
        if (ModuleFindHandle(pme, pge->hOwner))
            strcpy(wndproc_owner, pme->szModule);
        free(pme);
    }
    free(pge);

    // print information:
    // W  Task  hWnd   hTask  TaskQ  WndProc (owner)  Wnd Class  Wnd Text
    // for example:
    // 32 CAB32 0188h  1276h  207Fh  079F:3E66 (USER) 'Static'  "&Named:"
    for (i=0; i<level; i++)
        printf("  ");
    printf("%s %s %04Xh  %04Xh  %04Xh  %Fp (%s) \'%s\'  ",
        flag32 ? "32" : "16",
        taskname, hwnd, htask, htaskq,
        wndproc, wndproc_owner, classname);
    if (wndtext && *wndtext)
        printf("\"%s\"", wndtext);
    printf("\n");

    free(classname);
    free(wndtext);
}

void walkwin(HWND hwnd, int level) // recursive depth-first walk
{
    if (hwnd == 0)
        return;
    hwnd = GetWindow(hwnd, GW_HWNDFIRST);
    while (hwnd)
    {
        print_hwnd(hwnd, level);
        walkwin(GetWindow(hwnd, GW_CHILD), level+1);
        hwnd = GetWindow(hwnd, GW_HWNDNEXT);
    }
}

main(int argc, char *argv[])
{
    winio_setpaint(__hMainWnd, FALSE);
    printf("%s\n",
"W  Task  hWnd   hTask  TaskQ  WndProc (owner)    Wnd Class     Wnd Text");
    walkwin(GetWindow(GetDesktopWindow(), GW_CHILD), 0);
    winio_setpaint(__hMainWnd, TRUE);
    return 0;
}
```

This Win16 program can easily find the window handle, the TDB (from which it can extract the task name and message queue address), WndProc, class name, and window title not only of other Win16 applications but also of each running Win32 application. Here's a small portion of output from WALKWIN while I was running the Clock, WinBezMT, and FreeCell Win32 applications (along with WALKWIN itself):

```
32 CAB32 00D0h  1276h  207Fh  167F:0022 (KERNEL) 'tooltips_class32'
32 CAB32 00C4h  1276h  207Fh  167F:0022 (KERNEL) 'tooltips_class32'
32 CAB32 00B4h  1276h  207Fh  167F:0114 (KERNEL) 'Shell_TrayWnd'
  32 CAB32 00B8h  1276h  207Fh  079F:3E61 (USER) 'Button'
  32 CAB32 00BCh  1276h  207Fh  167F:01AE (KERNEL) 'TrayNotifyWnd'
    32 CAB32 00C0h  1276h  207Fh  167F:01C4 (KERNEL) 'TrayClockWClass'
  32 CAB32 00C8h  1276h  207Fh  167F:01DA (KERNEL) 'MSTaskSwWClass'
    32 CAB32 00CCh  1276h  207Fh  167F:007A (KERNEL) 'SysTabControl32'
16 MSGSRV32 0088h  13EFh  1677h  0797:06A2 (USER) '#32768'
16 MSGSRV32 0084h  13EFh  1677h  0777:0005 (USER) '#32771'
16 WALKWIN 05D0h  2787h  272Fh  2847:2B1B (WALKWIN) 'winio_wcmain'  "WALKWIN"
16 WINOLDAP 045Ch  1E07h  1CFFh  1227:0069 (COMMCTRL) 'tooltips_class'
16 WINOLDAP 0450h  1E07h  1CFFh  1EB7:0B07 (WINOLDAP) 'tty'  "COMMAND"
; ...
32 FREECELL 0128h  1B46h  1B1Fh  167F:05FA (KERNEL) 'FreeWClass'  "FreeCell
Game #5755"
32 WINBEZMT 014Ch  1A56h  1B4Fh  167F:0702 (KERNEL) 'winbezmt'  "32-bit
Multi-Threaded WinBez"
  32 WINBEZMT 0150h  1A56h  1B4Fh  07E7:0000 (USER) 'MDIClient'
    32 WINBEZMT 0228h  1A56h  1B4Fh  167F:0718 (KERNEL) 'ThreadClass'
"Thread Window 1"
    32 WINBEZMT 0224h  1A56h  1B4Fh  167F:0718 (KERNEL) 'ThreadClass'
"Thread Window 2"
; ...
32 CAB32 015Ch  1276h  207Fh  079F:3E70 (USER) '#32770'  "Find: All Files"
  32 CAB32 0184h  1276h  207Fh  079F:3E70 (USER) '#32770'  "Name & Location"
    32 CAB32 0188h  1276h  207Fh  079F:3E66 (USER) 'Static'  "&Named:"
; ...
32 CLOCK 0120h  1CAEh  1C6Fh  167F:04F2 (KERNEL) 'Clock'  "Clock"
32 BATMETER 00D8h  1F9Eh  1FA7h  167F:02F8 (KERNEL) 'BatteryMeter_Main'
"Battery Meter"
  32 BATMETER 00DCh  1F9Eh  1FA7h  079F:3E61 (USER) 'Button'  "Power Status"
; ...
32 CAB32 00D4h  1276h  207Fh  167F:016C (KERNEL) 'ProxyTarget'
32 CAB32 00B0h  1276h  207Fh  167F:016C (KERNEL) 'ProxyTarget'
32 CAB32 00A0h  1276h  207Fh  17D7:503E (DDEML) 'DMGFrame'
32 CAB32 009Ch  1276h  207Fh  17D7:5104 (DDEML) 'DMGClass'
  32 CAB32 0110h  1276h  207Fh  17D7:52EA (DDEML) 'DMGHoldingClass'
32 CAB32 0094h  1276h  207Fh  167F:00FE (KERNEL) 'OTTimerClass'
16 MSGSRV32 0090h  13EFh  1677h  13D7:0458 (MSGSRV32) 'Windows 32-bit VxD
Message Server'
16 TIMER 008Ch  130Fh  12CFh  1377:0332 (MMSYSTEM) '#42'
32 CAB32 0098h  1276h  207Fh  167F:012A (KERNEL) 'Progman'  "Program Manager"
  32 CAB32 00A4h  1276h  207Fh  167F:0156 (KERNEL) 'SHELLDLL_DefView'
    32 CAB32 00A8h  1276h  207Fh  167F:004E (KERNEL) 'SysListView32'
      32 CAB32 00ACh  1276h  207Fh  167F:0064 (KERNEL) 'SysHeader32'
```

WALKWIN uses the Win32 flag at offset 16h in the TDB to determine whether the window belongs to a Win16 or Win32 application. Apart from that flag (shown as 16 or 32 at the beginning of each line) and your knowledge of which applications are Win16 or Win32, there would be no way of knowing an application's "bitness" from looking at the other items WALKWIN displays. And that is the whole point here: As far as the Windows 95 windowing system is concerned, Win32 applications look much like Win16 applications, down to their use of KERNEL structures such as the TDB and task message queue.

To make it 100 percent clear that all windows belonging to Win32 applications really do have Win16 WndProcs, WALKWIN uses the ToolHelp API to retrieve the name of the owner of the segment in which each WndProc resides. As you can see from the WALKWIN output, the WndProcs for the built-in Win32 window classes such as Button, MDI-Client, and Static are located in the Win16 USER module, and the WndProcs for the Win32 application-specific windows belong to the Win16 KERNEL.

Win32 applications such as CAB32, WinBezMT, Clock, and FreeCell are all calling the Win32 version of RegisterClass from USER32.DLL, and all install 32-bit WndProcs. But WM_XXX messages in Windows 95 always go to 16-bit WndProcs. These 16-bit WndProcs thunk up to the 32-bit WndProcs installed by Win32 applications. (This message-thunk mechanism is explained in the September 1994 *Microsoft Systems Journal* article by Matt Pietrek.) Similarly, USER32 APIs such as GetMessage thunk down to their Win16 counterparts in USER.

This all looks fairly similar to the scheme used in Win32s. In Windows 95, if you trace through a message thunk, from the arrival of a WM_XXX message at a Win16 WndProc proxy to the delivery of the message to the Win32 WndProc, you'll encounter a call to function in KERNEL32 named W32S_BackTo32. For what it's worth, a function with the same name appears in the Win32s W32SKRNL.DLL module. Running WALKWIN with some Win32 applications under Win32s, furthermore, reveals the same basic approach we saw in Windows 95: In the case of the built-in window classes, Win16 WndProc proxies belong to USER; the Win16 proxies for application-specific Win32 WndProcs belong to WIN32S16. For example:

```
32 WINBEZMT 256Ch  1D67h  1D2Fh  1F07:0042 (WIN32S16) 'winbezmt'  "32-bit
Multi-Threaded WinBez"
  32 WINBEZMT 25C0h  1D67h  1D2Fh  06FF:1062 (USER) 'MDIClient'
32 CLOCK 2468h  1DFFh  1DD7h  1F07:002C (WIN32S16) 'Clock'  "Clock - 9/9/94"
32 FREECELL 1ED8h  125Fh  1167h  074F:0429 (USER) '#32770'  "About FreeCell"
; ...
  32 FREECELL 22E0h  125Fh  1167h  074F:2313 (USER) 'Static'  "Memory:"
  32 FREECELL 2328h  125Fh  1167h  074F:2313 (USER) 'Static'  "8,048 KB Free"
```

```
  32 FREECELL 2370h  125Fh  1167h  074F:2313 (USER) 'Static'
"System Resources:"
  32 FREECELL 23B8h  125Fh  1167h  074F:2313 (USER) 'Static'  "85% Free"
  32 FREECELL 2400h  125Fh  1167h  074F:1A12 (USER) 'Button'  "OK"
32 FREECELL 1E98h  125Fh  1167h  1F07:0016 (WIN32S16) 'FreeWClass'  "FreeCell
Game #7260"
```

Despite important changes such as input desynchronization, the messaging system in Windows 95 remains resolutely 16-bit, much as it was in Windows 3.*x*. The scheme for supporting Win32 messages looks much as it does in Win32s. Win32 applications participate in Windows 95 messaging by virtue of their Win16 proxies.

Now, the Win16 USER messaging system is totally dependent on Win16 KERNEL data structures, especially the task message queue. As *Undocumented Windows* (p. 380) notes, it is sometimes hard to decide where USER ends and KERNEL begins:

> Because messages are really posted to a task, not a window, it makes sense that the Task Queue itself is a KERNEL rather than a USER data structure. On the other hand, many routines inside USER have intimate knowledge of the Task Queue structure; these include ReplyMessage(), InSendMessage(), GetMessageTime(), GetMessagePos(), and PostQuitMessage()....
>
> Actually, it is difficult to decide whether the Task Queue is a KERNEL or a USER data structure. Really, it's shared between the two modules, and in fact provides most of the glue between KERNEL and USER. The GetTaskQueue() and SetTaskQueue() functions are in KERNEL, but the Task Queue itself is created by the InitApp() function in USER.

Put together these two facts — Win32 message support depends on Win16 message support, and Win16 message support depends on Win16 KERNEL data structures — and it is clear that Win32 support in Windows 95 *must* rest on the Win16 KERNEL. The idea that USER32 thunks down to USER but that KERNEL32 doesn't thunk down to KRNL386 is absurd. Indeed, in a Windows 95 system running only Win32 applications, a data-access breakpoint (BPR in Soft-ICE/Windows) placed on the TDBs and task queues will be triggered all the time.

Well, so what? Win32 applications need Win16 TDBs for compatibility with the Windows messaging system. And in any event, Windows 95 needs the Win16 kernel to run Win16 applications. What's wrong if KERNEL32 sometimes uses the code that already exists in KRNL386?

There's nothing at all wrong with it, except that Microsoft claims that, unlike USER32 which almost always thunks down to Win16 USER, and GDI32 which frequently thunks down to Win16 GDI, supposedly KERNEL32 never thunks down to KRNL386:

> Most of the code in USER32 is little more than a layer that accepts 32-bit API calls and hands them off to its 16-bit counterpart for processing.... [This is] a sensible way of using tried and trusted code — after all, the 16-bit API implementations have to be there for compatibility. GDI32 offers come significant performance improvements. Consequently, the 32-bit GDI handles a lot of API calls directly.
>
> The KERNEL32 module is completely independent of its 16-bit version. There is some communication from the 16-bit to the 32-bit side, but the 32-bit KERNEL never calls across to the 16-bit side. This is as you'd expect, since most of the code (for example, memory allocation and thread management) is quite different.
>
> — Adrian King, "Memory Management, the Win32 Subsystem, and Internal Synchronization in Chicago," *Microsoft Systems Journal*, May 1994, p. 58.

The statements that KERNEL32 is "completely independent" of the 16-bit KRNL386 and that "the 32-bit KERNEL never calls across to the 16-bit side" are simply untrue, as we'll soon see. And, as with the similar "never" statements regarding Windows and MS-DOS quoted in the preceding chapter — such as "if you only run Windows-based applications, you'll never execute any MS-DOS code" — what comes to mind are a few lines from Gilbert and Sullivan's *HMS Pinafore*. The ship's captain sings that he never, ever swears, and the chorus questions whether this is really true:

> Chorus: What, never?
>
> Captain: No, never.
>
> Chorus: What, never?
>
> Captain: Well, hardly ever.

Unfortunately, the computer trade press often performs as a quite different kind of chorus: When Microsoft mentions some Windows 95 compromise, such as Win16Lock (see "Win16 Everywhere" in Chapter 14), the press gets all bent out of shape. However, if Microsoft tells the press something it wants to hear, such as that some piece of 16-bit code is gone, there seems to be little attempt made to verify whether this is true. The PC trade press sometimes seems like a chorus of parrots with inverted priorities.

Instead of beating Microsoft up over necessary compromises such as Win16Lock, and then turning around and wholeheartedly believing the company when it says that real-mode DOS is gone or that the Win32 kernel doesn't rely on the Win16 kernel, it would be better to neither second-guess Microsoft's architectural compromises, nor believe the company when it claims that it has eliminated such necessary compromises.

The computer trade press has dutifully repeated Microsoft's claims regarding the Win32 kernel's supposed total independence of the Win16 kernel. As one example, *Windows Magazine*, in "A Revealing Look at the Architecture" (July 1994, p. 186), presents a diagram purporting to show that thunks in Chicago go USER 32->16, GDI 32<->16, but KERNEL 32<-16, and asserts that "All Chicago kernel components (task management, memory paging, file systems) are implemented using 32-bit protected mode."

No one who tried to independently verify Microsoft's statements could possibly say this. Even without disassembling the code, readily available debugging tools such as Soft-ICE/Windows and WinScope show, for example, that Windows 95 task management requires both 16-bit protected-mode code and some real-mode code. Once you see that every Win32 process has a Win16 task database and real-mode DOS PSP, everything else falls into place. KERNEL swings both ways (32<->16): Certainly KRNL386 calls up to KERNEL32, but KERNEL-32 calls down to KRNL386 as well (as we already saw with the LoadLibrary16 and GetProcAddress16 calls, and as we'll soon see in more detail). There's no good reason it shouldn't. Later, we'll look at the not-so-good reasons for *claiming* it doesn't.

King's point about using the "tried and trusted code" in USER is an important one. This point is valid even if you don't believe that all the bugs have been shaken out of this code. (I once had an opportunity to glance at the USER source code and was frankly appalled.) As Matt Pietrek puts it:

> USER.EXE is what's sometimes referred to as 'legacy code.' It's been modified, tinkered with, and otherwise tweaked for more than half a decade...there are, no doubt, peculiarities within USER.EXE that applications have come to rely on as normal behavior. It's likely that no one person can fully keep a working model of USER and all its assumptions and quirks in his or her head. If USER's code were ported to completely 32-bit code, existing applications would break.
>
> — Matt Pietrek, "Investigating the Hybrid Windowing and Messaging Architecture of Chicago," *Microsoft Systems Journal*, September 1994, pp. 15-16.

In other words, the devil you know is generally preferable to the supposed angel you've never met. The USER code has been banged on for years by millions of users out in the real world. This (and not the supposedly independent oversight of an easily confused, cajoled, and hoodwinked trade press) is the highest scrutiny of all. It's unlikely that any of the supposedly "genuine" operating systems favored by the operating system purists and pundits could survive such mass-market pounding.

But there's one thing I don't get: If the point applies to USER, then why not to KERNEL too? Adrian King says that the supposed independence of KERNEL32 from the Win16 KERNEL "is as you'd expect," but

I don't see this at all. We already know that Win16 USER handles WM_XXX messages for Win32 applications, and it is well known that the USER messaging system is heavily dependent on KERNEL task management. (See the earlier quote regarding the task queue from *Undocumented Windows*, p. 380, and see *Windows Internals*, Chapter 7.) Since Windows 95 uses Win16 for WM_XXX message handling, it is to be expected that Win32 would need the Win16 KERNEL at least to give each Win32 process a USER-compatible task queue and TDB. Given that USER32 APIs such as GetMessage thunk down to their Win16 USER equivalents, and given that message queue management continues to be the responsibility of Win16 USER, it logically follows that Win32 KERNEL32 must use some services from the Win16 KERNEL.

From Explorer to Create PSP in Six Easy Steps

It's okay if you didn't quite follow my logic just now, because the fact is that Windows 95's KERNEL32 *does* use services from the Win16 kernel.

Recall the following important line of WSPY21 output, which appears whenever CAB32 launches an application, even another Win32 application:

```
<CAB32> *(55) (Undoc) Create PSP 7503 (1D4Fh), 256 (0100h)
```

How do you get from clicking an application's icon in the Explorer to generating an INT 21h function 55h that is sent down to real-mode DOS? Interestingly, the path goes right through the Win16 kernel:

- When you select an application to run from the Explorer, CAB32 calls the ShellExecuteEx API in SHELL32. This API in turn calls the Win32 version of WinExec in KERNEL32. Win32 applications are supposed to use CreateProcess rather than WinExec, so WinExec is now just a compatibility layer around CreateProcess.
- Tracing through CreateProcess (actually, CreateProcessA), we eventually get to the following block of code:

```
0137:BFF91A67   MOV    CL,31                  ; thunk #
0137:BFF91A69   PUSH   EBP
0137:BFF91A6A   MOV    EBP,ESP
0137:BFF91A6C   PUSH   ECX
```

```
0137:BFF91A6D   SUB     ESP,+3C
0137:BFF91A70   PUSH    WORD PTR [EBP+08]       ; 0A7h
0137:BFF91A74   PUSH    DWORD PTR [EBP+0C]      ; 810FD9A4h
0137:BFF91A77   PUSH    WORD PTR [EBP+10]       ; 1E97h
0137:BFF91A7B   CALL    [BFF9181A]              ; BFFB7C44h
0137:BFF91A81   MOVZX   EAX,AX
0137:BFF91A84   LEAVE
0137:BFF91A85   RET     000C
```

- Tracing into the CALL [BFF9181A], we get to the following (incidentally, some of this code looks like output from Microsoft's thunk compiler):

```
0137:BFFB7C44   XOR     ECX,ECX
0137:BFFB7C46   MOV     CL,[EBP-04]                 ; 31h   thunk#
0137:BFFB7C49   MOV     EDX,[00030464+4*ECX]        ; 0117653Fh (see below)
0137:BFFB7C50   MOV     EAX,BFF71247
0137:BFFB7C55   JMP     EAX
```

Notice that the code is using 31h in CL as an index into a table of DWORDs. We'll look at this table more closely in a few minutes. Right now, what matters is that slot 31h in the table contains the value 0117653Fh and that the code has moved this value into the EDX register.

- Next, we jump to BFF71247h, which, it turns out, is the routine QT_Thunk in KERNEL32:

```
KERNEL32!QT_Thunk
0137:BFF71247   TEST    BYTE PTR FS:[0000001C],01
0137:BFF7124F   JE      BFF71320
0137:BFF71255   POP     DWORD PTR [EBP-24]
0137:BFF71258   PUSH    DWORD PTR [BFFB7CD8]
0137:BFF7125E   PUSH    EDX                 ;; Win16 addr to call
; ...
0137:BFF712B4   RETF
```

- When QT_Thunk issues the RETF, we suddenly are no longer in KERNEL32. Instead, QT_Thunk "returns" to the (phony) return address that was pushed on the stack. Note the PUSH EDX near the top of QT_Thunk; recall that EDX holds the value 0117653Fh extracted from slot 31h in the table of DWORDs at 30464h. Executing the RETF at the end of QT_Thunk takes us to the segment:offset address in EDX that was pushed on the stack:

```
0117:0000653F   PUSH    BP
0117:00006540   MOV     BP,SP
0117:00006542   PUSH    WORD PTR [BP+0C]
0117:00006545   PUSH    DWORD PTR [BP+08]
0117:00006549   PUSH    WORD PTR [BP+06]
; ...
```

Segment 0117h belongs to the Win16 kernel. Thus, through the miracle of QT_Thunk and that table at 30464h, KERNEL32 has called down to some code in the Win16 kernel. (Well, not quite a miracle: QT_Thunk jumps to a piece of 16-bit code by pushing its full 48-bit address on the stack and then "returning" to it.)

- If we trace through this KERNEL code, we eventually arrive at the call to INT 21h function 55h:

```
011F:0000411E   MOV     DX,[BP+08]
011F:00004121   MOV     SI,[BP+06]
011F:00004124   MOV     AH,55
011F:00004126   INT     21
```

So where in KERNEL are we? Recall our earlier discussion, based on Matt Pietrek's *Windows Internals*, about the internal CreateTask function in KRNL386,which calls BuildPDB, which calls INT 21h function 55h. We're somewhere in CreateTask; KERNEL32 thunk #31h provides a way for Win32 code such as CreateProcess to call KERNEL's 16-bit CreateTask function.

Those innocent-looking MOV AH,55h and INT 21h instructions are hardly the end of the trip. The trip has barely begun, in fact. Since KERNEL has called INT 21h in protected mode, the call will go to the protected-mode INT 21h chain. KERNEL's own INT 21h handler is typically at the front of this chain. KERNEL passes the call down to what we've called KernelDosProc, which is the previous owner of the INT 21h vector, usually a VxD. If no one on the protected-mode INT 21h chain absorbs the function 55h call (and it is likely no one will), the INT 21h is sent to the V86 INT 21h hook chain (where VxDs such as IFSMgr and DOSMGR will see it) and thence to the actual V86 interrupt chain, where various device drivers and TSRs will get a peek at the INT 21h before DOS sees it and creates a PSP.

The outgoing part of the trip looks like this:

```
Click on icon in CAB32 ->
SHELL32!ShellExecuteEx ->
KERNEL32!WinExec ->
internal KERNEL32!CreateProcess ->
thunk #31h ->
KERNEL32!QT_Thunk ->
internal KRNL386!CreateTask ->
internal BuildPDB ->
INT 21h function 55h ->
PM INT 21h chain (KERNEL -> KernelDosProc -> etc.) ->
V86 INT 21h hook chain (IFSMgr -> DOSMGR -> etc.) ->
V86 mode INT 21h chain (V86TEST -> IFSHLP.SYS -> etc.) ->
real-mode DOS
```

That provides a quick answer to the question posed earlier about how clicking an application's icon in the Explorer can produce a Create PSP call down in real-mode DOS. The return value from INT 21h function 55h must now travel all the way back to CreateTask, and eventually CreateTask must return to its KERNEL32 caller.

We've just looked at one thunk, #31, through which KERNEL32 causes KRNL386 to issue (among other things) a call to INT 21h function 55h. It's worth looking at some of the other routines in the thunk table located at offset 30464 in the System VM. We can dump out the whole table with the PROTDUMP utility:


```
C:\UNAUTHW\PROTDUMP>protdump #1 30464 -dword 0x100
C4430464 | 011F66CE 011F0B5B 011F4396 01272364
C4430474 | 0127258B 0127253B 01272527 01272513
C4430484 | 01170105 01177544 011765AB 011703D0
C4430494 | 01270525 01270233 0127017F 01270155
C44304A4 | 011775FD 011775D6 0117764B 01177624
C44304B4 | 011F04CD 011F041D 011F0317 011F048D
C44304C4 | 011F0387 011F045B 011F0355 011F03DF
C44304D4 | 011F02BD 011F03AD 011F023D 011700F1
C44304E4 | 01170144 01170175 01170158 011700D4
C44304F4 | 01170119 011700B8 011F01EF 011F0074
C4430504 | 01270533 011F4062 0117470C 01176580
C4430514 | 011760A7 0117607B 0117605A 0117604B
C4430524 | 01176553 0117653F 01176568 01174956
C4430534 | 01176432 011F0018 011F00EB 0117019D
C4430544 | 01170189 0117022C 01170218 01271331
C4430554 | 01271430 01271D73 01271CE6 01271D95
; ... don't know quite where table ends ...
```

Every one of these sixty or so entries represents a thunk from KERNEL32 down to KRNL386: you know, the stuff that supposedly never happens. Not every thunk in this table is necessarily still used in Windows 95; some of it could be just scaffolding that will be removed or ignored when the commercial release of Windows 95 is ready. To figure out what some of these KERNEL32 -> KRNL386 thunks do, and whether there are any more that are useful or important besides the few we've stumbled across already (LoadLibrary16, GetProcAddress16, and the CreateTask thunk we just examined), it's sometimes easier to look for code in KERNEL32 that employs the thunk, rather than at the KRNL386 code whose address appears in the preceding table. Huh? Well, here's what I mean:

```
KERNEL32!FindAtomA
0137:BFF825E9   PUSH    EDI
;;; param validation stuff
0137:BFF91D4E   MOV     CL,06
0137:BFF91D50   JMP     BFF91D60
```

```
KERNEL32!LoadLibrary16
0137:BFF91D52    MOV     CL,36
0137:BFF91D54    JMP     BFF91D60

KERNEL32!DeleteAtom
0137:BFF91D7F    MOV     CL,05
0137:BFF91D81    JMP     BFF91D9D

KERNEL32!GlobalFree16
0137:BFF91D8B    MOV     CL,23
0137:BFF91D8D    JMP     BFF91D9D

KERNEL32!GlobalDeleteAtom
0137:BFF91D97    MOV     CL,11
0137:BFF91D99    JMP     BFF91D9D

KERNEL32!InitAtomTable
0137:BFF91DE6    MOV     CL,03
0137:BFF91DE8    JMP     BFF91DEC
```

This all makes sense. For example, LoadLibrary16 is thunk #36; entry #36 in the table is at 30464+36*4 = 3053Ch, which points to 011F:00EB. This is the address of the LoadLibrary API in Win16 KERNEL. Similarly, FindAtomA is thunk #6; entry #6 in the table points to 0127:2527. This is the address of a routine in KERNEL that calls FindAtom.

In short, there are all sorts of circumstances in which KERNEL32 calls down to KRNL386. The table we've examined provides KERNEL32 with the 16-bit selector:offset address for various routines in KRNL386; KERNEL32 uses QT_Thunk to call the routines. It's difficult to believe that anyone would deny that KERNEL32 thunks down to KRNL386. We've just seen that there's a fairly elaborate mechanism whose sole purpose is to do just that.

A similar mechanism allows Win16 code in KRNL386 to thunk *up* to the Win32 code in KERNEL32. For example, I noted earlier (in the "Where's the Windows 95 Current Directory?" section) that KRNL386 contains functions such as SetCurrentDirectory and GetCurrentDirectory that thunk up to the equivalent functions in KERNEL32.

Now, there's absolutely nothing wrong if KERNEL32 needs to call down to the Win16 KERNEL. Microsoft surely knows that KERNEL32 *does* thunk down to the Win16 KERNEL and that, if nothing else, this follows logically from the combination of USER32's dependence on Win16 USER and Win16 USER's dependence on the Win16 KERNEL. So why the big claims that KERNEL32 doesn't need the Win16 KERNEL?

One reason, I think, is psychological. Microsoft is known for being a tremendously innovative marketing organization that is fantastically good at exploiting whatever opportunities come along. But not many in the software industry think of the company as particularly innovative technically. Microsoft has an inferiority complex about its most successful operating systems, MS-DOS and Windows. For years, the company has been trying to show that it, too, can build what might in some circles be called a "real man's" operating system, and what others might simply dismiss as a case of "second system syndrome." Perverse though it may sound, Bill Gates keeps trying to act like Steve Jobs.

Microsoft has produced wonderfully successful operating systems which have become the de facto standards for mass-market desktop computing (and the UNIX community, with its boutique-sized installed base, talks of "open systems"!), but this isn't good enough. From Bill Gates on down, Microsoft wants everyone to think that its products not only dominate the desktop but also meet some artificial purist criteria for operating system goodness.

Hence at least some of the exaggerated claims regarding Windows 95's independence from the old, wildly successful, "tried and trusted," DOS and Windows code base. And hence, too, Microsoft's doth-protest-too-much assertions that "Chicago is not Win32s!" (referring to a much-despised but perfectly workable add-on that allows Windows 3.1*x* to run some Win32 executables; see Chapter 14). While Microsoft keeps trying to assert that it has produced "new technology," I feel a lot safer knowing that it hasn't.

But aside from purely psychological motivation, there are also some firmly practical issues here. For one thing, much of the misinformation surrounding the Windows 95 architecture comes from Microsoft's natural desire (discussed in detail in Chapter 1) to portray Windows 95 as integrated, and therefore as a no-excuses alternative to the highly integrated, appliance-like Apple Macintosh.

Another reason, probably less important, has to do with Microsoft's strange relationship with the computer trade press. The same trade press that won't attempt to independently verify Microsoft's claims also likes to deride Microsoft over relatively silly issues. In the case of Windows 95, all the partisans of operating system purity have been complaining that Windows 95 isn't sufficiently like Windows NT.

The following quotations aren't perfect examples, because their author is a superb journalist whose articles frequently hit the nail on the head, but they are somewhat representative of the heat that Microsoft takes simply because Chicago isn't NT:

> Chicago's Win16 support is a potential Achilles heel....
>
> If you use Chicago to run Win32 applications only, it will more closely approximate an 'NT lite'....
>
> Chicago, when running a mixture of DOS and Win16 applications, will behave much like Windows 3.*x* with a few improvements....
>
> Even at its best, though, Chicago is not the pure 32-bit operating system that NT is. Instead, it is a 16- to 32-bit hybrid. At the December conference in which Microsoft distributed its second preliminary developer kits, programmers who hadn't yet worked with NT were, in general, more impressed with Chicago than those already familiar with NT.
>
> — Jon Udell, "Chicago: An Ambitious Compromise," *Byte*, March 1994, p. 23.

Notice that, while obviously critical of Microsoft's quite sensible plans not to model Windows 95 after the lacklustre NT boutique operating system, Udell's article appears to fully accept Microsoft's distinction between a Windows 95 running only Win32 applications and one also running a mixture of DOS and Win16 applications. The suggestion is that there is a qualitative difference between these two environments.

In another article ("The Fix Is In for Chicago," *Byte*, September 1994, p. 193), Udell states that "Chicago systems running Win32 applications should prove much more stable than Chicago or Windows 3.*x* systems running mostly DOS and Win16 applications." Although it's likely that he's referring here primarily to Windows 95's capability to give each Win32 application its own private address space, I think it's important to realize that a Windows 95 system, at least as presently constructed, is *never* purely running Win32 applications. For one thing, MSGSRV32, a Win16 task, is always running. If you take a Windows 95 machine running only Win32 applications and then start a Win16 application, there isn't much of a qualitative change that takes place.

As one example, below I listed all the loaded modules on a Windows 95 system running nothing except the Explorer. I've dropped font files (which are modules) from the following list, which was produced with the MOD command in WinICE:

```
:mod
hMod PEHeader       Module Name       .EXE File Name
010F                KERNEL            C:\WINDOWS\SYSTEM\KRNL386.EXE
024F                WSSYS             c:\ws_chi\wssys.drv
0297                SYSTEM            C:\WINDOWS\SYSTEM\system.drv
0167                KEYBOARD          C:\WINDOWS\SYSTEM\keyboard.drv
0257                MOUSE             C:\WINDOWS\SYSTEM\mouse.drv
029F                DISPLAY           C:\WINDOWS\SYSTEM\vga.drv
02FF                SOUND             C:\WINDOWS\SYSTEM\sound.drv
038F                COMM              C:\WINDOWS\SYSTEM\comm.drv
03EF                GDI               C:\WINDOWS\SYSTEM\gdi.exe
```

```
075F               USER       C:\WINDOWS\SYSTEM\user.exe
17E7               DDEML      C:\WINDOWS\SYSTEM\DDEML.DLL
13FF               MSGSRV32   C:\WINDOWS\SYSTEM\MSGSRV32.EXE
13A7               MMSYSTEM   C:\WINDOWS\SYSTEM\mmsystem.dll
132F               TIMER      C:\WINDOWS\SYSTEM\mmtask.tsk
13AF               POWER      C:\WINDOWS\SYSTEM\power.drv
1317               SHELL      C:\WINDOWS\SYSTEM\SHELL.DLL
123F               COMMCTRL   C:\WINDOWS\SYSTEM\commctrl.dll
206F               SHELL16    C:\WINDOWS\SYSTEM\shell16.dll
1E77               WIN87EM    C:\WINDOWS\SYSTEM\WIN87EM.DLL
1DE7               COMMDLG    C:\WINDOWS\SYSTEM\COMMDLG.DLL
018E 013F:BFF70080 KERNEL32   C:\WINDOWS\SYSTEM\KERNEL32.DLL
06D6 013F:810F8564 GDI32      C:\WINDOWS\SYSTEM\GDI32.DLL
06DE 013F:810F8820 ADVAPI32   C:\WINDOWS\SYSTEM\ADVAPI32.DLL
071E 013F:810F8A8C ICM32      C:\WINDOWS\SYSTEM\ICM32.DLL
1686 013F:810F8D3C USER32     C:\WINDOWS\SYSTEM\USER32.DLL
131E 013F:810F9A80 WINMM      C:\WINDOWS\SYSTEM\WINMM.DLL
12AE 013F:810FA55C MPR        C:\WINDOWS\SYSTEM\MPR.DLL
12F6 013F:810FA878 MSPWL32    C:\WINDOWS\SYSTEM\MSPWL32.DLL
1296 013F:810FAB18 NETLIB32   C:\WINDOWS\SYSTEM\NETLIB32.DLL
125E 013F:810FAF08 CAB32      C:\WINDOWS\CAB32.EXE
1256 013F:810FB8F8 COMCTL32   C:\WINDOWS\COMCTL32.DLL
124E 013F:810FBB34 SHELL32    C:\WINDOWS\SHELL32.DLL
1F5E 013F:810FC71C LINKINFO   C:\WINDOWS\SYSTEM\LINKINFO.DLL
1F06 013F:810FD264 BATMETER   C:\WINDOWS\BATMETER.EXE
1F0E 013F:810FD60C CRTDLL     C:\WINDOWS\SYSTEM\CRTDLL.DLL
```

So this is our Windows 95 "steady state," at least in the current implementation. Notice the large number of modules for which the PEHeader field is blank; these are Win16 DLLs.

Next, I started three Win32 applications: Clock, WinBezMT, and the Win32 version of FreeCell. The following additional Win32 modules showed up:

```
27CE 013F:81103908 CLOCK      C:\WINDOWS\CLOCK.EXE
27D6 013F:81104164 COMDLG32   C:\WINDOWS\SYSTEM\COMDLG32.DLL
26C6 013F:811043E0 WINBEZMT   C:\WINDOWS\WINBEZMT.EXE
232E 013F:81100294 MSNET32    C:\WINDOWS\SYSTEM\MSNET32.DLL
1C3E 013F:811052D8 FREECELL   C:\WIN32APP\FREECELL\FREECELL.EXE
0BCE 013F:81105D04 CARDS      C:\WIN32APP\FREECELL\CARDS.DLL
27DE 013F:81105F40 SHELL32    C:\WINDOWS\SYSTEM\SHELL32.DLL
```

Next, I started WSPY21, which is a Win16 application. No additional modules showed up other than WSPY21 itself:

```
276F               WSPY21     C:\UNAUTHW\BINW\WSPY21.EXE
```

No new Win16 modules were required to run this program. Finally, I started the WinScope debugger. This loaded three WinScope modules and dragged in three Win16 DLLs — WIN87EM, TOOLHELP, and COMMDLG — that didn't show up when we were running only Win32 applications:

```
1EBF            WINSCOPE        C:\ws_chi\winscope.exe
1E77            WSCD            C:\ws_chi\WSCD.DLL
1E57            WSMISC          C:\ws_chi\WSMISC.DLL
1E2F            WIN87EM         C:\WINDOWS\SYSTEM\WIN87EM.DLL
1E4F            TOOLHELP        C:\WINDOWS\SYSTEM\TOOLHELP.DLL
0A8F            COMMDLG         C:\WINDOWS\SYSTEM\COMMDLG.DLL
```

I was particularly concerned to see the effect of loading WinScope because another test I did for 32-bit purity employed this debugger. While running the standard set of Win32 applications already listed countless times in this chapter — Clock, Explorer, FreeCell, and WinBezMT — and no Win16 applications besides WinScope itself, I had WinScope hook calls *from* all DLLs *to* all APIs in the Win16 KERNEL DLL. After two or three minutes of this, I sorted the WinScope log and had an AWK program count the number of calls to each Win16 KERNEL function:


```
14367   total calls to KERNEL

02422   GlobalUnlock            02278   GlobalLock
01263   lstrlen                 01167   LocalAlloc
01091   LocalFree               00823   GetCurrentTask
00747   PrestoChangoSelector    00424   GetExpWinVer
00371   LocalUnlock             00371   LocalLock
00294   IsBadReadPtr            00250   WaitEvent
00250   PostEvent               00250   GetExePtr
00247   hmemcpy                 00241   FindAtom
00198   GlobalAlloc             00188   GlobalFree
00155   OldYield                00144   LockResource
00141   LoadResource            00141   FindResource
00132   lstrcpyn                00126   GetAtomName
00108   IsBadHugeReadPtr        00081   FreeResource
00078   LocalSize               00056   lstrcpy
00052   GlobalReAlloc           00050   GetAppCompatFlags
00046   AddAtom                 00040   IsBadStringPtr
00037   IsBadCodePtr            00032   NoHookDOSCall
; ...
```

The significance of this list is that no Win16 applications other than WinScope itself were running, yet in just two or three minutes there were over 14,000 calls to the Win16 KERNEL API. Assuming that WinScope isn't skewing the results too badly (which we'll get into in a moment), this would show that the whole notion of a pure Windows 95 system that runs only Win32 applications is fairly meaningless.

It was easy to confirm that the vast majority of these calls occur whether a Win16 application such as WinScope is loaded or not. I used WinICE (which runs *outside* Windows) to put breakpoints on some of the Win16 KERNEL functions that WinScope detected in the semi-pure Win32 configuration. I then unloaded WinScope, so no Win16 applications were running. I couldn't get rid of the TIMER and MSGSRV32 Win16 tasks, but these are built into Windows 95. Therefore, this is probably as pure a Win32 setup as one could hope for, at least in the current implementation of Windows 95. Here's what the configuration looked like:

```
:task
TaskName    SS:SP       StackTop  StackBot  StackLow  TaskDB  hQueue  Events
WINBEZMT  * 0000:0000   00737000  00740000            26E6    26C7    0000
CLOCK       0000:0000   00737000  00740000            279E    2777    0000
BATMETER    0000:0000   00737000  00740000            1F1E    1EF7    0000
CAB32       0000:0000   00756000  00760000            1276    207F    0000
TIMER       12E7:1F88   00B2      201C      201C      130F    12CF    0000
MSGSRV32    13CF:327E   00E2      3314      30C0      13EF    1677    0000
KERNEL32    012F:1218   000348B0  000448AF            0097    1677    0000

:thread
Ring0TCB  ID    Context   Ring3TCB  Process   TaskDB  PDB   SZ   Owner
C0FE55F0  0014  C0FD48E8  810FFC6C  810FF188  26E6    26DF  32   WINBEZMT
C0FE53A0  0013  C0FD48E8  810FFA2C  810FF188  26E6    26DF  32   WINBEZMT
C0FE5150  0012  C0FD48E8  810FF7EC  810FF188  26E6    26DF  32   WINBEZMT
C0FD5194  0011  C0FD48E8  810FF52C  810FF188  26E6    26DF  32 * WINBEZMT
C0FD3F30  0010  C0FE02F4  810FE7D8  810FE438  279E    27A7  32 * CLOCK
C0FDD140  000D  C0FDCB9C  810FD960  810FB30C  1276    126F  32   CAB32
C0FDDD74  000C  C0FE011C  810FD024  810FCC74  1F1E    1F2F  32 * BATMETER
C0FDF9F4  0008  C0FDCB9C  810FC224  810FB30C  1276    126F  32   CAB32
C0FDE21C  0007  C0FDCB9C  810FB6B8  810FB30C  1276    126F  32 * CAB32
C0FDC8B4  0006  C0FE8B1C  810FA26C  810F9F18  130F    1307  16 * TIMER
C0FDBE74  0005  C0FE8B1C  810F9820  810F726C  0097    00AF  32   KERNEL32
C0FDBAC8  0004  C0FE8B1C  810F95E0  810F928C  13EF    13E7  16 * MSGSRV32
C0FD916C  0003  C0FE8B1C  810F8FDC  810F726C  0097    00AF  32   KERNEL32
C0FD0E14  0002  C0FE8B1C  810F82C4  810F726C  0097    00AF  32   KERNEL32
C4520298  0001  C0FE8B1C  810F7344  810F726C  0097    00AF  32   VM 01
C0FE57F4  0018  C0FDCB9C  811002B0  810FB30C  1276    126F  32   CAB32
C0FD53D8  0016  C0FDCB9C  811000E4  810FB30C  1276    126F  32   CAB32
```

In this configuration — no 16-bit tasks or threads running other than TIMER and MSGSRV32 — I put breakpoints on some of the Win16 KERNEL calls that WinScope had detected.

It turned out that WinScope had skewed the results a bit. For example, many (though by no means all) of the calls to GetCurrentTask simply disappeared when WinScope wasn't running. These calls came from ToolHelp, which was present only because WinScope required it.

However, the vast majority of the Win16 KERNEL calls logged by WinScope did continue to occur when no Win16 application was running. Here are a few examples:

- All those calls to PrestoChangoSelector (see *Undocumented Windows*, pp. 39-40, 343-346) occur whether or not any Win16 applications are loaded. PrestoChangoSelector can turn a code selector into a data selector or vice versa. It is used to implement self-modifying code or executable data. The DISPLAY driver's BITBLT module calls PrestoChangoSelector to compile bitblts on the fly. (See the sample source code in the Windows DDK, such as \DISPLAY\4PLANE\BITBLT\BITBLT.ASM.)

- GetExePtr is called from FindResource and LoadResource, which are called from LoadString, which in turn is called via QT_Thunk from USER32!LoadStringA. (Which begat...) LoadString appears to be called constantly in Windows 95, perhaps to produce those clever bouncing "Hint:" items at the bottom of the screen. At any rate, there are constant calls to the Win16 GetExePtr function, which, given almost any kind of global handle, will find the module handle with which it's associated. (See Pietrek, *Windows Internals*, pp. 474-476: "GetExePtr() is one of my favorite undocumented functions.")
- The 32 NoHookDosCalls all come from the InquireSystem function in SYSTEM.DRV (see *Undocumented Windows*, pp. 339-340, 608-609). This in turn is called by the GetDriveType API in KERNEL.

We could go on and on, examining each Win16 KERNEL call that appears in a "Win32 applications only" Windows 95 environment, but you get the idea: Even in the purest case, there are tons of calls to the Win16 KERNEL. This is perfectly logical, given that the Win16 versions of GDI and USER both call down to KERNEL.

More and more, it seems that Microsoft's claim that the 32-bit KERNEL never calls across to the 16-bit KERNEL is not only false, but possibly even meaningless. Think about it for a second: Even if you accepted Microsoft's claim (which we know to be false) that KERNEL32 never directly calls across to KRNL386, Microsoft has said that USER32 calls USER and that GDI32 calls GDI. It's obvious from inspection with a tool such as Microsoft's EXEHDR or the EXE Quick View in the Windows 95 Explorer that USER and GDI both call KERNEL. For example, they rely heavily on the GlobalLock, GlobalUnlock, LocalAlloc, and LocalFree memory-management services. Thus, even when running only Win32 tasks, the Win16 KERNEL is in constant use because USER32 and GDI32 call USER and GDI, which in turn rely on KERNEL.

So, even if KERNEL32 didn't directly thunk down to the Win16 KERNEL, or even if you wanted to dismiss as unimportant the cases in which it does, the Win16 KERNEL remains a crucial part of Windows 95, *even if you run only Win32 applications*.

By claiming that even though USER32->USER and GDI32->GDI, at least KERNEL32 !-> KRNL386, Microsoft is obviously trying to win over operating system cognoscenti ("armchair OS designers," as Udell refers to them) who believe there is something inherently preferable about a pure 32-bit operating system.

Surely developers at Microsoft know that there's nothing inherently preferable about a brand-new operating system that doesn't rely on the "tried-and-trusted" (though far from bug-free) DOS or Win16 code base. And surely Microsoft knows that many of the claims made about Windows 95 — that it eliminates real-mode DOS, that the Win32 kernel doesn't rely on the Win16 kernel, that running only Win32 applications presents a qualitatively different configuration from one running a mixture of DOS, Win16, and Win32 applications — are simply untrue.

But perhaps Microsoft can brush all this off: "Oh, that didn't quite make it into Windows 95; we'll take care of it in Windows 96." Indeed, with each version of Windows, Microsoft can remove, and has removed, more and more dependence on real-mode DOS. Microsoft can start on the same path away from dependence on Win16 code.

So if one day the last drop of 16-bit or real-mode code is gone from Windows ("hey, we finally got around to creating PSPs in protected mode and storing them in extended memory"), is that some kind of important transformation? No. The real transformation occurred with Windows 3.0 Enhanced mode in May 1990.

And, although important, the crucial aspect of this transformation in 1990 wasn't the technical change of basing Windows on a protected-mode DOS extender. Recall that a similar important technical change took place in 1987-88 with Windows/386 2.*x* (which forms the basis for much of VMM), without transforming the PC desktop. Far more important than the new technology in Windows 3.*x* was the fact that Windows sales took off in 1990. On the other hand, this explosion in sales would never have happened had Windows not incorporated a protected-mode DOS extender that finally provided sufficient memory to make Windows useful.

With massive sales, all things become possible. There's an interesting parallel here to the ongoing historians' debate over the Industrial Revolution: Was it a "wave of gadgets," or was it more importantly an explosion in sales, consumption, population, and market size?

When Udell says "programmers who hadn't yet worked with NT were, in general, more impressed with Chicago than those already familiar with NT," I have to wonder what these programmers already familiar with NT are thinking about. What is impressive about Windows is not this or that technical feature, but its installed base. If you want technical excellence, I'm sure you can do a lot better than

Windows. If you want to develop applications that will potentially be used by millions of people, Windows is the way to go. In other words, a massive installed base will get you through times of unimpressive technology better than impressive technology will get you through a small installed base.

Windows 95 will outsell NT by at least an order of magnitude. Microsoft knows that this is what matters most about Windows 95. The coolest features matter little without the massive presence on the desktop required to make developing for the operating system worthwhile. As the StarKist commercial puts it, "We don't want tuna with good taste; we want tuna that tastes good."

Windows 95's reliance on DOS and on Win16 code is not an "Achilles heel." Instead, eliminating real-mode and Win16 code would be a Pyrrhic victory. Windows would attain 32-bit nirvana and lose a large number of customers. The movie *Field of Dreams* has it all wrong: You can build it but they won't necessarily come.

The WSPY21 Code

This long tirade of mine, you may dimly recall, was inspired by a few scant lines of WSPY21 output. I had originally intended WSPY21 to illuminate the DOS-Windows relationship, but it turned out to be at least as useful in shedding light on the possibly more important (and by now certainly more interesting) question of the Win32-Win16 relationship. As we'll see, WSPY21 also clarifies some otherwise-confusing features of the protected-mode INT 21h handler that lives inside the Win16 KERNEL.

So let's look at the code that produced those few lines of output that we've pored over for so long. Figure 13-3 shows a calling tree for WSPY21.

```
main
    INIT_REQUBUF
    GetCurrentTask
    get_vect
    set_vect (install IntHandler)
        _dpmi_set_pmode_vect (INT 31h AX=0205h)
        _dpmi_get_pmode_vect (INT 31h AX=0204h)
    GetSetKernelDosProc (install IntHandler2)
    display_ints
        winio_openwindows
        wmhandler_yield (GetMessage, etc.)
        read_data
```

```
            IS_REQUEST
            BEGIN_CRIT_SEC
            _fmemcpy, _fstrncpy
            END_CRIT_SEC
            SET_NEXT
        display_dos_int
            printf

IntHandler
    GetCurrentTask
    write_data
        BUFFER_FULL
        BEGIN_CRIT_SEC
        _fmemcpy, _fstrncpy
        GetTaskName
            verr
            sel_size (GetSelectorLimit)
        MAYBE_COPY
        verr
        sel_size
        SET_NEXT
        END_CRIT_SEC
        PostMessage
    _chain_intr

IntHandler2
    GetCurrentTask
    SAME_CALL
    write_data (see above)
    _chain_intr
```

Figure 13-3: Calling tree for WSPY21.

As the calling tree suggests, the program consists of three semi-independent pieces:

- The main function installs the interrupt handlers and calls display_ints, which calls read_data to retrieve items from a circular buffer. (WSPY21 is a WINIO application, and so starts off in main rather than in WinMain.) If not spying on INT 21h (you can specify an alternate interrupt on the WSPY21 command line; INT 31h for DPMI is particularly interesting) or on encountering an unknown INT 21h call, WSPY21 produces a plain register dump.
- IntHandler is the primary INT 21h hook. For each INT 21h call IntHandler sees, it calls write_data to place a packet of information about the call in the same circular buffer from which display_ints reads. This information includes the name of the current task at the time of the INT 21h; the interrupt handler in WSPY21 runs as part of this other task. (As explained earlier, this is why GetCurrentTask

doesn't get WSPY21's own task handle.) IntHandler posts a WM_NULL message to WSPY21's window, so that wmhandler_yield (which calls GetMessage) will return and display_ints can display the next INT 21h call. IntHandler chains the interrupt to the previous handler, which is generally KERNEL's INT 21h handler.

- IntHandler2 is almost the same as IntHandler, except it installs with GetSetKernelDosProc and therefore sees INT 21h at a slightly lower level than IntHandler. IntHandler2 uses a SAME_CALL macro to determine whether IntHandler has already seen(referring to a much-despised but perfectly-workable add-on that allows Windows 3.1*x* to run some Win32 executables) a call and therefore that it need not be displayed again (unless you run WSPY21 -SHOWALL; see below).

Listing 13-5 shows the code for WSPY21. This code is based loosely on the WISPY (I Spy for Windows) program from *Undocumented Windows* (pp. 180-188). A major difference is that WISPY used only GetSetKernel-DosProc to install a single INT 21h handler, but WSPY21 installs two INT 21h handlers. WISPY therefore missed all calls, such as function 4Bh (EXEC), that are absorbed in KERNEL's INT 21h handler, but WSPY21 sees these calls. The very fact that KERNEL can absorb or change some protected-mode INT 21h is significant; we'll get to that soon.

Listing 13-5: WSPY21.C

```
/*
WSPY21.C
Andrew Schulman, 1994
Based loosely on WISPY.C from Undocumented Windows
*/

#include <stdlib.h>
#include <dos.h>
#include <string.h>
#include "windows.h"
#include "wmhandlr.h"
#include "winio.h"

#pragma pack(1)

typedef struct {
#ifdef __BORLANDC__
    WORD bp,di,si,ds,es,dx,cx,bx,ax;
#else
    WORD es,ds,di,si,bp,sp,bx,dx,cx,ax;     /* same as PUSHA */
#endif
    WORD ip,cs,flags;
    } REG_PARAMS;
```

```
/************************************************************************/

// This gives us about 550 entries in the buffer
// Unfortunately, there are still frequent buffer overflows
#define BUF_SIZE    (0xFFFF / sizeof(REQUEST))
#define MAX_STR     40
#define MAX_REQU    (BUF_SIZE-1)

typedef struct {
    REG_PARAMS r;
    char taskname[9], char dsdx[MAX_STR], dssi[MAX_STR];
    int type, flag;
    } REQUEST, FAR * LPREQUEST;

#define REQU_FREE        'f'     /* request block not in use */
#define REQU_USE         'u'     /* in use */

#define BEGIN_CRIT_SEC()         _asm cli
#define END_CRIT_SEC()           _asm sti

#define SET_NEXT()      { if (next==MAX_REQU) next=0; else next++; }
#define IS_REQUEST(buf)          (buf[next].type != REQU_FREE)
#define BUFFER_FULL(buf)         IS_REQUEST(buf)

/************************************************************************/

#ifndef MK_FP
#define MK_FP(a,b)  ((void far *)(((DWORD)(a) << 16) | (b)))
#endif

#define INT21           ' '
#define KERNELDOSPROC   '*'

#define COPY_DSDX       1
#define COPY_DSSI       2
#define CHECK_AL        3
#define FIRST_FUNC      0x3b
#define LAST_FUNC       0xa0

// Instructions for WRT_REQUEST on how to handle each INT 21h function
static char copyflags[1 + LAST_FUNC - FIRST_FUNC] = {
    /*3b*/ COPY_DSDX, COPY_DSDX, COPY_DSDX, 0, 0, 0, 0, 0,
    /*43*/ COPY_DSDX, 0, 0, 0, 0, 0, 0, 0,
    /*4b*/ COPY_DSDX, 0, 0,
    /*4e*/ COPY_DSDX, 0, 0, 0, 0, 0, 0, 0, 0, 0, 0, 0,
    /*5a*/ COPY_DSDX, COPY_DSDX,  0, 0, 0, 0,
    /*60*/ COPY_DSSI, 0, 0, 0, 0, 0, 0, 0, 0, 0, 0, 0,
    /*6c*/ COPY_DSSI, 0, 0, 0, 0,
    /*71*/ CHECK_AL,  0, 0, 0, 0, 0, 0, 0, 0, 0, 0, 0, 0, 0, 0,
    /*80*/ 0, 0, 0, 0, 0, 0, 0, 0, 0, 0, 0, 0, 0, 0, 0, 0,
    /*90*/ 0, 0, 0, 0, 0, 0, 0, 0, 0, 0, 0, 0, 0, 0, 0, 0,
    /*a0*/ COPY_DSDX,
    } ;

static REQUEST far *requ;
static int show_all = 0;
```

```
static DWORD calls = 0, lost = 0, already = 0, mine = 0;

#define sel_size(sel)       (GetSelectorLimit(sel)+1)

WORD verr(WORD short sel)
{   _asm {
        mov ax, 1
        verr word ptr sel
        je short okay
        dec ax
    }
    okay:;
}

char far *GetTaskName(HANDLE hTask)
{
    static char none[2] = "";
    if (verr(hTask) && (sel_size(hTask) > (0xf2+8)))
        return (char far *) MK_FP(hTask, 0xf2);
    else
        return none;
}

int WRT_REQUEST(REQUEST far *buf, REG_PARAMS far *pr,
    HANDLE task, int flag)
{
    static int next = 0;
    unsigned char ah;
    void far *fp;

    if (BUFFER_FULL(buf))
        return 0;
    BEGIN_CRIT_SEC();
    _fstrncpy(&buf[next].taskname, GetTaskName(task), 8);
    buf[next].taskname[8] = '\0';
    _fmemcpy(&buf[next].r, pr, sizeof(REG_PARAMS));
    buf[next].type = REQU_USE;

#if 1
    #define MAYBE_COPY(str, r1, r2) { \
        _fmemset(str, 0, MAX_STR); \
        if (verr(r1) && (sel_size(r1) > r2)) \
            _fmemcpy(str, MK_FP(r1, r2), \
                     min(MAX_STR-1, sel_size(r1)-r2)); \
    }
#else
    // IsBadStringPtr works by causing GP faults which KRNL386 catches
    // But this seems to cause unexpected page faults in Win32s!
    #define MAYBE_COPY(str, r1, r2) { \
        _fmemset(str, 0, MAX_STR); \
        fp = MK_FP(r1, r2); \
        if (! IsBadStringPtr(fp, 256)) \
            _fstrncpy(str, fp, min(_fstrlen(fp), MAX_STR-1)); \
        }
#endif
```

```
    ah = pr->ax >> 8;
    if (ah >= FIRST_FUNC && ah <= LAST_FUNC)
    {
        ah -= FIRST_FUNC;
    top:
        if (copyflags[ah] == COPY_DSDX)
            MAYBE_COPY(&buf[next].dsdx, pr->ds, pr->dx) //;
        else if (copyflags[ah] == COPY_DSSI)
            MAYBE_COPY(&buf[next].dssi, pr->ds, pr->si) //;
        else if (copyflags[ah] == CHECK_AL)
        {
            ah = (pr->ax & 0xff) - FIRST_FUNC;
            if (copyflags[ah] != CHECK_AL)
                goto top;
        }
    }

    buf[next].flag = flag;
    SET_NEXT();
    END_CRIT_SEC();
    PostMessage(__hMainWnd, WM_NULL, 0, 0); // just to keep moving!
    return 1;
}

int RD_REQUEST(REQUEST far *buf, REG_PARAMS *pr, LPSTR ptaskname,
    LPSTR lpdsdx, LPSTR lpdssi, int far *pflag)
{
    static int next = 0;
    if (! IS_REQUEST(buf))
        return 0;
    BEGIN_CRIT_SEC();
    _fmemcpy(pr, &buf[next].r, sizeof(REG_PARAMS));
    _fmemcpy(ptaskname, &buf[next].taskname, 9);
    _fstrncpy(lpdsdx, &buf[next].dsdx, MAX_STR);
    _fstrncpy(lpdssi, &buf[next].dssi, MAX_STR);
    *pflag = buf[next].flag;
    buf[next].type = REQU_FREE;
    END_CRIT_SEC();
    SET_NEXT();
    return 1;
}

REQUEST far *INIT_REQUBUF(void)
{
    LPREQUEST buf, p;
    int i;
    if (! (buf =
        (LPREQUEST) GlobalLock(GlobalAlloc(GMEM_FIXED | GMEM_ZEROINIT,
        BUF_SIZE * sizeof(REQUEST)))))
        return 0;
    for (i=BUF_SIZE, p=buf; i--; p++)
        p->type = REQU_FREE;
    return buf;
}
```

```
FARPROC (FAR PASCAL *GetSetKernelDosProc)(FARPROC DosProc) = 0;

typedef void (_interrupt _far *INTRFUNC)();

INTRFUNC _dpmi_get_pmode_vect(int intno)
{
    INTRFUNC iv;
    _asm {
        mov ax, 0204h
        mov bl, byte ptr intno
        int 31h
        jc error
        mov word ptr iv+2, cx
        mov word ptr iv, dx
    }
    return iv;
error:
    return (INTRFUNC) 0;
}

void _dpmi_set_pmode_vect(int intno, INTRFUNC iv)
{   _asm {
        mov ax, 0205h
        mov bl, byte ptr intno
        mov cx, word ptr iv+2
        mov dx, word ptr iv
        int 31h
    }
    // _asm jc error
}

#define get_vect(intno)     _dpmi_get_pmode_vect(intno)

int set_vect(WORD intno, INTRFUNC handler)
{
    // Don't use INT 21h function 25h (Set Interrupt Vector), because
    // KERNEL's INT 21h handler prevents setting INT 1Bh, 1Ch, 21h, 24h.
    // So use DPMI instead. However, could also use undoc NoHookDOSCall,
    // which bypasses most of KERNEL's special INT 21h handling.
    _dpmi_set_pmode_vect(intno, handler);
    return (_dpmi_get_pmode_vect(intno) == handler);
}

void _interrupt _far IntHandler(REG_PARAMS r);
void _interrupt _far IntHandler2(REG_PARAMS r);

static HANDLE wspy21_task;
static int intno = 0x21;    // INT 21h default
static INTRFUNC old = 0;
static FARPROC old_dos = (FARPROC) 0;

void on_close(HWND hwnd)
{
    int i;
```

```
    winio_warn(FALSE, "WSPY21",
        "%08lu\tintercepted\n"
        "%08lu\talready seen in first handler\n"
        "%08lu\tabsorbed in first handler\n"
        "%08lu\tlost through buffer overruns\n"
        "%08lu\twere my own calls\n",
            calls, already, (intno == 0x21) ? calls - already : 0,
            lost, mine);

    if (! set_vect(intno, old))
        winio_warn(FALSE, "WSPY21",
            "Couldn't restore Int %02Xh", intno);
    if ((intno == 0x21) && old_dos)
        GetSetKernelDosProc(old_dos);
    }

void display_int(REG_PARAMS *pr)
{
    printf("AX=%04x BX=%04x CX=%04x DX=%04x DS=%04x SI=%04x DI=%04x "
           "CS:IP=%04x:%04xh",
        pr->ax, pr->bx, pr->cx, pr->dx,
        pr->ds, pr->si, pr->di, pr->cs, pr->ip);
}

#define PRINT_STR(s)             printf("%s", (s))
#define PRINT_2_STR(s1, s2)      printf("%s \'%s\'", (s1), (s2))
#define PRINT_STR_WORD(s, w)     printf("%s %u (%04Xh)", (s), (w), (w))
#define PRINT_2_WORD(s, w1, w2) printf("%s %u (%04Xh), %u (%04Xh)", \
                                    (s), (w1), (w1), (w2), (w2))
#define PRINT_STR_BYTE(s, b)     printf("%s %u (%02Xh)", (s), (b), (b))
#define PRINT_STR_FP(s, fp)      printf("%s %Fp", (s), (fp))

#ifdef SHOW_IOCTL
void print_ioctl(REG_PARAMS *pr)
{
    int al = pr->ax & 0xFF;
    int bl = pr->bx & 0xFF;
    printf("IOCTL (%02X) ", al);
    switch (al) {
        case 0x08: PRINT_STR_BYTE("Is Drv Removeable?", bl); break;
        case 0x09: PRINT_STR_BYTE("Is Drv Remote?", bl); break;
        case 0x0E: PRINT_STR_BYTE("Get Log Drv Map", bl); break;
        // ... boring list of IOCTL functions ...
    }
}
#endif

void display_dos_int(REG_PARAMS *pr, char *dsdx, char *dssi)
{
    int ah;
top:                 // IDoBelieveIUsedAGoToStatement
    ah = pr->ax >> 8;
    printf("(%02X) ", ah);
    switch (ah)     // ICantBelieveIUsedASwitchStatement
    {
```

```
        case 0x00:  PRINT_STR("Exit"); break;
        case 0x0E:  PRINT_STR_BYTE("Set Disk", pr->dx & 0xFF); break;
        case 0x19:  PRINT_STR("Get Disk"); break;
        case 0x1A:  PRINT_STR_FP("Set DTA", MK_FP(pr->ds, pr->dx)); break;
        case 0x25:  PRINT_STR_BYTE("Set Vect", pr->ax & 0xFF); break;
        case 0x2A:  PRINT_STR("Get Date"); break;
        case 0x2C:  PRINT_STR("Get Time"); break;
        case 0x2F:  PRINT_STR("Get DTA"); break;
        case 0x30:  PRINT_STR("Get DOS Vers"); break;
        case 0x32:  PRINT_STR_BYTE("Get DPB", pr->dx & 0xFF); break;
        case 0x35:  PRINT_STR_BYTE("Get Vect", pr->ax & 0xFF); break;
        case 0x36:  PRINT_STR_BYTE("Get Disk Space", pr->dx & 0xFF); break;
        case 0x3B:  PRINT_2_STR("ChDir", dsdx); break;
        case 0x3C:  PRINT_2_STR("Create", dsdx); break;
        case 0x3D:  PRINT_2_STR("Open", dsdx); break;
        case 0x3E:  PRINT_STR_WORD("Close", pr->bx); break;
        case 0x3F:  PRINT_2_WORD("Read", pr->bx, pr->cx); break;
        case 0x40:  PRINT_2_WORD("Write", pr->bx, pr->cx); break;
        case 0x41:  PRINT_2_STR("Delete", dsdx); break;
        case 0x42:  printf("Lseek%d %u %04x%04x",
                    pr->ax & 0xFF, pr->bx, pr->cx, pr->dx);
                    break;
        case 0x43:  PRINT_2_STR("Get/Set File Attr", dsdx); break;
#ifdef SHOW_IOCTL
        case 0x44:  print_ioctl(pr); break;
#else
        case 0x44:  PRINT_2_WORD("IOCTL", pr->ax & 0xFF, pr->bx); break;
#endif
        case 0x47:  PRINT_STR_BYTE("Get Curr Dir", pr->dx & 0xff); break;
        case 0x4b:  PRINT_2_STR("Exec", dsdx); break;
        case 0x4c:  PRINT_STR_BYTE("Exit", pr->ax & 0xff); break;
        case 0x4e:  PRINT_2_STR("Find First", dsdx); break;
        case 0x4f:  PRINT_STR("Find Next"); break;
        case 0x50:  PRINT_STR_WORD("Set PSP", pr->bx); break;
        case 0x51: case 0x62: PRINT_STR("Get PSP"); break;
        case 0x55:  PRINT_2_WORD("(Undoc) Create PSP", pr->dx, pr->si); break;
        case 0x57:  PRINT_STR_WORD("Get/Set File Date/Time", pr->bx); break;
        case 0x59:  PRINT_STR("Get Extended Error Info"); break;
        case 0x5A:  PRINT_2_STR("Create Temp File", dsdx); break;
        case 0x5B:  PRINT_2_STR("Create New File", dsdx); break;
        case 0x60:  PRINT_2_STR("Truename", dssi); break;
        case 0x65:  PRINT_STR_BYTE("International", pr->ax & 0xFF); break;
        case 0x68:  PRINT_STR_WORD("Commit", pr->bx); break;
        case 0x6C:  PRINT_2_STR("Open/Create", dssi); break;
        // for 21/71XX, do what IFSMgr does:  mark as an LFN function
        // and then turn into 21/XX.
        case 0x71:  printf("LFN "); pr->ax <<= 8; goto top;
        case 0xA0:  PRINT_2_STR("Get Volume Info", dsdx); break;
        case 0xA1:  PRINT_STR("Find Close"); break;
        default:    display_int(pr);
        }
}

void display_ints(void)
{
```

```
    REG_PARAMS r;
    static char modname[16];
    static char dsdx[MAX_STR];
    static char dssi[MAX_STR];
    int flag;

    // This loop looks for, extracts, and displays messages queued
    // up by the interrupt handler. The only way we know to
    // terminate the function is that the window closes
    while (winio_openwindows())
    {
        wmhandler_yield();
        while (RD_REQUEST(requ, &r, &modname, &dsdx, &dssi, &flag))
        {
            printf("<%s> %c", modname, flag);
            if (intno == 0x21)
                display_dos_int(&r, dsdx, dssi);
            else    // Could do formatted display of other INT like DPMI
                display_int(&r);
            printf("\n");
        }
    }
}

main(int argc, char *argv[])
{
    char buf[128], num[8];

    if (__hPrevInst)
        fail("Sorry, only one WSPY21 at a time");
    winio_setbufsize(__hMainWnd, (WORD) 32768, TRUE);
    if (! (requ = INIT_REQUBUF()))
        fail("INIT_REQUBUF fail!");
    winio_about("WSPY21");
    winio_onclose(__hMainWnd, (DESTROY_FUNC) on_close);
    wspy21_task = GetCurrentTask();

    if (argc < 2)
        intno = 0x21;
    else
    {
        int i;
        for (i=1; i<argc; i++)
            if (argv[i][0] == '-')
            {
                if (strncmp(strupr(&argv[i][1]), "SHOWALL", 4) == 0)
                    show_all++;
                else
                    fail("usage: wspy21 [-showall] [intno]");
            }
            else
                sscanf(argv[i], "%X", &intno);
    }

    old = get_vect(intno);
```

```
    if (! set_vect(intno, (INTRFUNC) IntHandler))
        fail("SetVect failed!");

    #define GET_PROC(mod, func) \
        GetProcAddress(GetModuleHandle(mod), (func))
    if ((intno == 0x21) && (GetSetKernelDosProc =
        GET_PROC("KERNEL", "GETSETKERNELDOSPROC")))
        old_dos = GetSetKernelDosProc((FARPROC) IntHandler2);

    sprintf(buf, "Windows Interrupt Spy: INT %02Xh", intno);
    winio_settitle(__hMainWnd, buf);

    display_ints();
    return 0;
}

static REG_PARAMS prev_r = {0} ;
static int was_prev = 0;

// CS:IP can be different
#define SAME_CALL(r1, r2)  \
    (((r1)->es == (r2)->es) && ((r1)->ds == (r2)->ds) && \
    ((r1)->di == (r2)->di) &&  ((r1)->si == (r2)->si) && \
    ((r1)->bx == (r2)->bx) &&  ((r1)->dx == (r2)->dx) && \
    ((r1)->cx == (r2)->cx) &&  ((r1)->ax == (r2)->ax))

void _interrupt _far IntHandler(REG_PARAMS r)
{
    HANDLE task = GetCurrentTask();

    if (! show_all) { prev_r = r; was_prev = 1; }

    if (task != wspy21_task)     /* don't show my own ints */
    {
        if (! WRT_REQUEST(requ, &r, task, INT21))
            lost++;     /* buffer overflow */
        calls++;
    }
    else
        mine++;

    _chain_intr(old);
}

void _interrupt _far IntHandler2(REG_PARAMS r)
{
    HANDLE task = GetCurrentTask();

    if ((! show_all) && was_prev-- && SAME_CALL(&r, &prev_r))
    {
        already++;
        goto done;  /* saw this already in IntHandler */
    }

    if (task == wspy21_task)    /* don't show my own ints */
```

```
    {
        mine++;
        goto done;
    }

    if (! WRT_REQUEST(requ, &r, task, KERNELDOSPROC))
        lost++;     /* buffer overflow */
    calls++;

done:
    _chain_intr((INTRFUNC) old_dos);
}
```


The most important point about WSPY21 is that, unlike V86TEST, it sees INT 21h calls generated in protected mode by Windows applications in the System VM. WSPY21 won't see INT 21h calls made from DOS boxes, nor will it see any that are first generated somewhere in VxD-land and then sent down to V86 mode. (For this, see the WLOG-212F program discussed in Chapter 1.)

To install a handler for INT 21h calls issued in protected mode, a program running under a DOS extender such as Windows would normally call the same DOS function that a real-mode program would call to hook INT 21h in real mode: Set Interrupt Vector (INT 21h function 25h). The purpose of a DOS extender is to provide a familiar INT 21h interface to protected-mode functionality and to make DOS seem to be a protected-mode operating system. (Although perhaps *seem* is no longer really the right word here; see the sidebar titled "The DOS extender: Still a great pretender?")

The DOS extender: Still a great pretender?

Imagine for a moment that you don't know anything about protected-mode INT 21h or DOS extenders. When you open a document in WinWord, open a spreadsheet in Excel, or do something similar in any protected-mode Windows application, either the application itself or a DLL it calls generates the equivalent of an INT 21h File Open call — *in protected mode*. Yet MS-DOS, as we all know, is a real-mode operating system. How then is protected-mode INT 21h handled?

The naive conception among a surprising number of Windows and DOS programmers is that since the request involves an INT 21h, Windows must therefore service the request "by calling down to DOS." As a random example of this widespread misconception, one programmer asserted (*Windows/DOS Developer's Journal*, April 1994) that a certain technique for watching DOS file I/O calls "is possible because all file opening is done through the real-mode DOS INT 21h services."

I hope it is clear from examples such as TEST21 in Chapter 8 that this ain't necessarily so, even for interrupts coming from real-mode DOS programs in V86 mode. Thus, there is certainly no reason why it should be true for protected-mode Windows programs. If Windows has complete discretion over how to handle interrupts coming from real-mode DOS programs that know nothing about Windows or protected mode, imagine what it can do with interrupts — even supposed DOS interrupts such as INT 21h or INT 2Fh — coming from applications that were designed for protected mode and that know about Windows.

To request 0FFFEh pararaphs of memory, a Windows application could issue the following request:

```
    _asm mov ah, 48h      ; DOS function 48h: Allocate Memory
    _asm mov bx, 0FFFEh   ; 0FFFEh * 16 = 1,048,544 bytes
    _asm int 21h          ; "DOS call" (but not necessarily call DOS!)
    _asm jc alloc_error   ; carry flag set indicates error
    _asm mov segment, ax  ; save away address of allocated memory
    ; ...
alloc_error:
```

Win16 applications are supposed to allocate memory not by calling INT 21h function 48h but with a Windows API function such as GlobalAlloc or LocalAlloc. Humor me for a moment. The preceding code *can* be placed inside a Win16 application. What's more, when placed inside a Win16 application, this code *succeeds* in allocating 0FFFEh paragraphs (1,048,554 bytes) of memory.

What's so strange about that? Well, if you think back to the days of real-mode DOS, you might recall that requesting a large number of paragraphs such as 0FFFEh or 0FFFFh was *guaranteed* to fail. Calling INT 21h function 48h with BX set to such an "impossibly high" number was the standard technique to determine the size of the largest block that could be allocated. Even if there were megabytes of free memory in the machine, real-mode DOS could only allocate substantially less than a megabyte of so-called conventional memory.

But INT 21h function 48h doesn't behave this way when called by a Win16 application. To demonstrate, Listing 13-6 shows DOSMEM.C, a tiny Windows program that calls the DOS Allocate Memory function.

Listing 13-6: DOSMEM.C

```
/*
DOSMEM.C
bcc -W dosmem.c
*/

#include <stdlib.h>
```

```
#include <stdio.h>
#include "windows.h"

#define MK_FP(seg,ofs) ((void far *)(((DWORD)(seg) << 16) | (ofs)))

int PASCAL WinMain(HANDLE hInstance, HANDLE hPrevInstance,
    LPSTR lpszCmdLine, int nCmdShow)
{
    char buf[80];
    DWORD huge *fp, huge *fp2;
    DWORD limit, size, i;
    WORD segment, avail;

    /* call DOS Allocate Memory function */
    _asm mov ah, 48h
    _asm mov bx, 0FFFEh
    _asm int 21h
    _asm jc alloc_error
    _asm mov segment, ax
    fp = (DWORD huge *) MK_FP(segment, 0);

    /* ask Windows how big it is:  limit = last valid byte offset */
    limit = GetSelectorLimit(segment);

    /* touch every byte of the allocated block */
    size = (limit+1) / sizeof(DWORD);
    for (i=0, fp2=fp; i < size; i++, fp2++)
        *fp2 = i;

    sprintf(buf, "Allocated %lu bytes at %Fp", limit + 1, fp);
    MessageBox(0, buf, "DOSMEM", MB_OK);

    /* don't free block until user clicks OK */
    _asm mov ah, 49h
    _asm mov es, segment
    _asm int 21h
    _asm jc free_error
    return 0;

free_error:
    MessageBox(0, "Error: couldn't free block!", "DOSMEM", MB_OK);
    return 1;
alloc_error:
    _asm mov avail, bx
    sprintf(buf, "Only %04Xh paragraphs available", avail);
    MessageBox(0, buf, "DOSMEM", MB_OK);
    return 1;
}
```

Figure 13-4 shows that DOSMEM can allocate nearly a megabyte of memory via a single call to INT 21h function 48h. DOSMEM only deallocates the memory (via protected-mode function 49h) when you click OK. As a result, running multiple copies of DOSMEM allocates multiple megabytes of memory at one time.

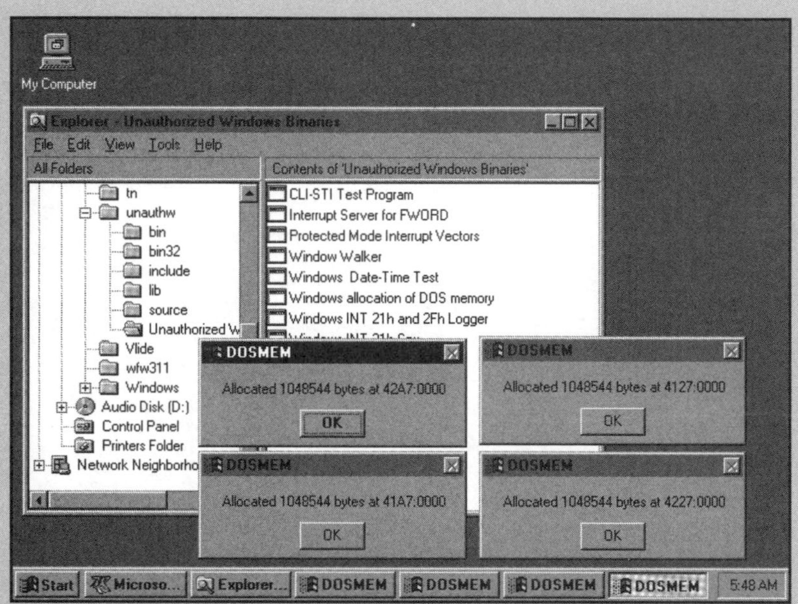

Figure 13-4: You can allocate megabytes of memory via INT 21h function 48h.

These results show that there is something very different about INT 21h in protected-mode Windows. We already know from our examination of the V86 INT 21h chain in previous chapters that this DOS interface undergoes radical changes under Windows. The changes are even more extreme when INT 21h is issued from protected mode. In this example, function 48h manages to not only allocate over one million bytes in one go, but also return a protected-mode selector to the newly allocated block.

But why is this such a far cry from the naive "Windows handles INT 21h by calling down to DOS" conception that many programmers continue to have? Because INT 21h function 48h in real-mode DOS *can't* allocate this much memory, much less in a single call. Nor does it return protected-mode selectors. Nor can it allocate extended memory above one megabyte, which is what we've done in Figure 13-4 because more than a megabyte has been allocated and at least *some* of it must be extended memory. The Windows DOS extender *can't* pass this call down to DOS. No amount of protected-mode-to-real-mode translation will make DOS allocate megabytes of readily accessible extended memory.

I say "readily accessible" extended memory because DOS programs can allocate tons of memory via the XMS and EMS interfaces. However, look at the block of code in DOSMEM.C following the comment "touch every byte of the allocated block." DOSMEM can immediately use the memory (*fp2). A program couldn't do this with memory allocated via XMS or EMS; those interfaces require that the memory first be mapped in with a function such as Move Extended Memory Block (XMS function 0Bh) or Map Extended Memory Page (EMS function 44h). You can see in Listing 13-6 that DOSMEM doesn't do anything like this; it just *uses* the memory.

If a Windows program *does* want to allocate DOS conventional memory and get back a real-mode segment address, it cannot do so using INT 21h function 48h. Instead, it must use a special function, such as GlobalDOSAlloc in the Windows API or Allocate DOS Memory Block in DPMI (INT 31h function 0100h).

This somewhat unusual behavior of INT 21h function 48h in protected mode is a good example of what the term *DOS extender* means. A DOS extender is an environment that, like Windows, provides INT 21h services in protected mode. Function 25h sets a protected-mode interrupt vector, function 48h allocates extended memory and returns a protected-mode selector, and so on.

Usually, the DOS extender concept (if one can call it that) is further explained by saying that a DOS extender makes it appear as though MS-DOS were a protected-mode operating system, in other words, that the DOS extender is the author of a fiction or the creator of an illusion.

For example, consider INT 21h function 3Fh (Read File). In real mode, this function expects that the DS:DX register pair will point to a buffer into which DOS will place data read from a specified file; the DS:DX pointer is a real-mode address, and the buffer is located in conventional memory. But under a protected-mode DOS extender, DS:DX must be a protected-mode address and the buffer can be located in extended memory. In general, a DOS extender would implement the protected-mode version of function 3Fh by allocating a conventional-memory buffer, switching to real (or V86) mode, and reissuing the function 3Fh call with DS:DX pointing to the conventional-memory buffer. When DOS returned, the DOS extender would copy the data from the conventional-memory buffer to the original extended-memory buffer specified by the application.

This scenario, in which the DOS extender translates protected-mode INT 21h requests into real-mode terms, reissues the INT 21h in real or V86 mode, and then translates any return value, is the foundation for the "Windows must call down to DOS" misconception. Certainly, DOS extenders such as Windows generally *do* handle many INT 21h functions in the way just described. The DOS extender makes real-mode DOS think it has a plain old real-mode caller, yet it also makes protected-mode programs think that DOS is a protected-mode operating system. In other words, the DOS extender is a deceiver.

But what about the examples of function 25h and 48h? As we've seen, to provide a reasonable protected-mode implementation for these functions, the DOS extender *can't* pass the call down to DOS. The DOS extender must handle these calls by itself, entirely in protected mode, because no amount of deception will convince real-mode DOS to set protected-mode interrupt vectors or allocate extended memory.

Here, there is no deception on the DOS extender's part. If it handles an INT 21h call entirely in protected mode, without calling real-mode DOS,

> then the DOS extender acts as a true protected-mode operating system — at least for that function.
>
> If over time a DOS extender such as Windows comes to handle more and more INT 21h functionality in protected mode without calling DOS, then over time the DOS extender becomes less of a DOS extender and more of a full-blown protected-mode operating system that happens to provide a familiar INT 21h interface. But notice how gradually this transformation can occur: with every release of the DOS extender, the authors can take a few more functions, stop passing them down to DOS, and instead implement them in protected mode. There is a smooth transition from the illusion of protected-mode DOS to an actual protected-mode DOS.
>
> Hmm, sounds a lot like what's been happening over the years in Windows.

Since real-mode programs hook real-mode interrupt vectors with function 25h, it makes sense for the DOS extender to provide a protected-mode INT 21h function 25h that hooks protected-mode interrupt vectors. Windows does provide this protected-mode function 25h. Yet, WSPY21 hooks INT 21h not with DOS INT 21h function 25h but with DPMI INT 31h function 0205h (Set Protected-Mode Interrupt Vector). Don't be thrown by the presence of the phrase *Protected-Mode* in the DPMI function's name and its absence in the DOS function's name. When called from a protected-mode application under Windows, the DOS function sets the protected-mode interrupt vector, just as the DPMI function does.

So why use the DPMI function? Because the Win16 KERNEL contains a protected-mode INT 21h handler that provides special handling for several DOS functions, one of which is function 25h. As we'll soon see, KERNEL ignores any attempt to hook certain interrupts; one of these interrupts is INT 21h! Thus, a Windows application *can't* use INT 21h AX=2125h to hook INT 21h. The solution is to use the DPMI function.

KERNEL's INT 21h Handler and KernelDosProc

In addition to the INT 21h hook installed via DPMI, WSPY21 has a second hook installed via GetSetKernelDosProc that I've mentioned several times. Why the two hooks? Having figured out that you must hook INT 21h via DPMI rather than via INT 21h, why bother with

GetSetKernelDosProc? Because many Windows programs and DLLs issue DOS calls without issuing an INT 21h, and the second hook installed with GetSetKernelDosProc will see these other calls.

Take, for example, the Dos3Call API (please!). The Windows SDK suggests that if you must make DOS calls, you should do so using Dos3Call. Dos3Call is *not* a wrapper around an INT 21h call; it does not generate an actual INT 21h that would be seen by WSPY21's INT 21h handler. Instead, as we saw in the preceding chapter (in the section titled "Win32 FindNextFile is INT 21h Function 714Fh"), Dos3Call is a wrapper around KERNEL's own INT 21h handler (that is, around the code to which WSPY21's IntHandler will most likely chain):

```
KERNEL!DOS3CALL
0117:000081C3   PUSHF               ;; push flags to simulate interrupt
0117:000081C4   PUSH    CS          ;; phony far call:  /FARCALLTRANS
0117:000081C5   CALL    7F38        ;; call KERNEL INT 21h handler
0117:000081C8   RETF
```

There are also many places where KERNEL calls this INT 21h handler directly, without going through Dos3Call. An example of this was also shown in the preceding chapter, in the code for _lopen:

```
KERNEL!_lopen:
0117:000093E9   MOV     AX,716C     ;; LFN Open/Create
0117:000093EC   PUSHF
0117:000093ED   PUSH    CS
0117:000093EE   CALL    7F38        ;; call KERNEL INT 21h handler
```

An undocumented function, NoHookDosCall (see *Undocumented Windows*, pp. 339-340 for a not entirely accurate description), provides another way that Windows can generate a DOS call without an INT 21h. WSPY21's IntHandler2, installed with GetSetKernelDosProc, will see these NoHookDosCalls too.

But what does *no hook* mean? Why would a part of Windows use NoHookDosCall rather than Dos3Call? And, if a handler installed with GetSetKernelDosProc will see these non-INT 21h DOS calls such as Dos3Call and NoHookDosCall, why does WSPY21 even need the higher-level INT 21h hook? Why not just use GetSetKernelDosProc?

I noted earlier that WSPY21 is based on the WISPY program from *Undocumented Windows*, but that WSPY21 installs two INT 21h handlers, whereas WISPY installed only a single INT 21h handler, using GetSet KernelDosProc. As a result, WISPY never saw some important INT 21h calls, such as function 4Bh (EXEC). This is important, not so you understand how WSPY21 works and why WISPY didn't (you could survive quite nicely without understanding that, thank you), but because this WISPY problem and its WSPY21 solution illuminate some important aspects of Windows. In addition, hooking INT 21h from a Windows applications appears to be a perennial topic, at least in the pages of one programmer's magazine (see Paul Bonneau's Windows Q&A column in *Windows/DOS Developer's Journal*, April 1994, June 1994, September 1994).

Even before the advent of Windows protected mode in version 3.0, KERNEL's INT 21h handler handled some DOS calls from Windows applications without passing them down to DOS. A prime example is function 4Bh (EXEC):

```
<PROGMAN>  (4B) Exec 'write.exe'
```

DOS doesn't know how to start Windows executables (NE files) such as WRITE.EXE, so KERNEL *can't* pass function 4Bh down to DOS. When issued by a Windows application or DLL (such as by the WinExec function in KERNEL), KERNEL turns function 4Bh into a LoadModule call (see *Windows Internals*, pp. 229-231). Even for the WinExec of a real-mode DOS program, KERNEL *still* can't pass function 4Bh down to real-mode DOS, because DOS unfortunately doesn't know how to start a Windows DOS box.

If you use function 4Bh in real-mode to try to run a Windows program, you usually just get a message to the effect that "This program must be run under Microsoft Windows." DOS runs the real-mode stub in the NE file, which can do what it wants (even launch Windows) but which generally just prints this message and exits. In Windows 95, you can (finally!) launch Windows applications from the DOS box, but this involves hooking INT 21h function 4Bh, seeing whether you've tried to start a Win16 or Win16 executable, and if you have, keeping the function 4Bh call away from real-mode and turning it into a WinExec. So real-mode DOS really doesn't know how to launch Windows applications. (This means that Windows itself requires a bootstrap stub-loader to start up from DOS; see Pietrek, *Windows Internals*, pp. 10-13.)

Furthermore, INT 21h function 4Bh in Windows can even launch .PIF files:

```
<PROGMAN>  (4B) Exec 'C:\WINDOWS\EDIT.PIF'
```

A moment's reflection should convince you that there's no way that Windows can pass this call down to real-mode DOS; DOS doesn't how how to launch .PIF files.

As another example, KERNEL absorbs most INT 21h function 0Eh (Set Drive) and 19h (Get Drive) calls from Windows applications. The reason is simple: Each Windows application has its own current drive/directory, stored in the Task Database (TDB) associated with its PSP (see "Where's the Windows 95 Current Directory" earlier in this chapter). You can have one Windows application parked at C:\FOO and another application (or another instance of the same application) at D:\BAR. Each VM in Windows also has its own current drive/directory, but this involves instance data (see Chapter 4) and, as noted earlier in this chapter, is no help to the multiple applications within the System VM. The System VM has a single instance of the DOS Current Directory Structure (CDS). Since KERNEL multiplexes this single CDS among multiple Windows applications, it must handle DOS Set Drive and Get Drive calls from Windows applications by manipulating the TDB.

KERNEL's special handling of some INT 21h calls also explains why WSPY21 wasn't able to hook INT 21h using DOS Set Interrupt Vector (INT 21h function 25h). As mentioned earlier, KERNEL *rejects* wholesale any attempt to use DOS function 25h to change four interrupt vectors. These are INT 1Bh (Ctrl-Break), 1Ch (Timer), 21h (DOS), and 24h (Critical Error). Notice that INT 21h is included. This means that a Windows application *cannot* use INT 21h function 25h to hook INT 21h.

KERNEL also provides special handling for several interrupts that are held in the TDB on a per-task basis (see *Undocumented Windows*, pp. 365-366):

Interrupt	Description
INT 0	Divide by zero
INT 2	Nonmaskable interrupt (NMI)
INT 4	Interrupt on overflow (INTO)
INT 6	Invalid opcode
INT 7	Coprocessor not available
INT 3Eh	Used by floating-point emulators
INT 75h	Coprocessor error

WSPY21 has a -SHOWALL option that shows some of the absorption of INT 21h calls inside KERNEL. The -SHOWALL option tells WSPY21's KernelDosProc handler not to filter out calls that have already been reported by the higher-level INT 21h handler. By reporting all calls seen at the INT 21h handler and all calls seen at the KernelDosProc handler (which WSPY21 marks with an asterisk), the -SHOWALL option makes it moderately easy to spot the calls that were absorbed by KERNEL. For example:

```
<SH>  (19) Get Disk
<SH>  (47) Get Curr Dir 3 (03h)
<SH> *(1A) Set DTA 2E07:0080
<SH> *(47) Get Curr Dir 3 (03h)
```

Here, KERNEL's INT 21h handler saw an INT 21h function 19h (Get Disk) call, and that's the last anyone saw of it. KERNEL handled it. Next, after KERNEL's INT 21h handler saw a function 47h (Get Current Directory) call, it generated a function 1Ah (Set DTA) call before sending the function 47h call down to KernelDosProc. KERNEL not only absorbs some INT 21h but may also inject some extra INT 21h calls after a task switch to guarantee that the newly switched-in task has the correct DTA, PSP, drive, and directory (as we saw much earlier in this chapter):


```
<SH> *(47) Get Curr Dir 8 (08h)
<CLOCK>  (71) LFN (4E) Find First 'C:\WINDOWS\clock.ini'
<CLOCK> *(1A) Set DTA 00AF:0080
<CLOCK> *(0E) Set Disk 2 (02h)
<CLOCK> *(71) LFN (3B) ChDir '\BORLANDC\BIN'
<CLOCK> *(71) LFN (4E) Find First 'C:\WINDOWS\clock.ini'
```

Immediately after a task switch from SH to CLOCK, KERNEL's INT 21h received a call to function 714Eh (LFN Find First). Before passing this call down to KernelDosProc, KERNEL had to inject calls to functions 1Ah (Set DTA), 0Eh (Set Disk), and 713Bh (LFN Change Directory).

So you can see that KERNEL will absorb some INT 21h calls (occasionally generating other calls in their place), and keep these calls away, from not only the real-mode DOS code, but also from any VxDs that have hooked INT 21h in protected mode. To see these calls that KERNEL absorbs, you need an INT 21h handler that sits in front of KERNEL's.

Again, I can't expect readers to care much about the vicissitudes of WISPY and WSPY21. But the question of how to see INT 21h calls before KERNEL absorbs them is illuminating because it shows that even before Windows 95, even before 32-bit file access in WfW 3.11, even before the introduction of protected mode in version 3.0, even — to make a long story short — way back in the days of version 2.*x*, Windows was already starting to do a number on the INT 21h interface.

Okay, so WSPY21 has seen an INT 21h call and passed it to KERNEL; KERNEL has performed any special processing of the INT 21h and will now pass the call (if it's not one of the INT 21h calls that KERNEL absorbs) down to real-mode DOS. Well, not quite. Actually, not at all. (Just wanted to see if you were paying attention.) KERNEL will pass the DOS call down to the previously installed protected-mode INT 21h handler, which in turn can chain the interrupt to the previous handler or not, as it sees fit.

KERNEL's INT 21h handler chains to the previous INT 21h handler using an undocumented KERNEL function called NoHookDOSCall. (Finally, we got back to NoHookDosCall!) To bypass the special treatment that KERNEL gives some DOS calls, some other parts of KERNEL, and some DLLs such as SYSTEM.DRV, use NoHookDosCall. For example, a sequence of three IOCTL calls show up frequently in WSPY21 logs; these calls come from SYSTEM.DRV's InquireSystem function (see *Undocumented Windows*, p. 609), which is in turn called by the GetDriveType API in KERNEL:

```
<CAB32> *(44) IOCTL (09) Is Drv Remote? 3 (03h)
<CAB32> *(44) IOCTL (08) Is Drv Removeable? 3 (03h)
<CAB32> *(44) IOCTL (0E) Get Log Drv Map 3 (03h)
```

Such use of NoHookDosCall won't be seen by a Windows program that hooks only INT 21h. Well, the name of the function *is* NoHookDosCall.

NoHookDOSCall doesn't bypass all of KERNEL's special handling. It still must check for the function 0Eh and 19h Get/Set Current Drive calls, for example. However, NoHookDOSCall is fairly simple and quickly chains to the previous proteced-mode INT 21 handler, which KERNEL saved away at startup in offset 1Ah of one of its code segments:

```
0117:0000814B    CALL    FAR CS:[001A]
```

So who owned INT 21h in protected mode before KERNEL started? Probably some VxD. (SHELL VxD is generally the last statically-loaded VxD, and it loads KERNEL.) But let's see where the INT 21h call goes when NoHookDosCall chains to the previous handler:

```
:dd 117:1a
003B:0396

:u 3b:396
003B:00000396    INT     30
```

Each protected-mode INT 21h in Windows, if not absorbed in KERNEL, will in turn generate an INT 30h! That INT 30h is all there is to KernelDosProc (well, not quite, but we'll get to that in a moment when we discuss the GetSetKernelDosProc function).

Using a utility such as IDTMAP from the *Unauthorized Windows 95* disk, you can see that about ten other protected-mode interrupts also lead via Trap Gates to this same selector 003Bh. (Incidentally, a Trap Gate is the same as an Interrupt Gate, except it leaves interrupts enabled; if you're interested in the significance of this, see the Windows DDK documentation for Set_PM_Int_Type.)

```
C:\UNAUTHW\IDTMAP>idtmap | find "003B:"
0010    INTR    0028:C0003DF4 (3)      TRAP16  003B:00000342 (3) PMCB
0013    INTR    0028:C0003E0C (3)      TRAP16  003B:00000324 (3) PMCB
0015    INTR    0028:C0003E1C (3)      TRAP16  003B:00000326 (3) PMCB
001C    INTR    0028:C0003E54 (3)      TRAP16  003B:00000328 (3) PMCB
0021    INTR    0028:C0003E7C (3)      TRAP16  003B:00000396 (3) PMCB
0025    INTR    0028:C0003E9C (3)      TRAP16  003B:00000390 (3) PMCB
0026    INTR    0028:C0003EA4 (3)      TRAP16  003B:00000392 (3) PMCB
002F    INTR    0028:C0003EEC (3)      TRAP16  003B:00000388 (3) PMCB
0031    INTR    0028:C0003EFC (3)      TRAP16  003B:00000210 (3) PMCB
0033    INTR    0028:C0003F0C (3)      TRAP16  003B:00000320 (3) PMCB
```

Each of these protected-mode interrupts generates an INT 30h. In fact, segment 03Bh in its entirety contains nothing but INT 30h instructions. As explained briefly in the discussion of the WINBP program in Chapter 8, INT 30h is a protected-mode (PM) callback to make the transition from Ring 3 protected mode to Ring 0 32-bit protected mode. VxDs hook protected-mode interrupts by passing the address of a 32-bit Ring 0 handler to VMM's Allocate_PM_Callback service and then passing the callback address returned from that service to Set_PM_Int_Vector.

In Windows 3.0, you wouldn't have seen INT 30h. Instead, this segment was filled with HLT instructions. That's right: every protected-mode INT 21h in turn generated a HLT. This at first sounds strange: every INT 21h would halt the processor? But the Intel manual page for HLT notes that in protected mode HLT is a privileged instruction that causes a GP fault if the current protection level isn't 0. In Windows 3.0, protected-mode applications ran at Ring 1, so the HLT wouldn't shut down the processor; it would cause a GP fault.

So every INT 21h from a Windows application would generate a GP fault? This doesn't sound much better than shutting down the processor. However, consider that the ominous-sounding GP fault is really just another interrupt (INT 0Dh), which can be caught by VMM or a VxD. Thus, by executing a HLT, a protected-mode application under Windows 3.0 would end up transitioning (what an awful word) from Ring 1 to Ring 0. By pointing a protected-mode interrupt vector at a HLT instruction, the caller (a Windows application that has called INT 21h, for example) would "haltingly" (you may groan now) make the transition to Ring 0.

That Windows 3.1 and later uses INT 30h in the same situation for which Windows 3.0 used HLT tells us that there's something interesting going on here. This use of HLT instructions in protected mode sounds a lot like the use of ARPL instructions in V86 mode, which was discussed in Chapter 8. In fact, these two schemes are similar. ARPL is used for V86 callbacks and breakpoints. Windows 3.0 used HLT for PM callbacks; Windows 3.1 and later uses INT 30h for PM callbacks. As the WINICE manual notes, "The change to INT 30h not only improves performance, but slightly simplifies a very complicated GP handler."

So where does the INT 30h go? We can see by running IDTMAP 30:

```
0030    INTR    0028:C0001A2C (3)    same
```


This address (28:C0001A2C) is located in the Windows VMM. Thus, INT 30h is another example of what Microsoft sometimes (not quite accurately) calls a thunk. By executing an INT 30h, a user-level (Ring 3) protected-mode program miraculously jumps into VMM, which is privileged (Ring 0) 32-bit protected mode. VMM's INT 30h handler will use the address from which the INT 30h came (such as 3B:396) to locate the handler for this PM callback (that is, the address originally passed to Allocate_PM_Callback). This is quite similar to VMM's use of ARPL in V86 callbacks.

VMM will call the most recently installed protected-mode INT 21h handler. In Windows 95, this will generally be IFSMgr. If IFSMgr isn't interested in the INT 21h call, it will jump to the previous handler in the chain, which is generally DOSMGR. DOSMGR is the Windows DOS extender. It handles most protected-mode INT 21h calls using small "scripts" that it passes to the V86MMGR_Xlat_API service. In most cases, V86MMGR reflects the call down to V86 mode using Begin_Nest_V86_Exec and Exec_Int 21h. (This process is described in some detail in *Undocumented DOS*, 2d ed., pp. 122-128.)

When it's said that V86MMGR reflects the INT 21h call down to V86 mode using Begin_Nest_V86_Exec and Exec_Int 21h, one crucial point must be made: This isn't quite true! Exec_Int will send (or reflect) the call to the V86 interrupt hook chain, which consists of 32-bit protected-mode code installed by VxDs using the Hook_V86_Int_Chain service. Windows will reflect the call to V86 mode only if no VxD absorbs it. Furthermore, even if the INT 21h call *is* reflected down to V86 mode, we know from previous chapters that Windows is using real-mode DOS just as a helper and that calls made by DOS in V86 mode frequently bounce back into VMM- and VxD-land (due to implanted V86 breakpoints, for example).

As noted earlier, KernelDosProc is nothing more than an INT 30h — except if a program such as WSPY21 has come along and replaced KernelDosProc with its own routine. The address of the previous INT 21h handler can be manipulated by Windows applications using yet another undocumented function, GetSetKernelDosProc. *Undocumented Windows* (pp. 188, 271-273) discusses this function, but unfortunately fails to explain that GetSetKernelDosProc manipulates nothing more than the *previous* INT 21h handler to which KERNEL's INT 21h handler chains and that, by using GetSetKernelDosProc, an INT 21h handler is essentially pretending to be the INT 21h handler that was installed before KERNEL:

```
;;; code for GetSetKernel DosProc
mov     ax, [bp+6]          ; take DWORD param
xchg    ax, [001A]          ; exchange with DWORD at 0117:001A
mov     dx, [bp+8]
xchg    dx, [001C]
```

GetSetKernelDosProc thus lets you insert an INT 21h hook *below* KERNEL but above any VxDs that have hooked INT 21h. It is similar to the INT 2Fh function 13h interface discussed in Chapter 8, where it was said that it would be nice to have a similar INT 2Fh function 21h interface, the role of which is currently played by IFSHLP. GetSetKernelDosProc sort of plays this role for protected-mode INT 21h.

We can see that the name KernelDosProc is confusing, in that the handler is *not* located in KERNEL. It is simply the handler to which KERNEL's INT 21h handler will chain (via NoHookDosCall).

To see as many protected-mode INT 21h as possible, WSPY21 uses GetSetKernelDosProc. When WSPY21 is running, KERNEL will pass the INT 21h calls it doesn't absorb to WSPY21, which will in turn pass them to the PM callback. At the same time, WSPY21 also hooks INT 21h (using DPMI rather than DOS, for reasons explained earlier), so WSPY21 will also see the INT 21h *before* KERNEL does. WSPY21 thus acts as a sandwich surrounding KERNEL's INT 21h handler.

Aside from examining KERNEL's INT 21h in order to show that, from its very beginnings, Windows has had to bypass certain DOS functions, this chapter has mostly examined the Win32 kernel's relationships with the Win16 kernel and with DOS. This chapter discussed some Win32 kernel issues such as thunking and Win16Lock, but didn't go into much detail. The next chapter, which you will be relieved to hear is the final chapter of this book, goes into a variety of Win32 kernel topics, including thunking, memory-mapped file I/O, the undocumented VxDCall API, and Win32 services, in more detail.

Chapter 14

Clock: Mixing 32-Bit and 16-Bit Code

In this final chapter, we'll focus almost entirely on one tiny, otherwise insignificant program that comes with Windows: the Clock. Because Microsoft produces it in both Win16 and Win32 flavors, and because both flavors run under both Windows 3.*x* and Windows 95, the Clock applet is handy for exploring various aspects of the Win16/Win32 relationship such as larger file handles and WIN32s:

Version of Clock	Windows 3.1*x*	Windows 95
Win16	16/16: 32BFA	16/32: WIN32 file handles
Win32	32/16: Win32s; CALL FWORD PTR	32/32: Memory-mapped EXE loading; Win16Lock

We'll start with one last look at the question of how Windows applications both call down to and bypass MS-DOS. We'll end with a discussion of a wide variety of items involved in the mixing of Win32 and Win16 code: CALL FWORD PTR, QT_Thunk, Win32 services, Win16Lock, _EnterSysLevel, the similarity between Win32s and Windows 95, and more.

16/16: The Win16 Clock under WfW 3.11

Under WfW 3.11 with 32BFA, I started the Clock applet that comes with Windows, let it run for a little while, and closed it. With the Show Changes option enabled, WV86TEST showed the following DOS calls, logged by the resident DOS version of V86TEST loaded before Windows:

```
139 seconds elapsed

INT 21h calls:
2A: 402     2C: 2201     4C: 1   50: 15  55: 2
```

This gives us a nice, concise list of some key INT 21h calls that are typically sent down to MS-DOS, even when 32-bit file access (32BFA) is enabled:

- Functions 2Ah and 2Ch get the date and time. Whenever the Win16 version of Clock receives a WM_TIMER message, it calls INT 21h functions 2Ah and 2Ch. WV86TEST shows that these calls are passed down to DOS. There are more calls to function 2Ch than to 2Ah here because the Win16 version of Clock issues a large number of calls to function 2Ch when it starts up. If you do a WV86TEST Show Changes and Refresh while Clock is already running, there will be exactly as many calls to function 2Ah as to function 2Ch; generally the number is about three times the number of elapsed seconds.
- Function 4Ch terminates the current DOS program; the standard Windows startup code calls this function after WinMain returns. Yes, Windows applications exit by calling the *DOS* exit function! This is documented in Microsoft's Windows 3.1 SDK (*Programmer's Reference, Volume 1: Overview*, Chapter 22: "Windows Application Startup").
- Functions 50h sets the current PSP; function 55h creates a PSP. When Windows task-switches between Windows applications, it usually ends up switching the DOS PSP too.

Ever get the sense that Windows applications are little more than fancy-looking protected-mode DOS applications? Clock's employment of DOS functions to get the date and time, the Windows startup code's exit via function 4Ch, and Windows' reliance on the PSP seem to confirm that impression.

Notice, though, that every time you start Clock, it has to find out whether you prefer an analog or a digital watch; if you prefer a digital display, Clock needs to know your preferred font. To get this information, Clock reads in CLOCK.INI. This in turn involves not only INT 21h calls to open, write, and close CLOCK.INI but also Find First and Get and Set DTA calls. As shown by WV86TEST, DOS doesn't see any of this file I/O. Even when I changed the Clock settings from analog to digital, browsed the Font list, selected a new font, and exited (which saves the changed settings in CLOCK.INI), the results logged by V86TEST and displayed by WV86TEST weren't terribly different:

```
56 seconds elapsed

INT 21h calls:
2A: 139     2C: 788 4C: 1   50: 63  55: 1   62: 23
```

For all the extra work of selecting a new font and writing out the changed CLOCK.INI settings, all DOS saw were some extra Get PSP calls (function 62h).

Of course, this is the 32BFA effect, whereby most DOS calls are never sent down to DOS. In contrast to the seven different INT 21h calls that WV86TEST displayed for Clock, here's just a little bit of what WSPY21 saw:


```
<PROGMAN> *(4B) Exec 'C:\WFW311\CLOCK.EXE'
<PROGMAN>  (50) Set PSP 183 (00B7h)
<PROGMAN>  (3D) Open 'C:\WFW311\CLOCK.EXE'
; ...
<CLOCK> *(25) Set Vect 0 (00h)
<CLOCK> *(2F) Get DTA
<CLOCK>  (50) Set PSP 4287 (10BFh)
<CLOCK>  (1A) Set DTA 10BF:0080
; ...
<CLOCK> *(4E) Find First 'C:\WFW311\WIN.INI'
<CLOCK>  (3D) Open 'C:\WFW311\CLOCK.INI'
<CLOCK>  (44) IOCTL (09) Is Drv Remote? 3 (03h)
<CLOCK>  (44) IOCTL (08) Is Drv Removeable? 3 (03h)
<CLOCK>  (44) IOCTL (0E) Get Log Drv Map 3 (03h)
<CLOCK>  (57) Get/Set File Date/Time 5 (0005h)
<CLOCK>  (42) Lseek2 5 00000000h
<CLOCK>  (42) Lseek0 5 00000000h
<CLOCK>  (3F) Read 5 (0005h), 89 (0059h)
<CLOCK>  (3E) Close 5 (0005h)
; ...
<CLOCK> *(2C) Get Time
<CLOCK>  (50) Set PSP 4287 (10BFh)
<CLOCK>  (2C) Get Time
<CLOCK> *(2A) Get Date
; ... plenty of 2A, 2C ...
<CLOCK> *(2F) Get DTA
<CLOCK>  (1A) Set DTA 10BF:0080
<CLOCK>  (3D) Open 'C:\WFW311\SYSTEM\TIMES.TTF'
<CLOCK>  (3F) Read 5 (0005h), 28 (001Ch)
; ... browsing fonts here ...
<CLOCK>  (3D) Open 'C:\WFW311\CLOCK.INI'
<CLOCK>  (57) Get/Set File Date/Time 5 (0005h)
<CLOCK>  (40) Write 5 (0005h), 87 (0057h)
<CLOCK>  (40) Write 5 (0005h), 0 (0000h)
<CLOCK>  (3E) Close 5 (0005h)
```

By contrasting this fragment of the WSPY21 log with the WV86TEST log, we can see that a whole series of DOS functions — including 1Ah (Set DTA), 2Fh (Get DTA), 3Dh (Open File), 3Eh

(Close), 3Fh (Read), 42h (Lseek), and 44h (IOCTL) — were generated by CLOCK but never sent down to DOS.

On the one hand, Windows applications seem like DOS programs in that they employ the DOS interface far more heavily than most Windows programmers seem to realize. Even in Windows 95, they require the real-mode DOS code. (Recall the Microsoft document quoted in Chapter 8: "On default all INT 21 interrupts, except file API INT 21s, are passed down to any hooker present in the system.")

On the other hand, Windows applications also require real-mode DOS far less than it would at first appear. When you see an INT 21h or a DOS3Call in an application, you can no longer assume that this is really a DOS call. It might just be a convenient way of calling into a VxD.

Well, if you've made it this far through this book, the fact that Windows both employs and bypasses MS-DOS is getting to be old news. So let's turn to the Win32 version of Clock that comes with Windows 95. Both the similarities with and the differences from the Win16 version are striking.

32/16: The Windows 95 Clock under Win32s

We can take the Win32 Clock applet from Windows 95 and run it under WfW 3.11 using Win32s. It's true that it doesn't work perfectly (only the digital watch face works), but the mere fact that this Win32 program from Windows 95 runs at all under Windows 3.1 shows that Win32s was perhaps a bigger deal — and Windows 95 perhaps something less of a radical change — than we have been led to believe.

Here's what WV86TEST shows for the Win32 Clock under WfW 3.11 with Win32s:

```
177 seconds elapsed

INT 21h calls:
2A: 1482     2C: 1482   30: 2   4C: 1   50: 146 51: 58  55: 2   62: 6

INT 2Fh calls:
11: 2
```

Note that there are as many calls to get the date (function 2Ah) as the time (function 2Ch). The Win32 version of Clock, whether running under Win32s or Windows 95, generates about 8 pairs (1482 / 177) of Get Date/Time calls per second. Considering that even an old 386SX/20 can execute about two million instructions per second, executing even a several-thousand instruction sequence, eight times a second, at worst constitutes perhaps a 1 percent overhead. On the other hand, this is just one operation: Accumulate enough similar tiny bits of overhead, and Windows might have a serious performance problem.

Anyway, WV86TEST shows that the Win32 version of Clock made pretty much the same set of DOS calls that we're used to seeing from the Win16 version of Clock. But in contrast, here's a small sample of the INT 21h calls that WSPY21 logged during the same period:

```
<WINFILE> *(4B) Exec 'C:\WINDOWS\CLOCK.EXE'
<WINFILE>  (50) Set PSP 175 (00AFh)
; ...
<WINFILE>  (3D) Open 'C:\WFW311\SYSTEM\W32SYS.DLL'
; ...
<WINFILE>  (3D) Open 'C:\WFW311\SYSTEM\WIN32S\WIN32S.EXE'
; ...
<WINFILE>  (3D) Open 'C:\WFW311\SYSTEM\WIN32S16.DLL'
<WINFILE>  (3D) Open 'C:\WFW311\SYSTEM\DDEML.DLL'
<WINFILE>  (3D) Open 'C:\WFW311\SYSTEM\OLECLI.DLL'
<WINFILE>  (3D) Open 'C:\WFW311\SYSTEM\OLESVR.DLL'
; ...
<WINFILE> *(47) Get Curr Dir 3 (03h)
<W32SXXXX>  (50) Set PSP 175 (00AFh)
<W32SXXXX>  (42) Lseek0 10 0001da00
<W32SXXXX>  (3F) Read 10 (000Ah), 2687 (0A7Fh)
; ...
<W32SXXXX> *(3D) Open 'C:\WFW311\SYSTEM\win32s\w32skrnl.dll'
; ...
<W32SXXXX> *(3D) Open 'C:\WINDOWS\CLOCK.EXE'
; ...
<W32SXXXX> *(3D) Open 'C:\WFW311\SYSTEM\win32s\comdlg32.dll'
<W32SXXXX> *(3D) Open 'C:\WFW311\SYSTEM\win32s\KERNEL32.dll'
<W32SXXXX> *(3D) Open 'C:\WFW311\SYSTEM\win32s\USER32.dll'
<W32SXXXX> *(3D) Open 'C:\WFW311\SYSTEM\win32s\GDI32.dll'
<W32SXXXX> *(3D) Open 'C:\WFW311\SYSTEM\win32s\NTDLL.dll'
<W32SXXXX> *(3D) Open 'C:\WFW311\SYSTEM\win32s\SHELL32.dll'
<W32SXXXX>  (3D) Open 'C:\WFW311\SYSTEM\USER.EXE'
; ...
<W32SXXXX>  (3F) Read 6 (0006h), 6755 (1A63h)
<CLOCK> *(2F) Get DTA
<CLOCK>  (50) Set PSP 6799 (1A8Fh)
<CLOCK>  (2F) Get DTA
<CLOCK> *(1A) Set DTA 31C7:8B8E
<CLOCK> *(4E) Find First 'C:\WFW311\WIN.INI'
<CLOCK> *(1A) Set DTA 1A8F:0080
<CLOCK>  (3D) Open 'C:\WFW311\CLOCK.INI'
; ...
<CLOCK> *(2A) Get Date
<CLOCK>  (50) Set PSP 6799 (1A8Fh)
<CLOCK>  (2A) Get Date
<CLOCK> *(2C) Get Time
```

```
<CLOCK>  (2A) Get Date
<CLOCK> *(2C) Get Time
; ...
```

To run a Win32 application, Windows 3.1*x* must load the Win32s subsystem. This process is described in my *Microsoft Systems Journal* (April 1993) article on Win32s (see especially the "How Does It Work?" section on pp. 24-29) and in Matt Pietrek's *Windows Internals* (pp. 244, 292-293).

Briefly, here's how Win32s loads: Whenever you select a program to run under Windows 3.*x* (for example, by clicking an icon in Program Manager), whatever shell you're using calls the WinExec API function, which in turn calls LoadModule. LoadModule has an error return code indicating that the specified module was a Win32 Portable Executable (PE) file rather than a Win16 New Executable (NE) file. When WinExec sees this error return, it calls a function in KRNL386.EXE that's called ExecPE. Yes, Windows 3.1 had built-in knowledge of Win32 PE executables; Win32s was not tacked on later as an afterthought.

This is an important point because if Win32s was in some way "integrated" into Windows 3.1, then suddenly Windows 95 looks a lot less like a brand-new version of Windows and a lot more like a vastly-improved version of Win32s. When someone makes this point, the programmers working on Windows 95 at Microsoft protest that "Chicago is not Win32s!" This was a frequent refrain at the December 1993 Win32 developer's conference at Disneyland, for example. They assert that in contrast to Win32s, Windows 95 is integrated, seamless, and all sorts of other good things.

But Microsoft doth protest too much. When Win32s first came out in late 1992, the company whistled a different tune: "Win32s and Windows 3.1 system-code are tightly coupled. Win32s is a true system extension to the Windows 3.1 operating system code" (Microsoft KnowledgeBase article, "Coordination Between Windows 3.1 and Win32s," 1992). It's a stretch to call a small hook in WinExec "tightly coupled," but this is the same stretch that Microsoft makes with each new system software release. The new software is always "integrated," "seamless," and "tightly coupled," and its predecessor suddenly turns out not to have been.

Perhaps we will one day be hearing how Windows 2000 is truly integrated and how Windows 95 wasn't. I predict that at the December 1998 developer's conference (which I further predict will be held at the Coney Island Cyclone at Astroland Amusement Park; see *Microsoft Systems Journal*, July 1994), Microsoft developers will tell the assembled 20,000 ISVs (all writing Microsoft Office add-ins in Visual Basic), "Windows 2000 is not Windows 95!"

Returning to reality, and to the WSPY21 log, ExecPE loads W32SYS.DLL (a Win16 DLL), which in turn loads WIN32S.EXE. This is a tiny Win16 executable, which acts as the proxy for a PE file in the 16-bit world. Another Win16 DLL, WIN32S16.DLL, contains the 16-bit side of the Win32s kernel. In addition to code that can load PE files into memory under Windows 3.1, resolve their fixups, and so on, WIN32S16 also contains the 16-bit side of the code that allows Win32 APIs to be implemented on top of the existing Windows 3.1 16-bit DLLs. WIN-32S16 loads W32SKRNL.DLL, which is a Win32 DLL.

With the fundamental 16/32-bit communication portion of Win32s loaded, WIN32S16 can now proceed to load the Win32 executable (here, CLOCK.EXE) and any Win32 API DLLs it uses (here, COMDLG32, KERNEL32, USER32, GDI32, NTDLL, and SHELL32). For example, KERNEL32.DLL contains the GetSystemTime and GetLocalTime Win32 API services that Clock will need to call when it receives a WM_TIMER message.

Now, the WV86TEST log shows that DOS sees almost none of this furious activity involved in bootstrapping the entire Win32s subsystem. The combination of 32BFA and Win32s turns WfW 3.11 into something that begins to look like a genuine 32-bit protected-mode operating system, much like Windows 95. Indeed, as will be discussed in detail at the end of this chapter, Windows 95 looks a lot like a Win32s "done right"; it certainly isn't the "NT Lite" that some in the computer trade press have wishfully thought.

Now, WV86TEST sees INT 21h function 2Ah and 2Ch calls from the Win32 version of Clock. Remember that this is the CLOCK.EXE that comes with Windows 95. It is unlikely that this executable contains direct INT 21h calls. Actually, it's more than unlikely; it's impossible: putting an _asm int 21h in a Win32 executable causes a GP fault under both Win32s and Windows 95. So how does WV86TEST see INT 21h function 2Ah and 2Ch calls coming from Clock?

As just noted, Clock's WM_TIMER handler calls the GetSystemTime and GetLocalTime Win32 API functions, which are exported from KERNEL32.DLL. If you use the Win-ICE BMSG (breakpoint on message) command to set a watch WM_TIMER messages going to Clock and, when the breakpoint is hit, trace (F8) through the code, you eventually get to this block of code in KERNEL32:

```
MOV     AH,2Ah
CALL    80BDC3E4h
; ...
MOV     AH,2Ch
CALL    80BDC3E4h
```

The numbers being moved into the AH register, 2Ah and 2Ch, should look familiar: These are the numbers of the INT 21h Get Date and Get Time functions. It's a safe bet that the function at 80BDC3E4h does INT 21h calls on behalf of Win32 applications. Jumping through several more levels of code, you get to a 32-bit instruction in W32SKRNL.DLL:

```
2197:80B927B3 FF1DF4D0B980    CALL FWORD PTR [80B9D0F4]
```

The odd-looking FWORD PTR refers to a *far pointer*. In 32-bit code, a far pointer is 48 bits, in the form 16:32 (16 bits for the selector and 32 bits for the offset). FWORD PTR indicates that the processor will use a 48-bit address (16-bit selector and 32-bit offset). As we'll see later, Windows 95 uses the same instruction when 32-bit code has to call down to 16-bit code. Windows NT uses the same mechanism as part of its WOW (Windows on Windows) subsystem for running Win16 applications. For an excellent discussion, see Jim Finnegan's article on WOW in the June 1994 *Microsoft Systems Journal*, especially the sidebar on CALL FWORD PTR (pp. 34-35).

In our current example, the CALL FWORD PTR instruction will interpret the six bytes at 80B9D0F4h as a 16:32 address to call:

```
:dw 80b9d0f4
2197:80B9D0F4 02C5 0000 1137 ...
```

In other words, executing CALL FWORD PTR [80B9D0F4h] will generate a far call to 1137:000002C5. In this configuration, selector 1137h contains 16-bit code, belonging to WIN32S16:

```
:ldt 1137
1137  Code16    Base=80B3A620  Lim=0000057F  DPL=3  P    RE
:heap 1137
Han./Sel    Address    Length     Owner       Type       Seg/Rsrc
1136        80B3A620   00000580   WIN32S16    Code       03
```

Thus, when the 32-bit part of Win32s executes the CALL FWORD PTR instruction, it calls into the 16-bit part. If you use a debugger to trace through the single CALL FWORD PTR instruction in W32SKRNL, you suddenly find yourself looking at 16-bit code in WIN32S16. The code at 1137:02C5 generates an honest-to-goodness INT 21h on behalf of its 32-bit caller.

Thunking: Mixing 16- and 32-bit code with CALL FWORD PTR

CALL FWORD PTR (opcodes FFh 1Dh) is Win32s's way of letting 32-bit code call down to 16-bit code. Microsoft somewhat incorrectly uses the term *thunk* to describe this mixing of 32- and 16-bit code.

You can use FWORD.C (Listing 14-1) and INTSERV.C (Listing 14-2) to experiment with these 32-to-16 thunks. FWORD is a simple Win32 program that does little more than make a CALL FWORD PTR to the address you specify on the program's command line, using whatever values you specify for EAX, EBX, ECX, and EDX.

Listing 14-1: FWORD.C

```
// FWORD.C - Win32 app
// cl fword.c
#include <stdlib.h>
#include <stdio.h>
#include "windows.h"

void fail(const char *s) { puts(s); exit(1); }

#pragma pack(1)

typedef struct {
    unsigned long ofs;
    unsigned short seg;
    } fword;

int PASCAL WinMain(HANDLE hInstance, HANDLE hPrevInstance,
    LPSTR lpCmdLine, int nCmdShow)
{
    // Microsoft C startup per MSJ, May 1991, pp. 135-6
    #define argc __argc
    #define argv __argv

    extern int __argc;
    extern char **__argv;

    char buf[80];
    fword addr;
    unsigned reax, rebx, recx, redx;
    int i;

    sscanf(argv[1], "%04X:%08lX", &addr.seg, &addr.ofs);
    sscanf(argv[2], "%08lX/%08lX/%08lX/%08lX",
        &reax, &rebx, &recx, &redx);

    sprintf(buf, "Calling %04X:%08lX %08lX/%08lX/%08lX/%08lX",
```

```
        addr.seg, addr.ofs, reax, rebx, recx, redx);
    MessageBox(0, buf, "FWORD", MB_OK);

    // Any pointers would need to be translated, of course.
    // Could translate e.g. via thunked calls to DPMI (INT 31h).

    // generate a lot so it's easy to see in WSPY21
    for (i=0; i<100; i++) {
        _asm {
            mov eax, reax
            mov ebx, rebx
            mov ecx, recx
            mov edx, redx
            call fword ptr [addr]
            mov reax, eax
            mov rebx, ebx
            mov recx, ecx
            mov redx, edx
        }
    }

    sprintf(buf, "Returned %08lX/%08lX/%08lX/%08lX",
        reax, rebx, recx, redx);
    MessageBox(0, buf, "FWORD", MB_OK);

    return 0;
}
```

INTSERV.C (Listing 14-2) is a Win16 program that includes three functions that issue interrupts: INT 21h (DOS), INT 2Fh (multiplex interrupt for assorted services), and INT 31h (DPMI). INTSERV displays the addresses of the three functions so that you can specify one of them on FWORD's command line.

Listing 14-2: INTSERV.C

```
// INTSERV.C -- Win16 app
// bcc -W -3 -B intserv.c

#include <stdlib.h>
#include <stdio.h>
#include <dos.h>
#define NOGDI
#include "windows.h"

static char dummy;  // just something to take seg of

// yuk! static vars:  only one caller at a time
#define SERVER(calls,intno) { \
    static char stack[1024]; \
    static unsigned stack_seg; \
    static unsigned prev_seg; \
    static unsigned long prev_ofs; \
```

```
    static unsigned prev_ds; \
    _asm { \
        push ax; \
        push bx; \
        mov ax, ds; \
        mov bx, seg dummy; \
        mov ds, bx; \
        mov stack_seg, bx; \
        mov prev_ds, ax; \
        pop bx; \
        pop ax; \
        mov prev_seg, ss; \
        mov dword ptr prev_ofs, esp; \
        mov ss, stack_seg; \
        mov sp, offset stack; \
        add sp, 512; \
    } \
    calls++; \
    _asm { \
        int intno; \
        mov ss, prev_seg; \
        mov esp, dword ptr prev_ofs; \
        mov ds, prev_ds; \
        db 66h; \
        retf; \
    } \
}

unsigned long calls21 = 0, calls2F = 0, calls31 = 0;

void server21(void) { SERVER(calls21, 0x21); }
void server2F(void) { SERVER(calls2F, 0x2F); }
void server31(void) { SERVER(calls31, 0x31); }

int PASCAL WinMain(HANDLE hInstance, HANDLE hprev21Instance,
    LPSTR lpszCmdLine, int nCmdShow)
{
    char buf[120];
    int len;

    len = sprintf(buf, "INT 21h server @ %Fp\n", (void far *) server21);
    len += sprintf(buf+len, "INT 2Fh server @ %Fp\n", (void far *)
           server2F);
    len += sprintf(buf+len, "INT 31h server @ %Fp", (void far *) server31);
    MessageBox(0, buf, "INTSERV", MB_OK);

    // servers are active until click MB_OK above

    len = sprintf(buf, "%lu calls to INT 21h server\n", calls21);
    len += sprintf(buf+len, "%lu calls to INT 2Fh server\n", calls2F);
    len += sprintf(buf+len, "%lu calls to INT 31h server", calls31);
    MessageBox(0, buf, "INTSERV", MB_OK);
    return 0;
}
```

Figure 14-1 shows one example of how the 32-bit FWORD and 16-bit INTSERV programs work together. INTSERV displays a message box indicating that its INT 21h server is at 1D4F:0170, INT 2Fh at 1D4F:01AE, and INT 31h at 1D4F:01EC. I wanted the FWORD Win32 program to get its PSP via INT 21h function 62h (Get PSP), so I ran the following command:

```
FWORD 1D4F:0170 6200/0/0/0
```

FWORD generates 100 calls so that it's easy to spot in WSPY21's log. Sure enough, WSPY21 shows the FWORD program making Get PSP calls. Finally, FWORD displayed the returned EAX, EBX, ECX, and EDX registers, with EBX=01EB7h. FWORD's PSP is 1EB7h.

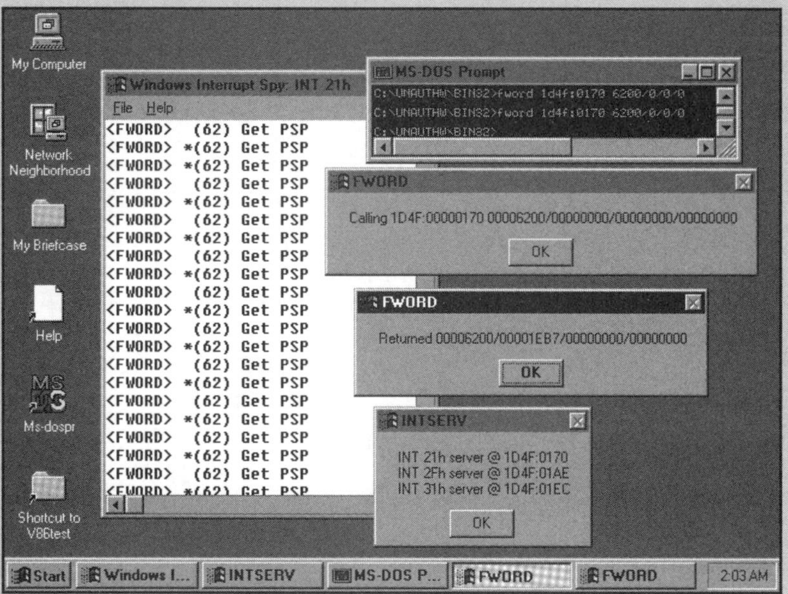

Figure 14-1. The 32-bit FWORD and 16-bit INTSERV programs demonstrate thunking in Win32s and Windows 95.

FWORD and INTSERV work in both Win32s and Windows 95. As you can see from Listings 14-1 and 14-2, there isn't much code involved. The only complexity is in INTSERV, which temporarily switches to a 16-bit stack to service the request from a 32-bit caller such as FWORD. On entry, INTSERV must save away the caller's 32-bit stack pointer, and it must restore the caller's stack pointer before returning. Because of the way I happened to implement this in INTSERV.C, the code is nonreentrant, supporting only one caller at a time. On the other hand, the interrupts to which INTSERV provides a gateway are themselves non-reentrant, so in a way all I did in INTSERV is create my own InDOS flag.

Everything interesting in INTSERV.C is located inside the SERVER macro. For example, the function that handles INT 21h calls from Win32 applications is nothing more than SERVER(calls21, 0x21). This expands to the following assembly language code:

```
push    ax                        ;;; save caller's AX and BX
push    bx
mov     ax, ds                    ;;; save caller's DS
mov     bx, seg dummy             ;;; SEG DUMMY is INTVECT's DS
mov     ds, bx                    ;;; set up our DS
mov     stack_seg, bx
mov     prev_ds, ax
pop     bx                        ;;; get back caller's AX and BX
pop     ax
mov     prev_seg, ss              ;;; save away caller's 48-bit stack ptr
mov     dword ptr prev_ofs, esp
mov     ss, stack_seg             ;;; set up new stack ptr
mov     sp, offset stack
add     sp, 512
inc     dword ptr calls21         ;;; increment counter
int     21h                       ;;; do it!
mov     ss, prev_seg
mov     esp, dword ptr prev_ofs   ;;; restore caller's 48-bit stack ptr
mov     ds, prev_ds               ;;; restore caller's DS
db      66h
retf                              ;;; 66 RETF: do 48-bit far return
```

Note that 16-bit INTVECT must save away and restore the full 48 bits of the 32-bit caller's stack pointer (SS:ESP rather than SS:SP) and must return to its 32-bit caller with a 48-bit (16:32) far return. Aside from these stack-related issues, calling 16-bit code from 32-bit code is a cinch. Actually, it might be even more of a cinch because Jim Finnegan, this book's technical editor, reminded me that "According to Intel, you don't have to do any of this stack fooling. If you futz with the DS B-bit, and your stack is top down in a <64K segment, you should be golden." The B-bit specifies the size of the stack pointer — the 32-bit ESP register or the 16-bit SP register — to be used for implicit stack references. (See the useful chapter on "Mixing 16-Bit and 32-Bit Code" in Intel's *i486 Microprocessor Programmer's Reference Manual*.)

Although Win32s (and as we'll soon see, Windows 95) uses CALL FWORD PTR to let Win32 applications make INT 21h calls, this isn't the only thunking mechanism available. In the 16-bit code just shown, notice the DB 66h RETF, which makes a 48-bit far return to a 32-bit caller. Now, by jiggling addresses on the stack, it's possible for a piece of code to use RETF to return to some piece of code from which it was never called in the first place. Thus, the capability to return from 16-bit code to 32-bit code is also a form of thunking. Skipping ahead a bit, KERNEL32 in Windows 95 uses RETF in its QT_Thunk routine, which is called by Win32 functions in USER32 and GDI32 that are implemented by thunking down to the old Win16 Windows DLLs. And, though Microsoft denies that KERNEL32 ever thunks down to the 16-bit kernel, KERNEL32 uses QT_Thunk too.

> In Windows 95, Win16 DLLs such as KRNL386.EXE use yet another thunking mechanism, 48-bit far jumps (DB 66h JMP FAR), to make Win32 calls. This is described in the "Win32 File Handles and Thunking" section later in this chapter.
>
> Microsoft's original intent was that applications in Win32s, NT, and Windows 95 wouldn't be allowed to mix 16- and 32-bit code. Period. After much screaming by developers who had Win16 code that was difficult or impossible to port to Win32 but that needed to be used in Win32 applications, Microsoft relaxed its principles about the purity of 32-bit code and published some thunking APIs. Unfortunately, there are three different thunking APIs:
>
> - Universal Thunk (UT) in Win32s. See Walter Oney, "Mix 16-bit and 32-bit Code in Your Applications with the Win32s Universal Thunk," *Microsoft Systems Journal* (November 1993).
> - Generic Thunk in NT. See James Finnegan, "Test Drive Win32 from 16-bit Code Using the Windows NT WOW Layer and Generic Thunk," *Microsoft Systems Journal* (June 1994).
> - Thunk Compiler in Windows 95. See THUNKME.TXT in the Windows 95 SDK. The thunk compiler, THUNK.EXE, accepts thunk scripts that contain C-style function prototypes, much as you would use with a Remote Procedure Call (RPC) compiler. The thunk compiler outputs an .ASM file to include on the 16-bit and 32-bit side of the call. What Microsoft persists in wrongly calling thunks are much more like a form of non-networked RPC.
>
> With all these different thunking APIs, it might be easier to build your own portable thunks using the native Intel instructions, such as CALL FWORD PTR, JMP FAR, and RETF.

We saw earlier that the Win32s implementation of GetLocalTime uses thunks to call down to Win16 code which, in turn, makes an INT 21h call to DOS's Get Date and Get Time functions. What a kludge, right? It's a good thing Windows 95 is a full-blown protected-mode operating system that doesn't require DOS to get the date and time, right? Well, let's see...

32/32: The Windows 95 Clock

Having run the Win16 and Win32 versions of Clock under WfW 3.11, let's next take the Win32 version of Clock and run it under Windows 95. (Yes, later on we'll run the Win16 version of Clock under Windows 95.) While Clock was running, WV86TEST logged the following DOS calls:

```
50 seconds elapsed

INT 21h calls:
2A: 451     2C: 451     4C: 1    50: 23   55: 1
```

There are the function 2Ah and 2Ch calls again. Naturally, WSPY21 shows Clock making many more DOS calls, including some of the new long filename functions (INT 21h function 71h):

```
<CLOCK> *(71) LFN (4E) Find First 'C:\WINDOWS\clock.ini'
<CLOCK> *(71) LFN (A1) Find Close
<CLOCK> *(71) LFN (60) Truename 'C:\WINDOWS\CLOCK.EXE'
```

But there's something much more interesting about the WSPY21 log for the Win32 version of Clock under Windows 95: *no* function 2Ah (Get Date) or 2Ch (Get Time) calls show up!

We've just seen that WV86TEST with Windows 95 sees function 2Ah and 2Ch calls while Clock is running. How can DOS see these calls when the higher-level INT 21h hook in WSPY21 doesn't? Where are these calls coming from?

As noted earlier, whenever the Win32 version of Clock receives a WM_TIMER message, it calls the GetLocalTime Win32 API function in KERNEL32.DLL. (Incidentally, that phrase, "the Win32 version of Clock receives a WM_TIMER message," hides a frightening amount of complexity; Chapter 13 briefly discusses how Win32 programs receive WM_XXX messages in Windows 95.)

In Win-ICE, you can set a breakpoint (BMSG) for WM_TIMER in Clock's window. When this breakpoint is triggered, you can trace through the code by pressing F8. After a bunch of code (including a call to KERNEL32!W32S_BackTo32, which sounds like a leftover from Win32s), you eventually reach Clock's call to GetLocalTime. Tracing through the code for that function in KERNEL32.DLL, you finally get to the following bit of code, which seems strangely reminiscent of the Win32s implementation of GetLocalTime:

```
0137:BFF71186   MOV     AH,2A
0137:BFF71188   CALL    BFF71E5F
; ...
0137:BFF7119C   MOV     AH,2C
0137:BFF7119E   CALL    BFF71E5F
```

The function at BFF71E5Fh in KERNEL32 must do INT 21h calls for Win32 applications. Examining this function in Win-ICE, we see:

```
:u bff71e5f
0137:BFF71E5F   PUSH    ECX
0137:BFF71E60   PUSH    EAX
0137:BFF71E61   PUSH    002A0010
0137:BFF71E66   CALL    KERNEL32!VxDCall0
0137:BFF71E6B   RET
```

We know from Chapter 13 that VxDCall0 2A0010h makes INT 21h calls on behalf of Win32 applications, but we didn't peer inside the code to see how it works. Let's do that now:

```
:u vxdcall0
KERNEL32!VxDCall0
0137:BFF71F10   POP     DWORD PTR [ESP]
0137:BFF71F13   CALL    FWORD PTR CS:[BFFB5004]
```

There's that CALL FWORD PTR again! Microsoft doth protest too much that "Chicago is not Win32s!" Although there are important differences between Windows 95 and Win32s (and although the Chicago team at Microsoft may not have reused much of the code written by the Win32s group at Microsoft Israel, that being the "not invented here" way that things often work inside Microsoft), there are nonetheless a lot of similarities between the two environments.

Remember that CALL FWORD PTR uses a 16:32 (48-bit) address. Examining the six bytes at BFFB5004, we see:

```
:dw bffb5004
0137:BFFB5004   03B6 0000 003B
```

Thus, the VxDCall function in KERNEL32 is little more than a fancy way of calling the code at 003B:03B6. This in turn is:

```
003B:000003B6   INT     30
```

Huh? After all that tracing, seeing this INT 30h is sort of like being told that the answer to Life, the Universe, and Everything is 42. What good is it to turn an INT 21h into an INT 30h? What's an INT 30h, anyhow?

Recall from Chapter 8 that INT 30h is a protected-mode (PM) callback. VxDs generate these PM callbacks with the Allocate_PM_Call_Back service, which is provided by VMM and documented in the Windows DDK. The INT 30h is basically a thunk that lets user-level protected-mode applications in Ring 3 jump to VMM and VxD code in Ring 0. Executing the INT 30h takes you to VMM's PM callback handler which, based on the offset within segment 003Bh from which the INT 30h came (such as 03B6h in this example), will jump to the appropriate PM callback.

Figure 14-2 shows what we have so far: VxDCall0 is an undocumented function exported by KERNEL32.DLL. VxDCall0 expects a VxD Win32 service number (such as 2A0010h), and any values for EAX and ECX on the stack (see the WIN32PSP.C sample program later in this chapter).

2A0010h indicates VxD ID #002Ah, Win32 service #0010h. The PM callback in VMM decodes such Win32 service requests. VxD 2Ah is VWIN32, and the PM callback in VMM will call its Win32 service #10.

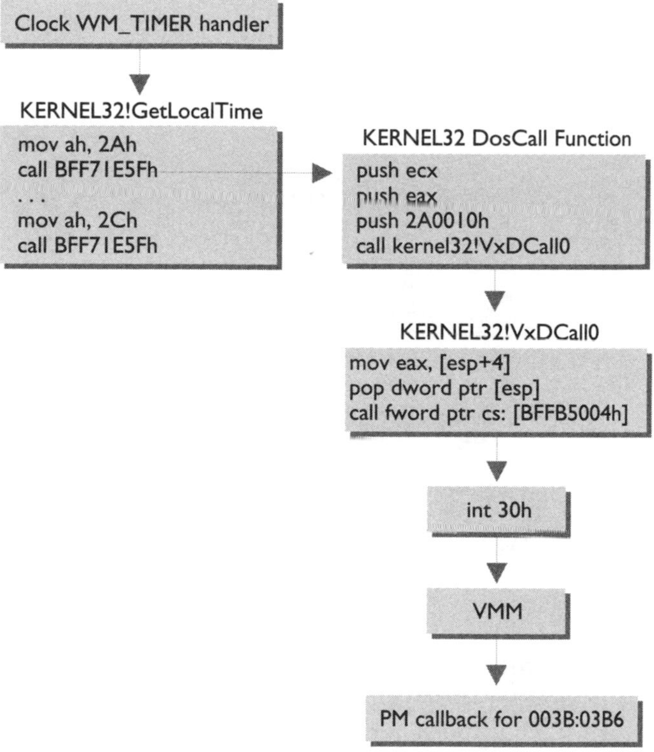

Figure 14-2: How the Win32 clock gets the date and time, part 1. Upon receiving a WM_TIMER message, the Clock calls the Win32 GetLocalTime function, which does a VxDCall0 2A0010h, with AH=2Ah and 2Ch. VxDCall0 eventually leads to the execution of protected-mode callback, which traps into VMM. See Figure 14-3 for part 2.

VWIN32's Win32 service #10h issues INT 21h on behalf of Win32 applications by calling Exec_PM_Int, a VMM service new to Windows 95, with the parameter 21h. Figure 14-3 shows the next part of the diagram.

Exec_PM_Int in turn is a wrapper around four other VMM calls:

```
Set_PM_Exec_Mode
Begin_Use_Locked_PM_Stack
Exec_Int
End_Nest_Exec
```

And Exec_Int in turn is equivalent to Simulate_Int followed by Resume_Exec.

Basically, then, calling Exec_PM_Int sends a simulated interrupt to the protected-mode interrupt chain. Thus, the whole VxDCall0 2A0010h mechanism is fairly similar to the FWORD/INTVECT code I cobbled together back in Listings 14-1 and 14-2.

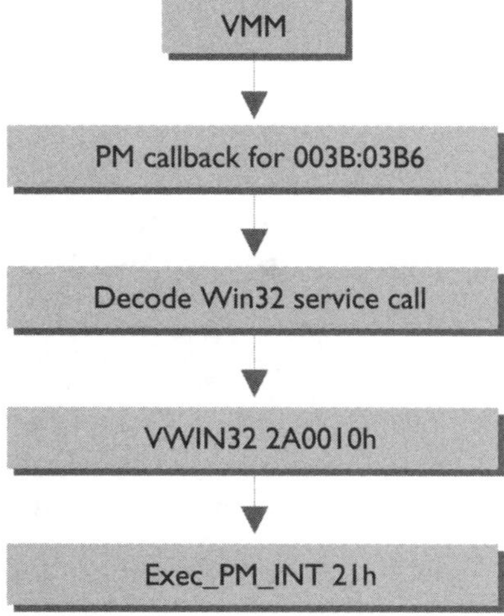

Figure 14-3: How the Win32 clock gets the date and time, part 2. The protected-mode callback executed at the bottom of Figure 14-2 is responsible for decoding Win32 service requests. Service 2A0010h is provided by the VWIN32 VxD, and uses the Exec_PM_INT service in VMM to make INT 21h calls on behalf of Win32 programs. See Figure 14-4 for part 3.

If no protected-mode interrupt handler absorbs the call, it winds up at VMM's default protected-mode handler, which reflects the call to the V86 interrupt hook chain (that is, the chain of VxD interrupt handlers established with the Hook_V86_Int_Chain service). If no VxD (such as IFSMgr) absorbs the simulated V86 interrupt, VMM's default V86-mode handler sends it down to the actual V86 interrupt chain (that is, the chain of real-mode interrupt handlers that Windows runs in V86 mode). It is crucial to understand the difference between the V86 interrupt chain (real-mode interrupt handlers, including DOS, device drivers, and TSRs) and what I'm calling the V86 interrupt hook chain (protected-mode handlers installed by VxDs).

If no VxD absorbs the INT 21h that VWIN32 simulated using Exec_PM_Int, the INT 21h is sent down to DOS, and V86TEST sees the call, even though WSPY21 doesn't. (WSPY21 doesn't see the call because it didn't start out life as INT 21h, Dos3Call, or NoHookDosCall, which is basically what WSPY21 traps.)

Figure 14-4 shows the next portion of the complicated path taken when a Win32 program asks for the date and time.

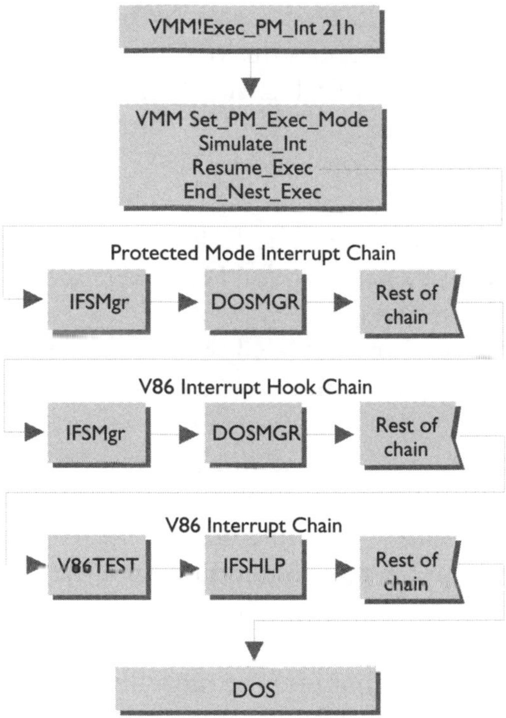

Figure 14-4: How the Win32 clock gets the date and time, part 3. The Exec_PM_Int service in VMM sends the simulated INT 21h function 2Ah and 2Ch calls to the protected-mode interrupt chain. If no protected-mode INT 21h handler services the calls, they are next sent to the VxD INT 21h hook chain. If no handler here services the calls either, they are sent to the V86 interrupt chain, and eventually to MS-DOS. See Figure 14-5 for the exciting conclusion, revealing what happens to the calls inside DOS.

Figures 14-2 through 14-5 certainly reveal a mechanism that is far more complicated and interesting than a plain INT 21h, but the result is still that DOS sees an INT 21h function 2Ah or 2Ch call — just as shown by the WV86TEST output that got us started on this subject in the first place.

Does Windows 95 Really Call Down to DOS? And What Does It Do When It Gets There?

By now, you must have a few nagging doubts and worries about whether Windows 95 really and truly calls down to MS-DOS to implement Win32 API functions such as GetLocalTime.

First, just because V86TEST has seen Windows issuing calls to INT 21h functions 2Ah and 2Ch, does this really mean that DOS sees these calls too? It's true that V86TEST chains all calls to the previous interrupt handler (see V86TEST.C in Chapter 10). But we know from previous chapters that IFSHLP.SYS sits between V86TEST and DOS, and that one of IFSHLP's main responsibilities is to divert DOS calls away from DOS and toward IFSMgr (see "The Role of IFSHLP.SYS and V86 Call-backs" in Chapter 8). So perhaps V86TEST sees the calls but DOS doesn't. I'll address this issue in a moment.

Second, there's what we might call the Heisenberg worry. As part of the explanation for his uncertainty relations (for example, that you can't determine simultaneously, for a given degree of certainty, both the position and the momentum of a subatomic particle), Werner Heisenberg came up with a "thought experiment" involving an imaginary gamma-ray microscope. Using Heisenberg's microscope, the very act of observing a particle diverts it from the position or momentum it would have had in its unobserved state. And the finer the resolution of the microscope, the more the act of observation perturbs its subject.

There's a nice analogy (but nothing more than that) to computing: When you use one piece of software to examine another piece of software with which it interacts, you must be careful not to build a Heisenberg microscope that changes the behavior of what you're trying to observe.

Now, is V86TEST a Heisenberg microscope? Does the mere act of loading V86TEST before Windows perhaps change the way that Windows interacts with DOS? Does the presence of V86TEST *cause* Windows to send INT 21h calls such as functions 2Ah and 2Ch down to DOS? If V86TEST were not present, would Windows still do this?

These questions are important because Microsoft has asserted for the longest time that Chicago would completely bypass DOS unless there was an INT 21h hooker (presumably other than DOS itself) on the system. The presence of even a single TSR that hooks INT 21h would then presumably cause Chicago to send all DOS calls down to the INT 21h chain. So perhaps V86TEST *is* that TSR and perhaps, without V86TEST, Windows would be behaving quite differently.

There are several ways to address all these concerns. First, though it does contradict other Microsoft statements intended for the *goyim* (that's "for public consumption" in Yiddish), Microsoft *has* explicitly stated that Windows will pass down all non-file I/O INT 21h calls. Once more, recall the Microsoft document titled "Chicago File System Features," quoted in Chapter 8: "On default all INT 21 interrupts, except file API INT 21s, are passed down to any hooker present in the system."

In this book, I could have perhaps just quoted this sentence a few more times — each time reminding you that DOS itself is an INT 21h hooker — and not bothered with any experiments. With this one sentence, Microsoft says that Windows 95 — including Win32 applications running under Windows 95 — calls down to DOS for non-file services, such as getting and setting the date and time. But the document's description of Windows interaction with INT 21h hookers doesn't really hit you (at least, it didn't hit *me*) until you've performed the experiments and seen what the document is getting at. This sentence is such a glaring contradiction with Microsoft's "Windows 95 doesn't require DOS" propaganda that most readers probably focus on the "except file API INT 21s" part and gloss over the broader statement being made about INT 21h in general. For all the talk of Windows 95 not requiring DOS, what Windows 95 actually does in relation to DOS is precisely what WfW 3.11 does: provide 32-bit file access.

At any rate, Microsoft's statement is consistent with our finding that Windows 95, like Win32s, implements certain Win32 API functions by calling (albeit in a highly baroque and circuitous style) down to the real-mode MS-DOS code (which Windows runs in V86 mode).

Second, by comparing output from WV86TEST and WSPY21, we've seen that many DOS calls are *not* passed down, even when V86TEST *is* loaded. Again, this is consistent with the Microsoft document on the Chicago file system: "The file API INT 21s are just passed to VM (local) hookers, but not to global (AUTOEXEC.BAT) type hookers." V86-TEST is a global INT 21h hooker. We've seen that, indeed, Windows does not pass it any file INT 21h calls. It seems a fair presumption, then, that the few calls that *are* passed down would still be passed down even if V86TEST weren't loaded.

Third, by running without V86TEST and putting a debugger breakpoint on the real-mode DOS code, we can confirm that the INT 21h calls seen by V86TEST, such as functions 2Ah and 2Ch, *really really are* sent down to DOS, even when V86TEST isn't running. It's worth looking at this not only to prove that V86TEST is not a Heisenberg microscope (were you really all that worried?) but also because it helps make a critical point about Windows-DOS interaction. Here goes.

I started Chicago without V86TEST and from a DOS box ran the INTCHAIN program (see the *Unauthorized Windows 95* disk), using it to locate DOS's INT 21h handler. Starting from when INTCHAIN issues the INT instruction given on its command line (such as "21/2A00" for INT 21h function 2Ah), until the interrupt returns to the line of code after the INT instruction, INTCHAIN single-steps through the interrupt chain, displaying key addresses such as when the segment changes or when another INT is encountered. I've added comments to the following output from INTCHAIN:

```
C:\UNAUTHW>intchain 21/2a00        ;; do INT 21h func 2Ah (Get Date)

Tracing INT 21 AX=2A00
494 instructions
Skipped over 5 INT

0337:04A8   IFS$HLP$               ;; IFSHLP.SYS
01EF:0023   D:
0498:1956   DBLSYSH$               ;; DBLSPACE.BIN
00A0:0FAC   DOS                    ;; low-memory stub for DOS in HMA (DOS=HIGH)
FE9E:4249   HMA                    ;; DOS's INT 21h handler in HMA
FE9E:4339   HMA INT 2Ah AX=8200h   ;; End critical sections 0-7
FE9E:5354   HMA INT 2Ah AX=8002h   ;; Begin critical section 2
0070:0166   IO                     ;; Device driver generic Strategy routine
FE9E:8979   HMA
0070:00EE   IO                     ;; CLOCK$ Interrupt routine in here
FFFF:0040   HMA
FFFF:08DA   HMA INT 1Ah AX=0000h   ;; CLOCK$ calls 1A/00 (Get System Time)
FE9E:8985   HMA
FE9E:5383   HMA INT 2Ah AX=8102h   ;; End critical section 2
```

We'll examine this DOS -> CLOCK$ -> INT 1Ah chain in more detail momentarily. Right now, we need only one piece of information: FE9E:4249 is the location of DOS's INT 21h handler. We can use Win-ICE to set a breakpoint on this V86-mode address (BPX &FE9E:4249).

Sure enough, the breakpoint is triggered, showing that Windows really does call down to DOS. This answers the first question, about whether IFSHLP perhaps ships all INT 21h calls to IFSMgr — it doesn't. Well, why would it? IFSMgr handles only about forty different INT 21h functions. In the absence of other VxDs that handle INT 21h, such as my CURRDRIV.386 and INTVECT.386 from Chapter 8, the remaining sixty or so less frequently used and less expensive INT 21h functions must be sent down to DOS; the Win-ICE breakpoint on DOS's INT 21h handler shows that they are.

So we now know that Windows 95 really does call down to DOS, even in the absence of an INT 21h hooker such as V86TEST. We could leave it at that, treating DOS as a monolithic black box. But rather than rest content with a vague statement like "Windows calls down to DOS," let's peer inside ("drill down" seems to be the current Microsoft lingo) DOS's INT 21h handler. By seeing what happens inside DOS during an

INT 21h function 2Ah call from Windows, we'll see why it's so important to remember that Windows runs DOS in V86 mode rather than in real mode, and why this is like taking the real-mode DOS code and running it in protected mode.

If you trace through DOS's INT 21h handler, you eventually hit something that looks like this:

```
FE9E:000042F1   MOV     BL,AH
FE9E:000042F3   SHL     BX,1            ;; BX = 2 * INT 21h func number
;;; ...
FE9E:00004354   MOV     DX,CS:[BX+3FE1] ;; index into table
FE9E:00004359   XCHG    BX,SS:[05EA]
FE9E:0000435E   MOV     DS,SS:[05EC]
FE9E:00004363   CALL    SS:[05EA]       ;; call handler for INT 21h func
```

This crucial bit of DOS code is explained in excruciating detail in the "Disassembling DOS" chapter of *Undocumented DOS* (2d ed., pp. 291-297). Briefly, the BX register holds the INT 21h AH function number (such as 2Ah) multiplied by two. This number is used to index into a table, here located at offset 3FE1h in the DOS code segment. This table holds near function pointers to DOS's handlers for each INT 21h function. The preceding code retrieves and calls this function pointer. With a utility such as FTAB (the real-mode version of PROTTAB), you can dump out this table and locate the handlers for the INT 21h Get/Set Date/Time functions:

```
C:\UNAUTHW>ftab fe9e:3fe1 73 i21 2 ;; show 73h words at FE9E:3FE1
...
FE9E:48B8   i21_2A          ;; Get Date
FE9E:48D5   i21_2B          ;; Set Date
FE9E:48F5   i21_2C          ;; Get Time
FE9E:4906   i21_2D          ;; Set Time
...
```

Now we can put a breakpoint on the INT 21h function 2Ah handler at FE9E:48B8 and go back to running Clock. If the breakpoint is hit, it means that Windows 95 calls down to DOS. Here's some of the WinICE trace, which I saved to a file, ran through the VXDNAME utility, and then decorated with my usual Talmudic commentary:

```
Break Due to BPX &FE9E:000048B8 C=01
FE9E:000048B8   PUSH    SS              ;;; hit DOS code that does 21/2A
FE9E:000048B9   POP     DS
; ...
;;; Prepare device-driver request packet. Device-driver function 4 (Read).
;;; Buffer points to a 6-byte CLOCK$ transfer record
; ...
FE9E:00008980   CALL    FAR SS:[0378]   ;;; DOS calls CLOCK$ dev driver
```

```
0070:000000EE   CALL    01AF             ;;; this is CLOCK$ Interrupt routine
; ...
0070:000001BF   JMP     FAR CS:[013A]    ;;; go to HMA (DOS=HIGH)
FFFF:00000040   PUSHA
; ...
FFFF:000008D8   SUB     AH,AH ;;; CLOCK$ calls INT 1Ah fn 0 (Get Sys Time)
FFFF:000008DA   INT     1A
```

Thus, Windows 95 *is* calling DOS. In turn, DOS's handler for function 2Ah is calling the Interrupt routine for the CLOCK$ device driver. This in turn (assuming you haven't supplied a new CLOCK$ driver) gets the current date and time for DOS by calling ROM BIOS INT 1Ah function 0 (Get System Time).

Why doesn't CLOCK$ just consult the BIOS data area, which includes a tick counter at 46Ch (0040:006C) and a midnight flag — unfortunately for those who leave their machines running for days at a time, this really is a flag and not a counter! — at 470h (0040:0070)? The source code for CLOCK$ included in Microsoft's DOS 5.0 OEM Adaptation Kit (OAK) has the following comment:

```
;  11/26/91 NSM   M101: We lose date sometimes under windows. To fix this
;           do Int 1a's to get tick count instead of looking at 40:
;           6ch and if we get rollover, then go & update date
;           and time from CMOS.
```

This is from PTIME.ASM, which is the source for the power-management version of CLOCK$ in POWER.EXE. But the standard version of CLOCK$, in MSCHAR.ASM, also calls the ROM BIOS INT 1Ah to get the time, presumably for the same reason.

Well, at least CLOCK$ *thinks* it's calling the ROM BIOS. In fact, because we're running in V86 mode under Windows, all interrupts vector through the IDT (see Chapter 9). The IDT entry for INT 1Ah points to VMM. Thus, when the DOS CLOCK$ device driver calls INT 1Ah, it's actually calling into VMM. Windows might have called down to DOS in V86 mode to handle the INT 21h function 2Ah, but DOS (without knowing it) is going to call right back into Windows to handle the INT 1Ah function 0. If you press F8 (trace) to drill down through the INT 1Ah instruction in Soft-ICE, you can see a dramatic demonstration of this. From the INT 1Ah inside DOS's CLOCK$ device driver, you suddenly switch into 32-bit protected mode and wind up at the next instruction inside VMM:

```
FFFF:000008DA   INT     1A              ;;; VMM hooks INT 1Ah via IDT
;;; INT takes us from V86 mode DOS right to 32-bit protected mode VMM!
0028:VMM+2E44   CALL    VMM+000         ;;; return addr is VMM+2E49
```

When it receives this INT 1Ah call from DOS, VMM does some generic interrupt-handling setup, and then walks the V86 interrupt hook chain:

```
0028:VMM+000    CLD                          ;;; in VMM generic INT handler
0028:VMM+001    PUSHAD
0028:VMM+002    MOV     EAX,[ESP+20]         ;;; return address (2E49h)
0028:VMM+006    SUB     EAX,VMM+2D79         ;;; sub base of INT handlers
0028:VMM+00B    SHR     EAX,03               ;;; (addr-base)/8 = intno (1Ah)
0028:VMM+00E    MOV     EBP,ESP              ;;; make Client Register Struct
0028:VMM+010    MOV     BX,0030
0028:VMM+014    MOV     DS,BX                ;;; get VMM data seg
0028:VMM+016    MOV     ES,BX
0028:VMM+018    MOV     EDI,[VMM+F670]       ;;; EDI = current thread handle
0028:VMM+01E    XCHG    ESP,[EDI+48]         ;;; switch to thread's stack
0028:VMM+021    MOV     EBX,[VMM+F6E4]       ;;; EBX = current VM handle
0028:VMM+027    STI                          ;;; re-enable interrupts
0028:VMM+028    PUSH    VMM+2E0              ;;; push return address (see below)
0028:VMM+02D    JMP     [VMM+D228+4*EAX]     ;;; go to V86 INT 1Ah hook chain
0028:C0FCE1BC   CALL    VTD+1C0              ;;; V86 int hook chain
```

VxDs install themselves on the V86 int hook chain by calling, naturally enough, Hook_V86_Int_Chain. During Windows initialization, the Virtual Timer Device (VTD) calls Hook_V86_Int_Chain with EAX=1Ah and ESI=VTD+1C0h. So now that VMM has received a V86-mode INT 1Ah, it's going to call the routine at VTD+1C0h:

```
0028:VMM+02D    JMP     [VMM+D228+4*EAX] ;;; go to V86 INT 1Ah hook chain
0028:C0FCE1BC   CALL    VTD+1C0          ;;; V86 int hook chain
```

Thus, an INT 1Ah function 0 call, from deep inside DOS's CLOCK$ device driver, ends up at the Windows Virtual Timer Device's 32-bit protected-mode handler for INT 1Ah:

```
0028:VTD+1C0    CMP     BYTE PTR [EBP.Client_AH],10
0028:VTD+1C4    JB      VTD+1C8                 ;;; INT 1Ah func < 10h?  Yes.
0028:VTD+1C8    CMP     BYTE PTR [EBP.Client_AH],01
0028:VTD+1CC    JA      VTD+1F8                 ;;; INT 1Ah func > 1?  No.
0028:VTD+1CE    JB      VTD+1E2                 ;;; INT 1Ah func < 1?  Yes.
0028:VTD+1E2    MOV     EAX,[VTD+3A4]           ;;; handler for INT 1Ah func 0
0028:VTD+1E7    MOV     [EBP.Client_DX],AX      ;;; ret CX:DX=ticks since midnight
0028:VTD+1EB    SHR     EAX,10
0028:VTD+1EE    MOV     [EBP.Client_CX],AX
0028:VTD+1F2    MOV     BYTE PTR [EBP.Client_AL],00  ;;; midnight flag = 0
0028:VTD+1F6    CLC                             ;;; handled it -- don't chain
0028:VTD+1F7    RET
```

The Windows 95 version of VTD handles the INT 1Ah call entirely in 32-bit protected mode by loading the client register structure from a variable (VTD+3A4h) that holds the current time in clock ticks since midnight.

How does VTD maintain this tick counter? The variable is set by VTD's handler for INT 1Ah function 1 (Set Time), which is called from DOS functions 2Bh (Set Date) and 2Dh (Set Time). But VTD can't rely on these functions to keep the tick counter updated, because they are called only when the user changes the date or time (with the Control Panel, for example).

As mentioned earlier, the BIOS data area includes a tick counter at 46Ch (0040:006C) and a midnight flag at 470h (0040:0070). You might think that VTD could maintain its own tick counter and midnight flag by reading the BIOS data area. But VTD reads these values only once, during initialization. In fact, the relation between VTD and the BIOS works the other way around: While Windows is running, VTD is responsible for keeping the BIOS data area updated (via its V86 INT 1Ch hook).

So where does VTD's tick counter and midnight flag come from? During initialization, VTD calls the Virtual Programmable Interrupt Controller (PIC) Device's VPICD_Virtualize_IRQ service to register a HW_Int_Proc handler for IRQ 0. Interrupt request 0 is the timer hardware interrupt, usually associated with INT 8. VPICD relocates the IRQs to INT 50h through 5Fh (see the FAULTHKS program on the *Unauthorized Windows 95* disk), so under Windows an actual timer hardware interrupt will come in as an INT 50h. About 18.2 times a second, VPICD receives one of these timer interrupts.

Among many other things, VPICD will call VTD's Hw_Int_Proc. The Hw_Int_Proc increments VTD's tick counter, sets the midnight flag (VTD maintains a midnight flag rather than a counter), and so on. One of its other responsibilities is to call the VMM Update_System_Clock service, which in turn can trigger a preemptive task switch if a VM or thread has used up its time slice.

Thus, VTD not only handles the INT 1Ah call from CLOCK$ entirely in protected mode but (in conjunction with VPICD) also manages the timer hardware interrupt. This is just one example of a more general point: VxDs now play much the same role that the ROM BIOS once did. (See the HOOKINT program in the "What about BIOS Calls?" section in Chapter 11.)

It's only a slight exaggeration to say that VxDs are now the ROM BIOS! And just as IBM's BIOS source listings were the foundation for a phenomenon variously described as the PC revolution, the formation of the PC industry standard architecture, or the commoditization of the PC, it's possible that similar accurate, complete listings for the entire VMM and VxD subsystem could be the foundation for a new industry standard architecture. I would argue that VxDs already constitute a de facto industry standard architecture. Unfortunately, this de facto architecture is not widely understood.

Wider understanding of VMM and VxDs could pave the way for radical improvements in the PC architecture. One possibility is to completely replace the BIOS with 32-bit protected-mode VxDs, and then put the entire VMM/VxD layer in ROM so that it is present from the moment you boot your machine. Now, *that* would be an integrated Windows PC. The tangible benefits of such an arrangement, however, are less clear.

At any rate, we've seen that even when Windows does send calls down to real-mode DOS, these calls can bop back into VxD-land. Here, Windows has reflected all function 2Ah and 2Ch calls down to DOS. As Figure 14-5 shows, DOS calls CLOCK$, and CLOCK$ calls INT 1Ah function 0, which is handled entirely inside VTD.

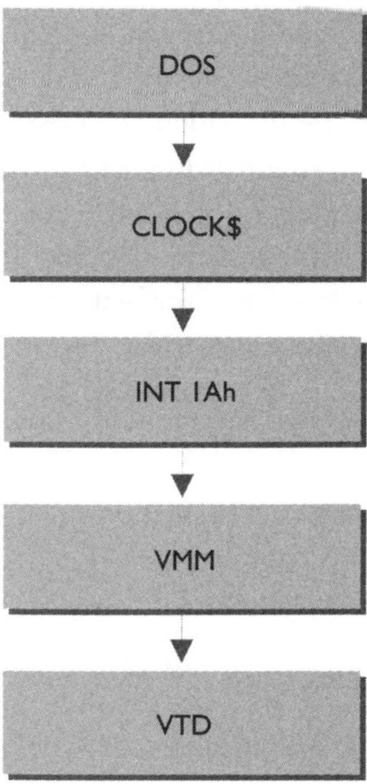

Figure 14-5: How the Win32 clock gets the date and time, part 4. Although Windows sends INT 21h function 2Ah and 2Ch calls down to DOS, when the DOS CLOCK$ device driver turns around to make an INT 1Ah call, this call traps back into Windows. The VMM sends the INT 1Ah call to the Virtual Timer Device (VTD).

Figure 14-5 answers the questions that began this section: "Does Windows 95 Really Call Down to DOS? And What Does It Do When It Gets There?" Yes, Windows 95 really calls down to DOS. But it's a significantly-altered DOS that Windows is running in V86 mode. When Windows calls down to DOS, DOS may (unknowingly) call back into Windows.

What happens when VTD returns from its INT 1Ah function 0 handler? VTD was called from VMM, and so it returns to VMM. VMM checks the carry flag, which VTD cleared to signify that VMM doesn't pass the INT 1Ah call along to any other handlers:

```
0028:C0FCE1C1   MOV     EAX,0000001A        ;;; back in V86 int chain
0028:C0FCE1C6   MOV     EBX,[VMM+F6E4]      ;;; EBX = cur VM handle
0028:C0FCE1CC   JB      VMM+1424    ;;; JB=JC. Carry clear, so INT handled
0028:C0FCE1D2   RET                 ;;;     already. Done!
```


The DDK documentation for Hook_V86_Int_Chain notes that "If the hook procedure services the interrupt, it must clear the carry flag to prevent the system from passing the interrupt to the next hook procedure." This bland remark has tremendous implications. By clearing the carry flag, a VxD's V86 interrupt hook keeps not only other VxDs but also any real-mode INT 1Ah handler from seeing the interrupt!

Let me repeat: Any real-mode INT 1Ah handler will *never* see this INT 1Ah call. That is the flip side (and possibly downside) to the point that VTD handles the call entirely in protected mode.

Entirely means that your DOS TSR, expecting for whatever reason to see INT 1Ah function 0 calls, won't. It also means that a lot of diagnostics tools for DOS (such as Quarterdeck's Manifest, to select one example at random) are hopelessly out-of-date. If you run one of these tools, it will tell you where INT 1Ah is handled:

```
INT 1A: System Timer        F000:FE6E System ROM
```

But this is totally wrong. When DOS calls INT 1Ah, the call goes to VMM, which passes it to VTD, which returns to VMM, which (as we'll see in a second) issues an IRETD to return to DOS. The call *never* goes to F000:FE6E. Tools such as Manifest (or the INTVECT program on the *Unauthorized Windows 95* disk, for that matter) get this F000:FE6E address by calling INT 21h function 25h or by directly inspecting the low-memory IVT. But those are no longer good techniques to find where interrupts are handled. In fact, they haven't been since May 1990, when Microsoft introduced Windows 3.0 Enhanced mode. Since then, VxDs have silently but surely taken over the role of the System ROM.

If you find this hard to believe, try some experiments with the HOOKINT program from Chapter 11. For example, in plain-vanilla DOS, you can load HOOKINT and then issue the DATE and TIME commands provided by DOS. If you change the date and time,

HOOKINT will show about twenty calls to INT 1Ah function 0. Now perform the same operation under Windows Enhanced mode — even Windows 3.0 Enhanced mode from 1990. HOOKINT won't see any INT 1Ah calls. The ROM BIOS won't either. Where were they handled? In VTD, of course.

Once VTD has handled the INT 1Ah call and returned to VMM, VMM gets ready to return to whatever called INT 1Ah in the first place (in this case, the DOS CLOCK$ device):

```
0028:VMM+2E0    MOV     EBX,[VMM+F6E4]        ;;; get cur VM handle
0028:VMM+2E6    MOV     EDI,[VMM+F670]        ;;; get cur thread handle
0028:VMM+2EC    CLI                           ;;; disable interrupts
0028:VMM+2ED    XOR     EAX,EAX
0028:VMM+2EF    CMP     EAX,[VMM+DC88]        ;;; Any pending events?
0028:VMM+2F5    JNZ     VMM+304               ;;; No.
0028:VMM+2F7    TEST    BYTE PTR [EBX],20     ;;; VM status & PM_Exec?
0028:VMM+2FA    JNZ     VMM+358               ;;; No. VM in V86 mode.
0028:VMM+2FC    XCHG    ESP,[EDI+48]          ;;; switch stacks back
0028:VMM+2FF    POPAD
0028:VMM+300    ADD     ESP,+04
0028:VMM+303    IRETD                         ;;; return to V86 mode
FFFF:08DC       TEST    BYTE PTR [0008],80    ;;; back in CLOCK$ after INT 1Ah
```

These two lines are particularly important:

```
0028:VMM+2EF    CMP     EAX,[VMM+DC88]        ;;; Any pending events?
0028:VMM+2F5    JNZ     VMM+304               ;;; No.
```

Just before returning to its caller (in this case, DOS's CLOCK$ device, which unknowingly called VMM by issuing an INT 1Ah in V86 mode), VMM always checks if there are any pending events. These events should not be confused with the events that Windows applications receive in the form of WM_XXX messages, nor with the events that VxDs receive in the form of System Control messages. Events are functions that VxDs ask VMM to call when it's safe for VMM to do so. It's safe to do so right at the spot of code just before VMM returns to whichever VM called it. As long as there are pending events, VMM services them before returning to the VM.

Notice that the events that VMM processes before returning to the VM bear no relationship to whatever the VM was doing when it called VMM. For example, the VPICD_Set_Int_Request service, which reflects hardware interrupts into VMs, does so using Schedule_Global_Event and Schedule_VM_Event. Every time you press a key, or there's a timer tick, or something comes in from a serial port, chances are that the VxD that owns the hardware will call VPICD_Set_Int_Request, which in turn will schedule an event.

Thus, a tremendous amount can happen in this event-processing loop, and it's a mistake to think that VMM will return simple-mindedly to the same VM that called it. In the case of CLOCK$ and INT 1Ah, VMM might have many events to service, and many highways to walk down, involving many VM or thread switches, before returning to CLOCK$ from the INT 1Ah. Any call to VMM — even an unwitting call such as an INT, or a GP fault caused by accessing a hooked I/O port, or a page fault caused by virtual memory — is a potential place for VMM to switch to another VM (or in Windows 95, to another thread). It may be a long time before VMM returns to the instruction following that innocent-looking INT 1Ah.

The magic of Call_Priority_VM_Event

Events reveal a crucial fact about Windows: VMM is a nonreentrant operating system. Because VMM is nonreentrant, VxDs that are called asynchronously (for example, because of a hardware interrupt) can use only a small subset of VMM services. However, among these few always-callable, reentrant services are Schedule_Global_Event, Schedule_VM_Event, and Schedule_Thread_Event. A VxD that is called asynchronously but that needs to call some nonreentrant VMM service, can schedule an event; that event can, when it occurs, call the service. Just before returning to the calling VM, VMM calls each function in the event list. These functions in turn can call any VMM function (including, possibly, Schedule_XXX_Event, so that VMM can stay in its service-event loop for some time before returning to the VM).

The DDK's documentation on events suggests that they are useful only in interrupt service routines. But events play a role in Windows that isn't limited to hardware interrupt handling. This becomes clear if you carefully read the DDK documentation for the Call_Priority_VM_Event service:

> *The Call_Priority_VM_Event service either calls the callback procedure immediately or schedules a priority event for the specified virtual machine. This service schedules the event if the virtual device is processing a hardware interrupt that interrupted the VMM, or the current virtual machine is not the specified virtual machine, or the Flags parameter specifies the PEF_Always_Sched value. In all other cases, the service calls the callback procedure and returns without scheduling an event.*

Notice the situations under which Call_Priority_VM_Event will schedule (rather than immediately call) an event: not only if the VxD is processing a hardware interrupt but also *if the current VM is not the specified target VM*. In other words, A VxD can be called in the context of one VM, and schedule an arbitary piece of code to be called in the context of some other VM. This forms the whole basis for inter-VM communications in Windows. In addition to Call_Priority_VM_Event and Schedule_VM_Event in Windows 3.*x*, Windows 95 adds Schedule_Thread_Event.

Events, particularly the Call_Priority_VM_Event service provided by VMM, can be used in many situations that require interprocess communications:

- VNETBIOS: The NetBIOS INT 5Ch interface includes an option to issue "no wait" network commands. For example, rather than wait for completion when you send a packet of data over the network, NetBIOS can return to you immediately. You can then poll a completion byte in the NCB, but it's often preferable to install a post routine. NetBIOS will call your post routine when the command completes. Meanwhile, you can go off and do other things. A server that uses NetBIOS could handle multiple clients in this way, for example. VNETBIOS has to make this work in the multitasking Windows environment, where the VM in which the no-wait NetBIOS call was issued might no longer be the current VM when the command completes and it's time to call the post routine. The solution? VNETBIOS uses Call_Priority_VM_Event to schedule an event to be called in the context of the original VM in which the no-wait command was issued. This event in turn calls the post routine. (VNETBIOS goes away with NDIS 3.0, but the implementation of NetBIOS post routines are still a good example of Call_Priority_VM_Event.)
- Many programmers have wondered about the strange-looking INT 2Fh function 1685h (Switch VMs and Callback) service that Windows provides. To use this function, you specify a target VM ID in BX and a far V86 procedure in ES:DI. (You can specify that interrupts be enabled in the VM, or that the VM not be in a critical section.) When the target VM is next scheduled, VMM calls your procedure. DOS programs running under Windows can use this as a quick-and-dirty way to make remote procedure calls into other VMs. Unfortunately, the function is not supported from protected mode, and it can't be used to call protected-mode code either. You also can't pass any parameters to the called function! But these are arbitrary limitations because INT 2Fh function 1685h is nothing more than a Call_Priority_VM_Event of a procedure. When the target VM is next scheduled, and has whatever VM state you specified, the procedure performs a nested-V86 exec (Begin_Nest_V86_Exec, Build_Int_Stack_Frame, Resume_Exec, End_Nest_Exec) of the function you specified in ES:DI.
- A better Switch VMs and Callback function could readily be built. For an excellent example, see Thomas Olsen's PIPE VxD in "Making Windows and DOS Programs Talk," *Windows/DOS Developer's Journal*, May 1992. Olsen's pipe uses Call_Priority_VM_Event.

- The SHELL VxD gives DOS applications programmatic access to the Windows Clipboard, via INT 2Fh function 17h. For example, function 1701h is equivalent to the OpenClipboard Windows API call, function 1703h is equivalent to SetClipboardData, and function 1705h is equivalent to GetClipboardData. How does SHELL arrange for you to effectively make remote Windows API calls from the DOS box? With Call_Priority_VM_Event, naturally. SHELL schedules an event that uses SHELL_Event, when the System VM is running, to pass the Clipboard requests onto WINOA386 (WinOldAp), which acts as a kind of Clipboard RPC server.
- In Windows 95, the SHELL VxD provides an extensive set of so-called "Appy Time" services (the name is supposed to be a play on *application* and *happy*) that allow other VxDs to make Windows API calls. These VxDs can then pass these Windows API services along to DOS applications. For example, when you type the name of a Windows executable in a DOS box under Windows 95, instead of the old "This program requires Microsoft Windows" message ("But I am running!"), Windows 95 will run the Windows application — what a concept! Although this is the way Windows should have behaved years ago, how *does* Windows 95 turn a DOS program's INT 21h function 4Bh (EXEC) into a WinExec? Simple: a function is scheduled with _SHELL_CallAtAppyTime. SHELL calls this function at 'appy time, when it is safe for it to make Windows API calls, that is, when the System VM is the current VM. At 'appy time, the function uses other services, such as _SHELL_PostMessage, _SHELL_ShellExecute, _SHELL_CallDll, _SHELL_LoadLibrary, and _SHELL_GetProcAddress, to load whatever Windows executable the user requested (and, optionally, to wait for it to complete). So how does _SHELL_CallAtAppyTime arrange for the 'appy time function to get called when the System VM is ready? By using the VMM service Call_Restricted_Event, which in its current implementation is identical to Call_Priority_VM_Event.
- Long before Microsoft woke up to the idea that typing the name of a Windows application in the DOS prompt might possibly mean that the user wanted to *run* the Windows application, several third-parties had developed Windows extensions that would turn a DOS box EXEC of a Windows application into a System VM call to WinExec. The best known of these extensions (well, I *would* say that, since I worked, albeit briefly, on this product) is probably Phar Lap's FrontRunner. Phar Lap gets a DOS box's INT 21h function 4Bh of a Windows application turned into a System VM WinExec with Call_Priority_VM_Event.

This is all very interesting, but what, aside from the name, does Call_Priority_VM_Event have to do with the event-processing loop mentioned in connection with VMM's return to CLOCK$? Simply this: If a VxD (acting possibly on the direct behalf of an application that has called a function such as Switch VMs and Callback) specified a target VM that differs from the current VM, Call_Priority_VM_Event must schedule (rather than immediately call) a VM event. This event will be processed the next time VMM is about to return to the target VM, possibly in connection with some entirely different operation. Windows really is a multitasking operating system and has been since Windows 3.0, when these interfaces were introduced.

Win32 File Handles and Thunking

We've already used WSPY21 to examine three of the four possible mixtures of executable and environment: 16/16 (the Win16 Clock under WfW 3.11), 32/16 (the Win32 Clock under WfW 3.11, with Win32s), and 32/32 (the Win32 Clock under Chicago). Running the Win16 Clock under Chicago (16/32) will complete the matrix.

When using WSPY21 to examine the Win16 Clock in Windows 95, one thing immediately jumps out from the WSPY21 log. Check out the file handles that are being passed to the DOS Read and Lseek functions:

```
<CAB32> *(4B) Exec 'C:\wfw311\clock.exe'
; ...
<CAB32>  (3F) Read 574 (023Eh), 64 (0040h)
<CAB32>  (42) Lseek0 574 00000400
<CAB32>  (3F) Read 574 (023Eh), 64 (0040h)
<CAB32>  (3F) Read 574 (023Eh), 277 (0115h)
<CAB32>  (42) Lseek0 574 000005a0
<CAB32>  (3F) Read 574 (023Eh), 13888 (3640h)
; ...
<CAB32>  (50) Set PSP 4831 (12DFh)
<CLOCK>  (50) Set PSP 175 (00AFh)
<CLOCK>  (42) Lseek0 574 00003f30
<CLOCK>  (3F) Read 574 (023Eh), 240 (00F0h)
<CLOCK>  (50) Set PSP 2735 (0AAFh)
; ...
<CLOCK>  (3E) Close 574 (023Eh)
```

What sort of file handle is 574? Although this could conceivably be a valid DOS file handle, it's difficult to produce such a large handle except under contrived circumstances. (FILETEST.ASM, which appears later in this chapter, is a good example of such a contrivance.) In real-mode DOS, file handles are indices into a per-task data structure called the Job File Table (JFT; see *Undocumented DOS*, 2d ed., pp. 472-474). Each task's PSP contains (at offset 34h) a far pointer to the task's JFT. The JFT's size is indicated by the WORD at offset 32h in the PSP. A valid DOS file handle of 574 would require a JFT with at least 575 entries (numbered 0 to 574).

Although such a swollen JFT can be created with INT 21h function 67h (Set Handle Count) or by juggling pointers in the PSP (*Undocumented DOS*, 2d ed., pp. 485-488), none of the PSPs displayed by WSPY21 have such an enlarged JFT. The next section provides a demonstration of this, as well as a brief example of Toolhelp32 and some more Win32 back-door programming with VxDCall.

Reading the PSP from Win32

TH32.C in Listing 14-3 is a simple Win32 Console (character-mode) application that uses the Process32First and Process32Next APIs from Microsoft's Toolhelp32 API (TLHELP32.H) to enumerate all Win32 processes. For each process, TH32 shows the address of the PSP and the size of the JFT. TH32.C unfortunately didn't make it onto the *Unauthorized Windows 95* disk. The program is short enough that hopefully you won't mind having to type it in.

Listing 14-3: TH32.C

```
/*
TH32.C
Win32 app uses Toolhelp32 and VxDCall to locate Win32 PSPs and JFTs

Sorry, this did *NOT* make it onto the Unauthorized Windows 95 disk!

from Schulman, Unauthorized Windows, 1994
*/

#include <stdlib.h>
#include <stdio.h>
#define  WIN32_LEAN_AND_MEAN
#include "windows.h"
#include "tlhelp32.h"

void fail(const char *s) { puts(s); exit(1); }

main()
{
    PROCESSENTRY32 pe32;
    MODULEENTRY32 me32;
    BOOL ok, ok2;
    HANDLE snap;
    char *name;

    DWORD (WINAPI *VxDCall0)(DWORD srvc, DWORD eax, DWORD ecx);
    HANDLE k32 = GetModuleHandle("KERNEL32");
    #define GET(func) func = GetProcAddress(k32, #func)
    GET(VxDCall0);
```

```
    #define VWIN32_INT31_CALL    0x2A0029
    #define DPMICall(eax, ecx)  VxDCall0(VWIN32_INT31_CALL, (eax), (ecx))

    if (! (snap = CreateToolhelp32Snapshot(TH32CS_SNAPALL, 0)))
        fail("Can't create Toolhelp32 snapshot");

    printf("Process    Module     Parent     PSP (#Files)   #Threads\n");
    printf("-------    ------     ------     ------------   --------\n");

    // walk process list
    pe32.dwSize = sizeof(pe32);
    for (ok=Process32First(snap, &pe32); ok; ok=Process32Next(snap, &pe32))
    {
        // PSP is currently at offset 28h in Process
        WORD psp = *((WORD *) (pe32.th32ProcessID + 0x28));
        DWORD psp_base, jft;
        WORD max;
        _asm mov bx, psp
        DPMICall(0x0006, 0);
        _asm mov word ptr psp_base+2, cx
        _asm mov word ptr psp_base, dx
        max = *((WORD *) (psp_base + 0x32)),
        jft = *((DWORD *) (psp_base + 0x34));

        // Walk module list, looking for this one
        name = "";
        me32.dwSize = sizeof(me32);
        for (ok2=Module32First(snap, &me32); ok2;
             ok2=Module32Next(snap, &me32))
            if (me32.th32ModuleID == pe32.th32ModuleID)
            {
                if (! (name = me32.szModule))
                    name = me32.szExePath;
                break;
            }

        printf("%08lX   %08lX   %08lX   %04X (%d)\t%d\t%s\n",
            pe32.th32ProcessID,
            pe32.th32ModuleID,
            pe32.th32ParentProcessID,
            (DWORD) psp, (DWORD) max,
            pe32.cntThreads,
            name);
    }

    CloseHandle(snap);
}
```

For each process, Toolhelp32 fills in a PROCESSENTRY32 structure containing the process handle, the handle of its parent, its module handle, and so on. There are similar Toolhelp32 functions to enumerate all threads and modules and to walk Win32 memory heaps. Because Win32 programs are preemptively multitasked in Windows 95, the system could change out from under a program while it was walking these lists; for this reason, a CreateToolhelp32Snapshot function must be called before other Toolhelp32 functions.

The PROCESSENTRY32 structure isn't Windows 95's internal process structure. Instead, it's a sanitized structure that contains a copy of the aspects of the internal process structure that Microsoft thinks are okay for you to know about. Unfortunately, the structure doesn't include the PSP that goes along with the process. However, the process handle returned in the PROCESSENTRY32 structure can be used as a 32-bit flat pointer to Windows 95's actual internal process structure, and in Beta-1 at any rate, this structure contained at offset 28h a protected-mode selector to the process's PSP.

This protected-mode PSP selector isn't immediately usable to a Win32 program such as TH32. To access the PSP, TH32 needs the PSP's 32-bit linear address. Given a selector, the base address can be retrieved with DPMI INT 31h function 6 (Get Selector Base Address). Win32 programs can't directly call DPMI. But the VWIN32 VxD provides a Win32 service (2A0029h) that makes DPMI INT 31h calls. Win32 programs can access these Win32 services by calling the VxDCall0 API exported by KERNEL32. This API isn't mentioned in the Chicago header files or libraries, but the GetProcAddress API makes it easy to dynamically link to VxDCall0 at run-time.

Having dynamically linked to VxDCall0, TH32 can use this function to call Win32 service 2A0029h, which it in turn uses to call DPMI function 6. TH32 takes the PSP selector from offset 28h in the process structure, and passes this selector to DPMI function 6; DPMI returns the base address of the PSP. With this base address, TH32 can proceed to examine the PSP to determine the size of its JFT (which, you might recall, was the purpose of this exercise).

Because TH32 is a 32-bit flat-model program, it can immediately use the PSP's base address as a *near* pointer. A Win32 process can use a near pointer to access any memory in a 4GB address space, as long as the memory is mapped into the address space of the process. A far pointer is neither necessary nor, in most cases, even allowed.

The size of the JFT is kept in the WORD at offset 32h in the PSP. A pointer to the JFT is kept in the DWORD at offset 34h. Once it has the base address of a PSP, finding the size of that PSP's JFT is simply a matter of:

```
WORD jft_size = *((WORD *) (psp_base + 0x32));
```

Figure 14-6 shows output from TH32. Notice that none of the Win32 processes have DOS JFTs large enough to accommodate file handles such as 574. The largest JFT, belonging to process 81100268h (PSP 00A7h), has room for only 128 DOS file handles.

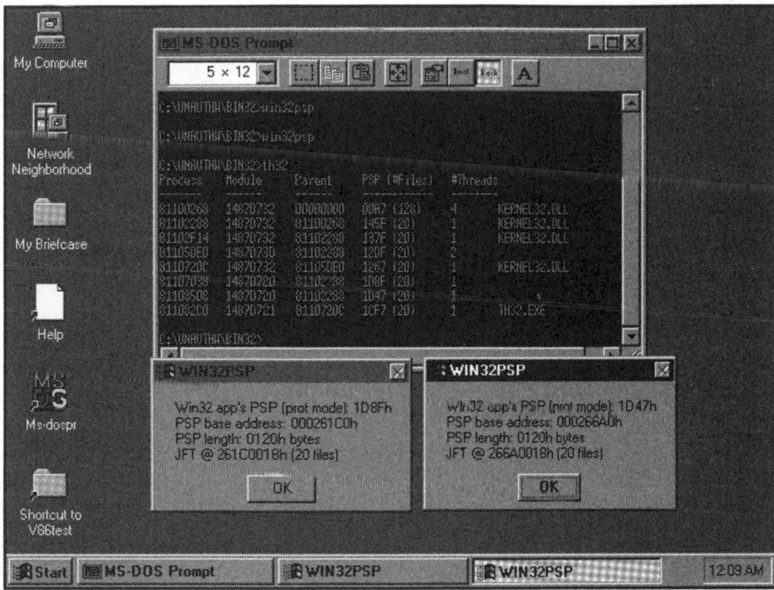

Figure 14-6: TH32 and WIN32PSP are Win32 programs that show the PSP and JFT associated with Win32 processes. (TH32 is a character-mode Win32 Console application.)

Besides the TH32 program, Figure 14-6 also shows two instances of the WIN32PSP program, the code for which appears in Listing 14-4. This is a Win32 program that accesses its own PSP. In addition to Win32 service 2A0029h for calling DPMI, WIN32PSP also uses Win32 service 2A0010h for calling DOS (or at least for making INT 21h calls — which, as we know, isn't the same thing as calling DOS). Although WIN32PSP, unlike TH32, is provided on the *Unauthorized Windows 95* disk, the version included on the disk is wrong: It mistakenly uses the EDX return value from DPMI function 6 rather than CX:DX, and it neglects to display the JFT's size which, again, was the ostensible purpose behind these programs.

Listing 14-4: WIN32PSP.C

```
/*
WIN32PSP.C
Win32 app accesses its own real-mode DOS PSP
Using VxDCall0 to make INT 21h (DOS) and INT 31h (DPMI) calls
```

```
from Schulman, Unauthorized Windows, 1994
*/

#include <stdlib.h>
#include <stdio.h>
#define  WIN32_LEAN_AND_MEAN
#include "windows.h"

#define MSG(s)           MessageBox(0, s, "WIN32PSP", MB_OK)

void fail(const char *s) { MSG(s); exit(1); }

DWORD (WINAPI *VxDCall)(DWORD srvc, DWORD eax, DWORD ecx);

#define GET_PROC(mod, func) GetProcAddress(GetModuleHandle(mod), (func))

DWORD lsl(WORD sel)
{
    if (! sel) return 0;
    _asm lsl eax, sel
    // retval in EAX
}

int PASCAL WinMain(HANDLE hInstance, HANDLE hPrevInstance,
    LPSTR lpszCmdLine, int nCmdShow)
{
    char buf[512];
    MEMORY_BASIC_INFORMATION info;
    WORD psp, *pmax;
    DWORD base, *pjft;
    int len;

    // init
    if (! (VxDCall = GET_PROC("KERNEL32", "VxDCall0")))
        fail("Cannot link to VxDCall");

    #define VWIN32_INT21_CALL       0x2A0010
    #define VWIN32_INT31_CALL       0x2A0029
    #define DosCall(eax, ecx)       VxDCall(VWIN32_INT21_CALL, (eax), (ecx))
    #define DPMICall(eax, ecx)      VxDCall(VWIN32_INT31_CALL, (eax), (ecx))

    // Call DOS INT 21h function 62h (Get PSP)
    DosCall(0x6200, 0);
    _asm mov psp, bx
    // returns protected-mode selector to PSP
    len = sprintf(buf, "Win32 app's PSP (prot mode): %04Xh\n", psp);

    // Pass prot-mode PSP to DPMI INT 31h function 6 (Get Sel Base)
    _asm mov bx, psp
    DPMICall(0x0006, 0);
#if 1
    // we're really a 16-bit DPMI client!!
    _asm mov word ptr base+2, cx
    _asm mov word ptr base, dx
#else
    // this is wrong on the disk!!
    _asm mov base, edx
```

```
#endif
    len += sprintf(buf+len, "PSP base address: %08lXh\n", base);

    // Pass prot-mode PSP to LSL (Load Selector Limit) instruction
    len += sprintf(buf+len, "PSP length: %04Xh bytes\n", lsl(psp) + 1);
    // Win32 app PSP is 120h bytes, not 100h!

    // Locate JFT, #files: this isn't in WIN32PSP.C version on disk
    pmax = (WORD *) (base + 0x32);
    pjft = (DWORD *) (base + 0x34);
    len += sprintf(buf+len, "JFT @ %08lXh (%u files)\n",
        *pjft, (DWORD) *pmax);

    MSG(buf);

    return 0;
}
```

WIN32PSP and TH32 are more interesting for their source code than for their output. Although the Toolhelp32 API has some limitations (see Matt Pietrek, "Investigating the Hybrid Windowing and Messaging Architecture of Chicago," *Microsoft Systems Journal*, September 1994, pp. 28-29), it's an improvement over Microsoft's earlier intention to provide no Toolhelp support for Win32 applications in Chicago.

The VxDCall0 function provided by KERNEL32 is a valuable API. There doesn't appear to be documentation for any Win32 services that are provided by VxDs and made accessible to Win32 applications by VxDCall0, but some of the services are easy to figure out.

The VXDLIST program included on the *Unauthorized Windows 95* disk shows the number of Win32 services provided by each VxD and sets these off from the "normal" VxD services with an exclamation mark:

```
C:\UNAUTHW\BIN>vxdlist | find "!"
VMM      4.00  0001h  C000EC28  C00023DE  C0002A11   C0002A11*  377 ! 39
REBOOT   2.00  0009h  C0074D94  C0074C64             C0259750*  0 ! 2
VWIN32   1.02  002Ah  C0063234  C006228C             C0239FB0*  21 ! 65
VCOMM    1.00  002Bh  C0063D44  C0063A94  C023D588   C023D588*  35 ! 27
VCOND    1.00  0038h  C0073B10  C0073ACC  C0252C3C*  C0252D46*  2 ! 52
```

VXDLIST's output shows there are about 175 Win32 services. To see more details on these services, run VXDLIST -VERBOSE.) Some of these, like the 2A0010h and 2A0029h services used by TH32 and WIN32PSP, are themselves gateways for other functionality (in this case, the entire DOS INT 21h and DPMI INT 31h interfaces). Over time, these Win32 services will probably become well-known in the Windows 95 developer community, just as happened with undocumented functions in the DOS developer community in the 1980s.

Using Win32 File Handles

So, CAB32 and CLOCK have default-sized JFTs with only twenty entries. They nonetheless successfully called the INT 21h Read and Lseek functions with a file handle of 574. How did they do this?

To answer this question, we need to understand what the low-level Lseek and Read calls displayed earlier by WSPY21 represent in terms of higher-level Windows operations.

Win16 CLOCK.EXE doesn't contain the actual INT 21h Read and Lseek calls we see at the end of the WSPY21 log. Instead, Clock is calling Windows API functions that, in turn, are generating the INT 21h calls. The Lseek to offset 3F30h (16176), followed by a Read of F0h bytes, matches a resource item in CLOCK.EXE itself, as revealed by Borland's TDUMP utility:

```
;;; Excerpt from WSPY21 output
<CLOCK>  (42) Lseek0 574 00003f30
<CLOCK>  (3F) Read 574 (023Eh), 240 (00F0h)

;;; Excerpt from TDUMP of \WFW311\CLOCK.EXE
type: DATA
Identifier: CLOCK
offset: 03F30h  length: 00F0h
```

Given that 0F0h (240) is evenly divisible by 60, which in turn is the number of positions assumed by the hands in Clock's analog clock face, it's likely that Clock's user-defined resource stores precomputed sine or cosine values. At any rate, the File Lseek/Read operation seen by WSPY21 is the low-level reflection of resource manipulation by Clock. Clock is calling KERNEL APIs such as FindResource and Load-Resource, and these APIs eventually translate into the INT 21h calls seen by WSPY21. Resource loading is one of the major ways that Windows applications interact (although indirectly) with DOS. By loading resources, Clock is reading from its own executable file. File handle 574 thus corresponds to CLOCK.EXE itself.

WSPY21 also showed that after launching CLOCK.EXE, but before Clock became the current task, the Chicago Cabinet (CAB32) also read from this same file. Launching an executable involves reading at least some of the executable file into memory; what CAB32 might view as a high-level WinExec looks to WSPY21 like low-level INT 21h calls. Sure enough, we can match CAB32's INT 21h calls with the format of CLOCK.EXE, as revealed by TDUMP. For example, what WSPY21 sees as just another Lseek/Read operation, TDUMP reveals is CAB32 reading in CLOCK.EXE's gangload area:

```
;;; Excerpt from WSPY21 output after EXEC CLOCK.EXE
<CAB32>  (42) Lseek0 574 000005a0
<CAB32>  (3F) Read 574 (023Eh), 13888 (3640h)

;;; Excerpt from TDUMP CLOCK.EXE
Start of Gangload Area                  05A0h
Length of Gangload Area                 3640h
```

Instead of reading an executable file's segments one at a time, a gangload area allows multiple segments to be ganged up and read in one gulp. There's a good explanation of the gangload area (which the Windows 3.1 SDK documentation calls the fast-load area) in Matt Pietrek's *Windows Internals* (pp. 243, 248). Matt shows that an internal LoadExeHeader function in the Win16 KERNEL uses the _hread function to bring in the gangload area.

CAB32 doesn't get directly involved in such low-level details as reading the gangload area. What to WSPY21 looks like an INT 21h Lseek/Read of this part of the file is for CAB32 just a tiny part (of which it knows nothing) in a much larger, higher-level operation: starting an application from the Run menu item on the shell's Start button.

Whenever you use the Windows 95 shell to run a program, CAB32 calls the ShellExecuteEx API in SHELL32.DLL. This API in turn (among many other things) calls the Win32 WinExec API in KERNEL-32.DLL. KERNEL32!WinExec, having figured out that it's been asked to run a Win16 executable, thunks down (via QT_Thunk, with CL=26h) to the Win16 WinExec API in KRNL386.EXE. Again we see that Microsoft's claim that KERNEL32 never thunks down to KRNL386 isn't true and doesn't even make much sense: For one thing, how else would the Win32 WinExec be able to launch Win16 executables?

At this point, we can pick up the story from Pietrek's *Windows Internals* (pp. 229-231): The Win16 version of WinExec issues an INT 21h function 4Bh (EXEC), just like the one seen at the top of the WSPY21 log. KRNL386's handler for INT 21h function 4Bh calls LoadModule, which calls an internal function named LoadExeHeader, which among many other things uses _hread to load the gangload area.

So, the INT 21h calls seen by WSPY21 represent the Windows 95 Shell loading CLOCK.EXE, which in turn is loading resources. The big file handle, 574, represents the open file CLOCK.EXE. This file handle exceeds the size of the shell's JFT, so something other than DOS will have to deal with INT 21h calls that the Win16 APIs such as LoadModule and LoadResource make with this big file handle.

So what might that something be? The IFSMGR.INC file included with the Chicago beta DDK briefly describes a service called IFSMgr_Win32MapExtendedHandleToSFT that sounds like it might have something to do with these big file handles. The VCOND (Virtual CON Device) uses this IFSMgr service when you run a Win32 Console (character-mode) application and redirect its stdout or stdin:

```
;** IFSMgr_Win32MapExtendedHandleToSFT - map an extended handle to a SFT
;
;   This service allocates a free SFT and maps an extended handle to this
;   SFT. It returns the index to the SFT back to the caller. This api is
;   for the purpose of redirection for Win32 apps when they spawn DOS apps.
;   The SFT and the extended handle track one another from this point on.
;   This service MUST be called in the context of the DOS VM the SFT is
;   going to be in.
```

Another function that sounds relevant is Win32HandleToDosFileHandle, which is exported by KERNEL32.DLL. This API isn't mentioned in WINBASE.H, but it's easy enough to access in the same way that TH32.C and WIN32PSP.C accessed VxDCall0: with the run-time dynamic linking API, GetProcAddress. Listing 14-5, W32HAND.C, shows a small Win32 Console program that calls this API in a loop over a reasonable number of possible Win32 file handles, trying to see if any of them correspond to DOS file handles.

Listing 14-5: W32HAND.C

```
// w32hand.c
#include <stdlib.h>
#include <stdio.h>
#define  WIN32_LEAN_AND_MEAN
#include "windows.h"

void fail(const char *s) { puts(s); exit(1); }

unsigned short (WINAPI *Win32HandleToDosFileHandle)(HANDLE h);
HANDLE (WINAPI *DosFileHandleToWin32Handle)(unsigned short h);

#define GET_PROC(mod, func) GetProcAddress(GetModuleHandle(mod), (func))

main(int argc, char *argv[])
{
    unsigned short fu;
    int fh;

    if (! (Win32HandleToDosFileHandle = GET_PROC("KERNEL32",
        "Win32HandleToDosFileHandle")))
```

```
        fail("Cannot link to Win32HandleToDosFileHandle");

    printf("Win32\t\tDOS\n"
           "-----\t\t---\n");
    for (fh=0; fh<0x100; fh++)
        if (fu = Win32HandleToDosFileHandle(fh))
            printf("%0u (%0Xh)\t%0u (%08Xh)\n", fh, fh, fu, fu);

    return 0;
}
```

If you run W32HAND and redirect its output and its (unused) input, sure enough the program outputs something that looks like the big file handles that have shown up in the WSPY21 log:


```
C:\UNAUTHW\BIN32>w32hand > w32hand.log < tmp.tmp

C:\UNAUTHW\BIN32>type w32hand.log
Win32       DOS
-----       ---
2 (2h)      713 (000002C9h)
3 (3h)      714 (000002Cah)
```

It appears, then, that the big file handles seen by WSPY21 are some sort of dummy, or placeholder, DOS equivalent to a Win32 file handle. When Windows 95 launches a Win16 application, it must do so using a Win32 file handle. This shows up at WSPY21 as a big DOS file handle.

But how was a Win32 file handle created for a Win16 application in the first place? Let's return to the Win16 version of WinExec to which the Win32 version of WinExec thunks when presented with a Win16 executable. WinExec, as also mentioned, calls INT 21h function 4Bh, which the Win16 kernel's INT 21h handler turns into a call to the Load-Module API.

Matt Pietrek can again be our tour guide, at least for part of the trip. As shown in *Windows Internals* (p. 241), LoadModule relies on a number of internal helper functions, a small number of which are shown in the following chopped-down calling tree:

```
LoadModule
    LMAlreadyLoaded -- if module is not already present...
    LMLoadExeFile
        MyOpenFile
    LoadExeHeader -- loads NE header
        _hread -- load gangload (discussed earlier)
```

After determining with LMAlreadyLoaded that a specified module isn't already loaded (in our example, that you're not already running an instance of Clock), LoadModule calls the internal LMLoadExeFile routine. Matt shows that this uses another internal routine, MyOpenFile, to open the executable file for a Win16 program such as CLOCK.EXE. MyOpenFile is a wrapper around the documented OpenFile API.

Windows Internals describes Windows 3.1. Things are slightly different when loading Win16 programs under Windows 95. (We'll see in the next section that they're totally different when loading Win32 programs under Windows 95.) Instead of calling the OpenFile API, MyOpenFile instead calls the following simple-looking routine:

```
0127:00003368   MOV    CX,00B0
0127:0000336B   JMP    33D4
```

Although it's part of the Win16 kernel, the code at 0127:33D4 contains 32-bit code and a 48-bit far JMP (opcode 66h EAh):

```
0127:000033D4   MOV    AX,013F
0127:000033D7   MOV    ES,AX
0127:000033D9   MOVZX  ECX,CX
0127:000033DD   MOV    EDX,ES:[ECX+BFF90FF8] ;; use CX (B0h) as index
0127:000033E6   JMP    0137:BFF7217E         ;; 48-bit far jump
```

As soon as a task executes the 48-bit far jump, it leaves the Win16 kernel and enters the Win32 kernel. Yes, it's another thunk! Earlier in this chapter ("Thunking: Mixing 16- and 32-bit code with CALL FWORD PTR"), we saw KERNEL32 use CALL FWORD PTR to thunk down to KRNL386; now we see KRNL386 using 48-bit jumps to thunk up to KERNEL32. As you can see, the value in CX (here, B0h) is used as an index into a table of DWORDs that selects the specific KERNEL32 routine to which KRNL386 wants to thunk.

Eventually, the KERNEL32 code that is called by MyOpenFile in KRNL386 does something that should look familiar from the "32/32: The Windows 95 Clock" section earlier in this chapter:

```
0137:BFF711DD   MOV    EAX,0000716C    ;;; AX=716Ch (LFN Open/Create File)
0137:BFF711E2   CALL   BFF71E5F ;;; do INT 21h via VWIN32 2A0010
0137:BFF71E5F   PUSH   ECX
0137:BFF71E60   PUSH   EAX
0137:BFF71E61   PUSH   002A0010 ;;; call VWIN32 service #10h
0137:BFF71E66   CALL   BFF71F0C ;;; VxDCall routine
VxDCall:                        ;;; expects Win32 svc# on stack
0137:BFF71F0C   MOV    EAX,[ESP+04]
0137:BFF71F10   POP    DWORD PTR [ESP]
0137:BFF71F13   CALL   FWORD PTR CS:[BFFB5004]  ;;; thunk down to callback
003B:000003B6   INT    30       ;;; PM callback
0028:C0001A2C   SUB    ESP,+04  ;;; Now in VMM PM callback handler
...
```

KERNEL32 is using the VxDCall0 API to call Win32 service #2A0010h, which is provided by the VWIN32 VxD. As we saw earlier, this service issues INT 21h calls on behalf of Win32 code. In this case, KERNEL32 wants to call INT 21h function 716Ch, which is the long filename (LFN) Extended Open/Create function. As seen earlier in Figures 14-3 and 14-4, VWIN32's Win32 service 2A0010h uses the Exec_PM_Int service provided by VMM, which in turn uses the Set_PM_Exec_Mode, Begin_Use_Locked_PM_Stack, and Exec_Int services.

So, CAB32 has effectively thunked down to KRNL386, which has thunked up to KERNEL32, which has thunked down to a PM callback, which has taken us to Ring 0, where the fun just starts. Perhaps the following calling tree will make the code path a little clearer. Because the tree kept sliding off the right hand edge of the page, I restarted the tree on the left hand side whenever I encountered a major level-change (thunk):

```
CAB32
    SHELL32!ShellExecuteEx
        KERNEL32!WinExec
            QT_Thunk #26
                KERNEL!WinExec

WinExec
    INT 21h function 4Bh
        LoadModule
            LMLoadExeFile
                MyOpenFile
                    KERNEL32 thunk #B0h
                        48-bit far jmp to KERNEL32

KERNEL32 thunk routine #B0h
    VxDCall 2A0010h EAX=716Ch (LFN Extended Open/Create File)
        call PM callback (INT 30h)

VMM INT 30h handler
    jmp Win32 service callback handler
        jmp Win32 svc 2A0010h
            VMM Exec_PM_Int 21h
                Set_PM_Exec_Mode
                Begin_Use_Locked_PM_Stack
                Exec_Int
                    Simulate_Int
                    Resume_Exec
                    ... eventually get to IFSMgr INT 21h handler
                End_Nest_Exec
```

This seems like a convoluted way to make a protected-mode INT 21h call. But eventually IFSMgr does open the executable file CLOCK.EXE, and a big file handle works its way back up to LoadModule. In addition to using the file handle to read the executable header, gangload area, and so on, LoadModule also puts the handle into a cache. Later on, LoadResource and other APIs that access the in-memory module will call an internal routine called GetCachedFileHandle (*Windows Internals*, p. 233) that, given a module handle, tries to return the corresponding cached file handle.

We were wondering how the Win16 version of Clock can successfully call the DOS Read and Lseek functions with a file handle such as 574 that exceeds the size of its JFT. Now that we know that these large file handles come from IFSMgr, we next need to look inside IFSMgr to see what happens when an API such as LoadResource makes a DOS call such as Lseek or Read on one of these handles.

One thing that's clear from even a quick glance at IFSMgr is that 200h is the cut-off point Microsoft has chosen between DOS file handles and extended file handles. Throughout IFSMgr (including the version released with WfW 3.11), there are numerous comparisons of file handles with 200h, subtractions of 200h from file handles, and so on. The 32BFA code assumes all file handles >= 200h refer to a separate IFSMgr file table. This can be seen in the following fragment from a Soft-ICE/Windows trace through an INT 21h function 3Fh read on an extended file handle:

```
IFSMgr2+7A60   MOV   ESI,[EBP+0C]          ;; fhandle
IFSMgr2+7A63   CMP   ESI,00000200          ;; a normal file handle?
IFSMgr2+7A69   MOV   ECX,[EBP+08]
IFSMgr2+7A6C   JL    IFSMgr2+7A80        (NO JUMP)
;;; From here on, IFSMgr dealing with fhandle >= 200h
IFSMgr2+7A6E   MOV   [ECX+06],SI           ;; fhandle
; ...
IFSMgr2+661    MOVZX EAX,WORD PTR [EDX+06] ;; fhandle
IFSMgr2+665    SUB   EAX,00000200          ;; minus 200h
IFSMgr2+66A    JB    IFSMgr2+6AE          (NO JUMP)
IFSMgr2+66C    MOV   EBX,EAX
IFSMgr2+66E    SHR   EBX,08                ;; find which table it's in
IFSMgr2+671    MOV   EBX,[IFSMgr+3B18+4*EBX]  ;; table of tables
IFSMgr2+678    OR    EBX,EBX
IFSMgr2+67A    JZ    IFSMgr2+6AE         (NO JUMP)
IFSMgr2+67C    XOR   AH,AH
IFSMgr2+67E    LEA   EBX,[EBX+8*EAX]       ;; each entry 8 bytes
IFSMgr2+681    MOV   EAX,[EBX]
```

This test for 200h is frighteningly easy to break. Geoff Chappell examined this in WfW 3.11, where IFSMGR assumes that all handles >= 200h must have been created through ServerDOSCall. Chappell wrote a short test program (shown in Listing 14-6) that uses Dup (DOS function 45h) to create more than 200h file handles. This program is contrived, perhaps, but it's legal and uses only documented DOS functionality. The program works fine in DOS, but under 32BFA (WfW 3.11 or Chicago) it outputs the message "Invalid handle error while reading file with handle >= 0200h." (Unfortunately, this program too failed to make its way onto the *Unauthorized Windows 95* disk in time.)

Listing 14-6: FILETEST.ASM

```
comment $
FILETEST.ASM
Geoff Chappell (geoffc@cix.compulink.co.uk)
8 March 1994

Assemble, link and use EXEHDR to set maxalloc to the minimum:
    ML FILETEST.ASM
    LINK FILETEST;
    EXEHDR /MAX:0 FILETEST.EXE
$

.MODEL                  SMALL, FARSTACK
.STACK                  0100h
.DATA
config                  db      "c:\config.sys"
buffer                  db      ?
no_problem              db      0Dh, 0Ah,
                                "Just to confirm everything worked OK",
                                0Dh, 0Ah, "$"
something_wrong         db      0Dh, 0Ah,
                                "This shouldn't happen. Something's gone ",
                                "wrong with the test rig.", 0Dh, 0Ah, "$"
something_very_wrong    db      0Dh, 0Ah,
                                "Invalid handle error while reading file ",
                                "with handle >= 0200h.", 0Dh, 0Ah, "$"

.CODE
.STARTUP

;   Use DOS function 67h to increase this program's file handle count to
;   more than 0200h.
                        mov     bx,0400h
                        mov     ah,67h
                        int     21h
                        jc      no_increase

;   Open a file. CONFIG.SYS in the root directory of drive C is taken as
;   a convenient hard-wired name.
                        mov     dx,OFFSET config
                        mov     ax,3D00h
                        int     21h
                        jc      no_open
                        mov     bx,ax

;   Duplicate the file handle 0200h times. This is just so that we can
;   eventually end up with a handle >= 0200h.
                        mov     cx,0200h
```

```
@@:
                        mov     ah,45h
                        int     21h
                        jc      no_dup
                        loop    @b

;   Try reading, but using the last handle. The test could be varied to
;   open a new file and read -- just as long as the handle >= 0200h.
                        cmp     ax,0200h
                        jbe     not_enough

                        mov     bx,ax
                        mov     dx,OFFSET buffer
                        mov     cx,0001h
                        mov     ah,3Fh
                        int     21h
                        jnc     ok

                        cmp     ax,0006h
                        jz      invalid_handle
no_increase:
no_open:
no_dup:
not_enough:
                        mov     dx,OFFSET something_wrong
                        mov     ah,09h
                        int     21h
                        jmp     done
invalid_handle:
                        mov     dx,OFFSET something_very_wrong
                        mov     ah,09h
                        int     21h
                        jmp     done
ok:
                        mov     dx,OFFSET no_problem
                        mov     ah,09h
                        int     21h
done:
.EXIT                   00h

END
```

If you run this program outside Windows, or under Windows 3.1, you'll get the OK message ("Just to confirm everything worked OK"). But if drive C: is a 32BFA drive, you'll get the following message:

```
Invalid handle error while reading file with handle >= 0200h
```

This error occurs not only in the betas of Chicago (which would be entirely understandable), but also in the shipping commercial product, WfW 3.11.

Really Bypassing DOS: Executable Loading and Memory-Mapped Files

Apart from the use of Win32 file handles, which ensures that DOS is bypassed for all file I/O required for loading an executable file or its resources, Win16 programs and DLLs otherwise appear to load fairly normally under Windows 95.

Not so with Win32 executables. Win32 programs and DLLs use the Portable Executable (PE) file format. When Windows 95 loads a Win32 executable into a process's address space, it uses a *memory-mapped file*. Unlike a lot of what we've seen in other parts of this book, memory-mapped files aren't just a wrapper around a layer around a series of indirections to an INT 21h call. Memory-mapped files *really and truly bypass DOS.*

A memory-mapped file, as its name suggests, is a file that's mapped into memory. Okay, so that's not a particularly helpful explanation. But the essential point about a memory-mapped file is that you access the file using, not read and write and lseek calls, but instead memory stores and loads (what a BASIC programmer would call peeks and pokes). To a program, a memory-mapped file looks like an array.

To try to make this simple but unfamiliar idea more concrete, Listing 14-7 shows a small Win32 Console program, MAPFILE.C. This program merely prints out the contents of whatever file you name on its command line.

Listing 14-7: MAPFILE.C

```
// mapfile.c -- Win32 Console app

#include <stdlib.h>
#include <stdio.h>
#include "windows.h"

void fail(const char *s) { puts(s); exit(1); }

main(int argc, char *argv[])
{
    DWORD size;
    unsigned char *p, *p2;
    HANDLE f, f2;
    int i;

    // Open file:
```

```
    // Yes, in Win32 you open files with CreateFile(OPEN_EXISTING).
    if ((f = CreateFile(argv[1], GENERIC_READ,
        FILE_SHARE_READ, NULL, OPEN_EXISTING,
        FILE_ATTRIBUTE_NORMAL, NULL)) == INVALID_HANDLE_VALUE)
        fail("CreateFile failed");
    size = GetFileSize(f, NULL);

    // Get handle to read-only memory-mapped file
    if ((f2 = CreateFileMapping(f, NULL, PAGE_READONLY,
        0, size, NULL)) == NULL)
        fail("CreateFileMapping failed");

    // Map in entire file, get pointer
    if ((p = MapViewOfFile(f2, FILE_MAP_READ, 0, 0, 0)) == NULL)
        fail("MapViewOfFile failed");

    // file I/O (drive light on, etc.) happens in here!
    for (i=0, p2=p; i<size; i++, p2++)
        putchar(*p2);

    CloseHandle(f2);
    CloseHandle(f);
}
```


Although three Win32 API calls — CreateFile, CreateFileMapping, and MapViewOfFile — occupy the bulk of MAPFILE.C, and although a chapter on memory-mapped files in a standard book on Win32 programming would naturally focus on these three calls, I instead want to draw your attention to the fact that MAPFILE.C is extremely curious-looking for a program that's supposed to display the contents of a file: *There are no read calls!*

Yet I assure you that the program does display the contents of a file named on its command line. How does it display the contents if it doesn't read them in? Here's how:

```
for (i=0, p2=p; i<size; i++, p2++)
        putchar(*p2);
```

Dereferencing the *p2* pointer (**p2*) reads in the file. Instead of an explicit file read, we have a pointer dereference. That's the essence of memory-mapped files.

Now, you might suspect this is some sort of parlor trick because *p2* starts life equal to *p*, and in MAPFILE.C *p* is returned from the MapViewOfFile API call. Without knowing anything more about this Win32 function, it would seem obvious that it reads an entire file into memory, and returns a pointer to the first byte of the in-memory buffer.

This would be a futile parlor trick, but this is *not* how MapViewOfFile works. When MapViewOfFile returns, no file I/O has yet occurred. In MAPFILE.C, all file I/O occurs *within* the expression **p2*.

How does this work? How does Windows 95 "know" to read in part of a file the first time that a Win32 program reads or writes to a certain pointer? It knows to do this for exactly the same reason that demand-paged virtual memory in Windows knows to read memory in from a swap memory.

Let's say a program has a pointer, *p*, to a block of memory that's been swapped out to a virtual-memory paging file. When the program reads or writes to this memory (**p* or *p[i]*), a Page Not Present fault occurs. A virtual-memory operating system such as Windows installs a handler for the Page Not Present fault (which on Intel microprocessors is just an INT 0Eh). When one of these faults occurs, because a program has tried to access ("demand") memory that the operating system has paged out to disk, the operating system reads the memory back in from disk, very likely swapping something else out to make room for it, and then restarts the instruction that caused the fault.

Memory-mapped files work the same way. The memory-mapped file is just a demand-paged virtual-memory swap file. Instead of restricting you to a single swap file selected by the operating system, such as WIN386.SWP, the CreateFileMapping and MapViewOfFile functions let you use any files you want as virtual-memory swap files.

If MAPFILE used array indexing rather than pointers, the expression **p2* would instead be *p[i]*, and the underlying 32-bit assembly language would look something like this:

```
;;; c = p[i]
0137:0040124C   MOV    EAX, _p
0137:0040124F   MOV    ECX, _i
0137:00401252   MOV    AL,[EAX+ECX] ;;; where fault will occur
0137:00401255   AND    EAX,000000FF ;;; one-byte character
```

Notice that MOV AL, [EAX+ECX] has now become an interface to read a byte at offset ECX (i) from a file/array in EAX (p). Similarly MOV [EAX+ECX], AL would write to the file (if MAPFILE hadn't opened and mapped the file with read-only flags).

But how does this really work? I've said that Windows 95 uses memory-mapped files to load Win32 executables. When CAB32 loads the Win32 version of CLOCK, somehow parts of CLOCK are read in from the disk using expressions such as **p* and *p[i]*. How do these translate into the file I/O that must still be occurring somewhere?

As noted earlier, reading or writing to a not-present memory page causes an INT 0Eh fault. To see where this fault is handled in Windows 95, I ran the FAULTHKS program from the *Unauthorized Windows 95* disk. FAULTHKS is just a wrapper around the Get_Fault_Hook_Addrs service provided by VMM; FAULTHKS.C uses the generic VxD (also provided on the disk) to call this VMM service.

```
C:\UNAUTHW\BIN>faulthks
INT     V86         PM          VMM
; ...
0E      C00077B0    C00077B0    C00077B0
```

The handler for INT 0Eh is the same for V86 mode, protected mode, and VMM — no matter what mode the machine is in when INT 0Eh occurs, the fault will always go to the same handler at C00077B0. A brief examination of this handler shows that the first thing it does is read the processor's CR2 register. As explained in countless books on the Intel architecture, CR2 is the page fault address register: It holds the linear address that most recently caused an INT 0Eh fault.

Now, if you trace through an INT 0Eh that has been caused by access to a memory-mapped file in Windows 95, you'll find something interesting: From deep inside VMM's page-not-present handler, we suddenly call into KERNEL32.DLL.

You wouldn't normally expect something so at the core of the operating system as the page-not-present handler to call up into a high-level DLL such as KERNEL32. But this is precisely how memory-mapped files work: Since memory-mapped files are really just user-selectable virtual-memory swap files, there must be a memory manager for this swap file. This memory manager is part of KERNEL32.DLL, which supplies the Win32 memory-mapped file API. VMM calls up into KERNEL32 because KERNEL32 is the installed memory-mapped file manager. KERNEL32 installs its memory-mapped file manager via a VMM service, _PagerRegister. KERNEL32 can't directly call this VMM function, but VMM provides a Win32 service, 10003h, that calls _Pager Register on behalf of a Win32 caller. This is one of several Win32 memory-management services that VMM provides:

```
Win32 service table @ VMM+ED20 (39 services)
   00010000h (0) @ VMM10+1C8h       _PageReserve
   00010001h (3) @ VMM6+1188h       _PageCommit
   00010002h (5) @ VMM6+119Dh       _PageDecommit
   00010003h (3) @ VMM5+165Ch       _PagerRegister
   00010004h (1) @ VMM5+1671h       _PagerQuery
   00010005h (2) @ VMM5+1686h       _PagerDeregister
   00010006h (1) @ VMM7+000h        _ContextCreate
   00010007h (0) @ VMM7+015h        _ContextDestroy
   00010008h (1) @ VMM7+02Ah        _PageAttach
   00010009h (4) @ VMM7+03Fh        _PageFlush
   ...
```

Thus, memory-mapped files differ from normal demand-paged virtual memory in that there's an installable memory manager. If you've been following operating system developments in the past ten years, you'll probably recognize that this notion of an installable memory manager fits nicely with the *microkernel* concept pioneered in the Mach operating system, in which many formerly privileged operating system features are offloaded to user-installable application software. Indeed, the _PagerRegister interface in the Windows 95 VMM is similar to what is called External Memory Management in Mach and OSF/1. Two excellent books on this subject (both of which are useful background to understanding memory-mapped files in Windows 95) are the Open Software Foundation's *Design of the OSF/1 Operating System* and *Programming under Mach* by Boykin, Kirschen, Langerman, and LoVerso.

The designer of Mach, Richard Rashid, is now head of Microsoft Research within Nathan Myhrvold's much-publicized Advanced Technology Group (ATG) at Microsoft (*Business Week*, March 21 and June 27, 1994). It's also worth noting that this microkernel idea of offloading operating system services onto applications is only superficially at odds with the company's strategy of pulling the general-purpose application domain into the operating system. Having a modular (that is, non-integrated) architecture makes it easier to keep expanding the operating system in the way Microsoft finds so important.

So, when a not-present portion of a memory-mapped file is accessed, VMM's INT 0Eh handler calls the pager registered by KERNEL32. KERNEL32 calls VWIN32, which in turn calls a function named IFSMgr_Ring0_FileIO. As seen in Figure 14-7, IFSMgr then does its usual 32BFA thing, such as calling the VFAT VxD. VFAT calls the I/O Supervisor (IOS), which calls either a FastDisk VxD or the real-mode mapper (RMM).

Notice that Figure 14-7 makes no mention of DOS. When Windows 95 loads a Win32 executable such as CLOCK.EXE, DOS quite literally doesn't enter the picture. Memory-mapped files are a perfect example of what bypassing DOS really looks like. However, this is in sharp contrast with how most of Windows 95 currently looks.

Win16 Everywhere: The Saga of Win16Lock

One of Microsoft's developer-marketing slogans is "Win32 Everywhere": Microsoft wants to promote the idea that the Win32 API is your safest bet for a portable API that will eventually run on every possible computing platform. When you look at the internals of Windows 95, though, one wonders whether an equally appropriate slogan might not be "Win16 Everywhere": almost every place you look in Windows 95, you see Win16 code. There are perfectly good reasons for Windows 95's reliance on 16-bit code; what's unreasonable are Microsoft's denials that Windows 95 relies on 16-bit code to the full extent that it does. This is particularly clear if you look at the infamous issue of Win16Lock.

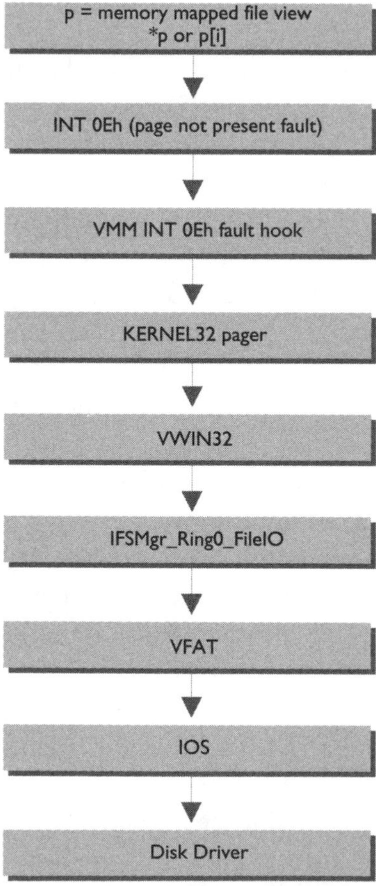

Figure 14-7: Dereferencing a pointer in a memory-mapped file can end up producing actual disk I/O by a Windows VxD.

In this chapter, I've loaded the Win16 Clock under Windows 3.1 and Windows 95, and loaded the Win32 Clock under Win32s and Windows 95. There's one final thing I'd like to do with the Win32 Clock: make it stop for a moment. No, Clock's ticking isn't giving me a pounding headache. I want to stop the Win32 Clock as a way to gain some understanding of Win16Lock.

First some background, though. To begin, Win16Lock is now called Win16Mutex. In one of his many enjoyable snide remarks about Microsoft, Adrian King (*Inside Windows 95*, p. 152) talks about "the awesome power of marketing. Win16Mutex used to be Win16Lock. After the early technical debates about Windows 95 multitasking effectiveness, the marketing group decided that Win16Mutex had fewer negative connotations than Win16Lock, and the name was changed."

So what is Win16Mutex nee Win16Lock? Mutex means *mutual exclusion:* it's something that allows a resource only one user at a time. In Windows 95, a lock/mutex is needed around the code for the Win16 API (primarily the USER and GDI modules but others too, including, as we'll see, even the Win16 KERNEL). The Win16 APIs were never designed to be reentrant, that is, to have multiple callers at the same time. This is probably why Windows 3.*x* never allowed the Windows GUI to be run in more than one VM at a time: VMs are preemptively multitasked, and the Win16 DLLs wouldn't be prepared for multiple callers.

In Windows 95, threads, as well as VMs, are preemptively multitasked, and threads are free to make Windows API calls. Only Win32 threads are preemptively multitasked, and the Win32 API has presumably been written with reentrancy in mind. However, as we know, many Win32 API calls just thunk down to their Win16 equivalent. Thus, two threads would be able to inhabit the Win16 DLLs at the same time, if some special provision weren't made to prevent this from happening.

Adrian King's *Inside Windows 95* (pp. 149-155) has an excellent discussion of the trade-offs involved here, such as why rewriting the entire Win16 code to be reentrant wasn't an option. Microsoft's solution was to come up with what is essentially the Win16 equivalent of the InDOS flag. This is known as Win16Lock, or Win16Mutex. All Win32 APIs that touch Win16 must first obtain the Win16Mutex; when they are finished, they release it. Because the crucial USER32 and GDI32 APIs rely on Win16, a task holding onto the Win16Lock can easily prevent Win32 tasks from running.

Win16Lock sparked a huge debate that went beyond the Chicago development team at Microsoft. As King notes (p. 149), "During late 1993, this topic became by far the most popular topic of debate in the Windows 95 CompuServe forums and at the various developer events organized by Microsoft."

Now, a lot of this debate was silly, and one has to agree with King's conclusion that Microsoft made the best trade-off possible. Much of the supposed debate was really nothing more than potshots from the NT and OS/2 contingents. Still, there remains a crucial issue here.

The general perception among developers appears to be that Win16-Mutex is a potential hazard only if you run Win16 applications. Of course, everyone *will* be running Win16 applications for a while, so in a way this is irrelevant. But let's think ahead to when Win32 applications start coming out in full force (that is, when they start showing up on the shelf at Egghead Software for $79.95). Does Win16Mutex cease to be a potential problem if you run only Win32 applications?

A number of experts say yes. For instance, my friend Matt Pietrek (*PC Magazine*, September 27, 1994, p. 307) writes that "...the sooner you move your application to 32 bits, the better. If a system doesn't have any 16-bit programs running, the Win16Mutex can't be a source of trouble...." And further, "None of the KERNEL32 functions become blocked by the Win16Mutex." Likewise, Adrian King (*Inside Windows 95*, p. 155) suggests that if there are no Win16 applications, there is no problem: "Both the shell and the print spooler are 32-bit applications, so the most commonly used components will avoid the problem altogether." And: "The possible drawbacks to this solution [Win16Mutex] when the user runs a mix of 16-bit and 32-bit applications are another incentive for application developers to concentrate their efforts on Win32 applications" (p. 155).

But we've seen elsewhere in this book that a Windows 95 system (at least Chicago Beta-1) always has two running Win16 tasks, TIMER and MSGSRV32. More importantly, it's not at all clear to me that the Win16Lock wouldn't still be a potential problem, even if no Win16 tasks were running. King writes (p. 153) that "A Win32 thread that does not thunk to the Win16 subsystem never blocks on Win16Mutex." But given that the most heavily used Win32 APIs in USER32 all thunk down to USER, and that many heavily used Win32 APIs in GDI32 also thunk down to GDI, King could be referring only to computation-intensive threads that don't make any Win32 API calls. Well, you'd fully hope and expect such threads wouldn't be blocked by Win16Lock.

However, most Win32 threads will have to grab and release the Win16Lock. Now as I understand it, the idea that Win16Lock "can't be a source of trouble" in the absence of any Win16 tasks (a condition that isn't met by current versions of Chicago) is simply based on the idea that the APIs can be trusted to be good citizens. For example: "The USER and GDI code will execute quickly and release the Win16Mutex. No 32-bit thread will ever hold and hog the Win16Mutex for any significant period of time" (*Microsoft Systems Journal*, September 1994, p. 23).

That this seems to be wishful thinking is shown by a small Win32 program, W16LOCK (Listing 14-8), which we'll use to make the Win32 Clock stop for as long as we want, based on a count specified on its command line. (Unfortunately, this program too didn't make it onto the *Unauthorized Windows 95* disk.)

Listing 14-8: W16LOCK.C

```
// w16lock.c
#include <stdlib.h>
#define  WIN32_LEAN_AND_MEAN
#include "windows.h"

#define MSG(s)          MessageBox(0, s, "W16LOCK", MB_OK)
void fail(const char *s) { MSG(s); exit(1); }

void (WINAPI *GetpWin16Lock)(DWORD *pWin16Lock);
void (WINAPI *_EnterSysLevel)(DWORD lock);
void (WINAPI *_LeaveSysLevel)(DWORD lock);

int PASCAL WinMain(HANDLE hInstance, HANDLE hPrevInstance,
    LPSTR lpszCmdLine, int nCmdShow)
{
    // Microsoft C code per MSJ, May 1991, pp. 135-6
    #define argc __argc
    #define argv __argv
    extern int __argc;
    extern char **__argv;

    DWORD Win16Lock = 0;
    int iter = (argc < 2) ? 10000 : atoi(argv[1]);
    int i;

    #define GET(mod, func) { \
        if (! (func = GetProcAddress(GetModuleHandle(mod), #func))) \
            fail("Can't link to " mod "!" #func); \
        }

    GET("KERNEL32", GetpWin16Lock);
    GET("KERNEL32", _EnterSysLevel);
    GET("KERNEL32", _LeaveSysLevel);

    GetpWin16Lock(&Win16Lock);
    if (Win16Lock == 0)
        fail("GetpWin16Lock didn't work");

    _EnterSysLevel(Win16Lock);
    for (i=0; i<iter; i++)
        (void) GetVersion(); // or any call that doesn't thunk to Win16
    _LeaveSysLevel(Win16Lock);
    return 0;
}
```

W16LOCK uses the undocumented GetpWin16Lock function exported from KERNEL32 to get the address of what still appears to be called Win16Lock. It grabs Win16Lock the same way all the thunking APIs do: by calling _EnterSysLevel. It releases the lock with _LeaveSysLevel. Notice that Win16Lock isn't a genuine mutex; it's one of several syslevels. W16LOCK uses run-time dynamic linking to access the GetpWin16Lock, _EnterSysLevel, and _LeaveSysLevel APIs.

After grabbing the Win16Lock, W16LOCK (which, let me remind you, is a Win32 program) goes into a loop, calling the Win32 GetVersion API for as many times as you specified on the command line (or 10,000 times if you didn't specify anything).

I selected GetVersion because it doesn't thunk down to Win16. Any Win32 API that also doesn't thunk down to Win16 would do just as well for the purposes of the W16LOCK program. Note, however, that some KERNEL32 APIs do thunk down to KRNL386, so it's wrong to assume that "Functions in KERNEL32 can be called by 32-bit threads without fear of blocking on the Win16Mutex, since KERNEL32 doesn't thunk down to KRNL386 at any point" (*Microsoft Systems Journal*, September 1994, p. 23). We've already seen in previous chapters that KERNEL32 certainly can thunk down to KRNL386.

During W16LOCK's loop, Clock — and other Win32 applications that use USER or GDI — is frozen out of Win16. The Clock stops. If you're running WinBezMT, the bezier curves stop curving. When W16LOCK completes the loop and calls _LeaveSysLevel, everything perks up again.

Why did Clock stop? What functions is it calling that depend on Win16Lock?

Actually, it's the ubiquitous QT_Thunk routine that calls _EnterSysLevel(Win16Lock). We examined QT_Thunk in Chapter 13 (see the "From Explorer to Create PSP in Six Easy Steps" section), though at that time I didn't mention _EnterSysLevel or Win16Lock.

So which Win32 APIs use QT_Thunk? Well, almost every routine in USER32 and GDI32 does. And we've seen in earlier chapters that a whole set of KERNEL32 functions do, too. I put a debugger breakpoint on QT_Thunk while starting the Win32 Clock, and found, for example, that the KERNEL32 GetProfileString, GetPrivateProfileString, and GetSystemDirectory APIs all call QT_Thunk, and hence potentially wait on Win16Lock. Importantly, calls to load 16-bit modules do too; these could take a while to execute, potentially blocking the system.

Now, just because something calls _EnterSysLevel(Win16Lock) doesn't mean that the current thread will block. Usually the caller will acquire the lock and return immediately. By tracing through _EnterSysLevel, however, you can follow the path taken when a thread must be blocked until some other thread releases the lock:

```
QT_Thunk
   _EnterSysLevel+0A  EDX=Win16Lock
      _VxDCall0 2A001Dh
      VWIN32+1A1h
            VMM Wait_Semaphore EAX=C0FD10E0
```


There are many early exits along this path. So will a thread ever really block on Win16Mutex in a pure Win32 system? Again, it's hard to say what a pure Win32 system means, but I suppose a Windows 95 system booted in fail-safe mode and running only the Explorer is as pure as you can get. In this configuration, I put a breakpoint on the following code in _EnterSysLevel:

```
0137:BFF71B9B 52                PUSH    EDX
0137:BFF71B9C 51                PUSH    ECX
0137:BFF71B9D 52                PUSH    EDX
0137:BFF71B9E 681D002A00        PUSH    002A001D
0137:BFF71BA3 E864030000        CALL    KERNEL32!VxDCall0
```

Was this ever hit because of Win16Lock? (Note that there are other locks passed to _EnterSysLevel.) Yes, it was. In fact, even when I was just dragging windows around in the Explorer, this code was hit constantly. Likewise when running WinBezMT.

But this still doesn't mean the thread will block. It all comes down to the Wait_Semaphore call in VMM, which is called by VWIN32 service 2A001Dh. At bottom, Win16Lock is a VMM semaphore. In many cases, Wait_Semaphore too can bail out early. But a breakpoint placed on the portion of Wait_Semaphore where a thread must truly wait is triggered pretty often, even when running only Win32 applications.

There's an interesting twist to Win16Lock. Recall that, in addition to Win32 thunks that travel down to Win16, there are also plenty of Win16 thunks that travel up to Win32. Whenever some Win16 code thunks up to Win32 (K32Thk1632Prolog), Win16Lock can be decremented. When it returns to Win16-land (K32Thk1632Epilog), Win16Lock must be incremented.

I'm convinced that the engineers at Microsoft made the right trade-offs in arriving at Win16Lock. Windows 95 is not NT. If customers and developers want NT, they'll get NT. But it's disturbing that Microsoft asserts that Win16Lock can't possibly be a problem in a pure Win32 system when there's no such thing as a pure Windows 95 Win32 system (nor does there need to be), and more importantly, when it seems obvious that Win16Lock will continue to be an issue for as long as the Win32 APIs thunk down to Win16.

We've seen that Microsoft is using Win16Lock as a not-so-subtle way of getting ISVs to switch their applications over to the Win32 API. (Win16-Lock is "another incentive for application developers to concentrate their efforts on Win32 applications.") This has been picked up by the trade press. ("The sooner you move your application to 32 bits, the better".)

This is rich in irony. The reason why Win16Lock exists in the first place is that Microsoft, quite correctly, did not want to do a fully 32-bit rewrite of the core Windows DLLs. And one of the main reasons for this is that 32-bit code is *fatter* than 16-bit code. As Adrian King (p. 150) puts it,

> Rewriting the entire Kernel, User, and GDI subsystems as 32-bit code would have dramatically increased the memory required for the system's working set. The User and GDI modules alone require a working set of about 800K [a footnote adds, "Out of a planned total working set of about 3 MB for the product — similar to that of Windows 3.1"]. Measurements indicated that a conversion to 32-bit code would have increased the memory requirements by close to 40 percent, which would have raised the working set requirements for User and GDI to well over a megabyte. Given the goal of running Windows 95 well on a 4-MB system, this increase in memory consumption wasn't acceptable.

Now, 32-bit code has tremendous benefits for programs that actually need to manipulate 32-bit quantities, but uncontrolled, profligate use of 32 bits will lead to bloated code. I don't know if this is a completely fair comparison, but the Win32 version of the FreeCell game that shipped with Win32s is 49,188 bytes, while the Win16 version that shipped with Beta-1 of Chicago is only 33,184 bytes. The Win32 Clock that ships with Chicago is 38,400 bytes, the Win16 version that ships with Windows 3.1 is only 16,416 bytes. I wrote a tiny Windows app that called MessageBox to display the string "hello world!" The Win16 executable was 3,668 bytes; the Win32 version was 9,216 bytes. Well, these comparisons are not quite fair, but notice King's figure of a 40 percent weight gain in Microsoft's own code. If Windows would swell up by 40 percent by switching to pure 32-bit code, then your application would too. If there's no compelling performance gain from going to 32 bits, then the increase in code size makes it a Bad Idea.

Microsoft knows that 16-bit code is often necessary. Keeping 16-bit code at the core of the Windows API is sufficiently important that Microsoft has introduced Win16Lock. It's a shame, then, that Microsoft then tries to use this very same Win16Lock as a motivational technique to artifically force developers to switch to 32-bit code.

Microsoft's other motivational technique to move everyone over to 32-bit code, whether or not this makes sense for a given program, is to deny the Windows 95 Compatible logo to any program that doesn't use the Win32 API.

There's a definite pattern here: Windows 95 makes a number of very sensible compromises, such as keeping a lot of Win16 code in the API and avoiding the use of OLE in the shell (see Chapter 2). At the same time, Microsoft says that other companies should not make these same compromises, and even denies that it has made them. Micro-soft's general approach is "Do as I say, not as I do." Developers might be much better off if they did as Microsoft does, and not as it says.

Epilog

Microsoft — It's Everywhere You Want to Be

I had been racking my brain for several days over how to conclude this book, when I was presented with a nearly perfect theme in the form of an article in the *Wall St. Journal* (October 14, 1994):

> Microsoft To Buy Intuit In Stock Pact
>
> Microsoft Corp., moving to capture one of the last key markets it has failed to dominate, reached an agreement to buy finance software specialist Intuit Inc. in a stock transaction valued at about $1.5 billion. The acquisition, approved by Intuit's board yesterday, would be the most expensive software acquisition, dramatizing an increasing pace of consolidation in a once free-wheeling industry.

In the "Industry Update" section that begins this book, I presented a gloomy picture of the future of PC software development: increasing consolidation of the software business, steadily growing domination by Microsoft, and the eventual withering away of the shrink-wrap software market into two- or three-person shops using Visual Basic for Applications to produce add-ins to Microsoft Office.

One of the few bright spots in the midst of this gloom was Intuit, makers of the popular Quicken financial software package. Intuit was one of the few companies that had succeeded against Microsoft — Quicken reportedly has 6 million active users, in contrast to perhaps 500,000 for Microsoft Money — and personal-finance software seemed to be an area where companies other than Microsoft could make a real impact.

But now, says the *Wall St. Journal*, "the PC software industry will lose one of its striking role models. For years, many in the industry looked to Intuit Chairman Scott Cook as a shining example that a small company could prosper in a market dominated by a few big players."

In a way, Intuit and Scott Cook are still positive examples. As Lawrence Fisher put it in the *New York Times* (October 16, 1994), Goliath didn't beat David: "Goliath dropped his weapons and picked up his checkbook." Cook started Quicken, a simple check-writing program; today he stands to acquire about $330 million in Microsoft stock.

This is a nice personal success story that shows someone other than Microsoft can still make money in the PC software industry. Unfortunately, though, the louder messages are negative ones: Microsoft has moved into yet another territory; there's one fewer competitor; fewer and fewer companies are in control of software. There's nothing particularly evil about Microsoft's goal of total control over general-purpose PC software — and the U.S. Justice Department's settlement with Microsoft seems to indicate that Microsoft broke few antitrust laws to get to its current position — but a Microsoft monopoly, like every other monopoly, will ultimately produce price-gouging and a glacial pace of genuine innovation.

Now, what could Microsoft want — and want so badly to pay $1.5 billion in stock — with a program that helps people balance their checkbooks? Why would Microsoft pay far more for Intuit than it paid for the excellent FoxPro database?

To understand this, you first have to understand that Microsoft is not simply taking over one application domain after another. Microsoft is taking over applications *and putting them into the operating system*. This is an important distinction. Microsoft is not really in the applications business. True, applications now account for 63 percent of Microsoft revenues, in contrast to only 42 percent in 1989 (*Economist*, September 17, 1994). But this is not necessarily a healthy trend from the company's perspective, because applications have a much narrower profit margin than operating systems.

The Windows operating system is Microsoft's core business, and this core must be continually redefined, enlarged, or both. The trick is to maintain a near monopoly on a ubiquitous standard. (Intel has not succeeded at this; it now has serious competition from AMD.) As Microsoft VP Brad Silverberg told me in October 1993, "Once Windows is frozen and no longer moving forward, it can easily be cloned and thus be reduced to a commodity. Microsoft doesn't want to be in the BIOS business."

To constantly change the operating system, Microsoft enlarges it with what were once applications. Microsoft doesn't want to be in the "BIOS business" (the business of making readily clonable systems software), but it also doesn't really want to be in the applications business. Even its applications suite, Microsoft Office, increasingly looks like part of the operating system. Microsoft Office is becoming a *platform*; it is systems software.

Microsoft may make most of its revenues from applications, but it is still fundamentally a systems software firm. So Microsoft isn't in the BIOS business, and it isn't in applications business. Its business is something in between: systems software that, like a combination of kudzu and the Energizer Bunny, just keeps growing and growing and growing...

That Windows 95 is a major step in this expansion of the operating system is noticeable even to those outside the industry. For example:

> Many products developed by smaller companies are now being subsumed into Microsoft's operating system dominance.... A look at an early version of the successor to Windows, Chicago, reveals built-in hooks to what could be a Microsoft on-line service. Later in 1994 [mid-1995, it now seems], Microsoft will have the ability to ship several million copies a month of a front end to potential online subscribers. America Online can't even think of numbers like that. It will have to move upstream, offering online content rather than just a connection service.
>
> — Andrew Kessler, "The monolith: Like the ominous black slab in '2001: A Space Odyssey,' Microsoft Corp. continues to expand its software line, leaving few vendors in its wake," *Forbes*, March 14, 1994

So where does the acquisition of Quicken fit into all this? To pay $1.5 billion in stock, the company must have far bigger ambitions than simply selling a lot of personal-finance software. Indeed, the *New York Times* observed that Microsoft VP Mike Maples "notably avoided calling Quicken an application." No, Microsoft has more systematic goals for this software.

What could a check-writing program have to do with systems software? The *New York Times* had a good explanation:

> The deal only makes sense when viewed in the broader context of the emerging market for online commerce. Quicken users can already pay bills electronically, and there is a Quicken Visa card that delivers an electronic monthly statement via disk or modem.
>
> While Intuit has lacked the clout to forge many links with major banks, Microsoft has the muscle to make Quicken the defacto standard for home banking services, via PC and modem today, interactive TV and cable systems tomorrow. Investment and insurance services would be natural extensions.

Microsoft hopes that Intuit will launch it into the world of online banking. Cook will become executive VP of Electronic Commerce at Microsoft. Notice the title: VP of Electronic Commerce at Microsoft. Is there a Microsoft Visa card in your future?

Online banking is just one new area that Microsoft is exploring. Cable TV, telephony, on-line services: we've heard it all. But it's important not to confuse Microsoft's daydreams with reality. Microsoft puts its eggs into many baskets. Only a few of these eggs hatch. For example, with all of Microsoft's talk of cable TV and telephony services, most of its cable and telephone deals were much smaller than it wanted. It's not clear what Microsoft brings to the "digital convergence" party other than a talent for alienating its potential dance partners.

Microsoft has had prominent failures, including OS/2 1.*x*, LAN Manager and, I would have to say, Windows NT. Microsoft is not a company with vision: it's a company with supreme opportunism (in the best sense of the word). Adrian King makes this point nicely in his *Inside Windows 95* (p. xxii) when he talks about the "seven-year overnight success of Windows." King says that Gates and Ballmer "would probably try to convince you it was planned that way. Don't believe it."

It's interesting to look at part of the story behind Microsoft's purchase of Intuit. *Newsweek* reporter Mike Meyer sat in on two "BillG meetings," first with the Microsoft Baseball team — they discuss purchasing — and then with the Microsoft Money group. Gates beats up on the Money group because they're losing badly to Intuit's Quicken. And,

> Then comes a strange moment, the sort of thing that happens often at Microsoft, which seemingly within moments turns disaster into salvation. Talk has turned to broader trends in banking. Where's it going, what's in it for us. Banks are dinosaurs, says Gates. We can "bypass" them. [The Microsoft Money product manager] is unhappy with an alliance involving a big bank-card company. "Too slow." Instead he proposes a deal with a small — and more easily controllable — check-clearing outfit. "Why don't we buy them?" Gates asks, thinking bigger. It occurs to him that people banking from home will cut checks using Microsoft's software. Microsoft can then push all those transactions through its new affiliate, taking a fee on every one. Abruptly, Gates sheds his disappointment with Money. He's caught up in a vision of the "transformation of the world financial system." It's a "pot of gold," he declares, pounding the conference table with his fists, triumphant and hungry and wired. "Get me into that and goddam, we'll make so much money!"
>
> Here is Microsoft in action. In just three hours, it laid plans to buy at least two companies, ditched an alliance with a major financial institution, opted for another and made major moves into "two incredible new worlds," as Gates put it — home banking and sports entertainment. Another company might take months to accomplish as much.
>
> — Michael Meyer, "Culture Club," *Newsweek*, July 11, 1994

This small episode speaks volumes about how Microsoft operates, and why it seems so much better than its competitors. The company has a tremendous capacity for snatching victory out of the jaws of defeat.

Anyone trying to survive in the software business should recognize that Microsoft now dominates the industry and will likely do so into the early 21st century. Don't bother trying to fight this domination, but realize that Microsoft doesn't know any more of what the future holds than you or I do. As Stephen Manes and Paul Andrews put it in their superb biography, *Gates*, the "Microsoft Everywhere" strategy looks almost as though the company "were placing a bet on every number on the digital roulette wheel."

Gates and Microsoft can afford to play the game this way because of the funding supplied by its MS-DOS cash cow. We, on the other hand, have to be more selective. We can't pay attention to everything that Microsoft tells us is important, such as NT, OLE, ODBC, TAPI, MAPI, WOSA, NDIS, MFC, VBA, and OCX (to name just a few). Not all of these will turn out to be important. As Manes and Andrews go on to say about Microsoft's saturation bet-placing, "To stockplayers who preferred to view Microsoft as a monolith able to enforce its will in the marketplace, a surprising number of these bets seemed to return small change."

At the same time, Microsoft is the reality of the PC software industry. Windows 95 will further dramatize its role. Therefore, developers need to understand Microsoft's systems inside and out. If you study even a speck of code in Windows, you're examining how tens of millions of computers work. This is not the same as studying every new interface that Microsoft claims is important. Again, Microsoft *doesn't know* what is going to be important and what isn't. But if you have a firm grasp of how Microsoft's systems work — as opposed to how Microsoft says they work (or perhaps even how most Microsoft employees think their own products work) — you'll be well equipped to understand Windows 95, Windows 96, Windows 97, and whatever else Microsoft sends our way.

Appendix A

Unauthorized Windows 95 Resource Kit

The *Unauthorized Windows 95* disk includes about sixty programs, several reusable function libraries, and about 20,000 lines of source code. Most of the programs are character mode, using the DOS Protected Mode Interface (DPMI), the Win32 Console API, or real-mode DOS.

When you run the setup batch file, it creates the directory C:\UNAUTHW with these subdirectories:

BIN	DOS programs, protected-mode DOS programs, and VxDs
BINW	16-bit Windows programs
BIN32	Win32 (including Console) programs
LIB	Libraries for Borland C++ 3.0
INCLUDE	C header files
SOURCE	C and assembly language source code

File Viewing Programs

Different versions of some of the file viewing utilities are also provided with the Windows Source disassembly toolkit from V Communications (800-648-8266, FAX 408-296-4224). If you have Windows Source, be careful not to overwrite the versions included with that product with the versions included on the *Unauthorized Windows 95* disk.

EXEDUMP displays information about 16-bit Windows (Win16) executables (EXEs, DLLs, DRVs, and so on), also known as New Executable (NE) files or Segmented Executable files. It shows the entry table (exports), relocation table (imports), segment table, NE header,module-reference table, and CodeView (R) information, if present. For example, you can use EXEDUMP to examine the core Win16 DLLs (KRNL386 .EXE, USER.EXE, and GDI.EXE), Win16 programs (SOL.EXE, WINWORD.EXE, TASKMAN.EXE, and so on), and 16-bit Windows device drivers (SYSTEM .DRV, KEYBOARD.DRV, and so on).

- To display information about a Win16 NE executable:
  Command: EXEDUMP [options] exe_file
  Example: exedump \windows\system\krnl386.exe

- To generate a listing of exports from an executable:
  Command: EXEDUMP -EXPORTS exe_file
  Example: for %f in (\windows\system*.*) do exedump -exports %f

- To display only the executable file type (MZ, NE, LE, W3, LX, or PE): -MAGIC

- To display only the description string: -DESC

W32DUMP displays information about a Win32 Portable Executable (PE) file. This information includes a list of the functions exported and imported by the executable. You can use W32DUMP to examine files such as the core Win32 DLLs (KERNEL32.DLL, USER32.DLL, and GDI32.DLL), the Windows 95 Shell/Explorer/Cabinet (CAB32.EXE), or other Win32 programs (such as WINBEZMT.EXE). You can also use W32DUMP to examine files from Windows NT (such as NTDLL.DLL) and Win32s.

- To display information about a Win32 PE file:
  Command: W32DUMP file_name
  Example: w32dump \win32\bin\ntdll.dll

- To show relocation information: -RELOC

Source code is provided on disk in W32DUMP.C. This requires NTIMAGE.H from Microsoft's Win32 SDK.

RESDUMP displays information about resources in a Windows .RES file, Win16 executable (EXE, DLL, DRV, and so on), or Win32 executable. Detailed information is provided for dialog boxes, controls, menus, string tables, accelerator tables, and version resources.

- To display resources in a Windows .RES or executable:
  Command: RESDUMP [options] res_or_exe_file
  Example: resdump \windows\winfile.exe

- To display resources only of a given type:
  Command: RESDUMP -TYPE [type] res_or_exe_file
  Examples: resdump -type menu \windows\cab32.exe
  resdump -type menu -type dialog -hex \foo\bar.exe

Types:	CURSOR	BITMAP	ICON
	MENU	DIALOG	STRINGTAB
	FONTDIR	FONT	ACCEL
	RCDATA	ERRORTAB	CURSDIR
	ICONDIR	NAMETAB	VERSION

- To also dump bytes (hex) for each resource: -HEX
- To disable ANSI to OEM conversion (Japan): -DBCS

Source code is provided on disk in RESDUMP.C and RESDMP32.C.

W3MAP displays information about the Virtual Machine Manager (VMM) and Virtual Device Drivers (VxDs) in a Windows 3.*x* Enhanced mode or 4.*x* WIN386-style (W3) file. You can use W3MAP to examine WIN386.EXE, VMM32.VXD, or various short-lived Microsoft W3 files such as DOS386.EXE and MSDPMI.EXE.

- To display a list of all VxDs in the WIN386 file:
  Command: W3MAP win386_file
  Example: w3map \windows\system\vmm32.vxd
- To display information on an individual VxD in the WIN386 file:
  Command: W3MAP -VXD vxd_name win386_file
  Example: w3map -vxd ifsmgr \windows\system\vmm32.vxd
- To display detailed information on each VxD in the WIN386 file:
  Command: W3MAP -VERBOSE win386_file
  Example: w3map -verbose \windows\system\win386.exe

Source code is provided on disk in W3MAP.C and LE2.C.

LEDUMP displays information about a Windows 3.*x* Enhanced mode or 4.*x* Virtual Device Driver (VxD), in a Linear Executable (LE) file. This includes DOS programs (such as EMM386.EXE, SMARTDRV.EXE, and DBLSPACE.BIN) with embedded VxDs. Source code is provided on disk in LEDUMP.C and LE2.C.

- To display information about a VxD:
  Command: LEDUMP vxd_file
  Examples: ledump \win31\system\vtdapi.386
  ledump \windows\system\iosubsys\rmm.pdr

Memory Viewing Programs

PROTDUMP is a protected-mode memory hex-dump program. It can display memory giving a 32-bit linear address, a real-mode segment:offset address, a protected-mode selector:offset address, or a physical address. You can specify that the memory is located in another virtual machine (VM). The memory can be displayed as an array of bytes (default), words, dwords, or far pointers, and you can adjust the width of the display. PROTDUMP also has an option to display all VMs and, in Windows 95, all threads.

- To examine memory at a 32-bit linear address:
  Command: PROTDUMP linear_addr num_bytes
  Example: protdump 80001000 128
- To display all VMs (and, in Windows 95, threads):
  Command: PROTDUMP -VM
  Note: This option requires the generic VxD; put device=\unauthw\bin\vxd.386 in SYSTEM.INI [386Enh]
- To examine a real-mode address in another virtual machine:
  Command: PROTDUMP #vm segment:offset num_bytes
  Example: protdump #1 00A0:0330 2 -word
- To examine part of the MS-DOS data segment in another VM:
  Command: PROTDUMP #vm DOS:offset num_bytes
  Example: protdump #1 DOS:0330 2 -word
- To examine a real-mode address in all VMs (instance data):
  Command: PROTDUMP -all segment:offset num_bytes
  Example: protdump -all DOS:0330 2 -word
- To examine a protected-mode address in another VM:
  Command: PROTDUMP -PROT #vm selector:offset num_bytes
  Example: protdump -prot #1 011F:0 2048
  Note: This option requires the generic VxD; put device=\unauthw\bin\vxd.386 in SYSTEM.INI [386Enh]
- To examine physical memory (uses DPMI physical to linear translation): -PHYS
- To treat a linear address as a pointer to a linear address (can be repeated): -PTR
- To treat a linear address as the beginning of a VMM linked list: -LIST
- To change the offset PROTDUMP uses for the LDT within a VM Control Block (114h in Windows 3.1): -LDT new_offset
- To dump words, dwords, or far pointers: -WORD, -DWORD, -FP
- To change the width (in bytes) of the hex dump (default: 16): -n
  Example: protdump -4 80001234 128

Source code is provided on disk in PROTDUMP.C, GDT.C, and VMWALK.C.

PROTTAB is a protected-mode program that displays tables from a given 32-bit linear address. It is particularly useful for examining VMM data structures (once you know their addresses). You can display tables of bytes, words, and dwords, specify an optional filter to suppress an uninteresting default entry in a table, and specify an optional name associated with a base address.

- To display a table at a linear address:
  Command: PROTTAB lin_addr num size [prefix] [filter] [name=base]
  Example: prottab c41db000 28 4 foo 0 VMM=C0001000

This example dumps out a table of 28h dwords (size: 4) located at C41DB000h. The entries are named foo_1, foo_2, and so on. All entries equal to 0 are suppressed. The value of each entry is displayed as "VMM+", relative to the address C0001000h (VMM+1234, VMM+5678, and so on). Source code is provided on disk as PROTTAB.C.

Structure Viewers

WINBP is a protected-mode DOS program that displays V86 breakpoints, V86 callbacks, and protected-mode callbacks in Windows 3.*x* Enhanced mode and in Windows 95. By default, WINBP displays only a few pieces of information, such as the current MaxBPs= setting and the location of the breakpoint table. To generate a list of all breakpoints and callbacks, run WINBP -VERBOSE. Source code is provided on disk in WINBP.C.

VXDLIST is a protected-mode DOS program that display the Virtual Device Driver (VxD) chain in Windows 3.*x* Enhanced mode and in Windows 95. By default, VXDLIST provides only one line of information for each VxD in the chain. If you run VXDLIST -VERBOSE, the program will generate a large amount of information for each VxD, such as a list of all the services it provides. In Windows 95, VXDLIST will show Win32 service tables. Rather than show the entire VxD chain, you can specify a particular VxD to examine.

- To display all services provided by all loaded VxDs:
  Example: VXDLIST -VERBOSE

- To display all services provided by a single VxD:
  Command: VXDLIST -VERBOSE vxd_name OR #hex_id
  Example: vxdlist -verbose DOSMGR

- To determine if a particular VxD is loaded:
  Command: vxdlist vxd_name OR #hex_id
  Example: vxdlist NDIS
  Example: vxdlist #28

The VxD name is case-sensitive. The return value from VXDLIST can be tested with the IF ERRORLEVEL statement in a DOS batch file. Source code is provided on disk in VXDLIST.C and VXDCHAIN.C.

There is a bug in the version on disk: Service names are output improperly for service 0 in each VxD: instead of something like DOSMGR_GetVersion or SHELL_GetVersion, the name comes out as something like "DOSMGR_~" or "SHELL_~". To correct this, all the "~~" entries in \UNAUTHW\INCLUDE\VXDFUNC.H should be replaced with "~GetVersion".

IDTMAP displays the V86 and protected-mode Interrupt Descriptor Table (IDT). By default, is displays both IDTs in their entirety. You can instead specify one or more interrupt numbers on the command line. Since IDTs are a per-VM structure, running a protected-mode DOS program like IDTMAP doesn't necessarily tell you how interrupts are handled in the System VM; see PMINTVEC (which is a Windows program) on disk. Source code is provided on disk in IDTMAP.C.

WINPSP is a 16-bit Windows program that displays the real-mode DOS Program Segment Prefix (PSP) structure belonging to each running Win16 and Win32 task. To use the program, just run it; its output can be saved to a file. Source code is provided on disk in WINPSP.C.

WALKWIN is a 16-bit Windows program that displays information about each WND (window) structure in Windows 3.*x* and Windows 95. WALKWIN is particularly useful for seeing how Windows 95 uses the Win16 USER and KERNEL modules to support windowing and messaging for Win32 applications. Source code is provided on disk in WALKWIN.C.

Programs to Examine the Windows-DOS Relationship

FAKEWIN is a DOS program that pretends to be Windows by issuing the same INT 2Fh function 16h broadcasts that Windows issues during its initialization. FAKEWIN displays the requests made by real-mode DOS programs and by DOS itself when starting up. These include requests to load VxDs and declare instance data. Source code is provided on disk in FAKEWIN.C, FAKEVXD.C, FAKETSR.C, FAKEEMM.C, and TEST1684.C.

TEST21 is a DOS program that hooks INT 21h and then issues some INT 21h calls. If the program's INT 21h handler doesn't see the program's own calls to INT 21h, someone is bypassing DOS for these calls. For testing Windows 95, use the -MYSETVECT option.

V86TEST is a DOS program that hooks INT 21h and INT 2Fh and then runs the program specified on its command line. Generally, this program will be Windows (WIN). V86TEST's interrupt handlers will keep count of the number of INT 21h and INT 2Fh calls made by Windows, whether the calls were made in real mode or V86 mode, what virtual machine they came from, and so on. When Windows exits, V86TEST will display the statistics. You can display the statistics from a DOS box, before Windows has exited, with -QUERY.

- To run Windows under V86TEST:
  Command: V86TEST Windows_path Windows_options
  Example: v86test win /D:C
- To query the V86TEST statistics while Windows is running:
  Example: v86test -verbose -query
  Note: Alternatively, you can use a Windows program, WV86TEST.
- To ignore all VMPoll broadcasts: -FILTER
- To run V86TEST if the machine is already in V86mode: -OKV86

WV86TEST is a Windows front-end to V86TEST. Source code is provided on disk in V86TEST.C and WV86TEST.C.

HOOKINT is a DOS program that hooks a number of BIOS interrupts (such as INT 10h for video services and INT 16h for the keyboard) and then spawns the program named on its command line. (If no program is named on the command line, HOOKINT runs COMMAND.COM or whatever command shell is named in the COMSPEC environment variable.) When the spawned program exits (or when you EXIT from the command shell), HOOKINT displays statistics on the number and types of interrupts generated. This is useful for examining how Windows interacts with the BIOS. Source code is provided on disk in HOOKINT.C.

WLOG212F is a Windows program that hooks INT 21h and INT 2Fh, in protected mode and (using a DPMI V86 callback) in V86 mode. By comparing the interrupts seen in protected mode with those seen in V86 mode, WLOG212F can determine which calls are sent down to DOS and which bypass DOS. WLOG212F has several menu items: Source code is provided on disk in WLOG212F.C.

WSPY21 hooks INT 21h in protected mode and displays a line of information about each INT 21h call. You can specify an interrupt number on the command line to watch a different interrupt, such as INT 2Fh or INT 31h. The text mentions a -SHOWALL option; this does not appear in the version of WSPY21 on the disk. Source code is provided on disk in WSPY21.C.

Libraries

DPMI Shell DPMISH.C, DPMISH.H, and CTRL_C.ASM provide a simple interface for writing small-model protected-mode DOS programs that can run under Windows 3.*x* Enhanced mode, Windows 95, or any other DOS Protected Mode Interface (DPMI) provider.

To use DPMISH, a program provides at least two functions, real_ main and prot_main. In real mode (or V86 mode), DPMISH will call the program's real_main function. If this function returns 0, DPMISH will switch to protected mode and call the program's pmode_main function. Once in protected mode, the program can use the Windows DOS extender or make DPMI calls.

The PROTDUMP, WINBP, VXDLIST, and IDTMAP programs all use DPMISH, and you can refer to the source code of these programs for examples of how to use DPMISH. Also see *Undocumented DOS*, 2d ed., Chapter 3.

Protected-Mode Functions PROT.C and PROT.H provide functions such as map_linear and map_real for working with protected-mode memory and functions such as real_int86x for generating real-mode (or V86-mode) interrupts from protected mode. PROT can be used both by 16-bit Windows programs and by protected-mode DOS programs (such as DPMISH). For protected-mode DOS programs, PROT also provides DPMI equivalents to Windows API functions such as AllocSelector, SetSelectorBase, GetSelectorBase, andGlobalDosAlloc.

PROTMODE.C and PROTMODE.H contain an alternate library, providing low-level protected-mode functions such as get_gdt (get a far pointer to the Global Descriptor Table), get_ldt (get a far pointer to the Local Descriptor Table), get_pagedir and get_pagetab (get far pointers to the Page Directory and to Page Tables). See PAGEWALK.C for examples of how to use these functions.

WINIO lets you write Windows programs with stdio functions such as printf. It is similar to, but more flexible than, the QuickWin library provided by Microsoft and the EasyWin library provided by Borland. WINIO programs can include menus and message handlers, can create multiple windows, and so on. The 16-bit Windows programs provided on the disk (such as WSPY21, WLOG212F, and WV86TEST) all use WINIO, so you can use the source files for these programs as examples of WINIO programming. WINIO is described in detail in *Undocumented Windows*, pp. 671-682.

Generic VxD VXD.386 is the generic VxD that provides Windows programs and DOS programs running under Windows with access to VMM and VxD functions. VXDCALLS.C and VXDCALLS.H provide a C interface to the generic VxD. VxDCall is the most important function provided by VXDCALLS. This function is used in the VMWALK.C, VXDTEST.C, VXDCHAIN.C, and FAULTHKS.C source files, which you can consult as examples of how to use the generic VxD.

Appendix B

Getting Started with The Programmer's Shop's CD-ROM

Smash Hits For Programmers™ is the first "try-before-you-buy" CD-ROM created exclusively for programmers. It lets you:

- Test drive new programming tools — before you buy
- Unlock software and install instantly
- Discover over 2,500 hard-to-find tools
- Browse articles from leading journals

It includes software from companies such as Powersoft, Computer Associates, IBM, Borland, and Symantec, plus Mega Guide from the Programmer's Shop.

Getting Started

1. Read the Programmer's Shop License Agreement printed in this book. By opening the CD-ROM envelope inside the back cover of this book, you indicate your acceptance of this License Agreement.
2. Place the Smash Hits For Programmers CD in your CD-ROM drive. In the Windows File Manager, click the icon for your CD-ROM drive. This displays a list of files on the CD. If the CD contains a README.TXT file, then double-click it to read important information that was not available at press time.
3. Double-click the SETUP.EXE file on the CD. Follow the Setup program's instructions. For details, see "About Setup."
4. In the Windows Program Manager, double-click the Smash Hits icon in the CD Select program group. After the opening animation, click Continue, unless you like endless loops.
5. Look at the Introduction and Frequently-Asked-Questions sections, then browse the on-screen catalog. Don't forget to check out MegaGuide! It's

right after the Free section. To read articles and code from programmer journals, go to the Information section.

6. If a product you're interested in has a demo, click its Demo button to launch the demo. If the button is grayed-out, the product does not have a demo. To see which products have demos, select "Products with Demos" from the Browse! menu.

How to Test Drive Products

1. If a product you're interested in has a test drive, click its Test Drive button and call 1-800-446-1185 for your test drive key. If the button is grayed-out, the product does not have a test drive. To see which products have test drives, select "Products with Test drives" from the Browse! menu.
2. When you click a product's Test Drive button, the Test Drive Order Form pops up with that product added to it. You can put multiple products onto your Test Drive Order Form by clicking their Test Drive buttons as well.

   (Note that each test drive takes up as much space on your hard drive as the corresponding full application. That's because each Test Drive is in fact an installation of the full application, except the files are encrypted. This lets you explore the full functionality of the product, not just a limited version. And it gives you a much more accurate gauge of performance than if you ran the application from the CD-ROM drive.)
3. With your completed Test Drive Order Form on screen, call CD Select at 1-800-446-1185. The CD Select representative asks for your name, address, and the catalog number, order number, and product numbers on your Test Drive Order Form. You then click the Unlock button. In the Unlock Test Drive dialog, enter the keys that the CD Select representative gives you. Click the Unlock button.
4. Each test drive is installed from the CD to your PC. The counter on the Test Drive button shows how many sessions you have left with that product. Once you quit the final session, the test drive is automatically uninstalled. To remove a test drive without using all its sessions, select "Delete Test Drive" from the Utilities menu.

How to Order Products

1. To order, click the Order button and call 1-800-446-1185, Monday through Friday, 8:30 a.m. to 8:00 p.m. EST. Note that prices and versions are subject to change. If you're ordering from MegaGuide, you don't have to click the Order button and can ignore the rest of this section.
2. When you click a product's Order button, the Order Form pops up with that product added to it. You can put multiple products onto your Order Form by

clicking their Order buttons as well. You can create, save, open, and print Order Forms from the File menu.

(Note that some products are available on this CD for immediate installation, while other products are available for shipment to you. If a product is available for immediate installation, it says "Available on this CD!" in the blackboard to the top left of the screen. To see which products you can install immediately, select "Available on this CD!" from the Browse! menu.)

3. With your completed Order Form on screen, call CD Select at 1-800-446-1185. The CD Select representative asks for your name, address, credit card or PO, and the catalog number, order number, and product numbers on your Order Form.
4. If you are ordering products for immediate installation, click the Unlock button. In the Unlock Products dialog, enter the keys that the CD Select representative gives you. Click the Unlock button. Each product is decrypted and installed from the CD to your PC. You're up and running right away! Depending on the product, the appropriate documentation and disks arrive in a few days.

System Requirements

- 386-based system or higher
- 4MB memory (8 MB recommended)
- Microsoft Windows 3.1 or later, in Enhanced Mode
- DOS 5.0 or later
- VGA monitor or better (Smash Hits is optimized for 256 colors)
- CD-ROM drive with MSCDEX.EXE 2.*x*
- 3MB available on your hard drive
- Mouse recommended

Technical Support

You'll find answers to most questions in the following resources: this section of the book, the ReadMe file in the CD Select program group, Smash Hits' own Introduction and Frequently-Asked-Questions sections, plus on-line Help. For further technical support, call 1-800-446-1185, Monday - Friday, 8:30 AM to 8:00 PM EST.

About Setup

Setup copies several files from the CD to your PC. These are program files that let you access the data on the CD. Product information, articles, and encrypted software stay on the CD until you need them.

Setup also gets your system ready for you to try-before-you-buy. To test drive software, two programs must be running before you start Windows: SHARE.EXE and REDIRECT.EXE (Redirector). Redirector uses 47K of DOS or base memory. Setup gives you three choices for running Redirector:

1. Have Setup add the necessary commands to AUTOEXEC.BAT. If you are a beginning user or not sure what's in AUTOEXEC.BAT, we recommend this option. The easiest way to run Redirector before you start Windows is to run it in AUTOEXEC.BAT. This is a file that runs every time you start up your machine. Setup backs up the original AUTOEXEC.BAT as AUTOEXEC.CD0.
2. Review changes before Setup makes them. If you use network drivers, we recommend this option. Setup shows you the commands to be inserted in AUTOEXEC.BAT, and lets you choose where to place them. We recommend you place them after any network drivers. Setup backs up the original AUTOEXEC.BAT as AUTOEXEC.CD0.
3. Have Setup put the necessary commands into a separate file. If you do not want to run Redirector every time you start your machine, or do not want to change AUTOEXEC.BAT, we recommend this option. Setup creates a separate file, MERGE_TD.BAT, that contains the necessary commands. When you want to test drive software, copy these commands into AUTOEXEC.BAT and reboot. Or run the commands by typing "MERGE_TD" at the DOS prompt before you start Windows.

For Users Outside the US and Canada

Due to restrictions on our ability to resell or support software outside the United States and Canada, The Programmer's Shop will not issue keys for test drives or for installation from this CD to users outside the US and Canada.

CD Select is a Programmer's Shop publication. A business unit of The Software Developer's Company, Inc.

The Programmer's Shop, 90 Industrial Park Road, Hingham, MA 02043-9845. Telephone 1-800-446-1185. Fax 617-749-2018. Monday - Friday, 8:30 AM to 8:00 PM EST.

For Further Reading

Walter Adams and James Brock, *Antitrust Economics on Trial: A Dialogue on the New Laissez-Faire*, Princeton NJ: Princeton University Press, 1991.

Rakesh K. Agarwal, *80x86 Architecture and Programming*, Volume 2: Architecture Reference, Englewood Cliffs NJ: Prentice Hall, 1991.

Prabhat K. Andleigh, *UNIX System Architecture*, Englewood Cliffs NJ: Prentice Hall, 1990.

Paul Andrews, "The Winds of Chicago," *Marketing Computers*, May 1994.

Russ Blake, *Optimizing Windows NT*, Redmond WA: Microsoft Press, 1993.

Paul Bonneau, "Windows Q&A," *Windows/DOS Developer's Journal*, October 1993, April 1994, June 1994, August 1994, and September 1994.

Paul Bonner, "Will the Real Operating System Please Stand Up?," *Computer Shopper*, October 1994.

Ed Bott, "Inside Windows 4.0," *PC/Computing*, March 1994.

Joseph Boykin, David Kirschen, Alan Langerman, and Susan LoVerso, *Programming under Mach*, Reading MA: Addison-Wesley, 1993.

Marshall Brain, *Win32 System Services: The Heart of Windows NT*, Englewood Cliffs NJ: Prentice Hall, 1994.

Geoff Chappell, *DOS Internals*, Reading MA: Addison-Wesley, 1994.

Nancy Winnick Cluts, "Getting Ready for Chicago," Microsoft Developer Network CD-ROM, January 28, 1994.

Amy Cortese, "Next Stop, Chicago," *Business Week*, August 1, 1994.

Helen Custer, *Inside Windows NT*, Redmond WA: Microsoft Press, 1993.

Ralph Davis, *Windows Network Programming: How to Survive in a World of Windows, DOS, and NetWare*, Reading MA: Addison-Wesley, 1993.

H.M. Deitel and M.S. Kogan, *The Design of OS/2*, Reading MA: Addison-Wesley, 1992.

Robert B.K. Dewar and Matthew Smosna, *Microprocessors: A Programmer's View*, New York NY: McGraw-Hill, 1991.

DOS Protected Mode Interface (DPMI) Specification, Version 1.0 (March 12, 1991). Intel Order no. 240977-001.

Ray Duncan, "Microsoft Windows/386: Creating a Virtual Machine Environment," *Microsoft Systems Journal*, September 1987.

Ray Duncan, Charles Petzold, Andrew Schulman, M. Steven Baker, Ross P. Nelson, Stephen R. Davis, and Robert Moote, *Extending DOS: A Programmer's Guide to Protected-Mode DOS*, Second edition, Reading MA: Addison-Wesley, 1992.

Dave Edson, "Seventeen Techniques for Preparing Your 16-Bit Applications for Chicago," *Microsoft Systems Journal*, February 1994.

Charles Ferguson and Charles Morris, *Computer Wars: The Fall of IBM and the Future of Global Technology*, New York NY: Times Books, 1993.

James Finnegan, "Hook and Monitor Any 16-Bit Windows Function with Our ProcHook DLL," *Microsoft Systems Journal*, January 1994.

James Finnegan, "Test Drive Win32 from 16-bit Code Using the Windows NT WOW Layer and Generic Thunk," *Microsoft Systems Journal*, June 1994.

Bill Gates, "Free Market Economics — Not Intervention — Drives Innovation," *InfoWorld*, August 16, 1993.

Douglas Greer, *Industrial Organization and Public Policy*, Third edition, New York NY: Macmillan, 1992.

Intel Corp., *80386 System Software Writer's Guide*, 1987.

Intel Corp., *i486 Microprocessor Programmer's Reference Manual*, 1990.

Adrian King, *Inside Windows 95*, Redmond WA: Microsoft Press, 1994.

Adrian King, "Memory Management, the Win32 Subsystem, and Internal Synchronization in Chicago," *Microsoft Systems Journal*, May 1994.

Adrian King, "Windows, the Next Generation: An Advance Look at the Architecture of Chicago," *Microsoft Systems Journal*, January 1994.

David Kirkpatrick, "What's Driving the New PC Shakeout," *Fortune*, September 19, 1994.

David Long, "TSR Support in Microsoft Windows Version 3.1," Microsoft Developer Network CD-ROM, October 1992.

Stephen Manes and Paul Andrews, *Gates*, New York NY: Doubleday, 1993.

John Markoff, "Microsoft's Barely Limited Future," *New York Times*, July 18, 1994.

Kyle Marsh, "Extending the Chicago Shell," *Microsoft Developer Network News*, July 1994.

Michael Maurice, "The PIF File Format, or, Topview (Sort of) Lives!," *Dr. Dobb's Journal*, July 1993.

Roger McNamee, "The PC Software Industry Sobers Up," *Upside*, March 1993.

Microsoft Corporation, *"Chicago" Reviewer's Guide*, Redmond WA, May 1994.

Microsoft Corporation, *Virtual Device Adaptation Guide* (Microsoft Windows 3.1 Device Driver Kit), Redmond WA, 1992.

Microsoft Corporation, *Windows for Workgroups 3.11 Resource Kit*, Redmond WA, 1993.

Michael Meyer, "Culture Club," *Newsweek*, July 11, 1994.

Klaus Mueller, "Think Globally, Act Locally: Inside the Windows Instance Data Manager," *Dr. Dobb's Journal*, April 1994.

Nu-Mega Technologies, *Soft-ICE/W Reference Guide*, Nashua NH, 1992.

Taku Okazaki, "The Windows Global EMM Import Interface," *Dr. Dobb's Journal*, August 1994.

Thomas Olsen, "Making Windows and DOS Programs Talk," *Windows/DOS Developer's Journal*, May 1992.

Walter Oney, "Mix 16-bit and 32-bit Code in Your Applications with the Win32s Universal Thunk," *Microsoft Systems Journal*, November 1993.

Walter Oney, "Unconstrained Filenames on the PC! Introducing Chicago's Protected Mode Fat File System," *Microsoft Systems Journal*, August 1994.

Open Software Foundation, *Design of the OSF/1 Operating System*, Englewood Cliffs NJ, 1993.

Matt Pietrek, "Investigating the Hybrid Windowing and Messaging System of Chicago," *Microsoft Systems Journal*, September 1994.

Matt Pietrek, "Stepping Up to 32 Bits: Chicago's Process, Thread, and Memory Management," *Microsoft Systems Journal*, August 1994.

Matt Pietrek, "Which Win32 Is For You?," *PC Magazine*, September 27, 1994.

Matt Pietrek, *Windows Internals: The Implementation of the Windows Operating Environment*, Reading MA: Addison-Wesley, 1993.

Jeffrey Richter, *Advanced Windows NT: The Developer's Guide to the Win32 Application Programming Interface*, Redmond WA: Microsoft Press, 1994.

Wendy Goldman Rohm, "United States v. Microsoft: The Inside Story," *Information Week*, August 1, 1994.

Stephen F. Ross, *Principles of Antitrust Law*, Westbury NY: Foundation Press, 1993.

Brett Salter, "An Exception Handler for Windows 3," *Dr. Dobb's Journal*, September 1992.

Jeffrey Savit, *VM/CMS Concepts and Facilities*, New York NY: McGraw-Hill, 1993.

F.M. Scherer and David Ross, *Industrial Market Structure and Economic Performance*, Third edition, Boston: Houghton Mifflin, 1990.

Andrew Schulman, "At Last — Write Bona Fide 32-bit Programs that Run on Windows 3.1 Using Win32s," *Microsoft Systems Journal*, April 1993

Andrew Schulman, "Call VxD Functions and VMM Services Easily Using Our Generic VxD," *Microsoft Systems Journal*, February 1993.

Andrew Schulman, "Exploring Demand-Paged Virtual Memory in Windows Enhanced Mode," *Microsoft Systems Journal*, December 1992.

Andrew Schulman, "Go Anywhere and Do Anything with 32-bit Virtual Device Drivers for Windows," *Microsoft Systems Journal*, October 1992.

Andrew Schulman, "LA Law," *Dr. Dobb's Journal*, May 1994.

Andrew Schulman, "Porting DOS Programs to Protected-Mode Windows with the WINDOS Library," *Microsoft Systems Journal*, September-October 1991.

Andrew Schulman, "Walking the VxD Chain in Windows (and Chicago)," *Dr. Dobb's Journal*, December 1993.

Andrew Schulman, Ralf Brown, David Maxey, Ray Michels, and Jim Kyle, *Undocumented DOS: A Programmer's Guide to Reserved MS-DOS Functions and Data Structures*, Second edition, Reading MA: Addison-Wesley, 1993.

Andrew Schulman and David Maxey, "Call Standard I/O Functions from Your Windows Code Using the WINIO Library," *Microsoft Systems Journal*, July 1991.

Andrew Schulman, David Maxey, and Matt Pietrek, *Undocumented Windows: A Programmer's Guide to Reserved Microsoft Windows API Functions*, Reading MA: Addison-Wesley, 1992.

Alex Shmidt, "RINGO: VxDs on the Fly," *Dr. Dobb's Journal*, March 1994.

Brad Silverberg, "Microsoft's Answer to AARD," *Dr. Dobb's Journal*, January 1994.

Bill Snyder, "The Great Escape," *PC Week*, April 4, 1994.

Mark Stahlman, "The Failure of IBM: Lessons for the Future," *Upside*, March 1993.

Tammy Steele, "How to Adapt an App for Chicago," *Microsoft Developer Network News*, July 1994.

John Steffens, *Newgames: Strategic Competition in the PC Revolution*, Oxford: Pergamon Press, 1994.

Andrew Tanenbaum, *Modern Operating Systems*, Englewood Cliffs NJ: Prentice Hall, 1992.

Paula Tomlinson, "The VDD Backdoor," *Windows/DOS Developer's Journal*, May 1993 (see letters to the editor in July 1993 issue).

Matt Trask, "Creating Virtual PCs on the 386," *Byte*, IBM Special edition, Fall 1990.

Jon Udell, "Chicago: An Ambitious Compromise," *Byte*, March 1994.

Jon Udell, "The Fix is in for Chicago," *Byte*, September 1994.

Jon Udell, "Windows for Workgroups 3.11," *Byte*, February 1994.

James M. Utterback, *Mastering the Dynamics of Innovation: How Companies Can Seize Opportunities in the Face of Technological Change*, Boston MA: Harvard Business School Press, 1994.

V Communications, *Windows Source Disassembly Pre-Processor*, San Jose CA, 1993.

G. Pascal Zachary, "Computer Industry Divides into Camps of Winners and Losers," *Wall St. Journal*, January 27, 1993.

Kelly Zytaruk, "The Windows Virtual Machine Control Block," *Dr. Dobb's Journal*, January 1994 (Part 1) and February 1994 (Part 2).

Index

32BFA (32-bit file access), 19, 31, 44–46, 77, 82, 95, 177–207, 291, 368
- additional VXDs required by, 178, 192
- bypassing DOS and, 12, 13, 15, 216–220, 237–238, 277
- CD-ROMs and, 274–276
- Clock and, 498, 543–544
- DblSpace and, 204–206
- vs. disk cache performance, 221–223
- effect of, 359–363
- FAKEWIN and, 136–137
- floppy disks and, 274–276
- IFSHLP.SYS and, 271, 272, 274
- IFSMgr and, 27
- INTRSPY and, 65–66
- INTVECT and, 240–241
- KRNL386.EXE and, 85–86
- long filename support and, 193–203
- networks and, 274–276
- TEST21 and, 214, 234–238
- V86TEST and, 339, 342, 352–363
- VFAT and, 79
- VMM32 and, 182–192
- WSPY21 and, 417–418, 492
- WV86TEST and, 371, 373–376, 378–383, 389, 394–396

386MAX, 99, 101, 146, 155, 159, 160, 170, 174, 288

A

_AddFreePhysPage, 128
_AddInstanceItem, 106–107, 120
Agarwal, Rakesh, 302
_AllocatedThreadDataSlot, 72
Allocate_PM_Callback, 494
Allocate Real Mode Callback Address, 33
Allocate_V86_Call_Back, 206, 250
AllocSelector, 414
Andrews, Paul, 144
ANSI.SYS, 122
API (Application Program Interface), 16, 20, 24, 33, 41, 44, 98, 294, 41432BFA and, 181, 275
- Cloaking, 288
- DOSMGR broadcast, 129–132
- IFSHLP.SYS and, 252–255, 265, 268–269, 273
- INT21h hookers and, 242–243
- long filename support and, 194, 200–201
- V86TEST and, 308, 340, 342
- VMM32 and, 192
- WSPY21 and, 419–420, 423, 424, 428, 445

APM (Advanced Power Management), 367
Apple Computer, 1, 2, 25, 465
architecture
- architectural diagrams, 20–23, 36
- integrated, 23–26

ARPL instructions, 206, 240, 250, 252, 255–258, 267–268, 270, 298, 337, 357, 495
Artisoft, 381
AUTOEXEC.BAT, 3–11, 27, 31, 35–36, 61, 96, 136, 293
- bypassing COMMAND.COM and,
- bypassing DOS and, 9–11, 19
- eliminating, 6–7
- INTRSPY and, 62–63

Award Software, 288
AWK, 421, 468

B

BACKUP, 204
Barrett, Phil, 249–250
Begin Exit, 97
Begin_Exec_V86_Mode, 225
Begin_Nest_V86_Exec, 228–229, 233, 345, 430, 495
BLOCKDEV, 177–178, 272, 349. *See also* IOS (I/O Supervisor)
BOOT, 49–51, 62
Borland, 84–85, 160, 304, 368
Build_Int_Stack_Frame, 270
BuildPDB, 16, 41, 442

C

CAB32 (Explorer/Cabinet), 15, 84–93, 383–386, 394, 396–397, 399, 401, 441–444
Calc, 374–378, 383, 421, 422, 424, 425, 441
CALL FWORD PTR, 504–510, 512
Call_Priority_Thread_Event, 83
Call_Priority_VM_Event, 82, 526–529
Call_When_Idle, 347
Call_When_Task_Switched, 390
Call_When_Thread_Switched, 72
Call_When_VM_Ints_Enabled, 324, 381
Call_When_VM_Returns, 227–228, 357, 368, 370
Cancel_Thread_Event, 72
CD-ROMs, 274–276
- MSCDEX (Microsoft CD-ROM Extensions), 58, 59, 60, 172, 275, 288
- MSDN (Microsoft Developer Network) CD-ROM, 98, 134, 172, 269

CDS (Current Directory Structure), 13, 42, 119–120, 340, 351, 491
_chain_intr, 210
Chappell, Geoff, 57, 97, 105, 119, 228, 242, 250, 270–273, 322
ChDir, 430

check_state, 308
CHGDIR, 446–452
CLI (clear interrupt flag), 297–298, 320–331, 336, 337
CLISTI.C, 328–329
CLITEST, 325, 326
Clock, 32, 35, 136, 332, 342, 345, 353, 355, 385, 407–408, 425, 435, 442, 455–456, 467–468, 500–557
Close File (INT 21h function 3Eh), 36, 182, 217, 235, 236
CodeView, 144, 368
COMMAND.COM, 27, 35, 61–62, 346,354–355
  32BFA and, 177, 179, 180,181
  bypassing DOS and, 5–11, 15,19
  IFSHLP.SYS and, 247
  MSDPMI and, 173–176
  VMM32 and, 185, 187
  WIN386.EXE and, 162, 165–166, 167, 172
COMMDLG, 467
CONAGENT.EXE, 451, 452
CONFIG$, 12, 56
CONFIGMG, 12, 56–57, 79
CONFIG.SYS, 4–5, 27, 31, 35–38,178
  bypassing DOS and, 9, 11, 19
  DEVICE= directives, 81
  DOS-ENHANCED switch in, 62
  INSTALL= directives, 63, 136
  Soft-ICE and, 50–51
  VMM32 and, 186
  WINBOOT and, 50–51, 57
Control Panel, 332, 425, 431
Control_Proc, 232
Control_RunDLL, 432–434
CopyFile, 340
COUNTDOS, 134–137, 342
CPL (Current Privilege Level), 319
CplApplet, 433
Create Directory (INT 21h function 39h), 398
CreateFile (API), 87–88, 194, 340
Create File (INT 21h function 3Ch), 179
_CreateMutex, 72
CreateProcess, 41, 444, 460–462
Create PSP (INT 21h function55h), 15, 16, 17, 38, 44, 374, 376, 420, 422, 425, 427, 430, 436, 441, 442, 460–472
CreateSystemTimer, 91
CreateTask, 16, 444, 462
CreateThread, 87–88
CreateWindow, 140
Ctrl-Alt-Del, 62, 188, 323, 325, 327
CURRDRIV, 233, 235, 238, 240, 377
CURRDRIV.386, 42, 36, 41, 233–234, 374
CURRDRIV.ASM, 230–232, 234

D

DblSpace compression, 35, 103, 198, 204–206, 248
  TEST21 and, 215–216
  VMM32 and, 182
DBLSPACE.386, 204, 205
DBLSPACE.BIN, 35, 51, 57, 103–104
DDB (Device Descriptor Block), 232
DDE (Dynamic Data Exchange), 56
DDK (Device Driver Kit), 54, 70–71, 82–84, 98, 338
DEBUG, 3, 13, 28–31, 102, 280, 322–323, 325, 326
Declare_Virtual_Device, 232
Deitel, H. M., 323, 324
DELWATCH, 172
_DestroyMutex, 72
DEVICE=, 60, 81, 186
Device_Init, 233
DIAGNOSE, 250
diagrams, architectural, 20–23, 36
DIR, 193, 200
disk driver terminology, 197–198
DiskTSD, 81–82, 196, 198
DISPLAY, 22, 368
Display Character (INT 21h function 02h), 354
DLLs (Dynamic Link Libraries), 16, 98, 99, 134, 140–141
  Explorer and, 65–66
  MEMLOOP and, 159
  PSPs and, 386, 388
  WSPY21 and, 386, 388, 417, 418, 424, 427, 489
Do_Device_Init, 233, 240
Do_Get_Vect, 241
DOS386.EXE, 62, 140–142, 165
Dos3Call, 401–402, 489
DOSDIR, 407, 408
Do_Set_Vect, 241
DOSKEY, 98–102, 113
DOSMEM.C, 484–485, 486
DOSMGR, 22, 79, 82, 105, 386–390, 445, 495
  broadcast API, 129–132
  FAKEWIN and, 120–122, 124, 126, 129–132
  DOSX and, 141, 151–152
  IFSHLP.SYS and, 252, 255
  WIN386.EXE and, 161
  WINBP and, 268–269
_dos_setvect, 217, 219, 235
DOSSHELL.EXE, 140–141
DOSX, 140–141, 146–156, 185, 207
  MEMLOOP and, 159
  WIN386.EXE and, 162, 168–169
DOSX.EXE, 61, 140, 142, 144–145, 150, 159
DPL (Descriptor Privilege Level), 319
DPMI (DOS Protected Mode Interface), 33, 39–40, 89, 135, 146–157, 161–173, 187–188, 414, 487. *See also* MSDPMI (Microsoft DPMI Server)
  32BFA and, 177, 207
  DOSX and, 146–152
  IOPL and, 328
  MEMLOOP and, 157, 159–160
  Shell library (DPMISH), 156–157, 168, 254, 326
  V86TEST and, 341, 342
  VMM32 and, 187
  WIN386.EXE and, 161–173
  WSPY21 and, 424
DPMICall, 449
DPMINFO, 167–173, 189
DPMINFO.C, 168–169
dpmi_init, 146
DPMISH (DPMI Shell library), 156–157, 168, 254, 326
DPMISH.H, 157
DPMITEST, 189
DPMS (DOS Protected Mode Services), 172
DRVSPACE.BIN, 51, 57, 103
DSWAP, 140, 141
DTA (Disk Transfer Area), 276, 355–356, 403, 422
DUMPBIN, 87–88
Duncan, Ray, 150–152
DYNLINK32.C, 433

E

EMM386.EXE, 5, 60, 98–99, 103–104, 154, 317
EMS (Expanded Memory Specification), 99, 100, 171, 289

Enable_VM_Ints, 367
Ergo Computing, 151, 170
errors. *See also* GP faults
  embedded VxDs and, 104
  Fatal_Error_Handler and, 178
  IFSMgr and, 13, 393
  INT 2Fh function 1605h and, 118
  IOPL and, 320
  USER and, 459
  V86 breakpoints and, 256
  viewing interrupts and, 277–278
  VMM32 setup and, 186
EXEC (INT 21h function 4Bh), 46, 47, 50, 63, 142, 157, 164, 179, 195, 422, 340, 418, 425, 441–444, 489, 490
Exec_Int, 228–229, 325, 345, 346, 392, 430, 495
Exec_PM_Int, 398
EXEDUMP, 85
EXEHDR, 84–85, 470
Exit Program (INT 21h function 4Ch), 38, 146, 374, 376
ExitWindows, 409
Explorer/Cabinet (CAB32), 32, 35, 64–66, 90–94.
  See also CAB32 Explorer/Cabinet)
  launching Win16 applets from, 420–424
  Quick View, 85, 90, 94
  WSPY21 and, 417–418, 420 441, 460–472
  WV86TEST and, 379, 383–385, 400, 403
Extended Open/Create, 50

F

fail-safe mode, 5, 187
FAKETSR.C, 107, 113, 132–134
FAKEVXD.C, 107, 113, 130–132
FAKEWIN, 97–113, 115–137, 296
  embedded VxDs and, 103–104
  V86TEST and, 309, 317
FastDisk, 238, 357, 368
Fatal_Error_Handler, 178
FAULTHKS, 546–547
file terminology, 197–198
FILETEST.ASM, 543–544
FindClose, 397–399
FindFirstFile, 402
FindNextFile, 397–399, 402–403, 418, 436, 489
FindResource, 470
FreeCell, 425, 442, 455, 456, 467, 468
FreeConsole, 452
_FreeThreadDataSlot, 72
FSNotify_HandleEvents, 92
FSNotify_Register, 92
FWORD.C, 505–506
FWORD PTR, 504–510

G

Gates, Bill, 25, 144, 288, 465
GDI (Graphics Device Interface), 23, 25, 44, 64, 90–91, 355, 434, 470
GDI32, 91, 457, 470
GDT (Global Descriptor Table), 265, 287–288, 304
GetCurrentDirectory (API), 194, 446, 448, 450, 464
Get Current Directory (INT 21h function 47h), 193, 194, 226, 248
GetCurrentTask, 423, 469, 473–474
GetCurrentThreadId, 448
Get_Cur_Thread_Handle, 69, 72
Get_Cur_VM_Handle, 69–70, 76
Get Date (INT 21h function 2Ah), 38, 43–44, 243, 340, 353, 378, 385
Get DOS Version (INT 21h function 30h), 12, 38
Get Drive (INT 21h function 19h), 38, 224–234, 235, 357, 374, 446, 490–491, 492
GetDriveType, 470, 493
GetExePtr, 470
GetFileSize, 340
Get Interrupt Vector (INT 21h function 35h), 219, 235, 238–242, 282
Get Keyboard Status (INT 21h function 0Bh), 247, 248, 270, 346, 354, 361
GetLocalTime, 41, 340, 385
GetMessage, 456, 460
GetOpenFileName, 275, 430
GetProcAddress, 432, 433, 434, 435, 449
Get PSP (INT 21h function 62h), 17, 27, 355–356, 383, 449
GetSaveFileName, 275, 423
GetSelectorLimit, 265
GetSetKernelDosProc, 33, 34, 402, 424, 474, 488–489, 496
Get_Set_Real_DOS_PSP, 390–391
get_stats, 409
GetSystemTime, 41, 340
Get_Sys_Thread_Handle, 72
_GetThreadTimeSlicePriority, 72
Get Time (INT 21h function 2Ch), 35–36, 38, 43–44, 340, 343, 353, 376, 378, 385
Get_VMM_Version, 68–69
GetWindow, 453
Gibson, Steve, 4
GlocalAlloc, 23, 84, 140, 484
GlobalDosAlloc, 444, 487
Global EMM Import, 100–101, 113, 128–129, 171
GOWIN386, 162–164, 170, 172, 176–179, 180–182, 185
GOWIN386.BAT, 163–164, 177
GOWIN386.INI, 162–163
GP faults, 289, 303, 320–321, 327, 330, 337, 381, 494
GUI (Graphical User Interface), 32, 140–141, 287
  VMM32 and, 184, 185, 186, 187
  WIN386.EXE and, 166

H

Heisenberg, Werner, 32, 516
Helix Software, 172, 275, 288
HIMEM, 6, 25, 57–58
HIMEM.SYS, 4, 5, 38, 57, 174
HLT instructions, 494–495
HMA (high memory area), 119
HOOKINT, 363–369, 371
Hook_V86_Fault, 290
Hook_V86_Int_Chain, 15, 17, 27, 36, 82, 219, 233, 235, 240, 290, 357, 363, 368, 389–390, 408, 524–525
Hook_VMM_Fault, 290

I

IBM (International Business Machines), 96, 160, 250, 299, 300, 323, 324
IBMBIO.COM, 51
IBMDOS.COM, 51
IDT (Interrupt Descriptor Table), 210, 218, 278, 280, 287–290, 297, 303–304, 321, 333, 336, 340, 357
IDTMAP, 218, 287–289, 493–494

IFS.H, 79
IFSHLP, 38, 60
IFSHLP.SYS, 4–5, 12–13, 22, 25, 38, 60–62, 178–179, 357
  32BFA and, 178, 182, 186
  IFSMGR and, 244, 249–252, 255, 257–258, 266, 270, 273, 280
  network redirectors and, 275
  role of, 244–274
IFSMgr (Installable File System Manager), 12–13, 17, 22, 27, 45, 60, 78, 105–106, 445
  32BFA and, 178, 181
  bypassing DOS and, 219
  DOSX and, 151
  Get/Set current-drive calls and, 224–230
  IFSHLP.SYS and, 244, 249–252, 255, 257–258, 266, 270, 273, 280
  INT 21h hookers and, 242–244
  INT 21h tables, and Chicago tables, difference between, 236–237
  INTVECT and, 240–242
  long filename support and, 194, 199, 203
  Microsoft's claims of integration and, 25–26
  network files and, 276
  PROTTAB and, 236
  PSPs and, 389–392
  V86TEST and, 347, 351–352, 357
  WIN386.EXE and, 161
  WV86TEST and, 378, 389–394, 399–403, 415
IFSMGR.386, 141, 178, 362
InDOS flags, 120, 392
InitApp, 134
InquireSystem, 493
INSTALL=, 63, 136
Install_IO_Handler, 76, 337, 357
Install_Mult_IO_Handlers, 76, 357
Install_V86_Break_Point, 43, 256, 357
instance data, 29, 97, 99, 101–102, 106, 119–123
InstDataStruc, 120
INT 6 functions, 249, 337
INT 8 functions, 91
INT 9 functions, 91
INT 0Dh functions, 320, 337
INT 10h functions, 367, 368, 369, 370
INT 13h functions, 272, 341, 368–370
INT 15h functions, 129, 341, 367
INT 16h functions, 367, 368, 369
INT 1Ah functions, 43
INT 20h functions, 69–70
INT 21h functions, 46–48, 294–296, 301. *See also* INT 21h functions (listed by number)
  32BFA and, 177, 179, 180–183, 207, 275–276, 278–279
  bypassing DOS and, 210–223
  hookers, global and local, 242–244
  IFSHLP.SYS and, 245–248, 252, 270–272
  IOPL and, 320, 321
  Long Filename (LFN functions), 186, 193, 194, 199, 200, 398, 446
  network redirectors and, 275
  simulating vs. reflecting
interrupts and, 334–335
  running TEST21 and, 234–238
  V86TEST and, 307, 309, 340–343, 346, 352–358
  VMM32 and, 199
  WSPY21 and, 417–496
  WV86TEST and, 371–372, 374,378–379, 382, 394–409, 415, 416
INT 21h functions (listed by number). *See also* INT 21h functions
  function 02h (Display Character), 354
  function 0Bh (Get Keyboard Status), 247, 248, 270, 346, 354, 361
  function 0Dh, 46, 47, 248
  function 0Eh, 38, 223–234, 228–230, 248, 375, 376, 490–492
  function 0Fh (Open File with FCB), 179
  function 1Ah (Set Disk Transfer Address), 355–356, 492
  function 2Ah (Get Date), 38, 43–44, 243, 340, 353, 378, 385
  function 2Ch (Get Time), 35–36, 38, 43–44, 340, 343, 353, 376, 378, 385
  function 3Ch (Create File), 179
  function 3Dh (Open File), 36, 63, 141–142, 179, 182, 195, 217, 235, 236, 375
  function 3Eh (Close File), 36, 182, 217, 235, 236
  function 3Fh (Read File), 36, 152, 182, 199, 217–218, 235, 236, 248, 340, 487
  function 4Bh (EXEC), 46, 47, 142, 157, 164, 179, 195, 422, 340, 425, 441–444, 489, 490
  function 4Ch (Exit Program), 38, 146, 374, 376
  function 4Eh (Find First File), 179, 195
  function 6Ch (Extended Open/Create), 63, 179
  function 19h (Get Drive), 38, 224–234, 235, 357, 374, 446, 490–491, 492
  function 25h (Set Interrupt Vector), 46, 47, 217, 219, 235–242, 282, 338, 483, 487–488, 491
  function 30h (Get DOS Version), 12, 38
  function 35h (Get Interrupt Vector), 219, 235, 238–242, 282
  function 39h (Create Directory), 398
  function 40h (Write File), 36, 152, 217–219, 235, 236, 248, 340, 343, 362
  function 42h (Move File Pointer), 248, 343, 382
  function 44h (IOCTL), 37, 80, 248, 356, 382
  function 45h (Duplicate File Handle), 38
  function 47h (Get Current Directory), 193, 194, 226, 248
  function 48h (Allocate Memory Block), 484, 486, 487
  function 50h (Set PSP), 27, 28–31, 38, 44, 276, 355–356, 374–376, 378, 383–387, 389, 390, 419, 422, 428, 429, 435
  function 51h (Get PSP Address), 17, 38, 276
  function 52h (Get Pointer to List of Lists), 233, 248
  function 55h (Create PSP), 15, 16, 17, 38, 44, 374, 376, 420, 422, 425, 427, 430, 436, 441, 442, 460–472
  function 57h (Get/Set File Date/Time), 248
  function 60h, 236, 248
  function 62h (Get PSP), 17, 27, 355–356, 383, 449
  function 71h, 26–27, 194, 236, 248, 398, 400–401, 446
  function 714Fh, 396–409, 418, 436, 489
INT 28h functions, 341, 345, 346, 347, 361, 363, 366
INT 2Fh functions, 33, 37, 97–101, 105, 155, 294–296. *See also* INT 2Fh functions (listed by number)
  32BFA and, 181, 275
  IFSHLP.SYS and, 255, 272–273
  network redirectors and, 275
  replacing real-mode code and, 278–281
  simulating vs. reflecting interrupts and, 333
  TEST2F16.C and, 281–291
  V86TEST and, 307, 308, 309, 317, 342–347
INT 2Fh functions (listed by number). *See also* INT 2Fh functions
  function 11h, 275, 374, 383
  function 13h, 272–273
  function 16h, 51, 52, 277, 281, 333

function 1600h, 278–281, 342
function 1605h, 97, 98–101, 105–106, 112, 118, 122, 134-135
function 1606h, 59, 105–106, 113, 123
function 1607h, 98, 129–130, 342, 343, 344
function 1608h, 113, 366
function 1609h, 113, 366
function 160Ah, 176, 342
function 160Bh, 98, 99, 342, 409
function 1613h, 51
function 1683h, 174, 281, 317, 333, 336, 341
function 1684h, 57, 67, 124, 125–126, 181, 255, 257, 259, 265
function 1687h, 146, 150, 155
function 1689h, 344–347
function 4310h, 267, 358
function 4B05h, 100
INT 30h functions, 254, 495
INT 31h functions, 33, 39, 149, 155, 424, 487
INT 33h functions, 367, 368
INTCHAIN, 27–29, 205, 244, 245,248, 280, 357, 517–518
Intel, 287–288, 319, 321
Interrupt Gates, 288, 290–291, 494
IntHandler, 473–474
INTSERV.C, 506–508
INTVECT, 277, 286–287
INTVECT.386, 36, 41, 241, 238–242
IOCTL (I/O Control), 37–38, 56, 80, 356
FAKEWIN and, 136
IFSHLP.SYS and, 60, 250
WV86TEST and, 382
IOPB (I/O Permission Bitmap), 297
IOPL (I/O Privilege Level), 319–331, 336
IOS (I/O Supervisor), 78, 81, 104, 177–178, 196–197, 272, 367, 368
IOS.INI, 104, 196
IOSUBSYS, 81, 196
IO.SYS, 3–4, 12, 49, 51–52, 60, 62
FAKEWIN, 124, 126
IFSHLP.SYS and, 272
INT2FAPI.H and, 52
VMM32 and, 185
IRET, 297–298, 321, 324, 330, 337, 368
ISWIN.C, 106, 107, 175
IVT (Interrupt Vector Table), 210, 218, 241, 280, 289, 290, 345

K

KERNEL, 15–16, 25, 44, 140–141
scheduler, idle loop in, 344–345
V86TEST and, 344–347, 355–356
WV86TEST and, 388–389, 401
KERNEL32.DLL, 15, 19–20, 23–24, 86–88, 89, 93, 192, 384, 399, 402–403, 424, 426–441
KernelDosProc, 34, 36, 491, 430, 492, 496
Keybd_Event, 91, 354
KEYBOARD, 22, 91, 368
KEYBOARD.DRV, 89, 91
King, Adrian, 1, 10, 11, 24, 34–35, 58, 66, 69, 81, 86–87, 378, 459–460, 551, 552, 556
Kogan, M. S., 323, 324
Kokkonen, Kim, 59
KRNL286, 140, 150, 152–153, 154, 156, 159, 162, 167
KRNL386, 23, 62–66, 82–94, 140, 176–177, 419–496
DOSX and, 150, 152–153, 154
MDPMI and, 176
MEMLOOP and, 159, 160

L

LANtastic, 81, 381
LASTDRIVE=, 13, 223
LDT (Local Descriptor Table), 75, 265, 287–288, 304
LEDUMP, 81
Letwin, Gordon, 254
LFN.C, 194, 201–203
LFNDIR, 407, 408
LFN.EXE, 203
LIDT, 288
Lin_CurDrv, 233
Lipe, Ralph, 249–250
LMSVCS, 18
LoadLibrary, 84, 432, 435, 463–464
LoadModule, 23, 490
LoadResource, 23, 84, 470
LoadString, 470
LOCAL=, 106
LocalAlloc, 484
LOCALTSRS=, 106
Locate_Byte_In_ROM, 255
LockFile, 340
Logitech, 288
Long, David, 98, 134, 172

M

Macintosh, 1, 2, 25
Manes, Stephen, 144
MAP.C, 107, 113
MAPEXE, 87
MAPFILE, 545–547
MapLS, 93
map_real, 414
MapViewOfFile, 87
Maritz, Paul, 93
MARK/RELEASE, 59
Marsh, Kyle, 93
Maxey, David, 62, 195
MEM, 5–7, 11–14, 17, 22, 268
MEMLOOP, 157–160, 172
VMM32 and, 189, 191
WIN386.EXE and, 164
Microsoft Office, 35, 135
MOUSE, 22, 91
MOUSE.DRV, 89
MoveFile, 340
Move File Pointer (INT 21h function 42h), 248, 343, 382
MRCI32.386, 204, 205
MRCI Get Version, 205–206
MSCDEX (Microsoft CD-ROM Extensions), 59, 58, 60, 172, 275, 288
MSDN (Microsoft Developer Network) CD-ROM, 98, 134, 172, 269
MSDOS.DOC, 398
MSDOS.SYS, 3–4, 12, 30, 51, 60
MSDPMI (Microsoft DPMI Server), 161, 173–176
MSGSRV32, 466, 469, 384
MSW (Machine Status Word), 302, 304
Mueller, Klaus, 99
MYDIR.C, 403, 404–407

N

NDIS (Network Device Interface Standard), 81
NetRoom, 172, 288
NetWare, 172, 274
Network Redirector Interface, 274–275
NETX (NetWare shell), 274
NMIs (nonmaskable interrupts), 324
NoHookDOSCall, 388, 429, 470, 489, 493
Novell, 96, 172
NTVDM, 324
Nuke_VM, 249
Nu-Mega Technologies, 31–32, 49–50, 68
NWCACHE, 172

O

OAK (MS-DOS OEM Adaptation Kit), 347
Okazaki, Taku, 101
OLE (Object Linking and Embedding), 41, 55, 56, 93–94
OpenDriver, 134
OpenFile (API), 142
Open File (INT 21h function 3Dh), 36, 63, 141–142, 179, 182, 195, 217, 235, 236, 375
Open File with FCB (INT 21h function 0Fh), 179
OS/2, 13, 25, 96, 149, 160, 257, 293–296, 301, 323–324

P

_PageGetAllocInfo, 268
_PageOutDirtyPages, 344, 347
PageSwap, 344, 347
PageSwap_Get_Version, 268
PageSwap_Test_IO_Valid, 268
patents, 204–205, 249–250, 254
PATH, 64
PDB (Process Data Block), 16, 442. *See also* PSP (Program Segment Prefix)
PE (Protect Enable) bits, 302–308, 316
PeekMessage, 346, 347
Petzold, Charles, 423
Phar Lap Software, 87, 151, 277
Pietrek, Matt, 16, 83, 84, 89, 159–160, 344, 347, 388, 441, 452
PIF files, 11–12, 490
PIPE.386, 117, 118–119
Plug and Play, 1, 12, 30, 184
    Configuration Manager (CONFIGMG), 56–57, 79
    removal functions and, 76
PM_INT21_PROC, 225
pmode_main, 157
POPF, 297, 319–322, 324, 330, 337
POWER.EXE, 345, 347, 367
PrestoChangoSelector, 469–470
PROCESSENTRY32, 534–535
Program Manager, 332
PROTDUMP, 258, 269, 463
PROTTAB, 225, 236
PSP (Program Segment Prefix), 7–8, 27–30, 41, 43, 324
    bypassing DOS and, 15, 16–20
    Create PSP (INT 21h function 55h), 15, 16, 17, 38, 44, 374, 376, 420, 422, 425, 427, 430, 436, 441, 442, 460–472
    FAKEWIN and, 123–124, 136
    Get PSP (INT 21h function 62h), 17, 27, 340, 355–356, 383, 449
    Set PSP (INT 21h function 50h), 27, 28–31, 38, 44, 276, 340, 355–356, 374–376, 378, 383–387, 389, 390, 419, 422, 428, 429, 435
    thread structures and, 74–75
    WV86TEST and, 385–396
PUSHF, 278–281, 297, 302, 319–322, 324, 330–331, 337

Q

QEMM, 99, 146, 149, 155, 288
    DPMI and, 170, 172
    V86TEST and, 317
    WIN386.EXE and, 163
QT_Thunk, 93, 429–430, 432, 433, 461–462, 464, 470, 497, 554
Qualitas, 101, 174
Quick View, 56, 85, 90, 94

R

Rational Systems, 151
ReadFile (API), 340
Read File (INT 21h function 3Fh), 36, 152, 182, 199, 217–218, 235, 236, 248, 340, 487
README.WRI, 26, 96
real_main, 157
REGEDIT, 55
RegisterClass, 456
RegisterShellHook, 92
Reynolds, Aaron, 249–250
RMM (Real Mode Mapper), 81, 198
    RMM.D32, 178, 179, 357
    RMM.PDR, 196, 198
RPL (Requestor Privilege Level), 319
RUNDLL32.EXE, 431–432
RUNDOSX.BAT, 152–156, 164, 167–168, 170
RUNVMM32, 196
RUNVMM32.BAT, 188–189, 196

S

Sargent, Murray, 144
SaveState, 450
Schedule_Thread_Event, 72
SCSI port driver (SCSI manager), 197
SDA (Swappable Data Area), 29, 42, 119–123, 230, 355, 386–387, 390–391, 392, 393
Set_Async_Time_Out, 72
SetCurrentDirectory, 446, 450
Set_Device_Focus, 269
Set Disk Transfer Address (INT 21h function 1Ah), 355–356, 492
SetFocus, 269
Set Interrupt Vector (INT 21h function 25h), 46, 47, 217, 219, 235–242, 282, 338, 483, 487–488, 491
Set_PM_Exex_Mode, 302
Set_PM_Int_Vector, 17, 27, 363, 494
Set PSP (INT 21h function 50h), 27, 28–31, 38, 44, 276, 355–356, 374–376, 378, 383–387, 389, 390, 419, 422, 428, 429, 435
SetSelectorBase, 84, 414
SetSelectorLimit, 414

Set_Thread_Time_Out, 72
_SetThreadTimeSlicePriority, 72
SetTimer, 91
Set_V86_Exec_Mode, 302
SETVER.EXE, 5–6, 38, 60
SetVolume, 450
SFT (System File Table), 42, 79, 340
SGDT (Store Global Descriptor Table), 304
SHARE_NET_PSP, 392
SHELL, 22, 76, 79, 82, 84, 86–87, 92
SHELL32.DLL, 92–93, 399, 432, 434, 460
SHELL_SYSMODAL_MESSAGE, 104
SideKick, 218
SIDT (Store Interrupt Descriptor Table), 288, 304
Silverberg, Brad, 26
Simulate_Int, 280, 345
Single Application Mode, 59–60, 106, 194
SIS_Next_Dev_Ptr, 101
SLDT (Store Local Descriptor Table), 304
SMARTDRV.EXE, 98, 103–104, 106, 113, 117, 178–179
  bypassing DOS and, 214, 216–217
  long filename support and, 199
Soft-ICE/Windows debugger, 32, 49–51, 57, 62, 256–257, 459
  IFSHLP.SYS and, 245–249
  TASK command, 383
  THREAD command, 75–76
Solitaire, 87, 160, 345
SPART.PAR, 164, 178
Stac Electronics, 4, 204–205
Stacker, 4, 51, 237
STI (set interrupt flag), 320–328, 330, 331, 336–337
STI_HANDLER, 327
STORAGE.DLL, 41
Swap_Always, 120
Swap_In_DOS, 120
SYSDM.CPL, 432–434
SYSINIT, 57
System_Control, 269
SYSTEM.DAT, 56, 186
SYSTEM.DRV, 89, 91, 470, 493
SYSTEM.INI, 80, 92, 106, 122, 163, 346
  32BFA and, 177, 179
  [386Enh] section of, 78
  [boot] section of, 87
  bypassing DOS and, 233–234
  damaged, 118–119
  DblSpace and, 205
  INTVECT.386 and, 241
  VMM32 and, 187, 189–191
  WIN386.EXE and, 162
System Message, 90
SystemROM BreakPoint=, 163, 255, 256–257, 266
SysVars, 233, 391

T

TASK, 383
TaskFirst, 442
TaskNext, 442
TDB (Task Database), 16, 423–424, 443–444, 446, 449, 452–457, 460, 491
TDUMP, 84–85
terminology, file/disk driver, 197–198
TEST13, 272
TEST1600, 278–279, 281–291
TEST1684, 105, 107, 124–126, 333
TEST21, 181–182, 200, 210–224, 227, 234–238, 241, 242, 244–245, 271, 274–277, 282, 287, 484
TEST2F16, 210, 281–291
Test_Cur_Thread Handle, 72
TESTFILE, 210
TestGlobalV86Mem, 332
TextOut, 140
TH32.C, 530–529
THCBs (Thread Control Blocks), 73–76, 448
Thielen, David, 161–162
THREAD, 75–76
Thread32First, 88
Thread32Next, 88
TIMER, 384, 469
TLHELP32.H, 88
TLS (Thread Local Storage), 76
ToolHelp, 88, 442, 456, 467, 469
Toolhelp32ReadProcessMemory, 88
ToolHelpNotifyRegister, 419–421
Trap Gates, 288, 494
TRUENAME, 236
TSR_Info_Struc, 132
TSRLDR.ASM, 100, 117–118
TSRs (terminate and stay resident programs), 31–32, 36, 78–84, 209, 296, 428–429
  bypassing COMMAND.COM and, 10
  bypassing DOS and, 16, 210, 220
  FAKEWIN and, 97–100, 105, 115–123, 132–137
  Identify function, 132–137
  IFSHLP.SYS and, 244, 272
  INT 21h function 34h and, 392
  INT 28h calls and, 347
  INTRSPY and, 62–65
  INTVECT and, 241
  long filename support and, 194
  TEST21 and, 234–238
  V86TEST and, 342, 344, 357
  WIN386.EXE and, 171–172
  WINSTART.BAT and, 175

U

Udell, Jon, 466, 471
UMBHEAD, 122
UMBs (Upper Memory Blocks), 99, 100, 122, 128, 317
Unix, 293–296
USEDPMI, 146–149, 153, 156–157, 164, 172
USEDPMI2.C, 156–157, 172
USER, 16, 23, 25, 44, 90–91, 134, 140–141, 354, 452, 459, 460
  KERNEL32 and, 434
  WndProc and, 453, 456
USER32, 24, 23, 74, 91, 456, 457, 458, 460, 464, 470–471

V

V86MMGR (V86 Memory Manager), 57–61, 79, 128–129, 170–171, 256, 267–268, 358
V86MMGR_GetPgStatus, 128–129
V86MMGR_Xlat_API, 495
V86TEST, 135, 198–199, 217–218, 234–237, 243–245, 281, 301, 307–319, 339–366. *See also* WV86TEST
  CHGDIR and, 451–452
  INT 2Fh function 1683h and, 333
  IOPL and, 322–324, 331–332
  pseudocode summary, 308

VBACKUP, 190
VCACHE, 45, 78, 104, 181, 199, 206, 237, 323, 378
VCACHE.386, 178, 179, 362
VCOND (Virtual CON Device), 79, 183, 451, 538
VDD (Virtual Display Device), 22, 78, 83, 368, 370
VDDINT.ASM, 369
VDHArmSTIHook, 324
VDK.ASM, 369
VDM (Virtual DOS Machine), 294, 296, 324
VDMAD (Virtual Direct Memory Access Device), 22, 78
VDMM (Virtual DOS Machine Manager), 53–54, 298
VDPX.SYS, 149
VFAT (Virtual DOS FAT system), 45, 78, 79, 178, 181, 273–274, 276, 378
Virtual Hard Disk Device. See IOS (I/O Supervisor)
VKD (Virtual Keyboard Device), 22, 78, 89, 368, 369
VMCBs (VM Control Block), 70–71, 74
VMD (Virtual Mouse Device), 22, 78, 89, 368
VMM (Virtual Machine Manager),
  basic description of, 66–77, 298–302
VMM32, 5–6, 140, 165, 182–192
  DblSpace and, 205
  long filename support and, 194–203
  setup, elements of, 186–187
  subdirectory, 187
VMM32.VXD, 61–62, 65–66, 78–80, 82, 140, 161, 182–192, 194, 339
VMM_AddInstanceItem, 120
VMMCreateThread, 72, 192
VMM_GetDDBList, 191
VMM.H, 70, 73–74
VMM.INC, 70, 343, 376
VMM_MMGR_Toggle_HMA, 268
VMPoll, 343–347, 361, 366, 380, 381
VMM_SelectorMapFlat, 430
VMSTAT_PM_EXEC, 227
VOLTRACK, 81–82, 196, 198
VPD (Virtual Printer Device), 368
VPICD (Virtual Programmable
Interrupt Control Device), 22, 67, 78, 82, 89, 324, 376, 381
VPICD_Set_Int_Request, 89
VREDIR, 276
VSHARE.386, 78, 178
VTD (Virtual Timer Device), 22, 41, 43, 78, 89, 368
VWIN32, 22, 79, 86–89, 183, 192, 390, 400
VXD86API, 252–255
VXDLDR, 79, 184, 191, 196
VXDLDR_GetDeviceList, 191
VXDLDR_LoadDevice, 184, 196
VXDLDR_UnloadLoadDevice, 184
VXDLIST, 191–192, 205

W

W16LOCK.C, 553–554
W32S_BackTo32, 456
W32HAND.C, 538–539
W386_Get_SYSDAT_Path, 52–53
W386_Int_Mulitiplex, 51–52
W3MAP, 65–70, 78–79, 182–184
WALKWIN, 443 453–456
WfW (Windows for Workgroups) 3.11, 31, 95, 96, 135–136, 416. *See also* 32BFA (32-bit file access)
  bypassing DOS and, 14, 19
  DOSX and, 141
  Get/Set current-drive calls and, 225–226, 230
  IFSHLP.SYS and, 250, 273–274
  IFSMgr and, 79
  INT 21h function handling in, summary of, 46
  INT 21h tables, and Chicago tables, difference between, 236–237
  INTRSPY and, 65
  INTVECT and, 286–287
  as a neglected operating system, 44–48
  Resource Kit, 81
  WIN386.EXE and, 161
  WV86TEST and, 377, 379
When_VM_Ints_Enabled, 327
WIN, 3, 5–6, 9, 25, 366–367, 375
Win16Lock, 497, 550–556.
WIN32PSP.C, 533
WIN386, 52, 161–176, 207
  FAKEWIN and, 118–119, 127
  the inner core of window and, 140–142
  as a memory manager, 170–172
WIN386.EXE, 61, 65–66, 97–98, 112, 161–180, 182, 298
  the inner core of window and, 140–142
  VMM32 and, 183, 187
Win386_Startup_Info_Struc, 100–101, 119
WINA20.386, 122–123
WinBezMT, 32, 35, 136, 425, 442, 456, 467, 468
WINBOOT.SYS, 3–5, 10, 12, 19, 22, 25, 30–32, 36, 38, 43, 48–54, 57, 65, 119, 293
  IFSHLP.SYS and, 60–62
  long filename support and, 194
  VMM32 and, 185
WINBP, 258–270, 494
WIN.COM, 4–5, 9, 32, 49–54, 60–66, 174, 176, 300
  32BFA and, 179–180
  VMM32 and, 185, 187, 188
Windows NT, 13–14, 17–18, 32, 274, 293–296, 324, 465–466, 471, 472
WinExec, 441, 460, 490
WinHelp, 374–378, 383, 421, 422, 441
WINHELP.EXE, 374
WINICE, 32, 346, 392, 393, 466–468
WINIO, 409, 414–415, 423, 438, 453, 473
WinOldAp, 129, 452
WINPSP, 7–9, 15, 17–18, 355, 385, 437–443
WinScope, 459, 467, 468, 469
WINSTART.BAT, 64, 82, 175–176, 196
WINWALK, 442
WISPY, 275–276, 489, 490
WLOG212F, 33–41, 45–48, 229–230, 276
WM_TIMER, 353, 385, 403, 498, 511
WndProc, 453, 455, 456
Word for Windows, 2, 55–56, 135, 332, 342, 345, 354, 355, 361, 373, 380–385
WordPad, 373, 383
WordPerfect, 294
WRITE.EXE, 490
Write File (INT 21h function 40h), 36, 152, 217–219, 235, 236, 248, 340, 343, 362
WSHELL, 129, 140
WSPY21, 372, 386, 399–400, 402,m 417–496, 499, 501, 517, 529, 538–539
  calling tree for, 472–473
WSWAP.EXE, 140–141
WV86TEST, 371–416, 417, 419, 421, 425, 427–428, 436

XMS (Extended Memory Specification), 55–60, 100, 152, 171, 177, 256, 267, 268, 358, 486–487

IDG Books' License Agreement

Important: Please read this carefully before opening the software packet. This is a legal agreement between you (either an individual or an entity) and IDG Books Worldwide, Inc. (IDG). By opening the accompanying sealed packet containing the software disk, you acknowledge that you have read and accept the following IDG License Agreement. If you do not agree and do not want to be bound by the terms of this Agreement, promptly return the book and the unopened software packet to the place you obtained them for a full refund.

1 *License.* This License Agreement (Agreement) permits you to use one copy of the enclosed Software program(s) on a single computer. The Software is in "use" on a computer when it is loaded into temporary memory (that is, RAM) or installed into permanent memory (for example, hard disk, CD ROM, or other storage device) of that computer.

2. *Copyright.* The entire contents of this disk and the compilation of the Software are copyrighted and protected by both United States copyright laws and international treaty provisions. The individual programs on the disk are copyrighted by the author of this Book, Andrew Schulman. You may only (a) make one copy of the Software for backup or archival purposes, or (b) transfer the Software to a single hard disk, provided that you keep the original for backup or archival purposes. None of the material on this disk or listed in this Book may ever be distributed, in original or modified form, for commercial purposes.

3. *Other Restrictions.* You may not rent or lease the Software. You may transfer the Software and user documentation on a permanent basis provided you retain no copies and the recipient agrees to the

terms of this Agreement. You may reverse engineer, decompile, or disassemble the Software except to the extent that the foregoing restriction is expressly prohibited by applicable law. If the Software is an update or has been updated, any transfer must include the most recent update and all prior versions.

4. *Limited Warranty*. IDG Warrants that the Software and disk are free from defects in materials and workmanship for a period of sixty (60) days from the date of purchase of this Book. If IDG receives notification within the warranty period of defects in material or workmanship, IDG will replace the defective disk. IDG's entire liability and your exclusive remedy shall be limited to replacement of the Software, which is returned to IDG with a copy of your receipt. This Limited Warranty is void if failure of the Software has resulted from accident, abuse, or misapplication. Any replacement Software will be warranted for the remainder of the original warranty period or thirty (30) days, whichever is longer.
5. *No Other Warranties*. To the maximum extent permitted by applicable law, IDG and the author disclaim all other warranties, express or implied, including but not limited to implied warranties of merchantability and fitness for a particular purpose, with respect to the Software, the programs, the source code contained therein and/or the techniques described in this Book. This limited warranty gives you specific legal rights. You may have others which vary from state/jurisdiction to state/jurisdiction.
6. *No Liability For Consequential Damages*. To the extent permitted by applicable law, in no event shall IDG or the author be liable for any damages whatsoever (including without limitation, damages for loss of business profits, business interruption, loss of business information, or any other pecuniary loss) arising out of the use of or inability to use the Book or the Software, even if IDG has been advised of the possibility of such damages. Because some states/jurisdictions do not allow the exclusion or limitation of liability for consequential or incidental damages, the above limitation may not apply to you.

Programmer's Shop License Agreement

The Programmer's Shop is a business unit of The Software Developer's Company, Inc. This is a legal agreement between you (either an individual or an entity) and The Software Developer's Company, Inc. Use of the SOFTWARE, as hereinafter defined, constitutes your complete and unconditional acceptance of the terms of this Agreement. If you do not agree to the terms of this agreement, promptly return the SOFTWARE and the accompanying items, including written materials and binders or other containers ("DOCUMENTATION"), for a full refund.

SOFTWARE LICENSE

1. *GRANT OF LICENSE.* The Software Developer's Company, Inc. ("SDC") grants you the non-exclusive right to use one copy of this CD-ROM disc ("SOFTWARE") on a single computer. If you are an entity, SDC grants you the right to designate one individual within your organization to have the right to use the SOFTWARE. The SOFTWARE is in "use" on a computer when it is loaded into memory (i.e., RAM) or installed into permanent memory (e.g., hard disk, CD-ROM, or other storage device) of that computer. However, installation on a network server for the purpose of distribution to one or more other computer(s) shall not constitute "use" for which a separate license agreement is required.
2. *COPYRIGHT.* The SOFTWARE, including any computer programs, images, photographs, animations, video, audio, music, and text incorporated in the SOFTWARE, is owned by SDC or its suppliers and is protected by United States copyright laws and

international treaty provisions. You may not reproduce or distribute the SOFTWARE or any written materials accompanying the SOFTWARE except as otherwise provided herein.

3. *OTHER RESTRICTIONS.* You may not rent or lease the SOFTWARE. You may make a permanent transfer of the SOFTWARE by providing SDC written notice of your name, company if appropriate, address, and the name, company if appropriate, and address of the person to whom you are transferring the rights granted herein. In the event of a transfer, you may not retain copies of the SOFTWARE and accompanying written materials and the recipient must agree to the terms of this Agreement. You may not reverse engineer, decompile or disassemble the SOFTWARE. If the SOFTWARE is an update or has been updated, any transfer of the license to use the SOFTWARE must include the most recent update and all prior versions. Any attempted sub-license, assignment, rental, sale or other transfer of the SOFTWARE or the rights or obligations of this Agreement in violation of the terms and conditions of this Agreement shall be void. This license will automatically terminate without notice to you, if you fail to comply with its terms.

LIMITED WARRANTY. You assume all responsibility for the selection of the SOFTWARE as appropriate to achieve the results intended by you. SDC warrants that the CD-ROM disc upon which the SOFTWARE is recorded shall be free from defects in material and workmanship under normal use and conditions, and that the SOFTWARE shall perform substantially as described in the DOCUMENTATION, for a period of sixty (60) days from purchase. EXCEPT FOR THE FOREGOING LIMITED WARRANTY, THE SOFTWARE AND DOCUMENTATION IS PROVIDED "AS IS" WITHOUT WARRANTY OF ANY KIND. SDC AND ITS SUPPLIERS DISCLAIM ALL OTHER WARRANTIES, EITHER EXPRESS OR IMPLIED, INCLUDING, BUT NOT LIMITED TO, IMPLIED WARRANTIES OF MERCHANTABILITY AND FITNESS FOR A PARTICULAR PURPOSE. This limited warranty gives you specific legal rights, and you may have others which vary from state to state.

LIMITATION OF REMEDIES. In the event of the break of the limited warranty set forth above, you shall be entitled to return the CD-ROM disc and, at the election of SDC, to have the purchase price refunded or to receive a CD-ROM disc containing the SOFTWARE which conforms to the above limited warranty. In no event shall SDC or its suppliers be liable for any damages whatsoever, including without limitation, damages for loss of business profits, business interruption, loss of business information, or any other pecuniary loss, or indirect, incidental, consequential or special damages of any kind, arising out of the use of or inability to use this SDC product, even if SDC has been advised of the possibility of such damages. In no event shall SDC's liability (whether based on a claim in contract, tort or otherwise) to any party exceed the purchase price of the SOFTWARE. The remedies set forth above are exclusive. Because some states do not allow the exclusion or limitation of liability for consequential or incidental damages, the above limitation or exclusions may not apply to you.

This Agreement sets forth the entire agreement between the parties. The terms herein may not be changed or modified except by an instrument in writing duly signed on behalf of both parties.

If any provision of this Agreement shall be deemed to be invalid, illegal or unenforceable, the validity, legality and enforceability of the remaining portions of this Agreement shall not be affected or impaired thereby.

This Agreement is governed by the laws of the state of Massachusetts.

Should you have any questions concerning this Agreement, or if you desire to contact SDC for any reason, please call or write: Software Developer's Company, Inc., 90 Industrial Park Road, Hingham, MA 02043-4399, telephone 1-800-446-1185.

Always get the very best products...For the

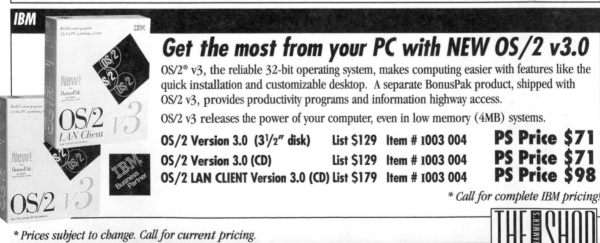

ACI

Object Master C++

The Object Master C++ programming environment offers tools for reducing development time.

- Project window for organization
- Browser window facilitates fast and easy navigation through code
- Class Tree window provides a graphical, hierarchical view of projects
- Powerful, scriptable Source Code editor

Object Master works seamlessly with all major compilation systems, and supports C and C++.

List $249 **Item # A442 001** **PS Price $235**

PRODEA

Prodea – Custom Solutions From Shrink-Wrapped Software

Develop business applications that automate everyday tasks without programming. ProdeaSynergy works with popular Windows applications and features variable passing and complex logic for advanced process automation.

List $199
Item # P291 001 **PS Price $165**

IBM

Get the most from your PC with NEW OS/2 v3.0

OS/2® v3, the reliable 32-bit operating system, makes computing easier with features like the quick installation and customizable desktop. A separate BonusPak product, shipped with OS/2 v3, provides productivity programs and information highway access.

OS/2 v3 releases the power of your computer, even in low memory (4MB) systems.

OS/2 Version 3.0 (3½″ disk)	**List $129**	**Item # I003 004**	**PS Price $71**
OS/2 Version 3.0 (CD)	**List $129**	**Item # I003 004**	**PS Price $71**
OS/2 LAN CLIENT Version 3.0 (CD)	**List $179**	**Item # I003 004**	**PS Price $98**

IBM Business Partner

** Call for complete IBM pricing!*

** Prices subject to change. Call for current pricing.*

CALL 1 800 421-8006 FOR YOUR *FREE* CATALOG! MON-FRI 8:30 - 8:00 EST

SOURCE CODE-IDP001 11/94